THE CAMBRIDG

THE ROMA

This book offers readers a comprehensive and innovative introduction to the economy of the Roman Empire. Focusing on the principal determinants, features, and consequences of Roman economic development and integrating additional web-based materials, it is designed as an up-to-date survey that is accessible to all audiences. Five main sections discuss theoretical approaches drawn from Economics, labor regimes, the production of power and goods, various means of distribution from markets to predation, and the success and ultimate failure of the Roman economy. The book not only covers traditionally prominent features such as slavery, food production, and monetization but also highlights the importance of previously neglected aspects such as the role of human capital, energy generation, rent-taking, logistics, and human well-being, and convenes a group of five experts to debate the nature of Roman trade.

WALTER SCHEIDEL is Dickason Professor in the Humanities and Professor of Classics and History at Stanford University. He is the author or editor of a dozen books on the ancient world, including *The Cambridge Economic History of the Greco-Roman World* (with Ian Morris and Richard Saller, 2007). His work, which has focused on ancient social and economic history, historical demography, and the history of empire, has been widely recognized for its innovative quantitative and comparative modelling, cross-cultural scope, and transdisciplinary breadth across the social sciences and life sciences.

THE CAMBRIDGE COMPANION TO

THE ROMAN ECONOMY

Edited by

WALTER SCHEIDEL

Dickason Professor in the Humanities and Professor of Classics and History, Stanford University

CAMBRIDGE
UNIVERSITY PRESS

University Printing House, Cambridge CB2 8BS, United Kingdom

Cambridge University Press is part of the University of Cambridge.

It furthers the University's mission by disseminating knowledge in the pursuit of education, learning and research at the highest international levels of excellence.

www.cambridge.org
Information on this title: www.cambridge.org/9780521726887

First published 2012
3rd printing 2014

Printed in the United Kingdom by Clays, St Ives plc.

A catalogue record for this publication is available from the British Library

Library of Congress Cataloguing in Publication data
The Cambridge companion to the Roman economy / edited by Walter Scheidel.
pages cm. – (Cambridge companions to the ancient world)
Includes bibliographical references and index.
ISBN 978-0-521-89822-5 – ISBN 978-0-521-72688-7 (pbk.)
1. Rome – Economic conditions – 30 B.C.–476 A.D. I. Scheidel, Walter, 1966–
HC39.C36 2012
330.937 – dc23 2012015664

ISBN 978-0-521-89822-5 Hardback
ISBN 978-0-521-72688-7 Paperback

Additional resources for this publication at www.stanford.edu/~scheidel/CCRE.htm

---

CONTENTS

List of Figures

Note on the Contributors

COLIN ADAMS is Senior Lecturer in Ancient History at the University of Liverpool. He specializes in the social and economic history of Roman Egypt and the broader Roman Empire, especially the role of transport in the ancient economy, and the dynamics of provincial administration.

PETER FIBIGER BANG is Associate Professor of History at the University of Copenhagen. He is a Roman comparative historian whose interests include social and economic history, state-formation, historical sociology, and world history.

PAUL ERDKAMP is Professor of Ancient History at the Flemish Free University of Brussels. He has published on the Roman grain market and food supply, the urban and rural economy, the Roman army, and Republican historiography.

CAMERON HAWKINS is Assistant Professor in the History Department at the University of Chicago. He has published studies on the organization of labor in the Roman world and on the economics of manumission, and is currently working on a book about artisans and the urban economy in the Late Republic and Early Roman Empire.

DENNIS KEHOE is currently Andrew W. Mellon Professor in the Humanities at Tulane University. His research interests are in Roman economic history and Roman law.

GEOFFREY KRON is Assistant Professor of Greek History at the University of Victoria. His research interests include democracy ancient and modern and its socio-economic and cultural impact, and the ancient economy, particularly agriculture, nutrition, housing, and living standards.

SIMON T. LOSEBY is Senior Lecturer in the Department of History at the University of Sheffield. He specializes in late antique and early medieval urbanism and exchange, and is currently completing a monograph on Marseille.

NEVILLE MORLEY is Professor of Ancient History at the University of Bristol. His research interests include ancient economic and social history and the reception of antiquity in modern social, economic, and political thought.

SITTA VON REDEN is Professor of Ancient History at the University of Freiburg. She has widely published on money in the Greek, Hellenistic, and Roman economy.

RICHARD SALLER is Professor of Classics and History and Dean of the School of Humanities and Sciences at Stanford University. His research interests include Roman social and economic history, especially the Roman household.

WALTER SCHEIDEL is Dickason Professor in the Humanities at Stanford University. His research focuses on ancient social and economic history, premodern demography, and comparative and transdisciplinary world history.

MORRIS SILVER is Professor Emeritus of Economics at the City College of the City University of New York. He specializes in ancient economies and is currently studying Roman institutions and economic policy with special emphasis on banking and contractual slavery.

PETER TEMIN is Elisha Gray II Professor of Economics Emeritus at MIT. One of his research interests is to bring economic tools into the study of the economy of the Roman world.

GLORIA VIVENZA is Professor of the History of Economic Thought at the University of Verona in Italy. Her research interests cover ancient history, economic history, history of economic thought, and the study of Adam Smith.

ANDREW WILSON is Professor of the Archaeology of the Roman Empire and Fellow of All Souls College, Oxford. His research interests include ancient water supply, ancient technology, economy, and trade.

Abbreviations

Abbreviations of ancient authors follow those used by the *Oxford Classical Dictionary* (3rd ed.).

AE	*L'Année Epigraphique*, 1888–.
BGU	*Ägyptische Urkunden aus den Königlichen Museen zu Berlin, Griechische Urkunden*, 1895–.
CIL	*Corpus Inscriptionum Latinarum*, 1863–.
FIRA	*Fontes Iuris Romani Anteiustiniani*, 1940.
IGRR	*Inscriptiones Graecae ad Res Romanas Pertinentes*, 1906–27.
ILS	*Inscriptiones Latinae Selectae*, 1892–1916.
Lewis and Short	C. T. Lewis and C. Short, *A Latin Dictionary*. Oxford 1879.
LTUR	E. M. Steinby (ed.), *Lexicon Topographicum Urbis Romae*, 1993–2000.
O.Petr.	*Ostraca in Prof. W. M. Flinders Petrie's Collection at University College*, London, in *Greek Ostraca in the Bodleian Library at Oxford and Various Other Collections, 1*. 1930.
OCD	S. Hornblower and A. Spawforth (eds.), *The Oxford Classical Dictionary*, rev. 3rd edn. Oxford 2003.
OGIS	*Orientis Graecae Inscriptiones Selectae*, 1903–5.
P.Bour.	*Les Papyrus Bouriant*, 1926.
P.Fouad	*Les Papyrus Fouad*, 1939.
P.Oxy.	*The Oxyrhynchus Papyri*, 1898–.
P.Panop.Beatty	*Papyri from Panopolis in the Chester Beatty Library Dublin*, 1964.
P.Princ.	*Papyri in the Princeton University Collections*, 1931–.
P.Ross.Georg.	*Papyri russischer und georgischer Sammlungen*, 1925–35.

P.Vindob.	*Papyri Vindobonenses* (in various editions).
PG	*Patrologiae Cursus Completus, Series Graeca*, 1857–66.
SB	*Sammelbuch griechischer Urkunden aus Ägypten*, 1915–.
SEG	*Supplementum Epigraphicum Graecum*, 1923–.
Sel.Pap.	A. S. Hunt, C. C. Edgar, and D. L. Page, *Select Papyri*. 3 vols., 1932–41.
SIG	*Sylloge Inscriptionum Graecarum*, 3rd edn., 1915–24.
TPSulp	*Tabulae Pompeianae Sulpiciorum*, 1999.

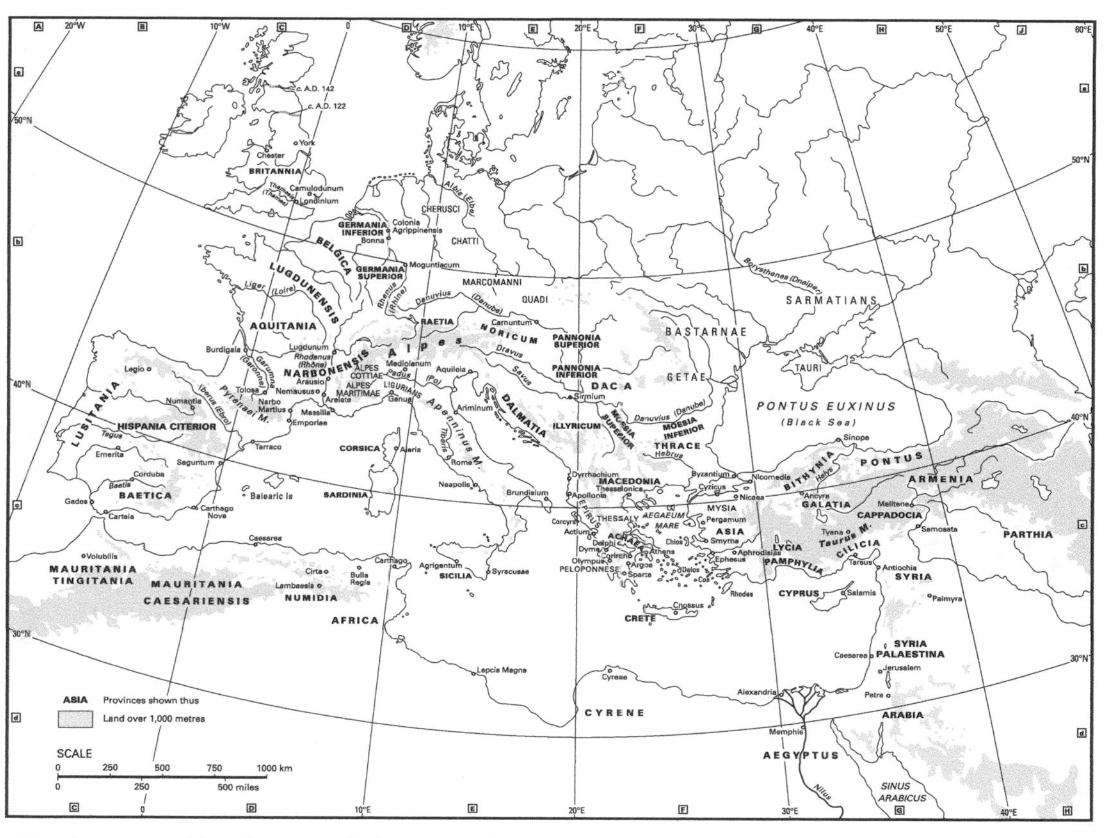

The Roman world at the time of Marcus Aurelius

1: APPROACHING THE ROMAN ECONOMY

Walter Scheidel

DEFINING THE ROMAN ECONOMY

What was the "Roman economy?" In this volume, we apply this term to economic developments that occurred within the Roman Empire, a polity that evolved from an alliance system in peninsular Italy into a large empire that from the second century BCE onward came to dominate and then rule the most densely populated parts of western Eurasia and North Africa west of Mesopotamia and Iran before it eventually experienced substantial contraction in the fifth and seventh centuries CE. Although many of the following chapters devote particular attention to conditions in Roman Italy, the original core of the empire, coverage extends across the varied territories under Roman control. More specifically, this volume seeks to relate economic structures and processes to the formation of the imperial state.[1]

Thanks to its exceptional size and duration, the Roman Empire offers one of the best opportunities to study economic development in the context of an agrarian world empire. Moreover, the fact that the Roman period was the only time when the entire Mediterranean basin was contained within a single political domain raises the question of how much the specific characteristics of the Roman economy owed to imperial unification. The Roman economy was a typical pre-modern economy in the sense that it depended on organic fuels and was dominated by agriculture and production within households. In developmental terms, it can be seen as the continuation and culmination of the expansion of the Hellenistic economies of the Eastern Mediterranean and Near East that in turn represented the mature phase of the political and economic recovery that had commenced in the Early Iron Age. The Roman period witnessed the extension of Near Eastern, Hellenic, and Hellenistic features such as urbanization, monetization, market exchange, taxation, and chattel slavery into the western peripheries of Eurasia.

Three things are necessary to understand Roman economic history: determine what happened, explain why it happened, and assess these developments comparatively by relating them to those of other times and places, thereby situating the Roman case in a global context of pre-modern economic performance. Explanations must be grounded in the empirical record but do not directly emerge from it: the evidence never speaks for itself. The study of causation benefits from an awareness of economic theory and from explicit comparison: both are vital tools in formulating logically coherent and historically plausible hypotheses that can be tested against specific data. Only an integrated approach that combines evidence, theory, and comparison has the potential to generate credible models of Roman economic development.

Performance

Our appreciation of Roman economic performance and its change over time rests on careful study of its visible manifestations. At the most basic level this requires the collection, analysis, and standardization of relevant data. Material remains are of crucial importance: consumer goods, technical devices and containers, remains of settlements, evidence of land use, building materials, human bones, plant and animal remains, coins, shipwrecks, and even traces of air pollution preserved in ice and sediment all shed light on economic life in the Roman world. In addition, we derive information from literary accounts and legal regulations and from large numbers of stone inscriptions and papyri as well as graffiti and wax tablets. Even though the scarcity of a potentially decisive type of documentation – that of ancient statistics – inevitably inhibits our efforts, on the whole the main challenge lies not so much in the amount of evidence, which is abundant and keeps expanding, as in its interpretation. In the near-absence of records of how much was produced, traded, and consumed, modern observers commonly interpret different kinds of data (such as those listed above) as putative proxies of Roman economic development. Temporal or spatial variation in the quantity or quality of such proxies is taken to reflect economic change.

In practice, however, the meaning of such variations is often ambiguous, which can make it difficult to relate them directly to economic performance. For example, evidence suggestive of population growth might reasonably be interpreted as a proxy of growing economic output – but only if it was not offset by a reduction in per capita levels of consumption. To complicate matters, demographic change is an elusive issue. Field surveys trace objects and not people: variation in surface scatter primarily reflects variation in the incidence of datable objects, which represents a different proxy of economic development. Urbanization may be interpreted in different ways, which are by no means mutually exclusive: as a sign of population growth, as an indicator of intensive economic growth and division of labor that increased the relative share of the non-agrarian sector, and of nucleation driven by social and political factors such as the emergence of an empire-wide city-based ruling class. The scale and direction of long-distance trade is often inferred from the frequency of ceramic finds, above all shipping containers and tableware, and from the distribution of shipwrecks: yet changes in the use of barrels or sacks may obscure actual trends, and shipwrecks only remain visible if they contain durable cargo. Whereas it would be hard to dissociate the appearance of large numbers of elaborate *villa* estates in late Republican Italy from increasing wealth and rationalization of production, it remains much more challenging to make sense of the later reduction of their numbers. Technological progress may be measured by tracking novel installations such as water-mills, but such devices can be very rare in the material record. Monetization through coinage may have been an index of economic development or more mundanely a function of increasing mining activity in previously underdeveloped areas. Moreover, coinage does not tell us about the scope of credit money and how it changed over time. Isotopic evidence of lead pollution reflects mining output but does not show how changes in metal use were related to overall economic growth or decline.[2] Contextual incentives or disincentives to economic activity also merit attention, yet their impact is even more difficult to gauge. They include evidence of institutional arrangements, such as laws and tolls, or signs of literacy.[3]

It is important to be specific about the limitations of the evidence. It would seem perverse to question the economic relevance of any given proxy individually, viewed in separation from others. Inasmuch as different types of data converge in distinctive ways, we may reasonably assume that they indicate at least the general direction of economic development. Thus, the combination of more or higher-quality goods being more widely distributed, of more or costlier infrastructure, and of more archaeologically visible settlement points to economic growth, and vice versa. At the same time, it is much more difficult to distinguish between extensive (aggregate) and intensive (per capita) growth. Once again, massive congruent changes in different indicators may well suggest not just the former but also the latter. However, such broad clues do not clearly translate to estimates of economic output in terms of per capita product or real incomes.

Historians are unable to establish Roman GDP without relying on exceedingly schematic extrapolation from select data for prices and wages. More generally, GDP estimates are to a significant extent determined by what we expect to have happened rather than by empirical measurements. They are useful mostly in establishing boundaries that constrain modern conjecture but far less capable of supporting cross-cultural comparison, of distinguishing among regions, or of discerning change over time.[4]

The distribution of GDP is at least as important as its size. Even if intensive economic growth could reliably be established, we would still need to ask how these gains were allocated. Indications of rising living standards in the general population are not incompatible with the notion of disproportionate elite enrichment: high-profile trade and urban monumentalization can easily be read in both ways. Slavery is an excellent example: just as it creates wealth by turning labor power into capital and is capable of increasing productivity, it is likely to exacerbate asset and income inequality within society. A wide range of material evidence, from house sizes to skeletal remains, can be marshaled to investigate such distributional effects.[5]

This raises an even bigger question, that of the relationship between economic development and human welfare. Information on real wages throws some light on the consequences of economic change but is relatively scarce and very unevenly distributed. Textual accounts, pollen data, and food remains can all help us obtain a better idea of Roman diets. The most immediately relevant evidence is preserved within the human body: stature and dental and bone health are powerful indicators of nutritional status and disease loads. Yet even physiological markers are by no means easy to interpret: economic growth may improve access to foodstuffs (thus favoring bodily wellbeing) but, by encouraging urbanization, may simultaneously increase the transmission of infectious disease (thereby causing the opposite effect).[6]

All this adds up to a thoroughly mixed picture of promise and limitations. On the one hand, the empirical record is abundant and continues to grow as new methods are developed: as always, natural science leads the way by enhancing our knowledge of the provenance of goods and people, of mineral extraction, and of human well-being. Not only will there be new data, but already existing data will also yield more information. Systematic analysis, greatly aided by information technology, will further contribute to this process. A growing amount of information will be available to test hypotheses and undertake comparisons with other times and places. On the other hand, some constraints will likely prove insuperable, as in the case of GDP estimates. But this focus on the level of economic performance and its consequences neglects what are perhaps the most interesting questions, those concerning the reasons for observed outcomes. Richer data help us address these questions but cannot answer them. The next two sections take a closer look at what is required to do so.

Comparison

The sheer size of the Roman economy creates a strong temptation to study it on its own terms by concentrating on conditions and developments within a clearly circumscribed space and period. This has always been and still is the dominant approach. Yet this exercise can only be a first step: by itself, it deprives Roman economic history of vital context. Comparison is not merely an optional bonus feature of historical inquiry: it not only gives us a better sense of how the Roman economy performed relative to that of other pre-modern systems, it also provides much-needed inspiration in the search for causation. Broadly speaking, comparison comes in three flavors: focusing on the same period, on the same space, or on the same type of social formation.[7]

The first kind of comparison would set Roman Italy against the Hellenistic East, or the mature Empire against economies in ancient Iran, India, and China. This approach is particularly useful if we are looking for factors that may have affected different economies concurrently. Candidates include connectivity, as proposed in the more ambitious versions of world-systems theory, or, more plausibly, exogenous forces such as climate change that acted more globally and thereby influenced the course of otherwise largely separate economies.[8]

The second kind privileges space by situating the Roman economy within the *longue durée* of a particular region or eco-system. Two recent attempts warrant particular attention. Peregrine Horden and Nicholas Purcell have focused on the Mediterranean properties of the Roman economy, stressing the nexus between physical connectivity and diverse micro-ecologies that favored mobility and exchange, as well as long-term continuities underlying phases of intensification and abatement. This perspective, which seeks to build a history *of* and not merely *in* the Mediterranean by taking proper account of ecological circumstances and basic structures, provides an important counterweight to the otherwise dominant preoccupation with the specifics of particular social formations. In a nutshell, it may help us determine how "Roman" the Roman economy really was. Instead of making us lose sight of the potential significance of the institutions of Roman rule – a likely but by no means inevitable corollary of this perspective – appreciation of the Mediterranean context ought to encourage explicit comparative analysis of different pre-modern economies in that region.[9] The other example is Willy Pleket's emphasis on continuities or rather functional equivalencies between the Roman economy and the later European economies of the Middle Ages and the *Ancien Régime*. This approach questions common notions that the structure of the Roman economy was substantially different from that of later periods of western history. Less interested in the ecological properties of a given region, it stresses similarities over discontinuities, assimilating the various economies of pre-modern Europe into a shared pattern of subsistence activities that were interspersed with niches of capitalist development tied to markets and long-distance trade. Once again, this perspective is useful in so far as it challenges preconceived notions of putatively "Roman" features but runs the risk of eliding potentially quite fundamental differences between the fusion of town and country or the dynamics generated by universal empire in the Roman period and contrasting conditions later on. As before, the principal value of this paradigm lies in providing a template for systematic diachronic comparison.[10]

The third and intellectually most stimulating kind of comparison transcends the constraints of time and space by focusing on institutional and organizational features. Thus, the Roman economy can fruitfully be compared to the economies of other large agrarian empires wherever and whenever they existed. This approach, still in its infancy, works best for formations that have generated comparable or, preferably, better data sets. Peter Bang's ongoing work on the Roman Empire and Mughal India is currently the most prominent example. China offers particularly rich opportunities: while the economy of the Han Empire has already begun to be considered in relation to that of the Roman economy, the economic efflorescence of the Song period (and its dramatic curtailment) may well constitute the closest analogy to Roman developments. In addition, the Umayyad and Abbasid Caliphates and especially the Ottoman Empire likewise offer suitable comparanda. But historical comparison is not merely about similarities: the study of contrasts can be instrumental in establishing the causal significance of specific variables in terms of observed outcomes. In the present case, the most obvious comparison is that between tributary integration in the Roman economy and the mechanisms of economic development in the very different political ecology of the Greek city-state culture.[11]

None of these different approaches is inherently superior to others, and all of them have something valuable to add. While consideration of concurrent developments may draw attention to otherwise obscure factors and the long-term study of the same environments may shed light on the influence of continuities or discontinuities, linkages are not necessary to justify comparison: temporally and spatially unrelated cases can equally well be brought together as long as this exercise improves our understanding of causation. The latter is perhaps the single most important element of a comparative approach to the Roman economy: our goal is not to rank it in some imaginary global league table but to explain why it developed the way it did.

CAUSATION

Markets and violence

In their critique of academic models of medieval (English) economic development, John Hatcher and Mark Bailey remark on the dominance of three competing 'supermodels' that focus on the role of demography (a Malthusian perspective), class relations (a Marxist perspective), and commercialization and consequently seek to explain the same historical processes "in exclusive and starkly conflicting terms." The contrast to the study of the Roman economy is striking: not only is there no need to respond to and bridge the gaps between competing 'supermodels,' historical interpretation has, with very few exceptions, barely advanced to the stage of explicit model-building.[12]

Instead, much existing scholarship has primarily been concerned with establishing facts, or otherwise accounting for them with the help of inchoate notions of plausibility that are heavily indebted to contemporary modes of economic behavior. Inasmuch as analytical framing devices are employed, the debate continues to be dominated by the contrast between 'primitivist' and/or 'substantivist' perspectives on the one hand and 'modernist' and/or 'formalist' ones on the other. Dating back to the nineteenth century, these are concerned with questions of scale (positing more or less economic development) but also, and crucially, with the structure of ancient economies. Put in a highly simplified manner, formalist positions stress similarities between ancient and modern economies by emphasizing the putative significance of price-setting markets, comparative advantage, and capitalist ventures, whereas substantivists emphasize discontinuities by focusing on how status concerns mediated economic behavior and generated specific dynamics that reflected elite preference for rent-taking and landownership and disdain for commercial enterprise that reinforced the fusion of political and economic power and marginalized independent merchants. De facto, if not in principle, these positions frequently tend to correlate with divergent assessments of the scale of economic development, with formalists keen to document growth and integration and with substantivists pointing out constraints.[13]

Both perspectives share a strong interest in the mechanisms and degree of economic integration, which is plausibly regarded as a yardstick of economic development in general: for economies to grow, they have to become more integrated.[14] Again very broadly speaking, the most recent generation of scholarship on the Roman economy has produced two competing visions of the underpinnings of its integration and hence the nature, scale, and sustainability of economic growth. Economic activities that extended beyond the household were framed by two types of relations, relations of the market and relations of domination. Historians of the Roman economy divide on whether they privilege market relations – characterized by trade driven by comparative advantage – or power relations such as tribute and rent-taking and slavery and their economic consequences.

According to market-centered narratives, Roman conquest created favorable preconditions for production and trade. Empire lowered transaction costs by reducing risk, easing the flow of information, and standardizing media of exchange at the same time as it facilitated an expansion of primary production (in farming and mining) that in turn encouraged urbanization, manufacturing, and production for the market. It enabled different regions to capitalize on their comparative advantage in producing goods for exchange. In this scenario, the imperial state plays an important role indirectly, by providing favorable framing conditions, and (in some versions) also directly, by issuing regulations or coinage or by investing in infrastructure that was conducive to trade or, at a later stage, by throttling markets through deleterious intervention. For much of the Roman period, these processes are thought to have created a conglomeration of interdependent markets.[15]

Others question whether market exchange and economic integration would automatically arise in that context. They assign critical importance to the need of the imperial state to process revenue and to the opportunities this created for political and landowning elites. From this perspective, integration was very much driven by tribute and rent collection and by the modes of exchange that it effectively supported. One of the most notable examples of this perspective is the Keynesian "tax-and-trade" model developed by Keith Hopkins: state demands for tax and elite demand for rent and their conversion and transfer impelled reciprocal flows of taxed and traded resources that encouraged urbanization, monetization, and the formation of exchange networks.[16] The counterpart to this model is Chris Wickham's account of the unraveling of the Roman economy, a process he explains with reference to the decline of the fiscal system and the elite network of market-oriented production and long-distance exchange that the state sector had sustained.[17] The most recent incarnation of this approach is Peter Bang's model of tributary surplus mobilization and portfolio capitalism (i.e., power elites' expansion of their economic activities into commercial ventures) that is based on both Roman evidence and explicit analogies to other agrarian empires where similar framing conditions prevailed.[18] In all these models, the Roman economy waxed and waned along with the power of the imperial state.

It would be a mistake to regard these perspectives as mutually exclusive causative interpretations.[19] In the most general terms, it is hard to see how Roman rule could have failed to lower transaction costs in ways that were, at least in principle, conducive to an increase in the volume of exchange. Yet this does not establish that any such development did not critically depend on the redistributive fiscal mechanisms of the state. At the same time, it is important to recognize that these two approaches do not merely represent two complementary sides of the same coin. The question which types of relations were essential or dominant in bringing about observed outcomes is not merely of intellectual interest but of vital importance for understanding the dynamics of Roman economic development and especially its limits and decline.

This debate underlines the pivotal role of comparison, theorizing, and model-building. Divergent modern reconstructions are ultimately shaped by analogies: with post-Roman Europe in the case of market-centered narratives or with other patrimonial empires in the case of coercion-based models. They are also indebted to different theoretical underpinnings and conceptualizations. One way forward that has the potential to bridge the gap between formalist or neo-classical notions of comparative advantage and a benign state and more substantivist or fiscalist models of commercial development is offered by the New Institutional Economics and Economic Sociology.[20] By demonstrating how social and cultural features shape economic activity, they alert us to the overriding significance of historically specific "rules of the game," the incentives and constraints that were instrumental in determining Roman economic development. Students of the Roman economy have recently begun to pay attention to these fields and one can only hope that this trend will continue.[21]

Ecology

Regardless of whether they emphasize markets and comparative advantage or tributary integration and coercion, currently dominant perspectives uniformly privilege human agency. However, we must not forget that economic behavior was embedded in a deep ecological context that constrained actors' choices and shaped outcomes. In marked contrast to the intensity of past and present debates about the institutional determinants of Roman economic development, historians have barely begun to take proper account of ecological factors. We have already noted recent work on the supposed commonalities of Mediterranean economies. Alternatively, one might focus on changes in the distribution and quality of crops and livestock, or explore the impact of soil erosion and deforestation. Due to constraints of space, this section will consider only two fundamental issues, namely the interaction of economy and demography and the role of climate change.[22]

Population is central to the economic history of later historical periods and despite its pervasive neglect by Roman economic historians can be expected to have played an important role in that period as well.[23] Both structural demographic features and population numbers are of great relevance. The former include low levels of overall and health-adjusted life expectancy that necessitated high fertility rates and thus restricted female labor participation, discouraged investment in human capital, and impaired asset management through the imposition of guardianship on orphans. Family and household structures mattered inasmuch as different patterns of marriage and residence – such as nuclear or extended families, age of first marriage, and levels of endogamy – helped condition economic behavior.[24]

The relationship between economic and demographic growth is perhaps the most important problem. If the Roman economy increased its output, it presumably also increased the number of consumers: the production and support of people is the core function of any economy. Although Roman natural population growth is not strictly speaking provable – in the technical sense that serial statistics referring to the same (breeding) population are lacking –, it is both logically compelling and made highly likely by the archaeological record that such a process occurred on a considerable scale. Being able to measure population growth would allow us to gauge extensive economic growth: unfortunately, scholars cannot even agree on the size of the population of Roman Italy, an uncertainty that has serious repercussions for any estimates of the demographic development of the Empire as a whole. Were Roman population numbers empirically known even in bare outlines, we would have a much better sense of the scale and direction of economic development.[25]

The Roman economy would not have been immune to the basic Malthusian mechanisms that applied across pre-modern societies and are set out in Chapter 3. While intensive, per capita growth in output would have encouraged population increases, the latter would eventually have put pressure on scarce resources and may have reversed earlier productivity gains, resulting in a larger population that was not necessarily more affluent than at the beginning of the cycle. At the same time, population pressure would have been an incentive to develop adaptations that made it possible to sustain growth. Technological progress was vital for this latter process, as was the population's desire and capacity for fertility control.[26]

In the most general terms, Malthusian effects are well documented in post-ancient Europe, where we observe a demographic recovery led by economic growth in the High Middle Ages, rising population pressure that was alleviated by the Black Death, a plague-induced demographic contraction that raised real wages and allowed renewed population growth, a process that once again caused real incomes to decline until modern economic development and the fertility transition, which uncoupled demographic from economic growth, provided a final release. Perhaps the biggest unacknowledged question of Roman economic history is whether population pressure was already mounting before the imperial power structure started to unravel or whether the epidemics of the second and third centuries CE provided temporary relief (or instead made matters worse). Empirical data are consistent with the presence of Malthusian mechanisms: real wages rose in the wake of epidemics and body height, a marker of physiological well-being, declined under Roman rule but recovered afterward. This suggests that in the long run, the Roman economy was unable to overcome fundamental demographic constraints on intensive economic growth.[27]

Demographic developments were also sensitive to climatic conditions. Comparative evidence shows that population growth is correlated with climate change in terms of temperature, precipitation, and the overall stability of weather regimes. The current surge of interest in past climatic variation has already begun to generate a growing amount of data pertaining to the Roman period. Even so, for the time being the only thing that we say with confidence is that the complexity of the evidence does not support a single straightforward reconstruction.[28] With this caveat in mind, it nevertheless seems very likely that the Roman Empire matured during a warm period comparable to the so-called Medieval Warm Period that coincided with massive population growth. An enormous variety of proxies has been brought to bear on this question, including tree-ring width, tree-line movement, glacier movement, analysis of stable isotopes and mercury deposits as well as pollen, algae, and mollusks recovered from ice cores and stalagmites and peat and lake sediment deposits. While no synthesis currently exists, a substantial series of data sets indicates an impressive convergence of trends all over Eurasia. These findings, summarized on the web site that accompanies this volume, reveal a warm period centered on the first century CE. Although the respective ranges vary by location and type of data, on average this period commenced in the second century BCE and ended in the third century CE.[29]

By increasing cultivable land and yields, warming can be expected to have had a positive effect on population growth, especially in the continental European parts of the Roman Empire.[30] The overall picture was of course more complex: in the southern and eastern reaches of the Empire, precipitation levels would have played a more important role than temperature. Once again, conditions were mostly favorable: while the Iberian peninsula, North Africa, and the Levant appear to have been wetter than today, the central Mediterranean may have experienced more arid conditions.[31] Climatic instability has already been observed for the third century CE but became more widespread in late antiquity, whereas the late antique cooling trend peaked in the sixth and seventh centuries CE, thus coinciding with a nadir of economic development in Europe.[32] The significance of climate for the evolution of the Roman Empire and its economic basis must not be underrated. Without wishing to advocate environmental determinism, there can be little doubt that climate history ought to occupy a much more central role in the study of the Roman economy than it has done so far.

Understanding the Roman economy

Overdetermination of outcomes and divergence of outcomes are among the most serious challenges to our understanding of the Roman economy. As for the former, the Roman economy can readily be said to have expanded for multiple and largely interconnected reasons. In Republican Italy, empire created capital inflows, checks on natural growth that were counterbalanced by slave imports, and novel opportunities for commercial exchange, elite enrichment, and violent redistribution of assets to commoners. In the long run, empire also yielded benefits for subject populations: peace reduced transaction costs, turned the entire Mediterranean into an 'inner sea,' and improved the ratio of natural endowments to labor; tributary integration mobilized resources and enabled portfolio capitalism; knowledge transfers improved productivity; and previously underexploited mines produced bullion that not only supported monetization but also enabled imports from beyond the empire. All these developments coincided with a climate optimum that sustained production and productivity growth and, at least for a while, with an absence of pandemics that might have weakened state power or commercial connectivity. In view of all this, it is hard to see how a substantial economic expansion could possibly have failed to occur.

This outcome was overdetermined in the sense that it was favored by numerous convergent factors. Although it seems plausible that these factors interacted and reinforced one another, we cannot simply assume that each of them was necessary or significant in producing observed outcomes. A more parsimonious model would be desirable for a number of reasons. It would help us avoid a profusion of alleged causes, such as those invoked to account for the so-called "Great Divergence" between modern European economies and the rest of the world, all of which are superficially plausible but rarely measured in terms of their relative significance.[33] If we do not know which factors mattered most in making the Roman economy grow, we are also unable to understand the reasons for its abatement.

Just as in the case of economic growth, multiple factors may have precipitated decline. Demographic growth could have raised Malthusian pressures and curbed the potential for further intensive growth, creating involution and what has been called a "low-equilibrium trap." Conversely, epidemics, which would have mitigated population pressure, could have undermined state power, which would have adversely affected economic integration inasmuch as it was sustained by the fiscal sector. Challenges to imperial rule would have raised protection costs. Climatic conditions became less stable or favorable. Whole lists of possible causes come to mind, reminiscent of the 210 different reasons (in)famously proposed for the fall of the Western Roman Empire.[34]

In order to understand both the expansion and the abatement of the Roman economy, choices have to be made. Not all explanations are equally valid. Some of them may not be compatible with others; others still may converge but need not be similarly significant. Some may only be relevant in conjunction with others: for instance, a favorable climate was likely to sustain demographic growth even in the absence of an imperial state, whereas certain forms of exchange may not have been feasible without the latter. Choices must be made on the basis of the empirical record but also, and critically, on the basis of what we expect to have mattered, an expectation that must be informed by historical analogies and social science theories to be at all defensible. Most important of all, explanations must ultimately cohere in logically consistent models. These requirements make for a challenging agenda, and go a long way in explaining the lack of recent syntheses that seek to take in the whole wide arc of Roman economic development.[35]

Diversity of outcomes poses another major challenge. Economic trends need not have matched trends in human welfare. Study of the Roman economy does not by itself reveal much about its impact on the participants unless we are prepared blithely to equate human well-being with mean income. Increasingly elaborate indices are being devised to measure human development in the world today, and historians need to be aware of these efforts if they want to make progress on their second key objective: not just to understand the dynamics of the Roman economy but also to understand what it accomplished and how it related to other forms of development.[36]

Roman economic history is rich in apparent contradictions. Violence, unleashed in campaigns of conquest and civil wars, was undeniably an evil that caused great suffering and dislocation, yet it also mobilized resources and protected real incomes by curtailing demographic growth. Slavery was another evil that fostered inequality but also spurred rationalization and productivity growth: it could simultaneously increase output and skew consumption, simultaneously benefit and harm society. The failure of the Roman Republic is usually viewed as a time of crisis: yet it also coincided with unprecedented economic development in the core of the Empire, and while the ruling class may have been the main beneficiaries of this process, the wealthy also contributed to the coercive redistribution to commoners prompted by the exigencies of civil war. Conversely, the prolonged peace of the first quarter-millennium of the imperial monarchy is usually considered as a period of prosperity: yet stability also facilitated rising inequality by allowing elites safely to accumulate assets and depressed real incomes by encouraging demographic expansion. Epidemics interfered with economic activities by disrupting trust-based commercial networks but also alleviated population pressure. Urbanization was beneficial in that it encouraged division of labor and human capital formation but also detrimental by boosting density-dependent diseases, which in turn could be beneficial by curtailing population growth.[37]

These events and trends do not contradict each other: they simply add up to the intricate dynamics that are typical of all historical processes. Awareness of these natural complexities will help us overcome the all too common notion that different elements of human development move in tandem: that the Roman combination of imperial peace and a larger population and greater economic output somehow represented an optimal state of affairs. Comparative evidence is vital in suggesting that this was probably not the case: real incomes of workers could fall as GDP grew; human bodies could shrink as the economy expanded. Tabulating the many ways in which the artifacts of the Roman economy were bigger, better, or more numerous than before or after is simply not sufficient to show that conditions were generally better: "intensification should not automatically and exclusively be identified with increasing prosperity and success." Conversely, evidence of abatement is not necessarily a sign of wholesale deterioration: it merely denotes change in the configuration of land and labor, of extraction and consumption, of local autonomy and interregional integration. The story of the Roman economy is not a simple story of rise and fall: it is a complex interplay of different determinants of human welfare in which economic output and its distribution played an important role. Economic history must be incorporated into the study of well-being to be at all worth doing.[38]

Parsimonious causal explanation and appreciation of diverse outcomes are basic requirements for being able to draw on Roman economic history to address bigger questions. Which kind of environment was more conducive to economic growth and human development more generally – large empires or fragmented political ecologies? And is this even a meaningful question? Much scholarship on the Roman economy conveys the impression that universal empire was a 'good' thing and its demise a 'bad' ending, whereas accounts of the ancient Greek economy or that of early modern Europe tend to reflect a rather different worldview. The study of the Roman economy as one of the most successful traditional imperial economies in history has a lot to contribute to our understanding of such broader issues. Current debates about the relative merits of the institutional foundations of Western economic development and the alternative 'Beijing consensus' suggest that such questions are not of purely historical interest. Roman economic history stands to make a contribution well beyond the confines of a long vanished past.

THE STRUCTURE OF THIS VOLUME

This is not a history of the Roman economy. For a chronological survey, readers are encouraged to consult the *Cambridge Economic History of the Greco-Roman World* (henceforth *CEHGRW*), published in 2007, which devotes eleven chapters to the Roman period. In addition, it contains five thematic chapters that discuss important determinants of economic performance in both the Greek and Roman worlds: ecology, demography, household and gender, law and economic institutions, and technology.[39] In order to avoid replication and overlap, these topics are not separately dealt with in the present volume. Instead, this companion expands the thematic approach that was taken, in a much more limited way, in the opening section of *CEHGRW*. Focusing exclusively on the Roman economy, the following fifteen chapters cover a wide range of closely interrelated themes and conclude with an essay on the aftermath of the Roman imperial economy, touching on a period that was beyond the remit of *CEHGRW*. Thanks to this setup, the present volume is meant to serve not only as a companion to the study of the Roman economy but likewise as a companion to the predominantly chronological narrative in *CEHGRW*. While both books were designed as free-standing projects, they should ideally be used and read side by side. By themselves, neither a chronological format nor a thematic focus that cuts across different periods and regions is capable of satisfying the need for a comprehensive and systematic assessment of the Roman economy. Only the combination of both approaches makes it possible to explore this topic in sufficient depth.

This volume opens with a section on theoretical perspectives, both ancient and modern. A discussion of ancient economic thought contextualizes the Roman experience within broader intellectual traditions (Chapter 2). Modern economic theory is introduced by explaining core tenets of Neoclassical Economics and illustrating them with reference to examples from the Roman period (Chapter 3) and by establishing the critical importance of human capital in economic development (Chapter 4). These two chapters should be read in conjunction with Bruce Frier's and Dennis Kehoe's chapter on legal and economic institutions in *CEHGRW*. Together, these brief discussions add up to the most substantial introduction to the relevance of modern economic theory to the study of the Roman economy that is currently available. (Needless to say, much more is needed.)

Much of this volume is concerned with the productive and distributive processes of the Roman period. Chattel slavery receives special attention, not because it was the quantitatively predominant form of labor (which it was not) but because it was one of the features that made the Roman economy specifically 'Roman' by distinguishing it from most other pre-modern economies (Chapter 5). Chapter 6 explores labor relations based on contract rather than force, represented by tenancy and wage labor.[40] The discussion then moves on to the production of goods, starting with the extraction of raw materials and energy generation (Chapter 7) and continuing with food production (Chapter 8) and manufacturing (Chapter 9). Among distributive mechanisms, predation is given pride of place (Chapter 10): an integral feature of early economies that to a significant extent relied on plunder, tribute, and rent-taking, it is all too often marginalized in treatments of economic history. Chapter 11 sheds light on the logistical foundations of the Roman economy and its circuits of exchange and integration, and the specific underpinnings and characteristics of Roman urbanism are discussed in Chapter 12. Exchange and extraction were greatly facilitated by monetization, the subject of Chapter 13. This section concludes with a 'forum on trade' (Chapter 14): long a particularly contentious issue in the study of the Roman economy (see above), it benefits from the diverse perspectives offered by five experts.

The final section considers outcomes, defined in two ways: as the benefits the Roman economy delivered to its participants in terms of physical well-being, arguably the most tangible manifestation of economic development (Chapter 15); and as the ultimate end product of Roman economy, that is, its contraction or disintegration in the wake of the failure of most of the Roman Empire in late antiquity (Chapter 16).

Our goal is not merely to provide information and interpretation but also to do justice to the manifold facets and complexities of Roman economic history. While ample room is given to the expansion of production, exchange, and consumption that is suggestive of Roman economic growth (Chapters 7, 8, 13, and 14 are good examples), we also keep track of the coercive basis of economic development (Chapters 5 and 10) and the limitations on the formation of capital and markets (Chapters 4, 9, and 12) and address the failures of the system (Chapters 15 and 16). All these elements were essential ingredients of the complex story of the Roman economic efflorescence, of its impetus, scale, and limits. Weaving all these strands together into a coherent argument that takes account of all the many moving parts is a task modern scholarship has yet to accomplish.

Supplementary material on the web site

Supplements to Chapters 1, 3, and 8 can be found on this volume's website at www.stanford.edu/~scheidel/CCRE.htm. Several footnotes in this print edition refer readers to these materials.

Notes

1 The three classic works of the twentieth century are Rostovtzeff 1957 (originally published in 1926), still the most sweeping narrative account; Frank (ed.) 1933–40, a rich five-volume survey of economic development in different regions; and Finley 1999 (originally published in 1973), the most incisive analysis of the nature of the Greek and Roman economies. See also De Martino 1979–80, regrettably never made available in English. In addition, Jones 1964 covers the late Roman economy, and McCormick 2001 and Wickham 2005 trace and seek to explain post-Roman transitions. Chapters 18–28 of Scheidel, Morris and Saller (eds.) 2007 are devoted to the Roman economy, which will also be covered by many of the chapters in Bresson, Lo Cascio and Velde (eds.) forthcoming. There are no recent monographical surveys in English (but see Garnsey and Saller 1987: 41–103) or comprehensive systematic bibliographies; for introductory surveys in other languages, see most recently Drexhage, Konen and Ruffing 2002; Andreau 2010. Single-authored collected studies are a popular format: noteworthy examples include Jones 1974; Duncan-Jones 1982, 1990; Lo Cascio 2009; Harris 2011a; Temin forthcoming a.

For surveys of pertinent scholarship, see Harris 1993; Andreau 2002; Bowman and Wilson 2009. Scheidel, Morris and Saller (eds.) 2007: 769–917 gather a substantial bibliography, and see also Bowman and Wilson 2009: 69–84 for scholarship more specifically on the Roman economy.

2 For the study of proxies, see especially Bowman and Wilson 2009. A number of recent discussions reveal the range, potential, and problems of particular types of proxy data: King 1999; Greene 2000; Kron 2002; Wilson 2002; MacKinnon 2004; De Callataÿ 2005; Jongman 2007a, 2007b; Silver 2007; Scheidel 2009a; Wilson 2009a, 2009b, forthcoming b; Launaro 2011.

3 For institutions, see below, in the second part of the fourth section. For literacy, see Harris 1989; for human capital in general, see below, Chapter 4.

4 The limitations of existing studies are underscored by their divergent results: see Hopkins 1980: 117–20; Goldsmith 1984; Temin 2006a; Maddison 2007: 11–68; Milanovic, Lindert and Williamson 2007: 64–9; Bang 2008: 86–91; Lo Cascio and Malanima 2009; Scheidel and Friesen 2009.

5 Work of this nature has mostly focused on ancient Greece: see Morris 2004, 2005; Ober 2010. Slavery and wealth in the United States: Wright 2006: 60. General changes in living standards at the end of the Roman period: Ward-Perkins 2005. For the complexities of measuring living standards in later periods, cf. Allen, Bengtsson, and Dribe (eds.) 2005. See also below, in the third part of the fourth section.

6 Real wages: Allen 2009b; Scheidel 2010. Nutrition: e.g., King 1999; MacKinnon 2004. Physical wellbeing: see below, Chapter 15.

7 Work that puts the Roman economy in context includes Goldsmith 1987; Jones 2000; Maddison 2007; Milanovic, Lindert and Williamson 2007; Morris 2010. Among more technical studies, Geoffrey Kron's work stands out for its strong comparative dimension.

8 See Frank and Thompson 2006 for a world-systems approach specifically to this period; but cf. Chase-Dunn, Hall and Turchin 2007. For exogenous forces, see below, in the second part of the fourth section.

9 The work in question is Horden and Purcell 2000; for debate, see especially Shaw 2001 and the contributions to Harris (ed.) 2005.

10 Pleket 1990, 1993a stresses premodern continuities. For criticism, see Bang 2008: 34–6. Temin 2004a; Rathbone and Temin 2008 compare Roman and early modern European financial institutions.

11 Rome and India: Bang 2008. Han China: Scheidel 2009b. For the Song economy, see Elvin 1973: 111–99; Jones 2000: 73–84; and especially Morris 2010 for the notion that premodern social development peaked in the Roman Empire and Song China, an observation that invites comparative analysis. For the inclusion of the Ottoman case in a three-way comparison with Rome and Mughal India, see http://tec.saxo.ku.dk/. Greek city-states: Ober 2010.

12 Hatcher and Bailey 2001, especially 11 for the three 'supermodels' and the quote. For the relative neglect of population in Roman economic history, see below. The only recent Marxist approach is de Ste Croix 1981.

13 For brief discussions, see Ian Morris in Finley 1999: XI-XXIII; Scheidel, Morris and Saller 2007: 2–5; Bang 2008: 17–36. Nafissi 2005 is now the most detailed general study.

14 For integration and growth (including decline) as the central themes of Roman economic history, see the mission statement of the 'Oxford Roman Economy Project' in Bowman and Wilson 2009: 15–53.

15 This perspective dates back, via Rostovtzeff 1957, to Eduard Meyer's work in 1896. Freyberg 1989 is the most sophisticated study in this vein, and while the most explicit recent statements are (not coincidentally) found in the work of two economists, Peter Temin and Morris Silver (most notably Temin 2001 and Silver 2007), a market-centered perspective is currently (at least implicitly) pervasive: see Bang 2008: 26–36 for discussion; and cf. also below, Chapter 15. For the underlying economics, see below, Chapter 3.

16 Hopkins 1980, 1995/6, and see also 2009. For criticism, see, e.g., Duncan-Jones 1990: 30–58; Silver 2008. Cf. Jongman 2006: 247–50 for the possibility of an alternative mechanism of economic integration (i.e, the geographical expansion of elite holdings) that was likewise spurred by taxation.

17 Wickham 2005, and see already Wickham 1994: 77–98; McCormick 2001: 25–119. Recent critiques include Haldon 2008 and Shaw 2008.

18 Bang 2007, 2008. Compare Silver 2009a for a critique that fails to engage with the key positive claims of Bang's model.

19 Lo Cascio 1991b seeks to combine both perspectives.

20 New Institutional Economics: North 1981 and 1990; Eggertson 1990; Furubotn and Richter 1997; Williamson 2000; Brousseau and Glachant (eds.) 2008 (especially Joskow 2008 and Nye 2008). Greif 2006 offers the most extensive application of NIE to premodern economies. Hass 2007 and the contributions to Smelser and Swedberg (eds.) 2005a provide the best introduction to Economic Sociology (among the latter, see especially Dobbin 2005, Nee 2005, and Smelser and Swedberg 2005b). Granovetter 1985 is a classic statement on the "embeddedness" (Polanyi 1957) of economic action in social relations; see also Granovetter 1992. Cf. Bourdieu 2000 for the cultural dimension of economic action.

21 For NIE and ancient economies, see Maucourant 1996; Lo Cascio 2006c; Frier and Kehoe 2007; Bang 2009a; for the economic sociology of the ancient world, see Morris and Manning 2005, and cf. also Verboven 2002; Maucourant 2004.

22 Sallares 2007 briefly introduces the ecological context of the Roman economy. Sallares 1991 is the most ambitious study, centered on ancient Greece but also touching on Rome. For the Mediterranean environment, see above, in the third section; for crops, see below, Chapter 8; for deforestation, see Harris 2011b.

23 See now Scheidel 2007a; and cf. Saller 2007 on household and gender. See also Hin forthcoming.

24 For living conditions, see below, Chapter 15. Demographic effects on households and investment: Saller 2007 and below, Chapter 4. Given that the intensity of infectious disease appears to be a determinant of cognitive ability (Eppig, Fincher and Thornhill 2010), the high disease loads documented for the Roman world can be expected to have had an adverse effect on human capital formation. Household types: Scheidel 2007a: 70–2. Evidence suggestive of relatively late Roman first marriage is relevant in this context but may be limited to urban settings: see Scheidel 2007c, qualifying work by Richard Saller and Brent Shaw.

25 Scheidel 2008a critiques the debate about the size of the population of Roman Italy. See also Lo Cascio and Malanima 2005 for the relationship between population and economy in Roman Italy.

26 For the interrelation of demographic constraints and incentives, see Lee 1986a, 1986b; Wood 1998; and the summary in Scheidel 2007a: 50–66. For technology and the Roman economy, see Greene 2000; Wilson 2002; Lo Cascio (ed.) 2006a; Schneider 2007. (The rate of diffusion of technological innovation is the critical variable: Persson 1988: 127–8.) For constraints on human capital formation, see below, Chapter 4. Scheidel 2007a: 66–74 considers fertility control. There was no Roman fertility transition: Caldwell 2004.

27 Real wages were generally low for unskilled workers (Scheidel 2010: 427–36, 444–7, 453) but increased in response to demographic contractions: see Scheidel 2002, forthcoming c (Antonine Plague); Findlay and Lundahl 2006; Scheidel 2010: 448–9, 456–7 (Justinianic Plague). Cf. Pamuk 2007 for analogous effects of the Black Death. For trends in human stature, see below, Chapter 15. Epidemics as a source of problems: Zelener 2003; Little (ed.) 2007. For a tentative Malthusian model of the Roman imperial economy, see Scheidel 2009a: 67–70; and cf. also Malanima forthcoming for a simple model of Roman growth and its limits.

28 Ljungqvist 2009, a survey of 71 studies of climatic variation from 1 to 2000 CE, conveys a good sense of the amount of variation among data samples.

29 See Table 1 and the references in the Supplement on the website, www.stanford.edu/~scheidel/CCRE.htm. Ljungqvist 2010: 345 fig.3 offers the most recent synthetic graph.

30 For comparative evidence, see, e.g., Galloway 1986; Koepke and Baten 2005a; Redman et al. 2007; Zhang et al. 2007.

31 See the references in the Supplement on the website.

32 See Haas 2006 on the third century CE, n.31 above on late antiquity, and Table 1 in the Supplement on the web site for late Roman and post-ancient cooling.

33 Allen 2009a exemplifies this approach: see esp. 106–31 for simulations of the relative significance of different variables.

34 "High-equilibrium trap:" Scheidel 2007a: 55–6. Two hundred and ten causes: Demandt 1984.

35 Bang 2007 may be the most ambitious attempt since Hopkins 1980; 1995/6. Cf. also Banaji 2001 for late antiquity. The end of the Roman economy has been well explained by Wickham 2005. For a different perspective, cf. Schiavone 2000. Yet all of these works neglect environmental factors.

36 Broad indices include the Human Development Index of the United Nations and the Gross National Happiness Index pioneered by Bhutan. Cf. also the 'Capabilities Approach' advocated by Nussbaum 2000.

37 Roman Republic: Scheidel 2007b. Demography: see above, in the second part of the fourth section, and below, Chapter 15. Turchin and Nefedov 2009 offer a wide-ranging survey of historical 'secular cycles' of peace and population growth that bred instability.

38 For pertinent comparative data, see Allen, Bengtsson and Dribe (2005), with Scheidel 2009a: 63–7. Intensification: Horden and Purcell 2000: 265 (quote). Intensification may well be interpreted as a response to pressures rather as evidence of net gains: note the contrasting perspectives of Chapters 8 and 15. For peace raising inequality, see Jongman 2006: 247–50.

39 Scheidel, Morris and Saller (eds.) 2007: 15–171 (topics), 487–768 (Roman economy).

40 Family labor within the household, the predominant form of labor in the ancient world, does not receive a separate chapter: the evidence is relatively poor, and it is unclear to what extent this type of labor in this period was distinctively 'Roman:' for debate, see, e.g., De Ligt 1990; Kron 2008b; Silver 2008.

Part I

Theory

2: Roman economic thought

Gloria Vivenza

The history of economic thought, rooted in (moral) philosophy and jurisprudence, is readily analyzed using general principles that equally apply to ancient and modern thought. It seems almost a platitude to say that ancient sensibilities differed from our own, or even from those of medieval Europe, shaped as it was by Christianity, and that we should not lose sight of this. This observation, however, is far from redundant considering that a great deal of (pseudo)history of thought has been done by adapting the work of one author to a theoretical grid worked out by another,[1] sometimes in a later period.[2]

The Romans, like the other ancients, lacked a systematic view of economics, either as an abstract theory or as an activity independent of politics. Though this may appear an endorsement of the Polanyian conception of economics "embedded" in other categories, the picture has now become more complex. After the traditional division into "primitivists" and "modernizers," and Finley's "new orthodoxy," the recent institutional approach raises fresh doubts. The basic principle that institutions are involved in economics as soon as transactions reach a relevant size (and cost) is acceptable; but to attribute "the fundamental assumption of scarcity"[3] of neoclassical theory to ancient economic thought appears excessive. Only in modern thought is the postulate of scarcity required to define an economic good;[4] at most, antecedents may be found in the medieval debates on value that inspired the analysis of exchange, reflected in the formulation of concepts such as *indigentia* (i.e., wants),[5] an idea destined to play an important role in later economic thought.

Ancient and modern approaches should therefore be kept distinct, yet implicit analogies between ancient and contemporary issues are sometimes evident even in the titles of academic works,[6] or in analogies such as the one drawn between the economic "model" of imperial Rome and the United States after the fall of the Soviet empire.[7] For centuries, economics was treated from a conceptual point of view as a moral discipline, one in some aspects related to jurisprudence at the practical level, and in this field the Romans were unrivalled.

An idea of how the Romans really valued certain economic activities can be gained from well-known facts, or from the policies they pursued. The notion, Greek in origin, that the Romans "officially" asserted the superiority of agriculture and were contemptuous of manufacturing and commercial activities contrasts both with the commercial law of the *Corpus Iuris*, which is clearly incompatible with policies hostile to activities of this kind,[8] and with attitudes that emerge indirectly from accounts of everyday life.[9]

True to the cliché that people who act don't brood and write treatises, the Romans apparently did not formulate any economic theories, yet their economic legislation reveals a mastery of the discipline on the one hand and is relatively free of prejudice and moralistic considerations on the other. The entire Roman legal system was designed, in reality, to preserve economic relations.[10] I believe that even these few clues reveal the importance of the Romans' contribution to economics: they had the ability to conceptualize and define; a strong tendency to systematize, albeit more from an empirical than an abstract point of view; and finally a solid cultural base: though derived in part from the Greeks, it was readily adapted to the traditions and needs of the Romans.

It would, perhaps, be more interesting to study in depth why the Greeks more than the Romans elaborated the analytical aspects of the discipline, and to go beyond contrasts between the "scientific spirit" of the Greeks and the "practical spirit" of the Romans. On the concept of value, for example, the Greeks conveyed to posterity the sophisticated observations of Aristotle[11] while the Romans offered the trivial *valet quantum vendi potest* of the Digest.[12] Both were destined to have a future, but there is no space to pursue this further here, other than to reiterate that in Greek thought certain fundamental economic concepts were expressed and defined both in theoretical terms (the theories of value, exchange, and price) and in practical terms (the best known example being Xenophon's *Oikonomikos*). It appears that the Romans allowed themselves to be influenced more by the practical than the theoretical literature, and did in fact write a number of treatises on agriculture and household administration. Not surprisingly, these works dominated the field even in the modern age: until the eighteenth century, the European ruling classes were made up of the very (aristocratic) landowners to whom the treatises were addressed. The same is true of the fundamental conception of economics as a private matter, an idea for which Plato is responsible and which was handed down through the centuries until the early texts on the economics of the "state" (political economy) appeared in the sixteenth century.[13]

Yet the Romans could well have written on economics. Claude Nicolet[14] has observed that Roman administration entailed copious documentation which, had it survived, would have been the joy of economic historians: provincial governors' reports, censuses of people and property; archives relating to direct and indirect taxation; customs registers; various types of accounting records. But there were no handbooks of trade or economics in a world that produced plenty of technical treatises.[15]

It was therefore left to modern scholars to produce an essay on Roman accounting methods,[16] as well as many other aspects of Roman economics such as credit and monetary techniques.[17] These works attest to the well-constructed and complex organization of an economy inspired by rationalistic empiricism and perhaps also – though caution is required – by the Roman military genius that must have developed forms of planning, organization, and resource management.

In the extant "theoretical" material, it is not always possible to isolate economic elements from moral, social, and political aspects, although this is true of all pre-industrial economic thought. In the case of the Romans, it is difficult to fully comprehend certain principles without taking into account factors such as the political character of the land regime or the military origin of certain aspects of economic organization. For example, the original bond between the farmer-soldier and his plot of land developed as part of a colonial policy, and resulted in the gradual and relentless seizure of land, albeit according to different criteria in different places.[18]

In a previous work[19] I have highlighted, among other themes, an agrarian approach underlying Roman economic thought, in the sense that all other wealth-generating activities, though practised widely by social classes in a position to do so, were considered discreditable if not downright ignoble. Exceptions were few in number. This is an old prejudice, one that in some ways survived to the cusp of the modern age: yet how much of its characteristically Roman and Republican essence persisted under the monarchy? In other words, the transformation of the citizen-soldier-elector (and originally small landowner) had already begun in the Republican period. Citizenship was retained and indeed progressively extended, through concessions granted for various reasons,[20] to all the inhabitants of the Empire by 212 CE,[21] though by then this no longer had the same meaning. The right to vote was lost with the advent of the Empire,[22] citizens become subjects, and despite the Augustan compromise that ably maintained a semblance of Republican institutions, the political structure had clearly changed. And not only the political structure: law came to be enacted by the administrative apparatus of the state, rather than by specialist jurists, the guardians of the discipline;[23] literary culture transformed into rhetoric certain genres that had carried a rather different weight in the past: the difference between Cicero's orations and those of the imperial period is significant in terms of their capacity to influence political choices.[24] This transformation was justified in abstract terms of peace and order, or even in more concrete terms in the sense that by then the vastness of the Empire demanded a change in the nature of power.[25]

Credit is due to Paul Veyne for underlining how the undisputed virtual superiority of agriculture and landownership was the product of a dual strategy involving security and profit: only landowners stood to gain on both fronts. Sporadic participation in mercantile activity had no impact on the social structure (the author rightly notes that only landed property qualified for the census).[26]

This supremacy of the countryside, even in a context where various forms of economic activity had reached significant levels, is undoubtedly a feature that distinguishes the Roman economy from those that followed, in which the most dynamic sector invariably prevailed, for instance in the late medieval " bourgeois" city-states (Florence, Bruges, and Antwerp).[27] At Rome, despite classes tied to commerce, manufacturing, and even the earliest forms of finance, landed wealth continued to represent the model, and with it the land-owning classes. The prestige of the *patres*, who had already been required to avoid (formal) involvement in commercial activities in 300 BCE,[28] once again needed to be defended from accusations of usury in 300 CE: senators were forbidden to lend money for interest, at least in certain periods.[29]

Considerable scholarly attention has been dedicated to the *villa rustica*, in the sense of an agricultural concern engaged not only in production but also in trade and possibly some form of manufacturing activity.[30] Archaeological data have been supplemented by clues from the great Latin agronomists, making it possible to reconstruct the theory and praxis of Roman farming, a profitable, well-developed activity integrated with other economic sectors. Hence the almost physiocratic claim of Pliny the Elder that all wealth derives from land comes as no surprise (*HN* 18.1; 2.154 ff.). Yet his attitude remains that of an ancient Roman, careful not to spend when he can avoid it, and opposed to the large estates.[31] As for Pliny the Younger, perhaps he did not speak out against the *latifundia* as openly as his uncle had done, yet we know that he was not in favor of extensive properties either, preferring small holdings in diverse locations that were not exposed to the same risks and offered a greater variety of terrain (*Epist.* 3.19.4).[32] He commended an interesting assortment of economic and aesthetic reasons to his friends: the farm should be of an appropriate size, "just enough to pleasantly disengage his thoughts from other things, but not enough to give him any worry"; he repeats the concept at *Epist.* 1.24: "learned schoolmen . . . ought only to have just sufficient land to enable them to get rid of headaches, delight their eyes, walk lazily round their boundary paths, make one beaten track for themselves, get to know all their vines and count their trees."

The *De Re Rustica*[33] treatises demonstrate that the Romans were conscious of the economic importance of the family-run enterprise, of its relations with the market, and of the role of the family as custodian, guardian, but also producer of wealth, particularly considering that from a legal standpoint slaves belonged to the family (*familia*). Importantly, as has recently been observed, this was the only type of treatise to assign a significant role to women.[34] There is no need to resurrect the old argument about the subordination of women or the well-known fact that Roman society was patriarchal. Rather, it is perhaps relevant to observe that the treatises taught to command,[35] or rather to direct people, together with managing wealth, and hence transferred to the modern age the figure of the head of the household as the manager and administrator of property, endowed with authority over persons and things. Nevertheless, some change can be seen between Cato and Columella despite the common agricultural theme: the concept of saving, for example, is considerably more restricted in Cato's work than in Columella's, the latter being more favorably disposed towards productive spending.[36]

In terms of relations between economic sectors, traditional attitudes remained firmly ingrained. Commercial activities took place on a broad front, one that was unified politically but not economically;[37] policies cannot be described as entirely liberal, even leaving aside questions of provisioning.[38] It seems incorrect to assert that commercial activities were never taxed until the time of Constantine:[39] the *centesima rerum venalium* was established at the dawn of the Empire.[40] It is true that few real barriers to trade survived, but those that did were deeply rooted in traditional culture. Indeed, it was since the time of Cato the Elder that the related interests of agriculture and commerce had brought to light the unique contrast, or rather discrepancy, between agricultural ideology and commercial vocation. It is well-known that Cato, though a traditionalist and an opponent of luxury, engaged in trade and lent for interest notwithstanding his criticism of usury. The important thing was that lending was not practised at a professional level: however, it was readily accepted as an activity to supplement agricultural income, and at times openly encouraged and considered almost preferable to mercantile activity.[41] In general terms, attitudes towards the economic foundations of existence, like attitudes towards work and the professions, did not change with the transition from Republic to Empire.

The literature on slave labor has witnessed considerable efforts on the part of politically oriented historiography,[42] and in the 1970s and 1980s it was not uncommon for the agricultural enterprises that I have referred to above to be defined 'slave villas.' Historians subsequently showed that the supply of labour to the *villa rustica* did not derive exclusively from slavery,[43] and argued that the contribution of free labor to other sectors should not be overlooked either.[44] Nevertheless, the Roman experience, with free men deprived of the opportunity of regular work on account of frequent wars and replaced by an abundant supply of slaves directed to agriculture and other activities, created a vision of a Republican and High Imperial economy resting to a large extent on the shoulders of slaves.

The related question of the presumed connection between technological stagnation and slave labor cannot be treated here in detail: this is an issue that has attracted a lot of attention and is not easily resolved, even though one now encounters a tendency to reject such an equation.[45]

Disdain for manual labour can certainly be attributed to both of the classical civilizations, and it may be unnecessary to recall the well-known Aristotelian distinction between men born to be masters and men born to be slaves,[46] a notion whereby slavery was, to a certain extent, taken for granted and legitimated. However, the Romans always showed respect for the work of the farmer, even if with economic progress landownership and labor took separate paths.[47] Agriculture had long been closely linked to a form of not exclusively agrarian technical expertise: land surveying, a technique that remained unrivalled until the modern land registries of the nineteenth century, bears witness to the Romans' unique approach to land and property. Established, paradoxically, to identify land that was *not* liable to pay tax,[48] it soon came to be used for the purposes of taxation in the provinces. It ended up producing a cornerstone of modern taxation: cadastral parcels unrelated to land ownership and landowner, associated with the reign of Diocletian. The link between political power and agricultural land reclamation was equally evident: the rapid increase in the availability of land that went hand in hand with the procurement of slaves was largely completed by the onset of imperial period. At that point, it was a question of organizing these holdings. To judge by their reflections upon law and economics (or what remains of them), the Romans realized that they were faced with a new situation, even in terms of manpower.

The Romans employed slaves in positions of prominence without undue concerns about status; properly freed, a slave became a Roman citizen.[49] The origins of Rome, after all, called for a massive presence of slaves; it is worth citing P. M. Martin: "Quel peuple en effet revendique d'avoir été constitué à l'origine par le rebut des autres?"[50] commenting on Livy's claim that, upon its foundation, Rome became a refuge for free and slaves from neighboring peoples (1.8.5–6; cf. also Plut. *Rom.* 9.3). It is no surprise that numerous sources refer to slaves as economic agents with contractual power, wielded on behalf of their owners.[51] Similarly, the figure of the *servus quasi colonus*, in other words the slave capable of independently managing a plot of land,[52] reveals a good deal about the less than completely subordinate position of such individuals. Despite their status as "objects" or instruments, as Aristotle would say, slaves performed functions of great responsibility in the Roman world, which grew further in importance in the imperial period.

The singularity of Roman slavery as an institution is significant: the slave was not *sui iuris* (i.e., legally competent), he could not perform any legally valid act, no more than a child of three, to use an example closer to our sensitivity. To the many explanations that have been offered, I would add that, despite their organizational genius, the Romans considered the running of the economy a *service*, a task to be delegated to designated categories of actors rather than to be performed directly. Thus slaves were afforded the legal power to perform duties from which their owners were to be relieved in order to devote themselves to other matters.

It is not easy to know to what extent slave labor replaced free labor; the related literature is endless, and prone to interesting mutations.[53] Here I want to stress only that ancient authors who address this topic tend to endorse the view that slave labor was unprofitable, or almost so. Writers of the Republican period already distinguished between the use of slave and free labor, albeit in a way that baffles the modern reader.[54] As for Columella and Pliny the Elder, both deplored slave labor,[55] but not for economic reasons: they longed for days gone by, when farming was the task (and the pride) of Roman citizens, before it had been entrusted to criminals, that is, the slaves of the *ergastula*. And we wonder, says Pliny the Elder (*HN* 18.19–21), that we do not obtain the same profit as when the land literally "enjoyed" being cultivated by heroes!

Recommendations for the humane treatment of slaves abound in the literature.[56] Pliny the Younger did not use slaves in plough stocks on any of his holdings but at the same time made it known that nobody else used them either in the part of the country where he was at that moment, namely in Tuscany (*Epist.*, 3.19.7). He also refers to his habit of freeing sick slaves[57] and allowing them to make a will.[58]

On the question of how the Roman world judged slavery,[59] suffice it to say that since Greek times slavery had been treated as a matter of subordination, with little distinction drawn between a slave laborer and a free man compelled to work to support himself: both, after all, obeyed orders. Aristotle defined the situation by asserting that the only difference between a free worker and a slave is that the former has several masters, the latter only one (*Pol.* 1278a11–13). Even the principle, upheld by Cicero, that slavery is a blessing to the slave ultimately derives from the Aristotelian idea that people "born to serve" should do precisely that, rather than demand changes that would not serve them well.[60]

The fact that no one, not even Christianity with its intention to renew society, ever dreamed of abolishing slavery is equally important.[61] This implies that slavery was considered inevitable, yet I find it significant that the Romans placed slavery within the legal framework of the *familia*. The very same jurisprudence that declared slavery against nature[62] categorized it among the "natural" relations of a biological family, next to children termed *liberi* precisely to set them apart from slaves. This construct shows not only the scope of paternal authority but how the family was perceived as an economic and productive unit.

Today's scholars of Greco-Roman slavery doubt that this mode of labor organization was as inefficient as has often been claimed.[63] Only Appian, the Greek historian of the early second century CE, observes how, in the Republic, slaves, being exempt from military obligations, were better suited to the great estates. In his view, the abundance of slaves ultimately harmed free farmers, who, oppressed by military service, taxes, and poverty, were unable to offer their labor to landowners who employed slaves.[64] Nevertheless, I do not detect in this phrase any sense of rivalry between free labor and slaves: this is a modern approach. If, for the Romans, having slaves was as normal as having children, they would never have contemplated abolishing slavery to save the work for themselves: work was certainly not considered a privilege.

On the whole, one might conclude that the conviction that slave labor was neither efficient nor advantageous originated well before Adam Smith. I do not wish to enter the debate on whether such a position was more philosophical than economic in nature[65] other than to observe that it would be pointless to accuse Seneca (and others) of failing to take an abolitionist stance on the grounds that he limited himself, in his famous letter 47, to paternalistic encouragement of the humane treatment of slaves. For a modern audience, such attitudes (including the Stoic position that considered the question from a predominantly moral standpoint[66]) avoid the key moral issue. But in the Roman world, the fact that certain institutions were deemed to be "against nature" was a philosophical argument that certainly did not produce any demands to abolish them through legal intervention.[67] The fact that slaves had a different legal status from free men was not considered particularly outrageous: women and minors shared diminished status. In reality, minors still do today, and western women achieved equal rights at the same time as, if not later than, slaves.

Modern interpretations that tend to present as paternalistic and self-interested the admonitions of Seneca (but also the legislation of the *Digest* that punished cruelty to slaves), and claim that all such expressions of "humanity" were designed to strengthen the system rather than to change it,[68] fail to take into account the fact no real change was seen until the Declaration of the Rights of Man (1789).[69]

The imperial administration is often considered to have been more rational and less disorganized than its Republican antecedents. Traditionally, Augustus is credited with a penchant for statistics borne out by the extension of the census and the land registry, previously limited to Rome and the Italian peninsula, to the entire Roman Empire.[70] Of course, this resulted in the progressive leveling of differences that characterized the political reality of the Empire in contrast to that of the Republic.[71] The fact that the provinces increasingly came to supply the "protagonists" in key sectors from the court to literary production is also evidence of greater cultural uniformity.

An awareness of these broadened and more cosmopolitan horizons emerges not only from Stoic philosophy but also from certain economic considerations. Among the praises that Pliny the Younger liberally bestowed upon the Emperor Trajan, we are told that peace and security fostered commercial activities, integrating the parts of the Empire and assuring the well-being of all in a rational and efficient manner.[72] This is little more than a commonplace, one that had already been expressed by Cicero, but if we add the idea of the "providential" nature of the diverse productivity of the various parts of the world, we may not be far from the intellectual roots of laissez-faire.[73]

Nevertheless, even acknowledgement of economic integration between the various parts of the Empire brought about by trade – though managed in certain cases by the state – was sufficient to induce an adequate awareness of the driving force of exchange. Pliny the Elder enthused, like his nephew, about the resources flowing from all parts of the world to Rome, yet he feared the spread of new spending habits.[74]

Roman literature has repeatedly produced surviving collections of letters, whether they were destined for publication or not; either way, epistolography may be the genre that most readily reveals the disposition of the author. The letters of Seneca and Pliny the Younger are the best-known collections from the imperial period. They are rather diverse. Seneca's letters are protreptic, letters of warning rather than a genuine form of private correspondence.[75] Conversely, Pliny the Younger owes his fame to two bodies of work that could well have brought him scorn: a panegyric on the ruling emperor and a collection of letters with countless requests of favours for friends and acquaintances.[76] Since Pliny occupied an eminent position, his letters also provide invaluable testimony of economic life, although he reveals little about his own preferences. There are no thundering phrases like that of Tacitus on the Romans' making graveyards of entire countries and calling it peace,[77] and just a couple of allusions to the fact that the senate carried practically no political weight.[78] His exchange of letters with Trajan contains a few curiosities: when Pliny proposes lowering interest rates to make bonds more attractive, Trajan agrees and adds that "forcing men to borrow money[79]. . . . is not worthy of the sense of justice of our time" (*Ep.* 10.54 (62) and 55(63)). More than once the Emperor stresses that he does not wish to damage the interests of private citizens that are equally worthy of attention as matters of state, and that it was necessary to control the distribution of monies for special occasions (*Ep.* 10.109–10, 111–12; 116–18). Pliny addresses the same theme in a letter to members of his family, praising those who bestow favors upon the needy instead of "those that can return them with still greater gifts" (*Ep.* 9.30.1).[80] Juvenal similarly deplored the abundance of benefits showered upon those who were already rich, coupled with the social success of those who made money from ignoble professions.[81] What seems to emerge from these topics is dissatisfaction with the 'nouveaux riches', together with the growing gap between rich and poor.

Our texts are also relevant to the debate about the relationship between commercial exchanges and other not strictly, or not solely, economic forms of exchange that many historians, from Polanyi onwards, have considered to have been of vital importance in ancient economies. In the Roman economy, non-economic forms of exchange included the institution of patronage.[82] It is interesting to note the concrete vein of the Roman "euergetic" gift: there is no lack of observations regarding the utility of donations in the public sphere.[83]

Many private transactions were presented within a context of mutual assistance between friends.[84] This matter has been treated so widely that a summary is no easy task. Seneca's letters contain several examples, as does his treatise *De beneficiis* which is entirely dedicated to this topic, a work in which he makes liberal use of economic metaphors, though in a critical way.[85] It is evident that when Seneca wishes to deplore or to describe an inappropriate attitude towards a benefactor, the first analogy that springs to his mind is that of a mercantile act. Most of the treatise describes "aristocratic" exchanges that are generous and disinterested in contrast to the miserly reckoning of debits and credits, of use in bookkeeping but not in the social life of a respectable man.

The question of whether the slave can "benefit" the master, to which Seneca responded affirmatively, is emblematic of the conflictual relationship between issues of status and contract, to use the terms of Sumner Maine. According to some, the inferior status of the slave might not have allowed him to perform an action that was appropriate only to those ranking higher in the social hierarchy.[86] This suggests that Seneca's attitude towards slavery is not exclusively paternalistic but shows genuinely liberal traits. The economic aspects of beneficial acts (encapsulated in the concept of *amicitia*) have received thorough treatment;[87] besides, it has often been remarked that Seneca was in no position to speak credibly about unselfish behavior.[88]

In his frequent hair-splitting over the distinction between a commercial and a beneficial act, Seneca helped to define matters both from a "euergetic" and an economic standpoint. He took a negative view of the fact that a commercial act "settled an account"[89] since this would have meant that an ongoing relationship of give and take, typical of friendship, was replaced by perfect parity, thereby ending the relationship. However, in so doing Seneca captured the essence of payment, in the sense of a release from a debt.

According to Miriam Griffin,[90] in the *de beneficiis* Seneca interprets the *princeps* as a *primus inter pares* in a society of equals – very few, of course – who mutually exchange benefits. In other words, it is a social ideal, in contrast to that of Pliny the Younger, whose use of *indulgentia*, together with the parallel he draws between the emperor and the father,[91] has been taken to symbolize a vertical relationship of authority and submission.

Nevertheless, it is worth noting that Seneca, unlike Pliny the Younger, says so much about the distinction between a gift and a commercial exchange. It is difficult to know to what extent such efforts to arrive at a definition reflect changes in society, but the very fact that they were made is significant in itself.

A rather controversial text by the third-century CE jurist Paulus (*Dig.* 18.1.1) seems to anticipate the controversy between metallists and nominalists, which in the history of economic thought dates back to Jean Bodin. Paulus provides one of the hypothetical reconstructions of the origin of money that, from Aristotle onwards, describe the transition from barter to commerce, the very purpose for which metal currency was invented. Yet Paulus's text goes a good deal further, anticipating many aspects of medieval and modern economic thought, from the issue of incommensurability to that of value.[92] These texts laid the foundations for the analysis of needs, exchange, value, and also of money as a medium of exchange, storage, and measure of value.

This passage has been joined to a number of literary texts, including two by Pliny the Elder,[93] to justify the claim that the Romans perceived a link between the increased supply of precious metals deriving from the conquest of new countries and secular price rises that can be detected in various sources.[94] Modern authors fail to agree whether the Romans could have been aware of long-term inflation: it is generally felt that any awareness they did have, coupled with their condemnation of luxury and their moralistic considerations, is not tantamount to a genuine understanding of economic factors.[95] I feel it is unnecessary, in this and in other cases, to identify an attitude *sub specie oeconomiae.* After all, not even the various medieval surveys of casuistry are unanimously considered to represent "economic thought", despite the existence of a "literature" that investigates all types of economic behavior and is far more copious than its Roman counterpart.

In conclusion, I wish to highlight certain Roman attitudes that reveal their way of "thinking" economics. For example, it has been said that private landownership was originally exempt from taxation: if the state wished to make money from land it had to subject the *ager publicus* to *vectigal*, in other words, charge for the use of public land.[96] If, however, we turn to the Roman technique *par excellence* of land surveying, we find that the land which was carefully measured, bounded and described on maps was private; originally, only the external perimeter of public land was bounded while the practice of dividing it into lots and mapping it came later. This situation did not last very long: taxes on (provincial) land became one of the characteristic traits of Roman dominion. Yet it is evident that land-surveying was not established for reasons of taxation: otherwise the state would not have surveyed (precisely) land that produced no public revenue. Despite all the criticism of the so-called principle of ownership-sovereignty – the notion that no one but the owner had any right to his land –,[97] I can find no better explanation for this paradox.

Let us now take another example, this time from the imperial period but relating to one of the most ancient Roman institutions: the census. As we know, the census counted people and things. The head of every household was called upon to produce an "income-tax return," of which the formal outline has survived.[98] The system was timocratic: access to high political offices was related to the census; the case of Aemilius Scaurus, who had to recover the wealth lost by his ancestors to enter the *cursus honorum*,[99] is well-known.

The Augustan restoration (apparently) left intact the principal Republican institutions, including the census. We know that possession of 400,000 sesterces was required to enter the senate, later raised by Augustus to one million.[100] After the devastation of the civil wars, many citizens of supposedly equestrian or senatorial status no longer possessed the requisite wealth. Augustus, who had reorganized the orders to admit those "who were worthy,"[101] decided to supply them with the riches necessary for the corresponding census class. Nicolet's comment is exemplary: it is not distinctions that spring from fortune, but precisely the opposite.[102] To this one might add a fundamental difference: in the Republican period, it was the dispossessed heir who struggled to rebuild his wealth: now this had become the task of the emperor.

These two examples show us that the Romans perceived economics, to which they attached the utmost importance, as a means to another end. This is not new: yet what is interesting is the fact that even though they considered economics only a means, they certainly did not ignore it. Even if *pecunia* was an *ancilla*, a servant, it served the most important purpose, the social and political distinction that entitled certain individuals to govern others. Unlike Aristotle, the Romans did not claim that some men were by their very nature destined to command and others to serve, but arranged such relations through their political and economic organisation and legislation that governed apparently "neutral" entities such as numbers, relationships of property, the census, and land survey data. They did not invoke nature, as money was sufficient.

All sources of wealth were arranged in a hierarchy, so to speak. Having taken possession of their rivals' land, the Romans subjected it to detailed and highly complex legal regulations. Thus even land had its own status, almost more so than people.[103] At the same time, intellectual tradition remained virtually intact: while estates had been increasing in size since the Republican conquests, it was in the first century CE that Pliny the Elder came up with his famous phrase *latifundia perdidere Italiam* ("large estates have ruined Italy:" *HN* 18.6[7].35) that remained an emblem of opposition to expansive landholdings.[104]

Today, there is a tendency to reconsider the notion that there is a certain economic logic to self-sufficiency.[105] Even so, rational agriculture necessarily takes place on a certain scale, and barely self-sufficient holdings put a structural brake on development. The Romans were quick to understand this, but the *mos maiorum* was too strong for them to admit it. Furthermore, the principle of self-sufficiency, associated for centuries with farming, can be interpreted in a number of ways: food independency in a limited sense, or the ability to produce for oneself all that is required for rich and sumptuous living. The mentality symbolized in Virgil's verse "he used to load his table with an unbought banquet" was handed down to Renaissance Europe.[106] It stood for a form of economic independence, one that nevertheless implied political independence and was echoed widely in modern "republican" thought.[107]

Literary documents from the imperial period do not make it possible to reconstruct any linear and systematic economic thought over and above what emerges from Republican texts. Historians, and Tacitus in particular, pinpointed the elements that were critical to the development of Roman society; but once again, we are presented with a political rather than an economic appraisal. Nevertheless, the change in political regime brought a greater awareness of fiscal – and hence economic – issues. It has been deemed excessive to relate this awareness specifically to the time of Augustus:[108] however, two centuries later Cassius Dio put into the mouth of Augustus' advisor Agrippa a sermon on taxation that not only underlined the difference between the Republic and the empire in matters of taxation[109] but also contained some revealing remarks. For instance, it was said to be necessary to be wary of citizens making "voluntary" contributions, possibly as a means of securing political support. This makes the attribution of the dialogue to the Augustan period not entirely implausible: civic freedoms were then so recent as to raise fears of this sort.

In the domain of "theorizing," few changes can be observed between the Republican and imperial periods. Attitudes to agriculture and trade changed very little, apart from awareness of the wider "market" and of greater affluence, perceived as ever from a moralistic standpoint. Certain observations on money and exchange were intuitions rather than complete formulations; but the fact that they were made at all is important insofar as they represented later economic thought in embryonic form. The same can be said of the use of economic metaphors in literature. A good example is Seneca's description (*QN* 5.15) of men crawling underground in order to obtain precious metals, as a perfect illustration of greed.

The tendency to preach "gentlemanly" behavior, without attaching excessive importance to money, can be tracked throughout Roman history: just as Cicero urges men to be *remissior* in the collection of debts (*Off.* 2.64), so Pliny the Younger "makes do" with lower income from his estates as much out of aversity to risk as out of a desire to lend a helping hand to his tenants.[110] The aristocratic *ethos* continued to color behaviors that may, with hindsight, have been dictated by practical motives.

To conclude, a certain awareness of how to construct economic arguments certainly developed in imperial Roman thought, even though it was not theorized. Romans probably felt the need to move away from the greedy practices of the Republican period that had been fuelled by the "drugged growth"[111] generated by warfare. Once the period of major conquest was over, a settlement was necessary and initially brought notable advantages.[112] All this called for reflection on a more "globalized" economy and on the essence of certain economic principles, a reasoning found in the definitions of jurists as well as in moralizing writings.

NOTES

1 I cannot say how many authors have been read "in the light" of what John Rawls affirms in his *Theory of Justice* of 1971.

2 A habit of the "deconstructionist" interpretations inspired by the philosophies of language in vogue in the 1970s, rarely applied, in general, to ancient history. An overview of historiographical trends can be found in Skinner 2009, especially 120–21.

3 The institutionalist thesis belongs to Douglas North, cf. Lo Cascio 2006c: 218–21. The phrase is cited on 218.

4 Cf. Vivenza 1998a: 69–79.

5 More precisely *indigentia communis eorum qui inter se commutare possunt*, the common wants of those able to trade amongst themselves. Cf. the careful analysis by Langholm 1979, particularly 114, 139–40.

6 Cf., e.g., Honoré 2002; Jones (ed.) 1998.

7 Zecchini 2005: 155–66. Bruce Hitchner is more cautious: the situation was "not repeated again until the rise of the European trans-Atlantic empires in the seventeenth and eighteenth centuries" (Hitchner 2005: 209).

8 Jean Andreau claims that the commercial legislation in the *Corpus Iuris* did not reflect any economic motivations, cf. Andreau 1994b: 86. But see also the objections raised by Harris 2003: 285.

9 An impressive bibliography exists on this; cf. recently Scheidel, Morris and Saller (eds.) 2007: Part VI.

10 *Dig.* 1.3.41. Cf. Alessio 1889: 406.

11 Vivenza 1999: 131–56.

12 *Dig.* 13.1.14, pr. and *passim*. Seneca had expressed this concept in *Ben.* 6.15.4. Cf. Langholm 1998: 78.

13 Cf. Brazzini 1988: 29–33; Frigo 1985.

14 Nicolet 1982: 877–960.

15 Nicolet 1982: 882.

16 Minaud 2005. But cf. also de Ste Croix 1956: 33–50.

17 Andreau 1984; Lo Cascio 1986; 1991a.

18 This aspect also receives thorough treatment in Part VII of Scheidel, Morris and Saller (eds.) 2007, to which I refer the reader for documentation.

19 Vivenza 1998b: 269–331.

20 Pugliese 1992: 164–5.

21 The limited echo of this measure has been noted by several authors. Cf. Spagnolo Vigorita 1993: 5–8. Nevertheless, it is considered to be of fundamental historical importance. See Sherwin-White 1972: 55–8; Zecchini 1998: 349.

22 Hopkins 2009: 181. More precisely, electoral assemblies were reduced to a formality from the time of Augustus, and later their function was taken over by the Senate, itself subsequently deprived of any effective power. Cf. recently Capogrossi Colognesi 2009: 299–301.

23 Schiavone 1992: 83–4; Wallace-Hadrill 1997: 16.

24 Gara 1992, especially 374–7, highlights a return to the tradition clearly seen in the first stage of the Empire, a sign of a conservative tendency.

25 Nicolet 1988b: 275.

26 Veyne 1991: 147, 158–9.

27 Schiavone 1996: 108.

28 With the so-called "Law of the 300 amphoras": see Vivenza 1998b: 284.

29 Maloney 1971: 93.

30 For example, in the production of terra-cotta amphoras for transport: Kehoe 2007b; Morley 2007b.

31 Today, we tend to emphasize the coexistence of the different management models rather than the linear development (small farm-*villa rustica*-*latifundium*) traced by earlier historiography. See Caliri 2005: 796, 801.

32 Martin 1967: 67–8. The author underlines that while Pliny the Elder's and Columella's opposition to *latifundia* was based on economic and moral motivations,

Pliny the Younger's objections were grounded in common sense, prudence, and experience.

33 Those of Cato, Varro, Columella, and Palladius survive but many others were written.

34 Mastrorosa 2006: 135–48.

35 Vivenza 2000: 95–6.

36 Capogrossi Colognesi 1981: 453–4.

37 A "globalized" market was never established, though Rome made efforts to link various markets by means of a dense network of relations between centre and periphery. See Schiavone 1996: 59–60; Gabba 1988: 102–3; recently Hitchner 2005: 218–19.

38 On this issue I refer the reader only to Lo Cascio 1991b: 326–7; 2006c. Cf. Schiavone 1996: 103–4.

39 Harris 2003: 292.

40 Tac., *Ann.* 1.78; cf. Vivenza 1994: 48.

41 Andreau 1994b: 91. The law authorized guardians to invest the wealth of their wards in lending activities, cf. Vivenza 1998b: 291 n. 38.

42 See, though by no means exhaustively, Milani 1972: 196–8; Raskolnikoff 1982: 51–5; and Andrea Carandini's preface to Kolendo 1980: IX-LX, with bibliography.

43 Garnsey (ed.) 1980; Capogrossi Colognesi 1981: 445–54; Gabba, 1988: 49–68; De Neeve 1990: 398; Garcìa MacGaw 2006: 27–41.

44 Lo Cascio 1991b: 330 ff.

45 Schiavone 1996: ch. IX.

46 Aristot., *Pol.* 1254 a13–17, 21–24; 1255a1–2.

47 Schiavone 1996: 148–51.

48 The *dominium ex iure Quiritium*, exempt in Rome and in Italy until Diocletian.

49 Westermann 1955: 79–80. I have already mentioned economic gain for the master, to the extent that there was talk of returning to slavery the freedman who did not render the services due, who was thus accused of a form of ingratitude (Vivenza 1998b: 298 with n. 61.); yet the proposal was not approved.

50 And he continues: "A notre connaissance aucun, à l'exception moderne des USA", Martin 2000: 65.

51 Schiavone 1996: 195–6. Cf also Garnsey 1996: 94.

"In such transactions the slave became a physical extension of his owner's legal person" (Westermann 1955: 83).

52 De Neeve 1990: 396, with note 181. Cf. Capogrossi Colognesi 1986: 344–8.

53 From the "removal" of the problem to classist interpretations, see only Finley 1999: ch. 3 and Gabba 1988: 58–64. A full bibliography would be very long.

54 Varro's recommendation to use free men in marshes, or for intensive work such a grape harvesting or reaping, is well known (Varr. *Rust.* 1.17.2). It is interpreted as a kind of "safeguard" for slaves by Whittaker 1987: 98.

55 Colum. *Rust.* 1. Praef. 3; Plin. *HN* 18.6(7).36; cf. Tozzi 1961: 338, 343, 363.

56 The best known exponent is Sen., *Ep.* 47; but also Plin. *Ep.* 5.19; Plut. *Mor.* 459C-460A. Moreover, imperial legislation weakened the authority of the *pater familias* over the slaves, whose defense Antoninus Pius took up directly (Casavola 1980: pp. 223–4).

57 *Ep.* 8.16.1–3. This allowed burial in the family tomb rather than in common graves. Cf. Veyne 1961: 221. Naturally, more egotistical explanations may also be put forward, as indeed Veyne does: it could be a way of continuing a name in the absence of heirs.

58 Slaves could not make a will; Pliny granted them this right and carried out their wishes *dumtaxat intra domum; nam servis respublica quaedam et quasi civitas domus est* – within the household, which is a country and a kind of citizenship for slaves (*Ep.* 8.16.2–3). Cf. Martin 1967: 85–7; Gonzales 1997: 364. Similarly humane behavior is seen in Pliny and Seneca, as Sherwin-White 1985: 350 underlines.

59 Vivenza 1998b: 296–300. A similar position is found in Westermann 1955: 74–5.

60 Cic. *Rep.* 1.34.51; 3.25.37; cf. Milani 1972: 207.

61 The influx of Christianity is not treated here. Interesting arguments can be found in Garnsey 1996: part II, section 2, and *passim*.

62 All the jurists of the Severan period declared slavery an institution *iuris gentium*, but contrary to natural law; cf. also Ulp. in *Dig.* 50.17.32. Milani hits the mark when he asserts that the slave had two roles in Roman law, as a man and a thing (Milani 1972: 203, 230). Cf. also Johnston 1999: 42–4.

63 Schiavone 1996:124–41, a position not far removed from that of Finley, who was notoriously convinced that had slavery not been worthwhile, it would not have been maintained, either by ancients or moderns (Finley 1999: 83–4.).

64 App. *BC* 1.7. This argument is peculiarly similar to that of Adam Smith's *Wealth of Nations* (IV.vii.a.3; IV.ix.47). On the relationship between slave and owner, cf. Whittaker 1987: 109–10. This relationship began to blur when the state was no longer able to impose military obligations.

65 Finley's reflections (Finley 1980) are still of interest.

66 Garnsey 1996: 131.

67 It seems that only the Sophists took this to the extreme: if slavery was contrary to nature, it was to be abolished (cf. Griffin 1976: 257).

68 Bradley 2008: 339–42; Milani 1972: 221; Rizzelli 1998–99: 235–9. Griffin alludes to the problem in Griffin 1976: 263–74. Cf. also Manning 1989: 1519, 1535.

69 Milani 1972: 206.

70 Augustus was also concerned with demographics, which is why he enacted legislation to strengthen the role of the ruling classes. Cf. Capogrossi Colognesi 2009: 303.

71 On the "provincialization" of the equestrian class, the army, and the class of freedmen under the monarchy, see Polverini 1964–5: 282–5, 455–8, 5–8.

72 Plin. *Pan.* 29.2–4; cf. also 25.4–5. Cf. Harris 2003: 290–2.

73 Pliny alludes to this in *Pan.* 32; cf. Viner 1960: 48.

74 Nicolet 1982: 935; Harris 2003: 293.

75 Sherwin-White 1985: 2. Cf. Habinek 1998: 137–50; Benoist 2006: 58; Mazzoli 1989: 1846 ff.

76 Letters of recommendation, in the definition of Pavis d'Escurac 1992: 55–69. Cf. also Aubrion 1989: 326.

77 *Agr.* 30.4. Tacitus was on good terms with Pliny the Younger, whom he also sent his works to read. Cf. Dupont 1997: 59. As well as with Tacitus, Pliny was also in correspondence with Suetonius, Martial, Musonius Rufus, and other notable intellectuals. Of particular interest is Pliny's letter 4.13.6–9 (to Tacitus): he says the same of teaching as Adam Smith was later to say in *Wealth of Nations* V.i.f.5–7,

namely that teachers should be paid by the families of their pupils, and not by the state – and for the same reason.

78 *Ep.* 3.20.10–12; 4.25,5; *Pan.* 72.1–2. Cf. Sherwin-White 1985: 262, 305.

79 It was the alternative proposed by Pliny: to make the decurions personally responsible, and then allow them to recover losses from the citizens. Cf. also Vidman 1960.

80 A frequent theme in the Latin moralists, cf. Cic. *Off.* 1.50–8; Sen. *Ben.* 1.4.2–3; 4.20.3.

81 Marache 1989: 620–3.

82 Summary in Griffin 2003a: 99–101.

83 Already in Cic. *Off.* 2.60, cf. Vivenza 1998b: 301. Frontinus explicitly states that an aqueduct is preferable to a statue, cf. Leveau 1993: 3; also Griffin 2003b: 104.

84 Michel 1962: 502–29 analyzes in this way Cicero's *De amicitia* and *De officiis* and Seneca's *De beneficiis*. Cf. also Nicolet 1982: 930–1; and also Vivenza 1998b: 312; Griffin 2003a: 107–8. The recent work by Verboven 2002 treats the entire issue.

85 Particularly in the *De beneficiis*, but also elsewhere, cf. Levick 2003: 216; Ker 2006: 35–7; Griffin 2003b: 99–102. Economic metaphors are found also in Pliny the Younger, e.g., in *Ep.* 1.13.6. Cf. Morley 2007a: 87–8.

86 Slaves could not give gifts (*benefacere*), only obey orders: Chaumartin 1989: 1719–22; cf. also Manning 1989: 1526.

87 Verboven 2002. Cf. moreover the criticism by Harris 2006.

88 Gabba 1991: 255–6; Grimal 1989: 1981–2; Levick 2003: 225 and *passim;* Veyne 2003: 159 with n. 3.

89 Vivenza 1998b: 313.

90 Griffin 2003a: esp. 116–19. The subordination of the aristocrat to the emperor (and his supremacy over other members of society: a hierarchy, in other words) is stressed by Habinek 1998: 13.

91 Likening a ruler to a father is a *locus classicus* of absolute monarchies; cf., though with reference to an entirely different political climate, Kaplan 1976: 5–7.

92 See Langholm 1979, 1983, 1984.

93 According to Zehnacker, it is no coincidence that Pliny deals with this issue in books 33 and 34 of his *Historia Naturalis*: supposedly, the Latin author focused his analysis deliberately on monetary metals, gold, silver, and bronze, as symbols of wealth, revealing a moralistic more than an economic standpoint (cf. Zehnacker 1979: especially 178–81).

94 Of the rich bibliography, I shall mention only Nicolet 1971; Crawford 1971; Lo Cascio 1978; 1981; Nicolet 1984; De Cecco 1985; Lo Cascio 1986; Harris 2006. I mentioned these problems in Vivenza 1998b: 292–4.

95 Nicolet defines the problem in terms of the Aristotelian definition of money (Nicolet 1984: 126–33). Cf. Crawford 1971: 1233. Veyne claims that the ancients were unable to distinguish between quantity of money and the money supply (by which I assume he means the supply of coinable metal): Veyne 1991: 149–50 n. 33; cf. also 163 ff.

96 And this was far from easy if the land had been occupied by private citizens; cf. Vivenza 1994: 87–92.

97 Bonfante 1976: 196–200; De Martino 1958: 18–21.

98 The *professio censualis*, cf. Ulp., *Dig.* 50.15.4.1–7.

99 Gabba 1988: 41–2. (cf. Cic. *Mur.* 16; Val. Max. 4.4.11).

100 Nicolet 1988b: 224–40, with discussion. Cf. id. 2000: 163–87; Capogrossi Colognesi 2009: 300.

101 As Cassius Dio, Tacitus, and Suetonius testify (cf. Nicolet 1988b: 233–4), as well as the lovable verse by Horace (*Ep.* 1.1.57–8: "You have sense, you have morals, eloquence and honour, but there are six or seven thousand short of the four hundred; you will be in the crowd", trad. H. Rushton Fairclough).

102 Nicolet 1988b: 239.

103 The cataloguing of the *ager* reflected its status: *publicus, privatus, occupatorius, censorius, quaestorius, vectigalis, tributarius, stipendiarius*, etc.

104 The definition of *latifundium* is controversial even today; it was not so much the size that mattered as the waste of land.

105 Morley 2007a: 92. Cf. Halstead 2002: 68.

106 *Georg.* 4.133; cf. Whittaker 1985: 49.

107 Here also the bibliography is endless; from Fink 1945 to Gelderen and Skinner 2002.

108 Nevertheless, if Augustus extended the census and the land registry to the provinces, he intended to assess and systematically impose taxes; this lends credibility to Agrippa's speech (and Maecenas's, cf. Dio 52.6, 27–29).

109 Vivenza 1998b: 318–20.

110 Which may, in part, have been calculated: Kehoe 1989: 584–5.

111 This expression is owed to Schiavone 1996: 203.

112 This is not the place to enter the discussion on whether economic growth occurred during the Empire; cf. the contributions by Bruce Hitchner (Hitchner 2005) and Richard Saller (Saller 2002 in Manning and Morris 2005 (eds.), and the comment by Avner Greif.

3: The Contribution of Economics

Peter Temin

Economics is about the allocation of resources. In the modern industrialized world, most goods and services are allocated through transactions, which in turn are mostly purchases and taxes. Goods are largely the outputs of early modern economies, while services – particularly labor services – are more typically the inputs. To understand how an economy works, we need to consider how inputs are directed to provide the outputs that people desire. There also are economic analyses of marriages and families, seeing marriage itself, fertility choice, and the raising of children as decisions that affect the allocation of resources. Ancient economies clearly differed from modern ones, but the principles of economics still hold true, and economics can bring clarity to the analysis of how resources were allocated in the ancient world.

I make this case in several steps. First, I describe the concepts of a market and of institutional economics. Second, I separate supply and demand and discuss the nature of economic incentives and equilibrium to show that economics may be useful even in the absence of market activity. Third, I introduce the concept of comparative advantage to explain trade. Fourth, I discuss possible economic growth as well as catastrophes like plagues. Fifth, I turn to money and prices. Sixth, I discuss the nature of information that can be used to test hypotheses about all these topics. The last two topics are discussed on this volume's web site.[1]

Markets

All economies larger than Robinson Crusoe's have to allocate resources among people. Even Robinson Crusoe had to allocate his time; adding other people makes the problems far more complex. Families need to decide who will work and in what activities. They need to decide how to divide the fruits of this labor among family members. Even if they do not consciously make choices – or even regard these decisions as choices – family decisions have consequences for both production and consumption. Larger groups have the same kinds of decisions to make, and the relations between people in tribes or states or other groupings affect the process by which they make these decisions as well as their outcomes.

Polanyi asserted that the main forms of integration in the human economy are reciprocity, redistribution, and exchange.[2] Reciprocity, as the term suggests, is a system in which people aim toward a rough balance between the goods and services they receive and that they give to others. The reciprocal obligations are determined by social obligations and tradition, and they change only slowly. Participants typically see themselves as following traditions or custom rather than as making choices. Redistribution is a system in which goods are collected in one hand and distributed by virtue of custom, law, or ad hoc central decision. This system is present in units as small as households, where it is known as householding, as well as in the taxation levied by modern states. The essential characteristic is that a central authority collects and distributes goods and services. Exchange is the familiar economic transaction where people voluntarily exchange goods for each other or for money.

This tripartite schema corresponds also to a division of individual behavior. People even today rely on a mixture of behavioral modes, choosing which one to use as a result of internal and external forces.[3] These forces can be represented on two dimensions. One dimension measures internal forces along an index of personal autonomy. The other dimension indexes the rapidity of change in the external environment. When people are less autonomous and change is slow, they typically utilize customary behavior. When change is rapid and personal autonomy is neither very high nor very low, then people use command behavior. When personal autonomy is high and the pace of change is moderate, people employ instrumental behavior, that is, they have explicit goals in mind and choose actions that advance their plans. These different modes of behavior correspond to the three types of organization used in economic life. Customary behavior generally is used for reciprocity. Command behavior is typical of redistribution. And instrumental behavior is used in market exchange.

There consequently are two types of tests we can use to discriminate between the various kinds of organizations. Prices are used in market exchanges. (They may be used in reciprocity, although they will not vary in response to economic conditions in that context.) In addition, people behave instrumentally in market exchanges, not customarily or by command; these two modes of behavior are typical of reciprocity and redistribution. Neither prices nor behavior are seen clearly in the historical record of ancient Rome, but the formulation of tests using varied fragments of information allows discrimination between alternative categories.

Markets are an important means of allocating resources, and they were prominent in the ancient world; it will ease later discussions to clarify what a market is. The problem is that there is a popular definition and an economic definition, sowing confusion in historical discussions. The popular definition of a market is a place at which trade is conducted. The *Oxford English Dictionary* notes that the Roman forum was designated as a market in medieval writing. Markets now include fish markets, farmers' markets and supermarkets for food. In the modern world, most trade is directed via stores – distinguished from markets by having uniform, posted prices. Department stores arose in the mid-nineteenth century, and the initial function of prices was to let the store know how much the customer had paid and therefore the amount to be returned, not to inform the customer how much he or she would have to pay.

The stock market is located in a specific place on Wall Street, even though news of stock-market activity is all around us. It is considered to be a paragon of markets by economists because stock prices change the way competitive prices are expected to behave. Current prices embody all information about the stock to date. Future prices depend on future information and cannot be predicted. The best prediction of tomorrow's stock's price therefore is today's price. In mathematical terms, stock prices move as a random walk, that is, tomorrow's price is today's price plus a random (with today's knowledge) movement. I have shown that agricultural prices in Hellenistic Babylon moved as a random walk, that is, that they behaved like modern market prices.[4]

Now think of selling a house. We speak of putting our house on the market, but there is no place to take a house – and of course no way to take it even if there were such a place. The market in this case is a virtual or disembodied market. It is defined by the nature of the goods or services being sold rather than by where they are sold. This is the key to the economic use of the term which focuses on the items being sold rather than the method of selling them.

People who anticipate buying or selling a house want to think about its price. To find a suitable range of prices, they look at the sale prices of other, similar houses. But what makes another house similar to this one? It might be location, the prime characteristic of all real estate, so that only local sales are relevant. Local sales might be those on the same street, in the same neighborhood, the same city, or the same country. It might be houses of the same size, or of the same age, or with the same kind of garden. It might even be houses of approximately the same putative value.

This highly ambiguous description is a key to how economists use the term, market. All houses are in some sense in the same market, but some are closer substitutes for the house being sold than others. Economists argue roughly that houses are in the same market if the price of one affects the price of the other. This is the general idea, but the statement is not quite accurate. On one hand, the price of any single house cannot affect the price of any other in a perfectly competitive market, because there are so many similar houses in this kind of market that the sale of any one house has no effect on the market as a whole. On the other, the price of nearby apartments might affect the price of houses. We do not have to be very precise here; we stay with the idea of a market consisting of goods and services that compete with each other. The boundaries of such a market are unclear, and setting them provides employment for economists, but not for ancient historians.

The term 'market economy' adds another level of complexity to the discussion. When Hopkins described Rome as a slave society, he did not mean that everyone was a slave.[5] Similarly, not every resource in a market economy is allocated through a market. In both cases, the terms indicate that slaves and markets were important, even dominant, institutions. In twentieth-century America – arguably the purest market economy in history – economists have estimated that one-third of economic activity in the United States today takes place within households, that is, in householding.[6] The proportion was even higher in the ancient world, but I argue that the economy of the early Roman Empire was a market economy because of the importance and prevalence of market activity.[7]

It is necessary here to distinguish between personal and anonymous exchanges. The former is negotiated between a buyer and seller, possibly with a broker to facilitate the transaction. Most house purchases and sales are of this type. Anonymous exchanges involve stated or posted prices that are available to any customers that come by. When we discuss the price of wheat in ancient Rome, we are referring to anonymous exchanges. Only if wheat had been sold in a bazaar for a different price to each purchaser would it be classified as personal exchange.

The consideration of societies can be made sharper by use of the New Institutional Economics (NIE). This body of thought grows out of a belated recognition by economists that institutions affect economic activity – and are in turn affected by economic pressures. Douglass North won a Nobel Prize for making this point over and over again.[8] A paragraph in the earlier of these books says that Rome fell when it could not longer maintain property rights. This paragraph illustrates a weakness of the NIE. No ancient historian can take such a paragraph seriously. Was a decline in property rights a cause or an effect of the "decline of the Roman Empire"? How do you define or measure either of these concepts to find out?

We should not throw the baby out with the bathwater. The New Institutional Economics is useful to ancient historians in two ways. It helps focus attention on the institutions that govern activities in the ancient world, and it has given rise to some basic hypotheses that may be useful to explore when considering ancient institutions. For example, property rights have been found to promote economic growth by more systematic studies than North's. Acemoglu, Johnson and Robinson made this assertion for modern colonies.[9] They argued that colonies differed initially by the healthiness of European colonists. Where the Europeans survived, they brought with them European institutions. Where Europeans died frequently from new (to them) diseases, colonial leaders instituted what are called extractive institutions that did not guarantee private property, condoned bound service of various types, and enriched a small elite at the extent of the general population. Acemoglu, Johnson and Robinson found that the effects of these initial conditions, indexed by European mortality, explain a substantial amount of income differences in former colonies today. This paper spawned an enormous literature, both because of its ideas and as a new indicator of institutions that avoided the chicken-and-egg problem in North's paragraph. (Economists speak of this chicken-and-egg problem as the identification problem, that is, the problem of identifying which is chicken and which is egg.)

Another aid to economic activity is education (see below, Chapter 4). Like property rights, it often is hard to determine whether education is a cause or effect of economic growth and prosperity. The same goes for governments that keep corruption at a minimum and for the protection of intellectual rights, that is, the application of property rights to new discoveries. While all of these institutional factors raise similar identification problems, it is useful to set them out separately in order to see what kinds of institutions dominated ancient societies. For example, chapters in Part VII of the *Cambridge Economic History of the Greco-Roman World* describe regions of the Roman Empire, distinguishing them by their initial institutional background and making progress toward solving the identification problem.[10] The western provinces contained few cities before the Roman conquest, and their economies were redirected after integration into the Empire. The eastern Mediterranean provinces by contrast built on previous urban patterns, and Roman Egypt developed from its previous well-developed organization and its peculiar geography.

Supply and demand

Economists divide their field into microeconomics (the study of individual markets) and macroeconomics (the study of economies as a whole). One of the foundations of microeconomic analysis is the separation of supply and demand. Both terms refer to schedules or curves relating the quantity supplied or demanded as a function of the relevant price. We have evidence of prices in the ancient world, and many of them appeared to vary as a result of changes in supply and demand. Some prices were fixed by administrative fiat of some sort, and some people were not aware of prices. I will discuss how to deal with the former; the latter can be dealt with by interpreting prices as an incentive to buy or sell. Economists speak of prices as shorthand for factors that provide incentives to supply or consume. University professors, for example, perform academic and administrative services for their departments and universities even when there are no explicit prices. The incentives to do so are informal, signifying reciprocity and customary behavior. Nevertheless, if the burden of doing these jobs gets large, professors will do less. If the rewards for these activities increase – say by enhancing chances for promotion or getting a better office – they will do more. This kind of enhanced price is harder to observe than a market price, but it functions in the same way.

We distinguish between supply and demand because it often is the case that different people are behind them. This was true particularly in Roman cities, where food was brought from farms located in the countryside and sometimes far away. It was true within cities when craftsmen made clothing or oil lamps for others to utilize. Robinson Crusoe was both supplier and demander, of course, but it even makes sense to distinguish him as producer (determining supply) and consumer (determining demand). The distinction helps to clarify the role of different forces affecting the allocation of resources even in such a simple economy.

The quantity demanded generally increases when the price falls. At lower prices, people can consume more; their money (in whatever form it takes) goes farther. In addition, people often want more when the price is lower; they may shift between goods to use more of the cheapest goods and leave some money left over for other things. If prices get much lower, then people may even think of new uses for a commodity. For example, the price of cotton fell dramatically in the Industrial Revolution, leading people to think of putting cotton sheets on the beds and cotton curtains on their windows.

These factors will differ in intensity for different goods, and economists use the concept of price elasticity to describe the extent to which the quantity demanded rises when the price declines. Unitary elasticity is defined to be when the proportional increase in the quantity demanded just equals the proportional decline in the price. Total expenditure stays the same. When the quantity demanded changes less than this, the demand curve is inelastic; when it changes more, demand is elastic. Demand is infinitely elastic if it is so elastic that even a very small change in price will lead to dramatic – even infinite – changes in the quantity demanded. In that case, the very high elasticity of demand keeps the price from varying. That is true in competitive markets, where the actions of any single person have no effect on the price. If the demand for houses, to return to the earlier example, is infinitely elastic, then the decision of any one person to put his or her house on the market will not have any effect on the price.

The quantity supplied generally increases when the price rises. As the price for a product increases, producers make and sell more. They can afford to use more inputs to produce their product, and they may enjoy greater return from the sale. The reasoning implicitly assumes that there are two inputs needed for production. Following a long tradition of classical economists, call them labor and land. If land is fixed, then increasing the number of workers will result in diminishing returns from each worker as more and more of them are added. It is diminishing returns that make the supply curve slope upward.

Supply and demand curves are shown in Figure 3.1. Economists normally draw the quantity on the horizontal x-axis and price on the vertical y-axis, and I have followed that convention here. Since the demand curve slopes down and the supply curve slopes up, they generally cross. This is shown in the figure as happening at Q* and P*. Let us ask what happens if the price is above P*. The quantity of this

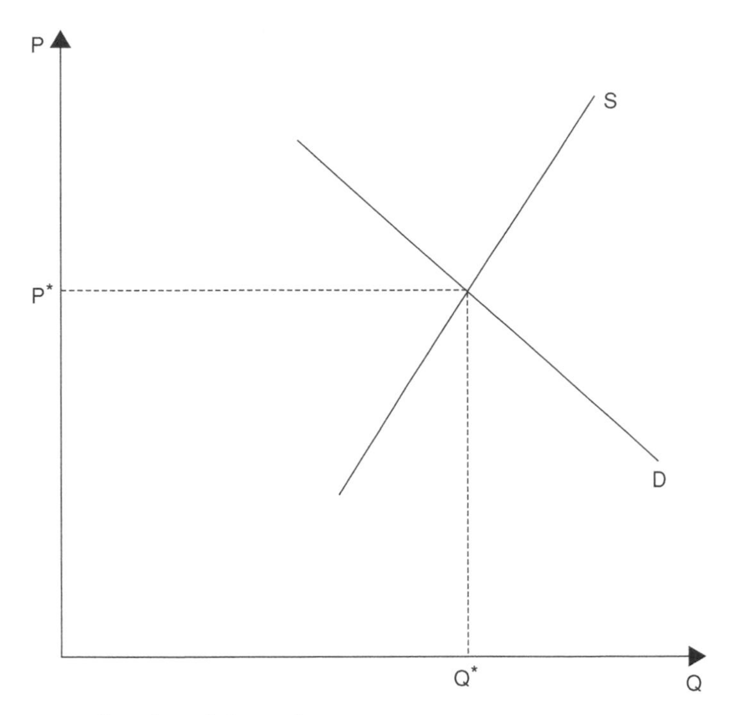

FIGURE 3.1 Supply and demand

good that producers want to sell is larger than Q*, while the quantity that people want to buy is less than Q*. Some of the goods produced will remain unsold, and producers will reduce their price to get rid of them. The price therefore will fall if it is above P*. Similarly, if the price is below P*, people will want to buy more of the good than producers want to sell. Producers will see that they can sell almost as much as before – each individual producer may expect to sell as much as before – if they raise the price. It will rise as long as the price is below P*. Only when the price equals P* will it stay at that level. We therefore speak of P* and Q* as the equilibrium level of this market.

Why do economists use this framework? The first reason is to understand *changes* in prices or quantities. For example, the production of wheat increased in Roman times. Looking at Figure 3.1, we see that the quantity is not likely to differ much from Q* while the supply and demand curves stay the same. If the quantity of wheat produced rose substantially, we then can ask why it rose. We can ask if the supply curve, the demand curve, or both curves shifted to move Q* to a new, higher level. Archaeological debates about innovations in agriculture focus on the supply curve, while thinking about feeding the city of

Rome is concentrated on demand. Thinking about supply and demand enables us to integrate these disparate analyses.

For example, a recent comparison of the supply and demand for wine and wheat in Republican Italy argued that there was not enough demand to support many large estates. It concluded that these markets were essentially competitive, earning limited profits for even large landowners and implying that, "We must remove the aristocracy's formation of large, commercial estates from the central role they have long played in reconstructions of the social and economic developments in the middle and late Republic."[11]

The forces of supply and demand operate even in reciprocity and redistribution. There are no explicit prices in these cases, but examples abound. The Roman senate gradually changed in the second century CE from a group of Italian senators to a group from the provinces.[12] The separation of supply and demand leads us to ask if this was due to conditions of supply (the scarcity of rich Italians) or instead to demand (a desire to have a wider representation in the Senate). Hopkins famously tried to estimate the GDP of the Roman Empire to show that the tax burden was light.[13] He clearly was motivated by the presumption that rising taxation would have led to disaffection from the empire, that is, that it would have been harder to maintain the tax rate as its burden increased.

A second reason to use this supply and demand framework is to describe the way in which people made decisions. While the demand for Roman wheat might have risen, each Sicilian or Egyptian farmer would only have known what price – or tax rate – he faced. We have several surviving comments about the prevailing price of wheat, some in normal times and more in unusual ones. The presence of these prices indicates that both farmers and consumers knew what the price was. We have no way of knowing how widespread this information was, but the quotations suggest strongly that this was general information. It makes sense therefore to see farmers as facing a competitive market in which their output was too small to affect the price. They then made their choices on the basis of what they saw as a fixed market price, just as farmers do today. We can use the tools of a competitive market to analyze the behavior of Roman farmers, even though we do not presume that they – or many more recent farmers – consciously saw themselves in what we now call a competitive market.

A third reason is to examine administrative decisions to see if they were effective or not. For example, wheat was given away in early imperial Rome under the *annona* for free or a very low price. This price almost certainly was below P*, the price that would have prevailed if the wheat was bought on some kind of free market. In that case, following the analysis of equilibrium, we expect that there should be pressure from consumers for more free distribution than the authorities planned to give away. The program expanded over time, and this analysis provides one reason why it did.

Two extreme cases are often spoken of by economists. The first one is the infinitely elastic demand curve. As noted already, this is a characteristic of a competitive market, where there are many producers all trying to sell their products in the same market. Transport and transaction costs in the ancient world kept many producers from competing head-to-head with others, but the abstraction gives us a benchmark against which to evaluate what we observe. Given that there were lots of farmers, vineyards, olive presses, makers of oil lamps, etc., the assumption of a competitive market can be very useful.

The second extreme case is when supply is completely inelastic, that is, the supply curve is vertical. A vertical supply curve says that the amount supplied is independent of the price. Paying a high amount or almost nothing will not affect how much is supplied. The most prominent example of this condition is agricultural land. When the Antonine and Justinianic Plagues struck the ancient world, they decreased the number of farmers, but they had no effect on the quantity of farmland. With fewer farmers seeking to work on the same amount of land, the price of land fell. Since the fall did not affect the quantity of land, we speak of this price as a rent, that is, a price that does not affect the allocation of resources. The more inelastically a good is supplied, the more its price resembles rent.

Rent seeking in the NIE consists of activities designed to capture economic rents. They do not encourage productive activity, but rather contest the returns to inelastically supplied goods and services. A thief, for example, does not produce anything; he steals things. In other words, he changes the ownership of existing resources, which is known as rent seeking. If we undertake activities like locking our houses or hiring body guards to deter thieves or assassins, that also is rent seeking. These preventive activities redirect activities that could be productive into unproductive pursuits; locks and guards are only used if thieves try to steal our possessions or others want to harm us. The existence of rent seeking causes the costs of purchasing to exceed the return from selling it; this discrepancy gives rise to what we call transaction costs, which include both rent seeking and anything else – like transport or information costs – that introduce a gap between the selling and buying price.

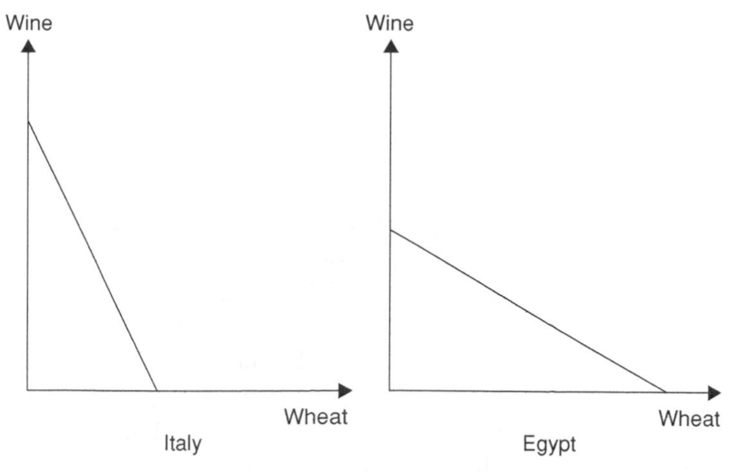

FIGURE 3.2 Production possibility curve

COMPARATIVE ADVANTAGE

David Ricardo presented the theory of comparative advantage 200 years ago; it has lasted as one of the most convincing argument in economics, showing how trade can benefit both partners. It is a simple theory, but it requires a little background to be understood.

Every country has what economists call a production possibility frontier, or PPF. The PPF shows how much of any one good or service can be produced, given how much of the other goods and services are being made. This relationship is best seen in two dimensions, assuming that a country makes only two products. Let us call them wine and wheat. If we put wine on the vertical axis and wheat on the horizontal axis, we can draw a country's PPF. It will touch each axis where the country devotes all of its resources to the production of either wine or wheat, that is, if it specializes in one or the other. The PPF connects these two points. Ricardo assumed it ran in a straight line, assuming that the amount of wheat that needed to be given up to produce an extra unit of wine was not affected by the amount of wheat and wine being produced. He assumed there was a single input to production – call it labor – which was easily switched between the production of various goods. There was no second input like land and no diminishing returns.

This relationship is shown in Figure 3.2. I show in this figure a PPF for each of two countries or regions that might trade with each other. The curves differ from one country to the other, even though both embody the same linear assumption. They differ in their slope. (The other possible difference – in height – will be discussed later.) One region, which we will call Italy, can make more wine more efficiently in terms of foregone wheat than the other region, which we will call Egypt. Egypt is well suited to growing wheat and needs to transfer a lot of resources from growing wheat to increase its wine production. The PPF for Italy therefore is steeper than the PPF for Egypt.

Consider the PPF for Italy. Where the PPF hits the vertical y-axis it shows how much wine would be produced in Italy if all the labor in Italy was used to produce wine. Where the Italian PPF hits the horizontal x-axis, it shows how much wheat would be produced if all the labor was used to produce wheat. If Italian agriculture was not completely specialized in wine or wheat, then total Italian production is shown by a point on the PPF between these extreme positions. The slope of the PPF shows the (constant) amount of one product that has to be foregone to produce more of the other. The ratio of the prices of the two goods is the *inverse* of this slope. Since Italy can make so much wine if it chooses to specialize in wine production, wine is cheap in Italy. The same reasoning applies to Egypt, where the PPF is flatter because Egypt is more suited to growing wheat. Wine therefore is more expensive in Egypt than in Italy because wine is scarcer – as represented by the flatter PPF.

It is the difference in the steepness of the PPF between the two countries that allows them to have comparative advantage and gains from trade. I have drawn the curves about the same level, but nothing rests on that. Assume for a minute that Italy is more efficient at producing both wine and wheat than Egypt. If the two PPF curves have different steepness, it still will be worthwhile to trade. For example, consider a lawyer who is the best lawyer in town and also the best typist. She has an absolute advantage over her secretary, even though the secretary has a comparative advantage in typing. The secretary can do a lot of typing for each unit of law services he omits, even though he does less legal work and typing than the lawyer in any time period. It makes sense for the lawyer to specialize in doing law and delegate her typing to her secretary, even though she is better at both. Despite the lawyer's absolute advantage in both activities, she still can gain by exploiting her *comparative* advantage in legal services.

Return to Figure 3.2. If there is a market, then the price of wine in terms of wheat will be higher in Egypt than in Italy, since the PPF is flatter. If farmers cannot sell wheat on any kind of market, they will make the choice of product by comparing the relative outputs they

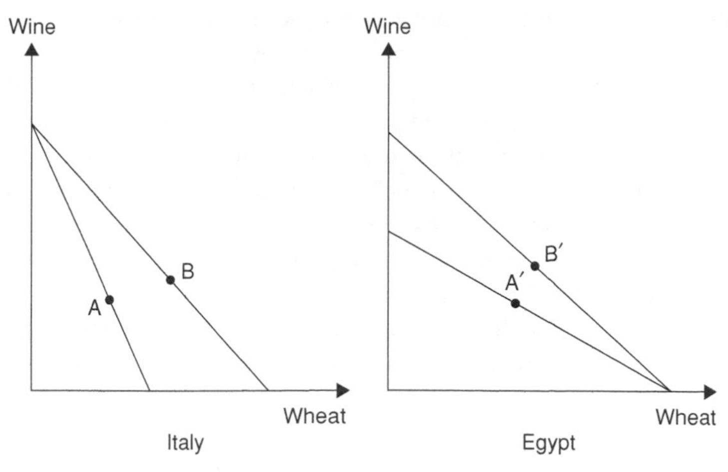

FIGURE 3.3 Effects of trade

can get from their limited resources. We can express this choice as expressing what economists call the "opportunity cost" of producing wheat or wine. That is the amount of the product *not* grown in order to produce the one that is grown. The opportunity cost functions exactly the way the price does in a market, and I use price as a generic term to include both market prices and opportunity costs. Egyptian farmers would like to produce wine due to its high price; the flat PPF shows that they cannot do so with Egyptian resources.

Now assume that trade is introduced between Italy and Egypt. Wine is more expensive in wheat units in Egypt because the opportunity cost of producing wine is larger than in Italy. Egyptians then will want to export wheat to get wine, which is relatively cheaper in Italy. Italians face exactly the opposite incentives. Wine can be produced easily in Italy, and the Italians will be happy to import wheat, which is harder to grow (relative to wine). Trade will make both countries or regions better off.

The benefits are shown in Figure 3.3. The price of wine was higher in Egypt before trade, and the price of wheat was higher in Italy. Once trade is allowed, both countries will have the same price ratio (in the absence of transport costs), which will be in between the initial price ratios in Italy and Egypt. The price of wine will fall in Egypt, allowing people there to get more wine for a given opportunity cost in wheat. Italy will use its resources to produce wine, getting its wheat by importing it. The initial consumption might have been at a point like A on the Italian PPF. With trade, Italy can now consume at point

B, above the PPF and unobtainable without trade. Similarly, Egypt will use its resources to produce wheat and increase its consumption of wine and wheat from A' to B'. The price of wheat in terms of wine will fall in Italy, and rise in Egypt. The price of wheat in terms of wine, or of wine in terms of wheat, will be the same in both countries.

Adam Smith wrote that the division of labor was limited by the extent of the market. Trade extends the market between countries or regions and thereby promotes the division of labor. This is one way in which the extension of trade increases the earnings of workers. Of course, if different regions or countries have resources unique to that locale, trade also allows these resources to be used for the benefit of the whole trading area.

Three extensions of this basic theory should be mentioned. First, what will be the new, common price of wine in terms of wheat? We know only that it must be between the original prices in Italy and Egypt, and the theory explained here does not contain enough detail to demonstrate where in this range it will lie. The position depends on the volume and elasticity of supply and demand for the two goods in the two countries or regions. In particular, large countries or regions that have large supplies and demands have much more effect on the eventual price than small countries. (This is where the height of the PPF is important.) When Britain was brought into the Roman trade network, it got many more gains from trade than the rest of the Roman world. Interregional trade benefits both regions, but taxes may offset some of the gains. For example, much of the wheat sent to Rome from Egypt was tribute. We clarify the effects of this tribute by dividing it into two parts. Trade improved access to all products in both Rome and Egypt. Tribute transferred some – or perhaps all – of this gain from Egypt to Rome.

Second, Ricardo drew the PPF as a straight line, but economists now generally draw it curving above a straight line. A convex PPF describes an economy in which there are diminishing returns to the production of wine and wheat. Here we consider two inputs to production, land and labor. If land cannot be transferred easily between different crops, there will be diminishing returns to labor in each activity. (This is the assumption that makes supply curves slope upward.) As the economy moves away from specialization in, say, wheat, it produces the first unit of wine by sacrificing only a tiny bit of wheat. In a position away from the axes where the economy is producing both wine and wheat, the economy has to give up a larger amount of wheat to free enough resources to make more wine. The gains from trade are the same as before with this complication, assuming that the internal price ratio of the goods differed initially in the two countries. The difference is that while countries will concentrate in the production of goods where they have a comparative advantage, they generally will continue to produce some of the other good as well. They will only specialize completely as shown in Figure 3.3 if the cost structures in the two countries are very different.

Third, the model as stated assumes that there are no transport costs when trade is allowed. That is why the price lines with trade in Figure 3.3 have the same slope in both graphs, indicating that the relative prices of wine and wheat were the same in Italy and Egypt. In antiquity, transport costs often were quite high, both because of the cost of transporting goods and because of administrative costs like duties and verification. If there are significant transport costs, the price ratios in the two countries will not approach equality. Instead, they will remain apart by the cost of the transport. If this wedge is large enough, it may preclude trade even if the costs of production in the two countries are different.

Transaction costs never completely eliminate trade. Very rare and expensive goods can be traded profitably even if transaction costs are high. Before the Pax Romana, jewelry and royal objects were traded around the known world. But high transaction costs prevented trade in cheaper goods, like wheat. Only when costs were low did trade extend to bulk commodities and the articles of common usage. This kind of trade flourished in the early Roman Empire, but it had existed earlier across the Mediterranean Sea. Two Phoenician ships sank in deep water during the eighth century BCE, each carrying 400 amphoras of wine. Their documentation has been lost, and we do not know why they were sailing, but it makes sense to infer that the people who sent 800 amphoras of wine into the center of the Mediterranean were engaged in interregional trade.[14]

The New Institutional Economics reminds us that transaction costs may be affected by institutions as well as transport costs. Trade requires not only shops or carts, but also ways to compensate prospective merchants for their efforts in bringing goods to strangers. The means of payments, the security of contracts – even implicit ones – are aspects of the institutions that promote trade. Kessler and Temin describe some of the ways Roman merchants made sure that goods shipped were the same as goods received, that bills were paid, and other aspects of trade were performed with relatively little cost to the people involved in trade.[15]

The extensive grain trade across the Mediterranean in the late Roman Republic and early Roman Empire is well known.[16] Using a complex version of the theory of comparative advantage, Geraghty showed that the growth of Mediterranean trade led Roman farmers in the Italian countryside to shift from wheat to wine.[17] This model allowed Geraghty to conclude that while free labor in Italy lost income as grain prices fell, their loss was largely offset by economic opportunities in the city of Rome and the *annona*. Kessler and Temin argued that the grain trade in the Mediterranean in this period led to the integration of prices across the whole area.[18] Wheat prices were lower in places far from Rome, such as Spain and the Middle East. In fact, the price discounts look like the cost of transporting wheat across the sea, implying that the price of wheat was equalized around the Mediterranean under the Pax Romana, subject only to the effect of transport costs.

ECONOMIC GROWTH

Hopkins proposed his famous taxes-and-trade model of the Roman economy in 1980. He argued that the Roman collection of taxes stimulated monetization and economic growth in the early Roman Empire.

> This simple model implies a whole series of small-scale changes in production, distribution and consumption, whose cumulative impact over time was important. There was a significant increase in agricultural production, an increase in the division of labor, growth in the number of artisans, in the size of towns where many of them lived, development of local markets and of long-distance commerce.[19]

Hopkins suggested a variety of ways to discern economic growth in this passage: the growth of agricultural production, non-agricultural production, towns, and trade. None of these indicators, however, indicates directly how fast economic growth progressed. They need to be inserted into some kind of framework to result in an estimate of Roman economic growth. Hopkins' accompanying estimate of the level of production does not help because it was derived by analogy with modern conditions and does not point toward the use of ancient evidence at all.

To provide evidence of economic growth, we need to define what we mean by this comprehensive term. The best measure is the growth of goods and services produced per person. This is a more restricted measure than changes in welfare because it looks only at the goods and services produced by the economy. All other things being equal, an increase in these goods and services should increase welfare, but other things may not have remained the same when economic production increased. The growth of goods and services produced per person also is a better measure of economic growth than the structural change used by Hopkins, for an economy can grow in many ways and with many different types of structural change. It is the results of structural change that are of interest to historians trying to discover the effects of events, institutions, and political decisions on the lives of ordinary people.

Economists speak of the growth in goods and services produced per person as intensive growth as opposed to extensive growth – the growth of *total* goods and services. Since population is in the denominator, growing population does not indicate economic growth. We use the product of economic growth and population growth to discuss military power, but discussions of economic growth typically take population to be determined by other factors. The interaction of population and economic growth will be discussed more in the context of the Malthusian model.

Goods and services are produced by workers and other factors of production like land and capital. These factors of production must be paid, perhaps by wages and rents, perhaps by other less formal means. Economic growth therefore can be measured either by examining the goods and services produced or the incomes received. Taxes and other charges by landowners or warlords may interfere with the equation of goods and services with incomes, but this is more of a concern for large modern governments than ancient ones. The terms 'per capita income' and 'per capita production' can be used interchangeably when discussing ancient economies.[20]

The growth of trade discussed in the last section clearly increased Roman incomes. Exploiting the gains from trade brings only temporary economic growth as the gains are realized over time, but these temporary gains might have lasted over a century to produce gains that are apparent even now. Increasing the efficiency of production, particularly in agriculture, also led to economic growth. Terracing was common, extending the range of land on which crops, particularly grapes and olives, could be grown. Wine and oil presses also used the Archimedean screw, enabling grapes and olives grown on new land to be processed more efficiently. The screw was used widely in cereal agriculture to drain land, extending the range of land that could be used for this crop as well. Our evidence is spotty, but evidence from many different areas suggests that these innovations had diffused over large ranges of the Roman Empire.[21]

Evidence of widespread improvements in consumption is accumulating, and Roman citizens must have had increasing incomes to buy the enhanced food and consumer durables. Jongman cited a variety of estimates showing that real wages, that is, the purchasing power of wages, increased in the late Republic and early Empire.[22] He surveyed the occasional evidence of documented wages, subsistence annuities, and slave prices – as an index of wages of free workers with whom Roman slaves competed. The data for any one of these measures is spotty, but the pattern of all of them is the same. This common pattern suggests that the occasional observations are capturing underlying trends whose existence is attested to by the variety of evidence that fits the pattern. Real wages rose after the Antonine Plague and fell unevenly after that. Labor income was the major part of total income in the agrarian society of ancient Rome, and an increase in real wages is a good index of an increase in total income.

How could there be economic growth in a basically Malthusian world? To answer this question, it is necessary to explain how the Malthusian model works. Malthus argued two hundred years ago that the size of a population was limited by the resources available to feed it.[23] By resources, most people mean land, understanding that the way land is used and other resources may be relevant as well. This Malthusian relation is known to economists today as the declining marginal product of labor when the number of workers on a given plot of land increases. Economics is called the dismal science because of this limitation on the ability of land to support a growing population. A larger population means that each person has less food and other products, that is, each person is poorer than he or she would have been with a smaller population. This is the same assumption used to generate an upward-sloping supply curve and convex PPF earlier.

For most workers near a Malthusian equilibrium, their diet consisted largely of grain in one form or another. We therefore approximate their real wage by looking at the ratio of the money wage to an index of the price of goods workers bought, giving grain a heavy weight in this index. If we divide money wages by the price of grain alone, we get a measure of the marginal product of labor, since farmers typically hire workers up to the point where the last (marginal) worker produces just enough grain to pay for the wages he earns. For ancient times, the real wage and the marginal product of labor can be taken as equal since farm workers often based their diet on the products they produced and we lack data to differentiate the two magnitudes.[24]

Return to Figure 3.1 and interpret it as showing the supply and demand for labor. The marginal product of labor is the demand curve for labor. An employer will hire workers up to the point where the marginal product – the increase in production gained by adding the last worker – equals the wage. If the employer hires more workers, the increase in production does not pay for the added workers. If the employer hires fewer workers, the last worker hired contributes more than his or her wage and the employer can see a way to increase output (production) more than input (wages) by hiring more workers. While the figure shows the total supply and demand of workers to the market, each farmer sees only the price he can get for his product. He faces a horizontal demand curve for his output, and he hires workers up to the point where the marginal product of workers equals this price. In ordinary markets, competition between workers will ensure that the decisions of individual farmers lead to the equilibrium of supply and demand in the labor market.

This explanation is for a profit-maximizing employer hiring workers in a market economy. This setting may have been the exception rather than the rule in the ancient world, but the logic of labor demand still holds. A Roman farmer or owner of a large estate had to consider how many workers, free or slave, to employ on his land. While he did not use the same language we use today, he saw the same gains and losses from using more or less labor. Given the imperfect recording of production long ago, we cannot expect any precision in the farmer's decision, but we expect the reasoning from modern markets to indicate the direction in which ancient employers tended to move. In particular, following the model of supply and demand explained earlier, we can expect ancient farmers to respond to changes in the environment in predictable ways.

Malthus needed an additional relation to find an equilibrium point on this line. Malthus did this by specifying a relation between worker's wages – taken to be their income – and their birth and death rates. Births rise with income, both as nutrition rises and as younger marriages become feasible. Death rates fall as income rises, infant mortality declines, and plagues, wars, and pestilence become less frequent. Modern research has confirmed the first of these relations, while generally failing to find convincing evidence of the latter.[25] For most purposes, only one relation is needed, provided the other one does not operate in the reverse direction.

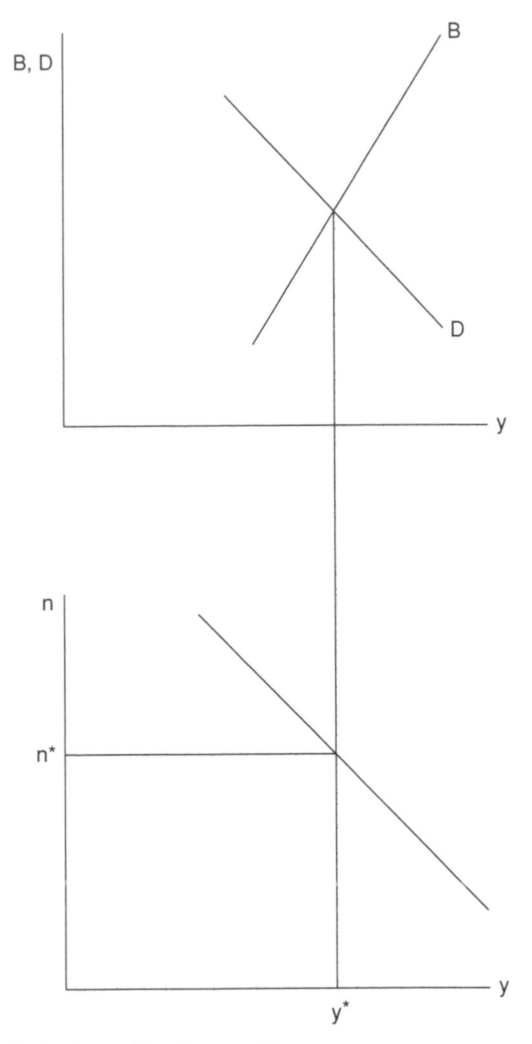

FIGURE 3.4 The basic Malthusian model

The preceding discussion is summarized in Figure 3.4. The horizontal axis on both graphs is the same: per capita income, represented by y. (Isn't it odd that economists often graph income, represented by "y," on the x-axis?) The top graph shows the determination of population size. Population grows if births exceed deaths; it falls if births fall short of deaths. The equilibrium is where the birth and death rates are equal, at y*. The bottom graph shows that the resource constraint permits only a limited population size, n*, at this income. Note that the model works well even if there is no relation between income and the death rate. If the curve marked D in the top graph is horizontal – that is, if it shows the death rate unaffected by income – y^* is still the equilibrium, and the analysis proceeds as before. The full Malthusian model was taken to restrict the range of early history. Clark's description is clear: "Anything that reduced the death rate schedule – advances in medical technology, better personal hygiene, improved public sanitation, public provision for harvest failures, peace and order – reduced material living standards [by increasing population]."[26]

Consider the effect of a plague, like the Antonine or Justinianic Plagues, in this model. Let us assume that the population fell by approximately one-third, without aiming for spurious precision. The effects are shown in Figure 3.5. Population fell from n^* to n_1. As population fell, income rose above the previous equilibrium income, y^*, because the marginal product of labor rises as population falls. Birth rates exceeded death rates at this higher income, as shown in the upper graph. Population grew as a result. It continued to grow until income was reduced to its previous level, y^*, where births and deaths were once again equal. As can be seen in the lower graph, per-capita income was unchanged at the new equilibrium, and the population returned to its former size.

Figure 3.5 shows two arrows. The horizontal one shows the effect of the plague, which reduced the population rapidly. The economy moved quickly along this arrow to the new point on the PPF. Then the excess of births over deaths slowly began to move the economy along the second arrow and bring the economy back to its equilibrium. Even though the two arrows look the same on the graph, they describe very different processes, one fast and one slow.

How long did this whole process take? We do not have much evidence from the Roman plagues, but we know more about the aftermath of the Black Death of 1349 in England. Immediately after the plague, money wages of farm workers shot up. For the Malthusian model, however, we need to know the path of real wages, that is, the extent to which the rise in money wages exceeded the rise in the price of grain and other consumables.

Real wages did not rise nearly as fast as money wages in the immediate aftermath of the plague. Instead they rose gradually and peaked a century after the plague, in the middle of the fifteenth century. It took a very long time for the Malthusian system to return to its equilibrium. It cannot be surprising that the return to the Malthusian equilibrium took a long time. Higher incomes after the Black Death may have resulted in earlier marriages, which in turn led to more children. But it took a generation or more for the effects of this change

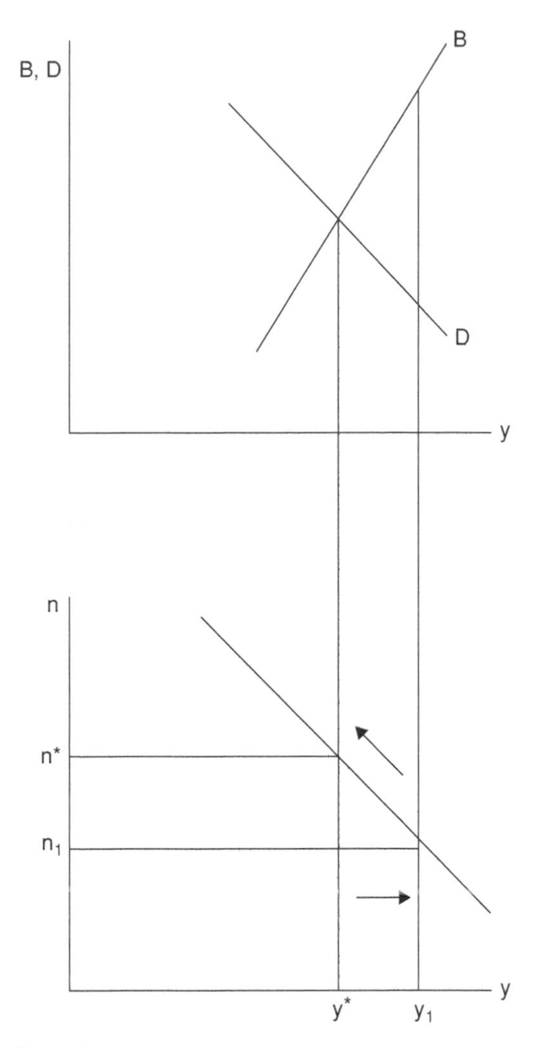

FIGURE 3.5 Effect of a plague

to become apparent in the agricultural labor market. If women changed their behavior slowly, it might have taken several generations to lead to population expansion. And when we start talking about generations, it requires only a few generations to make a century of delay. While we do not know much about family dynamics in the late fourteenth century, we do know that real wages did not start to fall until a century after the Black Death.[27]

This is consistent with the limited evidence from the Antonine Plague. Scheidel collected fragmentary wage and price data from

Roman Egypt in the second and third centuries.[28] The ancient sources are not frequent enough to provide the detailed timing evidence of the Medieval data, but they suggest a long period after the plague when wages were high. If we regard the observations as random draws from records of wages and prices in the two centuries, we are implicitly assuming that the effects of the population decline in the Antonine Plague lasted as long as the decline after the Black Death. The rise in the real wage, that is, the ratio of wages to commodity prices, was smaller in the ancient world, however. Real wages were less than half again as large in the third century as in the second century, while real wages peaked at twice the pre-plague level in the 15th century, suggesting that the Antonine Plague was not as severe as the Black Death.

Consider now a different "shock" to the Malthusian system. Instead of assuming that the size of the population changed, assume that the Malthusian resource constraint shifted outward. This change could come from trade and regional specialization permitted by the Pax Romana. It could come from technological change that allowed land to be used more efficiently. It shifts the line in the bottom graph of Figure 3.5 to the right. For any given population size, the available land now allows the marginal product of labor and income of farm workers to be higher than before.

As shown in Figure 3.6, this sets up a population expansion. In the short run, the effects of this "shock" on per capita income are the same as the results of a plague shown in Figure 3.5, but for different reasons. The population changed dramatically during a plague, but it changes more slowly under normal conditions. Per capita income can change more rapidly, and it increases in the short run, leaving population unaffected. In the longer run, however, the equilibrium has changed. The excess of births over deaths causes population to rise. Equilibrium is reached when income returns to its previous level in the upper graph, y^*. Looking at the lower graph, we see that the population is larger at the new equilibrium than before, at n_2 instead of n^*. The effect of technical change has been to increase the size of the population, not per capita income, in the Malthusian equilibrium. As in Figure 3.5, the initial movement shown in the initial horizontal arrow was much faster than the subsequent movement shown in the diagonal arrow.

Note the differences between Figures 3.5 and 3.6. In both of them, income increases, setting off a rise in population. This is a rightward shift in both graphs. Although population grows in both graphs, the relation of this growth to the prior level of the population is different. In Figure 3.5, the population is always lower than n^*, and the growth

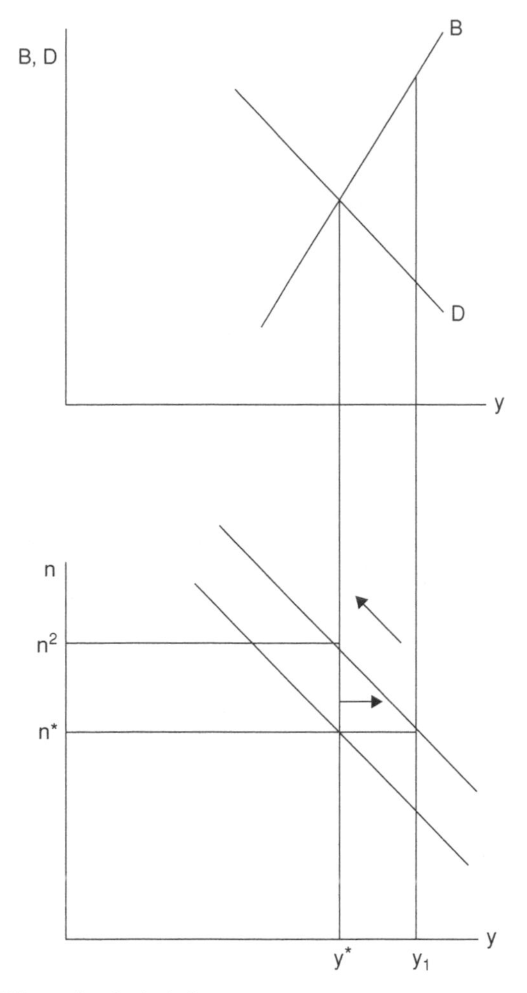

FIGURE 3.6 Effect of technical change

is only to regain the losses from the plague. In Figure 3.6, by contrast, population is always larger than n*, as improved technology allows for a larger population. If the shift in the resource constraint is a one-time movement, then the population settles down to a new equilibrium level, n_2, larger than n*.

As before, the economy will not move instantly to this new equilibrium. It will take a long time, perhaps more than a century. During that time, per capita income will be high and population will be growing. If the new technology diffuses slowly or perhaps continues to improve, then the resource constraint curve will continue to shift outward for a while instead of simply jumping from one position to another as shown in Figure 3.6. In that case, both incomes and population will continue to increase for quite a while before the pull of the Malthusian equilibrium is felt. If the resource constraint continues to shift outward for a while, then income can stay above y*, Malthusian subsistence, for more than a century. If productivity continues to advance indefinitely, income can stay above y* indefinitely.

Equilibrium in the Malthusian model shows constraints that operate on agrarian societies in the long run. The slow transition to a new equilibrium after a shock shows how Rome could have experienced economic growth for well over a century. Economics provides a coherent theoretical basis for debates about Roman economic growth.[29]

CONCLUSION

This paper summarizes a variety of economic models and techniques that can help ancient historians interested in economic affairs. Illustrations of existing uses of these tools have been noted, and readers of this essay are encouraged to read them, gather more details about these tools, and extend the use of these tools in ancient history. The aim of these tools is to clarify the economic basis of Roman and other ancient cultures; they do not presume that these societies operated like modern economies, as noted throughout the discussion. Even without explicit market activity, supply and demand, comparative advantage, and Malthusian influences were very important in the ancient world. These models and regression analysis are useful additions to the tool boxes of ancient historians.

NOTES

1 At www.stanford.edu/~scheidel/CCRE.htm.
2 Polanyi 1977: 35–40.
3 Temin 1980.
4 Temin 2002.
5 Hopkins 1978: 99–102.
6 Eisner 1989: 26.
7 Temin 2001.
8 North 1981, 1990.
9 Acemoglu, Johnson and Robinson 2001.
10 Scheidel, Morris and Saller (eds.) 2007: 651–741.
11 Rosenstein 2008: 23.
12 Eck 2000.

13 Hopkins 1980.
14 Temin 2006b.
15 Kessler and Temin 2007.
16 Rickman 1980; Erdkamp 2005; Morley 2007a.
17 Geraghty 2007.
18 Kessler and Temin 2008.
19 Hopkins 1980: 102.
20 Temin forthcoming b.
21 Wilson forthcoming a.
22 Jongman 2007a.
23 Malthus 2004.
24 Clark 2007a.
25 Lee 1980.
26 Clark 2007b: 27.
27 Clark 2007a.
28 Scheidel 2002.
29 Millett 2001; Saller 2002; Jongman 2007a; Scheidel 2009a.

4: HUMAN CAPITAL AND ECONOMIC GROWTH

Richard Saller

Economists seeking to explain the unparalleled economic growth of the nineteenth and twentieth centuries have paid increasing attention to human capital – that is, the education, training, and health of the labor force. Over the past two centuries higher levels of education have provided the foundation for discovery of new knowledge and the resulting technological advances needed to sustain growth over long periods at unprecedented rates. Training and education of the work force has enabled the technology to be used in economic production. And the life span and health of the population have improved to permit longer life spans and more intensive use of the skills. The magnitude of these gains is striking, as the average life span has more than doubled and the productivity per worker has increased by an order of magnitude in the most developed economies.

Roman historians have considered various aspects of the subject, but none has conceptualized a study of the Roman economy based on human capital. This is not surprising, since only in the second half of the twentieth century, when investments in human capital have come to dominate investments in physical capital, has it become clear to economists that the quality of labor is a major driver of growth. In the absence of reliable quantitative data for Rome, this chapter aims to provide a description of the levels of education and training of various sectors of the Roman labor force, an analysis of the extent of institutionalization of education and training, and some broad comparisons with other pre-industrial economies in order to assess Rome's level of economic development. The challenge is to add precision to the assessment of Keith Hopkins (1995/96) of "modest, though significant growth" of the Roman economy.[1] While it is not possible to calculate a growth rate with any confidence, it is possible to assess Roman institutions for education and training against those of other pre-modern economies. I will argue that Roman imperial levels of urbanization, education, and literacy (unsurprisingly) exceeded those of previous societies, but fell noticeably short of the most advanced societies of early modern Europe before the industrial revolution. On the one hand, Rome benefited from the more intense exchange of knowledge and differentiation of labor that generally comes with higher levels of urbanization; on the other hand, Rome was not able to break out of the contradiction that more intense urbanization also brought higher mortality.

HUMAN CAPITAL IN THE ROMAN IMPERIAL ECONOMY

Before turning to training and education, I want to signal the relevance of the more basic investments in food and shelter, the subject of a later chapter. Investment in nutrition and health enables labor, however unskilled, to put in the energy needed to produce. Robert Fogel has estimated that perhaps twenty percent of the population of pre-revolution France was too poorly fed to be able to work full days.[2] In the course of the nineteenth century the western European economies began a basic shift toward longer life expectancy through public health improvements, longer working lives, warranting greater investments in the education of fewer children who could be expected to survive. Debate continues over the adequacy of nutrition in the Roman empire, but there is no doubt that the Roman empire never experienced the shift of the demographic transition. The expected working life of a Roman entering adulthood was on the order of thirty years, in contrast with nearly forty-five years today.[3] That difference changes the calculation about how many children to bear and how much to invest in the nutrition and education of each.

The institution of slavery provided Roman slave owners with stark considerations of how much to invest in the food, clothing, and shelter for their servile human capital. For owners like Cato, this was a matter of conscious calculation. His *De Agricultura* (56) advised a greater investment of nutrition in fieldhands during the labor-intensive summer months than in the domestic and supervisory staff – an understanding of the need to invest in the calories necessary for work. And of course, Cato notoriously recommended that old, depreciated slaves be sold in order to off-load the costs of maintenance. Varro's *De Re Rustica* (1.17.3) shows an awareness that the risk of mortality varied by region, and with it, the rate of depreciation of slaves. The recent research of Sallares and Scheidel on the striking impact of malaria in dramatically increasing death-rates in certain regions has important consequences for the returns to human capital – an issue to which I will return in thinking about urbanization.[4]

Even when the calculation about investment in the human capital of slavery was not overt, the costs arguably influenced behavior – for example, in the phenomenon of the exposure and enslaving of newborns. Why, given the risk of childhood mortality, would anyone have picked up a newborn as a slave, and invested food and shelter in him or her until the age of productive work? It is possible to use data from Roman Egypt on the cost of wet nurses and food, together with the price of teenage slaves, to calculate that the present value of the investments in a foundling, including the probability of death before adulthood, came close to the market price of a young adult slave.[5] Why invest in the nurture of the foundling? I can think of two reasons: for an owner of modest means the investment was more gradual, and the owner would have had the equivalent of a *verna* who was regarded as more loyal.

What was the level of investment in the education and training of Roman workers? Not to ignore the obvious, the level of education as exemplified by literacy was higher in the Roman empire than at any time before and any time for centuries after. Having said that, is it possible to get a sense of scale in a comparative perspective?

Since we have no quantitative data, we will need to make estimates based on qualitative descriptions and assumptions about Roman society. First, there were the differences of social class between children of the leisured elite, the free working class, and slaves; and also the difference between rural and urban. In real life the distinctions were not always clear-cut; nevertheless, they are explicit and implicit in the ancient evidence.

In terms of institutional sophistication and size of investment, one may imagine three levels of training and education of children in the skills of production: (1) traditional learning from parents and family, (2) apprenticeship, and (3) formal education. The first level, learning by imitation and instruction within the family, is the one that I would assume to be the earliest in evolutionary terms – in fact, not unique to humans. My understanding of family farming throughout antiquity envisages this as the primary form of training of the next generation. Scattered references in the ancient texts suggest that young children, like old women, were thought suited to light tasks.[6] Presumably as they reached physical maturity, boys learned basic agricultural skills from fathers and other relatives and neighbors.

The complexity and subtlety of this learning, in which useful knowledge continues to accumulate from experience in later adult years, are evident from sophisticated studies of peasant agriculture in India based on unmatched data sets. Mark Rosenzweig found in India that the decline in production in bad years was forty percent in households where the head was under forty years old, in contrast to a decline of only fifteen percent on farms with a head over sixty.[7] Similarly, profits were multiples higher on farms with older heads. In other words, human capital from learning from experience continues to grow through the adult years. This has non-trivial implications for the Roman world, where some young men lost years of agricultural learning to army service, especially during the Republic, and where, to judge from the household census returns of Roman Egypt gathered by Bagnall and Frier, fewer than twenty percent of households had a head over sixty and forty percent had a head under forty.[8] Thus, Roman peasant households were generally held back by a double restraint of a high-mortality society: early death both cut short the application of knowledge gained through experience and also limited the further accumulation of knowledge.

In large-scale agriculture on the estates of the wealthy, work was more differentiated, though learning took place through imitation and experience. The pivotal figure organizing the production on these estates was the *vilicus* (bailiff), who should in Columella's view be experienced in the work of the farm, but need not be literate or formally educated. Carlsen's study of *vilici* identifies the moral virtues of honesty, sobriety, and self-restraint as the primary qualities sought in the ideal *vilicus*.[9] This is sensible in a context riddled by principal-agent problems. Of course, we know from the papyri of Roman Egypt that the skills of literacy and numeracy were deployed in the management of large estates, but it is interesting that Columella does not regard these beginning elements of formal education as essential in a *vilicus*. Furthermore, the example of Horace's Sabine estate shows that farm experience was not thought necessary, as trusted urban slaves were sent out to manage the farm. Rosenzweig's findings about the importance of experience to productivity are worth remembering.

The conclusion is that the overwhelming majority of the rural workforce relied on skills and knowledge gained through the first level of learning, and that the learning accumulated through a lifetime. This is not surprising, but it is worth contrasting with developments around the beginning of the industrial age, when the rise of agricultural schools and journals began to disseminate the results of the first organized experimental science in agriculture.[10] Columella lamented that, in contrast to rhetoric, mathematics, surveying, and other skills, agriculture "lacks both students and teachers" (1 pr.5). It is an important observation that whereas there were *officinae* (workshops) for the most contemptible vices – for example, the preparation and serving of luxurious foods – there were no schools dedicated to the dominant form of production, agriculture.

The urban economy of the empire – craft production, trade, and retail – presents a more varied picture of human capital. Certainly in the cities many children's education was no more than informal learning from parents. Plato (*Republic* 467A) referred to sons of potters learning their craft by watching their fathers, and Vitruvius (6 pr.6) alluded to the past practice of architects training their children. There was an analogous intergenerational transfer of skills when young slaves were purchased to work and to be trained in workshops by their masters.

APPRENTICESHIP

In addition, there were institutions of contractual apprenticeship and more formal education in several types of settings. For apprenticeship the papyri of Roman Egypt gathered by Keith Bradley provide the evidence.[11] Like Bradley, I assume that the fact that our examples of apprenticeship contracts come from Roman Egypt is a result of survival, not of the original geographical distribution of apprenticeship around the empire.

Why did apprenticeship make sense as an alternative to parent or master training in the household or workshop? A substantial minority of sons would not have had fathers alive to transmit their skills, and slaves did not always have a master with the skills. But the demographic explanation is not sufficient, to judge by the Egyptian weaver-father who contracted out his sons as apprentices to other weavers.[12] Cameron Hawkins, in his study of the craft economy, found that craftsmen were much less likely to receive funerary dedications from sons than other segments of the urban population – a pattern that would be hard to explain on the model of sons perpetually following fathers into their occupations.[13]

Why was apprenticeship used, even in situations where a skilled father existed? I think we need to imagine the variation in conditions that must have existed from one shop to the next. Apprenticeship was a mechanism that allowed labor to be moved from the natal family to a household where it was needed and could be supported with food for a limited term. The apprenticeship contracts usually included provision for the master craftsman to provide very basic subsistence for the apprentice. Given these terms, a household under financial pressure – perhaps because of poor sales or seasonal declines or too many children – could unload maintenance costs of a child to a more prosperous craft shop through apprenticeship. And if the prosperous shops were more successful because of the better skills or business sense of the master craftsman, then apprenticeship as an institution stood to improve the economy as a whole by allocating more students to the more skillful. But unless we believe that there were large differences in skill levels, economic growth derived from the institution of apprenticeship was limited.

The Egyptian contracts provide some insight into the age of the apprentice and the duration of the arrangement. Bradley deduced that apprentices were usually minors in their early teens, and this has a logic based on human capital. In order to derive the greatest return on the investment in training, it should be provided at that developmental moment after the ravages of childhood diseases when children have the physical and mental capacity to learn the skills and pull their weight in the workshop. An apprenticeship in the early teens fits pretty well with the implications of the schedule of Diocletian's maximum prices for slaves, which reach a peak value at age sixteen: this is the moment when the labor skills have been acquired and life expectancy to use those skills is longest.[14]

The extant apprenticeship contracts vary in length from a year or less up to six years. Most are for only a year or two. This means that the investment in human capital through apprenticeship was small by both early modern and contemporary standards, both because the duration of training was relatively brief and because the apprentice did not completely forgo wages in the course of training.[15] Contracts were structured so that the compensation – bare subsistence in the first year or two – gradually increased with increased skills and productivity – another reflection of a basic principle of human capital.

The fact that apprentices did not give up income during training distinguishes the economics of apprenticeship from formal education and raises a question. If an apprenticeship transformed an unskilled youth into a skilled *artifex* (craftsman) and as a result doubled his daily wage, to judge from several broad statements in our sources (for example, *Dig.* 17.1.26.8), why did more parents and slave masters not apprentice their sons and slaves.[16] It would seem that the investment was modest and the returns clear. I have no answer. In later eras guilds restricted the entry into crafts in order to limit supply, but there was no such organizational constraint in the Roman world.[17]

A second question for which I have no answer is why the Egyptian apprenticeship contracts are so heavily dominated by weaving and cloth production. The eighty percent or more of apprenticeship contracts in cloth production cannot reflect the distribution of workers among skilled crafts.

FORMAL EDUCATION

When economists today calculate the human capital investment in education, one of the biggest costs is that of the student's lost work time – i.e., forgone earnings. The Roman empire did have formal education of several types that took children and youths away from work. The literary and rhetorical education for the elite is best attested and most studied, though that type of education probably did not take that group away from much productive work in the conventional sense. Indeed, studies of modern education systems in developing economies argue that such elite education with little application to production can have a dampening effect on growth. The less elevated types of education that developed basic skills of literacy and numeracy for work as managers, stewards, surveyors, bankers, scribes, shorthand writers, and so on, are far more important as a positive influence on productivity.

In the Roman empire this basic education was transmitted in at least three settings. One was apprenticeship, but with the difference that the student paid a fee. One of the contracts from Egypt apprenticed a male slave to a shorthand writer for a fee. The fee compensated the *notarius* (shorthand writer) for his time lost in the course of teaching, in contrast to the master weavers who were able to use the apprentice's labor productively.[18]

The second setting was the class of the *magister*, who derived an income from teaching, sometimes in physical spaces as makeshift as the street. Alan Booth described the arrangement in the following terms: "there is cause to believe that in first-century Rome the *ludi magister* (the *calculator* and *notarius* too) ran a lowly type of technical school which peddled craft literacy to children, slave and free, to enhance their employability, but that the elements were usually acquired elsewhere by children embarking upon a liberal education."[19] Booth's language here reflects an aristocratic point of view; from the viewpoint of ordinary working Romans, such formal education, even if meager, was not "lowly." To judge by Diocletian's Price Edict it would have cost a laborer two day's worth of wages per month to have one child taught for a month. It would have been beyond the means of most working-class families to have more than one child in a class of this type for any length of time.

The third setting was the *paedagogium* (training school for young slaves) of the great aristocratic houses, where urban slave children were taught the elements of letters and numbers, as well as the finer arts of elegant domestic service.[20] The institution of the *paedagogium* made economic sense in two ways. First, it was the great houses of the Roman empire that had a clear need for the skills of reading, writing, and arithmetic for purposes of management of a large organization. The large *domus* (households) were the largest private productive units in the early empire, requiring coordination, monitoring, and record-keeping. Second, wealthy masters used slaves in managerial roles for good reason. Not only could slaves be held accountable through painful physical coercion, but they were not free to walk off with the human capital invested in them. One of the dilemmas faced by modern corporations is that if they invest in training their workers and raising the value of their skills, it is difficult to prevent those workers from taking that investment away to a competitor who has not borne the costs. Ownership of human chattel avoided that dilemma in Rome. As Sandra Joshel's tabulation of occupations by slave, freed, and freeborn status in funerary dedications shows, slaves are most overrepresented in administrative positions; freedmen are most overrepresented in manufacture; and the freeborn are most overrepresented in building occupations.[21]

A master could reap a profit from raising his slave's education level either by directly employing him or by selling him. In the late Republic both Crassus and Atticus were known for investing in this sort of human capital. Indeed, Plutarch writes in his *Life of Crassus* (2), "though he owned numberless silver mines, and highly valuable tracts of land with laborers upon them, nevertheless one might regard all this as nothing compared with the value of his slaves; so many and so capable were the slaves he possessed – readers, amanuenses, silver-smiths, stewards, table-servants; and he himself directed their education, and took part in it himself as a teacher, and, in a word, he thought that the chief duty of the master was to care for his slaves as the living implements (*organa empsucha*) of household management." Plutarch's phrase *organa empsucha* might be translated, with some license, as "human capital." My interpretation of this passage is that Plutarch wanted to acknowledge Crassus' appreciation of the value of human capital investment, and regarded Crassus as unusually shrewd in this regard.

The inclusion of "table-servants" in the list of educated slaves, alongside stewards and readers, might seem out of place to the modern reader, but it is a reminder that the *paedagogium* trained slaves not only in what we would consider basic productive skills, but also in the skills that supported the luxurious lifestyle of the grand *domus* – that is, the vices denounced by Columella in his lament over the lack of schools of agriculture.

The largest institution in the Roman world was the army. In the twentieth century the United States armed services figured substantially in enhancing the skills of the population, and it is reasonable to ask what role the Roman army may have had in the development of human capital. The army depended on the skills of literacy and numeracy, as well as on crafts, engineering, and medical expertise. At times, that expertise was loaned to civilian projects. There surely were informal development and transmission of skills within the army, but no formal institutions – for example, no military academies – to educate soldiers. The famous Roman training described by Vegetius was physical. To the extent that the army required educated specialists, they seem to have recruited them.[22] Overall, recent studies have concluded that the level of literacy in the army should not be exaggerated. J. N. Adams inferred from the Greek script and words in army documents "low rates of literacy and the shortage of learned scribes capable of doing a job properly".[23]

THE LABOR OF WOMEN

So far, this chapter has been focused on sons, slaves, and soldiers – an implicitly male orientation. But the potential for economic growth depends on the configuration of investment in women as well as men. The evidence from the city of Rome and from Roman Egypt suggests that freeborn women were not completely barred from the training and education that enhanced men's life chances; on the other hand, they seem to have received much less training than males. From the list of Egyptian contracts, Bradley made an important point about the absence of freeborn women in apprenticeships. Though there is some argument about a couple of cases, I think he is right, and certainly his general point stands. The contrast with female slaves is noteworthy: as many female slaves as male slaves appear on the list – a reminder that owners were willing to develop the value of their slaves, female or male. This is an illustration of how the institution of slavery allowed fuller exploitation of female human capital as compared with later Europe when apprenticeship was an exclusively male institution.[24]

If the rarity of freeborn women in apprenticeships was also true of Rome, it would provide one reason why women appear in so many fewer occupational categories in Roman funerary dedications: only 35 as compared with more than 200 for men.[25] One might argue that this is an illusion of funerary representation that preferred to refer to women as wives, but the heavy underrepresentation of women in jobs requiring education is corroborated by Setälä's brickstamp catalogue of 335 *officinatores* (shop managers), only 20 of whom were women.[26] On the other hand, the number of women is not zero, and we know that some women did learn letters and numbers, and more.

URBANIZATION AND HUMAN CAPITAL

The level of urbanization of a society is a broad indicator of economic development insofar as part of the population is engaged in non-agricultural production beyond subsistence. Urbanization in Europe, which peaked in the pre-modern era under the *Pax Romana*, also had diverse and cross-cutting implications for human capital.

Cities facilitate education and, more generally, the exchange of information and ideas, because denser populations generate more interactions. To take an illustration, Augustine's education progressed through a hierarchy of larger towns and cities, as his training advanced to higher levels of specialization. The letters of Pliny suggest that his hometown, Como, was of a size to be on the cusp of having enough children from families of sufficient means to employ a teacher (*praeceptor*), whereas much larger cities such as Rome, Alexandria, Antioch, and Carthage brought together enough teachers and students to generate the most sophisticated level of intellectual discourse of classical antiquity.[27] The larger cities also housed the large urban *familiae* with their *paedagogia* to train slaves, the largest of which was the imperial household. Only these very large *domus* would have had an urban slave staff of a size to warrant a *paedagogium*.

Beyond formal education, cities were sites of concentrated demand that encouraged the development of specialization and sub-specialization. Given the limits of formal education and information technology, most skills had to be transmitted by face-to-face interactions, which were facilitated by concentrations of population. Thus, the urban setting stood to increase the stock of human capital.

Here the insights of Jane Jacobs's classic book, *The Economy of Cities*, are worth exploring. Her fundamental point is that "economies that do not add new kinds of goods and services, but continue to repeat old work, do not expand much nor do they, by definition, develop." This process of "new work" being added to "old work" "is of the essence in understanding cities because cities are places where adding new work to older work proceeds vigorously."[28] In a sense, Hopkins was using this insight when he noted the differentiation of labor reflected in the number of occupational titles in the inscriptions from Rome and other cities.[29]

This seems to me to be an area that would repay further research. How much growth does the Roman occupational inventory represent over the occupational lists from the ancient Near East? In what sectors does "new work" appear? In analyzing the occupational structures of Roman cities, we should remember Jacobs's further observation about division of labor. "Division of labor, in itself, creates nothing . . . [It] is a device for achieving operating efficiency, nothing more. Of itself, it has no power to promote further economic development . . . All further increases in efficiency, once existing work has been suitably divided into tasks, depend upon the addition of new activities."[30] In this respect, it is not immediately clear to me how to evaluate, say, the *fabri ocularii* (makers of eyeballs for statues) as evidence for "new work" in a growing economy. In any case, a systematic comparison of the Roman imperial occupational inventory with those of earlier and later pre-industrial economies might yield valuable qualitative insights about the stock of human capital, and the inventories will be centered, not coincidentally, on cities.

But if Rome and other major cities were generators of development of human capital, they were also heavy consumers of human capital for intended and unintended reasons. One of the most striking features of Roman urban culture was the deliberate destruction of human capital in the arena. From late in the reign of Marcus Aurelius comes the *senatus consultum de pretiis gladiatorum minuendis* (Senatorial Decree on Lessening the Prices of Gladiators) providing information on the sale, taxing, and training of gladiators.[31] The text indicates that Marcus decided to forgo the blood money that had been flowing into the imperial treasury at a rate of 20 to 30 million sesterces per year from taxes on the sale of gladiators (25 to 33 percent) and revenues from the sale of convicted criminals to be put to death in the arena for the pleasure of audiences in cities across the empire. Several economic features of these practices warrant attention. First is the implied scale of the business at more than 100 million sesterces per year to generate this level of taxes, and then the accompanying level of deliberate destruction of human capital in the thousands or possibly even tens of thousands per year, including condemned criminals. Second is the elaborate categorization of gladiators by level of skill and by specialist training, with prices ranging from 3,000 sesterces to 15,000 sesterces for trained combatants and 600 sesterces for convicts sold for execution in the arena. The curious and telling feature to the modern eye is that the most highly differentiated sector in the civilian labor economy, with its five skill levels and several subspecialties, may have been killing for the purpose of entertainment.

Roman cities also had the unintended effect of being population sinks. Dense concentrations of population facilitated the transmission of knowledge and productive skills, and also the transmission of infectious diseases in an era before effective public health infrastructure. Walter Scheidel has guessed, based on the extraordinarily high excess seasonal mortality documented by Roman funerary inscriptions, that mortality in the capital may have been 50 percent higher than in the population as a whole (60 per 1,000 per year, as opposed to 40 per 1,000 per year).[32] For a slaveowner Rome might be the place where her artisanal slave could earn the highest wages as a return on the investment in skills, but also the place where the life expectancy of the slave was shortest. Sachs and Malaney have noted with respect to contemporary sub-Saharan Africa that "the impact of malaria on economic growth rates through the mechanism of depressing the rate of human capital accumulation could be considerable".[33] The possibility of a similar phenomenon should be taken into account in considering the human capital dimension of the demography of ancient Mediterranean cities. Not until the nineteenth century did the public health revolution begin to liberate humanity from the terrible contradiction that the same urban concentrations that enabled efficient exchange of ideas and skills also enabled efficient exchange of microbes.[34]

COMPARATIVE ASSESSMENT OF ROMAN INVESTMENT IN HUMAN CAPITAL

What does all of this add up to as to the impact of formal education and the investment in human capital? There cannot be much doubt that the levels of literacy and education were higher in the Roman empire than before or for centuries after, just as the early imperial economy was probably more productive than before or immediately after. To assess the impact on the economy, it is useful to estimate how much more. There is a rich debate over the causal relationship of education to economic growth. Clearly, the relationship is complex and not monocausal. And yet it is also clear that broad formal education is generally a prerequisite for sustained growth. There is a strong correlation between the breadth of primary education in Europe between 1600 CE and 1900 CE and growth. In the early modern era the Netherlands was the leader both in economic growth, with an annual rate of 0.2 percent in the seventeenth century, and in literacy, with rates of the order of 60 to 70 percent of adults, male and female.[35] The reason for the very high rate of education was that the Reformed Church mandated universal education and made provision to pay for poor orphans. Similarly, a recent study of Prussia argues that Protestant counties experienced faster growth than Catholic counties in the nineteenth century precisely because of the Protestant emphasis on universal education for purposes of literacy to read the Bible.[36]

In assessing the educational level of European countries in the early to mid-nineteenth century, Easterlin used the measure of proportion of the total population in primary school at any given time. Countries with low levels of education had fewer than 4 percent in primary school, whereas those with high levels were in the range of 10 to 20 percent, yielding literacy rates in excess of 70 percent.[37]

For the sake of comparison, today the leading economies have average education levels of up to twelve years per person and per capita Gross Domestic Products of more than $25,000 per year. Countries such as India and Pakistan have levels of education around five or six years and per capita Gross Domestic Products (GDP) at purchasing power parity (PPP) in the range of $2,000 to $3,000. The poorest countries of sub-Saharan Africa have education levels of one to two years and per capita GDPs at PPP of $700 to $1,400.[38]

Let me offer a tentative estimate of Roman education levels based on some rough assumptions. These assumptions are open to discussion and criticism, but they would have to be wildly wrong to change the general conclusion. First, I assume that formal education was largely the preserve of the cities and that the cities accounted for an eighth of the population of the empire.[39] Second, I assume that in the cities the skilled class of craftsmen and merchants had a basic education, but the unskilled did not because they could not afford to pay for it. And

I further assume that the skilled artisanal class amounted to half of the urban population. In addition, I assume that a basic education in letters and numbers could be acquired in three years. Finally, I assume that all members of the senatorial, equestrian, and curial orders received at least a basic education. These rough assumptions both underestimate and overestimate. They underestimate to the extent that the rural population was not utterly illiterate.[40] They overestimate to the extent that no discounting is done for girls, though it is clear that they received less schooling than boys. The oversimplifications will be partially offsetting. The chief point is that the Romans did not attempt mass publicly funded education, restricting basic education to children of families with enough surplus income to pay teachers.[41] Much of the imperial support for education went to the more refined levels, which did not contribute much to economic production.

On these assumptions, I estimate that the average number of years of formal education across the whole population was less than a half year per person and that at any given time perhaps one-half of one percent of the population over the age of five were receiving basic education. That is, Roman levels of formal education were more than an order of magnitude lower than in developed countries today and, more telling, a fraction of the levels seen in the least developed countries today and the fastest developing countries of the early nineteenth century. And, finally, the breadth of basic education and literacy was markedly lower than in the Netherlands in the seventeenth century with its literacy rate of sixty percent.[42]

How great was the investment in basic education in the empire? Setting aside elite education in literature and rhetoric, I would very roughly estimate on the basis of these assumptions a student population at any given time in the range of 250,000 taught by 10,000 teachers (of the order of 0.1 percent of the urban population). If these teachers had incomes at roughly the level of skilled craftsmen as suggested by Diocletian's Price Edict, then the total expenditure in the empire for basic education would have been of the order of ten million sesterces per year, or about 0.1 percent of the minimum Gross Domestic Product estimated by Hopkins.[43]

These very crude estimates of numbers of students and teachers and of investment could be multiplied several times and still lead to the same conclusion: Roman investment in education, and the resulting literacy, were high by pre-modern standards, but lower than those of the early modern economic leaders, and exceedingly low by contemporary standards. This assessment of human capital in the Roman economy corresponds with Temin's conclusion regarding the level of development of financial intermediation in the Roman Empire.[44] Neither the level nor the configuration of investment in human capital was sufficient to produce the steady stream of technological innovation required to sustain economic growth.[45]

NOTES

1 Hopkins 1995: 57.
2 Fogel 2004: 8–18.
3 Roman life expectancy at age fifteen was around thirty-five years, of which about six years would have been lost to ill health (W. Scheidel, personal correspondence, 19 July 2010).
4 Sallares 2002; Scheidel 2003.
5 Though the prices for sale of slaves in Roman Egypt are scattered and do not amount to a meaningful series, it appears that prices for a young female slave (outside Alexandria) centered around 1200 drachmas. If so, to spend 204 drachmas (8.5 drachmas per month times 24 months, including the oil allowance) to nurse a foundling would make sense on the following calculation. The investment entailed a substantial risk (perhaps 50 per cent) that the child would not survive to productive or reproductive adulthood; that sum, invested in loans at interest would have roughly doubled in value over the twelve to fourteen years of rearing; and the child would have required an additional investment of about 50 drachmas per year in maintenance after infancy. During the later years of childhood, enough return on the investment could have been realized in the form of household service to offset the cost of food (to judge by the apprenticeship contracts). The resulting total value of the investment ([204 drachmas X 2 (for risk) X 2 (for forgone interest)] + [50 drachmas per year (maintenance) X 5 years X 1.5 (forgone interest)]=1191 dr.) is comparable to the cost of an adult female slave. Of course, this calculation is extremely crude, but it does answer the argument of some historians that it would have made no financial sense to raise foundlings, especially females. For wetnursing contracts, see Manca Masciardi and Montevecchi 1984: 32–5; for slave prices, see Drexhage 1991: 249–79 and Johnson 1936: 279–81, especially *P.Bour.* 16 and *P.Oxy.* 95, and for wages, Johnson 1936: 306–10 especially *P.Oxy.* 736 and *BGU* 894.
6 Wiedemann 1989: 153–5.
7 Rosenzweig 1994: 63–90.
8 Bagnall and Frier 1994. From the appendix of household census returns, I surveyed the ages of the oldest males in complete returns: of 109 households, 49 had an oldest male under age 40, and 19 had an oldest male over the age of 60.
9 Carlsen 1995: 59–63.
10 True 1929: 2.
11 Bradley 1991: 103–24.
12 Bradley 1991: 107, Table 5.1, nos. 8, 10, 13.
13 Hawkins 2006 and below, Chapter 9.
14 Scheidel 1996b.

15 Smuts and Stromback 2001 discuss evidence for early modern apprenticeships ranging from three to four years in Germany to seven years in England.
16 As a point of comparison, Smuts and Stromback 2001: 9 report that in eighteenth-century England, the ratio of wages of apprentices to unskilled labor to journeymen craftsmen was 40:70:100 with apprentices at bare maintenance for one person.
17 Smuts and Stromback 2001: 9.
18 Bradley 1991: 107 no. 20.
19 Booth 1979: 19.
20 Bonner 1977: 45.
21 Joshel 1992: 127.
22 Nutton 1969.
23 Adams 2003: 634, endorsed by Phang 2007: 301.
24 Smuts and Stromback 2001: 5.
25 Joshel 1992: Table 3.1 illustrates the asymmetry of men and women in the occupations inscriptions: in the categories of "sales," "banking," "professional," and "administration" she counts 538 men as against 38 women.
26 Setälä 1977: 108.
27 Plin. *Ep.* 4.13, on which see Rawson 2003: 164.
28 Jacobs 1969: 49–50.
29 More than 200 from Rome, according to Treggiari 1980.
30 Jacobs 1969: 82.
31 *CIL* 2.6278 = *ILS* 5163= *FIRA* 1.295–97, with Carter 2003.
32 Scheidel 2003: 175.
33 Sachs and Malaney 2002: 683.
34 Meltzer 1992: 10.
35 De Vries and Van Der Woude 1997: 170.
36 Becker and Woessman 2007.
37 Easterlin 1981.
38 International Monetary Fund 2010; Barro and Lee 2010: 32–3.
39 Following Scheidel 2007a: 80.
40 Hezser 2001 suggests a literacy rate in rural Palestine of three percent or somewhat more.
41 See Kleigwegt 1991: 81, who estimates illiteracy at 90 percent – that is, slightly lower than my rough estimate. My estimate could be doubled and still leave the literacy rate in Roman Empire well below that of the early modern leaders. Rawson 2003: 165 implies elite access to education when she refers to the importance of the *paedagogus* accompanying the student.
42 See De Vries and Van Der Woude 1997: 694 for the substantial early modern Dutch investment in basic education in human capital, even in orphans.
43 Hopkins 1995/96.
44 Temin 2004a.
45 See Galor 2005 for the broad theoretical understanding of this transition in the nineteenth century.

Part II

Labor

5: SLAVERY

Walter Scheidel

Building on Greek and Hellenistic institutions, ancient Rome created the largest slave society in history.[1] There are several reasons for defining the Roman Empire as a slave society, above all in its Italian core but also to varying degrees in its subject territories. Slaves, numbering in the millions and widely dispersed, accounted for a non-trivial share of its total population. In key areas, slaves were not merely present but supported what has been termed a 'slave mode of production,' a mode that rested both on an integrated system of enslavement, slave trade, and slave employment in production, and on "the systematic subjection of slaves to the control of their masters in the process of production and reproduction."[2] Most importantly, Rome counts as a slave society in terms of the structural location of slavery: dominant groups, once again above all at the core, relied to a significant degree on slave labor to generate surplus and maintain their position of dominance.[3] Since the role of slavery in central productive processes turned Rome into a 'slave economy,' just as the widespread domination of slaves as a primary social relationship made it a 'slave society,' these two terms may be used interchangeably, especially in those strata where slaves and ex-slaves continuously enveloped owners and patrons and mediated their interaction with the freeborn population. In short, Rome was a 'slave society' to the extent that without slavery it would have looked profoundly different.[4]

In keeping with the theme of this volume, this chapter focuses on the economic dimension of Roman slavery.[5] It addresses the three principal questions of 'what,' 'why,' and 'how.' What was the Roman slave economy like – what did slaves do, where, and for whom? How many were there and where did they come from? And how did Roman slavery compare to other major slave systems in world history? Why did Romans employ slave labor the way they did? How did the Roman slave system develop over time? The overall objective is to assess the economic importance and consequences of Roman slavery, its contribution to the formation of the Roman economy as a distinctively imperial system of domination, production, and exchange.

Slavery in the Roman Empire

Throughout the centuries that have produced the most evidence, from the late Republic to late antiquity, slavery is amply documented. This documentation primarily conveys the impression that slavery was important and ubiquitous without enabling us to quantify its scale and contribution: it is much easier to establish the presence of slaves in the record or to encounter sentiments that consider their presence common than to measure their numbers, origins, and spatial and occupational distribution. For this reason, any modern assessments of the overall importance of Roman slavery are bound to remain uncomfortably vague, at least by the standards of the study of modern slave societies.

Relevant information comes from a wide range of sources, such as literary accounts, legal sources, inscriptions, papyri, and (albeit often more tenuously) from material remains.[6] Class bias permeates many of these sources: literature was composed by and for elites, law catered to them, and inscriptions recording slaves and freedpersons frequently emanated from the social networks of the propertied. In some sense this is not a serious problem: evidence of elite interest and involvement in slavery is critical for establishing the structural location of Roman slavery. At the same time, the nature of the evidence, with relatively few exceptions, makes it more difficult to answer questions about the spread of slavery into sub-elite groups and into more peripheral regions. Occasional references offer tantalizing glimpses of a world that may have been thoroughly permeated by the institution of slavery: in 214 BCE, middling Roman citizens could be expected to own slaves; in surviving census records from Roman Egypt during the first few centuries CE, some 13 per cent of adequately documented households owned slaves; and literary sources repeatedly portray slaveownership as a common feature well beyond elite circles.[7]

Slaves were engaged in an enormous variety of activities, as estate managers, field hands, shepherds, hunters, domestic servants, craftsmen, construction workers, retailers, miners, clerks, teachers, doctors, midwives, wetnurses, textile workers, potters, and entertainers. In addition to private sector employment, they worked in public administration and served in military support functions. They were owned by private individuals as well as the state, communities, temples, and partnerships.

As *servi vicarii*, slaves were put at the disposal of fellow slaves. Their responsibilities ranged from the most basic tasks of footmen and water-carriers to the complex duties of stewards and business managers. Slaves could be kept in chains or placed in positions of trust, resided in their owners' homes or were apprenticed or rented out. They are attested in every part of the Empire. Freed slaves were active in a similarly wide range of occupations, and in addition rose into the most senior echelons of private and public administration.[8]

As already noted, it is difficult to translate this powerful impression of ubiquity into a demographic assessment. Roman sources do not report the number of slaves in any particular community, let alone in entire regions or the Empire as a whole. The only apparent exception, Galen's casual claim that his hometown of Pergamum in Asia Minor was inhabited by 40,000 (adult male) citizens and 80,000 'wives and slaves' makes us wonder how children fit into this scheme. A number of texts refer to large-scale slaveowning in Italy and the provinces: 4,116 slaves bequeathed by a rich freedman; 400 slaves each in the households of a Roman aristocrat and a North African landowner; 2,000 slaves owned by a pretender; imperial legislation addressing owners of more than 500 slaves; more than 500 slaves repairing buildings in the city of Rome and 700 slaves taking care of its aqueducts; more than 152 slaves owned by a single landowner on a small Aegean island; 107 public slaves appropriated from an Anatolian town; 1,000 or 2,000 slaves ascribed to each of the wealthy of Antioch in Syria; 3,000 and 6,000 slaves held by two Cappadocian temples; and 2,400 or more rural slaves freed by a late Roman aristocrat.[9] Although some of these figures may well reflect rhetorical stylization or hyperbole, they are probably just the tip of the iceberg.

Nevertheless, isolated numbers do not readily support broad generalizations. Modern estimates of overall slave numbers are logically related to our assumptions about slaves' presence in different occupations, whereas the latter are also a function of the former: we are dealing with an equation replete with known unknowns. All we can confidently posit are logical corollaries: if slaves had been very numerous, slavery had to have been widespread, not limited to the rich and urban settings but extending into the general population and/or the countryside – which is just another way of saying that for slaves to have played an important role in farming there had to be very many of them.

The only proper statistics come from the census returns of Roman Egypt in the first three centuries CE. Close to 15 percent of urban residents and more than 8 percent of villagers, mostly in Middle Egypt, were slaves, but only 7 percent of the residents of a town in Upper

Egypt. This points to significant variation even within a putatively fairly homogeneous region, and higher rates of slaveownership are plausible but not attested in Alexandria.[10] The evidence is consistent with a rough estimate that between 5 to 10 percent of the population of Roman Egypt was made up of slaves.[11] Much more limited and fragmentary data from fourth-century CE census inscriptions from the Aegean point to a significant slave presence on rural holdings but do not permit more general estimates.[12]

Modern attention has traditionally centered on Italy, which may well have been the most slave-rich part of the Empire. Given that blanket guesses at overall tallies are of no value, the only even remotely promising way of getting some sense of the overall size of the Italian slave population is by estimating likely demand for slave labor.[13] This approach, for what it is worth, works best for rural slavery, an area where slave numbers can be more reliably linked to labor requirements. Estimates of rural slavery are highly sensitive to our assumptions about slaves' involvement in grain production, ranging from around a quarter of a million slaves (for low involvement) to perhaps three times as many (for high involvement). The scale of urban slavery is even more difficult to assess because it is very difficult to determine demand for services. A proposed range from half a million to one million urban slaves reflects these uncertainties.[14] It is quite possible but by no means certain that slavery was, in numerical terms, a predominantly urban phenomenon: an epigraphic roster from Herculaneum makes it hard to avoid the conclusion that a very large part and perhaps the majority of its inhabitants were current and former slaves, an observation that indicates the potential for extraordinary levels of slaveownership in the very core of the imperial system.[15]

Complicating matters further, abiding uncertainties about the size of the free population of Roman Italy make it difficult to convert any estimate of overall slave numbers into a proportion: 1 to 1.5 million slaves might represent 15 to 25 percent of the population of imperial Italy (see Chapter 1), and their share may have been even larger in western central Italy. Empirical information for the bulk of the imperial population, the 80-odd percent residing outside Italy and Egypt, is non-existent and even conjectures are therefore fraught with great hazards. A speculative reconstruction bounded by the estimates for Italy and Egypt suggests a share of slaves in the imperial population of somewhere around 10 percent, a figure that should best be taken as an order of magnitude in the sense that much lower (<5 percent) or higher (20+ percent) would seem much more difficult to defend.[16]

Estimates of slave numbers are logically connected to those of the slave supply and the incidence of manumission. Both of these features are well documented in qualitative terms but usually impossible to measure empirically. Ancient texts mention various sources of slaves from capture in warfare and kidnapping by pirates and brigands to penal slavery, the enslavement of abandoned or sold children, self-sale, foreign imports, and birth to slave women. Roman historiography emphasizes violent seizure especially during the Republican period: from 297 to 167 BCE alone, some 700,000 persons were reportedly enslaved in military campaigns, a tally that does not lay claim to completeness, and millions of slaves were supposedly created in later wars. Other types of seizure and imports would have added to these totals.[17]

While capture was clearly an important means of building up a large slave population in Roman Italy and Sicily, natural reproduction had probably always been of considerable importance and eventually became the dominant source of slaves. This observation cannot be directly derived from ancient sources, which mention home-born slaves (*vernae* or *oikogeneis*) but not do normally allow quantification. Under Roman law, the children of slave women retained the status of their mothers. The rate of natural reproduction of a slave population is a function of servile sex ratios, (de facto if not formal) family formation, and manumission rates, none of which are adequately documented. Yet although these multiple uncertainties may seem to forestall any estimate of the relative contribution of natural reproduction to the Roman slave supply, there can be little doubt about its overall significance. Due to the sheer size of the imperial slave population, running in to the millions, sources other than natural reproduction would have been demographically insufficient to maintain this system for centuries. Claims to the contrary inevitably entail implausible rates of capture in war or child enslavement. Moreover, capture in warfare most likely produced a surfeit of slave women, thereby already facilitating natural reproduction early on, and comparative data show that imbalanced servile sex ratios in any case tend to even out over time. Recent scholarship has stressed the economic contributions of slave women and children.[18]

What little empirical evidence happens to exist supports this evaluation. The sex ratio of slaves recorded in Roman Egyptian census returns is fairly balanced up to age thirty, when differential manumission practices appear to have released men but retained women of childbearing age; slave children were common. Similar impressions can be gleaned from a census inscription from the Aegean island of Thera.

The fact that in Diocletian's Price Edict of 301 CE, slave women reached their peak value already as teenagers is consistent with appreciation of their reproductive capacity. Possible counterexamples are ambiguous at best. If it could be ascertained whether the overrepresentation of males in the skeletal record from Herculaneum reflects the structure of the local population of slaves and freedpersons, we would have to surmise that this particular environment was not conducive to adequate rates of natural reproduction. The acquisition of highly skilled male slaves by elite households would have skewed sex ratios in favor of males. However, high (i.e., male-heavy) sex ratios of slaves and freedpersons found in clusters of epitaphs such as the *columbaria* of aristocratic households may, albeit to an unknowable extent, merely be a function of commemoration practices that disfavored women.[19]

Manumission rates are mostly unknown. The prominence of freedpersons in Italian funerary epigraphy has convincingly been attributed to 'epigraphic habit,' represented by that group's unusually strong desire for a particular form of commemoration. Cultural preferences for specifying the age at death of those who died young may well account for the fact that the majority of freedpersons in Rome and Italy are reported to have died before they turned thirty.[20] The best evidence for the frequency of manumission in Roman Italy is furnished by epigraphic rosters that list the members of associations (*collegia*) or other entities and by the wax tablets recording business dealings that have survived in Pompeii and Herculaneum: freedmen are strongly represented in all these documents.[21] As already noted, frequent male manumission is implied by Egyptian census returns. Other sources refer to young as well as elderly slaves but cannot be used for quantification.[22] It remains unclear if the concentration of references to freedpersons in urban settings reflects actual imbalances between town and country.[23]

If millions of slaves lived in the Roman Empire, as seems very likely, many had to be the offspring of slaves because alternative sources would not have sufficed to sustain the whole system. If many slaves descended from slaves, manumission could not have been very common at most ages because it would have simultaneously increased demand for replacements and interfered with their supply. In the final analysis, therefore, the four variables of slave numbers, societal penetration by slavery, servile natural reproduction, and manumission rates are inextricably interrelated, and none of them can be considered in isolation: assumptions about any one of them inevitably entail assumptions about the others. While an appreciation of this nexus does not reveal actual conditions, it very helpfully constrains our imagination by narrowing our choices to particular scenarios: a smaller slave population with concomitantly limited societal penetration would be compatible with a greater importance of various forms of capture and habitual manumission, whereas a larger slave population requires higher natural reproduction rates and less manumission. Regardless of our hunches and preferences, the debate necessarily has to acknowledge this matrix in order to retain a measure of intellectual respectability.[24]

The preponderance of the evidence favors the notion of a Roman imperial slave system that was sufficiently large in scale for natural reproduction to have been its most important means of maintenance and manumission to have been fairly limited. High slave prices likewise speak against indiscriminate manumission (see below, next section). Then again, regional variation may have been significant, and a wide range of sources of supply would have been required to support the system once it had reached its apex, mitigating shortfalls arising from locally skewed sex ratios, manumission, flight, and health hazards connected perhaps not so much with slave labor per se as with urban residence and attendant exposure to infectious disease.

This leaves the question of how Roman slavery compared to other major slave systems in history. Ancient Greek and Roman slavery – or more precisely conditions observed in classical Athens and Roman Italy – were in many ways very similar. Both systems were primarily intrusive (that is, dependent on the enslavement of outsiders) and formally treated slaves as chattel; engaged in both capture and purchase; imported slaves into densely settled cores; and employed them in a wide variety of occupations in both town and country, including on slave estates. Access to land rather than labor was the critical variable. Apart from issues of scale, which are not relevant to the consideration of structural features, and minor variations in style, the only main differences lie in the frequency of manumission and especially in the manner in which freedpersons were integrated into society. Although conditions in other regions may have varied, in focusing on the best-documented areas it is fair to say that with only relatively slight modifications, Roman slavery effectively *was* Greek slavery. This need not be a coincidence: just as the Roman imperial economy is best seen as an extension and maturation of the Hellenistic economy, Roman chattel slavery might be regarded as an extension and adaptation of Aegean forms of slavery, mediated perhaps by (generally poorly known) practices among the western Greeks and Carthaginians (see below, in the third section).

These similarities are thrown into sharp relief by comparison between Roman slavery and the modern slave systems of the New

World, which differed much more significantly. American slaveries were peripheral, characterized by less manumission or integration (even in Brazil), focused on agricultural slavery, and constricted the range of slave activities, a restriction that was strongly associated with racial bias. Slavery was fully commercialized, in the double sense that slaves almost exclusively produced for markets and were purchased rather than captured. Labor, not land, was scarce. Despite some similarities – such as the higher valuation of male slaves, the organization of plantations, or the influence of Roman law on some of the American slave systems –, differences dominate. Indeed, among post-ancient slave systems, slavery in the Sokoto Caliphate in nineteenth-century West Africa offers the most parallels to the Roman experience. Similarities include the wide range of servile occupations, urban and rural employment, intrusiveness and frequent capture, and the centripetal movement of slaves. Higher valuation of women (in part a function of African labor regimes), a higher degree of non-market allocation of slaves and non-market production, and the critical importance of labor rather than land represent the main differences.[25] Even so, when one controls for ecologically contingent differences (in terms of gender and the ratio of land to labor), observed organizational similarities outweigh the differences, which are primarily a consequence of lower commercial development. Comparative approaches to Roman slavery, which have thus far privileged the New World, need to adopt a more global perspective.

THE ECONOMY OF ROMAN SLAVERY

There are three basic preconditions for the employment of slave labor. Two of them concern supply: slavery must be institutionally acceptable, and slaves must be effectively available. The third and ultimately most important one is that there must be demand for slave labor because alternative sources of labor are – or are considered to be – insufficient or otherwise inadequate. The third variable subsumes several preconditions that are commonly regarded as separate but are actually components of demand: significant asset inequality (creating demand for non-family labor), accumulation of capital (allowing the acquisition of slaves) or military power (allowing their capture), the existence of markets (allowing the sale of the products of slave labor), constraints on the free labor supply, and employers' tastes.[26]

While the three basic preconditions must be met to facilitate slave labor, a large-scale system such as the one that existed in the Roman

Empire depends on an additional condition to be viable in the long term. Slaves must, on average, produce enough to justify the capital input associated with their purchase and maintenance. This condition, which does not strictly speaking require slave labor to be more profitable than free labor, applies for the simple reason that in a system where millions of slaves were kept for centuries, it is not credible to view slavery primarily as a mean of surplus consumption: although not all slaves had to earn their keep, and although the importance of status value of slaveownership and path dependence should not be underrated, it is difficult to see how such a system could have survived on such a large scale and for such a long time if it was burdened by structural deficits. The notion that in this very fundamental sense, slave labor must have been 'profitable' receives further support from the observation that slave prices were considerable (see below).

The property rights over labor that the institution of slavery bestowed on slaveowners required them to make a capital investment that was not necessary for the employment of free labor. The fixed capital invested in slaves diminished as slaves aged, and further depreciation was caused by the probability of loss due to death, flight, or manumission. High and unpredictable mortality at all ages added considerably to the total cost of slaveownership (see Chapter 15). The incidence of defection cannot be measured but appears to have been non-trivial, as was the incidence of manumission. We also have to allow for the possibility of costly avoidance or resistance behavior that might have been specific to slave labor as opposed to work for others more generally.[27] In addition to bearing the cost of acquiring slaves, owners had to pay wages in the form of maintenance, provide for supervision, and might also incur additional tax liabilities.

From a narrowly economic perspective, slave labor was sustainable if, for a given output, slaves' 'wages' were lower than free wages by an amount that was at least equivalent to the depreciation of the fixed capital invested in the slaves, or if slaves' output was greater by at least the same amount than that of free workers. For a number of reasons, it is impossible to test this assumption for the Roman world. First, although we are sometimes able to compare free wages and subsistence costs, this exercise would not tell us about the ratios of inputs to outputs: if slaves could be made to work more for the same wage, comparisons between wages and subsistence levels would not tell us about marginal productivity.[28] Second, even the most basic slave wages may generally have differed from bare physiological subsistence, and would almost certainly have done so to the extent that their tasks favored the application of reward incentives (see below). Third, we have to take account of transaction costs such as those associated with the potential for higher turnover rates for free labor. Fourth, we cannot assume simple substitutability: owing to lack of skills or other reasons, free labor need not have been available to perform particular tasks. Fifth, Roman slave labor was organized in very different ways, from quasi-familial domestic service to rationalized large-scale production, yet owners were required to make equivalent capital investments in slaves regardless of how they used them, which means that we would have to find ways to ascertain the average profitability of slave labor across a wide range of contexts. I labor this point to show that the profitability of Roman slave labor cannot be empirically determined.[29] This, however, does not mean that it did not matter. Faced with the large-scale and long-term slave system of the Roman Empire, we must proceed on the assumption that slavery was, indeed, profitable.

This raises the question which factors could have accounted for this outcome. In the absence of measurements, the best we can do is to weigh probabilities whose relative significance is open to debate. Labor may become scarce for various reasons. They include a shift in the ratio of labor to resources, especially land, for instance when the Black Death raised real wages in late medieval Europe or when colonial plantation farming opened up land in the New World after the indigenous population had been decimated by epidemics. Commitments of the free labor force to public service such as war, whether compulsory and/or (at least potentially) more rewarding than civilian employment, may also contribute to labor scarcity.

In the case of Republican Rome, the seizure and reallocation of arable land during the Italian conquests suggest that labor had not originally been scarce, even though these redistributions may have raised the price of labor at the center. Massive attrition during the first two Punic Wars would have had a similar effect. Both demographic and institutional developments that reduced elite access to and control over labor were intimately related to war-making and empire-building. The Roman Republic and its Italian allies shared high military participation rates, a situation that can be traced back to the fourth century BCE and continued into the early monarchical period.[30] Military service put pressure on the labor supply not only by increasing attrition by death or migration: it also served to destabilize and 'thin out' labor markets by raising unpredictability and turnover costs (see below). This process primarily affected young adults, the healthiest segment of the labor force and the one most amenable to migration in search of resources and skills acquisition. Roman military mobilization was facilitated by the abolition of debt-bondage and other forms of state-society bargaining that enhanced the freedom of citizens which, in turn, diminished the elite's capacity for controlling labor outside slavery and favored the rise of non-coercive contractual tenancy and wage labor arrangements (see Chapter 6). All these developments coincided with ongoing expansion of (generally successful) warfare which triggered capital inflows and facilitated the capture and purchase of slaves, and with Italy's integration into Hellenistic economic systems, where rational organization of slave labor had long been established. Taken together, these processes converged in creating an environment that was highly conducive to the employment of slave labor.[31]

However, while this may explain the rise of slavery in Roman Italy, we also need to explain how it was sustained and why it was apparently not uncommon in other parts of the Empire. These questions are lent urgency by the fact that throughout the monarchical period, Roman slave prices were high in terms of subsistence costs and probable per capita GDP. Existing price data are far from satisfactory but sufficient to establish that from the first to the early fourth centuries CE, the price of a young adult male slave without special skills, expressed in wheat equivalent, normally fell in a range of 4 tons plus/minus 40 percent, equivalent to between 4 and 8 times mean annual per capita GDP in the Roman Empire. Real prices remained at comparable levels until the sixth century CE. In this respect, Roman slave prices resembled those in the United States around 1850, when a comparable slave was valued at the equivalent of 7 times mean annual national per capita GDP. In terms of labor, the initial capital outlay for a Roman slave was very roughly worth 1,000 daily wages for an unskilled rural laborer. In so far as slave prices reflected the value of slave labor, slaveownership that regularly required considerable capital outlays (or entailed equivalent opportunity costs if slave offspring were retained) ought to have generated considerable benefits as well.[32]

How did owners obtain such benefits? Because of its reliance on fixed capital, slave labor is particularly suited to economic activities with relatively steady employment opportunities.[33] These may be divided into effort-intensive and care-intensive types of work. The former are amenable to close supervision and the application of pain incentives, and include mining, lumbering, field labor performed by gangs, and basic construction work. The successful performance of the latter depends to a greater extent on the ability to motivate workers with the help of reward incentives. They tend to be characterized by a higher degree of autonomy and include artisanal, commercial, and management activities, domestic service, herding, and specialized forms of agricultural labor. Effort-intensive activities involve more supervision costs than costs for rewards, and vice versa for care-intensive work. In practice, we encounter a spectrum from effort-intensive to care-intensive labor matched by a spectrum of treatment from harsh and closely monitored to autonomous and more benign, a spectrum that also reflects the overall likelihood of manumission (from low to high).[34] Unlike in the New World, where slaves were concentrated in effort-intensive activities, Roman slaves were successfully employed and managed across the entire spectrum.

Slave labor for effort-intensive tasks makes sense both for unpleasant or dangerous activities such as mining and whenever labor markets are 'thin' in the sense that turnover costs are high and labor cannot readily be substituted over time, as in farming. Differences in the supply of free labor help account for variation in the employment of slaves in such activities in different parts of the Roman Empire.[35] Effort-intensive slave labor also allows rationalization that generates economies of scale, as in gang labor.[36] The employment of slaves in care-intensive tasks makes sense when human capital is scarce, which generally appears to have been the case (see Chapter 4), but also requires owners to be legally and culturally capable of applying the appropriate reward incentives. Therefore, this type of slave labor flourishes most in 'open' slave systems where institutional arrangements and cultural norms allow slaves to be granted autonomy, assume positions of trust, and to be freed and become socially integrated upon manumission. In contrast to the more racialist 'closed' slave systems of the New World and to a lesser degree even to the more exclusive Greek polis, all these preconditions were met by Roman law and practice.[37] Roman institutions maximized owners' flexibility in managing their slaves: just as secure property rights enabled ruthless exploitation, societal inclusivity supported the use of reward incentives and created opportunities to continue to benefit from slaves after their manumission (see below). This flexibility accounts for the employment of slave labor in an extraordinarily wide range of settings, from the use of chained slaves and gangs in effort-intensive tasks to the existence of highly autonomous slaves who were endowed with their own sub-slaves (*vicarii*) and business accounts (*peculia*) and subsequently flourished as freedmen, with some of their descendants even joining the political ruling class.[38] Unfortunately, the evidence does not allow us to measure the relative prevalence of these various types of occupations.[39] The gradual integration of local elites into an empire-wide ruling class, accompanied by the spread of Roman law and custom, may well have encouraged employers to embrace and adapt these highly flexible arrangements outside the core areas of Greco-Roman chattel slavery.

Manumission was an integral element of the reward-incentive system.[40] Like slavery itself, it was a multi-faceted practice, not merely a benefit but also a powerful source of anxiety and thus social control both during slavery (as an outcome that was always possible but never guaranteed) and beyond, especially when the freedperson's kin were retained in bondage.[41] Although manumission may not have been an indispensable strategy given that alternative benefits – wages, autonomy, *peculium*, *vicarii*, and quasi-familial relations – could be employed to manipulate slave behavior, it was attractive to owners because it did not merely represent a reward but also a means of continuing to draw on a former slave's labor. The latter was made possible by a lasting bond between patrons and freed slaves.[42] This relationship was constructed in pseudo-kinship terms, advertised by the freedperson's assuming elements of the name of the former owner. Freed slaves commonly continued to belong to the patron's *familia*, merely adjusting their status, and sometimes were not only married to or buried with other members of that household but even continued to reside with their former owners. As Henrik Mouritsen puts it, "manumission did not mark the end of a process but represented a point on a broad continuum of incentives that covered the entire working life of the slave/freedman."[43]

In working with and through their freed slaves, patrons continued to be able to apply both reward incentives – such as benefits from agency arrangements and investment – and (moderate) pain incentives, especially if kin remained enslaved. Moreover, immediate pecuniary gains from manumission might accrue to owners. Manumission fees equivalent to the replacement value of a freed slave and the imposition of service obligations (*paramone*) are well documented in the Hellenistic East. Payments for manumission are also attested in Roman society but it is unclear how common they were.[44] Continuing bonds between former owners and slaves may often have been the most important benefit to both parties. Wealthy Romans were said to operate *per servos atque libertos*, with the help of slaves and freedmen.[45] Through the latter, individual Romans as well as the state extended the relationships of slavery into the sphere of the free citizenry. Unlike more reciprocal kin networks or patron-client relationships, freedpersons' dependence on their former owners created networks of subordination and trust that could not readily be replicated among those who had not passed through slavery. From a social perspective, slavery and manumission made it possible to convert material resources into personal power and domination, commodifying labor relations and familial relations. From an economic perspective, manumission helped owners to balance the costs and gains of slave labor.

Gains from slavery relative to the employment of free labor accrued from lowered transaction costs, control over human capital, the rationalization of labor arrangements, a possible muting of gender constraints on labor, the reproductive capacity of slaves that renewed the fixed capital they represented, and the creation of appropriately socialized and skilled free(d) agents. They also included any additional utility derived from the direct domination of other human beings, such as sexual services and status enhancement. Costs were incurred by fixed capital outlays, depreciation including unpredictable attrition risks, supervision costs insofar as slaves required monitoring beyond working hours, the need to maintain idle workers or find lessees, and tax liabilities.[46] While we cannot blithely assume that the former consistently exceeded the latter, they must regularly have done so across a wide range of occupations in order to account for the scale and duration of the Roman slave system. The tremendous flexibility of management strategies from brute force to ample rewards made slavery a highly versatile and adaptable institution, thereby ensuring its success in a variety of contexts.

THE DEVELOPMENT OF ROMAN SLAVERY

We do not know when Rome became a slave society. The Law of the Twelve Tables, if it does indeed date from the fifth century BCE, merely documents the existence of slavery at that time. The annalistic tradition, unreliable as it may be, indicates that slavery was already common in the fourth and third centuries BCE.[47] Early references must be treated with caution, such as the claim of mass enslavement following the conquest of Veii in the 390s BCE, the introduction of a manumission tax in 357 BCE, and political conflict over the tribal enrolement of freedmen in 312 BCE. While the abolition of debt-bondage (*nexum*) in 326 or 313 BCE may have been facilitated by elite access to slave labor, any such connection must ultimately remain conjecture. We move onto somewhat more solid ground with the large tallies of enslaved captives in the final stages of the wars that established Roman hegemony over peninsular Italy in the early third century BCE and the provision that Romans provide slaves for public service during the Second Punic War.[48]

That all of this predates the emergence of the Italian villa system and the massive urbanization of the late second and first centuries BCE should not be considered a serious problem. First of all, there is no need to assume that all war captives were employed by Romans. In the earliest stages of Roman expansion, slaves may have been sold to Greek and Punic traders. It is hardly unreasonable to conjecture significant demand for slaves in the more developed regions to the south: we hear about Greek enslavement of other Greeks in Sicily and of Africans, and the treaty of 346 BCE between Rome and Carthage mentioned the Carthaginian slave trade in Italy.[49] Just as the Gauls, Dacians, and Germans who later sold slaves to the Romans, the early Roman state occupied a semiperipheral position relative to a more developed (Greco-Punic) core, and there is no compelling reason to believe that it did not sell slaves merely because our much later sources did not write (or know or care) about it.

More importantly, however, military commitments by the citizenry were already high, thereby curbing the civilian labor supply and raising turnover risks. As colonists left Latium to settle conquered and redistributed land, slaves may have taken their place.[50] It is at least possible that precursors of the later villa, the so-called 'Hellenistic' farms that appear to have produced for the market, already employed slave labor.[51] Moreover, we do not know how commercialized Roman slavery was in this period: if war captives had been allocated to citizens, capital outlays would have been avoided, and slaves could usefully be employed in small-scale units of production.[52] Unlike other ancient states such as Pharaonic Egypt and Assyria that imported large numbers of war captives, the Roman Republic did not control them collectively but earmarked them for private use through purchase and, perhaps, other means. In a period of little regular state income and primitive accumulation through plunder, slaveownership represented one of few opportunities for elites to privatize of the gains from empire.[53]

The notion that slavery was already widespread in the late third and early second centuries BCE receives support not only from the aforementioned provision that citizens commit slaves to the war effort in 214 BCE and reports of slave uprisings in the early second century BCE but also from events such as the mass enslavement of the population of Epirus in 167 BCE which, however inflated by the record, is hard to understand except in the context of an existing large-scale system of slave labor and concomitant demand for labor replacement and augmentation.[54]

In the Italian core of the growing empire, this system continued to expand under the late Republic, a period of unusually dynamic economic development that witnessed unprecedented capital inflows; high mobility engendered by migration and at times extraordinary military commitments of the free labor force, both of which would have destabilized labor markets; and growing access to slaves through war and trade. Both the demand for and the supply of slaves soared. Rapid urbanization and the spread of villa estates – perhaps a new style rather than a new system of labor but surely indicative of increases in scale (and attendant economies of scale) – were closely linked to the expansion of slavery in this period.[55] It would be moot to argue whether this process was the result of Roman imperialism or of new commercial opportunities: inasmuch as Roman economic development was a consequence of empire (see Chapter 1), empire was both the ultimate cause of economic expansion and the proximate cause of slave imports.

To the east and south of Italy, conquest brought slave-rich regions under Roman control. There is no good reason to regard this as an expansion of Roman slavery except in the trivial sense that local slave-owners came to be subject to Roman rule. It makes better sense to view this as a process of integration or, more boldly, even as a step in the incorporation of Italy into the Hellenistic slave system: if anything, urbanization and slaveownership made Roman society look more Greek. The probable Greek and Punic roots of the Roman villa illustrate this premise.[56]

Outside Italy and Sicily, net growth of slavery as a result of Roman expansion occurred in the first instance farther west and north. Owing to the scarcity of regional textual documentation prior to late antiquity and uncertainty about the status of the labor forces of provincial villa estates, it is extremely difficult to gauge the scale and chronology of this process. We may conjecture that Roman-style slavery extended at least to the nodal points of provincial development. The extent of slave labor in the countryside remains an intractable issue: most of the relevant evidence is fairly late, and the modalities of labor organization are obscure.[57]

During the first two centuries of the monarchy and perhaps also later, population growth might be expected to have put downward pressure on the cost of labor while a reduction in the scale of warfare curbed the slave supply, and the congruence of these two developments would have reduced the appeal of slave labor.[58] Although the logical premises of this model are sound, this suggested outcome is hard to reconcile with the apparent stability of slave prices noted above

(n. 32). More specific empirical testing poses great challenges. In the western regions, there would have been ample scope for economic development (including the adoption of slave labor) before Malthusian constraints made themselves felt (see Chapter 1). In more developed regions, such as Italy and the Eastern Mediterranean, slavery may very well have stopped expanding but we cannot simply assume major contractions. Established slaveholdings would have generated large numbers of slave children. The imperial integration of slave markets favored regions with high nominal incomes, such as Italy, giving it a comparative advantage in the competition for slave labor.[59] The fact that the net expansion of the Italian villa system peaked in the first century BCE does not prove a subsequent decline in the slave mode of production because the archaeological record may merely reflect changes in elite residential patterns or concentration of landownership. The apparent decline in some agricultural exports might just as well reflect growing local demand as reductions in rural slave labor. We cannot be sure whether rural slavery contracted and/or came to be differently organized.[60]

In principle, slave labor remained suitable for higher-risk, higher-investment ventures that required supervision and produced commodities for the market. It is therefore telling that adult male slaves continued to be more highly valued than their female counterparts, a historically uncommon feature that suggests the heavy involvement of slaves in productive activities.[61] The apparent long-term stability of slave prices in the monarchical period (see the previous section) is potentially of great importance to our understanding of Roman slavery but difficult to interpret. It is logically compatible with stable demand and supply, diminished demand and supply, and increased demand and supply, which seems to be the least likely scenario. If the price of labor fell thanks to demographic growth, slave prices could have remained high even if imports declined relative to the demand for replacements.

Kyle Harper has argued against the notion of a massive decline of Roman slavery in the fourth century CE. Qualitative evidence, for what it is worth, and a sprinkling of census data point to substantial levels of slaveownership. It is unlikely that the emerging 'colonate' eroded the status of free workers to the extent that it undermined slave labor, and there is no sign that lots of slaves were transformed into quasi-tenants. While villas boomed in many regions, we cannot be sure about the composition of their labor force.[62] Insofar as the employment of slaves was associated with elites' commodity production and exchange, and insofar as elite profits from such ventures and from their involvement in the state sustained elite access to the services of slaves, there is no obvious reason why the slave system should have been greatly weakened prior to the fifth century CE. By the same token we would expect it to have contracted during the fifth and sixth centuries CE as these favorable preconditions began to disappear in the west and more radical forms of constraining workers' freedom emerged in the east.[63]

Rising nominal slave prices under the early Caliphate may have been related to labor shortages caused by the plague and/or inflows of African bullion.[64] By that time, the economic center of gravity in western Eurasia had once again shifted back to the Aegean and especially the Near East, both of which Europe took to supplying with slaves.[65] The Roman system of slavery, centered on Italy, had come to an end and, like the Roman Empire itself, was never rebuilt.

Conclusion: slavery, empire, and the nature of the Roman economy

The Roman economy was made distinctively 'Roman' by the institution of empire which, both directly and indirectly, mobilized resources in novel ways and ultimately accounted for the economic expansion we observe in the historical record (see Chapter 1). Empire facilitated a system of exchange that favored production for the market, a feature which in turn favored the employment of slave labor and the slave mode of production with its comprehensive control and rationalized organization. Just as most production and consumption were contained within households, most economic activities continued to be performed by free or semi-autonomous workers. Nevertheless, in terms of its intrinsic character and its structural location, slavery occupied a central position in the Roman economy.

By nature, empire and chattel slavery were very much alike, constituting analogous systems of violent and asymmetric domination and predatory appropriation that mobilized and allocated resources and created, sustained, and reinforced inequality and hierarchy. It was not by coincidence that slavery and empire flourished and declined together. Complementing imperial power over collectives, slavery ensured elite power over individuals. The fact that both empire and slavery were rooted in violent domination did not require violence to be continuously expressed or exercised: by necessity, state rulers and slaveowners both relied on the effective sharing of claimed resources and ostensible acts of beneficence in the management of their affairs. None of this altered the essence of imperial rule or slavery, nor did it diminish rulers' and owners' entitlement to and capacity for violent intervention.

The structural location of Roman slavery was not primarily a function of scale. A vital component of the households and ventures of the dominant groups (be they rulers, landowners, or even merchants), slave labor occupied a central position in the creation, management, and consumption of elite wealth and social power. Slavery and manumission enabled elite members to create distinctive networks of subordination and economic control that increased their autonomy from the free commoner population.[66]

Slavery had mixed effects on labor markets and the economic standing of the freeborn working population. On the one hand, access to enslaved outsiders may have curbed the elite's desire to control non-slave labor with the help of institutions such as debt-bondage. One the other, elite reliance on slaves and freedpersons would have disfavored freeborn workers by constricting their access to employment in the households and businesses of the wealthy and discouraging investment in human capital beyond the confines of these households and businesses.[67] Slavery also distorted labor markets. While it is true that slaves participated in labor markets in that they effectively received wages (in the form of maintenance and reward incentives) and their compensation levels were sensitive to their tasks, the extent of owners' claims to their slaves greatly raised the costs the latter faced in changing employers and consequently reduced slaves' bargaining power.[68]

One might object that all forms of labor for others involve asymmetries and coercion. Even so, chattel slavery, farm tenancy, wage labor, and serfdom differ in many ways, including owners' capacity for violence against workers and direct control over their labor. The specific configuration of labor regimes that underpinned the position of the dominant groups matters a great deal to our understanding of a given economic system. Slavery may be regarded as the 'dominant exception' of the Roman economy. Wherever slave labor was organized in a rational fashion, on a large scale and geared to production for the market, it arguably represented the most advanced – the most 'capitalist' – segment of the Roman economy. As such, it was the leading edge of intensive growth, making it possible to reorganize manufacturing processes and colonize the countryside with capital. Unlike in the slave societies of the New World, Roman slave labor never dominated market production in quantitative terms but created vital pockets of development.[69] Scholarly fashion swings like a pendulum: the study of the Roman economy has moved from sweeping claims about the absolute centrality of slave labor to a growing lack of enthusiasm for this topic.[70] Adjustment of what may have been an excessive emphasis on slavery among previous generations of scholars has led to indifference that is now itself in need of adjustment. Slavery is critical to our understanding of the Roman imperial economy as a product of organized violence and coercive integration.

NOTES

1 If the Roman Empire contained several million slaves (see below, in the first section) for twenty or more generations, anywhere from 100 to 200 million individual slaves would have existed during the Roman period, depending on overall numbers and the incidence of manumission. By comparison, the transatlantic slave trade involved no more than 10 million people, and although the total slave population of the New World around 1860 may briefly have approximated that of the Roman Empire, the underlying slave system was less long-lived and for the most part more modest in scale. This is not to say that 'Roman slavery' should be regarded as a single unified institution: the Roman Empire encompassed a conglomerate of (perhaps increasingly interrelated) 'slaveries.'

For general surveys of Roman slavery, see Bradley 1994 and chapters 11–22 of Bradley and Cartledge (eds.) 2011. Westermann 1955 is still useful as a survey of the evidence while Finley 1980 (now also in 1998) remains the most incisive discussion of the nature of Greco-Roman slavery. For slavery in the Roman Republic, see Hopkins 1978: 1–115 and Dumont 1987; for the Later Roman Empire, see Harper 2011. Bellen and Heinen (eds.) 2003 provide the most comprehensive bibliography. For world-historical context, see Patterson 1982; Finkelman and Miller (eds.) 1998; Turley 2000; Flaig 2009.

I owe thanks to Keith Bradley, Kyle Harper, Marc Kleijwegt, Elio Lo Cascio, and Henrik Mouritsen for comments on this chapter and/or sharing unpublished work with me.

2 See Lovejoy 2000: 10 for the former and Wickham 1994: 85; 2005: 260–2 for the latter.

3 For the concept of 'slave society,' see variously Hopkins 1978: 99–102; Finley 1998: 147–50, 274 (originally published in 1978 and 1982); Patterson 1982: 353 (for the equivalent notion of 'large-scale slave system'); Oakes 1990: 36–9; Bradley 1994: 12–14; Turley 2000: 4–5, 62–3, 76–100; and cf. also de Ste Croix 1981: 509. I use the terms 'society' and 'economy' in a generic sense without wishing to imply unity or high levels of integration.

4 Oakes 1990: 37–8 introduces the useful criterion of counterfactual outcomes. In this respect, ancient Rome was much more of a slave society than most other societies in history, yet markedly less so than New World slave systems, which would simply not have existed in any even remotely comparable form without slavery. This suggests that the notion of a spectrum is more appropriate than the often-invoked and deceptively neat dichotomy of 'societies with slaves' and 'slave societies.'

5 For this reason, notwithstanding slavery's primary and universal quality as a system of domination (Patterson 1982: 1–101, especially 13), it is treated here in the first instance as a labor system (cf. Lovejoy 2000: 5).

6 'Roman' is defined very broadly, with emphasis on Italy and citizen society but encompassing all areas under Roman rule. In keeping with the overall perspective of this volume, I focus on the economic properties of the imperial system (see Chapter 1).

7 Rosenstein 2008: 5–7 on Livy 24.11.7–8 (214 BCE); Bagnall and Frier 1994: 70, with Bagnall, Frier and Rutherford 1997: 98 (31 of 234 households, but the record is skewed in favor of slave-rich urban settings). Harper 2011: 38–60 gathers dozens of late Roman references suggestive of widespread slaveownership.

8 Bradley 1994: 57–80 and Bodel 2011 are the most accessible discussions of Roman slave labor. Public slaves: Weaver 1972 (state); Weiss 2004 (cities). *Vicarii*: Reduzzi Merola 1990. Slaves in the military sector: Welwei 1988. Staerman and Trofimova 1975; Staerman et al. 1987; Marinovic et al. 1992 provide geographical surveys of the evidence. Hezser 2005, on ancient Jewish slavery, also covers the Roman period. For freedpersons, see below.

9 Galen 5.49 (ed. Kühn); Plin. *HN* 33.135; Tac. *Ann.* 14.43; Apul. *Apol.* 93; SHA *Firmus* 12.2; Gai. *Inst.* 1.43 (cf. *ILS* 2927); Plut. *Crass.* 2; Frontin. *Aqu.* 116; Harper 2008: 107 (Thera); *IGRR* 4.914; Ioh. Chrys. *Homil. in Mt.* 63.4 (*PG* 58.608); Strabo 12.2.3 and 6; *Vita Melaniae* (*L*) 18.3. Cf. also Athen. 272e and, perhaps, Jos. *Ant.* 13.359. For references to large but unspecified numbers of slaves, see Harper 2011: 46, 52.

10 Bagnall, Frier and Rutherford 1997: 98. For Alexandria, see esp. *P.Oxy.* 44.3197. Biezunska-Malowist 1977 discusses slavery in Roman Egypt.

11 See Scheidel 2011b for the computational process, implying a target rate of 7 percent.

12 Harper 2008: 101–4 (on Tralles, Lesbos, and Thera).

13 Scheidel 2005a: 64–6, rejecting Brunt 1987: 124–5 and earlier guesses.

14 Scheidel 2005a: 66–71, for a total of 1–1.5 million slaves in Italy. See also De Ligt 2004: 745–7 for lower numbers than previously assumed. Jongman 2003: 113–16 emphasizes the limits of slave employment in Italian agriculture, but see now Harper 2011: 144–200 on agricultural slavery more generally. That grain cultivation by slaves was feasible in principle (Spurr 1986: 133–43; Scheidel 1994) does not tell us whether it was common.

15 *CIL* 10.1403, with Mouritsen 2007.

16 Scheidel 2011b, for an estimate of 7–13 percent. Harper 2011: 59 posits a similar total.

17 For discussions of the sources of Roman slaves, see Bradley 1987b; 1994: 31–56; Scheidel 2011b; Harper 2011: 67–99. Enslavement tallies: Scheidel 2011b: 294–6. Slave trade: Boese 1973; Harris 1980; 1999; Bodel 2005.

18 For supporting argument, see Scheidel 1997; 2005a (*contra* Harris 1999); 2011b; and cf. McKeown 2007: 124–40 on the debate. *Vernae*: Herrmann-Otto 1994. Roth 2007 and Laes 2008 emphasize labor by slave women and children; and note also the former's attractive argument that female labor would have greatly increased the profitability of Roman *villa* estates. At the same time, slave labor remained sensitive to gender norms: Saller 2003.

19 Scheidel 1997: 160–3 (Egypt); Harper 2008: 106–19 (Thera); Diocletian's Price Edict § 29 with Scheidel 1996b: 72–3 (prices); Camodeca 2008 with Capasso 2001: 956–71 (Herculaneum); Scheidel 2005a: 73 and Mouritsen 2011: 191 (inscriptions). Burial niches in *columbaria* were often unmarked. Saller 2003: 203 and above, Chapter 4, estimates that it would have made financial sense to raise foundlings as slaves.

20 See Mouritsen 2005 and 2011: 120–41, finally laying to rest the notion of frequent and early (urban) manumission propounded by Alföldy 1986: 286–331.

21 See Mouritsen 2011: 206–47.

22 Old slaves: Wiedemann 1996. Constraints on manumission: Wiedemann 1985.

23 Rarity of rural manumission is often assumed but hard to substantiate: the epigraphic record mostly reveals absence of evidence (but see now Harper 2008: 115–16 for some indirect epigraphic evidence). The relative neglect of manumission by the Roman agronomists and the preponderance of effort-intensive tasks in the countryside (see below, in the second section) support the traditional view; it seems that even estate managers were rarely manumitted (Carlsen 1995: 96–100). For various reasons, such as skills, proximity to owners, and employment opportunities for ex-slaves, urban slavery may very well have been more conducive to manumission.

24 For this reason alone, the recurrent condemnation of parametric models is misguided. Their purpose is not to show 'how it really was' but to establish the logical implications of modern reconstructions, and they are therefore inevitably less arbitrary than improperly contextualized claims advanced on the basis of particular source references or individual preconceptions.

25 See Lovejoy 1979; 1981.

26 This refines my earlier statement in Scheidel 2008b: 115–16. For different disaggregations of the third factor, see Finley 1998: 154; Cartledge 2002a: 162.

27 Slave flight: Bellen 1971; Bradley 1994: 118–21. It is much easier to document and argue about slave resistance (see especially Bradley 1989; 1990; 1994: 107–31; 2011a) than to relate it to baseline levels of malfeasance and counterfactuals (i.e., how wage laborers or serfs would have behaved).

28 For higher outputs relative to inputs in slavery, see Barzel 1977.

29 For the same reason, *contra* Jongman 2007a: 601–2, we cannot readily infer free wages from slave prices.

30 See Scheidel 2004a (migrations); Brunt 1987 (attrition). Service commitments: Hopkins 1978: 31–5; Scheidel 2007b: 325 fig.1. For the nexus between high mobilization levels and slavery in city-states and beyond, see Scheidel 2008b: 117–23.

31 While this array of contributing factors may seem to overdetermine outcomes, we lack the necessary data to create a more parsimonious explanation. Compare Finley's famous model (Finley 1998: 157–8; cf. Morris 2002: 29–41) of the rise of chattel slavery in ancient Greece that emphasizes the nexus between the abolition of debt bondage, private landownership, and citizen rights that made the free population less susceptible to exploitation and created a binary opposition between free and slave (for which see also Ste Croix 1981: 141; Patterson 1991). This dichotomy was one of the basic determinants of social identity: Cartledge 1993: 118–51. As Finley 1981: 165–6 intimates, an analogous process may have occurred

in fourth-century BCE Rome. Hopkins 1978: 1–98 develops a comprehensive model of the growth of slavery in Roman Italy driven by the mobilization of citizens and capital inflows.

32 For nominal and real slave prices, see Scheidel 2005b; Harper 2010; and cf. also Ruffing and Drexhage 2008. (I define 'real' prices in relation to other goods: what one might call the 'effective' slave price is the price of purchase minus the resale value plus the opportunity cost of capital, maintenance, and depreciation.) Manumission fees recorded in Delphi in the last two centuries BCE, which may but need not reflect actual slave prices (see below, n. 59), mostly fall in the same range (see Scheidel 2005b). For the Republican period, see below, in the third section. For Roman GDP: see Chapter 1, n. 4. American slave prices and GDP: Scheidel 1996b: 74, with www.measuringworth.org/usgdp/. Harper 2010, drawing on comparative evidence, elucidates the economic significance of ancient slave prices.

33 Anderson and Gallman 1977: 26. Fixed capital cannot be varied, unlike circulating capital such as wages. Eggertsson 1990: 203–13 provides a useful brief survey of the economics of slave labor.

34 Fenoaltea 1984. Canarella and Tomaske 1975 and Findlay 1975 discuss the balance between coercion and rewards.

35 See Hanes 1996 for turnover costs, and Scheidel 2008b: 111–12.

36 E.g., Metzler 1975; Toman 2005.

37 Scheidel 2008b: 112–15, drawing on Watson 1980; Temin 2004b.

38 Backhaus 1989 (*servi vincti*); Kaltenstadler 1978; Carandini 1988: 19–108, 287–326 (rational organization). For privileges, see Bradley 1987a: 39–112.

39 Joshel 1992: 173–82 lists occupational designations and measures their representation in the epigraphic record of the city of Rome. The representational dominance of certain sectors (manufacturing, domestic service, and administration) may be a function of the intensity of association with elite owners, even though less prominently documented occupational fields (such as construction and transportation) may well have involved less slave labor. Silver 2009b considers the relationship between terminological specificity and the frequency of occupations.

40 Mouritsen 2011: 120–247 is now the fundamental treatment. Valuable earlier work includes Treggiari 1969 and Fabre 1981.

41 Manumission was functionally analogous to slave families, which likewise served as a reward, a means of control, and a source of profit: see Bradley 1987a: 47–80, for familial relations as a means of control, and above n.18 for the importance of slave reproduction.

42 Mouritsen 2011: 220, 226–8, and also Los 1995. This was a globally common pattern: Patterson 1982: 240–61. Genuinely independent freedmen (cf. Garnsey 1998: 28–44) may have been (much?) rarer.

43 Mouritsen 2011: 152 (quote). Co-residence: see ibid. 149 and Fabre 1981: 131–62. Marriage: ibid.: 163–215; Bürge 1988.

44 Straus 1973 (Egypt); Hopkins 1978: 131–71 (Delphi). Mouritsen 2011: 159–80 holds that payment for manumission was less common in Rome; insofar as it severed bonds it may have been more of an alternative to than an element of continuing patron-freedman relations. Days of service (*operae*) ex-slaves owed their patrons (Waldstein 1986) may not have been particularly profitable.

45 Gai. *Dig*. 40.9.10. For their employment in top elite households, see Treggiari 1975; Hasegawa 2005; Mouritsen forthcoming. See also Kirschenbaum 1987 for their role as agents in commerce.

46 For attrition, see above. Steady employment was more important for slaves than in other labor systems: Anderson and Gallman 1977. Leasing was a viable option but incurred transaction costs and risks of impairment. Slaveownership established property tax obligations, for instance through the poll tax attested in Roman Eypt and the inheritance and manumission taxes imposed on Roman citizens.

47 For the early stages of Roman slavery, see Welwei 2000; Bradley 2011b. The notion that slavery used to be a characteristic of Mediterranean societies is correct (Horden and Purcell 2000: 388–91, following F. Braudel) but unhelpful inasmuch as it neglects the critical importance of organizational variation (cf. above, Chapter 1).

48 Rosenstein 2008: 5–7, on Livy 24.11.7–8 (but cf. Welwei 1988: 35, 37). It is unfortunate that we are ignorant of the participation of slaves in the large naval campaigns of the First Punic War: Welwei ibid. 29–34.

49 Volkmann 1990: 57, 148 (Greeks); Polyb. 3.24 (treaty). It is unclear to what extent the western Greeks employed indigenous serfs, but that institution may have been in decline: Van Wees 2003, especially 45–6 on Syracuse.

50 Centrifugal mobility and high commitments: Scheidel 2004a: 10–12; 2007b: 325 fig.1.

51 Rathbone 1983: 162; Terrenato 2001. Rosivach 1993 provides instructive comparanda for the possible role of smaller-scale slavery.

52 References to allocation of war captives in the sixth and fifth centuries BCE (Volkmann 1990: 37) need not be true but might reflect actual later practice. See also Caes. *B Gall*. 7.89.5. The evidence from Sokoto, whilst not necessarily germane to the Roman case, is suggestive.

53 Contrast Oded 1979; Gundlach 1994.

54 Bradley 1989: 41–3 (uprisings); Ziolkowski 1986 (Epirus).

55 E.g., Carandini 1988: 19–326; Marzano 2007: 125–53. Expansion: Giardina and Schiavone (eds.) 1981; Morel 2007. Mobility and commitments: Scheidel 2004a: 10–13, 21 fig.1; 2007b: 323–9. Capital inflows: Chapter 1. Gains for commoners: Scheidel 2007b: 329–33.

56 Fentress 2001.

57 The prominence of freedmen in the epigraphic record of Narbo (Narbonne) may reflect the replication of Italian practices of slavery and manumission: Woolf 1998: 99. For slavery in the western provinces in general, see Staerman et al. 1987; Morley 2011; Harper 2011: 182–98. Finds of chains on rural estates in Roman Gaul might be linked to slave labor: Thompson 2003: 217–44; Henning 2008. For other forms of labor, see, e.g., Whittaker 1993: ch. 1–2, and below, Chapter 6.

58 Lo Cascio 2009: 189 and 2010, a more sophisticated version of the 'conquest thesis' (critiqued by Harper 2011) that accords critical importance to changes in the slave supply. The incorporation of a demographic dimension is important and all too rare in Roman economic history: see Chapter 1.

59 Slave prices of the Republican period are virtually unknown but ransom rates are sporadically documented: see Prachner 1995. Higher fees for unconditional release in Delphi during the transition from republic to monarchy, albeit conceivably a reflection of rising slave prices (Hopkins 1978: 162–3), are difficult to interpret

due to changes in sample size and our ignorance of their circumstances (cf. Duncan-Jones 1984). Although the enslavement of war captives continued under the monarchy (Bradley 2004), its relative contribution to the slave supply probably declined given that campaigns became less extensive at a time when the overall slave population was probably larger than before. The catchment area for slave imports was relatively sparsely populated: Scheidel 1997: 159–60. Nominal slave prices appear to have been fairly homogeneous outside Egypt (where regulations constrained slave exports, depressing nominal prices). For higher nominal incomes and prices in Italy, see Freyberg 1989.

60 Marzano 2007: 199–222.

61 Scheidel 1996b: 72–73 (on Diocletian's Price Edict); Harper 2010.

62 See Harper 2011. Shaw 1998: 31–43 is more nuanced. MacMullen 1987 and Whittaker 1987 are among the most salient earlier studies. Quantitative data: Harper 2008. For villas, see Lewit 2004; cf. Vera 1995. For the nature of the colonate, see, e.g., Grey 2007, and below, Chapter 6.

63 See in general Wickham 2005, and cf. above, Chapter 1. *Adscripticii* may have been similar to slaves: Harper 2011: 155, 506.

64 See Harper 2010. High real wages due to labor shortage: Scheidel 2010: 456–7.

65 Harper 2010; McCormick 2001: 733–77; Henning 2008; Rotman 2009: 57–81.

66 This is a variant of the more global thesis advanced by Miller 2008 that throughout world history, slavery empowered owners relative to competitors who lacked access to slaves, thereby allowing the former to effect innovations. In the Roman case, slaveownership did not create a new dominant class but redefined the relationship between slaveowning dominants and the bulk of the freeborn population.

67 For example, Aubert 1994: 417–20 observes that the link between Roman business management and slavery was closer than legal institutions would lead us to expect if employers had been indifferent to their agents' status. Preference for unfree agents and attendant career opportunities may help explain the phenomenon of voluntary enslavement: Ramin and Veyne 1981.

68 On slavery within labor markets, see Temin 2004b, who notes that premodern 'free' labor was often subject to serious constraints on mobility and choice (cf. also Banaji 2003); but see below, Chapter 6, for Roman free labor institutions. Slaves could defect to seek new employment (Bellen 1971), but attendant risks were considerable.

69 See especially Carandini 1988: 318–23; Schiavone 2000: 63–5, 108–64.

70 See Morley 2009: 150–2 for choice quotations from Hume, Marx, Engels, and Weber, or more recently the work done in the 1980s (such as Finley 1998, first published in 1980; Giardina and Schiavone (eds.) 1981; de Ste Croix 1981; Carandini 1979), and contrast the effective absence of slavery from the 82-page mission statement of the current Oxford Roman Economy Project (see above, Chapter 1, n. 14). For abiding interest in the overall importance of ancient Greek slavery, cf. Cartledge 2002a; 2002b.

6: Contract labor

Dennis Kehoe

The role of slave labor has rightfully been a focus of historians assessing the performance of the Roman economy. But to develop a comprehensive picture of economic relationships in the Roman Empire, one must assess the situation of the empire's vast class of small-scale landowners, tenants, artisans, and people engaging in various forms of wage labor. Often these groups overlapped. So a basic question is the degree to which economic growth in the Roman Empire benefited the vast class of working people in the Roman economy.[1] Did the legal and social institutions surrounding the use of contract labor encourage the efficient use of resources, or did they simply promote the interests of the empire's elite at the expense of the vast majority of its population, including both farmers and urban laborers?[2] As comparisons with later societies will show, it is unlikely that Roman workers ever escaped Malthusian constraints, so that population remained a decisive factor in determining the welfare of workers. In the Roman Empire, workers faced increasing competition as population grew over the first two centuries CE, at least until the Antonine Plague in 165 CE, which apparently caused widespread loss of life and arguably substantial economic disruption.[3] Indeed, documentary papyri from Egypt, which provide some detailed information about wages and prices, suggest that wages and prices remained relatively stable in Egypt until in the 160s CE, when they doubled over a period of thirty years, quite possibly as a result of the loss of population. This sudden change, after a long period of stability, suggests how important population pressure was to the welfare of the empire's workers. After the 190s CE prices and wages remained stable until about 270 CE, when serious inflation set in.[4]

The growth of urbanism, fueled by a transfer of wealth from the countryside to the cities, brought profound changes to the Roman economy, and the recent study of Scheidel and Friesen over income levels and the distribution of wealth in the Roman Empire puts these changes in a useful perspective.[5] In their study, Scheidel and Friesen suggest that while a small elite (about 1.5 percent of the population) controlled a disproportionately large share of the wealth, perhaps one-fifth of the total income, that is not the whole story. The empire also saw the growth of a 'middling' class (about one-tenth of the population) that had considerable wealth of its own, perhaps another fifth of total income, while the largest class (80–85 percent of the population), including farmers living at close to subsistence level, also cumulatively accounted for considerable wealth and income. These estimates are clearly conjectural, but they give us a broad perspective within which to consider the role of contract labor in the economy. The institutions surrounding contractual and dependent labor would affect both the economic opportunities for the 'middling' class as well as the amount of wealth in the hands of the lower classes.

FARM TENANCY

To begin with contract labor in the rural economy, farm tenancy in the Roman Empire represents a broad range of relationships, including wealthy lessees of estates, small-farmers who contributed their own resources to cultivating individual farms belonging to other landowners, as well as tenants with few resources of their own cultivating their land under what can be viewed as labor contracts. Farm tenancy of the last two types represents an alternative to the employment of slave labor and long-term of permanent wage laborers. Slaves were used to cultivate estates in parts of Italy and in other regions of the empire, such as Baetica.[6] Wage labor was also an important means of exploiting estates in some parts of the empire, most notably Egypt, where it is well documented (see below). But tenancy was almost certainly found in some form throughout the Roman Empire, and it could be complementary, rather than an alternative, to slave and wage labor. Tenants cultivated lands that could not be incorporated within the management of a larger estate, and, along with small landowners, they provided a source of occasional labor at the busiest seasons, such as the harvest.[7] Indeed, in his recent study of twenty-seven rural surveys in Italy from the second century BCE until the second century CE, Alessandro Launaro shows that the construction of villas, presumably cultivated with slave labor, was often accompanied by an increase in smaller farmsteads, occupied by owner cultivators or tenants.[8]

One of our most important sources for understanding farm tenancy consists of Roman legal texts as preserved in the Digest and

Code of Justinian. Although legal texts do not describe land tenure arrangements, they do help us to understand how the Roman legal authorities responded to broad policy issues affecting the Roman agrarian economy.[9] Consequently, they offer us evidence for the changing dynamics in landowner-tenant relationships that are difficult to recover, say, from the numerous leases preserved on papyri that provide rich documentation of tenancy in Egypt.

The farm lease in classical Roman law, a form of *locatio-conductio*, 'lease-hire,' came to be recognized as a valid contract that could be protected in a court of law in the later Roman Republic, probably in the late third or early second century BCE.[10] This was the same period in which Roman law recognized the other consensual contracts, including *emptio-venditio*, sale, *societas*, partnership, and *mandatum*, mandate, and it is also the period that saw the development of precise rules for the allocation of water rights to respond to the needs of landowners engaging in increasingly commercialized agriculture.[11] As Luuk de Ligt argues, it is likely that some form of farm tenancy existed from the earliest Roman Republic, since it is basic to pre-industrial agrarian economies.[12] In the classical Roman farm lease, the tenant paid a fixed rent in cash, and generally leased the farm on a short-term basis, for five years. The landowner was expected to provide all fixed assets, not just the farmland, but any storage buildings, and other heavy equipment attached to the farm, such as wine presses or olive presses, or large storage jars fixed in the ground. The tenant, for his part, provided movable property, including tools, slaves, and livestock. The property that the tenant brought onto the farm, the *invecta aut illata*, was pledged as security for the rent and the condition of the farm. Theoretically, this method of leasing protected the landowner against risk, since the tenant, by paying a fixed rent in cash, assumed the risk for both the size of the harvest and for the market price of the crops. At the same time, the landlord enjoyed a great deal of flexibility, since he could dismiss an unsatisfactory tenant at the end of the lease period, and could use this possibility as well as the right to confiscate the property pledged by the tenant and sell it to pay off arrears to enforce the tenant's fulfillment of his contractual obligations. Landlords and tenants could freely bargain for other terms. For example, although the normative lease is for a cash rent, the Digest also recognizes a sharecropping contract as legally enforceable under Roman contract law (Gai. *Dig.* 19.2.25.6).

The reference to sharecropping suggests that the jurists, when developing rules for farm tenancy, considered the situation of a broad spectrum of tenants, rather than the wealthiest ones, as has often been assumed. Indeed, one recent study of the process of petitioning the emperor concerning matters of private law demonstrates that people outside the elite, at the very least, from the 'middling' class discussed above, could seek rescripts from the emperor to strengthen their cases in local courts.[13] These considerations suggest two important points for understanding farm tenancy: (1) that leases involving tenants of relatively humble status could be enforced through Roman legal institutions; and (2) that the classical farm lease provided a set of legal conventions within which the Roman legal authorities, when faced with the task of resolving disputes, interpreted leases whose terms were based on local customs or other traditions in origin quite different from classical Roman law.

In the late Republic in Italy, it is tempting to see the developing law surrounding tenancy as serving the interests of landowners taking advantage of growing commercial opportunities, fueled by a massive transfer of wealth from the provinces to Italy. Although many landowners used slaves to staff intensively cultivated compact estates to produce cash crops, notably wine and olive oil, as Launaro suggests, it is not likely that all of this land could be cultivated with slaves. Rather, some landowners leased lands to tenants primarily as a way of managing labor rather than sharing in the management of and investment in the land. In this scenario, tenants would have brought few resources of their own, and they would have been economically dependent on their landlords for the investment necessary to cultivate their land.[14]

As the boom in agriculture in the late Republic began to subside in the early principate, it is likely that the fundamental relationship between landowners and tenants changed. There is no reason to think that large landowners became less wealthy, but their sources of wealth changed. Rather than investing to increase the commercial capacity of their estates, they instead tended to gain their wealth by capturing some portion of the surplus that their tenants produced.[15] Both landowners and the Roman legal authorities demonstrated a willingness to adapt the classical farm lease to provide tenants with greater security and more of an incentive to invest in the long-term productivity of their farms. This was the experience of Pliny the Younger, whose income depended on his ability to keep his tenants cultivating their land productively. Consequently he sought to protect them from losses caused by droughts, first by granting remissions of rent, and then by instituting sharecropping.[16]

To create needed flexibility in the lease relationship, landowners and tenants had to bargain around some of the disincentives for investment that the classical farm lease created. One disadvantage was the burden of risk that the tenant bore. Legally, the tenant was only entitled to a remission of rent, or *remissio mercedis*, when the most extreme risks, that is, exogenous, unforeseeable disasters, such as an earthquake, an invasion of an enemy army, or an extreme and unforeseeable drought, made the farm impossible to cultivate.[17] The tenant bore the risk for other types of disasters, including the droughts that were a normal feature of Mediterranean agriculture.[18] These could leave the tenant unable to pay the rent, with disastrous consequences not only for the tenant, but also for the landowner, if the tenant could no longer cultivate the estate productively. The legal authorities recognized that social concerns would compel landowners to grant remissions to alleviate the tenant's risk for drought, and they responded by defining what rights and duties would arise for landowners and tenants as a result of such concessions.

Another potential disincentive to investment was the tenant's lack of possession rights.[19] The tenant's tenure was legally insecure, in that he could be expelled from his farm, say when a landowner sold or otherwise alienated the land, and his only recourse would be to sue the original landlord for monetary damages. In this area of the law as well, the Roman legal authorities showed great flexibility, recognizing as legally enforceable tenure arrangements that gave tenants much greater security of tenure than would be recognized in conventional Roman lease law. The Roman legal authorities could define open-ended tenure arrangements in terms of Roman conventions by applying the principle of the tacit renewal of the lease. According to this principle, if a tenant remained on his farm without the landlord's objection, the lease was considered renewed for one year under the same terms of rent and with the same property pledged as security.[20] A long-term lease, then, could be defined in Roman terms as a lease renewed year after year. Such an arrangement did not in and of itself give tenants security of tenure; rather, it provided a way in which to describe in terms of Roman conventions lease arrangements in which landowners had already provided this security. However, the legal authorities went one step further by recognizing the customary rents that formed the basis of these tenure arrangements as legally binding. Thus the emperors Valerian and Gallienus ruled that landowners could not raise the rents in tacitly renewed leases (*CJ* 4.65.16, 260 CE).

The process of according customary tenure arrangements the full force of law reached its logical conclusion under Constantine in the early fourth century, who recognized customary rents as legally binding and created a legal remedy for tenants whose landlords raised these (*CJ* 11.50.1, *c*.325 CE). Constantine's enactment is seen as the adoption by the Roman government of provincial or 'vulgar' law, but at the same time it was consistent with a policy to promote the undisturbed cultivation of the land by small farmers.[21] So important was the continued presence of small farmers on the land that, in the early fourth century, Constantine legislated that creditors could not seize property from farmers that they needed to cultivate their land (*CTh* 2.30.1; C. 8.16.7, 315 CE). The binding of *coloni*, tenant farmers registered for fiscal purposes on the land of (generally larger) landowners, represents another facet of this policy. To maintain its tax revenues, the imperial government imposed increasing responsibilities on local landowners to collect them, and, as part of this policy, the government sought to assure that landowners could meet their tax obligations by binding to their estates tenants who were registered there.[22] The binding of *coloni* does not mean that all tenants were bound to the land, and the *coloni* affected by this legislation represented a legal rather than an economic class. The legal sources documenting the colonate indicate that it was implemented gradually over the course of the fourth century. But it was not universally applied; in Egypt there is little trace of it in the fourth century, and it appears that farmers there were bound to their land only much later.[23]

To return to the Roman government's policy in regulating farm tenancy, the legal authorities' recognition of the legal validity of long-term tenure arrangements suggests that, in much of the Roman Empire, landowners profited from their estates largely by skimming some portion of the surplus that their tenants produced. Under this scenario, landowners were not first and foremost interested in making strategic investments in their estates to respond to changing market conditions. Rather, they were much more oriented toward achieving predictable and stable incomes from their estates. This was much the same approach that the Roman administration took in managing state-owned land, including imperial estates in North Africa and public land in Egypt. All of these lands formed part of a widespread network of properties under the control of the imperial treasury, or *fiscus*, and they supplied important revenues that supplemented those attained from taxation.[24] On the imperial estates of North Africa, where the conditions surrounding land tenure are documented in a famous series of inscriptions, the primary cultivators were small-scale farmers, *coloni*.[25] They were sharecroppers, generally paying one-third of their crops as rent, and they were given incentives to bring unused lands under cultivation, first through enactments extending the application of the *lex Manciana* (the lease regulation that defined their terms of tenure), and then by a more general enactment of the emperor Hadrian, the *lex Hadriana de rudibus agris*, or "the law of Hadrian concerning unused lands." One of the most important incentives the *coloni* received consisted of perpetual leaseholds, but to enforce their obligation to pay their share rents, the imperial administration set over them middlemen, or *conductores* ("lessees"), who held five-year leases for the imperial estates, collected the rent from the *coloni*, and used the labor and draft animals of the *coloni* to cultivate certain lands within the estates. In Egypt, the imperial administration also relied on small-scale farmers to cultivate state-owned lands, which were divided into various categories. The tenants on this land enjoyed substantial security of tenure. Other evidence for the exploitation of imperial estates comes from Asia Minor in the third century, and there it is also apparent that the estates were cultivated by small farmers, often living in villages on the estates.[26]

The papyrological evidence from Egypt provides us with detailed information about leases that helps to clarify important aspects of private farm tenancy.[27] In Egypt, and probably in other parts of the empire, the lines between farm tenants and small owner/cultivators were blurred, as small landowners also leased in land, both from private landowners and from the state. Private leases were generally set for short terms, from as little as one growing season, but often for several. Rents varied in accordance with the type of crop. The most common rents for grain land, *ekphoria*, were fixed amounts of grain for each unit of land. The amount of rent would vary depending on many factors, and it is difficult to determine what portion of the crop the farm tenant typically had to pay as rent. For vineyards, rents were often shares of the harvest. In some leases, in particular for vineyards, the tenant would be paid a wage; this would be a form of tenancy that would shift the risk entirely on to the landowner.[28] In late antique Egypt, long-term leases, often set at the owner's discretion, are documented.

The long-term nature of many tenancy relationships in the Roman Empire raises an important question as to the social relationship between landowners and tenants. To be sure, classical Roman lease law operated on the assumption that landowners and tenants could freely enter into contractual relationships, and the evidence for tenancy from Egypt suggests that the ranks of small landowners and tenants overlapped. At the same time, it is clear that a wide social gulf existed between many landowners and their tenants, such as between Pliny the Younger and his tenants. The inherent social dependency in many tenure arrangements certainly affected how the parties would use legal institutions to protect their rights.[29] This was clearly the case in other areas of the law. Creditors often exercised a great deal of latitude, including self-help, in dealing with debtors who were social inferiors.[30] There were, however, factors that mitigated the social domination of landowners. For one, the Roman government, as a broad policy, opposed the exercise self-help to settle debts, and, beginning at least by the reign of Marcus Aurelius, consistently sought to promote its courts as authoritative to settle disputes.[31] It is impossible to know to what extent more humble tenants had access to the protection of legal institutions, but the constitution of Constantine discussed above concerning customary rents indicates the emperor's expectation that they did. The legal authorities' practice of interpreting local custom in terms of Roman legal conventions points to their continuing efforts to keep tenancy under the control of the law. Moreover, even if the prominent role of the state as an economic actor could not disrupt relations of patronage in rural communities, the very favorable terms of tenure that tenants on imperial property enjoyed necessarily affected what private landowners had to offer to retain their tenants. So there were contradictory forces at work in the rural Roman world: elite landowners, at least the wealthiest among them, tended to become wealthier over the course of the early empire, but the growing role of the state as an economic actor mitigated their economic power.

WAGE LABOR

In agriculture, seasonal laborers, especially at the harvest time, were a ubiquitous feature. But long-term wage labor, documented in Roman Egypt, is also likely to have been a widely used way to exploit estates. Detailed evidence for the use of wage labor comes from the Heroninos archive, which documents the management of an estate in the Fayyum region of Egypt owned by Aurelius Appianus, an equestrian and member of the city council of Alexandria during the mid-third century. Dominic Rathbone has made a groundbreaking study of this estate.[32] The estate was divided into a number of divisions, or *phrontides*, organized around individual villages. These divisions had permanent salaried laborers, called *oiketai* and *metrematiaoi* (at one village, there were 11 of the former group and 15 of the latter in a particular year, but often the numbers were lower), supplemented by workers hired on a daily basis.[33] Both the *oiketai* and the *metrematiaioi* were of free status, but their relationship to the estate seems to have involved some dependence. The *oiketai* were paid modestly; their monthly wages included a cash stipend, which ranged from four to twelve drachmas, as well as one artab (*c.* 40 liters) of wheat. The cash payment was quite small, since laborers hired on a daily basis received around two drachmas, but the wheat allowance was more generous, much more food than an individual was likely to consume.[34] The status of the *metrematiaioi* was somewhat different.[35] They received the same monthly allowance of one artab (occasionally 1.5 artabs) of wheat as the *oiketai*, but their monthly cash salaries varied, from four drachmas to as many as 60 drachmas. They also tended to have somewhat more specialized functions, since many of them are designated as shepherds, donkey drivers, or oxen drivers, and often, though they were assigned to a particular village-based division, they worked for the central estate, going on assignment from one division to another. Both groups received accommodation within the estate, whether as part of their salary or something they rented, and, at least on occasion, clothing allowances. The estate also paid taxes on behalf of at least some of these workers. Unlike the *oiketai*, the terms of service for the *metrematiaioi* varied from several months to several years or more. As Rathbone suggests, they worked under conditions similar to those in so-called *paramone* contracts. These were arrangements in which one person agreed to remain with an employer for a set period, often for several years; the terms of employment might include a monthly allotment of grain, as well as some money.[36] In many cases, these contracts were antichretic in nature, in that they represented arrangements for the worker to pay off a debt. They can be seen as similar to antichretic leases, which involved a debtor's leasing land to a creditor rent-free as a way of extinguishing a debt.[37]

The remuneration of most of the permanent workers on the Appianus estate seems very modest, close to the subsistence level. But since they also apparently received housing and possibly also access to gardens to cultivate, they were paid a living wage. It is not known how common the form of labor organization was that is documented on the Appianus estate, but a similar pattern of employing permanent wage laborers housed within the estate is documented on the sixth-century estate of the aristocratic Flavii Apiones in the Oxyrhynchite nome, and it seems reasonable to infer that wage labor was employed in a similar fashion in many areas of the Roman Empire.[38]

But as important as the long-term wage laborers were on the Appianus estate, workers hired on a daily basis furnished much of the labor, according to the evidence of several monthly accounts, between about one-third and four-fifths of the labor, depending on how busy the season was.[39] The most common daily wage for occasional workers was two drachmas and two obols, whereas especially skilled or heavy labor was paid for at a higher rate of four drachmas. Children were also employed as laborers, and they were paid one drachma and five obols. Rathbone estimates the annual cost of living for an adult male as 420 drachmas, which would require being hired for around 200 days. In reality, the daily wage must be considered as part of a family's income, which might also include labor from children (but not, apparently, from women), as well as from land the family cultivated, whether as tenants or small-scale owners. The casual laborers could well have been better off, if somewhat less secure, than the permanent laborers.[40] In other parts of the empire, the wages earned by casual laborers, whether working in agriculture or in other trades, supplemented the living most people made from agriculture, which provided for their basic subsistence.[41]

The Appianus estate exercised a great deal of economic influence on the villages surrounding its divisions, and many people there must have been dependent on it for their livelihoods. The question is the extent to which the estate's relationships with the surrounding community were shaped by the social dominance of the landowner, as Andreau and Maucourant suggest.[42] However, the estate's economic domination should not be overstated, since there were many independent skilled workers, including carpenters and irrigation workers, whom the estate hired on a short-term basis.[43] The estate in fact depended on the continued viability of these skilled workers, and they clearly had other sources of income, which would mitigate the social domination of the estate.

Construction and other industries

Certainly construction represented one of the most important industries in which wage labor played a prominent role. Public building programs at Rome potentially employed thousands of workers at any one time, and, in addition, private building also represented a steady source of employment, for both masons and skilled artisans as well as ordinary construction workers.[44] The same will have been true in other cities in the Roman Empire, albeit on a lesser scale. In private building, the contractual relationship between the property owner or employer, who desired the construction project, and the actual builder, might take two forms. One was a stipulation, a formal promise by the builder to the employer to complete a construction project, generally within a specified time. Potentially complex construction projects were probably more likely to have been arranged through a form of lease, *locatio operis*, in which the owner of the building site, or employer, was the *locator*, or lessor, and the building contractor was the *conductor* (or *redemptor*).[45] To judge by the juristic sources, the contractors themselves were apparently financially independent, with sufficient resources to manage expensive projects. They were ordinarily paid in two installments, one-half at the beginning of the contract and the balance after the final approval of the project. This suggests that builders had to have resources to pay workers and buy materials. Of course, in more complex projects, employers might call on the services of a variety of contractors, who could even be responsible for small aspects of the job. Builders had their own professional organizations; one is known at the *collegium fabrum tignariorum*, both at Rome and Ostia.[46] Like other *collegia*, this body served primarily a social function, but it could also, at least in theory, have provided a way to organize skilled labor for a large-scale building project.[47] In the later empire, *collegia* of builders may have exercised more influence over the construction business. At least the emperor Zeno legislated against price-fixing by building contractors, among other trades.[48]

We can gain some appreciation of the economic impact of major construction projects from Janet DeLaine's study of the building of the baths of Caracalla in Rome, certainly one of the most ambitious public building projects from antiquity. In DeLaine's analysis, the construction of these baths took at least six years and involved the employment at any one time of between 1,900 and 13,100 workers, including hundreds of skilled artisans, hundreds of oxen drivers, and thousands of ordinary workers.[49] In addition, many of the materials used in this project were drawn from the countryside surrounding Rome, including stone from quarries, and bricks produced from clay pits on estates near the city.[50] Certainly a huge project like the Baths of Caracalla would represent an extreme example of the profits that might accrue to the rural economy from urban construction, but it is logical that in other cities in the Roman world, monumental construction, as well as the construction of private residences and apartment blocks, would likewise provide a significant if sporadic stimulus to the rural economy as well as employment in the cities. Unfortunately, we have little information about the pay of construction workers in the Roman world, either specialized artisans or ordinary workers.

To turn to wage labor in the manufacturing sector, as Cameron Hawkins points out in his essay in this volume, most types of manufacturing were organized around small workshops, under the control of an individual artisan. Many labor relationships in this setting would tend to revolve around a master artisan's employing a small number of slave assistants, who might eventually use the training they acquired to earn their freedom and establish their own workshop.[51] In Egypt, it was common for artisans to provide training for free apprentices, who would be paid a wage that increased with time. But, as Hawkins points out, instead of maintaining a staff of permanent employees, artisans would hire sub-contractors on a short-term basis as business warranted. Like the construction industry, the production of consumer goods was seasonal, and it seems likely that in Rome and in other large cities, workers migrated between the countryside and the city in search of seasonal employment.

THE WELFARE OF WORKERS

The evidence from the Appianus estate suggests that the cash wages earned by temporary workers, who had other sources of income, provided a mild stimulus to the rural economy. But this leaves unanswered the larger question about the standard of living that workers in the Roman Empire achieved. As discussed at the outset, population posed a basic constraint on the standard of living of laborers. Although we do have some information about wages and their purchasing power in the Roman Empire (see below), the data are far from complete. However, we can learn a great deal about the likely situation of Roman workers by comparing the purchasing power of known wages in the Roman Empire with purchasing power of wages in later, better documented periods of history. The economic historian Robert Allen has made a careful examination of the purchasing power of wages of workers in twenty cities in Europe from the fourteenth to the nineteenth centuries; the purchasing power is measured in terms of a basket of goods that would approximate a respectable standard of living, as well as another, more 'bare bones' consumption basket.[52] In essence, these consumption baskets measure the extent to which workers could purchase items beyond what they simply required for basic subsistence.

Allen's conclusions about wages in Europe suggest some basic limits on what we can expect the experience of workers in the Roman Empire to have been. In general, the purchasing power of wages was tied to demographic factors: wages were relatively high in the period following the Black Death in the fourteenth century, but as population increased in the sixteenth century, real wages tended to fall. The only exception to this rule was in England and in the Low Countries, where wages began to rise in the eighteenth and nineteenth centuries. If the ability to purchase the respectable basket of goods represents a welfare factor of 1, workers in these areas were able, because of their increasing productivity, to achieve welfare ratios that doubled this level.[53] The experience of England and the Low Countries represents a break with the Malthusian checks on the economy, but elsewhere in Europe real wages fell as population increased, and in many areas workers experienced grinding poverty. It is not likely that workers in the Roman Empire shared the good fortune of their counterparts in early modern England. Indeed, in applying his approach to the legal maxima for wages and prices in Diocletian's wage and price edict of 301 CE, Allen has determined that the wages and prices represented in this document would have given workers a welfare ratio of 0.56.[54] The purchasing power of Roman workers, however, did allow them to achieve a 'bare bones subsistence,' but even so, Roman workers would still have been poorer than workers in early-modern Europe, and even in Delhi and Beijing.[55] Scheidel has applied Allen's approach to the purchasing power of wages in Roman Egypt. The welfare ratios arising from this exercise are between approximately 0.25 and 0.4 for a 'respectability basket' and 0.7 and 0.9 for a 'bare bones basket.'[56] As Scheidel points out, to meet its basic subsistence needs, let alone have any money left over for discretionary purchases, a family would have required more income than what a single worker could provide, and it is likely that women and children also contributed to the family income.[57] To compare wages from Roman Egypt with those of other ancient economies, Scheidel measures their purchasing power in terms of wheat, a basic staple in most ancient societies. According to Scheidel's calculations, workers in Roman Egypt earned enough to purchase 4.9 liters of wheat per day. These wages are in the middle of Scheidel's database for societies in the Ancient Near East and Europe from 1800 BCE to 1300 CE.[58] Scheidel's data suggest that demographic factors were crucial to the welfare of pre-industrial workers. For example, workers in Egypt in the sixth century had wages of 7.7–13.4 liters per day, which may have been the result of labor shortages caused by periodic outbreaks of the plague.[59]

It seems unlikely that wages rose much as the Roman economy grew in the first two centuries CE. Certainly military wages remained stable.[60] At the time of Augustus, a legionary soldier received an annual salary of 900 sesterces.[61] It is not possible to offer a meaningful calculation of what this wage would represent in wheat per day, since the price of wheat surely varied considerably, depending on the locations in which the legions were stationed. The salaries of soldiers remained stable until Domitian raised them by a third in 85 to 1,200 sesterces, but they remained stable again until the time of Septimius Severus (193–211 CE). In 214, Caracalla raised the basic salary for a legionary soldier to 3,600 sesterces. Certainly soldiers had suffered a relative decline in the period after the Antonine Plague, when wages for other workers are likely to have risen as a result of population losses. Some troops were much better paid than rank-and-file legionaries: the urban cohorts in Rome received one and a half times the salary of ordinary legionaries (although prices were surely higher in Rome than in the provinces), while soldiers in the praetorian guard received three times as much. Officers were paid a great deal more than ordinary legionaries, fifteen times or more the base salary. So centurions received 13,500 sesterces annually before Domitian, and 18,000 afterwards. Despite their apparently modest pay, however, soldiers were able to accumulate some wealth, to judge by several wills made by soldiers that have been preserved.[62] Some of their wealth came from retirement bonuses and land grants.[63] In addition, third-century rescripts addressed to them indicate that soldiers did own property and have business dealings during the terms of their service.[64]

The information for wages in the Roman Empire and their purchasing power suggest that the fortunes of Roman workers were closely tied to demographic factors, and they never escaped Malthusian constraints. A larger issue is the significance of the purchasing power of daily wages for determining the relative prosperity of the working people of the Roman Empire. As mentioned previously, many wage workers had additional sources of income, primarily from agriculture. The daily wages paid to such workers surely supplemented what they gained from their other sources of income, and many of them produced much of the food that they consumed. From this perspective, the daily wages, modest as they were in comparison to those of urban workers in early modern Europe, may have provided some income above subsistence, and so increased the purchasing power of the lower classes in the Roman Empire. This observation seems all the more true for soldiers. Legionary soldiers, together with the auxiliary forces, whose pay was somewhat lower (auxiliaries received perhaps five-sixths that of legionaries), sailors, and urban guards represented perhaps 400,000 people receiving cash wages on a regular basis.[65] Although much of the soldiers' pay was withheld, the cash they did receive, including bonuses upon retirement, arguably represented an enormous infusion of money that stimulated commerce in the military zones. At the same time, the large number of people that the military employed had to affect the private market for labor. If the terms of service soldiers gained were favorable, which they must have been since so many sons of soldiers also entered military service, the military, much like the *fiscus* in administering imperial estates, offered stable terms of employment that, on the whole, must have helped to improve the situation of workers generally.[66] On the other side of the coin, much of the labor performed by wage earners in early modern Europe was carried out by slaves in the Roman Empire, and it is likely that their 'wages' (what they received over bare subsistence) would have been modest and so would have acted as a constraint on the wages of free workers. Still, the prosperity of free workers was largely dependent on agriculture, and the fortunes of small farmers were inexorably tied to population pressure and the demand for land.

NOTES

1 Morley 2007b; Lo Cascio 2007; Hitchner 2005.

2 For the role of law and legal institutions in the ancient economy, see Frier and Kehoe 2007.

3 See especially Scheidel 2002, and, for a very different interpretation, Bagnall 2002, with the response by Scheidel forthcoming c. For discussion of the population of the Roman Empire, see Frier 2000; Scheidel 2007a.

4 Rathbone 2009: 305; Scheidel 2010: 428.

5 Scheidel and Friesen 2009. On urbanism as an indicator of economic change, see Scheidel 2009a; Wilson 2009b. For the transfer of wealth from the countryside to the cities, see especially Erdkamp 2001, as well as Horden and Purcell 2000 175–297.

6 For a re-assessment of slave numbers in Italy, see Scheidel 2005a. For Baetica, see Haley 2003.

7 For this relationship between free and slave labor at Cosa in Italy, see Rathbone 1981.

8 Launaro 2011.

9 The principal legal sources for farm leases are in *Dig.* 19.2, on *locatio-conductio*, as well as in the corresponding section of the Code of Justinian, *CJ* 4.65.

10 A consensual contract is one in which obligations are created by the mutual agreement of the two parties, rather than, say, by a transfer of property. See Mayer-Maly 1956; Kaser 1971; 562–72, and, for the basics of Roman lease law, Frier 1979b; Kehoe 1997: 137–56, and, for a review of approaches to the subject, Lo Cascio 2009: 91–113.

11 Bannon 2009.

12 De Ligt 2000; for the development of tenancy in Roman law, see also de Neeve 1984.

13 Connolly 2010; her understanding of the 'middling' class would include many people in Scheidel and Friesen's 2009 lower class. For the upper-class orientation

of the jurists, see Zimmermann 1990: 348–50, following Frier 1979a: 39–47; cf. Kehoe 1997 139–42.

14 Launaro 2011. For the economic dependence of tenants without resources, see Foxhall 1990.

15 See especially Kehoe 2007a: 93–129; for a similar understanding of tenancy in the early imperial period, Launaro 2011. Cf. also Erdkamp 2005: 23–33, who emphasizes the tenant's access to credit from the landlord.

16 See Kehoe 1988a; de Neeve 1990.

17 For remission of rent in Roman law, see especially Frier 1989–90 and du Plessis 2003, as well as Kehoe 1997: 221–34; 2007a: 109–19.

18 Horden and Purcell 2000: 175–230.

19 On the tenant's lack of possession, see Mayer-Maley 1956: 53–5.

20 On *relocatio tacita*, see Mayer-Maly 1956: 218–21, who links the application of this principle with imperial efforts to address declining agriculture in the third century.

21 On vulgar law, see Levy 1951, 1956.

22 See most recently Grey 2007; Carrié 1983, 1997; Kehoe 2007a:165–73.

23 Bagnall 1993: 148–60.

24 Lo Cascio 2007: 630–1, 642–6.

25 Kehoe 1988b; 2007a: 56–79.

26 For Egypt, see Rowlandson 1996: 70–101; for Asia Minor, see Hauken 1998.

27 See especially Rowlandson 1996.

28 For work contracts for vineyards, see Jördens 1990.

29 For social dependency in labor relations, see Garnsey 1998: 77–87.

30 See Bürge 1980.

31 For fuller discussion, see Kehoe 2007a: 148–60.

32 Rathbone 1991.

33 Rathbone 1991: 91–102.

34 Rathbone 1991: 106–16; the amount of grain represents 3,350 calories/day.

35 Rathbone 1991: 116–47.

36 Rathbone 1991: 116–17. For a general introduction to labor contracts in Egypt, with literature, see Rupprecht 1994: 124–8; for *paramone* contracts, see also Jördens 1990: 284–95.

37 Rupprecht 1994: 127.

38 Rathbone 2005; for the Flavii Apiones and wage labor there, see Banaji 2001: 171–212.

39 Rathbone 1991: 148–66.

40 Rathbone 1991: 165–6.

41 Erdkamp 2005: 81–105.

42 Andreau and Maucourant 1999.

43 Rathbone 1991: 166–74.

44 For the use of free labor in public building projects at Rome, see Brunt 1980.

45 Martin 1989: 73–136.

46 Martin 1989: 65–9.

47 DeLaine 1997: 204.

48 *CJ* 4.59.2, 483 CE. Cf. also Zeno, *CJ* 8.10.12.9, and Garnsey 1998: 134–50.

49 DeLaine 1997: 175–94.

50 DeLaine 1997: 195–205.

51 See Fülle 1997, for the *terra sigillata* industry.
52 Allen 2001.
53 Allen 2001: 432–5.
54 Allen 2009b: 337–8; Allen adjusts the basket of goods to account for Roman conditions, e.g., with wine substituted for beer and olive oil for butter.
55 Allen 2009b: 339–42.
56 Scheidel 2010: 430–4.
57 Scheidel 2010: 433–5.
58 Scheidel 2010: 453, Table 4.
59 Scheidel 2010: 456–7.
60 For the details, see Rathbone 2009: 310–12.
61 Rathbone 2009: 311.
62 The most famous is the will of Gaius Longinus Kastor, a sailor who settled in Karanis in Egypt (*Sel.Pap.* 1.85, 189–94).
63 Webster 1998: 254–68.
64 Rescripts to soldiers often involve lending and borrowing money, or inherited property. But a soldier could be a lessor of agricultural property (Alexander Severus, *CJ* 4.65.9, 234 CE). See, more generally, Connolly 2010: 74–5. Soldiers were expressly forbidden from being business managers for private individuals (Diocletian, *CJ* 4.6.5, 290 CE).
65 Webster 1998: 268; Hassall 2000.
66 For the factors inhibiting the formation of a labor market, see Temin 2004b.

Part III

Production

7: RAW MATERIALS AND ENERGY

Andrew Wilson

RAW MATERIALS

Introduction

The extraction, supply, and trade in raw materials was of course fundamental to the non-agricultural sectors of the Roman economy. While the view that Roman trade was characterized more by the movement of raw materials than finished goods is wildly overstated, there was certainly a large trade in raw materials across the Roman world, with almost empire-wide distribution of materials from some sources. Long-distance trade in raw materials was of course a phenomenon that long pre-dated the Roman empire, with Bronze Age Aegean trade in copper ingots and raw glass represented in the fourteenth-century BCE Uluburun wreck, and Phoenician trade in metals from Iberia to the Levant. Particularly noteworthy features of the Roman world are the direct state interest in and control of the extraction and supply of certain types of metal and stone; the corporate organization of specialist suppliers of some materials such as timber, and, in the glass industry, the overwhelming dominance of a small minority of sources of raw glass that supplied glass-blowing workshops all around the Mediterranean.

Metals

The Roman state took a strong interest in the mining of precious metals needed for the trimetallic currency used throughout the empire, either operating mines directly (under military supervision, and sometimes using slaves, condemned criminals, or tributary labor as part of the workforce), or by contracting operations to lessees. There is evidence for state control or supervision of the extraction of gold, silver, and copper; one might expect a similar interest in tin, the other main element in copper alloys, but there is no direct evidence. Lead, since it often occurs in the same ores as silver, was also often extracted under state control. In southern Britain (the Weald) it appears that iron was mined under the supervision of the Classis Britannica, probably on an imperial estate. *Procuratores ferrararium* for Gaul and Pannonia are attested in inscriptions.[1]

The principal gold mines of late Republican Italy were near Bessa in the Biella Alps (second/early first century BCE), exploiting alluvial deposits by hydraulic means on a massive scale[2] – legislation was introduced to forbid mine contractors employing more than 5,000 people. Gold mines were also worked in the Limousin region of Gaul, but largely abandoned by the late first century BCE.[3] The Roman conquest of northwestern Spain under Augustus was followed swiftly by the development of large-scale hydraulic opencast mining of both alluvial and hard rock deposits, apparently using the local population as tributary labor under procuratorial control, with military supervision and technical expertise.[4] Over 500 sites are known. There was also hydraulic opencast mining of alluvial gold deposits in the Spanish and French Pyrenees, and in Dalmatia (certainly during the first century CE).[5] There were important gold ores in Upper Moesia (Kosovo and the Upper Timok valley), which probably became of key significance after the Spanish mines ceased to be exploited on a large scale in the early third century CE, and these Balkan mines continued to be critical to the Byzantine empire.[6] Mines in Dacia, especially the large complex of mines at Roşia Montană, were important gold and silver sources for the Roman world from soon after the conquest in 106 CE until the abandonment of the province under Aurelian, but there are strong indications that operation was disrupted by and diminished after the twin shocks of the Antonine Plague and the Marcomannic invasions of 167.[7] The Eastern Desert of Egypt also had a number of gold mines that were exploited in the Roman period.[8]

For silver, the most important sources were in the southwestern Iberian peninsula – the Sierra Morena until the first century CE, and the southwestern Iberian pyrites belt, including Rio Tinto, Tharsis, San Domingos and Aljustrel (*Vipasca*). These latter mines were developed from the first century BCE onwards, under state control but with concessions leased to contractors; they bid for exploration rights at auction and were then obliged to give half of the ore they extracted to the state.[9] Silver mines in Upper Moesia (especially Kosovo, the Upper Timok valley and the Kosmaj region to the south of Belgrade) were also important, from perhaps as early as the first century CE and certainly in the second to fourth centuries.[10] Dacia was an important source of silver in the second and third centuries, and there were argentiferous lead mines in Britain. Lead was extracted chiefly in SW Iberia and in Britain, especially in the Mendips and the Pennines.[11] This activity started soon after the Roman conquest, initially under military control and then worked by civilian contractors – an ingot of Mendip lead stamped by the Second Legion bears a date of 49 CE; mines in Flintshire were in operation by 74 and in Yorkshire by 81 CE, swiftly in the wake of the Flavian advance into northern Britain.[12] Pliny, writing around 77 CE, notes that the ease and extent of lead extraction in Britain, by comparison to that in Spain and Gaul, led to restrictions on the quantities mined, presumably to preserve the market price of Spanish and Gallic lead – an early example of the state setting a quota in what was primarily an industry operated by *privati*.[13]

The main sources of copper were again the southwestern Iberian peninsula until the late second century CE, Cyprus, which had a large number of major copper mines,[14] and the Wadi Faynan (ancient Phaeno) in Jordan, which was particularly important in the late Roman and Byzantine periods.[15] Iron was much more widespread (it is the most common metal in the earth's crust) and found in some quantity in many provinces, with especially high-quality resources in Noricum, where the iron is naturally carburized to form a natural quasi-steel. The main sources of tin were Cornwall (probably worked by streaming), with some deposits in NW Gaul and in Lusitania.[16]

The most direct evidence that we have for trade in these metals is in the form of ingots, the majority of which come from shipwrecks. Ingots of lead, copper, iron, and tin have been found in wrecks, but none of silver or gold. Since many of the copper and lead ingots come from mines in Spain that also produced silver, the implication is that the lead and silver ingots were shipped separately from each other; Domergue's suggestion that the Roman state transferred gold and silver ingots from the mines to the mints at Rome or in the provinces overland under military escort, to avoid the risk of shipwreck, is persuasive.[17]

Apart from the clear evidence for trade in ingots, metal ores were also traded, particularly iron. Diodorus Siculus (5.13.1–2), writing around the middle of the first century BCE, describes how iron ore was quarried and smelted on Elba to produce raw blooms of iron which were exported to Puteoli and other ports where they were made into metal artefacts. At the port city of Leptiminus in Tunisia there is evidence for primary iron smelting (from ores) in the Roman period; since there is no iron source within 200 km, this must imply that unsmelted iron ore was imported by sea, as return cargoes on ships exporting the agricultural produce and fish products of North Africa.[18]

Minerals

Minerals were used as agents in various stages of textile production – for example alum in mordant dyeing, Melian earth as an agent in fulling, or sulphur for bleaching fulled clothes – and as pigments. Many of these occurred as a result of specific geological formations only in particular regions. Sulphur, for example, was produced particularly in Sicily, where molds for sulphur cakes have been found, with stamps indicating the production of sulphur first probably by private contractors and then under imperial control from Commodus through to at least Constantine.[19]

A group of minerals known in Latin as *alumen* and in Greek as styptic earth, was used in mordant dyeing. These are not identical to our alum, but seem to be a family of iron sulphates. A key source for these was Lipari in the Aeolian islands off northeastern Sicily; Diodorus Siculus and Strabo both refer to the revenues this brought the Liparians and the Romans, Diodorus adding that this was because Lipari enjoyed a virtual monopoly on styptic earth and could raise the price, the only competitor being Melos, whose production was insufficient to satisfy widespread demand.[20] Pliny gives a wider range of sources for *alumen* (Spain, Egypt, Armenia, Macedonia, Pontus, Africa, and the islands of Sardinia, Melos, Lipari, and Strongyle),[21] but archaeological evidence suggests that Lipari was indeed the most important; 'Richborough 527' amphorae produced on Lipari, and identified as transport containers for *alumen*, are widely distributed in the western Mediterranean and also reached the Adriatic and Britain.[22]

Melos was also the source for 'Melian earth,' one of the brightest white pigments used in antiquity; it was extracted from both surface deposits and underground mines.[23] Cinnabar (an ore of mercury), used as a red pigment and also exploited for its mercury content,[24] was also extracted from subterranean mines, some of which could be large operations – a Roman cinnabar mine was discovered at Sizma (Turkey), in which a tunnel had collapsed killing nearly 50 people.[25] This mine is thought to have formed part of an imperial estate, reminding us once again of the state/imperial interest in natural resource extraction.[26]

Natron was exploited principally in the Wadi Natrun and al-Barnuj in Egypt, with lesser deposits also in the Eastern Desert of Egypt, and other sources at Lake Van in Armenia and Lake Pikrolimni in Macedonia. In antiquity it was used for a range of purposes from an ingredient in antiseptics, in the preservation of dried fish and meats and in mummification, and as a flux for glass production.[27]

Gems and precious stones

Little work has been done on the sources and extraction of the precious gemstones used in antiquity, and this is a topic ripe for research. Precious and semi-precious stones by definition came from select and rare geological deposits, some outside the Roman Empire (e.g., diamonds traded from India and Sri Lanka). A review of the main sources of exploitation of precious and semi-precious stones, with evidence for ancient workings and their chronology, is a key desideratum for any analysis of ancient gem use that moves beyond the antiquarian approaches that characterize most studies of ancient gems.[28] To what extent does the organized exploitation of such sources, or the empire's access to external sources of precious stones such as India, explain the apparent growth in the number of gemstones over the Roman imperial period? The issue is complicated by the fact that some gemstones occur as surface phenomena and can simply be collected without leaving archaeologically visible traces of extraction. It is nevertheless clear that the Eastern Desert of Egypt was an important source for numerous precious stones, both surface-picked and mined,[29] and one of only two sources for emeralds within the empire (the other being Habachtal in Austria), and it is surely significant that emerald and topaz mining were under the control of a procurator, based at Berenice on the Red Sea, who was also responsible for the gold mines and marble quarries of the Eastern Desert.[30] The Eastern Desert was also probably the most important source of amethyst located within the empire, although by the early fifth century CE these mines were being operated by the Blemmyes, who had been raiding the area for a while.[31] Carbuncles or garnets, a semi-precious stone, were traded by the Garamantes from the Sahara to first the Carthaginian realm and then to the Roman world.[32]

Clay

Clay was of course used for pottery, roof tiles, bricks, vaulting tubes and ceramic pipes, and forms of architectural decoration. Good clay beds were a valuable economic resource and might be exploited directly by a landowner's slaves or freedmen, or their use leased to specialist potters. Papyrus contracts from third-century CE Egypt document the rental of pottery workshops to potters in exchange for the obligation to provide a set number of amphorae for the landowner, who seems to have been producing wine.[33] The evidence from potters' stamps for the migration of potters from Arezzo to Gaul, and the number of different potters attested by stamps found in large-scale workshops such as those at Scoppieto (Upper Tiber Valley, first century CE) and Le Rozier (near La Graufesenque in southern Gaul), may suggest that some landowners with good clay resources established large pottery production facilities which they then leased to potters to provide a revenue stream.[34] In the lower Tiber Valley and around Rome clay beds were exploited to produce the millions of bricks needed for building projects in and around Rome and Ostia from the first century CE onwards; the evidence of brickstamps shows that by the late second century CE nearly all the key estates had come into imperial hands, either by marriage or confiscation, and the imperial house exercised a near monopoly over brick production in this region.[35]

While amphora and cookware production seems to have been principally located in coastal or riverine regions with good access to transport networks, the location of some of the major fine pottery production centres (Arezzo, Scoppieto, La Graufesenque) away from good transport corridors seems to have been determined principally by the availability of good clay and fuel resources. In the Mediterranean, where clay is easily available and cheap, its wide availability (and the scarcity of good timber) meant that ceramic amphorae were preferred as a container over the more efficient technology of wooden barrels.

Stone and building sand

Most building stone resources were used relatively locally – much of the Roman Empire, especially in the Mediterranean, had good local deposits of sandstone or limestone. In many cases building stone was quarried immediately locally to (or even within the limits of) cities (Sabratha, Tocra, Cyrene, Paphos); but where necessary there was local trade in such stone; further downstream than upstream along rivers, for reasons of transport cost.

Marble and granites were used for decorative and prestige architecture. Greek architecture had made extensive use of white marble from sources in Greece and Asia Minor; the Romans continued this practice with marble from the same sources, but under Julius Caesar new quarries were opened up at Luna in Italy, transforming the availability of white marble, and thus the extent of its use, in Italy. But from the late second century BCE onwards the use of coloured marbles for architecture, as columns and veneer, was becoming popular. Originally this began as a late Hellenistic trend – the Numidian kingdoms had begun exploiting Chemtou marble – but the process was accelerated by Rome's acquisition of the Mediterranean basin, to the point where exotic coloured stones did duty as symbols of Rome's control of space and of geographical resources – purple Phrygian columns, red porphyry and granite from Egypt, yellowish/pink marble from Numidia. These stones began to be traded widely for architectural purposes under Augustus, and in the Julio-Claudian period there was deliberate prospecting for exotic colored marbles in the Eastern Desert of Egypt, undertaken apparently at imperial command.[36] Many colored marble quarries seem to have been under imperial control; but this was not necessarily universal; the popularity of Troad granite, used in many private building projects, may be due to its being a close visual analogue of the imperially controlled granite from Mons Claudianus in Egypt, whose use was reserved for imperially controlled and funded building projects. Certainly the use of exotic coloured marble statues, especially those from the Egyptian quarries in the Eastern Desert, was an imperial prerogative.

White marble was traded more widely for statues, sarcophagi and architectural elements, and although the major quarries were under imperial control, there were clearly private quarries which escaped such monopoly. In many cases, both to reduce weight before transport and to add value, architectural elements, sarcophagi, and even in some cases honorific statues might be part-worked at the quarries and finished at receiving centers.[37]

Much Roman construction relied on artificial concrete, and a particularly durable variety, which could even set under water and was thus particularly used in harbor works, involved the use of volcanic sand or *pozzolana*, from the vicinity of Pozzuoli in the Bay of Naples. It was shipped in large quantities to Caesarea Maritima, for use in Herod's harbor there, probably transported in Alexandrian grain ships returning from Italy, as part of Rome's assistance to its client king.[38] The harbor at Chersonisos in northern Crete also uses Italian pozzolana, probably also transported as a return cargo;[39] but there is some evidence also that other ships carried part-cargoes of pozzolana, and it may have been more widely traded than is currently realized.[40]

Timber

The Roman jurists distinguished between *materia* – timber for building (construction, shipbuilding, furniture, mine shoring, barrels, etc.) – and *lignum*, firewood (discussed below under fuel).[41] Texts mention the use of silver fir particularly in construction and shipbuilding, and maple, boxwood, and citrus for furniture – the latter especially for the vastly expensive *mensae citreae* from Mauretania.[42] In fact, oak, beech, etc. are much more common in furniture from Herculaneum and Pompeii than we would expect from the ancient authors. The texts seem to mention luxury materials with the greatest frequency, and largely ignore the common materials; they give us a very distorted view of the frequency with which woods were used in furniture making.[43]

We may build on this emerging new picture with a re-analysis of the key evidence, overlooked by Meiggs in *Trees and Timber*, of dedications by *collegia* of *dendrophoroi* ("tree carriers") or their members or patrons.[44] Despite persistent attempts to see the *dendrophoroi* primarily as a religious phenomenon,[45] their occurrence in inscriptions alongside guilds of other traders, shippers, or woodworkers argues their involvement in trade and commerce. The distribution of Latin inscriptions mentioning *dendrophoroi* is very much what we might expect for the heavy timber trade – concentrated in Italy either side of the Apennines, around the southern Alps especially in the Po Valley, and in the Rhône Valley, and along major river systems for waterway transport.[46] Alpine fir and spruce have recently been identified archaeologically at both Herculaneum and Pompeii.[47] But there is also a notable concentration of *dendrophoroi* inscriptions in the wooded uplands of the Tunisian Tell and its export ports of Utica and Carthage,[48] and in northern Numidia at Cirta,[49] from where logs could be floated down the Oued Rhummel to the port of Rusicade. It is striking however that there seems to be absolutely nothing in Spain or western Gaul. The biggest concentrations are at the maritime import/export ports, and the major river port of Lyon. The *dendrophoroi* were lumberjacks or loggers, involved primarily in logging and shipment of timber for shipbuilding and construction rather than furniture – sources of expensive luxury furniture timber, such as citrus from Mauretania, are absent from the map. The location of major shipbuilding centers was of course primarily coastal but influenced by the possibilities of downstream logging transport from areas of good timber forests (e.g., Cadiz, not far from the estuary of the Guadalcuivir, and Minturnae on the Liris river).

Glass (sand, natron, raw glass)

The manufacture of glass involves heating sand with a flux in large kilns to produce slabs of raw glass. This raw glass is then heated in glass-blowing furnaces and blown into vessel form. Before the introduction of vegetable fluxes in the ninth century CE, natron was almost universally used as the flux in raw glass production. By far the most important sources of natron were in Egypt at Wadi Natrun, south of Alexandria.[50] There were furnaces for raw glass in Wadi Natrun, using the local sand and natron, but chemical analysis of Roman glass samples suggests that little or none of this was exported outside Egypt.[51] Rather, by far the majority of Roman glass has isotopic signatures indicating an origin in the Levant, and large late Roman/Byzantine glass furnaces have been found in Israel. Raw glass was produced in tank furnaces each yielding slabs of glass weighing several tons, which were smashed up into chunks or ingots, and then exported around the empire.[52] Raw glass has been found in several Roman shipwrecks, including the Embiez-Ouest wreck of the late second/early third century CE, sunk off southern Gaul, which was carrying 18 tons of raw glass ingots from the Levant.[53] There was some smaller-scale raw glass production apparently in Italy, North Africa (a tank furnace has been discovered at Carthage), allegedly in Spain, and certainly at Cologne, but the general pattern of glass production in the Roman world involved the necessarily large-scale export of natron from Egypt to the Levant, and its use there to make vast quantities of raw glass using the local silicate-rich sands.[54] This Levantine raw glass was then exported around the Mediterranean to supply innumerable glass-blowing workshops located at port cities and inland throughout the provinces. This domination of the glass industry by a single production region is an important feature of Roman glass production and one of the most powerful indicators of the integration of Roman trading networks.[55] Even those other raw glass production centers in the provinces relied on natron from Egypt to use as a flux.

Discussion

It appears that to some extent the degree to which the location of raw materials determined the location of industries that used them varied in inverse proportion to the value of the raw material. Generally, pottery industries were located relatively close (within a few kilometers) of the clay beds they used, although the shipment of raw clay from Pantelleria and North Africa to Sicily shows that there were exceptions. By contrast, precious metal ingots for coins were transported overland from NW Spain to the mint at Rome, and ingots of lead, copper, tin, and iron were shipped around the empire to urban and sometimes rural workshops to be turned into finished objects. On occasion, where transport costs were subsidized by the need for return cargoes, iron ore rather than ingots might be shipped between provinces (as at Leptiminus). Yet the picture is nuanced also by factors of availability of supply, and by questions of scale: for glass production, although natron was found primarily in Egypt, this did not prevent the development of a major primary glass industry in the Levant (exceeding in importance for exported glass the production within Egypt); and the Levant then exported this raw glass to glassblowing centres all around the Roman world. As Horden and Purcell note, much production is located within the medium of communication rather than necessarily at centres of either raw material origin or demand location.[56]

Between the Julio-Claudian period and the early or mid-third century there is an increasing concentration of particularly significant raw materials under state or imperial control. The Roman state moved very swiftly to exploit metal resources in newly conquered or acquired territories: large-scale gold mining was developed in Asturia and Callaecia immediately following the Augustan conquest; a lead-silver mine was in operation 100 km east of the Rhine already before the *Clades Varianae* of 9 CE; lead mines were operating in central Britain within 4 years of the invasion, and the development of gold mining in Wales and lead mining in northern Britain followed hard on the heels of the Flavian advances into these regions. This will have involved deliberate prospecting by specialists attached to the army, and this is indeed documented for the parallel process of developing the quarries of prestige colored marble, for imperial statuary and architectural display, in the Eastern Desert of Egypt. Procurators oversaw and controlled the exploitation of key metals and indeed some colored marbles and even gemstones, from the first until the early third century CE, although even during this period some mines and quarries were turned over to private operation if their yield did not warrant direct state exploitation.

ENERGY GENERATION

Sources of power

All pre-industrial economies are what Wrigley has termed 'organic' economies, whose energy requirements are ultimately supplied by solar radiation – either directly as heat, or indirectly via photosynthesis to produce vegetation that serves as food for animals and humans.[57] Even the currents of water and wind that provide power for various kinds of prime movers are dependent on climate, which affects rainfall and wind patterns. It was only with the Industrial Revolution that mankind learned to exploit fossil fuels (which effectively unlock concentrated solar-derived energy accumulated over millennia) on any large scale and harness them to mobile energy sources. For pre-industrial societies Wikander, in his review of sources of energy in the ancient world (to which the reader is referred for a fuller treatment than is possible in this chapter), identifies two major stages of development in the harnessing of energy.[58] The first is the Neolithic Revolution, in which animals were domesticated, allowing humans to use them as power sources in a limited array of tasks, and the second was the spate of mechanical inventions of the Hellenistic period, which included the water-mill and water-powered lifting wheel, opening up the development of machines driven by water-power, and extending the range of applications for which animal muscle power could be used.

Solar radiation

Because the sun is the basic source of energy for crops, understanding temperature fluctuations in climate over time is a key desideratum for the study of ancient economies, although one that is still far from having been achieved. Sunlight, besides being the ultimate energy basis for plant and animal life, provides direct warmth that can be used to heat buildings. Indeed, some buildings were designed to make maximum use of sunlight – the hot rooms of baths usually had windows that faced southwest to take advantage of the afternoon sun, and the effect might be intensified by the use of large glazed windows.[59] The sun's warmth was also used routinely for drying clothes; and the use of curved concentrating lenses to kindle fire was known.[60]

Human muscle power

Before the recent invention of complex robots, the performance of many complex tasks was limited to humans, who possessed the necessary dexterity and the capacity for learning and instruction. Human muscle power, however, is inefficient, as people use about three-quarters of their energy intake simply to stay alive, and the maximum output is limited.[61] Nevertheless, an enormous amount of labor in the ancient world was carried out by human muscle power, from agricultural ditch-digging to construction, mining, and quarrying. Humans were used also to perform tasks that could be carried out better by animals – milling grain, or carrying people in a litter. While the institution of slavery may have encouraged such use of human labor perceived as cheap, in the context of an economy's energy budget, "slavery is a zero-sum game that transfers surplus human energy from one group (the slaves) to another (the masters)."[62]

A variety of mechanical devices did, however, increase the potential of human muscle power. Most of the simple machines or mechanical powers – the wheel and axle, the lever, pulley, winch, and wedge – were known by the Archaic period. These enabled the multiplication of a force, or a change in its direction, to exert greater effort than muscular power alone could achieve. The rotary hand-quern and rotary mill, for example, allowed a more efficient use of human power to grind grain than did the saddle quern. Two more simple machines, the gear wheel and the screw, were invented in the Hellenistic period and, in combination with the others, transformed the possibilities for the development of machinery allowing human and animal muscular output to be harnessed for a greater range of more demanding, complex, and repetitive tasks.[63]

Animal power

Large quadrupeds – the ox, horse, donkey, mule, and camel – are more powerful than humans but less adaptable to complex tasks. In the simplest form, they can serve as mounts for human riders, or as beasts of burden. With suitable harnessing they can be made to perform simple tasks requiring linear movement, such as traction for ploughs, carts, and other vehicles. Around the third century BCE the potential uses of animal power were extended by the invention of several machines that could be driven by rotary motion, and besides transport and agriculture, these rotary machines constituted the most important use of animal power. Three main sizes of rotary mill were developed, the smallest for humans, and the larger two for donkeys and horses respectively. By the first century BCE the rotary dough-mixing machine had been developed for kneading dough, and was driven by animals, as shown on the relief from the Tomb of Eurysaces in Rome.[64] These machines were important for partially mechanizing the enormously labor-intensive task of bread production, freeing up human labor for other tasks, although it should be noted that human-powered rotary mills and hand querns remained in use, alongside animal-powered ones, for smaller-scale production or less capital-intensive operations. But of great importance for primary agriculture, especially in the drier parts of the ancient world, was the development of a family of water-lifting machines, known by their modern Arabic name as *saqiyyas*, which were used primarily for irrigation, and also for the supply of baths. These were driven by an animal walking around a drive wheel and a right-angle gearing converted the rotary horizontal motion into motion in a vertical plane to drive either a wheel that raised water in boxes or pots on its rim, in the case of shallow wells or cisterns, or a bucket chain or pot-garland for deep wells. The invention of these machines dates back to the third century BCE,[65] and by the first century BCE they had spread to Italy, and by the first century CE as far north as Britain. *Saqiyyas* with pot-garlands were widespread in Egypt by the later third or early fourth centuries CE, used particularly for the irrigation of vineyards. This machine had a transformative effect on agriculture in certain arid regions, allowing cash crop production through the ability to harness animal muscle power for irrigation.[66] These machines effectively increased the energy budget available to the ancient world.

Water-power

The current of flowing water facilitates transport downstream, and had been exploited ever since the first boat. Its importance can be seen in the Roman period from the differential distribution up- and downstream of, for example, stone from quarries situated near rivers.[67] The distribution of inscriptions by *dendrophoroi* (above) around major river systems strongly suggests the floating of logs downstream by lumberjacks.

A major addition to the energy budget of antiquity was enabled by the harnessing of water-power to turn wheels that could then be used to drive other machinery. This development, also a product of the inventively fertile Hellenistic world of the third century BCE, represents humanity's first efforts at harnessing the power of natural forces to do mechanical work (rather than for transport), and stands at the head of the sequence of developments that led ultimately (though not inevitably) to the mechanization of the Industrial Revolution. Its importance is therefore considerable, and this explains the ink that has been spilled in debates over the date of the origin and the adoption of the water-mill.[68]

The hydraulic *noria*, or water-driven water-lifting wheel, was one of the products of the extraordinary milieu of mechanical creativity fostered in Alexandria in the middle decades of the third century BCE.[69] Flowing water turned a wheel with paddles on its rim and hollow wooden box compartments in the rim, each with a hole at the leading edge. These filled up as they dipped under the surface of the river or stream and discharged their water near the top of the cycle into a trough or launder. This machine had the advantage of a high discharge and a high lift (medieval examples at Hama in Syria are up to 60 feet in diameter), and was driven automatically so long as the level of the watercourse was high enough. The more recent distribution of this technology suggests its use also in antiquity on perennial rivers in arid zones such as the Orontes (it is represented on a mosaic from Apamea in Syria dated to 451 CE), the Euphrates, and in the Fayyum in Egypt; but its use was probably much more widespread.[70] By the time of Lucretius the machine was known in Italy, and a sixth-century CE example is known from Salona.[71] The primary use of this machine was probably irrigation.

The water-mill is now generally thought to be a product of the same period, and combines the paddle-wheel of the *noria* with the right-angle gearing of the *saqiyya* to drive millstones.[72] All three main varieties – the geared overshot and undershot vertical-wheeled mills, and the horizontal-wheeled mills, which lack a gearing – seem to have been invented in the third century BCE, in the eastern Mediterranean (some types probably at Alexandria). By the first century BCE they were known in the western Mediterranean and by the mid-first century CE were common both there and north of the Alps. Large multiple-wheeled installations – veritable bread factories – existed from the Trajanic period onwards, as at Barbegal near Arles, with 16 wheels driven from an aqueduct.[73] Numerous large installations existed on the Janiculum Hill at Rome. The water-mill was found in both urban and rural settings, and the technology survived into the early Middle Ages, especially in monastic contexts.

The overshot and undershot water-mills convert the rotary motion of the water-wheel into rotary motion in a horizontal plane. A major breakthrough was also made probably as early as the third century BCE with the use of the cam to convert the continuous rotary motion of a wheel into reciprocating linear motion. This was demonstrated originally in automata, and seems to have been used in full-scale machines doing serious work by the first century CE.[74] Pliny, in a difficult passage, seems to describe the pounding of grains by water-powered pestles in Etruria.[75] The plausibility of this reading is enhanced by the archaeological evidence at some Roman mines in the Iberian peninsula and Britain for anvil stones of what are clearly water-powered ore-crushing stamps, of an apparently nearly identical design to ore-stamps illustrated by Georgius Agricola in 1557 and in use until the communist period at, e.g., Roşia Montană in Romania. Here, projecting cams or lugs on the axle of a water-wheel alternately raised and dropped several stamps with a heavy iron shoe mounted within a vertical framework; the stamps dropped onto lumps of ore on a stone block or anvil to crush them. The archaeological evidence consists of the worn anvil stones with the depressions caused by repeated stamping, and in the case of Dolaucothi in Wales the anvil stone is near a probable wheel-pit for a water-driven wheel.[76]

Water-powered saws are also attested in textual and archaeological evidence. A relief on a third-century sarcophagus shows a double frame-saw driven by a breast-shot water-wheel;[77] in the fourth century, Ausonius' *Mosella* certainly, and Gregory of Nyssa probably, mentions the sawing of stone with water-powered saws, and Ammianus Marcellinus refers to a *serratoria machina* ('sawing machine').[78] Actual installations survive from the Byzantine period: a late sixth-/early seventh-century overshot wheel driving a pair of single-bladed saws in Hanghaus II at Ephesos,[79] and a wheel driving a pair of four-bladed saws in the Sanctuary of Artemis at Jerash, thought to date from the fifth to seventh centuries CE.[80] In all these cases it seems that the rotary power of the waterwheel was converted to linear motion by a camshaft which alternately pushed the frame-saws to and fro.

A further use of the power of water was the harnessing of its erosive power in opencast mining, to erode overburden, exploit gold-bearing alluvial deposits, or sort gold particles from dross. All these techniques essentially mimicked the natural action of water in artificially controlled ways: hushing involved the sudden release of large quantities of water from reservoirs on the edge of an opencast, capable of eroding and transporting large quantities of earth and rock overburden to expose gold-bearing veins (or occasionally those containing silver and lead) beneath. Ground-sluicing involved the more continuous playing of a stream of water over a gold-bearing alluvial deposit, eroding it and funnelling the material out through an exit channel running over a stepped riffle, in which the denser gold particles could settle out while the lighter alluvial soil was carried away. This enabled the processing of vast quantities of deposits containing very small quantities of gold per m^3 of earth in a way that simply would not have been possible without the mechanical aid of water; in the Valduerna in Asturias in northwestern Spain some 25 km^2 of landscape on the southern bank of the river were worked to a depth of 2 to 10 meters by these means.[81]

Hydraulic mining techniques can be traced back to the fifth century BCE; in the Laurion region particles of lead-silver ore that had been crushed and ground to powder were sorted in special ore-washing establishments by the release of water from stand-tanks over stepped washing tables on which the crushed ore was spread out. Similar techniques were used in Ptolemaic Egypt, and these may have influenced the stepped riffles or washing channels used in Roman ground-sluicing opencasts. In the second century BCE the Salassi, a tribe of the Italian Alps, used ground-sluicing techniques to work gold deposits at Bessa near Vercellae; in the aftermath of the Augustan conquest of northwestern Spain such methods were developed and applied there on a massive scale (see above). Roman hydraulic gold mines using hushing and ground-sluicing have also been identified in the Spanish and French Pyrenees, Dalmatia, South Wales (Dolaucothi, active *c.*75–125 CE), and Dacia (where they should date between 106 and 270 CE). Hydraulic mining techniques were of major significance for enabling extraordinary levels of gold extraction from the late first century BCE to the early third century CE; but they required enormous investment in the associated infrastructure of long-distance aqueducts and reservoir tanks. When the mines of northwestern Spain were abandoned in the late Severan period, possibly because the deposits had been largely exhausted to the limit of economic viability with the technology and labor resources available, the sources of new gold available to the Roman state were dramatically reduced, with serious effects on the state finances at a time of increasing military spending and the need to buy off barbarians.

Wind

The wind was harnessed in antiquity chiefly to propel ships. This essentially free motive power had a great impact on the economy of transport; maritime sailing was far cheaper per unit of cargo than even downstream riverine transport, let alone any other form which required either human or animal muscle power to haul goods along tracks or roads or upstream along rivers. Moreover, the costs of carrying a part or a full load in the same ship were the same, in contrast to modern ships where fuel costs rise if the cargo is heavier.

The wind was also used in winnowing, to sort the threshed grain from the chaff by throwing it in the air and letting the wind carry the light chaff away, while the heavier grain fell back onto the threshing floor. Unspectacular as both these uses were, they were both fundamental for ancient societies, and particularly for the Roman Empire, since it was the wind that provided the key means of Mediterranean maritime connectivity.

Hero of Alexandria's wind-driven water-organ, in which the air pressure needed to play the organ is provided by a wind-driven wheel with cams on its axle which pump a piston in a cylinder, was probably more a demonstration of a principle than a practical device.[82] It is however intriguing that he says that the wheel should have vanes "like the so-called *anemouria*." What *anemouria* ('wind-whirls') were is unclear; a child's toy or a form of prayer wheel may be possibilities.[83] Although the basic components of both the later windmill and the wind pump were individually in existence in antiquity, there is no evidence that they were put together to create the windmill before the eighth century CE.

Fuels

Ancient fuels included firewood, dung, olive pits, and occasionally coal for ovens, furnaces, and kilns; and olive oil, animal fats, and occasionally other kinds of nut and vegetable oils for lighting.

One might assume that there was less trade in firewood (*lignum*) than in building timbers, since species was less important and almost any locally available wood could in theory be used. Woodland management would evidently have been necessary to supply the demand for *lignum*, and there is some evidence for donations of woodland to support the needs of major public baths.[84] But there clearly was a trade, perhaps relatively long-distance, in firewood. A mosaic from a burial chamber in the northern necropolis at Hadrumetum (modern Sousse, on the Tunisian coast), shows a scene in which logs of wood are unloaded from a ship through the shallows onto a beach, and weighed.[85] The logs, which are yellowish brown and knobbly, carried on the shoulders, and sold by weight, must surely be logs of firewood; and the mosaic therefore gives us evidence for the import, or at least the coastal transport from further north along the Tunisian coast (perhaps Cap Bon), of firewood to the region around Sousse. The scarcity of local timber supply in this region evidently raised the price to the point where a maritime traffic in firewood was economically viable.

Demand for firewood, or its alternatives, must have been enormous. Water has a specific heat capacity of 4.2 kilojoules (kJ), meaning that 4.2 kJ of energy are required to raise the temperature of 1 litre of water by 1°C. If we suppose that a typical set of baths used water whose starting temperature was 12°C, and that hot pools were heated to 40°C, then the energy initially required to bring *each cubic metre of water* in a hot pool up to this temperature is 117,600 kJ (= 117.6 MJ per m^3).[86] In fact, the furnace will have to supply much more energy than this, to overcome efficiency losses caused by dissipation and heat transfer to other parts of the structure. Taking a value of 14 MJ/kg for the energy latent in firewood,[87] and assuming (arbitrarily) 25 percent efficiency in the transfer to the water of the heat energy produced, we arrive at a fuel requirement of 33.6 kg of wood per m^3 of pool capacity to heat the water from cold (12°C) to 40°C. These calculations relate to the heating of the water alone; they ignore the energy required to heat the air space of the baths. Clearly, many of the parameters have been arbitrarily chosen – the firewood may have had a higher calorific value, efficiency might have been greater, the water may have been warmer to start with, or heated to a different temperature – but such calculations do help to give a rough idea of the quantity of fuel required.

With large public baths, often several sets, in every town, and hundreds of country villas with private baths, the aggregate demand for fuel simply for heating baths was massive. Deforestation as a result of this demand over several centuries is a real possibility,[88] and the trend towards much smaller pools in Byzantine baths may have been driven by the cost and availability of firewood as much as or more than by limited water supply. Large parts of the Roman world, especially regions of North Africa, Egypt, and some of the eastern provinces, were not well wooded, and local firewood would have been scarce. In North Africa – especially the coastal plain of Tunisia – the scarcity of firewood led to the use of the residues from olive pressings as fuel for kilns and bath furnaces.[89] A similar use of olive pits as fuel for baths of the mid-sixth century CE is attested at Androna (al-Andarin) in Syria,[90] and ongoing work on the bakeries of Pompeii is now also suggesting the use of olive pressings as fuel there in the late first century CE.[91] It has even been argued, with plausibility, that for the production of amphorae and cooking wares in Roman North Africa, co-location with olive processing activities to enable the cheap use of olive pits as kiln fuel was as important or more so than proximity to clay beds.[92]

Since charcoal is of course much lighter than the equivalent volume of wood, and burns hotter and cleaner, we might expect trade in charcoal to have been at least as extensive, if not more so, than trade in firewood. Dried animal dung would also have provided a cheap and readily obtainable fuel in wood-scarce regions such as the southern shores of the Mediterranean and the Near East. In Britain, some 200 sites have produced stratified evidence for the use of coal (including lignite) in the Roman period, and there is also evidence at some sites in Gaul and Germany.[93] Its use is attested in domestic hearths, hypocausts, in corn-driers, and in metal-working (particularly iron-working sites), but not in pottery kilns; it may also have been used on cremation pyres and in lime-burning for plaster and mortars.[94] Coal was transported beyond the regions where it occurred naturally, and the major study of Roman coal usage concludes that "the widespread use of coal may prove to be a reflection of increasing pressure on other natural resources in the face of their long-term exploitation by growing populations, being used to fuel hungry amenities such as hypocausted heating and the product of equally fuel dependent metallurgical industries."

Conclusion

The Roman world, like all other pre-industrial societies, was an organic economy, and suffered the same constraints; the available energy budget in each year was a fraction of the solar radiation emitted in that year that could be captured, principally via photosynthesis. Although we have seen that there was some use of coal in some of the northern provinces, without the large-scale use of fossil fuels to release the stores of solar energy accumulated over millions of years, there was never going to be a sustained period of massive, geometrically increasing growth of the sort that characterises modern industrial economies. Nevertheless, within these limitations the Hellenistic and Roman periods saw a number of changes in the energy budget that enabled greater use of the available energy of human and animal muscle power, water, and wind than was possible in the societies that preceded them, and even in some that succeeded them. The Hellenistic period, especially the third century BCE, saw the invention of a range of machines which enabled the harnessing of animal power to perform useful work via rotary motion: these included the rotary mill, the *saqiyya* family of water-lifting machines, and (by the late first century BCE) the dough-mixing machine. In parallel to these the use of water-power was developed, first with the water-mill and the water-powered water-lifting wheel, and (by the late first century CE) apparently for driving ore-crushing stamps, and by the third century CE for sawing stone. The first of these developments enabled livestock to perform a greater range of work than simply drawing ploughs, pulling carts or carrying loads; the second opened up an entirely new source of power. In addition, considerable progress was made between the second century BCE and the second century CE in harnessing the erosive force of water for mining operations. How far the scarcity of resources acted as a constraint on economic development is difficult to assess. The Roman Empire was sufficiently large and geographically diverse that to a very considerable extent, imbalances in resource availability between regions could be overcome by long-distance trade in raw materials. This might be either state-directed, as in the case of exotic marble for sculpture and architecture, or the supply of *pozzolana* to a client king for harbor construction, or market-driven, as is implied by the trade in gemstones, alum, and other minerals, timber, and, within Britain, in coal. The trade in firewood draws attention to the vast fuel demands created by Roman urbanism and particularly the bathing habit, and metallurgical and other industries, in places outstripping the supply of local resources; local deforestation around the state-controlled copper smelting site of Khirbet Faynan in Jordan is implied by paleoenvironmental studies, and the evidence for long-distance transport of coal in Britain suggests that a shortage of firewood was not restricted solely to the drier and timber-scarce areas of the Mediterranean. Yet there is no real evidence that extractive or productive activities actually ceased because of a shortage of timber or fuel; instead supplies were shipped in from further afield, which of course increased costs. Rather, the constraint was that faced by all organic economies, that considerable amounts of land had to be set aside as managed woodland to provide firewood, although as we have seen numerous other fuel sources were employed as well. Where a shortage of raw materials may have had a greater negative impact on the economy is in the extraction of precious metals. The productivity of the main gold mines of the Iberian peninsula was in large part due to techniques of hydraulic working of alluvial gold deposits and the use of tributory labor. During the first and second centuries CE the supply of new gold was sufficiently abundant to sustain very high levels of state expenditure both on the army and on public building. The apparent exhaustion of the Spanish deposits in the early third century – at least those deposits with gold concentrations which made their extraction economically worthwhile – coincides chronologically with a downturn in state expenditure on public buildings and civic infrastructure, and it is tempting to see a correlation between these events, as the state directed more of its reduced income to the army and cut back on other areas of expenditure.[95]

Notes

1 Hirt 2010: 136–9, 140–5.
2 Domergue 2008: 129.
3 Cauuet 2005; Domergue 2008.
4 Domergue 1990.
5 Cauuet 2005; Wilson 2007: 113.
6 Mladenović 2009: 70–81, 93–7.
7 The dated writing tablets from the mine galleries of Roşia Montană all cease in 167 CE (Russu 1975). Cf. Hirt 2010: 41–44; 192–6.

8 Schörle 2008: 32–47; Schörle 2010; Sidebotham, Hense, and Nouwens 2008: 213–26.
9 Domergue 1983, 1990; Hirt 2010: 260–9.
10 Mladenović 2009: 70–81, 93–7.
11 Jones and Mattingly 1990: 184–90.
12 Jones and Mattingly 1990: 184.
13 Plin., *HN* 34.164: *nigro plumbo ad fistulas lamnasque utimur, laboriosius in Hispania eruto totasque per Gallias, sed in Brittannia summo terrae corio adeo large, ut lex ultro dicatur, ne plus certo modo fiat.* ("We use dark lead for pipes and sheets. It is dug out with great effort in Spain and throughout all the Gauls, but in Britain it occurs to such a widespread extent in the upper layer of the earth that a law was recently passed that not more than a certain quantity be produced.")
14 Kassianidou 2004: 99; Graham, Jacobsen and Kassianidou 2006.
15 Barker, Gilbertson and Mattingly 2007.
16 Domergue 2008: 20–21, carte 3.
17 Claude Domergue, personal communication 2010.
18 Mattingly et al. 2001: 80.
19 Wilson 1990: 238–9; *CIL* 10.8044.1–11 (Agrigento); Salinas 1900 (Racalmuto).
20 Diod. 5.10.2; Strab. 6.2.10.
21 Plin. *NH* 35.52; cf. papers in Borgard, Brun and Picon 2006.
22 Borgard and Cavalier 2003; Borgard 2006.
23 Photos-Jones et al. 1999; Hall et al. 2003.
24 Vitr. 7.4–5; Plin. *NH* 33.36–42.
25 Myres *apud* Paterson and Broad 1909; Calder 1910: 242; Robinson 1924: 444. I am grateful to Kristina Glicksman for these references.
26 Calder 1913.
27 Shortland et al. 2006.
28 Cf. Henig 1988: 142: "it remains true that Roman gems . . . are the province of the antiquary."
29 Shaw and Jameson 1993; Shaw, Bunbury and Jameson 1999; Sidebotham, Hense and Nouwens 2008: 277–302.
30 Schörle 2008: 48–56; 2011.
31 Schörle 2008: 55–6; Olympiodorus fr. 37 (= Maisano 1979: 51 paragraph 50); Bowman 1986: 51. Cf. Murray 1914.
32 Mattingly 2003: 85, 351, 356, 358; Mattingly et al. 2010: 189–94, 202.
33 Cockle 1981.
34 Wilson 2008b: 397–400.
35 Harris 1993: 22; cf. Setälä 1977: 235–7, 239.
36 Schörle 2008: 8–10; the inscription of C. Cominius Leugas from Mons Porphyrites records the discovery of quarries of black porphyry and other coloured stones there in 18 CE (Van Rengen 1995).
37 Russell 2009.
38 Oleson 1988: 152.
39 Brandon et al. 2005.
40 E.g., the Madrague de Giens wreck, Liou and Pomey 1985: 559–67; Parker 1992: 249–50.
41 Ulp., *Dig.* 32.55 pr.
42 Meiggs 1982: 118–19, 287–93; Mols 2002.

43 Mols 2002: 230.
44 I am indebted to Katia Schörle for drawing my attention to the potential of this source of evidence.
45 Fear 1989: 201; Hemelrijk 2008: 121.
46 Based on analysis of the Epigraphische Datenbank Clauss-Slaby: www.manfredclauss.de/.
47 Kuniholm 2002.
48 Setif: *CIL* 8.8457; Carthage: *CIL* 8.12570; Mactar: *AE* 1892.18; Thugga: *CIL* 8.15527.
49 Cirta: *CIL* 8.6940–1 (dedications by a *curator dendrophorum* to Castor and Pollux).
50 Shortland et al. 2006.
51 Nenna 2003.
52 Foy 2003b; Nenna 2007.
53 Foy and Nenna 2001: 99–112; Jézégou 2007; Wilson, Schörle and Rice forthcoming.
54 Foy and Nenna 2001: 34–45, 99–112; Foy 2003b, 2003c; Nenna 2007; Shortland et al. 2006.
55 Wilson, Schörle, and Rice forthcoming.
56 Horden and Purcell 2000: 346.
57 Wrigley 2004: 30–32; Wrigley 2010.
58 Wikander 2008.
59 E.g., Baths of Caracalla, Rome; Large Baths, Hadrian's Villa at Tivoli.
60 Wikander 2008: 138.
61 Wikander 2008: 136, 140.
62 Wikander 2008: 137.
63 Wilson 2008b.
64 Wilson 2008c: 358.
65 Lewis 1997: 20–32.
66 Wilson 2003: 119–23; and forthcoming work by M. Malouta and me.
67 Russell 2009: 113–14.
68 E.g., Bloch 1935; Finley 1965; Greene 1990, 2000; Lewis 1997; Wikander 1981, 1984, 2000b, 2008: 141–52; Wilson 2002.
69 Lewis 1997; Wilson 2002: 7–8.
70 Oleson 1984: 325–50; 2000: 235–7; Wilson 2003.
71 Lucr. 5.516; Morvillez et al. 2005.
72 Lewis 1997; Wikander 2000b.
73 Leveau 1995.
74 Lewis 1997.
75 Plin. *HN* 18.97; Lewis 1997: 101–3.
76 Burnham 1997; Lewis 1997: 106–10.
77 Ritti et al. 2007.
78 Wikander 1981: 99; 1989. Amm. Marc. 23.4.4; Auson. *Mos.* 359–64; Gregory of Nyssa, *In Ecclesiasten* 3.656A *PG*.
79 Mangartz 2006.
80 Seigne 2002.
81 Jones and Bird 1972; Domergue and Hérail 1977; Matías Rodríguez 2006: 254–8.
82 Wikander 2008: 152–3.
83 Wikander 2008: 153; cf. Lucas 2006: 105.

84 Meiggs 1982: 237–8, 329; Fagan 1999: 163–4, cf. 313 (no. 241).

85 The cargo was correctly identified as logs of wood by Du Coudray la Blanchère and Gauckler 1897: 10; Pl. I.6. Bardo Museum, A.6; and by Meiggs (1982: 529–30). The common interpretation of this scene as showing the unloading of metal ingots is simply impossible from the iconography: Foucher 1957: 16 and fig. 8; 1960, 78; Pl. XLIa (No. 57.169); Yacoub 1970: 53 ('des barres'); Casson 1971: fig. 191 ('bars of lead'); Basch 1987: 481 ('cargaison de plomb'); Nieto 1997: 159 (figure caption: 'lingots de plomb (?)').

86 1 m^3 = 1,000 litres. The calculation is $1{,}000 \times 4.2 \times (40 - 12)$. For recent work on heating water (as opposed to air) in Roman baths, see Rook 1993a, b, with corrections in Rook 1994; Blyth 1995 (who uses the same assumptions, but whose calculation on p. 3 contains misprints).

87 Rook 1994 cites a range of calorific values for air-dry wood, which vary from 13–20 MJ/kg.

88 Cf. Meiggs 1982: 371–403.

89 Stirling and Ben Lazreg 2001: 227–8; Smith 2001: 434–5.

90 Marlia Mango, personal communication.

91 N. Monteix, Pompéi, recherches sur les boulangeries d'Italie romaine, *Fasti Online Documents & Research* www.fastionline.org/docs/FOLDER-IT-2009-166.pdf.

92 Leitch 2010.

93 Dearne and Branigan 1995.

94 Dearne and Branigan 1995: 81–5.

95 Wilson 2009b.

8: Food production

Geoffrey Kron

Although it would be attractive to offer a comprehensive survey of agriculture throughout the ancient Mediterranean, the Near East, and Western Europe, I intend to concentrate primarily upon the best attested and most productive farming regime, that of Italy, Greece, Western Asia Minor, North Africa, Baetica and Eastern Tarraconensis during the Principate and Early Empire.[1] Within this affluent urban heartland of the Roman Empire, our sources and archaeological evidence present a coherent picture of market-oriented intensive mixed farming, viticulture, arboriculture, and market gardening, comparable, and often superior, in its productivity and agronomic expertise to the best agricultural practice of England, the Low Countries, France (wine), and Northern Italy in the mid-nineteenth century. Greco-Roman farmers succeeded in supplying a large urban population equal to, if not significantly greater than, that of early nineteenth century Italy and Greece, with a diet rich, not just in cereals, but in meat, wine, olive oil, fish, condiments, fresh fruit and vegetables. The most striking evidence comes from ancient skeletal remains, which reveal robust mean heights for Greeks and Romans and a high standard of health and nutrition. Protein and calorie malnutrition, caused by an insufficient diet based overwhelmingly on cereals, was very acute throughout eighteenth- and nineteenth-century Western Europe, and drove the mean heights of the Spaniards, Italians, and Austro-Hungarians as low as 158–162cm, comparable to the heights of poor peasants in the Egyptian Old Kingdom. The evidence from Roman Italy, on the other hand, allows us to estimate a mean height of 168cm, equal to that of Italian males just after World War II, and the material from Hellenistic Greece suggests a mean height of 172cm, a level not reached in modern Greece until the late 1970s.[2]

TECHNIQUES, AGRONOMIC EXPERTISE, AND PRODUCTIVITY

The extant Roman agronomists, Cato, Varro, Columella, and Palladius are our most important and informative sources for ancient agriculture, despite the objections raised, mistakenly in my view, about their applicability to the farming of ordinary owner-occupiers.[3] Their rich storehouse of agricultural expertise, and that of many now lost works, was kept alive by the Arab agronomists of al-Andalus, culminating in the work of Ibn al-Awwâm, and in the rest of Europe they were constantly reprinted, admired, and studied from the moment urban life and intensive agriculture began to revive in thirteenth-century Italy, until the rise of a new scientific agronomy in the mid-nineteenth century.[4] The soundness of their advice is constantly lauded in the best recent accounts, particularly by those with comparable experience in organic farming, most notably, perhaps, in the comprehensive and insightful two-volume study of Adam Dickson, arguing for the superiority of Roman practice to that of England in the midst of its agricultural revolution.[5]

The loss of the extensive agronomic literature of the Greeks and Carthaginians, so admired by the Roman agronomists, which was specialized enough to boast entire books devoted to alfalfa and the medics, or the radish, is a significant problem for our understanding of Greek agriculture, even though outstanding work has been done by scholars such as Hodkinson and Amigues to extract information from scientific works, particularly Theophrastus.[6] The evidence which we do have suggests that Classical and Hellenistic Greek farming was at least as intensive and productive as that of Augustan Italy, provided we leave aside the Romans' development of mariculture in hydraulic concrete fish tanks, or their introduction of new fruits, vegetables, or grapevine cultivars as the result of conquest and expanded trade. But this absence of agronomic sources, and insufficient attention to the extant Roman agronomists, has encouraged the persistence, alongside more realistic assessments, of a still influential primitivist school of Greek agriculture.[7]

The best informed authorities have long acknowledged that Roman farming was both sophisticated and productive,[8] with clear evidence that the ancients had anticipated the critical innovations most responsible for the modern agricultural revolution: seed selection; effective tillage; hoeing and harrowing to destroy weeds; crop rotations; the suppression of bare fallow; the rotation of legumes, whether for human consumption, fodder or green manure; irrigation, particularly of meadows and garden vegetables; artificial leys sown with leguminous fodder crops; housing of livestock; improved manure management; careful grazing management for range and pasture land; and, most decisively, as I have argued in a number of publications, ley farming or convertible husbandry, still the most effective system of intensive mixed farming.[9]

Of all these innovations, the most significant were those which allowed farmers to keep more livestock, not only for the great profits to be made from their sale, but because, properly managed, their manure was the cheapest and most beneficial source of nitrogen, which is the critical limiting factor in the yields of most crops.[10] Until very recently, historians of ancient farming have ignored a critical index of the productivity of Greco-Roman animal husbandry and of mixed farming as a whole. As studies of livestock bones demonstrate, Classical Greek and Roman cattle were dramatically larger than those of the Bronze and Iron Age, and of the Medieval period, with cattle standing 20cm taller at the withers and weighing almost twice as much, and sheep were bred as large as modern animals, with wool as fine as the Merino. As late as the 1880s, cattle of comparable size could be found only in England, Holland, and in a few scattered regions of advanced farming. The nutritional needs of such large animals are such that their presence in large numbers is probably reliable evidence of the application of convertible husbandry or, at the very least, of improved pastures, meadows, and leguminous fodder crops. Although the smaller Celtic breeds remained dominant in Roman Britain, throughout most of Gaul and occupied Germany, improved Greco-Roman cattle had almost entirely supplanted the older breeds by the fourth century CE. Of course, some unimproved sheep breeds continued in widespread use, since they were inexpensive and hardy producers of generalized medium wool for coarse clothing, and some smaller cattle breeds were retained as prime milk producers, so improved methods of husbandry may well have been applied on many sites with smaller livestock.[11]

Not only did the Romans raise large livestock more consistently and over a broader geographical range than nineteenth-century Europeans, their use of fodder crops was arguably equal, if not superior, even to that of England and the Netherlands. In addition to fully exploiting alfalfa and most of the principal modern fodder crops, the ancients added a number of outstanding, but still little-known, fodder crops, such as shrub trefoil (*Medicago arborea*) a hardy drought-resistant shrub version of alfalfa, ideal for ovicaprines, particularly in semi-arid conditions.[12]

The integration of livestock into arable farming fostered heavy manuring and high yields. As was recognized long ago by Dickson, Roman techniques for managing compost and manure were sophisticated, dressing the land more heavily and protecting the value of manure more carefully than English farmers did at the end of the 18th century. In addition to farmyard manure and compost, we have evidence for the use, often extensive, of manures imported onto the farm, including night soil, potash and wood ash, bone, and marling with chalk or calcium carbonate.[13]

Unlike the high productivity of animal husbandry, which can be demonstrated archaeologically, direct evidence of ancient yields must rely on literary evidence. As Spurr, Erdkamp and Goodchild have recently demonstrated, Romans' wheat yields matched or exceeded the performance of the most intensive Medieval or Modern agriculture, or that of Italy as a whole in the 1970s.[14] Columella's claim that four-fold cereal yields were now common over a "great part" of Italy should be interpreted carefully. Columella regards such yields as derisorily low, but they are precisely what one would expect in extensive farming without adequate manuring, fallowing, or weeding, and significantly lower yields were normal from the Medieval period through the 19th-century. Since Columella's claim is part of a less than fair or candid argument for the profitability of viticulture, one is tempted to dismiss it, but given the vast imports of inexpensive wheat from Sicily, North Africa, and Egypt, it would not be surprising if many farmers reserved their labor and manure for more lucrative crops.

The most striking evidence of high yields comes from viticulture, a particularly demanding branch of intensive farming. Tchernia's comparison of contemporary and historical wine yields with those achieved by the Roman agronomists in well-managed vineyards, show that the Romans were able to match the performance of their counterparts in nineteenth- or even twentieth-century France. Columella's benchmark for the minimum production of a well-cultivated vineyard, 21 hectoliters/hectare, is almost exactly the same as the average productivity of 19th-century France, and his estimate of a normal yield of 31.5 to 42 hectoliters/hectare matches French figures for the early 1950s.[15] Some scholars question whether ancient vintners could match modern yields, but many modern vineyards using traditional techniques are very competitive, and the Roman agronomists reflected a long tradition of expertise, as Billiard demonstrates in detail in a classic work, based on a deep knowledge of the best French oenology at the turn of the twentieth century. In fact, as Billiard noted, the Romans kept sheep or other livestock on their farms, allowing them to manure their vineyards, whereas their French counterparts generally had to purchase manure, or, as Lachiver points out, declined to fertilize their vines altogether. It is therefore not surprising that French yields did not match the benchmarks of the Roman agronomists until after World War II, when winemakers began fertilizing their vineyards in earnest.[16]

THE INFLUENCE OF COMMERCIALIZATION, URBAN MARKETS, AND TRADE

The intensification of Greco-Roman agriculture depended upon the existence of prosperous urban mass markets for agricultural produce, integrated by vigorous trade networks. As Pleket's magisterial comparative survey reminds us, in *ancien régime* Europe, a system of intensive agriculture specializing in the production of more expensive and profitable crops such as meat, cheese, fruit, fresh vegetables, and wine, was well established in the highly urbanized trading states of Northern Italy and the Low Countries over the course of the later Middle Ages, with important pockets of development around Paris and London, but much lower standards of farming were normal where the bulk of the population remained overwhelmingly rural and poor: landless laborers, as in much of England or Southern Italy in the eighteenth and nineteenth century, or peasants struggling under the burden of heavy rents, taxes, feudal dues, bans, and corvées, as in pre-revolutionary France.[17]

The city-state cultures of Greece, Roman Italy, and Carthage were as highly urbanized as the Dutch or Northern Italian city-states,[18] but enjoyed with a much more vigorous tradition of democratic politics, and consequently, a higher level of social equality. The effect on agricultural productivity was powerful. The affluence of ordinary citizens, and the determination of their broadly democratic governments to encourage the large-scale import and distribution of cheap staple foods to the population, freed up income among ordinary people for the purchase of what in many other cultures would be considered luxury foods. This encouraged the sort of agricultural intensification one can see in sixteenth-century Holland, permitting greater livestock production and the sort of intensive mixed farming critical to improved agricultural productivity. The Greek and Roman diet was therefore much richer and more diverse, not just in cereals and legumes, but in meat, fish, shellfish, wine, olive oil, condiments, fruit, nuts, and vegetables, than that of the rural poor and working classes of eighteenth and nineteenth century Europe.[19] Wine, which we shall discuss in some depth, was the object of a true mass market,[20] and there is even less doubt that the same was true for olive oil. The unique dump of millions of Baetican Dressel 20 amphoras at Monte Testaccio shows that the state distribution of olive oil in the city of Rome, which is unlikely to have represented the whole of the market, would imply per capita consumption at twice the level of early twentieth-century Italy.[21] Although ancient historians often assume that olive oil has always been a staple of the Mediterranean diet, production on the scale so well attested in the ancient world is largely a phenomenon of the twentieth century.[22]

Rome was the wealthiest and most important urban market in the pre-industrial world, and the demand it created for agricultural produce spawned a dense network of villas and *horti* packing Rome's *suburbium*.[23] But Rome was hardly the only megalopolis of the empire, and would have represented only a modest proportion of the overall market for agricultural produce. Trade, cultural contact, and conquest linked the Mediterranean *koine* of Greek, Etruscan, Roman, and Carthaginian cultures with the civilizations of the Celts and Germans, the Near East, Africa, India, and even China.[24] As Pliny declared:

> For who would not admit that, now that intercommunication has been established throughout the world by the majesty of the Roman Empire, life has been advanced by the interchange of commodities and by partnership in the blessings of peace, and that even things that had lain concealed have all now been established in general use.[25]

The trade in condiments and spices, many of which had to be imported from the Near East, Arabia, India, and East Asia, confirms Pliny's boast. Despite the fragmentary nature of our sources, 142 different spices and condiments are listed in ancient texts, 84 of which can now be identified. Miller argues convincingly that ordinary Romans were eager to incorporate new condiments and spices into their diets from a relatively early stage, noting the fake spice names incorporated into Plautus' comedies, and the discovery of the monsoon winds led to a dramatic expansion of these imports and a reduction in their cost. Finds from the House of Hercules' Wedding at Pompeii show that pepper, oregano, rosemary, bay leaves, fennel, coriander, and capers were consumed, and, thanks to its desert climate, Mons Claudianus offers an even longer list, despite being populated entirely by laborers, legionaries, and a single centurion.[26]

One of the most expensive of the exotic spices, black pepper, was imported in massive quantities. Pliny puts the empire's annual imports of pepper at fifty million sesterces,[27] clear evidence, despite its cost, of an impressively broad market, as is Domitian's dedication of an entire warehouse to stockpile it in Rome. The importance of pepper in Roman cooking is attested by 482 citations in the ancient literature, rivaled only by *garum*. It was consumed by the laborers at Mons Claudianus, has been found in large quantities at the Red Sea port of Berenike, and, perhaps more surprisingly, at the German river port of Straubing, on the Danube.[28]

A look at the Roman wine trade will illustrate the importance of the empire-wide Roman trade in agricultural commodities, as well as the innovation it fostered as consumers and producers sampled the best produce from around the ancient world. Already by fifth-century BCE Greece, a tradition had developed ranking wines and other agricultural products by region, and the Roman sources reveal a comprehensive technical vocabulary to describe the qualities of fine wine, an elaborate hierarchy of *grands crus*, and a vivid literary and agro-touristic landscape of the country's wine-producing regions.[29] By the time of Pliny, Cato the Elder's advice on the varieties of grape available to a winemaker served only to show "how great an advance civilization has made in the past 230 years."[30] The pace of innovation is clear even from our abbreviated accounts of the grape varieties available to contemporary vintners. The constant quest to discover more productive, and better-tasting varieties spawned a significant trade in vines, including new creations like the Gallic Allobrogica and Biturica,[31] which were almost immediately transplanted into Italian vineyards. Although he and Columella only discuss 34 different vine cultivars, Pliny claims that there were at least 80 ancient grape varieties known to produce outstanding wine, two-thirds of them from Italy, more than the 50 or so modern grape varieties of interest to wine growers in the 1970s.[32] Roman winemakers were so willing to experiment because of the profits to be made should one produce a superior product. Wines from prestigious regions, like Falernian, could command four times the price of ordinary table wines, although Greco-Roman wine culture was more oriented to making good quality wine in large quantities for a broad market, rather than catering to the social snobbery of an elite, as in *ancien régime* France, where a Margaux or La Fite could sell for sixteen times the price of the product of a lowly peasant's vineyard.[33]

Several decades of amphora studies provide ample evidence that wine was traded on a massive scale throughout the Mediterranean and beyond, with production for export expanding from Greece into Italy, Spain, North Africa, even Egypt,[34] and, most significantly, into France, laying the foundation for one of the world's great wine cultures. Creating new vines suitable for Northern France was challenging, but the Romans were ambitious and confident enough to create vineyards in Germany, and even in Britain! Ausonius and Fortunatus lauded the fine wines of the Moselle, and recent excavations have uncovered twenty villas, each furnished with two large wine presses, along a 20 km stretch of the river. As Brun argues plausibly, cauldrons excavated at several wine-making villas were used to boil down *sapa* to trigger adequate fermentation of grapes, which had not ripened fully in this cold climate.[35] Certainly large scale wine production, most of it produced by peasants on small plots, is also well attested for *ancien régime* France, and wine represented one of the few high-value cash crops in what was otherwise an underdeveloped agrarian regime, but the poverty of the eighteenth- and nineteenth-century working classes offered far less scope for a mass trade. Even in the nineteenth century, when France was the world's dominant wine producer, with 40 percent of the world's vineyards, a remarkably small proportion of her wine production was exported, only around 2.6 percent in 1828, for example. It would be hard to conceive that the great Greco-Roman wine producers, island states like Thasos, Chios, Cnidus, or Rhodes, or even Baetica, Campania, or Southern Gaul, exported such a small proportion of their production.[36]

The production and trade of wine and olive oil is highly visible archaeologically, and therefore well known, but the economic importance of the trade in livestock, cheese, meat and fish products, fruits, nuts, and vegetables, to say nothing of cereals, will have been just as impressive. I have dealt elsewhere with the scale of the market for meat, which included not just domestic animals, but fowl, game, fresh fish, and shellfish, often farmed, to which one must add a massive trade, second only to that in wine and olive oil, in *garum* and salted or cured fish or meat.[37] It is worth reiterating, though, how effectively livestock can be transported great distances by sea, and by land, on the hoof.[38]

Regarding the other major products, we will content ourselves with one example. Fruit consumption, like that of meat, fish, and fresh vegetables, tends to be highly elastic, and is therefore dependent upon prosperous urban populations for much of their market, but fruit orchards, unlike market gardens, need not be located in the immediate suburbs of substantial towns or cities. Fruit trees are generally less labor intensive than vegetables, require less manure, are more tolerant of poor soil and arid conditions, and require only periodic watering rather than continuous irrigation.[39]

Even leaving aside the olive, fruit and nuts were the object of a highly developed trade over great distances in the Greco-Roman world. Fruit trees, vines, and olives were planted in such numbers that Varro could describe Italy as one vast orchard.[40] Figs were sometimes cheap enough to be fed to fish, or to geese or even for pigs to be raised for their 'fig-forced' livers,[41] and the fruit of Italy, Greece, Spain, Syria, and North Africa was shipped by river and sea through much of the Roman world.[42] In fact, Cato the Elder helped seal the fate of Rome's old enemy, when he held out a fig he had bought in a Roman market, picked just a couple of days before in Carthage.[43] A number of shipwrecks have preserved amphoras packed with fruit, particularly dates, which the Greeks and Romans never succeeded in cultivating domestically. Moreover, the Roman provinces reveal many fruit imported from the Mediterranean, and finds at the Red sea ports show that coconuts were brought from India.[44] Both Pliny and Columella give detailed instructions for the packing and storage of fruit, which are scientifically sound, and both practical and economically viable for transport to market, as is clear from the use of similar methods in nineteenth-century California.[45] A sealed amphora with the pits of 162 peaches, recovered at Aquileia, not only attests to the careful packing, transport and sale of what is a very delicate and perishable fruit, but the fact that all of the peaches, once analyzed, came from the same cultivar, suggests an orchard carefully selected and propagated from slips for uniform, presumably high-quality fruit.[46]

Although tolerable yields of mediocre fruit can be harvested with minimal inputs of labor, the competitiveness of the market demanded a much more professional and labor-intensive approach. Theophrastus's works, and the advice of the Roman agronomists, demonstrate a thorough mastery of principles of budding, grafting, and training fruit trees in order to breed new varietals, clone the best trees in nurseries, and maximize their yield. One Roman *pomarius* was so eager to show off his virtuosity, that he grafted a tree at Tivoli so that it "had nuts on one branch, berries on another, while in other places hung grapes, pears, figs, pomegranates and various sorts of apples." In addition to introducing new fruit trees from Africa and the Near East, including pomegranates, peaches, nectarines, quinces, sweet cherries, jujube, carob, damson, and citrus fruit, new species were created, like the apple-pumpkin, said to be a cross between the melon and the quince, or the apple-plum and almond-plum, and innumerable new cultivars were bred or selected, with Pliny listing 41 pear varieties, 28 fig cultivars, 22 types of apple, 8 of the cherry, 7 of the quince, and 5 varieties of peach and plum.[47]

The lists preserved for us are naturally rather selective, for, as Pliny points out: "The rest of the fruits produced by trees can scarcely be enumerated by their appearance or shape, let alone by their flavors and juices, which have been so frequently modified by crossing and grafting."[48] Although he claimed that the art of grafting and cross-breeding had long since been perfected by Greco-Roman growers, so that little technical progress was possible, he noted a number of successful new cultivars developed within the last thirty or even the last five years. Significantly, the creators of many of these fruit varieties, drawn from very diverse social backgrounds, from freedmen to senators, became famous for their innovation, with their names given to the Scaudian and Sceptian apples, the Dolabellian pear, and the Appian quince, to name just a few. The diversity of fruit grown in Italy, or imported by sea, is very impressive. In addition to the fruit already listed, literary sources or archaebotanical studies attest to the consumption of mulberries, blackberries, blueberries, myrtleberries, cornelberries, serviceberries, rowanberries, strawberries, figs, grapes, sorbs, apricots, citrons, bitter oranges, lemons, medlars, cucumbers, gourds, melons, including watermelons, and such nuts as acorns, hazelnuts, chestnuts, beechnuts, almonds, pistachios, walnuts, and pine nuts.[49]

The importance of fresh fruit in the Roman diet, and the skill of Roman *pomarii*, is clear from literary evidence as well as innumerable still lives and garden paintings.[50] As one historian of modern market gardening remarks: "In the National Museum at Naples is a mural from the ruins of Pompeii showing a bowl of grapes, pears and apples equal, it would seem, in size and quality, to anything that can be produced today."[51] Archaeobotanical evidence confirms that growers did indeed produce larger fruit, with many different species and cultivars, including several which would disappear from Central Europe for centuries with the decline of the empire. Nor was fruit a luxury in the Roman diet. It was widely consumed in households, legionary camps, and even desert quarries like Mons Claudianus.[52]

Roman trade networks stimulated agricultural production for export throughout the empire, even in underpopulated semi-deserts, which would be abandoned to small-scale nomadic pastoralism for centuries after the fall of the Empire. The scale of North African olive oil production is now famous from the remains of a dense network of massive press complexes,[53] but olive oil was only part of a rich mixed farming regime producing cereals, wine, livestock, wild and domestic fowl.[54] Less well known, perhaps, Mauretania built up a significant wine industry, with a surprising reputation for quality, and huge complexes such as that at Kherbet Agoub, the largest discovered so far, with 21 wine presses and the capacity to produce up to 5,000 hectoliters at one time. In the East, Egypt built its olive oil industry, launched by the Ptolemies in the Fayyum, into a major producer, and even succeeded in creating a *grand cru* centred on Lake Mareotis, suitable for export, and managed intensively using up-to-date equipment and methods, as confirmed by papyri. Even more remarkably, wine and olive oil production took off in the Jordanian desert, combining traditional run-off farming with Roman expertise in arboriculture and inspiring modern Israeli farmers in the Negev.[55]

The State, Infrastructure, and Subsidiary Industries: Drainage, Irrigation, and Tools

Although the high demand fostered by social equality, urbanization, and trade played the most important role in permitting Greco-Roman farmers to exploit the land to its full potential, the structure of their society also provided a powerful stimulus to agriculture in more indirect and subtle ways. Centuriation, which still marks the modern countryside of Italy, France, Tunisia, and Spain, is the most visible indication of the transformative effect of Roman culture upon the landscape, but similar systems had also had a long history among the Greeks, as we see at a number of sites, particularly Metapontum or Heraclea Pontica in the Chersonnese. Many historians have ignored or underestimated the agricultural significance of centuriation. For small farmers, who could struggle to drain their land and bring their produce to market otherwise, the state's organization and mobilization of the collective labor of the rural population in the broader public interest would have been invaluable. Such drainage works, which were typically extended throughout the countryside in the form of drainage ditches flanking the rectilinear road network dividing up the land into *centuriae*, were essential for the full agricultural exploitation of the countryside. Drainage was particularly important in low-lying or clay soils, or in rich river valleys, such as the Pomptine marshes, or the Po valley, which was transformed into one of Italy's richest agricultural regions, in large part through Aemilius Scaurus' important land reclamation initiative.[56]

Although lauded in Continental Europe for its model of large estates and capital intensive agriculture, systematic attention to drainage seems to have been far less common in England, where, even in the high farming period of the mid-nineteenth century, it was frequently restricted to the estates of select improving landlords, despite the serious effect poor drainage could have upon yields. The Roman agronomists explain the techniques of drainage in detail, and archaeological field-work provides ample confirmation that drainage was a constant concern of most ordinary Roman farmers, not just the agronomists. Ground-breaking interdisciplinary studies in Southern France have documented the careful maintenance of elaborate systems of drainage ditches, and tens of thousands of amphoras were buried to provide effective subsoil drainage.[57]

The Romans made great strides in irrigation as well. Centuriation helped a broad cross-section of the farming population, since drainage ditches can also channel water for irrigation, but dedicated canals and aqueducts were also built for large-scale projects. Our best evidence for large-scale irrigation now comes from the canal system of Roman Spain, better understood with the recent discovery of a detailed inscription regulating access to irrigation in several small rural communities.[58] Decisions were taken on a democratic basis, by majority vote, with water rights and labor and maintenance obligations apportioned according to the amount of land which owners or cultivators must irrigate.[59]

The most intensive irrigation was reserved for market gardening, but irrigated meadows were both productive and lucrative, and they are described in detail by the agronomists. Some arable and tree crops benefit from intermittent irrigation as well, primarily in times of drought, but most of our evidence for such irrigation, at least on any scale, comes from semi-arid regions such as Spain, North Africa, and certain parts of Greece, particular the Cycladic islands. Run-off irrigation in desert and semi-desert conditions is well attested among the Nabataeans, and in North Africa, as we have noted above. Although some have questioned whether irrigation was practiced on any scale in Classical or Hellenistic Greece, recent work on Delos has revealed an extensive infrastructure designed to capture and store the rainwater resources of this arid island, permitting the market gardening, viticulture, oleiculture, and mixed farming revealed by epigraphy and archaeozoological studies.[60] The success of irrigated agriculture in contemporary Greece has confirmed its viability and potential impact, and should warn us against underestimating its role in the more intensive ancient regime, particularly given the evidence for the importance of Greek market gardening.[61]

Transport infrastructure played a critical role in facilitating the large-scale trade in such bulky agricultural commodities as grain, wine, and olive oil so important to the intensification and specialization of agricultural production. Since most large Greco-Roman cities were on the sea or a navigable river, harbors were the most important link in the supply chain. The great harbors of the Peiraeus, Syracuse, Alexandria, Puteoli, Ostia, and Portus, among many others, dwarfed the crude small harbors which served the Mediterranean in the nineteenth century. Hydraulic concrete was used to great effect to build moles and breakwaters for artificial harbors throughout the Mediterranean, most ambitiously, perhaps, in creating the harbor of Caesarea Maritima along a stretch of ocean marked by powerful and potentially destructive currents. Rome, with its quays and *horrea* stretching for kilometers along the Tiber, was as great as many of these maritime harbors, but many other river ports were highly developed, as at Trier or Bordeaux, and the creation of navigable canals made for a relatively comprehensive and inexpensive system of transport.[62] While necessarily more expensive, land transport in the Roman era was as highly developed as in any preindustrial society, facilitated by the superb Roman road network, which was still a cause of wonder through the nineteenth century, and by the roads built into the centuriation grid, which, while unpaved, were presumably leveled and kept passable in winter by drainage ditches.[63]

In addition to this elaborate infrastructure of harbors, roads, canals, drainage ditches, rural aqueducts, cisterns, and dams, we should not neglect other smaller, but often more direct investments on the farm: agricultural terraces helped to prevent erosion, field fences, hedges, and plantings of trees, which served as boundary markers, windbreaks, and sources of fodder, brush, and lumber.[64]

The massive Greek, Carthaginian, and Roman investment in farm buildings likely represented the lion's share of the capital pumped into farming infrastructure – it has certainly left the most remarkable archaeological remains. Large, often superbly built, villas and farmhouses were lavished with store-rooms, granaries, stables, and sheepfolds, as well as processing facilities such as wine and olive presses, and wine cellars, and expensive facilities for *pastio villatica*, including massive maritime fishponds of hydraulic concrete, aviaries, game farms, and columbaria. As James Caird argued strenuously, nineteenth-century English landlords and tenant farmers failed to invest sufficiently in farm buildings or stables,[65] but this certainly was not the case in the ancient Mediterranean. The number, size, and standard of construction of Roman villas and farms, which has emerged from more than two centuries of excavation and intensive surveys is truly staggering for a pre-industrial society.[66] Archaeologists have generally ignored ordinary farmhouses, concentrating on luxury villas, which, as Roman social values demanded,[67] were also working farms, but enough *villae rusticae* have been studied to show that farmers of all social levels concurred with the high farming philosophy of Caird and the Roman agronomists. The villas and farms excavated to date suggest a tentative typology for Roman Italy of the late Republic and Principate, consisting of three broad classes: small farms, very rarely excavated, with a handful of examples as small as 55 m² attested, but generally ranging from 150 to 250 m², a middle rank of substantial *villae rusticae* of between 400 and 600 m², and larger villas of 1,000 m², often well over 2,000 m² in size. The signs of comfort and elegant decoration in many of the farmhouses, which fall within the two smaller classes, suggests that these belonged largely to owner-occupiers, occasionally helped by a few slaves. The evidence of Greek farmhouses, many of which can be clearly identified by the careful study of field divisions as small family farms intensively working a few hectares of land, further confirms the prosperity of these *autourgoi*, and the pride they took in their farm buildings.[68]

As we have seen, farmers benefitted from the rapid growth of the ancient building trades, with access to cheap mass-produced roof tiles and many skilled contractors with experience in quickly building solid structures in mud-brick and concrete. Likewise, we see a significant improvement in the quality of tools and in the application of machinery and labor-saving devices in agriculture. The sources and archaeological finds attest to a large range of ploughs, including the heavy *carrus*, with wheels, coulter, and moldboard, designed to work dense clay soils, and archaeological work shows the widespread introduction of a wide range of sturdy metal ploughshares and coulters. Agricultural implements seem to have been made overwhelmingly, if not exclusively, of iron, and, like Roman carpenters' tools, were professionally made and well-designed, with most virtually identical to modern implements for gardening, hand cultivation, or vine-dressing. As we can see from the wide range of such tools found in Pompeii, even relatively modest smallholders seem to have bought them from manufacturers, as recommended by Cato, rather than hand-crafting their own tools out of wood, as Tuscan *contadini* of the nineteenth and early twentieth centuries often did. Although these fine metal tools will have been somewhat more efficient, their use is arguably more important as an indication of the prosperity of Roman farms, and their integration into the urban economy, as buyers as well as sellers.[69]

Most attention has been given to the development of the *vallus*, a type of animal-powered harvesting machine, but the wine or oil press was surely a far more common and expensive machine. The deserts of North Africa have provided the most fertile environment for recovering ancient presses, but it is now increasingly clear that such machines were ubiquitous throughout the Mediterranean, Egypt, the Near East, and the Roman provinces of temperate Europe. We have already noted the complex at Kherbet Agoub with 21 presses. Another with 17 presses has been uncovered at Senam Semana in Tripolitania, and there is also a marked increase in their size and power. One press at the massive Lusitanian villa of Torre de Palma had a beam 12 m long and a 4500 kg counterweight capable, theoretically at least, of exerting a pressure of 29 tons.[70]

FOOD PROCESSING

The study of Greco-Roman food processing has received detailed attention in two excellent recent monographs,[71] so we can be relatively brief here. Thurmond has performed an extremely important service, showing that the advice of the Roman agronomists, particularly Columella, regarding food processing and preservation is generally consistent with the principles in the modern scientific literature.

Food processing and preservation played an increasingly important role as foodstuffs were traded over large distances. Although livestock, and even fish or shellfish, could be transported live, and some fresh and unprocessed produce could be traded long distances with appropriate packaging, as we have seen, perishable foods could be transported more safely, and preserved for consumption out of season, if dried, smoked, cured, or salted, or packed in wine, vinegar, brine, or sugar syrups using honey or boiled must.[72] Many of these techniques had been developed in the Near East, but in the Greco-Roman period we see innovation, not only in the diversity of products and the repertoire of techniques, but an increase in the scale of production and in the capital invested in new technologies and equipment. Massive water mills, capable of supplying thousands of people, as at the Barbegal complex, were used to mill flour and even to knead dough, allowing bread to be baked for popular distribution on an unprecedented scale and presumably at a much reduced cost.[73]

Wine production is arguably the most complex and demanding branch of ancient food processing, an art as well as a science, and one which confirms the expertise of the Roman agronomists, as Billiard has documented in great detail. Moreover, Thurmond addresses most of Billiard's criticisms of Greco-Roman practice, noting, to take just one example, that the addition of salt, which so outraged Billiard, is a well-attested practice among French winemakers today. In fact, the agronomists were aware of many of the methods used by modern wine-makers to protect or stabilize wine and ensure its quality, to restart a feeble fermentation process, or to restore wine which was in danger of spoiling. The acidity of wine, critical to its long-term health and stability, flavour, and effective fermentation, was regulated by adding either gypsum (calcium sulfate) in order to refine wine, precipitating its impurities, improve the colour, and reduce acidity, or marble dust or chalk (calcium carbonate) in order to increase acidity. Bentonite was used to clarify wine, and has been proven by modern research to be very effective in removing proteins, which can create offensive flavors, and sulfur dioxide was used to fumigate the tanks, *dolia*, and amphorae, which would come into contact with wine, destroying potentially harmful yeast cultures and microbes.[74]

The preservation of fish by salting or smoking, and the production of *garum* or fish sauce, is the other Greco-Roman food processing industry which was organized on a massive scale, comparable to the trade in wine and olive oil in its geographical reach, as we have already noted. Since fish can be salted and dried on a very large scale on crude reed platforms on the seashore, or brined in *dolia*, leaving little archaeological trace, we cannot read too much into the limited evidence discovered so far for the Classical and Hellenistic salt-fish industry in the Eastern Mediterranean and the Black sea, which is very well attested by literary sources. In the Western Mediterranean, however, in the Punic, late Republican, and early Imperial periods, concrete fish salting tanks were used, offering direct evidence that this industry was creating salt-fish products on a scale surely unprecedented at any time before or since. At Lixus in Mauretania Tingitania, a series of 10 factories, capable of producing *ca.* 1,013,000 m^3 of *salsamenta* and *garum* have been excavated. Smaller facilities varying from 3 to 20 m^3 capacity have been found at a wide range of sites, including the coasts of Italy, Mediterranean Gaul, and Libya, but the largest fish-salting vats have been found all along the coast of Southern Spain, Brittany, North Africa, and the Black Sea, with capacities ranging from 30 to over 100,000 m^3, with factories at Troia I/II reaching capacities of 600,000 m^3.[75]

Other processed animal products such as cheese, ham, and sausage were likely produced and exported on a comparable, if not even greater, scale. We know of considerable exports of hams and cheese from Northern Italy, in the region of Parma known to this day for these same products, as Thurmond points out. Literary sources as well as papyri make it clear that sausages and cheeses in particular were prime articles of trade, available in a wide range of regional specialties, with cheese from Turkey and the Cyclades and even Lucanian sausages imported into Egypt.[76]

Notes

For a more detailed version of this chapter, see the website for this volume, at www.stanford.edu/~scheidel/CCRE.htm.

1 Britain, Gaul, Germany, Moesia, Pannonia, even Egypt and Palestine likely enjoyed less intensive farming regimes, the result of lower levels of urbanization, cultural conservatism, or the effects of persistent social inequality and low demand. See the excellent overview in Marcone 1997: 175–203.

2 Kron 2005a. [For a different reading of the Roman evidence, see below, Chapter 15. (Ed.)]

3 For the productivity and vitality of peasant farming in Roman Italy, see Kron 2008b. For Greece, see Hanson 1999.

4 White 1970: 14–43; Marcone 1997: 206–17.

5 Dickson 1788; Billiard 1913; White 1970; Forni and Marcone 2002.

6 See, for example, Hodkinson 1988; Amigues 2007.

7 See Davies 2007: 339–52 for a survey.

8 See, e.g., Dickson 1788; Kolendo 1980; Pleket 1990; Forni 2006; Marcone 1997; 2006; Forni and Marcone 2002.

9 White 1970: 110–40, 202; Kron 2000; 2005c; 2008a; 2008b: 73–5; Ciaraldi 2007: 84–5, 158–9.

10 Allen 2008.

11 See, e.g., Kron 2002; 2008a; 2008b: 74–6.

12 Ambrosoli 1997; Kron 2004; Ciaraldi 2007: 75–85.

13 Dickson 1788: I 253, 273, 281–2, 289–90, 299–302; White 1970: 125–45; Spurr 1986: 128–31; Marcone 1997: 64–7; Kron 2005c: 293–6; 2008b: 76.

14 Spurr 1986: 82–8; Erdkamp 2005: 34–46; Goodchild 2007: 246–97, 337, 414–8.

15 Tchernia 1986: 359–60; cf. Lachiver 1988: 393–4.

16 Billiard 1913: 122; cf. Lachiver 1988: 178, 184, 393–4, 516–17, 556–9.

17 Pleket 1990; Allen, Bengtsson and Dribe (eds.) 2005; Kron 2008b: 98.

18 See, e.g., Pöhlmann 1884; Hansen 2006: 18–21.

19 See Kron 2005a; 2008b: 79–86 and cf. Burnett 1979.

20 Tchernia 1986: 21–7, 58–60, 172–9.

21 See Kron 2008b: 86.

22 Halstead 1997: 243–4.

23 Kolendo 1994; Quilici-Gigli 1994; Frass 2006: 163–73, 205–356; Goodchild 2007.
24 For trade in 'luxury' foods, see Papathomas 2006: 193 n. 3.
25 Plin. *HN* 14.3. Compare Aristid. *Or.* 26.9–13.
26 Miller 1969; Thurmond 2006: 263–71; Ciaraldi 2007: 114, 145–6.
27 Plin. *HN* 12.28 and 58.
28 Miller 1969: 82–3; Van der Veen 1998; Bakels and Jacomet 2003: 550; Cappers 2006; Ciaraldi 2007: 114–15.
29 Tchernia 1986: 184–93, 272–8; Dalby 2000: 21–81; Thurmond 2006: 155.
30 Plin. *HN* 14.45. Cf. Col. *Rust.* 3.9.4–6.
31 Plin. *HN* 14.26–8.
32 Billiard 1913: 70–8; André 1961: 165–76; Tchernia 1986: 322–41, 350–7; Johnson 1971: 22–5.
33 Tchernia 1986: 36–7, 116–19; Bouvier 2000: 128; cf. Lachiver 1988: 361–2.
34 See Peacock and Williams 1986; Tchernia 1986; Brun 2003; 2004a; 2004b; 2005 *passim* with references.
35 Lachiver 1988: 19–55; Brun 2005: 129–52.
36 Lachiver 1988: 244–7, 393–4, 582.
37 Kron 2002; 2008a; 2008b: 79–86. For *garum* and *salsamenta* see below, for salted or cured meats, see Leguilloux 2002; Thurmond 2006: 210–19.
38 Kron 2008b: 107 and n. 217.
39 Webber 1972: 50–3; Wickson 1891: 79–80, 207–29.
40 Varro *Rust.* 1.2.6.
41 Cappers 2006: 165.
42 Plin. *HN* 15.105.
43 Plin. *HN* 15.75.
44 Peacock and Williams 1986: 96, 106, 109; Bakels and Jacomet 2003: 547; Cappers 2006: 162–3, 166–7; Ciaraldi 2007: 146; Sadori et al. 2009: 47.
45 Plin. *HN* 15.59–67; Col. *Rust.* 12.10.1–16.5. Cf. Wickson 1891: 237–8, 285; Thurmond 2006: 174–86; Cappers 2006: 147–51.
46 Sadori et al. 2009: 47.
47 Plin. *HN* 15.35–117; Col. *Rust.* 5.10.1–11.15. White 1970: 228–9, 247–61; Flach 1990: 258–274; Farrar 1998: 67–71 (the quoted words are at p. 168); Brun 2003: 29–44; Thurmond 2006: 173.
48 Plin. *HN* 15.35.
49 Cato *Agr.* 7.2; 143.3; Col. *Rust.* 5.10.11; Plin. *HN* 15.49–50; 15.102–3; André 1961: 42–3; Thurmond 2006: 174–5.
50 De Caro and Boriello 2002; Ciaraldi 2007: 143–4.
51 Webber 1972: 19.
52 Van der Veen 1998; Bakels and Jacomet 2003; Sadori et al. 2009: 49–53.
53 Brun 2004b: 185–259.
54 See Marcone 1997: 183–93.
55 Brun 2004b: 138–51, 232–44; Evenari, Shanan and Tadmor 1982: 95–147, 179–219.
56 Quilici-Gigli 1992; Quilici and Quilici-Gigli 1995; Chouquer and Favory 2001; Kron 2005b: 478–82; Collin-Bouffier 2008.
57 Caird 1852: 256–7, 470–2; White 1970: 146–50, 190; Berger 2008.
58 Beltrán Lloris 2006.

59 White 1970: 151–72; Horden and Purcell 2000: 237–57, 585–8; Beltrán Lloris 2006; Bannon 2009: 249–61; Wilson 2009c.

60 Col. *Rust.* 2.16–7; Plin. *HN* 18.258–63; Varro *Rust.* 1.31.5; Pallad. 10.10; Brunet 2008; Bannon 2009: 258–9.

61 Hanson 1999: 60–3; Horden and Purcell 2000: 244–7.

62 Harbors: Blackmann 1982; 2008. Canals: Uggeri 1987: 337–47; Kron 2005b: 447–8 and n. 205.

63 Quilici 2008.

64 Kron 2005c: 297–8.

65 Caird 1852: 77, 89, 135, 152, 222, 430.

66 Rossiter 1978; Flach 1990: 233–45; Kron 2008a: 183; Higginbotham 1997; Franceschini 1998; Marzano 2007. For the density of farms and villas near Rome: Goodchild 2007: 80–120.

67 See, e.g., Cato *Agr.* 3.2; Varro *Rust.* 3.2.6; Col. *Rust.* 1.4.8.

68 Typology: Rathbone 2008. Luxury: Ortalli 2006. Greek farmhouses: Pecirka 1970; Brun 2004a: 118–21.

69 White 1967; Kolendo 1980: 71–84; 1985; Forni 2002; 2006; Marcone 2006.

70 *Vallus*: White 1970: 182–3; Kolendo 1980: 155–178. Presses: Brun 2003: 58–62, 148–56, 208–17; 2004b: 190, 300–2.

71 Curtis 2001; Thurmond 2006.

72 Thurmond 2006: 165–87, 212–9; Curtis 2008: 384.

73 Thurmond 2006: 37–72; Curtis 2008: 373–9.

74 Billiard 1913: 424–536; Thurmond 2006: 111–64.

75 Curtis 1991; 2001: 317–21, 403–17; 2008: 385–6, 403–16; Ponsich 1988; Bekker-Nielsen 2005; Wilson 2006a.

76 Frost 1999; Thurmond 2006: 193–207, 212–17; 220–2; Dalby 2000: 39, 67–8; 218–19; Papathomas 2006: 196.

9: Manufacturing

Cameron Hawkins

Our efforts to understand the way in which manufacturing was organized in the Roman world are necessarily hampered by the state of our evidence. Not only is this evidence fragmentary, it is also capable of supporting potentially conflicting conclusions about the dominant patterns of industrial organization and the degree to which these patterns may have changed over time.

On one level, the surviving material is capable of supporting an argument about modest development in the scale and organizational complexity of manufacturing. It is clear, for instance, that urban development and modest economic growth in Italy did create concentrated consumer markets in which demand became sufficient to provoke labor differentiation and specialization within several individual industries. Specialization is best attested in industries geared toward elite consumption, such as construction or the manufacture of durable goods in precious metals (both of which I explore in more detail below).[1] Specialization may also have existed at lower levels of the market: Xenophon notes that in the shoemaking industries in Athens during the fourth century BCE, some men earned a living by cutting out soles, others by fashioning the uppers, and more still by stitching the pieces together; there is no reason to doubt that the same held true in the Roman empire (Xen. *Cyr.* 8.2.5).

At the same time, our sources also convey a strong sense of continuity. While some entrepreneurs in Italy may have experimented with economies of scale made possible by labor specialization – most notably, the producers of the various series of Campanian ware, who arguably ran large units of production staffed by slaves – they appear to have been the exception rather than the rule: their efforts were typically possible only when low slave prices in the second and first centuries BCE aligned with ready access to overseas markets in which local producers could not deliver goods at comparably low prices. These industries aside, manufacture in both the republican and imperial periods is thought to have remained largely in the hands of independent artisans who toiled in small workshops, in which they could not necessarily accommodate extensive differentiations in labor.[2]

In this chapter, I pursue the problem of industrial organization in the Roman world in more detail. I argue two main points. One, that Roman manufacturers adjusted to modest growth and to an increasingly specialized workforce not by developing large and integrated businesses, but by organizing themselves into subcontracting networks in which they contracted with other specialists for intermediate goods and services. Two, that they did so not only because the nature of the demand for manufactured goods made integration costly, but also because labor market conditions and social institutions (in this case professional *collegia*) vitiated the main advantage of vertical integration, namely its ability to reduce certain kinds of transaction costs. In the process, I suggest that both the problems they faced and the solutions they adopted are comparable to those experienced by manufacturers in later periods of European history.

Specialization and industrial organization

I begin by addressing a fundamental question: does economic growth, even when it is sufficient to generate specialization in the labor force, inevitably stimulate the development of larger and more complex enterprises? Although the answer to this question will inevitably shape our preconceptions about what was plausible in the Roman context, it has not often been raised in such an explicit way. As we shall see, theoretical considerations and comparative evidence both suggest that the answer is 'no': growth and specialization can just as easily give rise to networks of small and specialized workshops in which artisans collaborate with one another in subcontracting relationships.

On the theoretical side, the work of Coase and his successors on transaction costs and the growth of firms remains foundational. The transaction-cost approach begins with the assumption that economic actors almost never have easy access to the information necessary in order to make decisions, and then elaborates on the ways in which this observation complicates economic exchange. Transaction costs are conceptualized as the time, energy, and resources that individuals must devote to specific activities in the process of conducting business because of their imperfect access to information: locating and vetting potential economic partners, negotiating contracts, and enforcing the terms of agreements. Recent discussions have placed particular emphasis on enforcement, stressing that some of the most severe transaction costs arise when one partner opportunistically reneges on an agreement or attempts to renegotiate the terms of a contract in his own favor when it is least convenient for the other partner to do so.

In classic formulations of this theory, economic actors develop firms as a response to high transaction costs. The firm subsumes transactions that would otherwise take place in the market between independent agents and incorporates them into a single organization, under the guidance of a clear managerial hierarchy. This process obviously entails costs: some arise from the need to supervise employees or to structure incentives capable of keeping them motivated; others are opportunity costs imposed by increasing complexity (large firms, for instance, can be less responsive than individual entrepreneurs to sudden changes in market conditions). But the benefits of creating integrated businesses can be substantial: thanks to its internal hierarchy, the firm eliminates most of the transaction costs that would normally impede market-based exchanges between its constituent members. Entrepreneurs can therefore be expected to develop firms when the savings generated by eliminating transaction costs outweigh the costs of integration.[3]

While this perspective treats integrated firms as an alternative to market-based subcontracting relationships, recent work has complicated the basic model by identifying a third organizational paradigm that exists alongside the other two: the private-order enforcement network. In this paradigm, the marketplace continues to be dominated not by integrated enterprises, but by individual entrepreneurs who contract with one another for intermediate goods and services. But rather than contract with anyone, they transact only with members of a well-defined network. Entrepreneurs in such a network do incur costs, both direct and indirect – they are often required to pay a membership fee, and they suffer opportunity costs when they refuse to consider non-members as potential economic partners. That said, private-order enforcement networks do make it possible for members to generate substantial savings in transaction costs, and in particular in those costs arising from the need to enforce contracts. Members rely on reputation in order to identify reliable partners, and also to signal to others that those guilty of negligent or opportunistic behavior are not to be trusted: the possibility that participants in the network who engage in questionable behavior might acquire a negative reputation offers them an incentive to honor their agreements and provides a measure of transactional security.[4]

The theoretical material strongly suggests that integration is only one possible response to increasing occupational specialization, and one which entrepreneurs will select only when its cost-benefit balance is superior to those of other available solutions. Comparative evidence from early modern Europe not only bolsters this conclusion, but also suggests that integration was not necessarily the preferred response to economic growth and expanding occupational specialization in pre-industrial societies. In the finishing trades in particular, most manufacturers eschewed large and integrated firms well into the eighteenth century (and sometimes beyond), even though slow economic growth over the preceding few hundred years had given rise to extensive divisions of labor. At the low end of the market, where artisans manufactured goods for clients who valued accessible prices above quality, they tended to put certain stages of work out to relatively low-skilled workers who based themselves out of their own homes. At the upper end of the market, on the other hand, where artisans manufactured high-quality goods for a discerning and wealthy clientele, they operated relatively small and specialized workshops, contracting with one another as necessary for intermediate goods and services. While coachbuilders, for instance, often constructed the chasses of the vehicles they sold, they also drew on the services of many other specialists: craftsmen who specialized in producing axles, wheels, and springs; leatherworkers who fitted out the harness and the trimmings; and other artisans who added painted, carved, or gilded decoration. Most coachbuilders, however, did not retain such specialists as permanent employees. Instead, they contracted with them as necessary for parts and services in response to orders from their clients.[5]

DISINTEGRATED PRODUCTION IN THE ROMAN WORLD

The preceding discussion offers a framework in which we can potentially contextualize the evidence from the Roman world. The main virtue of this framework is its ability to reconcile the apparent conflict in our source material: the possibility that Roman artisans accommodated an increasingly specialized workforce in subcontracting networks rather than in integrated firms would account for both the persistence of small workshops and the evidence for differentiation in the labor force. In this section, I argue that disintegrated subcontracting networks were indeed widespread in antiquity, particularly in certain industries that catered to wealthy clients and for which we consequently have good evidence. And, while our evidence is less comprehensive for other industries, a case can be made that disintegrated production was also prevalent at lower levels of the market.

In industries geared toward the manufacture of goods in precious metals, artisans tended to break production down into a number of specialized processes that gave rise to several distinct but closely related occupations. In the manufacture of gold and silver plate, for example, these included the *vascularii*, who raised the bodies of vessels from sheets of precious metal; the *caelatores*, who appear to have worked primarily as engravers; the *crustarii*, who manufactured decorative elements that were applied by *appliqué*; and craftsmen skilled in *ars toreutice*, which may have encompassed embossing, chasing, or *repoussé*. Other specialists who may have been involved in this industry include the *excusores* (or *exclusores*), whose precise function is unfortunately obscure; *inauratores* or gilders, who applied gold finishes to a range of products, including silver tableware; *flaturarii*, who specialized in casting metal and who may have produced components such as handles and bases for gold and silver vessels; and finally *tritores*, who polished objects made from precious metals.[6]

The funerary epigraphy from the city of Rome suggests that many of these specialists did not work as employees in large and integrated businesses but instead ran workshops of their own. In their inscriptions, some artisans identify themselves not only in terms of their occupation, but also with reference to that part of the city in which they worked. For example, the engraver Lucius Furius Diomedes, a former slave, put up the following monument on behalf of his wife and daughter: "Lucius Furius Diomedes, freedman of Lucius and engraver on the Sacra Via, [put up this monument] for his wife Cornelia Tertulla . . . " (*CIL* 6.9221). Diomedes' specific reference here to the location of his workplace seems intended to stress that he was a proprietor who owned or rented a shop of his own.[7] The same is true of a *vascularius* and two *flaturarii*, of whom we know thanks to their own comparable inscriptions (*CIL* 6.37824, 9418, 9419a).

The fact that these specialists ran establishments of their own is clearly consistent with the view that they were embedded in networks of production in which artisans were linked to one another by subcontracting arrangements. Likewise, the literary evidence that touches on the manufacture of goods in precious metals presupposes that disintegrated production and subcontracting networks were the norm. Augustine – an admittedly late source – offers a particularly interesting comment in the context of a discussion on traditional polytheistic religions. While criticizing the way in which practitioners of these religions parcelled out specific functions to individual deities, Augustine compares such gods to "craftsmen in the quarter of the silversmiths, where one vessel passes through the hands of many artisans in order to come out finished, even though it could have been completed by one perfect artisan" (August. *De civ. D.* 7.4). The locus of production that unites the various specialists in this description is the neighborhood rather than the workshop, and this seems more consonant with a model in which artisans collaborated in subcontracting networks than it does with a model in which entrepreneurs organized production in integrated firms.[8]

Comparable evidence from the early imperial period can be found in an anecdote from the New Testament, in which we can see disintegrated forms of production in the Ephesian metalworking industries of the first century CE. According to the author of *Acts*, a silversmith named Demetrios – who made a living by manufacturing miniature devotional shrines dedicated to Artemis – played a leading role in instigating a riot in opposition to Paul's efforts to proselytize in the city. He was able to do so because, as a wealthy entrepreneur who "furnished no small amount of business to the artisans" of Ephesus (*Acts* 19.24), he had the necessary social clout to gather together a number of other craftsmen from their individual places of work for an impromptu assembly. Once again, the details in this particular anecdote are easiest to understand if we imagine production taking place in a subcontracting network: Demetrios is associated with a number of artisans to whom he 'gives work,' but who nevertheless seem to maintain their own establishments.[9]

Our sources pertaining to the construction industry suggest that disintegrated production and subcontracting networks were just as common there as they were in metalwork. The Roman jurists certainly assumed that builders routinely subcontracted with other craftsmen for specialized services on the job site. Venuleius, for instance, believed that builders employed only minimal permanent workforces and recruited additional manpower by the job: in his view, the conscientious builder did "not hasten to collect craftsmen from all sides and employ numerous labourers" upon accepting a contract, nor remain "satisfied with one or two," but instead carefully considered his needs and recruited accordingly (Ven. *Dig.* 45.1.137.3; translation adapted from Alan Watson).

Like Venuleius, Cicero suggests that builders operated specialized and disintegrated businesses that were linked together by subcontracting agreements. In his correspondence with his brother Quintus, Cicero reveals that the initial stages of renovations to Quintus' house on the Palatine were in the hands of a contractor (*redemptor*) named Longilius. Two years later, however, the ongoing work had been entrusted to other contractors who specialized in finishing the interiors of houses.[10] Although we cannot tell in this particular case whether Cicero had contracted with these specialists individually or whether they had been recruited by the primary contractor Longilius, a piece of evidence from Aretaeus' medical corpus arguably describes a comparable situation in which builders subcontracted for specific services from a specialist: one of Aretaeus' patients, a carpenter who specialized in joinery or interior woodwork, regularly accepted contracts from clients (*ergodotes*) who are perhaps best interpreted as primary building contractors (Aretaeus 3.6.6).

Finally, the inscriptions of men who worked in the building trades point to independent specialists rather than employees of large firms. Many of these men signalled their independence by referring to themselves as contractors (*redemptores*) working in specific and relatively narrow branches of the building trades. Tiberius Claudius Celadus, either a freedman of the emperor Claudius or the descendant of one of Claudius' former slaves, identified himself on his funeral monument in Rome as a *redemptor intestinarius* – that is, as a contractor who specialized in interior finishing work (*AE* 1925.87). Caius Avilius December, on the other hand, worked in Puteoli as a *redemptor marmorarius*, a contractor who specialized in building projects that demanded worked marble (*CIL* 10.1549).

Our evidence is far less comprehensive for industries that were not so clearly oriented toward the needs of elite and wealthy consumers. That said, there are hints that disintegrated production and subcontracting may have been typical in a range of other industries at different levels of the market. Like metalwork, the manufacture of wooden furniture involved a number of discrete processes that could conceivably give rise to distinct specialties: the creation of a carcass or frame by a joiner or cabinetmaker; the production of turned elements on a lathe; and decorative processes, such as carving and inlay.[11] While we cannot demonstrate conclusively that these processes were in the hands of specialists, turners at least do seem to have maintained shops of their own, both in late Roman Egypt (*P.Genova* I.24 [4c]), but also in Africa during the second century CE (if, that is, we can rely for evidence on a metaphor in Apul. *De Mundo* 1).

Textile production offers greater scope for analysis. In urban textile industries, independent artisans appear to have been involved in several stages of the production process: dyers, fullers, and tailors all ran shops of their own in Rome during the early imperial period, and the same is likely to have been true in other cities during much of antiquity.[12] Moreover, at certain levels of the market, specific stages of the process were arguably devolved on to home-based workers: an anecdote in Apuleius' *Metamorphoses* suggests that the wife of a carpenter might find employment spinning thread at home (Apul. *Met.* 9.5). Textile production in rural contexts could likewise be managed in disintegrated networks: much of the textile production in the northwest provinces of the empire appears to have remained rooted in rural domestic contexts, and the Igel column of Trier may offer evidence of a network in which the Secundinii family converted wool into textiles by coordinating the labor of a number of home-based workers who specialized in particular tasks.[13]

The Structure of Demand and the Costs of Integration

How are we to understand the apparent proliferation of small workshops and disintegrated subcontracting networks? In his recent discussion of production in the early Roman Empire, Dennis Kehoe proposes a potential solution: because of a conceptual framework that not only stressed the prestige attached to land ownership, but also encouraged risk-averse patterns of investment, members of the elite were reluctant to invest heavily in manufacture, and thereby constrained the development of this sector of the economy.[14] While there can be little doubt that this was true, on its own this answer is not entirely satisfactory, since it leaves unexplored the failure of artisans and manufacturers to develop integrated businesses in the absence of elite involvement. Although they had far fewer resources at their disposal than did the wealthy, they were nevertheless able to capture some rewards from their work that they conceivably could have used to expand their businesses.

Here, the theoretical material introduced above proves useful. As we have seen, modern discussions of the ways in which businesses develop focus on a cost-benefit approach: entrepreneurs will tend to create integrated businesses if and when the savings they accrue by reducing transaction costs outweigh those imposed by integration. In the following two sections, I argue that this perspective can help us to understand the nature of manufacturing in the Roman world. I hope to show, first of all, that the costs of integration in the Roman world were relatively high; second, that transaction costs were mitigated in some industries by labor market conditions, and in others by the ability of manufacturers to embed their production in professional *collegia* capable of functioning as private-order enforcement networks. Manufacturers (along with elite investors) therefore had little incentive to create integrated businesses.

I begin with the costs of integration. Given the nature of our evidence, there is unfortunately no way to assess directly the magnitude of the costs that Roman manufacturers would have incurred by attempting to create integrated businesses. Comparative evidence from early modern Europe, however, suggests that these were likely to have been high. In particular, early modern artisans who sought to create integrated firms faced high costs because of two characteristics of the early modern economic environment: seasonality, and the importance of particularized consumption among wealthy consumers.

Seasonality ensured that early modern consumption patterns oscillated throughout the year, especially in large cities, where much of the demand for manufactured goods was concentrated. In part, this was so because annual cycles in the price of grain dramatically affected the purchasing power of much of the urban populace. Grain tended to be most affordable immediately after the harvest, when it was most abundant, and more expensive – twice as much was not unusual – some months later when stores had been depleted. Because the demand for grain was relatively inelastic, substantial increases in its cost could easily erode the ability of much of the population to consume other goods. But other factors were also in play. Major annual holidays like Christmas or Easter generated surges of demand at particular times of the year for the products of numerous manufacturers. So too did patterns of temporary migration, whether among the elite, many of whom retreated from cities into the countryside during the summer, or among members of the general population, whose movements were stimulated by the high demand for agricultural labor at certain critical times of the year. In London, temporary seasonal migration produced so noticeable an effect on consumer demand that residents could speak of 'the Season' – that is, the months between autumn and late spring when the political, social, and economic life of the city was at its busiest.

Within these broad seasonal fluctuations in demand, manufacturers also faced unpredictable and short-term fluctuations stemming from the particular consumption habits of wealthy urban consumers. Those who catered to the wealthy had to contend with a clientele that often sought goods made to their own individual specifications and whose needs were therefore always somewhat unpredictable. Even when bespoke production was not the rule, artisans producing for upper echelons of the market often needed to cope with periodic changes in fashion, which could quickly erode the profit margin of older pre-made goods.

As a consequence of both short-term fluctuations and broader seasonal changes in demand, most artisans in early modern Europe found that manufacturing strategies built around integrated enterprises imposed heavy costs. Integrated production usually entailed long production runs of relatively standardized products, so that workforces could remain steadily employed. In industries where much of the business was conducted on a bespoke basis, on the other hand, proprietors contemplating integration faced the prospect of permanently employing specialists whose services might be needed only occasionally, depending on the nature and frequency of orders placed by clients. Even in industries in which bespoke production was not the norm, the seasonal rhythms of economic life meant that manufacturers attempting to sustain production throughout the year would incur costs imposed by the lengthy turnover time between their initial investments in materials and labor and the final sale of their goods. Moreover, because fashions could change or a poor harvest could destroy the purchasing power of consumers in low-end markets, such manufacturers ran the risk that they would not recoup these costs at all. All things being equal, the structure of the market therefore created notable incentives not to integrate production.[15]

Comparable factors almost certainly shaped the demand for manufactured goods in the Roman world, ensuring that the costs of integration for Roman manufacturers were likewise high. At the most basic level, grain prices were no more constant throughout the year in antiquity than they were in early modern Europe, and the demand for grain was no more elastic than it was in later centuries. The ability of much of the empire's population to consume other goods therefore varied dramatically over the course of any given year.[16]

In urban contexts, seasonality shaped consumption patterns by generating waves of travel and temporary migration, thereby altering the size and composition of the local consumer base. Rome furnishes the best evidence for the nature and impact of this problem. Here, seasonality governed not only the timing of visits made by wealthy individuals who normally resided in Italy or in the provinces, but also the temporary migration away from the city of its resident elite. Members of the resident elite left Rome in the late summer and autumn for two reasons: first, to avoid the city's unpleasant and unhealthy climate, the product of malaria and other pathogens that were at their most dangerous at this time of the year; second, to oversee operations on their agricultural estates and rental properties during the harvest and the vintage, the most critical moments of the agricultural calendar. The same seasonal considerations also affected the timing of journeys to Rome on the part of wealthy visitors, who came for a variety of different reasons: to settle lawsuits, to participate in politics, or to attempt to tap into the networks of patronage that bound the upper strata of society together. Manufacturers who targeted the wealthier segments of the urban consumer market therefore faced much stronger demand for their products in the winter and spring than they did in the late summer and autumn.

Seasonality also generated high levels of temporary migration into and out of Rome on the part of the less affluent. Like peasant cultivators in other historical contexts, those in the ancient world faced a constant struggle to balance the labor supplied by the members of their household with the amount of productive capital at their disposal. While peasants often find additional farmland difficult to acquire, their households tend to expand and contract over time; as a result, many peasant households include at least some members who are chronically underemployed, particularly after the harvest, and who therefore turn to seasonal migration in order to increase their productivity and diversify their income streams. Rome arguably attracted tens of thousands of underemployed agriculturalists during the winter and the spring each year, many of whom came to work in the building industry. Moreover, when these cultivators returned to their farms for the harvest, they were likely joined by large numbers of laborers and craftsmen from Rome who temporarily left the city in search of harvest work, either in the city's immediate hinterland or further afield on large estates. Manufacturers who targeted sub-elite consumers therefore faced seasonal fluctuations in demand that paralleled those visible in upper segments of the market.[17]

Although much of the direct evidence for seasonality and its impact on consumption pertains to Rome, the factors that drove temporary migration into and out of the capital almost certainly generated comparable patterns of movement in other great cities of the empire like Carthage, Alexandria, and Antioch. These cities likely attracted temporary labor from the countryside during the agricultural low season, much as Rome did. Likewise, their elite residents maintained extramural agricultural estates that demanded their attention from time to time, particularly at crucial moments of the agricultural calendar. Many also had to contend with local seasonal outbreaks of disease and morbidity. Urban manufacturers across the empire therefore produced for markets that were subject to seasonal swings in demand.

The particularized consumption habits of wealthy consumers further complicated the strategies of manufacturers in the upper levels of the market, who were compelled to produce many of their goods to order. Several pieces of evidence show that manufacturers who produced goods for wealthy clients in urban markets often worked on a bespoke basis, filling individual orders in response to specific commissions. In his recent study of the remains of wooden furniture found in Herculaneum, for instance, Stephan Mols notes that much of it exhibited considerable variety in form and technique. This observation is not consistent with a model in which woodworkers in the city engaged in serial production, and Mols concludes instead that they tailored pieces of furniture to the particular needs and specifications of individual clients.[18] A valuable anecdote in our literary corpus shows a carpenter working on precisely this model, albeit not in the furniture trade: in his *Apologia*, Apuleius describes how he commissioned a number of decorative and devotional items from a carpenter in Oea after seeing sample goods on display in the carpenter's shop (Apul. *Apol.* 61).

Bespoke production was also the rule for manufactures who catered to wealthy clients in large cities like Rome. This was most obviously true in industries in which the final product was inevitably tailored to individual specifications, such as construction, portrait sculpture, or certain footwear industries in which shoes were produced to measure. But scraps of evidence indicate that manufacturers produced on a bespoke basis even in industries in which individual specifications were not so critical. According to Plautus, for example, goldsmiths worked mostly on commission during the late third and early second centuries BCE (Plaut. *Men.* 541–5), and the writings of the jurists strongly suggest that the same was true in the imperial period, whether artisans worked on raw materials supplied by their clients or procured materials themselves (e.g., Gai. *Dig.* 19.2.2.1).

TRANSACTION COSTS AND PRIVATE-ORDER ENFORCEMENT IN THE ROMAN WORLD

Given the apparent parallels between the structure of demand for manufactured goods in the Roman and early modern periods, it seems almost certain that Roman manufacturers faced high costs when seeking to create integrated businesses. As in early modern Europe, these costs were a consequence of the mismatch between long- and short-term fluctuations in demand and the kinds of production strategies to which integrated businesses were best suited: long production runs of relatively standardized products, in which workforces remained steadily employed. That said, the fact that the costs of integration were high need not necessarily have discouraged manufacturers from integrating their businesses, if by doing so they were able to circumvent high transaction costs.

In the remainder of this chapter, I attempt to develop some sense of the transaction costs with which manufacturers in the Roman world had to contend. I suggest that transaction costs in certain lines of production were simply not high enough to outweigh the costs of integration. In others, manufacturers were able to mitigate high transaction costs by using voluntary associations – particularly professional *collegia* – as private-order enforcement networks, thereby forestalling the need to create integrated firms. Roughly speaking, industries that depended on widely-dispersed and easily acquired skills fell into the former category, while those in which specialized training remained important fell into the latter.

In the early modern context, where underemployment was often endemic among much of the rural and urban populace, the market in unskilled labor tended to be thick, as did the market for workers who possessed skills that were readily and quickly acquired in the domestic context or on the job. Transaction costs in these labor markets were correspondingly low: because workers in these segments of the market were plentiful and could be replaced easily and at short notice, the consequences of broken contracts were not severe, and subcontractors had insufficient leverage to attempt opportunistic renegotiations of their contracts. Manufacturers who could draw on these labor markets – typically, those producing low-quality clothing or furniture – therefore saw little benefit in integration: instead, they were able to expand their production as and when necessary by putting work out to, or by purchasing intermediate goods and services from, individuals who worked in their own homes (including, increasingly, women).[19]

The degree to which the same was true in the Roman world depended partly on the specific time and place on which we focus. In Italy during the late Republic, markets in skilled and semi-skilled free labor were constricted by the political obligations of Roman citizens and the military obligations of both Romans and Italians. At the same time, slave prices may have been relatively low compared to later periods. All of this changed after the Augustan transition. Slaves became more expensive as the pace of imperial conquest abroad slowed, and free labor markets thickened as a professional army replaced the military levy of the Republic and as popular participation in the political process began to decline. As a consequence, transaction costs in markets for free skilled and unskilled labor were likely higher in the first century BCE, and slavery more appealing as a substitute, than was the case after the Augustan transition.[20]

During the late Republic, high transaction costs therefore meant that manufacturers who could employ unskilled or semi-skilled labor had greater incentive to integrate production than did those in the early imperial period. Likewise, because of the relatively low price of slaves, they had greater means to integrate production by acquiring coerced labor. Thus, if transaction costs were ever sufficient to impel integration in low-skilled segments of the market in spite of the obvious costs imposed by seasonality, then this was likely to have happened in the late Republic rather than in the first and second centuries CE. We should therefore not be surprised that the late Republic offers the best potential examples of integrated industries, such as the various lines of Campanian ware, in which production was broken down into simple and standardized processes carried out largely by slaves.[21] By contrast, such industries seem to have been much less common in the early Empire, when falling transaction costs in unskilled labor markets and increasing slave prices meant that integration offered fewer tangible benefits.

In industries demanding training in specialized skills that were not widely distributed throughout the population, labor markets were presumably always thinner than were those for unskilled labor, even if they did benefit somewhat from changes in prevailing levels of military and political participation during the early Empire. Transaction costs in these industries must therefore have been relatively high: subcontractors who were difficult to replace enjoyed greater scope for opportunistic behavior than did those with widespread skills, and since skilled specialists remained scarce and difficult to replace on short notice, even unintended breaches of contract could be costly for artisans who relied on subcontractors for intermediate goods and services. Given these potential problems, industries in which skilled labor was the rule conceivably offered fertile ground for experiments with vertical integration in spite of its potential costs.

Why, then, did disintegrated workshops predominate even in the high-skilled segments of the manufacturing sector? The most straightforward hypothesis is that manufacturers in these industries defrayed high transaction costs through some means other than vertical integration, with private-order enforcement standing in as an obvious candidate. Although no direct evidence exists to demonstrate that Roman manufacturers embedded their businesses in private-order enforcement networks, two general considerations at least suggest that they did. First, master artisans in early modern Europe appear to have relied on reputation in order to secure transactions with one another, pointing to the possible existence of private-order enforcement networks in a context in which manufacturing was (as in the Roman world) disintegrated.[22] Second, in the ancient world itself individuals demonstrably made use of reputation in a range of other economic transactions. The work of David Cohen and Paul Millett has drawn attention to the role of honor and shame in structuring not only social norms in a broad sense in classical Athens, but lending and borrowing in particular. Likewise, Koenraad Verboven has argued that social and economic exchange in the late Roman Republic were mediated by a matrix of important values grounded in *fides* – a complex value that carried connotations of trust, obligation, loyalty, and reliability. Because *fides* itself was undergirded by an individual's reputation (*existimatio* or *dignitas*), individuals who violated the norms with which it was associated – for example, by refusing to honor a debt to a patron or to a friend – ran the risk of tarnishing their reputations. Given the value attached to reputation, this risk discouraged opportunism and served as an incentive to ensure that individuals abided by their agreements.[23]

We can press this argument further by drawing on recent suggestions that private-order enforcement works best when embedded in social networks that meet three basic requirements. The first is that membership in the network is a privilege and is costly enough that participants remain invested in preserving that membership; the second is that there exists an organized reputation mechanism for transmitting information about defaulters to other members in the network; the third is that the community as a whole is capable of imposing costly and collective sanctions on those who break their agreements.[24] If artisans and manufacturers regularly belonged to networks like this in the Roman world, then there is a distinct possibility that they relied on them for private-order enforcement.

Professional associations – known by a range of terms in antiquity, and generally referred to as professional *collegia* in modern scholarship – are the most visible networks to which artisans and manufacturers belonged in the Roman world. These associations were widespread in the imperial period, particularly in large cities, and had likely enjoyed a long history in the Republic as well. While our evidence for professional *collegia* is patchy, it does show that they shared many basic structural and functional characteristics with other kinds of ancient associations, which could be based on residence in a particular neighborhood or organized around the worship of a specific divinity. All provided a social context in which their members could satisfy a number of important needs: they offered opportunities for sociability and conviviality, for communal religious celebrations, and for the articulation of hierarchies of honor and status. The degree to which professional associations also addressed specific economic needs is a more controversial question; while I cannot explore it fully here, I do wish to suggest that ancient associations in general – and professional associations in particular – were similar enough in structure to private-order enforcement networks that they likely functioned as such in practice.[25]

Distinctions between members and non-members are important in private-order enforcement networks because, when membership is a privilege, members are more likely to have a vested interest in maintaining a good reputation within the organization. In the ancient world, associations of all types established such distinctions. They did so in the first place by establishing criteria for membership, which often entailed the payment of a fee. Such fees could be substantial: in the late second century CE, applicants paid a fee of at least twenty-five denarii to join the Athenian Iobachhoi, an association devoted to the worship of Bacchus (*IG* 2^2 1368, lines 37–41); this amount represented almost a fifth of the annual gross earnings of artisans employed by the Roman state. Fees of this magnitude not only imposed a degree of self-selection on prospective members, but also increased the odds that members would be committed to long-term transactions within the network and invested in the quality of their reputations.[26]

Members of associations further reinforced the boundaries between themselves and non-members by engaging in a variety of regular and communal social and religious activities. Particularly important in this respect were ceremonial occasions that involved the creation of formal membership lists (*alba* or *fasti*) – monumental inscriptions that were prominently displayed in the meeting places of many associations. In Van Nijf's view, the creation of these lists offered a clear and public statement that the members named in them "had accepted the codes and values of the *collegium*."[27] The boundaries of an association, along with the identities of those whom they encompassed, could be expressed in no clearer way. Along with selection criteria and entrance fees, membership lists clearly expressed the fact that membership in a *collegium* was a privilege that "always distinguished 'ins' from 'outs'."[28]

In addition to erecting clear boundaries between members and non-members, strong private-order enforcement networks also possess organized mechanisms for transmitting information about personal reputations. These ensure that members of the network quickly learn of contractual breaches or opportunistic behavior on the part of their colleagues. In modern trade associations, arbitration panels often serve this function. By publicizing the results of their inquiries, they make public not only the details of contractual breaches, but also important information about the degree to which individuals are committed to the values of the network, since those who refuse to accept the decisions of arbitrators quickly acquire negative reputations.[29]

The best evidence for comparable mechanisms in an ancient association is found in the regulations of the Athenian Iobacchoi. The Iobacchoi insisted that certain disputes between members were to be resolved internally. Thus, members who became involved in a physical altercation with one another were compelled to argue their cases before the assembled membership of the association or face a fine and temporary exclusion from the association's events (*IG* 2^2 1368, lines 84–90). Arguably, this procedure served two basic functions. First, it ensured that the membership as a whole was quickly apprised of what was seen as a serious violation of the values of their community. Second, it gave them a first-hand opportunity to evaluate how highly both the victim and the assailant valued their reputations within the community: the refusal of either party to settle the matter internally set a clear message about his long-term commitment to the association.

A Roman funerary inscription from the imperial period hints at the existence of comparable mechanisms in at least one association of a primarily professional nature. In his epitaph, T. Flavius Hilario listed a number of offices and honors he had held in the *collegium fabrorum tignuariorum*, Rome's association of builders, during the late first and early second centuries CE. One of these entailed serving on a panel of twelve judges who were elected from among the junior and senior magistrates of the association, the *iudices inter electos XII ab ordine* (*CIL* 14.2630). While the inscription does not elaborate on the function of these judges, it is difficult not to see here an echo of the arbitrators in contemporary professional associations, who play such an important role in disseminating information about individual reputations and breaches of contract.

Finally, private-order enforcement networks function best when their members can impose costly and collective sanctions on colleagues who violate their agreements. At a rudimentary level, members do so by refusing to form contracts with those guilty of reneging on previous commitments. But the stakes for defaulters can be higher in a private-order enforcement network that incorporates religious and social functions in addition to narrowly economic ones: in these networks, members can further amplify the costs of undesirable behavior by barring defaulters from important communal celebrations.[30] Because associations in the ancient world offered so many opportunities for conviviality, religious expression, and status competition, their members were likewise able to use temporary exclusion or outright expulsion from an association as a powerful sanction against those who violated the norms of the community. Most of the evidence for punishments of this nature deals with procedural violations: the Athenian Iobacchoi punished those guilty of assault or of other infractions with temporary exclusion from social and religious gatherings (*IG* 2^2 1368, lines 48–53 and 72–95); the worshippers of Diana and Antinous in Lanuvium threatened to withhold funeral rites from those who died while delinquent in their dues (*CIL* 14.2112, col 1, lines 21–23); and the dealers in ivory and citrus wood in Rome threatened to expel *collegium* officers who fraudulently extended membership to those who did not work in their profession (*CIL* 6.33885, lines 4–6).

None of our evidence demonstrates conclusively that members of professional associations used temporary exclusion or outright expulsion to sanction colleagues who violated contracts. There are, however, strong if indirect indications that they likely did. In Artemidorus' manual on dream interpretation, written in the second century CE, we read of a man who was expelled from an association because he had disgraced himself in such a way that his colleagues considered him *atimos*, bereft of honor (Artem. 4.44). Reputation clearly played a role in his expulsion, and while Artemidorus is unspecific about both the nature of the association and the infraction that destroyed the man's reputation with his colleagues, Pliny the Younger shows that expectations about economic behavior loomed large in the minds of association members in antiquity. In his famous correspondence with Trajan concerning the prosecution of Christians, Pliny notes that the members of Christian groups swore oaths to one another that they would not only refrain from theft, robbery, and adultery, but also from violating agreements of a more economic nature, whether by reneging on obligations or by withholding deposits (Plin. *Ep.* 10.96.7). It would be surprising indeed had members of professional associations not expected the same of their own colleagues, and had they not made comparable use of reputation mechanisms and exclusion when those expectations were violated.

Thus, while our evidence on professional associations is indirect and based in part on comparisons with other voluntary associations in the ancient world, it does show that these associations had strong functional similarities to private-order enforcement networks. They were therefore ideal institutions in which manufacturers who relied on highly-skilled specialists could make use of reputation to mitigate transaction costs that may otherwise have stimulated vertical integration. This was particularly true in large cities, where occupational specialization was most acute, where *collegia* were organized around a number of different industries, and where specialists who worked in various branches of a given industry often belonged to the same association – the builders' association at Rome, the *collegium fabrorum tignuariorum*, consisted of hundreds of members, many of whom were arguably specialists in different aspects of the industry.[31] And while belonging to an association could be costly because of both membership fees and the pressure to impress colleagues through generosity, these were costs that many manufacturers were likely to incur in any case in order to participate in the social and religious life of associations.

If the preceding analyses are correct, then they show that most manufacturers in the Republican and imperial periods chose to organize their production in small workshops because of the way in which the structure of consumer demand interacted both with labor markets and with institutions that were capable of mitigating transaction costs. As long as the market for manufactured goods remained dominated by seasonal and erratic fluctuations in demand, manufacturers had good reasons to prefer the flexibility of small and specialized workshops to the costs of large and integrated firms. Any incentives they faced to integrate their businesses were further eroded by the way in which economic conditions and social institutions mitigated the costs of doing business, whether by ensuring ready access to labor in low-skilled sectors of the market, or by offering access to reputation-based mechanisms for securing transactions where training remained important. In that sense, manufacturers in antiquity faced challenges not at all dissimilar to those that characterized the early modern European economy, and devised solutions to those challenges that would have been recognizable to their early modern colleagues.

Notes

1 Von Petrikovits 1981 and Joshel 1992: 171–82 both provide some sense of the degree of specialization that existed in the Roman Empire.
2 Morel 2007; Kehoe 2007b: 559–66.
3 Coase 1988. See also Acheson 2002 for a brief introduction to many of these issues.
4 Richman 2004.
5 Farr 2000: 52–6; Sonenscher 1989: 135–8; Schwarz 1992: 31–3.
6 Strong 1966: 15–16.
7 Joshel 1992: 106–12.
8 Drexhage, Konen, and Ruffing. 2002: 247 offer an alternative interpretation.
9 Van Minnen 1987: 56–8. Cf. Drexhage, Konen, and Ruffing 2002: 111.
10 Martin 1989: 53–4.
11 Mols 1999: 91–110.
12 See, e.g., Ulp. *Dig.* 14.3.5.10; *CIL* 6.9969–6.9976; 6.37820.
13 Wild 1999.
14 Kehoe 2007b, especially 549–50 and 560–1.
15 The preceding model is based largely on Schwarz 1992: 31–73, 103–23, and on Sonenscher 1989: 99–173.
16 Erdkamp 2005: 147–55.
17 I offer a more detailed discussion of seasonality and survey the relevant evidence in Hawkins forthcoming.
18 Mols 1999: 112.
19 Schwarz 1992: 32–3, 179–207.
20 Scheidel 2005b; 2008b.
21 Morel 2007: 504–9.
22 Sonenscher 1989: 135; Rosser 1997.
23 Millett 1991, especially 24–52; Cohen 1991; Verboven 2002: 35–48, 170–8.
24 Richman 2004.
25 For recent discussions of professional associations, and their relationship to associations of other kinds, see Harland 2003: 25–87; Van Nijf 2002; Verboven 2007.
26 Cf. Monson 2006: 228–38, who makes this argument about membership fees and other entrance requirements in the context of a discussion of Ptolemaic religious associations. For wages paid to artisans by the state in the second century CE, see Cuvigny 1996. For more on entrance fees in antiquity, see Waltzing 1895–1900: I 450–1.
27 Van Nijf 2002: 332–4.
28 Verboven 2007: 882.
29 Richman 2006: 395–8; Bernstein 2001: 1737–9, 1766–9.
30 Bernstein 2001: 1750–2; Richman 2006: 398–408.
31 See Gai. *Dig.* 50.16.235.1, who suggests that *faber tignarius* (which can be interpreted in a narrow sense as 'carpenter' or 'framer') was generally used in practice to refer "not only to those who hew timber, but to all who work as builders."

Part IV

Distribution

10: Predation

Peter Fibiger Bang

> Then the state was strong and seasoned in the arts of war and peace.[1]
>
> (Livy 1.21: 6)

Rape – the rape or rather abduction of the Sabine women – is one of the most famous and popular tales of Roman history. It belongs among the rich stock of founding myths with which Roman historians embellished the distant origins of their city and explained the character of its social institutions.[2] After Romulus had founded the city and killed his impudent brother, his band of male herders was in need of women to create a durable society. But the neighboring polities all refused to grant them *conubium*, the right of intermarriage. Not one to take no for an answer, Romulus instead resourcefully lured them into visiting the new city for a religious celebration. During the festivities, his warriors, in blatant violation of the laws of hospitality, broke in on the party and abducted the young women of the visitors. An outrageous act of betrayal, this theft called for immediate revenge; the communities which had been wronged were all up in arms. Soon the Romans had to take to the field to defend their newly won possessions and prove the worth of their young state in the test of war.

Triumph was immediate, the story goes. The first army of avenging foes to face the Roman soldiers was roundly beaten and their commanding king killed in the heat of battle by Romulus himself. Sporting the armor of his slain opponent, Romulus returned to the city in triumph and dedicated this precious booty to Jupiter Feretrius, "the striker," and a temple to house it on the Capitol.[3] Taking the *spolia opima* by killing the enemy leader on the battle field came in the Roman tradition to signify the ultimate act of heroism and military prowess; and the Romans did not blush to attach to this rare feat an explanatory legend of how might so conspicuously had made right. "Anger without strength was vain," as Livy advised the reader of his history.[4] Roman society had prospered at the cost of neighbors and subjects. Empire was a question of military power which prised open other communities and made their resources available to the victors. The Romans were under few illusions in this respect; their society was built on predation.

How to preserve or generate the vigorous assertiveness, the *virtus*, that classical authors had celebrated in a lush undergrowth of myths and quasi-historical tales of the earliest Roman times, became a burning issue when during the early modern period the foundations of social science were laid. It was the central question which inspired Machiavelli's investigation into the nature of power and politics. The secret was held to lie in the ability of societal institutions to balance each other and thereby prevent the commonwealth from falling under the domination of a single, self-serving, faction.[5] This concern, too, was behind Adam Smith's attack on "the mercantile system" and call for laissez-faire; governments should not be held captive to a particular set of economic interests – an argument which J. A. Hobson repeated by the turn of the nineteenth century in his liberal indictment of colonial imperialism as the handmaiden of rent-seeking financiers.[6] At the heart of this theoretical tradition was a preoccupation with how to cultivate a firm fabric of social and political institutions to structure human existence. The question has lost nothing of its pertinence. Institutions and their importance for shaping the development of societies are back high on the agenda of social science, not least economics; and with institutions comes an interest in understanding historical divergence, the result of different modes of social organization. So, the time seems ripe and the ground well prepared for Classics to renew this longstanding dialogue. To the ancient economic historian, the so-called New Institutional Economics, in particular, attracts interest and offers a way of refertilizing our field by providing a sophisticated set of tools for understanding the interplay between economy and society.[7]

Much has already been achieved in the pioneering collective effort represented by *The Cambridge Economic History of the Greco-Roman World* (*CEHGRW*). In this first generation of work, focus tended to be on performance and on understanding how states provided the institutional foundations of economic activity. The culmination of this process in antiquity is understood as having been reached with the establishment in the Mediterranean of the Roman peace and dissemination of imperial law, which together are seen as lowering transaction costs and thus facilitating economic exchange.[8] Emphasis, in short, has been rather on another aspect of the Roman experience, also embodied in their civic mythology: that aggression might be followed by cooperation. The tale of the stolen Sabine womenfolk did not end where we left it. Severe fighting continued with more of the antagonized neighboring peoples. The conflict was only resolved when the maidens threw themselves in between their Roman husbands and their angry fathers and brothers. By their appeals to both sides, they brought reconciliation between their new and old families and enabled an alliance to be struck which strengthened the foundations of Roman society and produced peaceful collaboration.[9] In the long term, to cite the conclusion of the editors of *CEHGRW*, "Greek and Roman states on the whole stayed within a[n] (. . .) optimality band, strong enough to protect property rights, but too weak to predate on their subjects so viciously that they smothered economic activity."[10]

But this is a questionable way of phrasing the problem, in more ways than one. Few, if any, pre-industrial states were ever strong enough to smother the economy, and certainly not on the continental scale of the territory dominated by Rome.[11] Moreover, in modern experience, predatory activities of state personnel and political elites are often most rampant in weak states, which are insufficiently strong to guarantee property rights of individuals and groups that lose political power.[12] Finally, the assessment seems to lend too much weight to the arts of peace rather than war. Imperial conquests are relegated to the margins as of trivial significance to the economy. But the Roman state was above anything else a war machine, whereas the civilian apparatus of government long remained rudimentary.[13] King Numa, the lawmaker, took second place to Romulus, the founder of this ferocious breed which through centuries of relentless war-making pillaged, conquered, and subjected the greater Mediterranean world to its rule. At the triumph, the celebration of military victory was institutionalized as a festive time for the display of power and affluence. Booty, slaves, and allegories of tax-yielding provinces were all arranged in impressive tableaus to put on parade the blessings flowing from empire.[14] If the imposition of empire did not significantly depress economic activity in the Mediterranean, it was certainly not for lack of predation; the lesson from Roman history seems rather the opposite, slightly more disturbing and certainly challenging: predation worked.

Organized violence and its effects need to be thoroughly worked into our analysis of the institutional fabric of the ancient economy, that of the Romans in particular. Incidentally, New Institutional Economics readily supplies the tools. Customarily it conceptualizes the state as a predator.[15] To this may be added a general observation from the more institutionally inclined among economic historians: under pre-industrial conditions, where productivity is relatively low, violent conquest is a key economic parameter.[16] The following sections of this essay will trace the economic impact of Roman imperial predation, move on to a discussion of consolidated rule in terms of a so-called "stationary bandit" before the final section attempts to introduce, from the recent work on *Violence and Social Orders* by North, Wallis and Weingast, the concept of the "natural state" as a rent-producing aristocratic coalition to explain the character of the Pax Romana.

Predatory imperialism and the expansionism of Rome

From the late fourth century BCE when the Roman city-state slowly begins to emerge from the twilight realm of myth and prehistorical archaeology, warfare was a constant of its social life, perennial and all-pervasive. No other state was able to match its capacity to mobilize the citizenry in the army for years on end. Peace was abnormal. Plunder and raiding, on the other hand, were a staple of ancient warfare. Much campaigning boiled down to little more. Among the stipulations contained in the treaties of friendship between Rome and Carthage, the first clause tellingly sets out a demarcation line beyond which "the Romans shall not make raiding expeditions."[17] Following in the wake of the victorious legions, roaming ever more widely around the Mediterranean, a steady stream of movable wealth began to flow into Rome and Italy. Looted treasure, art works, and slaves by the thousands, many of them captured in Roman campaigns, were crammed into central-south Italian society during the three centuries of vigorous imperial expansion.

But these were only the, admittedly large, tip of the iceberg.[18] Many of the spoils of empire were not immediately transferable. Roman conquests were regularly followed by confiscation of choice agricultural lands in subjected communities. Across Italy, but also in the provincial parts of the empire, the Roman state began to draw proceeds from farming out to contractors its *ager publicus*. Other parts of the confiscated lands were developed into colonies, urban communities settled by Roman citizens and Latin allies who had been allocated parcels of land in the new territory.[19] Arable and grazing lands were not the only ones targeted. Areas endowed with particular natural resources were another favorite, such as quarries and, in particular, precious metal mines. In the Iberian peninsula, the voracious Roman appetite for silver and gold saw the new conquerors follow hot on the heels of the former Carthaginian masters to develop and intensify mining operations, often under direct military surveillance. Atmospheric lead pollution from Roman silver extraction registered as far away as Greenland.[20] The major parts of conquered territories, however, were subjected to a more indirect method of extraction: taxation. Imperial tribute was demanded based on the principle of obtaining as much as possible with the least effort. On Sicily, the first province of the empire, the old system of taxation developed under the tyrants of Syracuse was taken over wholesale.[21] After the kingdom of Macedon had been crushed at Pydna in 168 BCE, the territory, now divided into four self-ruling republics, had imposed on it a tax at half the rate formerly claimed by the kings. But the new masters had not all of a sudden grown soft-hearted; they just had no intention of garrisoning the area, which had to be left to its own devices in dealing with the military threat posed by querulous tribes living on its frontiers. The profits from empire were not going to be squandered on providing demanding, and potentially expensive, services to imperial subjects.[22]

It is difficult to exaggerate the scale of brutality, human suffering, and sheer ruthlessness involved in this process of expansive imperial predation, but harder to gauge the economic impact in precise terms. Yet, impressionistic and speculative as our analysis must remain, imperial conquest wrought profound economic change on the Mediterranean. Redistribution of wealth and economic resources was staggering and must easily have been the single most significant and dynamic factor shaping economic developments. The argument rests on both a set of proxy indicators and hypothetical quantification. Following the Macedonian triumph, the Roman state was able to dispense with collecting land-taxes from its own citizens in Italy.[23] For the next centuries, Rome nevertheless fielded armies of a size that during the military revolution of the early modern period beggared monarchs and forced them into a relentless quest to borrow enormous sums of money and drive up internal taxation. But Rome could soldier on, comfortably even, without all this – such was the fabulous wealth produced by Roman imperialism.[24] Indeed, the proceeds of empire allowed the Republic to introduce a strong and copious silver coinage, the denarius struck in quantities without any real comparison in the ancient Western Mediterranean.[25] Under Roman colonization schemes several hundreds of thousands of people were resettled and granted land-allotments.[26] To this voluntary movement of population must be added an enormous, yet statistically uncertain number of slaves. The best modern attempt to model the forced transfer of slaves into Italy hypothesizes annual quantities to have averaged some 15–20,000 during the last two centuries BCE. A modest number, perhaps, but the accumulated weight adds up to a dizzying long-term forced relocation of some three to four million people, many of them the direct victims of Roman imperialism.[27]

Intense military activity financed by conquest, enormous mobilization of precious metals and giant population transfers – one would be hard pressed to identify any other factor of similar moment to predation in effecting economic change in the Mediterranean during the period of Roman expansion. In overall terms, however, the Roman state may be thought to have had only a relatively modest presence in the economy. Our best and most educated guesses would set the share taken up by the imperial state in the economy during the early empire at between 5 and 10 percent, and closer to the first than the second figure.[28] But this is less an argument for the insignificance of the imperial state than a reminder of the small scale and narrow limits set by pre-industrial economies. Most of the economy was relatively immobile, consumed within the households of peasant producers, and much of the rest only moved in relatively narrow local or regional circuits.[29] Among economic historians of early modern Europe it is equally often remarked that in terms of the total economy, foreign trade, colonial in particular, commanded only a relatively modest share. But its importance derived from the fact that it was one of the most dynamic and fastest growing sectors in Northwestern Europe.[30] The same applies, in parallel fashion, to our assessment of Roman imperialism.

Perhaps, the strongest macro indicator of the revolutionary economic impact of Roman expansion is provided by Rome the city itself. Widely held to have grown over three centuries to reach the million mark during the late Republic or reign of Augustus, the capital, feeding on the profits from empire, represented a colossal and unparalleled increase of consumer demand in the Western Mediterranean. We may try to clarify the proportions of this figure through some hypothetical quantification. If we generously set the population inhabiting the area that would become the western part of the Roman Empire at some 25–30 million in the last decades of the third century BCE and speculate the average urbanization rate to have been approximately 5 percent, the urban population would have been between 1.2 and 1.5 million.[31] In this scenario, the extraordinary expansion of Rome would have increased total urbanization by at least half and possibly almost doubled it. Even when the population of the empire is thought to have peaked, just before the outbreak of the Antonine Plague, by the middle of the second century CE, a recent estimate still sees Rome to have equalled the entire urban population of all the Western provinces north of the Mediterranean (excluding Italy of course) from the Balkans to Hispania and across Gaul to Germania and Britain.[32]

No other economic force could credibly be claimed to have matched the impact and structural transformation produced by predatory imperialism in the Mediterranean world of the last centuries before our era. There is simply not enough room left within the narrow confines of a pre-industrial economy. The process was merciless. Enormous destruction was left in the wake of the progress of the Roman legions. The year 146 BCE marks something of a high-point or nadir, according to the chosen perspective. In this year Carthage and Corinth were crushed and razed to the ground. Both these cities were famed as centers for Mediterranean commerce, and their fall came shortly after Rhodes, another commercial hub, had been chastised by Rome for its wavering support during the war with Macedon. But much as commercial life was disrupted by these events, the strength of predatory mobilization seems to have outweighed its adverse effects.[33] Resources continued to be harnessed on a steadily increasing scale, lifted out of local communities and thrust into circulation. Predatory imperialism cut across the obstacles to integration and unlocked the economic potential of the Mediterranean world to a degree which markets left on their own were as yet unable to do.[34] Indeed, both the sale and consumption of the spoils of empire began to spawn the formation of new markets that developed to service the process of predatory mobilization.

PREDATORS, STATIONARY BANDITS, AND CORPORATE ENTERPRISE

Fame, or notoriety, is attached to the groups of state contractors which emerged to service the needs of Roman imperialism to have armies supplied and subjects taxed. These 'publicans' would bid at auctions for building contracts, delivery of military equipment and food rations, mining concessions, and the right to collect customs as well as the land taxes in a select number of rich provinces in return for a stipulated annual sum. Senators being legally barred from these activities, the publicans were drawn from the affluent layer just below the senatorial *ordo*. Most of them were wealthy landowners, a necessary requirement since holders of government contracts had to offer land as security for the fulfilment of terms.[35] Many of these contracts were in any case far too large to be underwritten by a single person; publicans regularly had to band together in larger companies.[36] This was the high-point of ancient "capitalism," as Max Weber realized.[37] In connection with their activities developed a complex web linking credit and land in Italy to the political exploitation of provincial societies. "For we know that when numerous people have experienced great losses in the province of Asia, credit collapses in Rome, since repayment of debts has become difficult." Here was Cicero, evoking the unpleasant spectre of a disruption of tax collections in Asia Minor to advocate to his Roman audience the appointment of Pompey to lead a campaign to put an end once and for all to the threat posed by king Mithridates of Pontus to the Empire's eastern possessions. Imperial taxation had become big business, a key avenue of elite investment.[38]

One might even play with the idea that the largest tax-farming companies were an institutional precursor of the modern business corporation and joint-stock company;[39] they were organized with something resembling an executive, a board of directors, and a wider group of passive investors and partners; they also acquired a corporate existence. Normally, in the eyes of the law, a *societas* was dissolved on the death of or withdrawal of consent by one of the partners.[40] But this arrangement was too fragile to ensure the interests of the Republic in steady and stable performance of the vital tasks it had contracted to private individuals. So an exemption was made, in this case, to give the companies of the *publicani* greater permanence and possibly invest them with a legally sanctioned corporate status for the duration of the contract.[41] It has even been suggested that they developed some form of ownership akin to shares. But here we really are clutching at straws. The transferable 'parts' that are alluded to occasionally in late Republican sources are only vaguely described. At any rate, they seem to belong to a realm of semi-clandestine operations designed to enable members of the senatorial aristocracy to invest in the lucrative business of provincial exploitation.[42]

Direct comparison with those institutional innovations of the early modern period that are normally claimed as the origins of the modern business corporation will bring the character of the Roman *societas publicanorum* into sharper relief. These developed as vehicles for European overseas commerce, in particular the East India trade pioneered by the Portuguese in the sixteenth century, followed by the Dutch and English in the seventeenth. A set of brilliant ideal-types enabled the historian Steensgaard to differentiate between the first and second generation of commercial developments.[43] The Portuguese *Estado da India* behaved more like an "old-fashioned," predatory imperial power. Its empire in the Indian Ocean exploited its superior war-craft to tax ships sailing on the open seas. Unless these had bought a Portuguese "passport" granting safe passage, they risked being boarded and plundered by the Portuguese men-of-war plying the Oriental waters. The novelty of the Portuguese establishment was to have transferred the logic of imperial taxation from the land to the sea. Compared to this, the efforts of the Dutch United East-India Company, the VOC, were concentrated on developing its trade in Eastern spices; these were the mainstay of its activities and enabled it to prosper for many decades as the first fully fledged business corporation. Critics have rightly objected that the Portuguese also engaged in a great deal of commercial enterprise. Conversely, the Dutch also earned money from selling passports in the Indian Ocean.[44] As with all ideal types, we are dealing with a (useful) simplification designed to enhance our perception of shades of difference: the one more of a tax collector, the other more of a merchant. Rather than absolutely distinct in character, the two establishments may be ranged on a spectrum with the two kinds of activity marking out the opposite poles. For the historian of the Roman tax-farming corporation, however, the finer details matter less. It is clear that the most significant of the *societates publicanorum* were closer, even than the Portuguese *Estado da India*, to the imperial taxation end of the spectrum. They earned their keep, based on land, by collecting and extracting customs, tribute, and minerals from subject communities.

Nevertheless, even if the family relationship to the modern business corporation is tenuous, the institutional innovations represented by the large companies of the *publicani* are still testimony to the complexity and sophistication of the processes linking Republican Italy with the political exploitation of the provinces. But impressive organizational talent and substantial formation of "capital" was only part of the story: infamy was the other. "How great is the audacity, how great the insolence of the groups of *publicani*, everybody knows."[45] The activities of the companies and the hosts of private individuals following in their footsteps often came perilously close to outright plunder. Through the correspondence of Cicero we are allowed an intimate glimpse of the system in operation. Sordid and cynical, the details revealed in his letters almost seem to confirm even the worst prejudices that the historian might take away from the moralizing and rhetorically exaggerated stereotypes often found in the public discourse of speeches, philosophical treatises, and historical works.[46]

As governor of Cilicia, Cicero found himself approached by what was later revealed to be the agents of the same Brutus who would win immortal fame as the assassin of Julius Caesar and the upright hero of liberty.[47] These agents/businessmen were requesting that Cicero, like his predecessor, put at their disposal some contingents of cavalry to assist them in driving in the substantial debts owed to them by Ariobarzanes, the Roman client king of Cappadocia, and by the city of Salamis on Cyprus.[48] The first part of the request, concerning a matter outside his own jurisdiction, Cicero had few problems granting. But with Salamis the matter was different. The loan advanced to the city had been charged at the extortionate rate of 48 percent interest per annum. Cicero was doubly embarrassed. In the edict promulgated in the province to announce the principles on which he would base his term of office, Cicero had set the maximum rate of interest to be charged by anyone at 12 percent per annum. He was also reluctant to grant a businessman a cavalry command to be used for his private purposes inside the province. Immediately pressure was brought to bear on him. Atticus, the rich financier and trusted friend, wrote and advised him in no uncertain terms to forget his moral scruples and get on with the business. Before that, Brutus, to lean more heavily on Cicero, had already come clean as the true lender acting behind the two straw men; and in Atticus' book, relations with the Roman noble counted for far more than principled administration and provincial sighs of woe. Whether our Tully ever caved in to the pressures cannot be determined on the basis of the letters. Nor is it possible to know whether his administration really was more just than the norm such as he liked to boast. But such justice as even a sympathetically minded governor was able to dispense had to unfold within fairly narrow confines. It is characteristic that when the leaders of Salamis offered to deposit in a temple the repayment of Brutus' loan, calculated on the interest recognized in Cicero's edit, he nevertheless did not allow it and thereby did not free them of further obligations.[49] First and foremost, Cicero was in the province as the representative of Roman interests. A preferable solution, from his perspective, was for Brutus and the Salaminians to reach a compromise accord, presumably somewhere between the extortionate claims and the maximum rate of interest prescribed by the gubernatorial edict.

In the same missives to Atticus, Cicero congratulated himself on having facilitated a similar sort of compromise between the cities and the *publicani* in another district under his provincial jurisdiction.[50] There tax arrears had been building up owing, at least, from the five preceding years, and city finances were in a sorry state. In Cicero's version of events, he had managed to unlock the stalemate by a well-directed *double entendre*. By going through the urban accounts, he had identified considerable embezzlement, or so he claimed, and persuaded city-councillors to pay back these *furta*. Apparently, they had done so without complaint and thus enabled the cities to settle their tax debts. But here the versatile senator is himself taxing our credulity. It hardly seems credible that city-councillors should have voluntarily returned a sum of money amounting to five years' taxes for these urban communities without demur. The willingness of the urban notables had undoubtedly been spurred by Cicero's second measure. To all the cities had been given a fixed date before which they had to repay their mounting debt to the tax-farmers. If so, the debt would be calculated according to the governor's maximum interest rate, if not, the debt would be settled in accordance with the no doubt even harsher terms stipulated in their borrowing contracts with the publicans. Was this carrot or stick? It all depends on the perspective, of course, but it is hard to avoid the impression that the civic leaders had been subjected to a little polite arm-twisting and squeezed more tightly to allow a greater amount of the tax intake to flow to the Romans. The deal, in this case, was quite good enough also to earn him the gratitude of the tax-farmers, Cicero reported.[51] Possibly the Brutus affair stretched common practice, but it was a symptom of the wider system of exploitation. The ability of governors to curb predatory exploitation was reined in by their dependence on political networks centered in Rome.

The logic of tax-farming dictated a certain amount of ruthless extraction. Contracts stipulated an annual sum to be paid to the state by the *publicani*. Everything they could collect from subjects in excess of this amount they would keep as profit. Obviously this did not exactly invite restraint; on the contrary, it encouraged putting the squeeze on taxpayers; the business depended on it. This pattern of behavior was further exacerbated by the fact that companies normally only held their concession for a four-year period, the *lustrum*, after which they would have to compete for the right again with other bidders at a new auction. In these circumstances, the short-term interest of the publicans in extracting as much revenue as possible might well outweigh the interest of the state in a sustainable regime of taxation preserving the long-term capacity of subjects to pay. The goose that laid the golden eggs occasionally found itself at risk. With the transition to the imperial monarchy, this situation may have eased. The provinces where they had held the right to collect the land-taxes were taken away from the publicans and transferred to a system organized by imperial officials.[52] The balance of interests shifted in favor of the long term. From a theoretical perspective, one might describe the development as naked predation giving way to a regime of a so-called stationary bandit.[53] Monarchy had a greater stake in the continuous economic well-being of its subjects. "It was the task of a good shepherd to shear, not to flay his sheep," as the emperor Tiberius was thought to have instructed his governors. Plunder was replaced by a system of the 'quasi-voluntary' co-operation of provincial subjects.[54]

But the contrast is easily exaggerated. Again, and here even more, it is probably better to think in terms of movement along a spectrum where the two alternatives are marked out as opposite poles. The tax-farmers never held the right to collect the land-taxes in all the provinces acquired by the Republic.[55] Neither did the companies of the *publicani* nor the imperial authorities ever create an extensive provincial bureaucracy. Both regimes depended on subject communities to do most of the actual job of collecting the imperial tribute; their 'quasi-voluntary' co-operation had to be sought from the very beginning, opportunities offered to provincial 'middlemen' to profit from the involvement in the collection of taxes and conflict kept within limits. By the middle of the second century BCE, the imperial Republic responded to this need by the introduction of the so-called *actio de rebus repetundis* whereby aggrieved provincials were granted a legal avenue through which to seek redress against extortionate behavior. This remedy was far from perfect. Occasionally, it seems almost to have become a tool for the equestrian *publicani* to ensure that their activities went unhampered by 'overly conscientious' senatorial governors.[56] But the effects of random Republican rapacity have to be weighed against the greater intrusiveness of the imperial state under the caesars. From the time of Augustus, provincial censuses and land-surveys became a regular tool of government. Frequency and extent varied widely from province to province, though.[57] Even so, one may speculate that censuses made possible a more even and predictable distribution of the tax burden. But they certainly also represented a potent expansion of state controls over subject populations and their wealth. In several provinces, the introduction of surveys of land and people is known to have sparked rebellion.[58]

Extortion remained a feature even of the imperial monarchy. State personnel and other wielders of power still expected to profit from their positions of influence; and government had insufficient resources to offer the population systematic protection against such behavior and to control its officials.[59] Declarations by the governing authorities, roundly condemning abuse and extortion, remained episodic, prompted by particular conflicts, and never changed the basic pattern of conduct.[60] The underlying dynamic of power is well reflected in the reports of extortion trials confided to his literary epistles by the senator Pliny. His description of the trials in the senate against the governors Caecilius Classicus and Julius Bassus is illuminating – and sobering.[61] Consistently and without a blush, the Roman senator, who in both cases had appeared for the prosecution, nevertheless lashes out against leading members of the accusing provincial delegation. Even though the grounds of their complaint are well established and the governor convicted, these people are still portrayed with overt hostility, slandered and maligned. *Malus, pravus, audacia* are among the pejorative labels liberally stamped on their personalities. To the verbal opprobrium of the letters, the senate seems to have added vindictiveness. On both occasions attempts were made to bring charges against the 'victorious' provincials, once even successfully. The outcome was, as Pliny notes, quite remarkable – but in a higher sense well deserved, as we are implicitly led to understand. The leader of the provincial delegation – "of character bad and crooked" – was convicted of colluding with the wife of the condemned governor in hiding her share of the crimes committed in the province. But after this conviction the senate then proceeded to clear the wife of all charges. In short, "the defendant was acquitted, although her accuser was convicted of collusion with her." This was extraordinary but exemplary justice – material worthy to be dressed up in literary garb and preserved for posterity. Banishment from his province was the reward meted out to this 'wicked' man for successfully taking a governor to court. Most people would undoubtedly think twice before they would risk senatorial justice. While offering redress for grievances, it actually reinforced the ruling hierarchy; the imperial courts were inseparable from the games of power and political conflict.

Empire under the monarchy remained a question of dominance and political exploitation. This bears emphasis, not to evoke scandal or provoke moral indignation, but as a salutary reminder of the harsher realities of power undergirding most successful empires in history that still need to find a place within the evolving institutionalist interpretation of the Roman economy. Being in a position of power and influence was commonly accompanied by the capacity to divert resources to one's own advantage. Roman subjects can be found casually to include in their expense accounts very considerable sums – 'shake-downs,' 'bribes' – paid as protection money to office-holders and soldiers.[62] The latter can also be documented to have been habitually able to circumvent the imperial ban on owning property in the provinces where they were stationed.[63] Power accumulated profits under the emperors as under the Republic. What did change, however, was a stronger integration of provincials in the operation of the empire. More people in the conquered territories were admitted to a share of the privileges and benefits afforded by imperial rule.[64] Provincial councillors would less frequently have found themselves as hard pressed as described in the letters of Cicero, and would thereby have been able to pocket a larger part of the profits from tax-collection. The crowning achievement of this process was the entry of scores of provincial nobles into the senate and the equestrian order during the Principate. This was a visible demonstration that the accumulation of wealth in the hands of the powerful had proceeded apace or more probably been reinforced under the paternalistic care of the emperors.[65] Of all the many things that empire undoubtedly was, it was very much a network of rent-seeking elites.

Natural states and rent-seeking, creative destruction and imperial hegemony

Such a way of organizing society may seem inherently corrupt, and built on favoritism and special privilege it certainly is; but it also marks the imposition of a political order and lends shape to society. As North, Wallis and Weingast have argued in their recent book, pre-industrial statehood consisted in the establishment of a ruling coalition of rent-seeking elites. Such "natural states" existed to generate rents to the rulers by limiting "access to valuable resources" and make their enjoyment dependent on political privilege.[66] In classical economic accounts, rent-seeking is seen primarily as wasteful and destructive. Rents divert the allocation of economic resources away from the most efficient employment and distort the free operation of the market.[67]

Long ago, however, the Austro-American economist Joseph Schumpeter pointed out that in some circumstances rent-seeking may be productive. Industrial capitalism, for instance, had not produced a stable market regime where free moving actors could steadily improve the utilization of resources and approach an optimally efficient economic equilibrium. Quite the reverse, modern economic growth depended on a sustained revolution where new sectors constantly, but unpredictably, emerged to redefine the conditions of economic competition and wipe out established branches of industry. Already in the early stages of modern capitalism, the contours of this development become discernible. The Dutch had outdone the Portuguese in the Indian Ocean by creating a monopoly in fine spices and had in turn been eclipsed by the English East India Company's development of a new market in Indian cotton calicoes.[68] This process of 'creative destruction' was conducive to the formation of large business corporations. With their vast amounts of capital and organizational muscle they did not simply have to accept terms in the market, they were able to reshape conditions, affect or even manipulate prices and draw benefit from their market power. The monopolistic influence of such business corporations might be taken for a classic example of uneconomic rent-seeking. But, Schumpeter objected, when the wider market situation is highly dynamic and subject to radical change, the rents enjoyed by large corporations rather served to provide a measure of certainty and stability. They gave reassurance that the very large investments of capital which were required to push the industrial frontier forward could be expected to generate a return before everything changed again. In short, erected on shifting sand, these monopoly rents gave corporations something to hold onto in the 'perennial gale' of capitalist economic change.[69]

As we saw above, however, corporations did not shape the long-term development of Roman economic life. They emerged only in the sphere of state-contracting, during the middle to late Republic, and were scaled back under the early Principate. Schumpeter's insight is, thus, not automatically transferable to an analysis of the Roman imperial economy. In fact, North, Wallis and Weingast point out that the conditions prevailing under a natural state-regime generally make a continuous dynamic of 'creative destruction' impossible. The ruling rent-receiving groups are unwilling to accept the societal changes that would follow in its wake. A state of constant reform and economic revolution would undermine their position of privilege, which depends on restricting the access of other groups to economic resources.[70] Intense external competition between natural states, however, might force reform and push a society to the doorstep conditions of modernity by allowing opening access to unleash the process of perennial economic change, but only just. This is what is believed to have happened in Europe from, say, the seventeenth to the nineteenth century. Faced with foreign competition, ruling elites had continuously to explore new solutions, to strengthen the muscle of their states and avoid falling behind, or risk destruction – which quite a few of them actually suffered.[71]

Roman society, however, steered a different course; it conquered most of its rivals to impose a hegemonic and imperial peace on the Mediterranean world. With no serious competition left, there was little to challenge the continuous hold of the ruling, rent-drawing groups on society and no urgent need to introduce radical institutional changes. The economic history of the imperial monarchy is not one punctuated by a succession of organizational and commercial innovations.[72] Instead one is faced with a scenario where different provinces, at different times, make their entry to wider Mediterranean networks with the same types of goods. Italian exports of wine and ceramic tableware, for instance, were replaced by Gallic. Later, Spanish olive oil was eased out by North African exports of oil and tableware.[73] This was the key discovery of the great historian and archaeologist, Rostovtzeff;[74] but more of the same was not the economic tragedy that he made it out to be. It was a sign that landowners around the provinces gradually became able to benefit from the privileges offered by empire and introduce a more intensive exploitation of land and people to sustain urban lifestyles with conspicuous consumption in the imperial mode.[75] In the terminology of North, Wallis and Weingast, the natural state was maturing by co-opting a wider segment of powerful groups within the ruling coalition. Under the emperors, the frontier of urbanized society was pushed westward and northward.[76]

To explain the seemingly paradoxical coexistence of this productive development with the reaffirmation of rent-seeking privilege, it may be useful to turn back to Schumpeter once more. Rent-seeking might turn out to be productive if the market situation is volatile and unpredictable: this was his general proposition. He, of course, had the highly dynamic and competitive markets of American industrialism in mind. But uncertainty is not only the product of accelerating development, it may also be a result of weak integration of markets. Equally at work during the 1930s, Ronald Coase, the 1991 Nobel laureate in economics, offered a related explanation for the presence of firms in economic life. Had markets been operating perfectly and without friction, organization would not be necessary. Markets would take care of the division of labor and co-ordinate the activities of individual producers. In real life, however, it was often too cumbersome to obtain reliable information about external partners or ensure reliable supplies of materials needed for one's own production. It might, therefore, be more profitable to assemble a larger group of actors and place them under the same hierarchical command structure to organize their activities.[77]

By analogy, both Coase's concern about market friction and the potential value of hierarchical organization are easily transferred to the Roman case. The constraints of pre-industrial technology presented formidable obstacles to the integration of markets and their ability to mobilize economic resources.[78] There is some disagreement about the level of integration reached under the Pax Romana. But even those that favor a higher degree of integration than I do would by implication have to concede that the Mediterranean world before the imposition of the imperial peace was far from an integrated market.[79] Many resources, human and non-human, were left un- or under-exploited by the free operation of markets compared to what could have been achieved in a setting more akin to the low-friction universe of classical and neo-classical theory. The formation of empire radically changed the capacity of hierarchical organizations, aristocratic households and government in particular. They were able to impose greater demands on wider populations. Lands and mineral fields were confiscated, people enslaved or faced with higher demands for rents and taxes. In short, idle hands were put to work, immobilia set in circulation and leisure reduced. The creation of an imperial hierarchy of power intensified the mobilization of resources to a degree which markets could not achieve unaided by the muscles of political power.[80]

When under the imperial peace, the frequency of disruptive warfare declined and extraction became more routinized, Rome moved from a basic to a mature natural state. As the consumption of rents settled into a more stable pattern, markets may even have been able marginally to optimize the utilization of resources.[81] It is noticeable that the efficiency (the ratio of clay to contents volume) of transport amphorae improved noticeably from the middle and late Republic to the early and high Empire.[82] At the same time, factional conflict, atavistic and ruthless, regulated the access of rent-taking elites, at court and in provincial society, to economic resources. The spectacular outcome of one of the trials reported by Pliny was precisely an expression of rival factions seeking revenge for past conflicts over power, property, and status. For, as the senator explained, our ill-starred provincial delegate "gained no protection from legal procedure . . . So intense was the ill-will directed against this generally outrageous person. Like many others he had exploited the times of Domitian" – the emperor who fallen foul of a large segment of the imperial aristocracy and been assassinated – "and had been chosen by his province to collect evidence, not for his honesty . . . but because of his hatred of Classicus (who had previously banished him) . . . Two consulars hurt him [considerably] by testifying that he had likewise appeared for the court under Domitian among the accusers of Salvius Liberalis."[83] The imperial court served as an arena of aristocratic politics, struggle, and settling of longstanding scores. To quote, in conclusion, the assessment of North, Wallis and Weingast: "the Roman Empire over the next four hundred years moved back and forth along the dimensions of social organizations that define basic and mature natural states."[84]

Notes

1 Livy comments that, with the mythical reigns of Romulus and Numa completed, the Roman *civitas* had now learned to master both war-making and the organization of civic life. I am deeply grateful to Peter Garnsey, who generously read and commented on the first draft of this piece, and to Joe Manning and a seminar audience at Yale for helpful discussion.
2 See Raaflaub 1996 for an analysis of how and when the Romans developed a 'wolfish' imperialism.
3 Livy 1.10.6. His chapters 9–13 narrate the episode with the abduction of the young woman and the ensuing conflicts.
4 Livy 1.10.4.
5 Macchiavelli *Discorsi* 1.1–6, with Pocock 1975: ch. 7. In general: North, Wallis and Weingast 2009: 195–205, 244–5.
6 Hobson 1902, in particular Part I, Chapter 4, branding British imperialism as the product of a parasitical class of financiers. Smith 1976: Part IV contains a long assault on the "mercantile" system, with grants of privileges and monopolies to promote colonies and certain groups of traders at the expense of the commonwealth.
7 Bang 2009a.
8 Lo Cascio 2007.
9 Livy 1.13.
10 Scheidel, Morris, and Saller 2007: 11.
11 Crone 1989: ch. 3–4.
12 Clapham 1985: ch. 3–4; Fukuyama 2004: ch. 2; Kiser and Sacks 2009.
13 Garnsey and Saller 1987: ch. 2.
14 Cf. the description of Joseph *BJ* 7.132–52. See Beard 2007 for a recent discussion of the multifaceted and perennially changing character of the triumph, but the celebration of booty was a constant, well brought out by Östenberg 2009.
15 Levi 1988: ch. 2; Olson 2000.
16 Steensgaard 1981; Lane 1966: ch. 22–25.
17 Polyb. 3.24; Harris 1979: 59 and more generally ch. 2, also for what follows.
18 Finley 1978 offers a convenient "balance sheet" of Roman imperialism and the tributes it generated. Dmitriev 2009 and other attempts to resurrect Badian 1968: ch. 2 ignore the enormous wealth flowing from Empire, *cui bono?*
19 Broadhead 2007.
20 Lowe 2009: ch. 3–4.
21 Salmeri 2011.
22 Bang 2009b: 106.
23 Cic. *Off.* 2.76.
24 Hopkins 1978: ch. 1 for Roman army size and mobilization levels. Compare the discussions of early modern European state formation of Brewer 1989 and Tilly 1992.
25 Wolters 1999; Howgego 1995: ch. 3; Hopkins 1980 on the growth of the coin supply; Crawford 1970 for the basic study of the republican coinage.

26 Brunt 1987 is still fundamental.
27 Scheidel 2005a.
28 Scheidel and Friesen 2009; Lo Cascio 2007; Hopkins 1995/6.
29 Bang 2008: ch. 2.
30 Steensgaard 1990: 102–6, 151; further Braudel 1985: 453.
31 Frier 2000 and Scheidel 2007a for basic discussions of the population in the Roman Empire.
32 Wilson forthcoming b.
33 Cf. Gabrielsen 1997 who points out that the attempt to harm Rhodes had less disruptive economic effects than used to be thought.
34 As Scheidel 2009a observes, in terms of economic change, it is the Republican era, not the high empire which comes across as the most dynamic phase in ancient Mediterranean history.
35 Nicolet 1966: 285–312, 317–40 on landed property, the equestrians and the *publicani*.
36 On the *societates publicanorum*, see the studies of Badian 1972; Cimma 1981; Malmendier 2002.
37 Weber 1924: 28, analyzed by Love 1991: ch. 1 and Capogrossi Colognesi 2000, ch. 5, 8, 9.
38 Cic. *De imp. Cn. Pomp.* 7.19 (my translation).
39 So Malmendier 2005; followed by Hollander 2007: 49–51.
40 Gai. *Inst.* 3.151–2. The issue of whether the *societates publicanorum* were invested with a legal persona under the Republic is obscured by the fact that the surviving legal evidence dates from the imperial period and was only excerpted under Justinian, half a millennium after the great Republican companies had flourished. Legal scholars tend to see the strict juridical acquisition of corporate status, the right to *corpus habere* in the words of the second-century CE jurist Gaius (*Dig.* 3.4.1.pr.), as a development of imperial law under the emperors (Cimma 1981: 95–8; Malmendier 2002: 251–9). But it is in any case clear that the companies of the *publicani* were already differentiated from the normal private partnership (*societas*) during the Republic, and Badian (1972: 69) is probably right, based on Tac., *Ann.* 13.50.3, to argue that this also entailed a form of legal persona, though not fully in the sense of modern company law.
41 *Dig.* 17.2.59 (Pomponius).
42 Badian 1972: 100–6. The key evidence for the existence of something akin to shares is an oblique passage in Cicero's speech against Vatinius (*Vat.* 29): "... eripuerisne partis illo tempore carissimas partim a Caesare, partim a publicanis?" – not much to go by, since most of the argument has to be based on conjecture. Caution seems advisable.
43 Steensgaard 1973; Prakash 1999 (with the contrast more muted).
44 Chaudhuri 1985: ch. 3; Subrahmanyam and Thomas 1991.
45 Thus Ulp. *Dig.* 39, 4, 12: ("quantae audaciae, quantae temeritatis sint publicanorum factiones, nemo est qui nesciat"). See Van Nijf 2008: 281–5 on the opprobrium commonly clinging to tax- and customs collectors in the Roman world.
46 The classic examples of which would be Cicero's *Verrine Orations* (Prag 2007 for a recent collection of essays examining this set of speeches) and Sallust's *The War against Jugurtha*.

47 Cic., *Att.* 5.21; 6.1, 2 allow us to follow the affair. The best analysis is still Rauh 1986. It was normal for members of the Roman elite to invest in loans to provincials, see Shatzman 1975: 77–8, and 372–3 for a basic summary of the "facts" in Cicero's dealings with Brutus' loan.

48 A practice which was common and well established, see Verboven 2002: 312–14.

49 Cic., *Att.* 5.21.12; 6.1.7.

50 Cic., *Att.* 6.1.15–16; 6.2.4–5.

51 Badian 1972: 113–14 was uncharacteristically credulous in accepting Cicero's claims at face value.

52 Brunt 1990: ch. 17 for a basic discussion making the important point that publican companies continued to farm customs dues in some provinces for a long time into the imperial monarchy.

53 For the concept, see Olson 2000: ch. 1.

54 Suet. *Tib.* 32: "boni pastoris esse tondere pecus, non deglubere." Levi 1988: ch. 4.

55 As can be surmised for instance from Cic. *2 Verr.* 3.12–15 (recently discussed by France 2007).

56 Badian 1972: 90–2. More cautious was Shatzman 1975: 201–4, but his interest was mainly to undermine the idea that equites and senators were opposed to each other as groups. A governor who was too zealous would face the opposition also of senators with an interest in the exploitation of his province.

57 Neesen 1980: 25–86 brings out the wide regional variety in the regime of taxation still prevailing under the emperors. Nicolet 1988a is illuminating, even if he tends to underestimate this aspect in the ability of the government to have the empire recorded and registered.

58 Joseph *BJ* 2.117–18; *AJ* 18.1–10, with Goodman 1987: 43–4; Millar 1993: 46.

59 Cf. Van Nijf 2008: 293–7 on the weak controls put in place by the state to contain the activities of tax-collectors. Corruption was endemic and institutionalized.

60 Compare Oliver 1988: no. 254 with *OGIS* 669 (trans. in Sherk 1988: no. 80), an edict of the prefect of Egypt in which one can find the same practices reviled more than a century earlier.

61 Plin. *Ep.* 3.9 (quotation from §34) and 4.9. See Brunt 1990: ch. 4 on the continuing relevance of extortion trials under the emperors.

62 *SB* 6.9207 (*diaseismon*) (trans. in Campbell 1994, no. 297); *P.Raineri* 20.75 (an account from Hermopolis, a German translation of which can be found in Wessely 1894: 88, no. 289). The evidence was collected and discussed by MacMullen 1963: 88–9, most recently Adams 2007b: 217–29.

63 Adams 2007b: 222.

64 Rathbone 2008: 276–8.

65 Bang 2008: ch. 2.

66 North, Wallis and Weingast 2009: 30–41 (quotation from p. 30).

67 As Adam Smith argued in his classic *Wealth of Nations* (1976: 374–5 = Book II, Chapter V, Paragraph 37), mercantilist privileges had diverted capital away from its most productive employments in Europe and favored some groups at the expense of others (1976: 660–2 = Book IV, Chapter VIII, Paragraphs 49–54).

68 Chaudhuri 1985: ch. 3–4; Steensgaard 1990: 120–8; Landes 1998: ch. 9–11.

69 Schumpeter 2010 (1942), especially ch. 7 and 8, building on 5 and 6. The expression of "the perennial gale of creative destruction" occurs on pp. 73 and 76 of the 2010 edition I have used.

70 North, Wallis and Weingast 2009: 115–17.

71 Tilly 1992; Brewer 1989.

72 A point conceded, but explained away, by Rathbone 2003: 212, 225–6. More generally Scheidel 2009a.

73 Panella 1993; Panella and Tchernia 2002; Carandini 1983. Morley 2007b for an excellent recent discussion of the economic meaning of the observable pattern.

74 Rostovtzeff 1957: 162–77 (decentralization of economic activity, Italian products being replaced by provincial); von Freyberg 1989 for a discussion by a modern economist.

75 Bang 2008: ch. 2; Woolf 2001; Tchernia 1986; 2010.

76 Scheidel 2007a: 80–6.

77 Coase 1937.

78 Bang 2008, ch. 3; Erdkamp 2005. More generally about pre-industrial conditions, see Persson 1999; Braudel 1966.

79 Reger 1994 for an analysis of the limits to Hellenistic economic integration.

80 Wickham 2005 confirms this scenario for the late Roman world.

81 As suggested by the "taxes and trade" model advanced by Keith Hopkins (1980; 2000), positing a degree of integration for a thin veneer of the imperial economy.

82 Cf. the table in Peacock and Williams 1986: 52. On the other hand, integration was still not intense enough to force convergence. It is noticeable that two regionally very distinct traditions of oil amphorae design, with significantly different carrying efficiencies, the globular Baetican (Dressel 20) and the more cylindrical North African, co-existed for close to 200 years, with both enjoying wide dissemination in the Roman Empire.

83 Plin. *Ep.* 3.9.31–3 (translation modified from Betty Radice in the Loeb Classical Library).

84 North, Wallis and Weingast 2009: 48–9.

11: Transport

Colin Adams

The role of transport in the economy of the Roman world is far from clearly understood, and is a controversial issue in modern historical debate.[1] Our knowledge is hampered by two main factors: first, the nature of our evidence. Ancient authors were generally not interested in how commodities were transported, and really only comment on the exceptional. And second, our understanding of transport has arguably been hampered by both a failure of modern scholars to fully appreciate its complexities, and by, it has to be said, in some cases, willfully bending the facts, and more seriously evidence, to fit preconceived 'models.'[2] The purpose of this chapter is to review evidence for transport, survey modern views of its role, assess the still prevailing orthodoxy that it restricted economic growth, and suggest a way forward to understanding its real capacity and function in the Roman economy. It can only scratch the surface of a very large and complex topic, which deserves a full treatment.[3]

Conditioning factors

The geographer Strabo makes the following comment on the Mediterranean, but more importantly its relations with the lands on which it bounds: "It is the sea more than anything else that defines the contours of the land and gives it its shape, by forming gulfs, deep seas, straits, and likewise isthmuses, peninsulas and promontories; but both the rivers and the mountains assist the seas herein."[4] While it is clear that for Strabo the sea is the principal factor, he raises the important point that rivers and mountains are the points of connection to inland regions. Indeed, an essential part of how Strabo viewed his world is how specific points (cities, ports) and wider regions are connected with each other:

> But it is above all worthwhile to note again a characteristic
> of this region (Toulouse) which I have spoken of

> before – the harmonious arrangement of the country with reference not only to rivers, but also to the sea, both the outer sea and the inner alike; for one might find if he set his thoughts upon it, that this is not the least factor in the excellence of the regions – I mean the fact that the necessities of life are easily interchanged by everyone with everyone else and that the advantages that have arisen therefrom are common to all.[5]

The Mediterranean as a region is defined by its connectivity. It displayed similar climatic features – hot summers and mild winters – but we should not exaggerate uniformity as many scholars have done, as this is one of geographical conception rather than reality.[6] One of the principal themes brought out by Horden and Purcell's *Corrupting Sea* is that of a 'pronounced local irregularity', of the differences between micro-regions within the Mediterranean.[7] This regional diversity is important, for it naturally undermines one of the two key limitations placed on the ancient economy by primitivist approaches, that due to the similarities of climate and topography, areas adjoining the Mediterranean had the same needs and surpluses, thus there was little stimulus to trade. This notion depends on us imagining, as Harris has pointed out, widespread autarky, but would specifically rule out a regional nature to the Mediterranean.[8] The reality was quite different, there was short and long range trade, *cabotage*, ferrying, and long voyages, both by land and sea.[9]

The Mediterranean Sea offered easy communication, albeit determined by the patterns of winds and weather. As we shall see, rivers provided easy access to regions inland, where they were navigable. As time went on, the Romans constructed a complex system of roads, further extending transport and communication, and often improving on pre-existing local infrastructure. But just as the geography of sea and rivers determined possibilities for transport, the topography of inland regions also had a profound effect. Arid, mountainous terrain is bound to have limited the construction of roads to some extent. Indeed it has been suggested that the topography of Mediterranean countries generally was ill-suited to the use of wagons, which prefer flat and easy terrain.[10] While this argument cannot be pressed too far – the Greeks had built impressive roads through mountainous Achaea, and Roman roads traversed some impressively difficult terrain – terrain that encouraged the use of pack animals, which were by far the most widely used form of transport by land.[11] Even in Egypt, for example, the use of pack animals was necessary given the highly irrigated land, where canals and drainage channels cut up the countryside.[12]

Before considering these matters in more detail, it is necessary to establish the orthodox view of the role of transport in the Roman economy.

Orthodoxies

Most discussions of the limitation of Roman transport concentrate on the inefficiency of land transport and trace their arguments back to Cedric Yeo, who argued that long distance land transport in the Roman empire was economically unviable, except in the case of luxury goods: after making the bold claim on the "singular extent" of our knowledge about manufacture and agriculture, "we know practically nothing," he states, "about the equally important problem of transportation beyond the fact that it was costly and difficult."[13] The fundamental issues, however, can be traced further back. Linn Westermann, in a more thoughtful paper than Yeo's, raised a number of central issues: time and capacity.[14] The speed of travel was slow, and the capacity of ships, wagons, and animals was small – but the main issue is relative; time (the length of journeys) had to be reduced, while capacity had to be increased, in order for significant progress to be made.

The other key limiting factors, according to this orthodox view, were methods of transport themselves. Transport has been described as the greatest failure of ancient technology.[15] Limitations in the effectiveness of transport, the seasonal nature of Roman seafaring, made the long distance transport of commodities impossible except where they were connected to the supply of food to the city of Rome or its armies. Major technological advances, however, although they certainly took place, took a long time to be accepted, and Westermann argues that even if steam power had had a very early introduction, it is unlikely it would have encouraged speedier change.

In terms of technology, the ineffectiveness of animal harnessing systems has been adduced as one of the main limiting factors on Roman land transport. The arguments go back to the influential study of Lefebvre des Noëttes, who suggested that the design of harnesses limited the load a team of two horses could pull to 500kg.[16] His argument is based on the Theodosian Code, which stipulated 500kg to be the maximum allowable weight carried by wagons of the *cursus publicus*.[17] But this, surely, is not a measure of what animals could pull, rather an attempt to limit possible abuse of the *cursus publicus*. His arguments are also 'hippocentric,' and therefore his whole thesis is a red herring; most heavy loads would have been pulled by oxen (or sometimes camels, at least in Egypt and Africa). Lefebvre des Noëttes's theories are now largely discredited, and recent work by Spruytte and Raepsaet in particular has shown conclusively that good traction could be obtained and that animals in the Roman period were capable of pulling significant loads.[18]

Dwelling on the limitations of ancient transport technology is a recurring feature of works on the ancient economy. This emphasis is misguided, and we should instead focus on the real innovation that took place during a millennium. Animals' efficiency can only have improved with the development of the Roman road system. The construction over many years of the principal roads of Italy, the *Via Appia*, *Via Flaminia* and *Via Aemilia*, gradually led to the development, over a long period, of road systems throughout the provinces.

To time and capacity must be added cost. For Yeo, this was the most serious obstacle, and he has been followed by a long list of scholars.[19] It is necessary here to set out Yeo's calculations of land transport costs in detail, for they form the basis of calculations on the relative costs of transport contained in subsequent studies. They were based on figures in Cato's *De Agri Cultura* and Diocletian's *Edict of Maximum Prices*. Cato's discussion of the cost of transporting an olive press has famously been deployed in many discussions.[20] He gives the cost of transporting a mill bought in Suessa, 25 miles from his estate, and one bought in Pompeii, 75 miles away; transport from Suessa adds 11 per cent to the cost of the mill, while 39 per cent would be added if the mill were transported from Pompeii.[21] But further comparison of the overall cost suggests only a 15 per cent difference (95 sesterces) in the cost – not of much significance to someone like Cato. Two basic points further obscure proper understanding. First, an olive press is a high-cost item designed for long use, a considerable capital investment, and the cost is necessarily spread over time. Second, Yeo goes on to convert costs for the olive press directly into equivalent costs for grain; hardly credible.

A letter written by the younger Pliny, as governor of the province of Bithynia-Pontus, to the Emperor Trajan is also commonly adduced as evidence for the high cost of land transport relative to water. It contains Pliny's request for the services of an engineer to act as a surveyor in a project to build a canal from Lake Sophon to the sea, for "marble, farm produce, wood and timber for building are easily and cheaply brought by boat as far as the main road; after which everything has to be taken on to the sea by cart, with great difficulty and increased expense."[22] Although there are some difficulties of interpretation with this text, and it is unclear if the project was ever undertaken, Pliny's statement seems clear. Pliny's justification for the project, however, should be regarded as a specific case, and not a general rule. Specific topographical and economic conditions may have underlain the project, and may not be generally valid, and we must also be mindful of Pliny's special remit in the province, carefully to inspect provincial building projects and their finances; this may have prompted and justified a more detailed study of this project.

As far as the *Edict of Maximum Prices* is concerned, the edict presents freight-rates by sea and land, and therefore, on the surface, might allow for an understanding of relative cost. The rates for sea transport are given as payable per *kastrensis modius* of wheat (and vary between specified destinations). The freight charge for land transport is dependant upon the cost of wheat and its transport by wagon (with a set load of 1,200 Roman pounds) for 100 miles. This allowed Duncan-Jones to speculate that the cost of shipping wheat from Alexandria to Rome would be 1.3 per cent of its value, while transporting wheat by land would be 55 per cent per 100 miles. However, there are problems here. Walter Scheidel has suggested that the maximum costs of goods (say wheat at 100 *denarii*) must have included freight charges in order for the whole transaction to be under the maximum permitted cost.[23] Additionally, the freight charges that are mentioned in the edict would, if applied, mean a much lower percentage cost for transport than has been suggested in the orthodox view. Whatever the case, it seems impossible to extract from the edict any clear indication of real transport costs. Further, the edict does not contain rates for river or canal transport, and our evidence is noticeably thin for this. A papyrus from Egypt preserves rates of transport by canal from Arsinoe to Ptolemais Hormou at 6.3 per cent of the cargo's value. The relative cost of the different modes of transport, then, according to the orthodox view, works out at 1; 4.9; 34–42.[24] As A. H. M. Jones puts it, "it was cheaper to ship grain from one end of the Mediterranean to the other than to cart it 75 miles."[25] This all seems confused, and a red-herring.

Jones goes on to discuss the slow speed of land transport in comparison to transport by sea, but although he does discuss the hazards of maritime transport, he does not stress this enough, and also fails to expand upon the effects that poor weather and seasonality had on the overall speed of maritime journeys, for as we will see below, the information we have on the speed of such journeys can be difficult to interpret. Jones notes the importance of riverine transport, and that rivers such as the Nile, Danube, and Rhone made transport of grain possible, especially where grain-producing land was close to ports and where markets (for Jones, mainly cities) were similarly situated. But too much is made of these arguments. We should not forget that grain and other commodities still need to be taken to port by land, as is certainly clear in the Egyptian evidence.[26] Surely it is the case that most settlements had reasonable access to either coasts or navigable streams, or to good roads connecting to them. Few were totally isolated, and even those that arguably were, for example, Sitifis in Numidia, found ways to cope, with a mixture of self-sufficiency (but not without the marketing of a significant surplus of agricultural and manufactured goods) and an economy stimulated by the presence of large imperial estates, the produce of which was taken to ports.[27]

Finley was largely supportive of Jones's view – arguing that "individuals could not move bulky merchandise long distances by land as a normal activity."[28] He further denies the economic importance of Roman roads, seeing them as purely military in character, stating also that the limitations of animal harnessing and traction were not improved by the presence of good roads. For Finley, rivers were more important, and he cites Gaul as important in this respect.[29] In Britain, for example, despite the presence of roads, and the development of villages and towns, the average distance traveled to markets given the limits and cost of transport was four or five miles.[30]

This view of transport remained prevalent until work by Keith Hopkins opened new directions. He developed the so-called "taxes and trades" model of the Roman economy.[31] Hopkins argued that the imposition of taxes on Roman provinces stimulated trade, necessary for the payment of such taxes.[32] Regional economies were stimulated, and this coincided with growing sophistication in production and manufacture and increased monetization. Most important for our purposes here, he argued that although maritime and riverine transport were important, land transport could not be seen as a poor relation, but must be seen as part of a wider system of transport. This idea will be developed later, when we consider how integrated transport was in the Roman world. But Hopkins goes further, not only does he attenuate the notion of the same needs and surpluses (which Finley and Jones would see as a limiting factor on trade), he also considers the scale of transport. First, he notes that there "were in fact different zones within the Roman economy, fertile zones, arid zones, river-accessible and land-locked zones, high cost and low cost zones, mining, pastoral and arable zones".[33] This along with the imposition of taxes and the need to generate income to pay them, provided a dynamic for trade. He gives estimates for the scale of transport. These estimates, certainly not accurate but effective notions of scale, suggest that very large amounts of staples (wheat, wine, and olive oil) were transported middle and long distances; perhaps something like 460,000 tons, which on his calculations based on the price of wheat represented some 210 million sesterces (higher prices for wine and oil would increase this).[34] As Pucci puts it, "the statement that ancient long distance trade concerned only luxury goods is quite simply untrue."[35]

Responding to orthodoxies

The arguments of Jones, Finley, and their followers who want to see an economy with little commerce and long distance transport sit very uncomfortably with the reality that another view of the evidence can provide. As already noted, there are problems with the interpretation of Cato's figures. Equally, the *Edict of Maximum Prices* as a whole is poorly understood, and this is especially the case with transport costs. On the misinterpretation of these figures, Horden and Purcell have this to say: "these figures do not concern economic costs but maximum permitted hauliers' rates. It would be an unwise industrial manager who estimated his transportation costs on a quotation from Pickfords."[36] As they note, it is not possible to calculate the relative costs of transport with any accuracy, as there are too many economic and social variables. Egyptian papyri provide perhaps our best evidence for this, but even they fall short of providing definitive answers.[37] Despite copious numbers of texts, we have little specific evidence for transport rates. But, more importantly, we have much evidence for the socioeconomic environment in which transport took place. On both large estates and peasant small-holdings, strategies were developed through which transport costs could be reduced. Utilizing their own animals, farmers could absorb the cost of transporting produce to markets. But price variations in markets also had to be factored in, and we have evidence that producers responded to this.[38] There was also a large transport pool. By this I mean there were a large number of animals, and a large number of available laborers within the agricultural economy, who could view transport as a negative opportunity cost. Animals had to be kept busy (and in Egypt they were probably busier than most), so they were deployed on transport tasks when not engaged in agricultural ones. This allowed their owners to supplement their income.[39] There is no reason to believe that these features of economic life were unique to Egypt, but were almost certainly widespread.

We need to think about transport in more sophisticated ways. In order to facilitate this, I want to discuss maritime, riverine, and land transport, before considering how these could come together into an 'integrated transport system.'

MARITIME

In a passage concerning Pompey's defeat of pirates in the Mediterranean, Cicero mentions maritime routes (*cursus maritimi*) which brought together the Mediterranean "as though it were a single harbor."[40] There certainly were shipping lanes that were favored, but Cicero obscures the difficulties of sailing in the Mediterranean, where winds and currents were often in opposition and imposed a fairly rigid seasonality on sea travel, and we should remember the limitations of Roman geographical knowledge. The inability of Roman ships to reach effectively (sails at 90 degrees to the wind) and to beat close to the wind also imposed restrictions.[41] But we should be wary of too rigid an approach, as Horden and Purcell have noted. Sailors certainly braved the winter months, and it is clear that local journeys, cabotage, and ferrying (*porthmeutice*) could take place at any stage of the year, weather permitting.[42] A strict seasonal approach may have been present in the transport of tax grain from Africa or Alexandria, where risk was not politically acceptable, but private merchants may have braved the winter months in search of good prices (demand for goods may remain constant, and if fewer goods are making it to market, prices will be higher).[43] We also need to factor in fluctuations in sizes and quality of harvests from year to year. "Economic and other factors constantly induced ships to voyage away from the main trunk route sea lanes," and we should add, frequently sail outside the summer season.[44] We should be mindful too of the role of cabotage. Coastal voyages are mentioned in our sources, and local conditions naturally affected patterns of travel. When Pliny the Younger traveled to his province of Bithynia-Pontus, he wrote to the emperor Trajan that his intention was to travel "partly by coastal boat and partly by carriage."[45]

We have some interesting information preserved in our sources about the speed of maritime transport, often adduced, but it is not without difficulty of interpretation. In the context of discussing the qualities of flax, Pliny praises sails made from it, and the consequent speed of sailing times:

> Is there a greater miracle than the flax plant which brings Egypt so close to Italy that of two governors of Egypt, Galerius, who reached Alexandria on the seventh day from the straits of Messina, and Balbillus on the sixth, and that in the summer fifteen years later the praetorian senator Valerius Marianus crossed from Puteoli to Alexandria in nine days with a very gentle breeze? That there is a plant which brings Cadiz within seven day's sail from the straits of Gibraltar to Ostia, and thither Spain within four days and the province of Narbonne within three, and Africa within two.[46]

But these figures must represent the fastest possible journeys, and do not reflect normal conditions or journey times.[47] Nor does Pliny here indicate how long it took to travel from Rome to Messina: the illustration does not detail the full journey time, but only part of it.[48] Other evidence, free from the exceptional, may be instructive, and Duncan Jones has attempted to assess communication speed using documentary sources – establishing how long it took residents of Egypt to learn of the accession of a new emperor.[49] He finds that journey times could be much slower, and were, in addition, hampered by seasonality.[50] There were other risks: difficulties of navigation, treacherous waters and straits, and, of course, piracy. For example, ships sailing from the eastern coast of Greece and Asia Minor, in order to avoid the open sea and the difficulties of navigation thus presented, had to negotiate the dangerous Cape of Malea at the southern tip of the Peloponnese.[51] A merchant from Phrygia, Flavius Zeuxis, celebrated his successful navigation around the Cape of Malea seventy-two times on his tomb inscription, such was the cape's notoriety.[52] The Straits of Messene between Sicily and Italy presented a similarly unavoidable challenge. An equally serious threat to sea travel was, of course, piracy. Certain seas and peoples were notorious, the Aetolians and Illyrians for example, but the problem lessened in the late Republic after Pompey's successful campaigns, and the *Pax Augusta* brought further improvements, as Strabo puts it (not without Augustan bias), "all pirates are eliminated, and hence all sailors feel wholly at ease."[53]

While the details of exceptional voyages and the exotic nature of sea travel attracted the attention of writers like Pliny, they show less concern with details of the speed of river or land transport, unless there was something remarkable about the routes traveled – Pliny gives details, for example, of the routes traversing the Eastern Desert of Egypt.

Despite clear limitations with ancient shipping, significant advances in ships and sailing were made during our period.[54] Developments were made in sail design and rigging, but most importantly, improvements in hull design allowed for much bigger ships; pumps were also introduced. Lucian's *Isis*, at somewhere between 1,200 and 1,300 tons, may not have been unique, but was clearly exceptional.[55] Legislation limited the smallest size of ships carrying grain for the *annona* to 68 tons (10,000 *modii*), but the average size of ships seems to have been about 340 tons (50,000 *modii*).[56] The transportation of stone and timber demanded large capacity, but in some cases necessitated the development of specifically designed ships and barges, the most famous being a ship commissioned by Caligula at *c.*1300 tons to carry an Egyptian obelisk.[57] Although exceptional, there must have been quite a number of these vessels, if we take into account the scale of imperial building projects, such as the Pantheon and its fifty-foot columns from Mons Claudianus.[58]

RIVERS

Rivers, as Strabo makes clear, provided navigable highways deep inland, further adding to this connectivity. Their tributaries, if navigable, extended their reach. Ports, whether on coast or on rivers, were met by roads, most of them major roads, but they in turn were connected to minor roads and tracks. Rivers provided easily accessible transport for communities (which often were located close to a river, for both drinking water, transport, and other reasons). Even when navigation became difficult further upstream, rafts, rather than boats could be used, and commodities like timber could be floated downstream.[59] Indeed, without rivers, trade in timber would have been severely hampered. But rivers did present problems of navigation: swift streams or currents, rapids, waterfalls, and narrows, presented difficulties, some rivers froze in winter months, such as the Danube, and others flooded, as the Nile famously did. Severe problems were presented by sailing in darkness, as unlike modern times, few lights would have been visible, except where rivers flowed through urbanized areas. Indeed, on the Nile at least, shipping contracts often specified that boats moored at safe points during the hours of darkness: "he (the ship's captain) shall anchor at the safest and designated anchorages at the proper hours."[60]

Rivers provided inland communication – for Pliny the Elder, they naturally offered connections between places, especially important in regions in which roads were absent. Strabo's well-known description of the rivers of Gaul illustrates just how much territory could be opened up and made accessible to ships. But importantly, he also shows how rivers are linked by roads: "But since the Rhodanus is swift and difficult to sail up, some of the traffic from here preferably goes by land on the wagons, that is, all the traffic that goes to the Avernians and the Liger river – albeit in a part of its course the Rhodanus draws close to these too; still the fact that the road is level and not long (about 800 *stadia*) is an inducement not to use the voyage upstream, since it is easier to go by land; from here, however, the road is naturally succeeded by the Liger; and it flows from the Cemmenus Mountain to the ocean".[61] For both Strabo and Pliny, rivers were important highways affording transport, trade and commercial activity, and employment. Pliny's description of rivers in Italy makes this clear, especially in the case of the Tiber and its tributaries, which were central to the prosperity and growth of Rome.[62] The Tiber was "navigable for vessels of whatever size from the Mediterranean, and is a most placid trader (*mercator placidissimus*) in the produce of all the earth, with perhaps more villas on its banks and overlooking it than all the other rivers in the whole world."[63] But rivers had varying levels of navigability and the uses of various forms of shipping to deal with this: the Baetis (Guadalquivir), which was one of Spain's most important rivers, was navigable as far as Hispalis "for merchant vessels of considerable size, that is, for a distance not much short of 500 stadia; the cities higher up the stream as far as Ilipa, for the smaller merchant vessels; and as far as Corduba, for the river boats."[64] Elsewhere in Hispania, the Cilbus (Guadalete) provided access inland from Portus Gaditanus, and on the Eastern coast, the Ebro provided vital access to the interior from the port at Dertosa.

Ports acted as nodal points, connecting maritime, riverine, and land routes – the notion of land routes as "the shortest distance between two prominent seamarks or navigable rivers" perhaps still underestimates their importance.[65] As Geoffrey Rickman has stated, ports "must be thought of as great clusters of facilities, set in wide webs of communication by road and by water."[66] Many good examples exist, but only a few can be presented here. Strabo celebrates the good fortune of the region of Turdetania in southern Baetica, for while it produced a wide range of commodities, its ports were served by the river Baetis and others, as well as navigable estuaries, which meant produce could be exported easily, including the valuable mineral resources of the mountains to the north.[67] At the head of the Adriatic, the cities of Ravenna and Patavium lay at the head of the great plain of the river Padus, which offered rich land, as well as riverine access to the interior, but also access to the *Via Aemilia*, linking Ariminum, Bononia, Mutina, Parma, and Placentia (the latter also served directly by the Padus). Communication was enhanced by the construction of a canal, the *Fossa Augusta*, which further integrated river and land transport routes with Ravenna as the terminal, further canals being added over time.[68] Further north, the port of Aquileia benefitted from easy access to the sea, a navigable river heading north, the Natiso, and good road communications: it was from here that the Illyrians "load on wagons and carry inland the products of the sea, and wine stored in wooden barrels, and also olive oil, and the former get in exchange slaves, cattle, and hides."[69] In Gaul, rivers formed essential highways, as we have seen. The port at Narbo offered road communication towards Toulouse and eventually the Atlantic coast. Most importantly, Arelete gave access to the Rhodanus, leading deep into central Gaul.

ROADS

The development over time of a complex road system, essentially connecting Hadrian's Wall with the cities of Roman Syria, extended connectivity beyond the Mediterranean region as the Roman Empire grew. Early Republican roads, however, should not be compared directly with the developed system of roads in the High Empire, but their basic rationale was the same – Roman control of geographical space.[70] While there is no doubt about the military importance of roads, and of their importance to state communication, they clearly had an economic function on a number of levels. They allowed an imperial power to exploit the resources of its provinces, but secondary economic activity naturally followed. It is no coincidence, as Purcell has pointed out, that roads naturally followed the annexation of new territory, and their importance to the domination of space is clearly demonstrated by the speed and energy characterizing their construction. A good example of this is the vast network of roads constructed in Anatolia during the reigns of Trajan and Hadrian, especially the road-building of the proconsul Caesennius Gallus at immense cost.[71] To their military and economic roles should be added their importance to government and their facilitation of legal jurisdiction as governors made their annual *conventus*.

Cities, towns, villages, villas, farmers, merchants, and professional transporters all benefitted from Roman roads. It is easy, too, to focus on the great *viae publicae* (largely built by emperors), and lose sight of local roads, private roads associated with villas, and tracks (largely built and maintained locally), which all had a part in the road system. A passage in the Digest of Roman Law nicely illustrates this, but also the fact that road use was open to all:

> We call a road public if its land is public. For our definition of a private road is unlike that of a public road. The land of a public road belongs to someone else, but the right of driving along it is open to us. But the land of a public road is public, bequeathed or marked out, with fixed limits of width by whoever had the right of making it public, so that the public might walk or travel along it. We mean by public roads what the Greeks call royal, and our people, praetorian and consular roads. Private roads are what some call agrarian roads. Local roads are those that are in villages or lead to villages.[72]

Finley stresses the military importance of roads, downplaying their importance to the economy. However, they afforded opportunities for easy and relatively quick travel, indeed, as Westermann has suggested, travel by land could, in some circumstances, be quicker than travel by water, especially in the winter months when poor weather or contrary winds might halt all sea travel.[73] For example, in Egypt, we know of round-trip journeys between Hermopolis and Panopolis (a total distance of *c.*240 km) being made within 24 hours, albeit by imperial messenger.[74] Normal travel times will have been much slower, but still impressive enough. Finley and his followers are always keen to criticize the slowness of wagons pulled by oxen, but fail to note realities. First, other animals could be and were used to draw wagons – donkeys, mules, and camels – at a considerably faster pace; second, that pack animals were the preferred mode of land transport, as pointed out above. In terms of speed, it is best to think in terms of distances traveled per day and loads transported: the reality is a much brighter picture than that suggested by a primitivist approach to the economy. Horses pulling loads were capable of covering distances of over 40 km per day, with loads of 680 kg; camels could pull more and travel further. Pack animals could cover similar distances, carrying loads of between 80 and 150 kg, depending on terrain, distance to be traveled, and the conditions of animals.[75]

TOWARDS AN INTEGRATED TRANSPORT SYSTEM

It is clear that we need to think about transport in the Roman world as an integrated system, combining land, river (and canal), and sea transport, rather than viewing them separately. To do so creates a false distinction, for in almost any transport operation involving maritime or riverine transport, this would have been preceded by at least a short journey by land – a fact which is clearly seen in the transport of grain in Egypt. Strabo, as we have seen, was clear in his view that seas, rivers, and land interacted. The clearest expression of this in Strabo is his description of the roads of Italy, which he claimed "could carry shiploads," suggesting not just the origins of the loads, but also the huge capacity for transport that the roads offered.[76] Horden and Purcell's notion of connectivity joins micro-regions in the Mediterranean, but also argues for the integration of sea and land, where rivers and ports, as we have seen, formed conduits.

To an extent, this was a natural, organic feature, which critics of the role of transport ignored or avoided. But one important question follows, one central to our understanding of the Roman economy: to what extent, if any, was this system of transport consciously developed in terms of infrastructure? "All roads lead to Rome." The second century orator Aelius Aristeides stated that safe travel was now possible under the Romans, throughout the empire, even in the most inhospitable environments.[77] Through the construction of roads, bridges, canals, ports, and the development of systems of communication, such as the *cursus publicus*, the Romans fostered connectivity.[78] It could be argued, for example, from the letter of Pliny to Trajan, previously discussed, and the plans for the construction of a canal at Nicomedia to improve transport infrastructure, that this was a matter of central importance to Rome. The development of canal systems in Aquileia and Northern Italy, also discussed, show an awareness of the advantages of connecting seas, rivers, and roads. The construction and development of major ports, most notably Portus, catered for an increased volume of maritime traffic. While many of these initiatives were centrally directed by the emperor – Claudius' and Trajan's construction at Portus, for example – it is simplistic and misguided to see in this a clear central direction of purpose or conscious development of infrastructure – in short, an imperial transport policy. The reality is implicit in Pliny's letter, that most of the initiative for the development of infrastructure was local, carried out with local knowledge of both topography and economic necessity, and that imperial involvement was characterized by a desire to control provincial finances, rather than promote a grand plan for the development of a transport infrastructure.

Customs duties and transit tolls

State interest in transport and its infrastructure can certainly be demonstrated, especially when connected to the supply of the city of Rome. This raises the question of its cost and relation to taxation. This is important to our understanding of the economy generally, for alongside a culture of autarky, inefficient transport techniques, high costs of land transport, all of which have now been discussed, another important aspect of transport and economic activity that the primitivist view of the ancient economy sees as a limiting factor was the ubiquity of harbor taxes.[79] It is perfectly clear from our evidence – literary, epigraphic, and papyrological – that harbor taxes, importantly charged on both imports and exports, were a standard feature of life in the Mediterranean from the archaic period in Greece onwards: as Andreades shows, customs dues were one of the principal sources of income for Greek states.[80] In the Roman world, direct taxes on land and persons may be the most obvious forms of tax, but indirect taxes and customs duties (*ad valorem* taxes and *portoria*) and transit tolls were exacted in ports and administrative boundaries throughout the empire.[81]

Our evidence then, on one view, suggests oppression: greedy tax collectors, extortion, abusive officials and soldiers. Such is clear from the New Testament, a neglected source for Roman historians, from literature, where abusive soldiers become a *topos*, from papyri, and from inscriptions, most notably the numerous edicts designed to stop such misconduct. The evidence is copious, but a second-century papyrus from Egypt preserving an edict of the *praefectus Aegypti* is especially instructive and will serve to illustrate the general picture: "I am informed that the customs collectors have employed fraudulent and clever tricks against those who are passing through the country and that they are, in addition, demanding what is not owing to them and are detaining those who are in urgent haste, in order that some might pay for a speedier release. I therefore order them to desist from such greed."[82]

Tax collectors were in a strong position; taxes had to be paid, they had the right of search, they could confiscate goods, additional charges could be made above and beyond the basic tax, but most importantly, as taxes were *ad valorem* (on the value of goods), and the collectors had the right to estimate value, the scope for abuse is obvious.[83] Further, taxes increased costs to the trader, and this could be substantial, as a text from Egypt shows: the tax imposed on a load of 550 artabas of wheat for the harbor of Memphis was 44 drachmas, but an extra 47 drachmas was imposed through a number of surcharges. *Portorium* charged on goods coming into the empire was charged at 25 percent, as is clear from a unique papyrus detailing an exceptionally valuable cargo at Myos Hormos, where the tax yield to the state from this one cargo was almost 290 talents.[84] Often, then, taxes and other duties represented to traders a cost that could outstrip transport costs considerably, which in itself further undermines arguments about the cost of transport being prohibitive. What is abundantly clear is that the negative effect of taxes was not significant; an important point is that such duties were placed not only on luxury goods, but also bulky staples, as the papyrus quoted above shows. Although the presence of taxes must have been on the minds of merchants, any suggestion that taxation limited trade to a significant extent should firmly be rejected.

Another aspect of taxation needs further unpacking; significant questions exist, answers are difficult to find. These taxes generated a considerable income for the Roman state. What happened to it? Was it re-invested in infrastructure?

TRADERS AND TRANSPORTERS

One of the main facets of recent discussion on the nature of the economy has been social status and, thus, embedded economies; with this in mind we need to turn to those engaged in transport.[85] We need to establish the relationship between traders and transporters, and explore their position within Roman society. We also need to think more about who the transporters were. Were they specialists, or were they drawn from the existing agricultural labor force? If the latter is the case, what effects might this have had on the agricultural economy?

There are of course different levels; it is clear that there were distinct status differences between two "distinguished matrons, *naukleroi*, and merchants of the Red Sea trade" and Nikanor, the owner of a small transport company operating out of Koptos in Middle Egypt.[86]

Social status was central to Finley's arguments – elites did not engage in commercial activity in a meaningful way: social status matters to economic history. The reality is more complex.[87] There can be little doubt that the majority of traders and transporters in the Roman world were not of equestrian or senatorial class, but two points must be made. First, that does not mean that equestrians or senators were not directly or indirectly involved in trade, and second, that people outside these top status groups could not be wealthy and move in such circles. John D'Arms, however, has argued that members of the social elites were heavily engaged in commercial activity. Keith Hopkins has suggested some tentative costs for trading ventures, which are worth setting out briefly, before turning to some concrete examples. Basing his estimates on comparative evidence, Hopkins suggests that the cost of a ship of some 400 tons burden would have been between 250,000 and 400,000 sesterces. Its cargo of wheat would have been valued at 185,000 sesterces. On the basis of his estimates of population size and demand for wheat on an annual basis, and that two sailings were made in a year, a minimum of 275 ships, with a hull value of 80 million sesterces, would have been required to supply the bare minimum of wheat alone to the city of Rome (the biggest, but certainly not the only consumer).[88] These figures must be taken as absolute minimums for the city of Rome alone. Cargos of wine and oil would have a much greater value, and we should not forget that much of the exceptionally valuable cargo from Muziris, mentioned below, would be destined for the imperial city.

Given this, there must have been a large number of individuals with considerable capital investment dedicated to shipping and transport, and importantly being able to invest in operations with some risk. For cargoes of wheat, the value of ship and cargo is not too far off the minimum property qualification for the senate.[89] Vast fortunes could be made, but by whom? By a *Lex Claudia* of 218 BCE, senators were restricted to owning only ships of less than 300 amphoras burden, for the purposes of merely moving around the produce of their estates.[90] We know there was opposition to this, and the fact that the law was promulgated in itself suggests that senators possessed larger ships. The law was essentially unenforceable, and resourceful senators could easily get around it by acting through agents, usually their freedman or slaves. It is probably not a coincidence that in the third or second century BCE, developments in Roman law, specifically laws concerning agency, were developed which promoted the interests of members of the Roman elite and may have allowed them to act through agents more efficiently.[91] The best-known example of this is Cato the Elder:

> Cato used to lend money in what is surely the most disreputable form of speculation, that is, the underwriting of ships. Those who wished to borrow money from him were obliged to form a large association, and when this reached the number of fifty, representing as many ships, he would take one share in the company. His interests were looked after by Quintio, one of his freedmen, who used to accompany Cato's clients on their voyages and transact their business. In this way he drew a handsome profit, while at the same time spreading his risk and never venturing more than a fraction of his capital.[92]

Claude Nicolet has summed this up nicely: "It looks as if the Roman governing class, for all that their property was in land and their supposed role military and civic, was also a financial class – bankers and money-lenders and slave-dealers, distinguished only by the veil of hypocrisy from the mercantile aristocracies of Carthage or of Venice."[93] The old view of a separation between the senators as landowners and the equites as a mercantile class has rightly been abandoned. We should really also abandon any real distinction, except of public status, between them and the propertied elites, who all benefitted from empire.

But such commerce was not restricted to the elite, and strategies, such as part shares in ships, could be adopted to make such ventures accessible to many more. But it would be a mistake to limit our discussion to the supply of Rome. In terms of wheat, the cost for a good proportion of it would be met by the state. What is striking is the diversity of interests among merchants. We need only think of the trade in wine in Gaul, an excellent example of a quickly growing phenomenon and response to market opportunities.[94]

An equally quick response to economic opportunities can be seen in Egypt, and it might be worth looking at some examples. The importance of the *Pax Augusta* to economic development cannot be stressed enough.[95] In Egypt, individuals quickly responded to changing economic conditions, most importantly private ownership of land. From an archive of documents from the Augustan period, we catch a glimpse of the activities of a man named Athenodoros. Well-connected and evidently wealthy, he was a landowner, owned his own ships, and sold his surplus produce in markets, not just locally, but importantly, where he could find the best price.[96]

The annexation of Egypt also opened up trade with the East, and it is no surprise that under Augustus, according to Strabo, we see a huge increase in this trade.[97] As mentioned above, wealthy metropolites from Egypt may have been heavily invested in the Eastern trade, and the wealth generated from it, to judge by a uniquely important papyrus, was enormous. In this text, part of the cargo of a ship, the *Hermapollon*, had a value of around 1,157 talents (roughly seven million sesterces).[98] Unfortunately, the names of principals are not preserved, but there can be no doubt as to their wealth. But interesting names turn up in other evidence concerning the eastern trade which can give us clues: agents of Marcus Julius Alexander are present in Myos Hormos, the port most associated with such trade at this time (along with Berenike). The brother of the Prefect of Egypt, Tiberius Julius Alexander, he was the member of an extremely rich equestrian family and clearly enjoyed imperial favor.[99] Further, Tiberius Claudius Epaphroditus, evidently a freedman of Claudius, was present, along with other imperial slaves. The presence of members of the *familia Caesaris* raises questions about imperial involvement in trade.[100]

We need to return to transport and transporters, for other interesting issues are raised. It is clear from the Muziris papyrus that transport is being arranged for the cargo between Myos Hormos and Koptos. Here was an opportunity for professional transporters like Nikanor to profit. His transport company carried goods under contract supplying the port communities on the coast, supplying soldiers under contract with the state, and was then well placed to carry luxury goods back to Koptos on the return journey. The point is that many individuals at different socioeconomic levels were involved in this trade. It allowed for Nikanor and others like him to specialize in transport as an economic activity. Similar specialists exist elsewhere. They appear in customs house receipts from the Egyptian Fayyum.[101]

Other individuals appear, with no real connection to Egypt except in economic ventures, but who are known historical characters. P. Annius Plocamus, linked to the Annii family from Puteoli, had tax farming interests in the desert.[102] Another more interesting character turns up. Gaius Peticius engraved his name twice at the *Paneion* at Wadi Hammamat between Myos Hormos and Koptos. But who was he, and what was he doing there? How does he relate to the Gaius Peticius who is mentioned by both Plutarch and Julius Caesar as a *negotiator* in grain at the Battle of Pharsalus in 48 BCE; to a Gaius Peticius who is named on a wine amphora from Byrsa in Carthage dating to the late first century BCE; to a Peticius Marsus whose name is found on a fragment of a wine amphora from the wreck of the Diano Marina off Liguria; and to M. Attius Peticius Marsus, whose name is on a bronze statuette dedicated at the sanctuary of Hercules Curinus in Sulmo in Italy? Can it be a coincidence that camels are present on a dedicatory inscription that may be linked to the family? Are we looking at generations of a family engaged in commerce and transport?[103]

CONCLUSION

This survey is necessarily brief, but hopefully brings out some of the main issues concerning transport and its role in the Roman economy. The views of Finley and others that transport was a severe limitation on economic activity must be firmly rejected. Careful consideration of the main tenets of their arguments concerning transport reveals a different picture. Rethinking the Mediterranean has certainly provided important ways of approaching the role of transport, and careful study of our evidence, both documentary and archaeological, as well as critical analysis of literary evidence (rather than taking it at face value) reveals a reality which is considerably more complex, showing high levels of mobility and commercial interaction, not just at local levels, but across the Roman empire and beyond.

NOTES

1 My thanks to Walter Scheidel for his invitation to contribute and for his patience. Brian Campbell kindly discussed rivers with me, and let me see chapters from his forthcoming book. My colleagues Graham Oliver and Claire Holleran generously read drafts. I would like to dedicate the chapter to the memory of Geoffrey Rickman, whose support in the early years of my academic career was so important, hoping that he would have approved of its intent, if not its content.
2 I am, of course, thinking primarily of Finley 1999 (first published in 1973), even though, as Bagnall 2005 suggests, Finley would have been uncomfortable with the concept of a 'model.'
3 I am currently engaged in the development of this project.
4 Strabo 2.5.17 (C121).
5 Strabo 4.1.14 (C189).
6 Horden and Purcell 2000 *passim* on thinking and writing the Mediterranean, and note the important *rethinking* in Harris 2005. Especially important is the chapter by Bresson, developing ideas of unity and connectivity after Horden and Purcell.
7 Horden and Purcell 2000: 13.
8 Harris 2005: 23.
9 Morley 2007a: 19–26 offers a sensible overview. See also Sippel 1987.
10 Sion 1935: 631 – a response to Lefebvre des Noëttes, see below for discussion.
11 On Greek roads, see Pikoulas 2007; on Roman, the basic treatment remains Chevallier 1976.
12 Adams 2007a: 26–9; Bagnall 1985.

13 Yeo 1946: 221.
14 Westermann 1928.
15 Brunt 1972: 156.
16 Lefebvre des Noëttes 1931: 164.
17 *CTh* 8.5.30. See Kolb 2000: 214–17; also Adams 2007a: 76; on law and transport, see Martin 2002.
18 Spruytte 1983; Raepsaet 2002. See the general comments of Schneider 2007: 151. Of older works, White 1984 remains important.
19 Most importantly Jones 1964; Finley 1999; Duncan-Jones 1982; *contra* Burford 1960.
20 Cato, *Agr.* 22.3. Yeo 1946, with Laurence 1999: 131–2, who notes mistakes in Yeo's calculations.
21 These percentage figures are corrected from Yeo.
22 Plin. *Ep.* 10.41.
23 My thanks to Walter Scheidel for pointing this out to me and letting me see a paper prior to publication.
24 Duncan-Jones 1982: 366–9; *BGU* 3.802 (42 CE), with Johnson 1936: 407. See also Adams 2007a: 78, 191.
25 Jones 1964: 842. Seventy-five miles does not reflect the *Edict of Maximum Prices*, but rather Cato's influence on the issue.
26 See Adams 2007a for discussion.
27 See Fentress 1990.
28 Finley 1999: 126.
29 *Contra* Purcell 1990.
30 Finley 1999: 127. For a recent account of the Romano-British economy, see Mattingly 2006: 491–528, rather different in its approaches and findings to Finley.
31 Hopkins 1980, with further discussion in Hopkins 1995/6.
32 For an important critique of Hopkins and earlier work, see Bang 2007.
33 Hopkins 1983: 95.
34 Hopkins 1983, an estimate he considers to be on the low side.
35 Pucci 1983: 111.
36 Horden and Purcell 2000: 377.
37 See Adams 2007a: 11–14; also 277–81 for an overview of the role of transport in the agricultural economy of Egypt.
38 *BGU* 16.2611 (10 BCE); see Adams 2007a: 250.
39 For similar points, but for eighteenth-century Spain, see Ringrose 1970.
40 Cic. *Cons. Prov.* 12.31, discussed by Horden and Purcell 2000: 134–5. On sea routes, Rougé 1966 remains important, especially 81–105 on maritime routes. See also Vélissaropoulos 1980.
41 The arguments of Pryor 1988 are central here.
42 On ferrying, see Constantakopoulou 2002.
43 On out of season sea travel, see Arnaud 2005: 26–8. See also, generally, Morton 2001.
44 Pryor 1988: 38, cited by Horden and Purcell 2000: 139.
45 Plin. *Ep.* 10.15, 10.16, 10.17a.
46 Plin. *HN* 19.3–4.
47 On the sailing times between Alexandria and Rome, see Casson 1971: 297–9, with Rickman 1980: 128–31.

48 Arnaud 2005: 131–2.
49 Duncan Jones 1990: 7–29.
50 There is a question about the comparative speed of sea travel in the Roman and medieval periods. It is widely argued that, as in the medieval period, sailing times in the Roman were slow. See Horden and Purcell 2000: 140–6 generally, also McCormick 2001: 481–500. Contra Arnaud 2005: 97–148, especially 117, who believes sailing was faster in antiquity (an average of 3 knots compared to 1 for the medieval), downplays the importance of cabotage, and that sailing in darkness was not uncommon (see, e.g., Plin., *HN* 2.128). Medieval sailing times are discussed by Udovitch 1978. See also Arnaud 2007.
51 Strabo 8.6.20.
52 *SIG*[3] 1229.
53 Strabo 3.2.5. For a similar theme, see Suet. *Aug.* 98.2.
54 Still fundamental is Casson 1971.
55 Lucian, *Navig.* 5 with Casson 1950 and Hopkins 1983: 99.
56 Gai. *Inst.* 1.32c on Claudius' restriction on size; *Dig.* 50.5.3 on 50,000 *modii* on one ship or a number of ships for exemption on the part of the shipowner from liturgies.
57 Pomey and Tchernia 1978; Plin., *HN* 16.201; on timber, see Meiggs 1982: 335–46, stressing the importance of rivers, but not blind to the importance of land transport.
58 Adams 2001a.
59 Meiggs 1982: 336 for this on the Tiber and its tributaries.
60 See Adams 2001a: 146, with *P.Ross.Georg.* 2. 18 (140 CE); on shipping contracts see Meyer-Termeer 1978.
61 Strabo 4.1.14.
62 Plin. *HN* 3.54.
63 Ibid.; see also Strabo 5.3.7.
64 Strabo 3.2.3. On routes of communication in Spain, see generally Sillières 1990.
65 Purcell 1990: 126.
66 Rickman 2008: 7.
67 Strabo 3.2.4.
68 Plin. *HN* 3.16.119–21.
69 Strabo 5.1.8. Purcell 1990: 9 rightly points out, however, that at least in Republican times, we should not assume a thorough geographical knowledge of the region on the part of the Romans.
70 Purcell 1990; Nicolet 1988a.
71 See Mitchell 1993: I 124–33.
72 *Digest* 43.8.21 (Ulpianus).
73 Westermann 1928; also Casson 1994: 166.
74 See the letters preserved in *P.Panop.Beatty* 2.109–60.
75 There is much useful material on the capabilities of animals in Cotterell and Kaminga 1990: 192–233, Raepsaet 2002: *passim*, and Adams 2007a: 77–81.
76 Strabo 5.3.8.
77 *Or.* 26.100–2.
78 Horden and Purcell 2000:133–43.
79 Finley 1999: 159, 164, 165, 175.
80 Andreades 1993: 297, cited by Purcell 2005: 207 n. 19.

81 De Laet 1949; Sijpesteijn 1987; Bang 2008: 202–38. The most significant development in the study of taxation recently is the publication of the Asian tax law, see Cottier et al. (eds.) 2008.

82 *P.Princ.* 2.20.

83 Bang 2008: 205.

84 See Rathbone 2000; Adams 2007a: 228–30.

85 Finley 1999 (drawing on Polyani); on social status in particular, see initially D'Arms 1977 and 1981, with more recent comments by Andreau 1995.

86 *SB* 5.7539 = *SEG* 8.703 for "distinguished matrons." See *O.Petr.* 220–304, for the so-called Archive of Nikanor, with Adams 2007a: 221–34. The status of the two matrons is in itself interesting, not least because they are women. If members of the metropolite elite in Egypt were involved in the expensive and risky trade in the East, what can we say of higher status groups in Roman Italy?

87 Pleket 1990 argues for a complete separation between social and economic matters, but pushes too far.

88 On all of this, Hopkins 1983. See also Garnsey 1983, and Mattingly and Aldrete 2000.

89 See Pleket 1983 on urban elites and business. Pleket argues that the number of self-styled merchants who also noted their magistracies epigraphically is small. However, it is not necessary to advertise one's economic interests in order to have them.

90 Livy 21.63.

91 See Frier and Kehoe 2007: 128.

92 Plut. *Cat. Mai.* 21.

93 Nicolet 1994: 634.

94 See Tchernia 1983; Woolf 1998 on consumption.

95 See Woolf 1992.

96 *BGU* 16.2600–72. Best price: *BGU* 16.2611 (10 BCE). A year previously, Athenodorus was criticized by his associates for not getting a good price, see Adams 2007a: 250.

97 Strabo 2.5.12, 17.1.13.

98 *P.Vindob.G.* 40822 = *SB* 18.13167 (second century CE). This is a much discussed text, see most importantly Rathbone 2000, with Adams 2007a: 229–32 for further comments and bibliography.

99 On agents, see *O.Petr.* 266, 268, 271; on the family, see Turner 1954. Discussion in Adams 2007a: 223–4. Tiberius was a crucial supporter of Vespasian.

100 Adams 2007a: 224.

101 Adams 2007a: 220–53 generally, with comments of Rathbone 2007: 709–12.

102 Plin. *HN* 6.24.84–5.

103 See the ingenious article by Tchernia 1992.

12: Urbanism

Paul Erdkamp

Introduction

After the armies of the eastern Roman Empire had conquered the Vandal Kingdom, the emperor Justinian (527–65 CE) decided to build a city on the location of a minor and insignificant town, close to where his army had landed. The account by the contemporary historian Procopius shows his wholehearted support of the undertaking:

> Justinian . . . conceived the desire to transform this place forthwith into a city which should be made strong by a wall and distinguished by other constructions as worthy to be counted a prosperous and impressive city; and the purpose of the emperor has been realized. For the wall and the city has been brought to completion, and the condition of the territory is being suddenly changed. The country-dwellers have thrown aside the plough and lead the existence of a community, no longer going the round of country tasks but living a city life. They pass their days in the market place and hold assemblies to deliberate on questions which concern them; and they traffic with one another, and conduct all the other affairs which pertain to the dignity of a city.[1]

This one passage offers occasion for several reflections on urbanism in the Roman world. To begin with, the ancients did not perceive a city as merely a concentration of many people in one place. To them it was a symbol of prosperity and civilized culture. Hence, peoples without towns and cities were uncivilized. Concomitantly, country-dwellers are often depicted by the urban writers as boorish and ignorant simpletons, at best as naïve and unspoiled.[2] Related to these ideas is the notion that a city is only a city if it contains the markers of civilized life: towns and cities had to be built around public monuments like temples, theatres, and baths, and contain halls and public spaces where councils and people assembled.[3] In the later Roman Empire, walls had become an important feature too. Without these monuments and features such settlements would indeed have been no more than many people living in the same place. Hence, it was the duty of rulers and of social elites to support urban society by building and maintaining public monuments. Rulers of the Roman Empire could of course go a step further and, in the tradition of Hellenistic kings, create a city were none had been before. At the end of Classical Antiquity Justinian founded Justiniana Prima near his birth place in modern Serbia. Apart from such imperial foundations, throughout the centuries Roman authorities stimulated the emergence of cities in the lands they conquered by the settlement of colonists and veterans and by imposing the administrative and political structures of the Mediterranean cities onto the new territories. However, Justinian's attempt to revive the grand old days of classical urban culture was bound to fail. As we shall see in more detail shortly, urban life was disappearing in Africa and by that time had already disappeared by and large in most of Europe. Cities in Islamic northern Africa did not build on classical traditions. Only the East still boasted many vigorous cities, but even here things were changing.

Procopius also emphasizes that urban dwellers do not work the land, but engage in different means to earn a living. The division of labor between agriculture in the countryside and manufacture, commerce, and services in the cities will be central to our economic study of urbanism in the Roman world. In fact, it has dominated the debate about the nature of Greek and Roman cities in the past decades, ever since Finley's *The Ancient Economy*, reviving the models of Bücher and Weber, argued that ancient cities were based on the political and social dominance of the city over the countryside, in contrast to medieval cities, which were based on production and exchange with a countryside that was politically independent. The subsequent debate has been dominated by the dichotomy between the so-called consumer and producer city. However, this debate will not be the focus of the current chapter, as much has already been written on this matter, and the debate will not be brought forward by yet another positioning in it.[4] Moreover, the consumer city and producer city are ideal types; they were developed as tools for the debate, but as ideal types they tend to present things in black and white, while this chapter will attempt to sketch the economic aspect of Roman urbanism in shades of grey. The consumer vs. producer city debate did point out, however, that the crucial question is: what was the economic basis of urbanization in the Roman world? This will be the main question of this chapter, and the conclusion will not be determined by allegiance to either the primitivist or modernist stance, although I may state at the outset that I hold much sympathy for both the consumer city model and the primitivist approach to the ancient economy.

This chapter starts with a very brief survey of the scale of urbanization and the size of towns and cities in the various regions of the Roman world and its development over time. For a long time towns and cities grew in most of the Roman world, in size as well as in geographical distribution. This leads to some brief remarks about the margins of the concept 'city' and to a consideration of the question in what ways 'city' is or is not a relevant concept for an economic analysis. This analysis, I hope, will shed some light on the economic functioning of the growing urbanization in the Roman world as well as its decline in many parts of it.

Size of cities and scale of urbanization

Statistical evidence on either the population of the Roman Empire as a whole or the populations of the various towns and cities is lacking, but archaeological data and historical (written) evidence allow rough estimates to be made. The population of what would be the Roman world increased slowly but steadily from the early first millennium BCE until the second century CE, when the so-called Antonine Plague caused significant population losses. According to one recent estimate, the population grew from the Augustan to the Antonine period from 45 million to 60 or 70 million. Later developments diverge: while the West seems to have experienced stagnation and further decline during subsequent centuries, the East recovered magnificently. Syria, Judea and Egypt experienced a peak in population levels in the fifth and sixth centuries CE; population densities in much of the region were not surpassed until the nineteenth century.[5] The growth of the size and number of cities did not merely reflect increasing population levels: it is generally agreed that during the early Roman Empire the number and size of cities grew more than the population at large. In other words, to a large extent population growth occurred in the towns and cities, and hence the scale of urbanization grew. The increase of both the population and the scale of urbanization is an indication of the economic growth in the Roman world during this period, as society was apparently able to support a larger share of urban dwellers.

Most of the towns were small, however, counting no more than one or two thousand inhabitants, and it is not always clear which population nuclei should be designated as urban and which not. Studies of urbanization in medieval and early modern Europe generally count only those settlements of more than 5,000 inhabitants as urban. It has been estimated that in the Roman world the proportion of people residing in towns and cities above this minimum (which is admittedly very arbitrary) was roughly of the same magnitude as in early-modern Europe. While in that sense the scale of urbanization may be said to have been similar, one could also point to a significant difference: the share of people living in *megalopoleis* was much larger in the Roman world than in later Europe.

Rome itself obviously surpassed any other city in size, reflecting its role as political centre and the vast resources from the entire empire that the Roman authorities could control on behalf of their capital. At the height of its power, in the second century, the city of Rome may have numbered one million inhabitants, surpassing by a wide margin all the other grand cities of the Mediterranean world. Alexandria may have numbered more than 500,000 inhabitants in the early Empire[6]; Carthage 300,000 in the third century CE, while Antioch is estimated at the same figure in the fourth century CE. A few other cities probably surpassed the level of 100,000, such as Pergamum and Ephesus.[7] The fact that the top ten includes cities that may have been less than one-tenth of the largest city indicates the exceptional position of Rome. The contrast was greatest within Italy itself: no other city came near 100,000. To give an indication: the harbor city of Puteoli is estimated at 50,000 inhabitants, Ostia at above 25,000, and Pompeii at 15,000.[8] As I said before, most towns were much smaller.

The difference between East and West is also significant. As we have seen, Egypt, Syria, Asia Minor, and Greece contained several great cities. As far as Gallia Comata, Britain, and the provinces along Rhine and Danube are concerned, none of the cities there surpassed the level of 50,000. Trier, Cologne, Lyon, Autun, and Augsburg are estimated at between 25,000 and 50,000.[9] The only exception may have been late Roman Trier, which as imperial residence in the fourth century CE possibly grew beyond this threshold.[10]

It is also the West that from the third century CE onwards saw the most serious decline in urbanization. It is a general phenomenon that the walls that were built as a result of the crisis of the third century enclosed a much smaller area than the earlier town. Expressed in hectares, the size of many towns in Gaul diminished to 10 percent of that of the second century. While those earlier towns may have included large uninhabited areas and the density of later walled sites may have been higher, the conclusion is unavoidable that the population of most towns and cities catastrophically declined.[11] In the fifth century CE towns had virtually disappeared from the scene in vast stretches of the former western Roman Empire. They remained, however, part of the human landscape in the Mediterranean region: in Italy, southern France, and Spain cities continued to exist and even flourish, albeit usually in reduced form. Rome itself was obviously the main victim of the political and military disturbances of this era and may have fallen below 100,000 inhabitants around 500 CE.[12] No such urban decline occurred in the late Roman East, with the exception of parts of Asia Minor. In Syria, Arabia, and Egypt, the classical city survived until the Islamic conquest.[13]

Two important issues emerge from our survey. First, the rank-size distribution reflects the political basis of the urbanization in the Roman world. Rome, Alexandria, Carthage, and Antioch were huge cities, partly because they were important political and administrative centers.[14] The same phenomenon is reflected in the emergence of Trier in the fourth century as the biggest city north of the Mediterranean region. Secondly, the answer to the question why and how towns and cities flourished throughout the early Empire should at the same time answer the question why cities continued to do so in the East, but failed in the West.

WHAT DOES 'URBAN' MEAN?

'Town' and 'city' are concepts with limited usefulness in economic analysis. For one, the division between town and countryside overlaps very imperfectly with concepts that are economically meaningful, such as agricultural versus non-agricultural, and food-producing versus non-food-producing labor. However, we shall postpone the discussion of the division of labor until later. Another limitation of the concept 'city' is that the distinction between 'urban' and 'rural' is impossible to define economically. There will always be a grey area around the idea of 'city.'

Whether a settlement of people was called a village or a town often depended on non-economic factors, such as political status. The ancient view was that one town (*polis*, *municipium*) was not subordinate to another town. It could be *de facto* dominated by a larger and more influential neighbor, but not be *de iure* part of another town's territory. Hence, some of the villages in the territories of big cities could be as populous as most small towns. A good example is the modern site of Shivta (Palestine), where the remains of a late antique village of some 2,000 inhabitants are well preserved. "The houses were mostly evenly sized between 250 and 550 square meters, implying a generally homogeneous population whose livelihood depended on livestock, cereal agriculture, vine and olive cultivation."[15] Prosperous and populous villages were part of the landscape in many regions of the East throughout the Roman and late Roman periods. It has been estimated that the limestone massif in late Roman north-central Syria housed some 700 to 800 villages, characterized by public monuments, where well-to-do farmers lived who sold agricultural products to the big cities in the region, such as Antioch. Similarly, Procopius (*Bell.* 2.25.2–3) says of Armenia that there were many populous villages where merchants conducted their business. In short, some of these villages had many economic and social features that we also meet in an urban context, even if they lacked the political status of a city.

It is a common estimate that 80 or 90 percent of the population in the Roman world worked the land, while 10 or 20 percent engaged in non-agricultural sectors of the economy. It should be emphasized, though, that the division between town and countryside does not completely overlap with the division between agricultural and non-agricultural sectors of the economy. First, many people living in towns worked the land. Generally speaking, the smaller the town, the larger the percentage of farmers who dwelled within the urban settlement and worked the surrounding land. As I said above, many towns in the Roman world had no more than a few thousand inhabitants, and while we cannot put figures on the number of agricultural workers living in such towns, we can safely say that a significant part of their residents were part of the agricultural sector. Even in a sizeable town such as Pompeii, whose population is estimated at roughly 15,000, a large number and a wide range of agricultural tools and farm implements have been found, which points to a significant number of Pompeians working as independent farmers or agricultural laborers in the town's immediate hinterland. Needless to say, the share of agricultural workers and farmers cannot have been significant in metropolitan centers such as Rome or Alexandria. The sheer size of the largest cities ensures that they accounted for a large share of the aggregate urban population, but the much greater number of small towns means that one should not underestimate the proportion of city-dwelling agricultural workers.

Conversely, it may be said that the predominance of non-agricultural sectors is a characteristic of the urban economy, but by itself this cannot count as a defining feature of a town. Take for example the marble quarry of Mons Claudianus in the Eastern Desert of Egypt. The exploitation of the quarry by the Roman emperors to support their building activities in Rome caused a settlement of some 900 laborers and soldiers to emerge at the site. The purple marble of Mons Porphyrius undoubtedly attracted a settlement of similar size.[16] Agriculture was impossible in the desert, so the entire population of these settlements was clearly engaged in non-agricultural activities. The same can be said of mining settlements. According to Polybius (34.9.9), in the second century BCE 40,000 men worked the silver mines at Carthago Nova in Spain, which is a good deal more than the population of an average town in the Roman Empire. In short, a large concentration of people not working the land does not make a city.

Second, many people living in the countryside were engaged in non-agricultural labor, either as a full-time profession or in part-time jobs. On the one hand, smiths, toolmakers, and potters lived in the villages, while the estates of the wealthy landowners contained brickyards or textile workshops, whose permanent workforce probably largely consisted of slaves. On the other hand, non-agricultural activities such as spinning were probably part of the daily work on peasant farms, while in the slack periods of the year the men from these households offered themselves for seasonal employment in transport or construction. In sum, one should not underestimate the contribution of the countryside to the non-agricultural sector nor the agricultural nature of much of Roman small towns. 'Urban' is impossible to define clearly in an economic sense.

The urban economy

While it is impossible to define a 'town' at the small end of the spectrum of settlements in economic terms, there is no doubt that the economy of a large city was different from that of a small settlement. Already in classical Greece the Athenian Xenophon (*Cyr.* 8.2.5) realized that the larger pool of consumers in big cities ensured a much larger degree of specialization:

> In small cities the same workmen make couches, doors, ploughs, tables, and often the same person actually builds the house, and is thankful if he finds enough employers to make a living. It is therefore impossible for a man who practices many crafts to do everything well. But in large cities because of the great demand for each particular trade, a single trade is enough to provide a living, sometimes even only a fraction of a trade. Thus one man will make shoes for men, another shoes for women, and there are even places where one man makes a living by stitching shoes together, another by cutting them, another by cutting only uppers, another by merely assembling all the pieces.

The situation in the Roman Empire was undoubtedly similar. Unfortunately, the sparse evidence on the urban economy of the small town is very limited and allows only very inadequate insight into the extent of specialization of artisans and merchants. Sometimes we catch a glimpse of the various trades, as in late Roman Korykos (Cilicia, fifth/sixth centuries CE), where grave-inscriptions mention boot-makers, potters, butchers, greengrocers, tavern keepers, stone masons, carpenters, fishermen, sail-makers, and doctors. Interestingly, 8.2 percent of the 456 inscriptions mentioning the deceased's occupation refer to a position as some sort of state official or councilor. It has been observed that late Roman Korykos owed its prosperity to its location on a well-traveled sea-route between Constantinople and the East. Nevertheless, it may be regarded as a typical coastal small town. The picture emerging from the grave-inscriptions is not very surprising: the urban community offered sufficient employment and business to a great many traders, workers, and artisans, but the degree of specialization is fairly limited.[17] The picture is obviously different in Rome or the busy ports that catered to its needs. More than 200 different occupations have been counted in the literary and epigraphic evidence for Rome, some of them reflecting an astonishing degree of specialization, in particular among the domestic staff of the urban elite.[18]

A detailed analysis of the various trades and industries within the towns and cities of the Roman Empire would obviously exceed the limited scope of this chapter. The largest sector of the economy in early modern Europe, apart from the production and distribution of food, was the textile industry, which reflects the ubiquitous demand for the product among all types and classes of consumers, the general availability of raw materials, and the possibility to produce and transport textiles cheaply. Although there remains much to be desired about the availability of evidence on the textile industry in the Roman world, it may serve as a case study of urban manufacture.

The production of textiles consisted of various stages, beginning with the production of raw material such as wool or flax. The spinning of wool and the processing of flax did not involve investment of much capital in tools or equipment, nor did it entail the cooperation of a large workforce or require much education or training. Hence, the raw material could just as well be processed in the context of rural households as in urban workshops. Weaving occurred either in urban workshops, in workshops that were part of rural estates, or in the households of smallholders. The relationship between the owner or producer of the raw material (wool, flax) and the owner or manager of the production unit could be diverse. Some smallholders probably processed their own wool into woven cloth. Egyptian estate owners rented out workshops on their estates to independent entrepreneurs. A different situation emerges from the evidence for the woollen industry in northern Gaul in the third century CE, in and around Trier to be precise, provided by a funerary monument of the Secundinii family. Drinkwater summarized his study of the organization of the activities of this family thus: "they produced these fabrics in and around Trier, by recruiting and organizing a large and specialized, and therefore highly dependent, workforce, of spinners, weavers, fullers, dyers, etc., paid by the piece."[19] In other words, the Secundinii family employed workers who did not produce or own the raw materials that they processed. Moreover, the workers were specialized in only one stage of the production process. From our perspective, it is particularly interesting that the distinction between 'town' and 'countryside' seems to have been quite irrelevant to the family's business.

A further stage in the textile production of woolen cloth consisted of the dyeing and fulling of the fabric (to which may be added the cleaning of togas and other woolen clothing). As these activities required heated vats and tubs and lots of water, unlike spinning and weaving, dyeing and fulling necessitated substantial capital investment in establishments of considerable size. Several *fullonicae* have been found in Pompeii, but also in the North African town of Timgad, where about twenty fulling establishments have been identified, mostly concentrated in the town's north-east quarter. Jongman has shown that the economy of Pompeii was not based on the textile industry, but now an important role is claimed for the "large-scale finishing and sale of cloth" in Timgad. Apart from the size and number of fulling establishments in Timgad, it has been noted that the town boasted two epigraphically attested market halls for textiles, possibly altogether too large merely to reflect local demand.[20] However, the evidence does not tell us how far the market for textiles from Timgad extended.

Epigraphic and literary evidence provides several examples of urban export production of textiles in the East and in northern Italy. Strabo (12.8) remarks that "the country round Laodicea produces sheep that are excellent not only for the softness of their wool . . . but also for its raven-black color, so that the Laodiceans derive splendid revenue from it." In a similar vein, he observes that the Tyrian dyeworking "makes the city rich through the superior skill of its inhabitants" (Strabo 16.2.23). Several textiles that are associated with a particular town or city are mentioned in Diocletian's Price Edict, such as Milesian purple wool (also mentioned in several other sources), linen from Alexandria, woolen garments from Mutina, and woolen clothing from Altinum.[21] Unfortunately, the evidence sheds little light on the scale of production and the sector's importance in relation to other urban activities. We have to rely on such impressionistic evidence as Dio Chrysostom's oration (34.21ff.) on behalf of linen weavers in Tarsus, who were being treated as second-class citizens by the local authorities. In Tarsus weaving was done by urban full-time workers rather than by rural labor. The city is also mentioned in other sources as an exporter of linen textiles.[22]

The main advantage of rural labor was that it was cheaper, as workers did not need to rely on income from manufacture for their entire sustenance. Quite typically part of the household's labor was employed in production, processing of raw materials and finished goods, while its subsistence needs were covered by the household's prime activity, that is, cultivation of the land. Economic history has devised the term 'externalization of reproductive costs' for this phenomenon, as a result of which rural labor was cheaper than urban labor. On the other hand, there were advantages to the employment of urban labor. The level of skill was higher among full-time professionals, and the division of the production process among several specialists was most feasible in physical proximity. Moreover, the concentration of workers and traders in one place was easier to manage and thereby reduced costs. The price level of the product presumably made a big difference. Labor costs played less of a role in the manufacture of expensive goods whose price-elasticity was very large. As Jones observed, "the great weaving centers produced in the main luxury garments, the best of which cost 20 times as much as those made for the poorest classes."[23] For such expensive products, skill and the availability of a market were more important conditions, and which may, therefore, have been undertaken primarily by 'professional,' urban textile workers.[24]

In short, textile manufacture and processing was a feature of all towns and cities in the Roman Empire. Activities related to the textile market were part of the rural as well as the urban economy. Specialized full-time workers in the textile industry were part of the urban workforce. In some towns, the textile sector catered to the needs of local customers, in others it was of more than local importance and was seen as a source of wealth for the entire community.

The general point to be emphasized is that many thriving activities in services, trade, and manufacture occurred in numerous towns and cities, the aggregate volume and complexity of which should not be underestimated. Some towns were famous for their textiles, other for ceramics (such as Arezzo). On the other hand, one should not too readily deduce flourishing export production from slim evidence. For example, on the basis of findings indicating irons melting and smithing in North African Leptiminus, it has recently been claimed that metalworking was a significant activity within the "industrialized suburban zone" of that harbor town.[25] To quote an earlier cautionary remark: "It is one thing to observe the traces of iron- or bronze-working in a town; it is another to assess the economic importance of the metal trade." The sparse, often fragmentary and one-sided evidence that we have does not allow quantification. Nevertheless, we can state with confidence that most of the urban dwellers worked for a living, even if it is impossible to say which part of the urban populace was employed in which sector.

One economic activity that should not be underestimated concerns the building sector and all its related activities, such as the making of bricks and the transportation of building material. That a significant part of the populace of Rome found employment in the building sector is confirmed by an anecdote concerning Vespasian:

> To a mechanical engineer, who promised to transport some heavy columns to the Capitol at small expense, he gave no mean reward for his invention, but refused to make use of it, saying: "You must let me feed my poor commons."
>
> (Suet. *Vesp.* 18.)

Whether true or not, the anecdote would have made no sense if few free people had been employed in the building sector. According to an estimate by Janet DeLaine, 4 to 6 percent of the total population of Rome worked in the building industry. However, even in this sector 'urban' and 'rural' cannot be completely differentiated. Much of the building material, such as bricks, was produced in the countryside. Bricks, mortar, timber, marble, fuel, etc. were transported using vast amounts of animal and human labor, much of which was offered seasonally by the male members of rural households and their animals. Construction itself involved two kinds of labor: on the one hand, skilled labor that was offered by a professional full-time workforce; on the other, menial labor offered by day laborers among the urban poor and seasonal migrants from the countryside.

Not only the transportation of building material but that of all goods involved much labor. The several hundred thousand tons of grain, olive oil, wine, meat, and all other kinds of foodstuffs that were brought into Rome, in particular from overseas but also down the Tiber, needed to be transferred from ships to boats, unloaded, moved to storage facilities, brought to distribution points and shops, and so on. Loading and unloading was done by hand, amphora by amphora, sack by sack, offering employment for thousands of stevedores in Puteoli, Ostia, and Rome itself. Furthermore, ships needed maintenance, requiring the services of rope- and sail-makers, carpenters, etc. The volume of labor involvement in the logistics of the capital may have been exceptionally large, but the demand for labor was not significantly different in smaller harbors and cities. Again, much of this labor was offered by seasonal workers from the countryside, but the transportation sector offered work to thousands of urban residents as well.

From our perspective, the distinction between free and servile labor is irrelevant. All the forms of labor mentioned above were performed both by slaves and free or freed workers. One of the largest sectors of work in early modern towns was domestic service. In the Roman world, this kind of work was virtually restricted to slaves and ex-slaves, who not only performed tasks but also enhanced the social status of their owners. The households of the extremely rich contained hundreds of slaves, among them doormen, hair dressers, masseuses, grammarians, lectors, secretaries, doctors, wet-nurses, different kinds of cooks, and the like. Wealthy Romans also employed slaves and ex-slaves as more or less independent entrepreneurs and managers. According to the epigraphic evidence the commercial and manufacturing sectors were dominated by freedmen, which may in part reflect reality and in part stem from the greater need of freedmen to advertise their social mobility publicly. Finally, the urban workforce included dancers, musicians, pimps and prostitutes. Even brothel-keepers mention their trade on their gravestones!

In sum, the people living in the cities earned their living in numerous trades and with all kinds of employment. The economy of more moderately sized towns may have been less varied, but even in such towns the majority of residents did not work in agriculture. For their survival they needed access to the food surpluses produced in the countryside.

DIVISION OF LABOR

The division between agricultural and non-agricultural sectors does not capture the essence of the division of labor. The point is that all people need food[26] and that therefore all people not engaged in food production live off the produce of those who do produce food. It is a basic characteristic of pre-industrial societies that, due to relatively low labor productivity, a large share of the population is engaged in food production. While almost all of food production is part of agriculture (fishing or hunting might be mentioned as exceptions), the reverse is not true: not all agricultural labor produces food. The cultivation of flax or flowers and the rearing of sheep for their wool are agricultural activities on the non-food-producing side of the equation. The dividing lines are not always clear, although they are significant: cattle are raised for their skin, bones, and hooves as well as for their meat; olive oil can be consumed, burned in oil lamps, or applied in gymnasia and bath houses. While the largest part of urban labor did not produce food, there was also a large non-food producing sector in the countryside. There is nothing inherently 'urban' about the non-agricultural and non-food-producing sectors. Non-agricultural and non-food-producing activities occurred in rural as well as urban contexts. Hence, a study of urbanism from an economic perspective should focus on the interaction between agricultural and non-agricultural sectors, and between food-producing and non-food-producing sectors.

It is crucial to understand how these entities economically interact and whether the relationships involved are reciprocal or not. Non-food-producing labor required access to the surpluses produced by food-producing labor. Obviously, one could sell one's product or service and use the income to buy food on the market. Numerous texts illustrate the sale of food by farmers and peasants, either to traders or directly to (urban) consumers. These channels are clearly reciprocal. However, both sectors were also connected by other means than commercial channels.

In some cases, non-food-producing labor is supported by food-production within the productive unit. Many rural households functioned as productive units whose members employed various subsistence strategies besides the cultivation of subsistence crops. For one, members of the household were engaged in processing the crops and/or making goods that were sold to merchants and on markets. Moreover, they not only grew food crops but also non-food crops on their land, and kept sheep for wool. In addition, part of the human and animal labor was employed for wages, in particular in the slack periods of the year, for example, in the transportation of fuel, building material, and raw material from the countryside to the city. It must be emphasized that smallholders often did not fully employ the labor within their household, as most rural households had limited access to land. The extent to which they employed their labor in other strategies depended on the one hand on the availability of employment and the demand for their goods and services, and on the other on the urge to do so. If they already enjoyed sufficient income to support their household, leisure was a viable alternative. Two important points emerge from this. Firstly, rural underemployment limited surplus production. Secondly, as far as the land meets the subsistence needs of the members of the household, non-food-producing labor is directly supported by food production within the household. In other words, smallholders contributed not only their surplus of food production to the non-food-producing sector, but also their surplus of labor.

Direct distribution within the productive unit is, however, not limited to smallholders. The activities on the estates of the landowners consisted of several interrelated enterprises, including the holding of animals (ranging from cattle to poultry and fish), the cultivation of food and cash crops, as well as the processing of natural resources and raw materials (ranging from textiles to bricks). The wealthiest Romans combined many enterprises spread over several provinces in one hand. Here too there was undoubtedly much shifting of labor between activities on the same estate: Columella (*Rust.* 12.3.6) advises against female slaves working the land on rainy days, while all hands were needed at peak times, such as the harvest. The economic interaction between holdings undoubtedly was very complex. Varro (*Rust.* 1.16.3) may refer to such intercourse when he writes: "For many have among their holdings some into which grain or wine or the like which they lack must be brought, and on the other hand not a few have holdings from which a surplus must be sent away."

In short, the non-food-producing activities on the possessions of the wealthy landowners were in part supported by the food produced on their estates, whether these were in the same location or not. It should be emphasized that it also made little difference whether the non-food-producing activities took place in the countryside or in town. The relationship may be either reciprocal or non-reciprocal, since production and consumption take place within the same entity, consisting of a household or of a rich person's holdings.

The transfer of food surpluses to the non-food-producing sectors by means of taxes and rents was clearly non-reciprocal. It has often been emphasized that the food supply of the city of Rome and of the Roman armies depended primarily on the distribution of grain that was acquired in the form of taxes-in-kind. Rents collected by landowners from tenants are a very similar case. While both rents and taxes were partly gathered in the form of money, which involved the transformation of surpluses into money, both the state and local landowners acquired much agricultural produce directly in kind.

We have observed an increase in the scale of urbanization during the Roman period. Such intensification may be the result of various changes. On the one hand, increases in the urbanization rate and growth in the non-food-producing sectors may reflect growth in surplus production as a result of an increase in the labor productivity in the food-producing sector, which may either be the result of technical innovation or of the structure of agriculture, or both. Changes in landholding may have resulted in the increased concentration of rural rents in the towns and cities. On the other hand, the growth of the size and number of towns and cities may also reflect a mere transfer of activities from the countryside to the city. If we take 'activity' in a broad sense, this includes also the very real possibility that rural underemployment was transferred into urban employment.

Urban production and consumption

At some unknown date the Greek orator Dio Chrysostom (*c.* 40–*c.* 120 CE) gave a speech in Celaenae in Phrygia and, as the custom was, he flattered his audience by extolling the prosperity of the town, which, he notes, served as a market and a place of meeting for the neighboring Cappadocians, Pamphylians, and Pisidians.

> And what is more, the courts are in session every other year in Celaenae, and they bring together an unnumbered throng of people – litigants, jurymen, orators, princes, attendants, slaves, pimps, muleteers, petty traders, harlots, and artisans. Consequently not only can those who have goods to sell obtain the highest price, but also nothing in the city is out of work, neither the teams nor the houses nor the women. And this contributes not a little to prosperity. For wherever the greatest throng of people comes together, there necessarily we find money in greatest abundance, and it stands to reason that the place should thrive.
>
> (*Or.* 35.15–16.)

Lots of people mean lots of customers, and the ensuing economic activity leads to prosperity. Dio undoubtedly raised at least a smile with his allusions to the sex industry, which apparently also experienced a boom when the courts were in session. The text raises some interesting points. Economic activity could be 'productive' in many different meanings of the word. Labor could be employed to produce goods that were productive in themselves, like ploughs or tools, or enhanced the productivity of others, like shippers or carters who transported the food that enabled others to work in non-food-producing sectors, and the workers who built the roads on which the carts moved. Labor could also be used for more consumptive purposes, such as literature, music – or sex.

A sign of the economic growth of the Roman period is the apparent increase in services and in the consumption of luxury goods. There were not only more people, but all the indicators show that per capita consumption had also grown. The material culture of the common people in the Roman Empire of the second or third century CE reflects more affluence and diversity than any earlier (and, for a long time, later) period. A well-to-do farmer or merchant of that time may not have had much political power, but materially he was as well off as the aristocracy of archaic Greece and Italy. The towns and cities themselves were more splendid than ever before, often boasting multistoried houses, aqueducts and sewage systems, bathhouses, theaters, temples, and public squares. In other words, luxuries and consumer goods were available to wider circles of society and were distributed over wider distances than ever, and this, one might say, constitutes the essence of economic growth in the Roman world.

The economic 'value' of these goods and services may be said to rest in the economic 'demand.' However, demand requires a lever – without this, it is merely wishful thinking – and the lever that turns 'demand' into 'value' is buying power. So, the question is: on what basis did the buying power (or entitlement) of the consumers of the goods and services of Celaenae, and all the other towns and cities of the Roman world, rest?

URBAN PROSPERITY AND RURAL PROPERTY

The elites of classical antiquity were mostly landowners who resided in towns. It is disputed to what extent the landowning elites of Roman cities invested their capital in urban commercial activities, but it may safely be said that for the majority their wealth was based on their rural properties. Of course, these possessions in the countryside included such rural industries as brickyards, potteries, and textile workshops, but the greater part of their rural holdings consisted of plots of land and farms spread over a wide region. The richest landowners owned land in several provinces. Our sources do not allow us to establish with any precision the extent of landownership by the urban elites in relation to that of other groups, such as peasants or well-to-do farmers, but it is clear that much of the land was concentrated in few hands. In the Later Roman Empire, for example, the wealthy Christian lady Melania is said to have owned 60 small villages, each housing 400 slaves. A few (fragmented and incomplete) inscriptions and papyri offer surveys of landownership in particular territories, on the basis of which Duncan-Jones concluded that landownership tended to be highly concentrated. He also observed that in some cases the largest single holding accounted for about 10 per cent of the surveyed area.[27] The concentration of landownership may not be adequately reflected in these sources, given that the richest owners held land in more than one town.

A brief calculation may serve to visualize the volume of production controlled by the upper layer of landowners. During the early empire C. Caecilius Isidorus is said to have owned more than 100,000 hectares (Plin., *HN* 33.134; 36.109–10). Even on a fairly conservative estimate (on the assumption that no more than 15 percent of his land was under cultivation of wheat each year, 5 *modii* were sown per *iugerum*

[= $\frac{1}{4}$ ha], and that the land yielded eightfold of the seed sown), the property of Caecilius Isidorus may have yielded 2,400,000 *modii* of wheat annually, enough to feed approximately 44,000 soldiers (who received rations of 4 *modii* per month) for a year. If we take into account that (1) labor productivity in commercial cereal farming may be estimated at between 450 and 700 *modii* of wheat per worker per year; (2) we have left out 85 percent of Isidorus' land; and (3) the average urban consumer ate less than a Roman soldier (i.e., a well-fed adult male), it is clear that the land of Caecilius Isidorus by itself may very well have provided a sizeable Mediterranean town with all the wheat, oil, wine, meat, etc. it needed. Of course, few landowners were as rich as Caecilius Isidorus. However, we have some idea of the number of senators, *equites*, and members of the municipal councils, and of the wealth that was required to hold such positions. On this basis Wim Jongman has concluded that the imperial and municipal elites "must have controlled almost the entire surplus above subsistence".[28] Moreover, wealthy landowners had much better access to the grain market than their poorer neighbors, hampering the latter's ability to sell their occasional surpluses.[29]

As noted above, the landowning elite tended to reside in towns and cities, and this is where they spent most of the income they derived from their estates. The towns and cities served as it were as the stage on which the landowning elite performed its social role, which encompassed much conspicuous consumption and acts of euergetism, that is, the expenditure on behalf of the community of citizens – primarily conceived as the citizens residing in the towns.

Elite income in kind was transferred into money through the market. Wealthy landowners transported part of the wheat, barley, wine, oil and other food stuffs produced on their estates to the towns in order to feed their sizeable urban households and to support their dependents. Much of it, however, was sold to local urban consumers or exported to distant markets, and the revenue was used to purchase luxuries and to finance their activities as local benefactors, which included the construction and maintenance of temples, theatres, bathhouses, and the like. The people who earned income by offering goods or services to the elites bought goods and services in turn, not only including the food produced on the estates of the urban elites, but also the goods and services produced by the urban economic sectors. In short, the distribution and redistribution of agriculturally based income provided the engine for a potentially complex urban economy.

This engine, fueled by the rural income of the urban elites, also worked beyond the confines of a single town or city. Whether they belonged to the class of wealthy landowners or those urban dwellers who depended for their employment on the spending power of the former, urban consumers bought their goods from local producers as well as from outside sources. For example, Patavium in Cisalpine Gaul is said to have exported clothing to Rome.[30] Hence, the textile industry in Patavium profited from the spending power injected into Rome. It makes no difference for our model of the urban economy whether urban consumers bought their clothing, ceramic ware, or perfumes from people living in the same city or from people outside that city, just as it makes no difference whether the landowners sold their surpluses to the neighboring town or to a distant metropolis. There is also no denying that many among the large-landowners profited from the economic activity that was the result of their own spending. Urban elites owned ships, brickyards, and urban workshops, and drew income from them. The crucial point is that much of the buying power that formed the basis of the urban sectors originated in the income that the urban elites derived from their rural properties.

The flow of spending power from the urban landowners' agricultural possessions to the urban sectors was largely one-way, and whether they received income in money or kind does not make much difference to our model. Their estates were partly worked by slaves, supplemented by free laborers at peak times. The slaves and free workers only saw a small share of the income derived from their labor, ensuring living standards that were little above subsistence level. Alternatively, the land was leased to tenants who either paid their leases as a fixed sum of money or in a fixed share of the crops (sharecropping). In the case of sharecropping the landowner clearly controlled a large part of the marketable surplus. In the case of money leases, the tenant needed to sell his surpluses first in order to pay the landowner, but much of the income of the land still ended up in the owner's hands. In either case, investment in food production was not proportionate to its share in earnings. From the viewpoint of the Roman landowners, there was little point in investing much money in basic food production. The practice of arable cultivation on commercial farms was characterized by relatively low input of capital. Earnings were high and – what may have been more important – stable without large investments. The alternative approach – increased exploitation of those working the land – was far more attractive.[31]

This is not to argue that the landowners did not invest capital in their rural possessions, but, as we have seen, these activities should partly be seen as belonging to the non-food-producing sectors. From our perspective it does not make a difference whether the urban elite participated in the textile industry by employing urban weavers (as in Tarsus) or by investing in textile workshops on their rural estates. In part, this investment was very direct: the workers employed in their non-food-producing activities were fed with the food produced either on the same or on other estates in their possession (thus Varro, *Rust.* 1.16.3). In short, the capital the elite earned by cultivating food crops was invested in non-food-producing activities both in the urban and in the rural context. This was not balanced by an equal flow in the opposite direction.

A similar role may be attributed to the emperor and the state, including the military, which distributed much spending power on the basis of its taxes in money and kind. The emperor was by far the largest landowner in the Roman Empire, and his expenditure was likewise aimed at fulfilling the political and social role that was expected of him. Spending by the emperor and the state likewise fueled the non-food-producing sectors.[32] A large part of the spending power that thus trickled down benefited the urban economy. This spending power was based on the social and political rights of the landowning elites, the emperor, and the state – in other words, their entitlement to a large part of the surpluses produced by the labor employed in the food-producing sector.

Was the entire urban economy based on one-way flows of resources? No, the agricultural workers, peasants, and small market-orientated farmers consumed goods and services too, and paid for them with the income of their labor. In other words, this constituted a two-way flow of resources. While the spending power of the majority of the rural population was quite low individually, the aggregate demand it generated was significant. Peasants bought goods that they could not produce themselves, such as iron tools or large ceramic vessels (*pithoi*), but also luxuries that became part of the expected living standard of the common people, such as clay figurines or *terra sigillata*.[33] Strabo (5.1.12) remarked that most Italian households wore clothes made of coarse Ligurian wool.[34] Egyptian papyri indicate that peasants bought mass-produced goods such as cheap jewelry and clothing.[35] One should also not underestimate the aggregate buying power of middling groups, such as estate managers and well-to-do farmers. The best example of the flow of spending power towards the countryside may be found in the prosperous villages of the East, which, as we have seen, profited from the sale of olive oil, wine, and other agricultural goods to the populous cities in the region.

However, not all the goods and services consumed by the rural populace should be seen as part of a reciprocal flow of resources between town and countryside. While it is true that the rural populace collectively consumed many goods, many of these goods were produced in the countryside and thus bypassed the urban economy. Moreover, rural households overall earned much income by employing their labor away from their farm, by processing goods, offering transportation, or acting as seasonal workers in towns and cities. To the extent that their consumption is based on this income it does not constitute a reciprocal relationship in the division of labor between food- and non-food-producing sectors. In short, the spending by the landowning elites, including the emperor, and the state of their income seems to have predominated sufficiently to justify the statement that the urban economy was founded on the base of their social and political entitlement to the produce of others.

We have seen that the urban population grew even more in Roman times than the population at large. The question is: how did the economy support this increasing urbanization? Growing levels of productivity in the food-producing sectors were not only the result of technological innovation but also of changes in the structure of agriculture. In fact, the share of the urban population (or rather, of the labor engaged in non-food-producing sectors) was not limited so much by technological constraints as by the structure of agriculture, characterized by high labor input, low labor productivity, and much underemployment in the countryside. It has been pointed out in regard to early modern France that "the share of the population strictly required to sustain a minimum level of subsistence was probably at most 40 percent; in agriculturally advanced regions it was about one-third."[36] In reality, the share of food-production was much higher than that. A similar picture prevails for much of Europe, and the same is undoubtedly true for the ancient world. The increase in urbanization reflected shifts in this regard: agricultural labor input was lowered by a shift from subsistence farming to slave-based estates and tenancy. In other words, high numbers of peasants were replaced by lower numbers of slaves and tenants. Concomitantly, labor input in agriculture was lowered, thus diminishing the level of underemployment. At the same time, the growth of non-food-producing sectors opened up employment opportunities for members of rural households, not least in the form of temporary or permanent migration to the cities. This is reflected in urbanization levels: the proportion (not size) of the rural population decreased as that of the urban populace increased. In that sense, rural underemployment was transferred into urban (and rural non-food) production. In short, owing to the large extent of underemployment there was much scope for growth even without technological advance.

One observation may be added: the Romans had less trouble mobilizing large armies in the third century BCE than in the third century CE. This seems paradoxical, in view of the economic growth in the meantime, but it is, in fact, quite logical. The high level of underemployment and low level of labor productivity characterizing the Italian countryside in the mid-Republic made it easier to withdraw part of the available manpower without detrimental effects on society. The intensification of the agricultural labor regime and the higher levels of labor productivity in the countryside in the Mediterranean region during the High Empire made it harder to withdraw rural labor without interfering with the surplus production that was necessary to maintain the expanded non-food-producing sectors. Together with other factors, this might explain the mobilization problems the Romans experienced and the shift in recruitment from Mediterranean lands to less urbanized regions.

EAST AND WEST IN THE LATER ROMAN EMPIRE

Finally, a look at the decline of the city in the western half of the Empire from the third century CE onwards. We may distinguish two aspects. In the first place, those elements that characterized the 'classical' city declined: the public spaces and monuments, the bathhouses and theatres deteriorated and literally fell apart, the stones often used for churches and walls. In late antique Leptiminus, an amphora workshop was located in one of the former bathhouses of the town, while metalworking taking place in basilicas in Silchester and Caerwent (Britain) indicates a shift in function rather than an absolute disappearance.[37] In this regard, the contrast to the eastern provinces is striking. In Syria, Palestine, and Arabia, for instance, large-scale building projects of a similar kind to those in the early empire continued. The social and political decay of urban life may be distinguished from the economic and demographic decline that affected the city in the period of the Later Roman Empire. As we have seen, many towns and cities in the West diminished in size or disappeared altogether, while similar developments hardly occurred in the East. The causes for this development should take into account the widening gulf between East and West in this regard.[38]

Neither the increasing concentration of landownership, nor any decreasing prosperity of landowners may be blamed for the decline of the city. Concentration of landownership would not necessarily have affected the city negatively, while there is no indication that large landowners were less wealthy than before. However, one cause contributing to the decline of the city in the West was the greater extent of the ruralization of the landowning elites. In the western provinces the upper layer of landowners tended to evade civic duties and claims by the state by withdrawing to the countryside. The city ceased to be the stage on which they played their social and political roles, and consequently conspicuous spending and beneficence ceased to constitute the means by which they infused buying power in to the city. Similar developments may have taken place in the East, but certainly not to the same extent. In fact, there is "no clear evidence that in the East landowners transferred their principal residence to the country in significant numbers."[39] Interestingly, the support shown by the imperial court and private benefactors to the Holy Land in the fourth to sixth centuries CE contributed to the prosperity of the towns and cities of Palestine.[40]

Towns and cities in the West also lost part of their economic functions. In Sicily, for example, agriculture in the countryside continued to prosper, but large landowners now exported their surpluses directly, bypassing urban channels. As a result, the three main harbors Syracuse, Catania, and Massana survived, while the other towns declined. Similar developments occurred in the *ager Tarraconensis* in Spain.[41] Significantly, the one city in the northern provinces that escaped urban decline in the fourth century was the imperial residence of Trier.

We end by concluding that the ruling landowners of the municipalities and the imperial elites, including the emperor, had been sufficiently wealthy and powerful to sustain the prosperity of the classical city. In the West, the city declined once rulers and landowning elite stopped spending their income in urban settings, a process that was as much a consequence of social and political developments as of economic changes.

NOTES

1 Procop. *Aed.* 6.6.13–16, quoted from Mitchell 2007: 348.

2 Dio Chrys., *Or.* 7, presents rustics as morally pure, but significantly his main character does not recognize a popular assembly or theater when he sees it.

3 See for instance Sperber 1998: 73–102 for an overview of public buildings in the towns and cities of Roman Palestine, which together boasted more than 30 theaters, at least 10 circuses, and possibly more than 6 amphitheaters (p. 78).
4 Moreover, I have already done so in Erdkamp 2001. But see also below, in the penultimate section of this chapter.
5 Scheidel 2007a: 42–9.
6 Manning 2007: 441. Rathbone 2007: 706 even estimates 750,000.
7 Alcock 2007: 677.
8 Pleket 1990: 81. On the Italian urban system, Morley 1996: 181–3.
9 Pleket 1990: 83.
10 Approximately 80,000 according to Mitchell 2007: 351. Cf. Scheidel 2007a: 78.
11 Jones 1987, 52; Faulkner 2000; Liebeschuetz 2001: 82–5; Depeyrot 2006: 229–30.
12 Holum 2005: 97.
13 Walmsley 1996.
14 Cf. Rathbone 1990: 119–21 regarding Alexandria's dominant position in Egypt. On the urban network in Roman Greece, Alcock 1993: especially 129–71.
15 Mitchell 2007: 334. On the distinction between cities, towns and villages in Roman Palestine, see Safrai 1994: 17–103.
16 Adams 2001b: 177.
17 Trombley 1987; Holum 2005: 94; Mitchell 2007: 337–8.
18 Treggiari 1979.
19 Drinkwater 2001: 298.
20 Wilson 2001.
21 Pleket 1998: 123–5; 1990: 123; Garnsey 1998: 47.
22 Pleket 1990: 35.
23 Jones 1974: 353.
24 Erdkamp 1999.
25 Mattingly et al. 2001: 79–80.
26 And also water or air, but, though crucial, these latter necessities are not meaningful elements of an economic analysis of urbanism as intended here.
27 Duncan-Jones 1990: 126ff.
28 Jongman 2006: 247–50. Similar, Bang 2008: 111–12. Scheidel and Friesen 2009 have estimated that elites (around 1.5 per cent of the imperial population) controlled one-fifth of total income, while middling households (10 per cent of the population) consumed another fifth.
29 Erdkamp 2005: ch. 3–4.
30 Strabo 5.2.5; 5.3.11; 12.8.14; 5.1.7.
31 Kehoe 1992: especially 2 and 168ff.; Pleket 1993b: 15.
32 See in particular Pollard 2000: 171–211 on early imperial Syria.
33 Woolf 2001: 54–8.
34 Garnsey 1998: 47.
35 Rathbone 2007: 709, 713.
36 Grantham 1993: 487. Cf. Allen 2000: 1: "Crop yields have received considerable attention. [. . .] However, labour productivity is arguably a more important variable in explaining the transition to an urban, industrial economy." Discussed in more detail in Erdkamp 2005: ch. 1.

37 Jones 2007: 188.
38 See also Wickham 2005: 591–692.
39 Liebeschuetz 2001: 37–8.
40 Holum 2005: 96–7.
41 Keay 1991: 79–87; Liebeschuetz 2001: 97.

13: Money and Finance

Sitta von Reden

The development of Rome and the Roman Empire would have been impossible without the development of money. The introduction of coinage was a direct consequence of Rome's expansion into Italy and soon formed a close relationship with Roman imperialism. Coined money was the medium with which the Roman armies were paid and most tributes from the provinces extracted, while imperial conquest secured control over a growing number of gold and silver mines as well as expanding the geographical radius of monetary relationships. Culturally, Roman money owed much to the Greek model, or rather, what it had grown into during the Hellenistic period: the idea of coinage; the idea of bronze coins as fiduciary money (money not backed up by 'absolute' value); the exchange of coins between different monetary systems; banks as places for money-changing, safekeeping of deposits, managing of payments, and making of loans; and, above all, some fundamental rules of contractual law that made credit and cashless transactions possible among a wide group of people. The Greek influence on Roman monetary practice is reflected in many Latin financial terms, such as *mensa* (table) for bank like the Greek *trapeza* also meaning table. Certain types of loan contract and banking procedures carried transliterated Greek names, such as *sungrapha* for witnessed loan contracts, and *chirographum* referring originally to an informal hand-written contract. Some terms were translated from the Greek, such as *perscriptio* for the Greek term *diagraphe*, meaning written order of payment.

Yet from about the middle of the second century BCE onwards, the Roman monetary economy began to grow into something quite notably different. Greek monetary economies had been largely regional and mostly subordinate to agricultural wealth and resources. Surely, the Athenian empire during the fifth century BCE had created an interregional coinage which was widely accepted and imitated far beyond the Greek-speaking world, and which remained a dominant coinage long after the Athenian confederacy had disintegrated. The conquests of Alexander the Great, in addition to mobilizing large amounts of Persian treasure, created an even greater imperial coinage and took it far into the Eastern empires. Both the development of extensive imperial coinages, circulating side by side with more local issues, and the massive increase of precious metal in circulation had affected the power of Greek monetary economies considerably. And yet, in the largest economies of the Hellenistic world – Egypt and the Near East – coined money formed only some part of vast agricultural systems that functioned on the basis of payments in grain and precious metal bullion. Even in the Aegean and the Greek mainland monetary wealth remained dependent on agrarian social structures. In this chapter, I wish to demonstrate how Roman money and finance transformed the Mediterranean economy, and how this transformation can be explained.

MONETIZATION

What does monetary development mean? The Romans had some form of money by the time of the Laws of the Twelve Tables, where penalties are reckoned in the monetary unit of the *as* (*Tabula* 8.3–4 [*c.* 400 BCE]). The so-called Servian census of the fifth century BCE is also – perhaps anachronistically – supposed to have been conducted on the basis of a calculation of *asses* of bronze (Livy 1.43; Dion. Hal. 4.16). The first Roman bronze coins and pre-weighed bronze bars (*aes signatum*), however, appear not before the end of the fourth or early third century BCE.[1] The issues were tiny in comparison to the monetary transactions that the Romans are likely to have made by means of uncoined metal. The first Greek-style silver drachms produced by Roman authority in Campania in the mid-third century BCE, too, can hardly have been central to the economy of the Republic, nor do they match the size of the indemnity payments that Carthage is supposed to have paid to Rome after the first Punic War.[2] They must have served a particular purpose for the Romans in dealings with Greeks in Magna Graecia.

An incontrovertible link between Roman monetization and coin production emerged by the end of the Second Punic War when Rome massively increased its silver coinage. In 214 BCE a monetary reform created a totally new monetary system in which the denarius first appears, replacing the silver didrachm minted so far for the Campanian coin system. The adoption of coinage as the dominant form of money in Rome must be linked to the new level of income and expenditure derived from tribute, indemnity payments, and predation, on the one hand, and the costs of warfare and imperialism (stipends, construction work, and subsidies to client kings) on the other. Precious metal, the backbone of the new denarius coinage, is believed to have been captured at first, but soon was derived from mining resources that came into Roman possession.[3] The districts of the Spanish silver mines were conquered in the course of the second century. Macedonia, both storing wealth and controlling gold and silver mines, became a Roman province in 146 BCE. Greece followed, and the province of Asia was created in 129 BCE. The impact of conquest on the money supply in Rome was immediate. Between 157 and 100 BCE Roman coin production quadrupled.[4] In a famous though controversial calculation, Keith Hopkins suggested that the number of Roman coins in circulation rose tenfold during the mid-second and early first centuries BCE.[5] According to Suetonius, the increase of spending power resulting from conquest could be so dramatic that it caused property prices in Rome to rise and interest rates to fall (Suet. *Aug.* 41; cf. Dio 51.21.5, related to the conquest of Egypt in 30 BCE).

We must be careful, however, not to infer from an increase of Roman coin production that monetization increased in absolute terms. Already by the second century BCE Roman coins virtually extinguished Greek coinage in Italy and Sicily. Native Spanish coins began to be replaced from about 70 BCE. Imperial expansion also led to a growing number of people with Roman citizenship and Latin rights, the growth of the city of Rome itself, and probably population increase in the Roman Empire as a whole. Thus quite simply, a larger number of people used Roman money. Despite the well-founded impression that the Roman economy became more monetized in the course of the second and first centuries BCE, we need to look for changes that increased monetization rather than noting that there were more Roman coins around.

The army was the first and foremost stimulus to monetization. By paying soldiers and the labor costs of military infrastructures in cash, the Roman government showed a firm commitment to its own monetary medium.[6] The Roman army, moreover, itself spread the practice of monetary exchange. It has frequently been argued that the stationing of troops in frontier provinces led to an increase of monetization there. But the influence of the army seems to have been a little less direct. Constantina Katsari has observed that numismatic finds concentrate less in military sites and fortresses than in the urban centers in their proximity. It was the growth of urban centers that was stimulated by the presence of troops, rather than army movement on its own.[7] Soldiers also, rather than just spending money, introduced monetary practice in the areas in which they lived or settled.[8] Soldiers mostly came from and were settled in rural areas, where household production and local social exchange shaped the economy. At times of war, however, their pay was supplemented by monetary donatives and above all booty. Ancient authors make a special point of emphasizing that Roman armies sold their share of booty on the spot (Polyb. 10.16. 4; Livy 10. 17. 4). Sallust tells us that Roman soldiers in North Africa sold the grain allotted to them and bought bread from day to day (Sall. *Iug.* 44). Claude Nicolet comments "commercial and military activity were not sharply opposed . . . Pillage and commerce were two complimentary and interconnected methods of exchange and . . . it was a long time before the ancient world established a clear distinction between them."[9] David Hollander argues that army service was what sociologists call a "bridging occupation," that is, one that affected subsequent economic accomplishment and social mobility. In rural areas traditional farmers lived side by side with their more commercially minded peers who had served in the army. The growth of towns created new demands on the hinterland of cities and fostered a transformation of the rural economy. This, as Hollander suggests, was driven by the innovative activities of soldiers and veterans. Veterans above all, who were settled in *coloniae* within hostile environments, introduced cash-cropping for urban markets and monetary exchange into areas yet unfamiliar with coinage.

Urbanization was thus another major stimulating factor for monetization. The argument that money was an urban phenomenon has bulked large in older accounts which linked the development of money to the development of markets.[10] The view has been qualified by site finds of large amounts of coins in rural Britain and Gaul, and above all by the highly monetized economies of the Greeks and Romans in rural Egypt.[11] Urbanization, moreover, is a highly flexible concept that does not imply necessarily a sharp contrast with rural habitation. The terms for city or town (*oppidum*, *municipium*, or *colonia*) conveyed to settlements a particular official status in the Roman administrative system rather than relating to size, population density, or economic function. Large Egyptian villages could be far more populous than Italian cities, and pre-Roman hill forts in Gaul appear to have been similar in size and population density as the Roman *oppida* that developed after the conquest.[12] Urbanization also does not necessarily go along with an increase of non-agricultural production. Since the Roman Empire grew out of a conglomerate of highly diverse sociopolitical formations, it did not develop a single unified system of towns. Small poleis of the Greek world typically had a large proportion of urban residents who farmed land in the surrounding hinterland. *Coloniae* were not just urban settlements in which residents lived in recognizably urban centers. The megacities of Antioch, Alexandria, and Rome itself come closest to modern concepts of cities developing a high degree of division of labor and dependence on markets. But their supply of food and services, too, was highly dependent on a class of resident agrarian *rentiers*, agrarian hinterlands extending into distant regions artificially linked to these cities, and on imperial tribute in kind. At least in principle we have to assume that in many cases the number of urban residents was well above the size of non-agricultural producers dependent on markets.[13]

And yet the large degree of urbanization that did take place above all in the Western provinces played a significant part in monetization, while urbanization itself was spurred by it. For it was in the Roman towns – large or small – where the Romanizing elites resided and where agricultural taxes and rents were converted into cash. As Walter Scheidel suggests, "by the early Roman imperial period many cities had come to function as nodal points of a larger system of exploitation and transfers, converting local taxes and rents into exportable items of trade and cash. Without the extraction of resources that was caused or facilitated by imperial authority, elongated lines of trade and the resultant network of cities that was ultimately centred on the capital would not have emerged in the same way."[14] The political life of urban elites in the cities of the eastern Mediterranean, moreover, was centered on self-representation and public expenditure (so-called *euergetism*), which also stimulated the transformation of agricultural surplus into cash.[15] In these functions, and as parts of an emerging urban network which can be studied particularly well in Roman Gaul, urbanization played an ever increasing role in the development of monetary relationships.[16]

The commercialisation of agriculture and the expansion of villa economies from the late Republican period onwards combine into a third important stimulus for monetization.[17] Villas were rural estates which functioned as agricultural enterprises and rural retreats of absentee landlords living in the cities of the Empire. We know much about villa economies through the literary works of the agrarian writers Varro and Columella, while archaeological remains add to our knowledge of the spread of villas and their spatial organization. Economically, villas were run by free or slave managers (*vilici*) and keenly supervised by absentee landlords who occasionally visited their estates. Large villas specialized in cash-crops, especially wine and oil. Experimentation with stock-raising for commercial purposes is evident from the first century BCE onwards and increased substantially in the subsequent two centuries. Part of the land of a villa was rented out to tenants in short-term tenancies. As these tenancies were subject to monetary rents, they encouraged cash-cropping and monetary exchange of small and great farmers.[18] Villas flourished above all in Italy and Campania due to the demand created by the growth of the city of Rome for which all Italy served as hinterland.[19] But they also spread into the provinces as both Roman agrarian holdings and Roman economic behavior expanded rapidly in the empire, especially in Africa, Gaul, and Egypt. Moreover, both here and elsewhere the flourishing of villa economies was intimately linked to the importance of agriculture for political careers. It can be regarded as a particularly enduring aspect of Roman civilization and its transformation under provincial influence in the late Republican and early Imperial periods.

For most of the time of the late Republic and early Empire the interdependent processes of military expansion, metal supply, economic development, and monetization seem to have been fairly balanced. The Julio-Claudian emperors managed to hold both silver and gold coins stable in weight and fineness until the middle of the first century BCE. Yet with an ever increasing demand for coinage in the military sector, and growing monetization in terms of coinage in the provinces, the Roman government began to stretch its financial resources by lowering the weight and fineness of the precious metal coins. Such reductions were made temporarily in the first century, but regularly from the mid-second century onwards. In 215 CE a double denarius (*antoninianus*) had 1.5 times the weight of the denarius but twice its value, but soon had to be abolished because it drove out of circulation the heavy denarii of the old weight. In 238 CE the *antoninianus* was reintroduced, this time in connection with the demonetization of the single denarius, and was further reduced in weight and fineness. Provincial currencies were adjusted, while the growing number of cities producing local coins may suggest that the increase of Roman coins in circulation increased the demand for small change in local economies.[20] By the third quarter of the third century, monetary manipulation combined with political disintegration had reached a scale that made people lose their confidence in Roman silver coinage.[21] Evidence for banks disappears between 260 and 330 CE.[22] After a period of massive price inflation, monetary units were fixed to a gold standard. Further reforms under the emperors Diocletian and Constantine followed, aiming to stabilize a system which for some reason had become impossible to stabilize. But many users turned away from coinage and reverted to a barter economy.

Imperial money

Money becomes a more powerful instrument of payment if it promises a broad transactional network. Nothing enhances a currency's acceptability more than the prospect of acceptability by others.[23] There are, however, constraints and objections to the development of broad currency networks: the desire of local governments to control their own currencies; the tendency of national (or civic) coinages to build a sense of collective tradition and memory; the identification of domestic currencies with popular sovereignty; its capacity to create trust and confidence in local government, and so on. The monetary consequences of the Roman conquests are a good example of the tension between local concerns and imperial power striving to foster monetary cohesion. At the time of the Severan emperors, the Roman historian Cassius Dio has Maecenas advise Augustus: "Let no one have currency and weights and measures of their own, but let them use ours instead" (Dio 52.30). If this was an imperative of the imperial policy of Augustus, or the Severan emperors, it had not been so from the beginning of Roman expansion.[24]

In Italy, Sicily, and Africa the Roman silver currency soon was the only precious metal currency after the Roman conquest. In Greece, however, despite the fact that the Romans became involved here from the beginning of the second century BCE, Roman silver coinage does not appear before the time of Sulla. In Asia Minor, Roman denarii became current around the late first century BCE and in Syria from the time of Augustus. In Egypt, the Ptolemaic currency based on the Greek tetradrachm continued to be the only valid coinage until 296 CE. Down to the Julio-Claudian period the *kistophoroi* of Pergamon and Ephesus remained important in Asia Minor, the drachms and didrachms of Caesarea in Cappadocia, and tetradrachms in Antioch.

In other areas, denarii were the dominant currency, but coexisted with local issues. In Spain, Iberian denarii, which had been minted in a large number of local mints from the second century BCE onwards, continued to be in use until the time of Augustus. In Western Macedonia, the denarius began to spread slowly, but was supplemented by silver coins of Dyrrhachium and Apollonia. In Gaul, natively produced silver coinages continued to play a role, as did surviving British issues in

Norfolk and Southern Britain. In addition, many cities in Asia Minor minted local bronze coinages, a practice which was prestigious, necessary for the high demand of coinage, and profitable.

Although other currencies circulated alongside the denarius, by the middle of the first century BCE there was no real currency competition any longer. The Roman denarius had become what economists call a top-currency in the Roman Empire.[25] Its exceptional role was, as just argued, due to the monetizing dynamics of the Roman army, urbanization, taxation, imperial control over currency production, and above all a new degree of mining. Whereas in the first 150 years of Roman expansion it seems to have been impossible for both economic and political reasons to interfere systematically with local production of coins, and to produce coinage on an imperial scale, these possibilities emerged gradually during the first centuries BCE and CE. As we mentioned above, the production of Roman denarii is reckoned to have increased fourfold from the mid-second century to the beginning of the first century BCE. In absolute terms, there may have been as many as 450 million denarii in circulation in *c.* 80 BCE as against 40 million in 157 BCE. This means that within eighty years more than 400 million denarii had been produced at irregular intervals, averaging 50 million per year. Although absolute numbers must be treated with caution, the figures support the impression that the massive increase in Roman wealth generated by successful warfare and provincial exploitation had direct effects on coin circulation in the Mediterranean.

Where local monetary traditions remained strong, currency consolidation was achieved by monetary coordination, that is, the regulation of exchange rates. Official exchange rates were introduced in order to integrate old coinages into new monetary systems. As we saw in the previous section, the major silver currencies in the late Hellenistic period were based on three standards: the Attic, the Chian and the Ptolemaic. On the Attic standard, on which the Seleucid coinages in Syria were still based, one tetradrachm was equivalent to four denarii. On the lighter Chian standard, to which the *kistophoroi* in Asia Minor came close, a tetradrachm was equal to three denarii. In Egypt, where the silver content of the tetradrachm was much reduced in the first century BCE, a tetradrachm was reckoned at 1.5, and by the time of Nero, at 1 denarius. Whether these rates were set officially, or developed in practice, is controversial.[26] In the course of the Empire, however, these relationships were subject to frequent change and led to a great degree of uncertainty about the value of money in transactions.[27]

In payments by and to the state, the denarius was usually the official accounting standard even when payments were made in other currencies, or in kind.[28] In some areas we know that reckoning in Roman units (rather than using Roman coins, as is often argued) was enforced by law. An inscription from Thessaly in Northern Greece refers to a directive of Augustus according to which customs and taxes had to be reckoned in denarii (*IG* IX.2 415, ll. 52–60).[29] Similarly, Germanicus laid down for the customs stations in Palmyra that taxes must be reckoned *pros Italikon assarion* ("in Italian *asses*," *OGIS* II 629, 16 ff.). In a subsequent reissue of that law under Hadrian, however, only larger dues were to be collected *eis denarion* (on the denarius standard), whereas those below the denarius were allowed to be exacted in local *kerma* (ibid. ll. 153–8). Scholars tend to believe that this meant that sums paid in local coins were unacceptable if above the amount prescribed. But it is also possible that *eis denarion* and *pros Italikon assarion* simply meant that this was the monetary standard on which the tax was assessed, whereas taxpayers could pay in any coinage provided the tax collector accepted local coinage, presumably for a fee.[30] In some cases local coins were countermarked with Roman denominations in order to be valid for payment. This practice is known from Caesarea, where a Greek coin was found marked with a stamp stating its Roman equivalent of two *quadrantes*. In Chios, where at one time value marks were put on coins, pieces of the same size and weight were inscribed with either *obolos* (1 obol) or *hemiassarion* (half *as*).[31]

The need of Roman emperors to incorporate, rather than extinguish, local monetary systems into their system, can also be inferred from the *kistophoroi* in Asia Minor. At times of independence, this coinage showed on the obverse the sacred chest (*cista*) encircled by a laurel wreath. In the early decades of Augustan rule, however, Ephesus and Pergamon produced *kistophoroi* with imperial iconography. Instead of the chest, coins now showed a portrait of Augustus and the Roman Pax on the reverse. The change may not even have been imposed by imperial directive, but by local response to Roman rule. For the next 150 years, Roman-style *kistophoroi* continued to be minted locally, while many other provinces used denarii imported from the Roman mints.

In Egypt, too, local currency was maintained. Since the introduction of a closed currency system under Ptolemy I, the Egyptian tetradrachm had been lighter than the Attic, although a high degree of fineness had been maintained well into the first century BCE, despite a perennial shortage of silver.[32] Ptolemy XIII (73–51 BCE), however, took the step of reducing the silver content of the Egyptian coins. By the time of Cleopatra VII, the tetradrachm contained less than fifty per cent silver. Under Tiberius minting of precious metal tetradrachms was resumed, but their silver content further reduced and a distinctly imperial design adopted. Egypt occupied an exceptional position in the Roman economy, producing much grain for the capital as well as other parts of the empire. The economic exploitation of Egypt had worked for centuries on the basis of a currency that was regulated not by circulation but administrative control. There was no reason for the Romans to change this. On the contrary, they still continued to devalue the silver coinage. Augustus is said to have stripped the capital and temples of their silver resources and prohibited any import of precious metal. By the time of Nero, the Egyptian tetradrachm contained a little more than 50 per cent of the silver of a denarius, but was exchanged at a rate of 1:1.[33]

Coin circulation reached an unprecedented scale as an ever-increasing portion of the Mediterranean came under the control of the Romans and their coinage. But the degree of monetary consolidation that was achieved under the Roman Empire cannot lead to the conclusion that the economy of the Roman Empire was integrated in terms of market prices and production.[34] There has been much debate over the question of what economic integration might mean.[35] There is no unequivocal evidence that there were interregional markets for goods, labor, or credit. At the level of monetary circulation, the cash flow was interrupted by uneven monetization throughout the Empire, and the interest of the Roman government in collecting tribute in kind.[36] The difficulty of policing an imperial currency across the geographical reach of the Empire added further problems for a unified monetary system. The Roman government continually legislated against counterfeit and adulterated coins produced both privately and officially by local mints.[37] This shows, on the one hand, the demand for Roman coins over and above their supply. On the other hand, it demonstrates that the administrative regulation required for maintaining an imperial currency was difficult to achieve.

A unified currency facilitated the collection of taxes and, in principle, benefited the flow of coins between Rome and the provinces. But, arguably, imperial finance remained decentralized, with most taxes being spent where they were raised.[38] Moreover, in local economies much cash took the form of bronze coinage which was produced locally and accepted only in the area of its issue. It has proved difficult to derive a general pattern of coin circulation from the composition of surviving hoards, but in the absence of clear evidence for empire-wide circulation it should be supposed to have been predominantly local or regional.[39] The monetary network that was created by the denarius in the first 250 years of Roman rule will have had massive effects on the degree of monetization, on the efficiency of the political economy of the emperors, and on the 'private' economy of those who benefited from public infrastructures and communication lines. Yet it remains open to further investigation whether the Roman currency network was able to transform the Roman economy into a market economy with an empire-wide consolidation of prices affecting local patterns of production and consumption.

Money beyond cash

For most of the last century scholars have insisted that monetary exchange was synonymous with the use of coinage in the ancient world. This orthodoxy has now been challenged. How could Cicero transfer 3.5 million sesterces which he paid for a house on the Palatine (*Fam.* 5.6.2)? Did C. Albinius, when buying an estate from a certain C. Pilius for 11.5 million sesterces, physically send him this sum in silver coins (Cic. *Att.* 13. 31. 4)?[40] Scholars have brought together many indications that by the Hellenistic period the circulation of money was not, and cannot have been, just based on coinage.[41] There were, first of all, forms of cashless payments for which the law of debt provided the legal frame. The commonest form was probably the use of *nomina* (credit or 'bonds'). Cicero alludes to the practice when mentioning the purchase of a house (*Off.* 3. 59: "He provides *nomina* and thus completes the deal"). *Nomen* was the term for a written entry made into an account-book when a loan was made or taken out. It could either refer to the entry made, or to the actual loan that the entry referred to. If a purchase was made by *nomen*, the purchase price was extended as a loan and paid later in the form of some monetary transfer, or in installments. Already by the mid-second century BCE, it was recognized that *nomina* (loans or their written testimony) could be transferred by *delegatio* or *transcriptio* to third parties (e.g., Cat. *Agr.* 149.2).[42] In 49 BCE, Quintus Cicero tried to pay off a loan to Atticus by assigning to him a debt owed to Quintus by Egnatius (*Att.* 7.18.4). In 45 BCE, Faberius wished to pay off a debt by assigning to Cicero several of his *nomina* (which, however, Cicero did not accept; *Att.* 13.3.1.). In principle, therefore, any large payment could be settled without the use of cash by constructing a loan, or by transferring a debt claim. During the Republic such transfers still required the consent of all parties involved, but by the second century CE they seem to have become less personal and quite standard.[43] Legal historians have explained such strategies as constructions to circumvent the general principle of cash exchange.[44] But a purely legal explanation downplays the impact of these practices on the development of money. They transformed a monetary economy based on cash into one based on both cash and monetary instruments.[45]

Another type of cashless transfer of money was *permutatio*, literally meaning the 'exchange of one thing for another.' The transaction has been variously translated as 'barter' or 'written order of payment between banks' or 'bill of exchange.'[46] It has also been suggested that it originally involved an exchange of different currencies.[47] Cicero alludes to the practice several times without explaining it.[48] In all cases, *permutatio* seems to have had the function of transferring money from one place to another by using money that was in one place, and the currency, in which it was needed. Thus Cicero, travelling to Cilicia where he served as governor in 51 BCE, stopped over in Laodicea to collect money owed to him by the administration. He refers to the operation as a *publica permutatio*, a transfer of public funds, and the money was handed over to him by a tax-collector. Subsequently he paid to the tax-collectors 2.2 million sesterces, which he had accumulated during his proconsular government of the province (Cic. *Fam.* 3.5.4). When sums were transferred for private purposes, no tax-collectors would be involved, and other channels had to be used. Cicero, once again not in Rome, asked Atticus to give to his son Marcus, who happened to be studying in Athens at the time, his stipend by *permutatio*. Atticus, who had many contacts in Greece, found a creditor who advanced the money to Marcus. The creditor in fact owed money to Atticus, and by paying the cash to Marcus, he paid off his debt to Atticus. Cicero, in turn, paid over to Atticus rents of houses that he leased out in some quarters of Rome.[49] *Permutatio* was thus a procedure, rather than a document or legal claim, involving a network of relationships and obligations built up over time and various transactions. Although its primary objective seems to have been to move public resources around the empire, individuals could make similar arrangements if their economic activities had reached a degree of complexity.

A third type of cashless payment was related even more closely to transactions across provincial boundaries. These payments were based on documents (loan contracts) called *chirographa* or *sungraphae*. The fact that these words derive directly from the Greek (*cheirographon* ['informal written contract'] and *sungraphe* [written contract witnessed by six witnesses]) shows their Hellenistic origin. At first they were used just for contracts with non-Roman citizens.[50] By the time of the first century BCE, however, both *chirographa* and *sungraphae* referred to debt claims transferable to third parties. The meaning is likely to have been derived from the fact that in Greek these documents served as proof that a debt was still outstanding (if the loan was returned, the creditor gave the note to the debtor). This had gone so far that in Rome loans based on a *sungrapha* could be reclaimed by the heirs of a deceased creditor on production of the loan document (e.g. *IG* XII 5, 860; *c.* 75 BCE). But in an exchange of letters with C. Trebatius Testa Cicero alludes to the possibility that *sungraphae* were also a means of cashing money (*Fam.* 8.2.2; 8.4.5; 8.8 and 10; 7.7.1). Reproaching Trebatius Testa for his eagerness to exploit the finances of a province too hastily, he writes: "For you were in a hurry to snatch up money and return home, just as if what you had brought the governor was not a letter of recommendation but a *sungrapha*" (*Fam.* 7.7.1). Cicero also mentions *sungraphae* in a brief fragment of a letter which he had written to Greek *negotiatores* who wished to cash these documents in the province of Achaia. According to a letter to Atticus, the city of Salamis in Cyprus had borrowed from Brutus 100 talents (2.4 million sesterces) for which a *sungrapha* had been issued (*Att.* 6.2.7). Some years later, M. Scaptius and P. Martinius, intermediaries acting on Brutus' behalf and resident in Cyprus, tried to reclaim the money on production of the document (*Att.* 5. 10 ff.). Some quarrel arose over the amount of interest to be paid, since the document specified a rate which had become illegal when Cicero became governor of Cyprus.

In comparison to the Hellenistic economy where cashless payment and credit money had first come into practice, there were some important developments. As the geographical radius of Roman imperial power was greater than that of Hellenistic kingdoms, the administrative and legal space in which cashless forms of money could operate was more extensive. A second development that may be noted is the increasing flexibility of cashless payments. Transfers of debt-claims to third parties are attested in Hellenistic Egpyt (where most of our Hellenistic material comes from) within the royal administration and that of large estates. This might be an accident of our evidence as it almost exclusively relates to these contexts. Yet the fact that Roman law, in contrast to Hellenistic principles, seems to have begun to recognize the transfer of *nomina* and written loan contracts to third parties by *delegatio*, renders it highly likely that loan documents became proper monetary instruments to be used among a wide social range of people and a wide range of transactions.[51]

CREDIT AND BANKING

The impact of credit, banking, and financial intermediation can be conceptualized in various ways, depending on the model of economic development one adopts. According to the neoclassical model, credit has economic consequences only if it is used as capital for investment into productive enterprise. So-called consumption loans taken out to cover deficits and personal expenses are of little significance in this approach. Lending and borrowing in Roman society took place at all social levels, and for a wide range of purposes.[52] Our evidence privileges lending and borrowing of large sums, and we may presume that in terms of volume of money, they formed the more significant part. Still, most examples we have for Roman credit fall in the category of consumption loans. In his comprehensive survey of the purposes of elite borrowing in Rome, Koenraad Verboven lists warfare, luxury items, purchases of houses and estates, building projects, dowries, travel and accommodation expenses, repayment of debts, bribery, unforeseen deficits, and general business purposes among the most frequently mentioned.[53] While it seems that elite borrowing was mostly for non-productive purposes in the neoclassical sense, credit mobilized coinage and extended the monetary economy where it was weak. We know that Roman citizens lent to provincials, despite certain prohibitions made by the *lex Gabinia* in 67 or 58 BCE.[54] Brutus, for example, lent to the Salaminians on Cyprus 2.4 million sesterces in 56 BCE (see above). The Gallic revolt in 21 CE is said to have been caused by debts incurred due to the pressure of Roman monetary tribute (Tac. *Ann.* 3.40). The revolt of Boudicca in Britain was also, according to hostile sources, caused by Seneca's recalling 40 million sesterces worth of loans all at once (Dio 62.2.1; Tac. *Ann.* 14.31); and the father of the emperor Vespasian is said to have turned from tax-collecting in Asia to lending money to the Helvetii (Suet. *Vesp.* 1.3).[55] It is in this sense that we must envisage the impact of credit on the Roman economy. Because large amounts of money were concentrated in the hands of very few, exceptionally wealthy people, the spread of the Roman monetary economy was predicated on credit.

A significant part of the imperial elite (including, as time went on, wealthy provincials) were lenders. Debt claims, rather than money, constituted the monetary part of the property of the wealthy. Eumolpos, a fictional character in Petronius' *Satyricon* (first century CE), pretends to have in Africa 30 million sesterces partly in land and partly in debt claims (*Sat.* 117). Seneca describes a fortunate man as one who was "sowing and lending a lot" (*Ep.* 41. 7), and he himself was known for "spreading estates and equally extensive lending" (Tac. *Ann.* 14.53). Pliny the Younger thought in the same terms when claiming that he was all in landed property, while having some money on loan (*Ep.* 3.19.8). Money was regarded as an asset when it was used productively (though not in the neoclassical sense) by being lent at interest.[56] Caesar's law on the restriction of credit provided that no more than one-third of the property that was situated in Italy (i.e., property which qualified for registration in the census), should be in loans rather than land (Tac. *Ann.* 6.16). The law is usually quoted to illustrate political restrictions on senatorial lending, but other aspects are equally noteworthy: the fact that a significant part of a senator's property was invested in loans, and that senatorial lending reached such a scale that it affected the census.

Loans were made and mediated in several ways: interpersonally, through middlemen, and through bankers.[57] The three categories overlapped in practice, and it is often difficult for us to distinguish them in the evidence. When Q. Considius, possibly a senator, is said to have held 15 million sesterces' worth of debt claims (Val. Max. 4.8.3), it can neither be expected that he did not use intermediaries, nor can we exclude that he was an intermediary himself.[58] One of Cicero's letters to Atticus shows that both Cicero and Atticus had intermediaries in Puteoli (*Att.* 6.2.3.). The tablets of the Sulpicii reveal that the emperor Claudius invested money of his *patrimonium* in loans through his freedmen and the Sulpicii.[59]

Intermediation could take different forms. M. Scaptius and P. Matinius, mentioned above, were *negotiatores*, businessmen who among other activities made money through mediating loans for a fee or share of interest. Elite lenders could also invest their money through mandated agents (*procuratores* or *institutores*) who invested money on behalf of their principals, and did other business for them as well.[60] Alternatively, masters (as well as the emperor) could set up their slaves or freedmen as *faenatores*, professionals who specialized in money-lending. Some such men did their work "around the middle Janus" in the Forum at Rome where independent moneylenders no doubt also set up their business. Making use of professional *faenatores* had the advantage of rendering financial affairs more discrete, and of profiting from the bargaining power of people whose skills as usurers were famed. Yet another alternative was to set up a legal business partnership (*societas*).

Cato the Elder is one of the earliest examples in Rome to have done so to invest his money in maritime loans (Plut. *Cat. Mai.* 21.6). The Sulpicii, too, are most likely to have been a *societas* of either bankers or *negotiatores*.[61] A *societas* was a partnership of two or more associates (Cato is said to have assembled 50) who pooled their resources and shared the profit. *Societates* could be set up for any business purpose (tax-collectors frequently formed *societates*), and their members did not have to have an equal share and status. Cato's partnership was set up for financing maritime commerce, while his financial assets were mandated to his freedman Quintio who also 'looked after' the loans of the others. Given that elite lending was part of a wide portfolio of financial, managerial, and political, activities, the strategies and purposes of elite lending would have varied.

Bankers formed a special type of credit institution. The first bankers (*argentarii*) appeared in Rome together with the first coins, but they are not well attested before the early second century BCE. In the comedies of Plautus they are money changers, assayers of coins, and deposit bankers. During the second half of the second century BCE they begin to surface in connection with public auctions, where they advanced credit to buyers. Several sub-categories of bankers existed, who seem to have provided some but not all services associated with banking. Yet by the first century, *argentarii* provided the range of services we expect from a high-street bank.[62]

Bankers differed from other professional moneylenders in that they took funds in deposit. For unsealed deposits they paid interest and were allowed to lend them to third parties. Despite this fundamental difference, and despite bankers being distinguished from *faenatores*, they are not easy to tell apart from other attested financial intermediaries. We cannot be certain whether the Sulpicii of Puteoli, whose records offer many insights into the complex nature of financial business, were bankers or businessmen (see n. 61). The Sulpicii were a circle of freedmen, or sons of freedmen, who in the first century CE formed a business alliance through which a range of banking services were provided. They extended loans against security in cash or kind, managed the assets of others (including at some point considerable sums of the emperor Claudius), kept documents safe, and mediated legal support. The four members of the association were two brothers and their associates who were official agents (*procurators*) of these brothers. To judge from the range of documents kept on file, both the brothers and their agents looked after affairs independently, and all three looked after the affairs of third parties. The fuzziness of their business profile (scholars are divided as to whether they were *negotiatores* or *argentarii*), the complexity of their dealings (lending, borrowing, fund-raising, arranging guarantees, dealing with legal affairs) and the vagueness of the contracts which they left in writing but which must have entailed additional verbal agreements (no loan contract, for example, specifies the rate of interest) suggest that financial transactions, even of bankers, were based to a large extent on oral communication and dealt with a mixture of financial, legal, and commercial purposes.

Given that bankers looked after the money of others, and given that they could take over some legal functions, their reputation for honesty was, and had to be, much higher than that of other professional creditors. In contrast to elite lenders, however, their power and status was lower and the sums they lent more modest.[63] Jean Andreau suggests that the significance and status of bankers declined with an increasing interest of members of the elite in lending out their assets, which roughly began by the time of Augustus. "This development worked increasingly against the emergence of a bourgeoisie, since the financiers situated above the professional bankers were already connected with the world of landowners with patrimonies. One of the features of this development was that the growing financial activity propelled the ancient economy into greater dependence upon the land-owning oligarchy."[64] There is also, and perhaps linked to this observation, no evidence that bankers were much involved in maritime finance.[65] Maritime loans were a special type of loan in that they were secured by the cargo of the ship for which the money was lent, and if this was lost, the creditor lost the full amount of the money invested. If extant information does not mislead us, it seems that this profitable but risk-laden business was embedded in the social business networks of the elite, who may have provided a better infra-structure to control its success and safety.

Although research of the past decades has concentrated on proving or disproving bankers' involvement in maritime trade, the impact of banks on the monetary economy must be seen somewhere else. Because of their regular and complex management of the assets of others, they developed in practice procedures that were very important for monetary flexibilty. Banks, rather than *faenatores* or elite lenders, can be shown to have spurred innovation by making legal principles adjust to their financial reality. Paper transactions from one deposit to another, for example, came to be recognized as loans, since bankers, transferring money between accounts by routine, did not record every transaction through a proper loan contract.[66] Bankers could also by convention make payments on a client's behalf without the client's account showing sufficient funds. The so-called *receptum argentarii* (responsibility of the banker) foresaw that legal claims of the beneficiary lay against the banker rather than the payer. So if there was sufficient trust between banker and client, a banker could accept 'overdrafts' or make a loan to his client without his being present.[67] Many bankers, furthermore, were individuals, but some formed *societates* (e.g. *Rhet. Her.* 2.19; *Dig.* 2.14.25 pr.; 14.27 pr.). As early as the first century BCE partners could contribute and profit asymmetrically, and a principal could by oral or written order give an agent unlimited or restricted competence over transactions, thereby limiting his own liability. Conversely, claims to recover deposits and loans could be made against any partner of a bank set up as a *societas*, not just the one with which the client had dealt. This gave the bank great flexibility in monetary dealings, and reduced the transaction costs of both bankers and clients.

CONCLUSION

It is now sufficiently proven that Roman money and finance were not too simple to have had any impact on the ancient economy.[68] Rathbone and Temin write "it seems that Rome did not miss industrialisation for want of adequate financial intermediation"; and similarly, Harris concludes that "shortage of money was not to any important extent a brake on growth."[69] From the second century BCE onwards evidence for credit and banking increases by the century until it declines again in the second century CE.[70] The Roman monetary economy had taken off when the Romans became engaged in Magna Graecia and the Hellenistic Mediterranean, which they gradually came to dominate. Right down to the conquest of Egypt the massive monetary wealth of the Hellenistic monarchies was appropriated by the Romans and became part of Republican social structures. It enriched the Roman nobility, probably at the cost of Hellenistic aristocracies, as is indicated by a decline in wealth of Hellenistic bankers.[71] Henceforth monetary expansion went hand in hand with imperial expansion, provincial exploitation, imperial administration of taxes, the spread of Roman agricultural property throughout the Empire, urbanization, and the spread of Roman currency itself. Monetization affected local economies more profoundly than had been the case in previous centuries, as can be seen from the monetization of Gaul, which was different in nature than the spread of coinage among the Celts in the Hellenistic period; and from the further monetization of Egypt, where monetary contracts become far more frequent and widespread than under the Ptolemaic kings.[72] Although the degree of monetization remained very uneven throughout the Roman Empire, its growth in some places stimulated further growth, in particular through the lucrative financial activities of the imperial elite. I have suggested in this chapter, that among the most fundamental developments of the Roman monetary economy must be regarded the growth of a currency network based on the Roman denarius, the development of monetary instruments based on Roman law and an imperial administrative infrastructure, and the development of Roman law that backed up an increasing range of monetary transactions and banking operations.

NOTES

1 For the beginnings of Roman coinage, Burnett 1987: 4ff.; and Crawford 1985: 1–25 with slightly different chronology.
2 Howgego 1992: 4f., with Frank 1933–40: I 74f. Whether these figures, taken from later literary sources, are trustworthy may be open to doubt.
3 Howgego 1992.
4 Crawford 1974: II.643–91.
5 Hopkins 1980: 107ff.; for discussion, e.g., de Callataÿ 1995; Wilson 2002; 2007 emphasizes the increase in Greenland ice-core lead as a result of a significant increase in mining activity during this period.
6 For the importance of such commitment, see Woodruff 1996.
7 Katsari 2008: 261–3.
8 Hollander 2005.
9 Nicolet 1980: 122, quoted from Hollander 2005: 233.
10 Thus above all Crawford 1970; and Burnett 1987: 96.
11 Howgego 1992: 20–2; and Katsari 2008: 243–4.
12 Woolf 1998: 106–42 for an excellent survey of the nature of urbanization in Gaul under Roman influence.
13 Scheidel 2007a: 74–80.
14 Scheidel 2007a: 80; see also Katsari 2008: 262.
15 Osborne 1991 for this link in Greek poleis.
16 Woolf 1998: 112ff.
17 Jongman 2003 has qualified the impact of villas on social and economic change in the Middle and Late Republic; but, however much villas mattered in the economy as a whole, they did matter for monetization.
18 Kehoe 1988b and 1997 provide the best surveys of the different kinds of tenancies in Italy and the Roman Empire.
19 Morley 1996.
20 For the monetary changes, see Harl 1996: 125–57; for the demand for local coinage, Katsari 2005.
21 Rathbone 1996b; also Burnett 1987: 104.
22 Andreau 1999: 33.
23 Cohen 2004: especially 11.
24 For the following, Burnett in Burnett et al. 1992: 2–10.

25 Cohen 2004: 14.
26 Wolters 1999: 373 for the former; Harl 1996: 98 for the latter.
27 Wolters 1999: 371–4.
28 Christiansen 1984.
29 Burnett 2005: 176, also for discussion of the following example. The Ephesian Customs Law, sections 25–6 (Engelmann and Knibbe 1989; 62 CE), may refer to a practice of taxing the transportation of coined money across provincial borders, but the evidence is inconclusive.
30 Maresch 1996: 121–7 for agios in Roman Egypt.
31 Burnett 1987: 46 for both examples.
32 Hazzard 1984.
33 Christiansen 1984: 292–6.
34 Bang 2008: 93–110 for the best recent discussion; Kessler and Temin 2008 build their argument on unconvincing evidence.
35 Woolf 1992; Howgego 1994; Wolters 1999.
36 Duncan-Jones 1990; Howgego 1992; Rathbone 1996a.
37 *Dig.* 48.13.1; Wolters 1999: 365–7.
38 Rathbone 1996a; Wolters 1999: 233f.
39 Howgego 1995: 102f. Duncan-Jones 1994: 172–9 argues against an empire-wide circulation pattern; von Reden 2010: 65–91 for the case of the Roman Empire in a wider diachronic perspective.
40 Harris 2008b: 175f.; Shatzman 1975: 22–4 for further examples.
41 Harris 2006; 2008b; Hollander 2007; Rathbone and Temin 2008; von Reden 2007.
42 Harris 2008b: 192; Hollander 2007: ch. 3, for a survey of cashless forms of payment and credit-money.
43 Hollander 2007 for the Republican period; Harris 2008b: 193 with *P.Fouad* I. 45 (153 CE) and *CIL* 3.934–5 V (162 CE) for Roman Egypt and Dacia.
44 The classic statement of this theory is that of Pringsheim 1950.
45 Andreau 1999: 1 denies that the Romans developed any "organized system of monetary instruments" beyond coins.
46 Kiessling 1924; Lewis and Short s.v. *permutatio*.
47 Andreau 1999: 132; see also Cic. *Att.* 11.1.2.
48 Hollander 2007: 40–1 with examples.
49 Cic., *Att.* 12.24.1, 27.2, 32,2; 13.37.1; 14.7.2, 16.4, 20.3; 15.15.4, 17.1, 20.4; 16.1.5; for which Andreau 1999: 21.
50 In theory, Roman contractual forms could only be used among Roman citizens, while other forms of contract applied in dealings with peregrines (foreigners). In practice, business agreements with non-Romans were quite indiscriminate, and many contracts used both Roman and Greek law; Rathbone and Temin 2008: 382.
51 For the lack of legal guarantees for written transfers, and even orders, of payment, see Bagnall and Bogaert 1975; von Reden 2007: 290–3; by contrast, Harris 2008b: 193 with *Dig.* 46.2 (*De novationibus et delegationibus*).
52 The vast majority of loans were oral agreements between friends and family, patrons and clients, or masters and slaves. It was morally most acceptable to charge no interest. In a society where a high value was placed on generosity, large amounts of money could be lent interest-free, or even donated, to entire communities.

Commonly, however, interest was charged, and there was no particular stigma placed on it. Probably from the early second century BCE the maximum legal rate to be charged per year was 12 per cent (*usura centesima*). In the late Republic and early Principate, this rate could also apply to provincials. Exception was made for maritime loans, where rates were higher because of the higher risk of loss.

53 Verboven 2002: 153ff.

54 M. Crawford in *OCD* s.v. *lex (Gabinia)* suggests that the law forbade lending to provincials just within Rome; by contrast, Rathbone and Temin 2008: 387 n. 46 suggest lending to provincials was generally forbidden for fear that such loans were made against future tax revenue.

55 Rathbone and Temin 2008: 391 for these and further examples.

56 This implies the observation that loans were a certain form of money, as Cicero takes for granted in 2 *Verr.* 5.17; Harris 2006: 7.

57 See for the following the excellent surveys by Andreau 1999 and Rathbone and Temin 2008, although the latter disagree with Andreau in several details.

58 Andreau 1999: 11, 15.

59 Rathbone and Temin 2008: 388.

60 Rathbone and Temin 2008: 403–4.

61 For discussion whether they were bankers or brokers, Andreau 1999: 76–8; Jones 2006; Rathbone and Temin 2008: 397–9 suggest that they were bankers.

62 Andreau 1999: 30–49; Rathbone and Temin 2008 disagree with Andreau's distinction between different types of banks each having a clearly defined range of functions.

63 Andreau 1999: 4; but see also his own qualifications (49).

64 Andreau 1999: 134–5.

65 We have just two hints of bankers mediating a maritime loan *TPSulp.* 23 (if the Sulpicii were bankers); and *SB* 14.11850 (second century CE), with Rathbone 2003.

66 Rathbone and Temin 2008: 400 with *TPSulp.* 60–5.

67 Andreau 1987: 597–602.

68 So Finley argues in Finley 1999: 53–4, 115–16, 141–3, 166–9, 174 and *passim*.

69 Rathbone and Temin 2008: 371; Harris 2008b: 207.

70 Andreau 1999: 136.

71 Andreau 1999: 134–5.

72 Woolf 1998: 44–5 for Gaul; Rathbone 1989: 165 and Forabosci and Gara 1982 for Roman Egypt.

14A: A FORUM ON TRADE

Andrew Wilson

Interstate treaties in Classical Greece normally specified reciprocal trading rights; Latin citizenship was defined partly in terms of trading privileges, and the Punic Wars were fought over the control of trading zones in the central Mediterranean. The persistent reluctance of many historians in the later twentieth century to admit the extent and importance of long-distance trade in the ancient world is therefore difficult to understand,[1] and indeed utterly incomprehensible when one considers the archaeological evidence in addition to the written record.

Long-distance trade, already important in the Hellenistic period, increased further with the gradual unification of the Mediterranean under Rome, and the virtual eradication of piracy by Pompey. By the Augustan period all the regions surrounding the Mediterranean were controlled either directly by Rome or indirectly through its client kings, and with this unified political control came a single currency throughout most of the region, common institutional frameworks in the form of laws, market supervision and regulation, and state investment in road networks, canals, and harbors.[2] All of these greatly reduced transaction and transportation costs and facilitated the growth of trade. Many of the goods available in the markets of any city, and especially in coastal ports, were produced in the territory of another city, and often in another province; this applies to staples as well as luxuries.[3]

The wide distribution of certain categories of goods is clearly evidenced by archaeology, but chiefly for ceramic and stone artefacts, which are archaeologically durable and can be provenanced to a source region. The scale of the wine trade between Italy and Gaul in the second and first centuries BCE is clearly shown by the distribution of Italian amphorae throughout Iron Age Gaul and even into Britain,[4] and by wrecks carrying cargoes of wine amphorae, notably the Albenga wreck (100–90 BCE, with up to 10,000 Dressel 1B amphorae) and the Madrague de Giens (60–50 BCE, with between 5,000 and 7,000 amphorae).[5] These amphorae stand proxy for the archaeologically less visible goods, principally slaves, against which they must have been exchanged. The widespread, and at times almost pan-Mediterranean distribution of table pottery (Italian terra sigillata, Gaulish Samian, and then African Red Slip wares) further shows the existence of intensive trading networks; amphorae containing fish products, olive oil, preserved fruits and minerals such as alum were also widely traded; even cooking pots were shipped in volume between provinces,[6] as was glass (both raw chunks and finished products).[7] These goods are just the tip of the iceberg, as they are the most archaeologically visible.

The trans-provincial or even empire-wide distribution of many goods implies high volumes of maritime trade. The chronological distribution of known shipwrecks is a poor guide to volumes of trade for numerous reasons, but principally because the pattern of known shipwrecks is affected by the intensity of research and the visibility of durable cargoes.[8] The gradual replacement of amphorae by barrels complicates the apparent picture of a decline in wreck numbers after the first century CE. Wrecks provide better information about the composition and loading of cargoes; while mixed cargoes are the norm, they emphatically do not imply a pattern of casual tramping. Rather, analysis of the arrangement of mixed cargoes in wrecks shows that they must have been loaded at emporia in a single go.[9] The dominant pattern of Roman maritime trade, in stark contrast to picture of cabotage tramping painted by McCormick for the early medieval period, is of directed trade between emporia, with coastal redistribution to lesser ports in their coastal foreland.[10] State investment in harbor infrastructure, through the construction of new harbor facilities and the dredging of existing harbors, enabled this directed trade.[11]

Riverine and overland trade, although more expensive than maritime trade, formed a part of most trading journeys and is amply attested through iconography and epigraphy. The Roman state created a handful of canals, and repaired others, but its interventions in transport networks are best exemplified by the empire's extensive road system.[12] Although the initial impetus for road construction was the need to control newly conquered provinces, roads and bridges greatly facilitated the commercial carriage of goods. No equivalent network was seen again in even a part of the Roman empire until the creation of turnpike roads in eighteenth-century England, and even these covered only a fraction of the area of the Roman system, and their usage was charged for.

State intervention went well beyond the creation of transport infrastructure, and extended to systems of food provisioning, principally for Rome but also for some other key cities. The *annona* or grain handout to citizens at Rome was created as a political tool by the Gracchi and reorganized by Augustus; Severus added olive oil to the handout, and by the time of Aurelian the grain handout had been upgraded to loaves of bread, and augmented by a ration of pork.[13] The political need to secure the food supply for Rome was a key reason for building the imperial harbor at Portus, and tax incentives were soon created to encourage private shippers to put their ships at the state's disposal. In the reign of Commodus a state merchant fleet for Africa was created.[14] The *annona* must have had a stimulating effect on private trade in other goods along routes between Egypt and North Africa,[15] providing a framework of regular traffic on which other goods could piggyback, but the scale of market demand was such that trade also throve along routes unconnected with this armature of state supply. In addition, the state intervened in the market in other ways: the creation of the vast olive oil amphora dump at Monte Testaccio began nearly two centuries before Severus added olive oil to the *annona*,[16] but the centralised discard at Testaccio, coupled with control marks written on the amphorae, show unmistakably that this was a state operation. It seems that the state was buying sufficient quantities of olive oil from producers chiefly in Baetica, and to a lesser extent Tripolitania, to guarantee the supply to Rome and avoid shortages and concomitant price fluctuations.[17] Until it was distributed free under Severus, this oil must have been sold at a fixed or subsidised price. Aurelian proposed a very similar arrangement for wine produced in southern Etruria, stored by the state in the Temple of the Sun and sold at a controlled price.[18]

Large-scale long-distance trade in marble, and especially colored marbles, for architecture had started in the late Republic but increased substantially from the reign of Augustus onwards, with large state-funded building programs both in Rome and the provinces making use of exotic colored marbles from quarries that increasingly came under imperial ownership. Marble from Numidia, Greece, and Phrygia, and granite and porphyry from the Eastern Desert of Egypt used in imperial projects symbolized the reach and control of the empire, and the expense of quarrying and transport lent extra potency to the message they conveyed. Some colored marbles were also made available to privately or muncipally funded building projects, and on the back of the imperially driven trade in colored and white architectural marbles a private trade developed in white marble sarcophagi, marble sculpture, and veneer panels, peaking in the second and early third centuries CE.[19]

Until recently, trade beyond the frontiers of the Roman Empire was considered to be of little significance, restricted to low volumes of luxury goods for a small elite market. Recent archaeological discoveries are leading to a reevaluation of this view: the quantity of Roman amphorae and table pottery found in excavation and survey work of settlement sites and tombs in the Fazzan indicate a substantial trade with the Garamantes of the Libyan Sahara, who were trafficking slaves northwards from sub-Saharan Africa.[20] New work in India and at the Red Sea ports of Myos Hormos and Berenice points to a thriving and intensive trade between Roman Egypt, the Arabian peninsula, and Egypt, exporting gold, wine, and fish products, and importing spices, cotton textiles, pearls, and sea turtle shells.[21] Pepper was imported in sufficiently large quantities that it was available throughout the empire to the social levels well below the elite, as far north as Vindolanda in Britain.[22]

The goods from Arabia and India imported through the Red Sea ports were conveyed across the Egyptian Eastern Desert via two main road routes, and then conveyed down the Nile to Alexandria for onward shipment to other provinces. The desert roads were equipped with watering points guarded by forts, and traffic was organized in caravans with armed escorts against desert nomads; the state charged a fee for the permits to use these roads.[23] In the mid-second century CE a detachment of troops was stationed on the Farasan Islands near the southern mouth of the Red Sea, well to the south of the Roman frontier, presumably as protection against pirates.[24] The state interest in the Red Sea trade which is evidenced by such measures is explained by the customs value of this trade, with a 25 percent import duty levied on goods imported or exported across the frontiers of the empire. The Muziris papyrus of the mid-second century CE gives a customs assessment of part of a cargo imported from Muziris (Pattanam, India) to Berenice, valuing the cargo after customs duties at nearly seven million sesterces.[25] The state's revenue on this one cargo was thus *c.* 2.2 million sesterces. With 100 such cargoes a year (a conservative estimate, as Strabo a century before speaks of 120 ships a year leaving Myos Hormos for India[26]), the customs revenue on the *import* trade alone through the Red Sea would have amounted to perhaps between a quarter and a third of the entire military budget for the empire.[27] This new appreciation of the potential importance of external trade to the state coffers is reinforced by Strabo's account of Augustus's reasons for not invading Britain; one was the projected loss in customs revenue if the cross-Channel trade ceased to be taxed at external rates and became subject only to the lower rates of inter-provincial transfers.[28]

The high levels of long-distance trade resulted in a partial convergence of the cultural package of material goods available in different provinces, increasing the variety of choice of goods, and contributing to a sense of belonging to a wider empire with goods available from its constituent parts. This geographically integrated trading network, sustained by the institutional support of a politically unified Mediterranean, began to come apart with the collapse of the Roman state, weakening in the west after the creation of Constantinople, which diverted much of the *annona* trade away from Rome, and the Vandal conquest of North Africa. In northern Europe, trade networks collapsed with the end of Roman rule, to the extent that markets in post-Roman Britain were no longer large enough to support the continued production of wheel-made pottery.[29] By the seventh century, even before the Arab invasions of Egypt and North Africa, trade reached a nadir in the central Mediterranean, and between the seventh and ninth centuries Rome's pottery came from within a radius of 30 km.[30] The importance of the Roman state to the functioning of trade networks is well shown by what happened when that state fell apart; but we are perhaps only just beginning to grasp the importance of that trade to the Roman state.

14B: A FORUM ON TRADE

Morris Silver

Archaeological data and texts reveal large-scale commerce (regional and local) in the late Roman Republic and Empire. Heavily traded commodities include grain, processed fish, table pottery, textiles, and especially well attested, wine and olive oil.

The Roman state stored grain and provisioned armies and cities. It contracted with shippers (*navicularii*) and benefited associations (*corpora*) of importers. Nevertheless, much grain was stored for future sale by producers (recommended by Varro *Rust.* 1.69.1), and after leaving farms much (most?) grain was entirely handled by private traders and speculators. Their customers might be private individuals or public agencies. After deducting tax-grain, an estimated two-thirds of first-century CE grain exports from Egypt to Rome were available for purchase by private individuals and government.[31] Some 84 tons of Alexandrian wheat were pledged as security in the Sulpicii texts, with comparable quantities in other commercial texts, and large grain purchases were undertaken by the state.[32] Notwithstanding an anti-speculator mentality and maximum price regulations, grain prices fluctuated notably in response to changes in market supply and demand.[33] State participation in imports increased in the Later Empire.[34] Nevertheless, charges for government services were expressed in terms of wheat's market price.[35]

Dated shipwrecks, mostly near the coasts of Italy, France, and Spain, index Italy's wine exports. Early eighteenth-century England's East India Company lost 10 percent annually of its tonnage (5 percent in Victorian times). Applied to about 670 discovered wrecks, ships in Rome's wine trade numbered no less than 13,400 (or 6,700). Thousands of amphorae findspots in France are widely distributed. In the last century BCE an estimated two million gallons of Italian wine were imported into Gaul annually.[36] Cicero (*Font.* 9) concedes the duty levied in Gaul on Italian "produce/fruits" amassed "a very large sum of money." The exports were part of a pattern of regional specialization, not "surpluses": individuals, including elites (e.g., the Sestii family), repetitively produced wine for sale and profit.

"All Gaul is filled with traders – is full of Roman citizens. No Gaul does any business without the aid of a Roman citizen, not a single sesterce in Gaul ever changes hands without being entered in the account-books of Roman citizens".[37] Italians invested capital (including expertise) in Gaul's economy.[38] "The Gallic people wear the *sagus*... The wool of their sheep, from which they weave the coarse *sagi*... is not only rough, but also flocky at the surface; *the Romans, however, even in the most northerly parts raise skin-clothed flocks with wool that is sufficiently fine*".[39] Romans worked (pastoral?) estates in Transalpine Gaul (Cic. *Quinct.* 3–4, 6). Fieldwork in Gaul's Crau plain suggests the scale of the Roman pastoral economy.[40] A Lyon production site reveals names of several potters active in Arezzo and clay analysis reveals molds made there. Possibly, Italian tableware-producing firms founded branches more than 300 miles away, a fact which suggests a substantial degree of integration and managerial hierarchy.

New wine markets transformed Italian agriculture: land was consolidated, skilled slaves imported, and independent farmers became dependent workers.[41] Several regions reallocated resources from cereal production to wine/oil estates ('villas'). The Campanian estate of Cato, which had supported seventeen wheat-growing families, was planted with olive trees and vines. At Settefinestre, near Cosa on the Etruscan coast, villas replaced small plots. Juvenal (14.256–84) testifies to the scope of Italy's wine trade, spread of villas, and profit-motivation. The contribution of wine and oil production to gross domestic product is not known, but this is the relevant measure rather than the proportion of raw land employed.

Technical and informational connections between Italy and Roman provinces are visible in agricultural manuals: "In many passages Varro [37 BCE] draws attention to diverse methods of cultivation in different parts of Italy, and further afield, surprisingly he often uses Spain as a parallel. This tendency to adduce areas other than Italy becomes even more marked in Columella's *De re rustica* dating to the 60s AD. Here Spain, Gaul, and North Africa are frequently mentioned, although the Italian peninsula is still at the centre of the author's attention."[42]

Economic forces caused vertically integrated villas to decline in importance relative to small farms while Italian wine production reoriented from export markets to Rome and other cities.[43] De Sena provisionally estimates that during the earlier Empire perhaps 33 percent of Rome's wine and 25 percent of its oil were produced in the city's hinterland.[44]

Italy imported wine and oil from Gaul and Baetica (southern Spain). Baeticans invested in olive trees and amphora production facilities. Rome's Monte Testaccio ("Pottery Mountain") is made from more than 50 million oil amphorae (about 35,000 shiploads for the smallest cargo ship or some 1.5 billion gallons), about 80 percent from Baetica.[45] Millions of discards over two centuries prior to Septimus Severus's regularized oil distributions testify to markets.[46] Names on amphorae attest participation by merchants even during the third century CE. Emptied olive oil amphorae were smashed rather than reused/recycled as per the pottery "life cycle." New oil jars cost about 8 drachmas and 4 obols per 100, about twice the daily wage of a potter, in mid-third century CE Egypt. Arguably, merchants (*negotiatores olearii ex Baetica*) feared that empties, with their structural associations and markings, would be refilled with local olive oil and marketed as Baetican. Wasteful precautions to prevent "spoiled" markets suggest a continuous and significant private component in Italy's oil imports.[47]

Evidence fails to confirm numerous Roman 'peasants' standing mainly outside the market economy. Small farmers certainly participated in urban markets.[48] Objections that 'peasants' did not exchange much because, by utilizing redundant agricultural labor power, they could fulfill their needs more cheaply than outside suppliers, fail to understand that specialization and trade are guided by comparative, not absolute advantage. What matters is not a difference between trading partners in the amount of productive resources required to produce a good, but rather a difference between them in the rate at which one good can be transformed into the other by reallocating resources.[49]

Occupational specialists who take advantage of economies of scale provide an index of marketization (volume of transactions). Morel cites "160 trades mentioned in texts and inscriptions (and 225 for the whole of the Roman West), as compared with 101 and more than 99, respectively, for thirteenth-century Paris and fifteenth-century Florence, which were centers of artisan work."[50]

North (1977: 710; 1984: 262) sees transaction costs as "an insuperable barrier to price-making markets throughout most of history" and adds: "Exchange was, for most individuals, a supplement to a largely self-sufficient life." Expectations based on elevated communication and transport costs mislead because it is easy to forget that ancient institutions drastically reduced contract enforcement costs, mainly through reliance on solemn contractual rituals and oaths. Where moderns rely on technology and third-party enforcement, the ancients relied on gods and ritualization to build market economies.

14C: A FORUM ON TRADE

Peter Fibiger Bang

BAZAARS, EMPIRES, AND ROMAN TRADE

> When I was consul for the thirteenth time, I gave 60 *denarii* to those plebeians who were then receiving the public grain dole; these included a little more than 200,000 people.[51]

In this boast of Augustus is contained a paradox: the paradox of Roman trade. It is evidence for the single largest and most concentrated form of exchange that we can document with a fair degree of precision in the Roman Empire in terms of annual quantities; and it was the result, not of free market trade, but of state redistribution of imperial tributes imposed on the provinces. The public grain dole, 5 *modii* a month handed out free of charge to some 200,000 citizens in Rome year after year during the Principate, would have required the annual supply to the capital of some 80,000 tons of wheat and sufficed to cover the grain consumption of perhaps 400,000+ people. This is easily the largest example of redistribution in recorded pre-industrial European history.

Yet, it is the very same figure that gives concrete shape to the conclusion both that Rome, the city, must have been the greatest market in the empire and that state-directed redistribution, in the way it was understood by Karl Polanyi, was of only marginal importance in the Roman world. Most exchange activities outside the household would have involved markets. The public grain dole was precisely an exception; no other city in the early Empire had anything comparable. As Finley once insisted, the Greco-Roman economy was one of markets.[52] Even in Rome a large part of the population still had, wholly or in part, to buy their basic grain or bread subsistence on the market, not to speak of wine, clothes, olive oil, meat, and other necessities of life not covered by the grain dole (at least not until under Septimius Severus handouts of olive oil and meat were added to the grain rations). The number 200,000 likely comprised the vast majority of free males in the capital. But when we add to these women, children, and a sizable population of slaves serving in the households of the elite and those of middling wealth, a plausible multiplier would set the population total in the range of some 700,000–900,000 or perhaps even as high as a million.[53] This also makes Rome the largest market concentration in pre-industrial European history.[54]

Lured by the specter of this giant market, it has become increasingly popular to argue that the empire constituted a unified market economy.[55] This is a mistake – and it is unrealistic. Certainly, redistribution in pure form may not hold the key to the Roman economy. After all, the concept hails from economic anthropology – a discipline which developed from the study of small so-called primitive, much simpler societies, whereas the Roman Empire was a vast agglomeration stretching from modern Scotland to Iraq. The concept of redistribution, a very visible aspect of Roman antiquity, is nevertheless still useful in reminding us of the imperial dimension in the Roman economy.[56] As ideal types, empire and free market may be thought of as contrasts. The latter operates by voluntary exchange, while the former depends on force and the ability to command in order to extract resources from subjugated societies. The enormous concentration of demand in Rome derived from the exploitation of empire and the expenditure in the capital of much of the vast amount of plunder, tribute, and profits that it generated. As already indicated, the state-redistributive grain dole helped underwrite the formation of markets by enabling a large pool of consumers to spend their incomes on more than basic staple food.[57] In short, the "free traders" both exaggerate the extent of the market and underestimate the institutional complexity of the Roman Empire. The real issue is not whether the Roman Empire constituted a unified market economy – it could not possibly have done so, given that no other continent-sized society managed to do that before the age of steam and industry[58] – but to understand how markets interacted and mixed with other forms of economic organization. To that purpose, we need to look to other complex agrarian societies, to get a better sense of the limits of the possible and seek out plausible parallels. The weaknesses of the "free market" school, to sum up, are three-fold in character: empirical, comparative, and theoretical. Let us consider them one by one in somewhat greater detail.

EMPIRICAL OBJECTIONS

Let me start by stating what is not at issue. It is beyond doubt that a lot of trade took place in the Roman Mediterranean and that some integration of markets did occur. The movement of commodities is amply documented by the diligent work of archaeologists who have uncovered millions of ceramic vessels and shards from amphorae, table ware and cooking ware many of which had travelled far from their place of production, by processes where market trade may often safely be assumed to have played a prominent part. But much of this material does not fit the pattern envisaged by those that think that the empire created a unified market.[59] According to this school, the gradual political integration of the Mediterranean under one government promoted and eased trade by creating peace and institutional unity through the spread of Roman law and coinage; the end result was an empire-wide integrated market. Come late antiquity, however, commercial integration began to suffer as the state apparatus expanded and intervention in the market sphere became more frequent.[60]

There are several problems here. Archaeologists have revealed vigorous commercial developments in late antiquity, with exports from Africa (Tunisia-Libya in particular) conspicuously expanding from the second century CE, followed by parallel developments, for instance in Syria, Palestine, and Greece.[61] It is also clear that the largest commercial expansion in the Mediterranean preceded Roman unification. The two largest cities of the Empire, Rome and Alexandria, both developed into giant conurbations between the third and first century BCE.[62] Between them, they represented an enormous expansion of demand in the Mediterranean world. In the same period, we also see a significant rise in the slave trade to supply estates in Italy and on Sicily, the flowering of Delos as a commercial, customs-exempt hub, and exports of Italian wine finding their way inside Dressel I amphorae to many locations in the Mediterranean and in vast quantities, not least to the parts of Gaul beyond the Roman province.[63] Finally, it has long been recognized that under the early empire, Italian exports declined as some of the newly "Romanized" provinces began to substitute their own versions of the previously imported product – Gaul being the classic illustration of this rise of the provinces, with the emergence of both extensive production of so-called terra sigillata, emulating the ceramic productions from Italy, and cultivation of wine. Trade and the interregional division of labor quickly ran up against a barrier, precisely in the period when it was supposed to have intensified and deepened.[64]

One answer to this riddle, of course, is to deny that this is what happened and speculate that Italy came up with new products to export which regrettably have left no or little trace in the historical record.[65] Absent from this analysis, however, is one item which Italy, as the seat of government, did continue to export: violence and protection, in return for which the state could claim taxes and privileged aristocracies could draw rent. State and empire formation with its increased mobilization of resources preceded Mediterranean political unity and lasted into late antiquity. This "predatory" or tributary aspect of empire cannot easily be left out of any attempt to explain the expansion of markets under Roman rule as well as their "failure" to deepen any further.[66]

Two other aspects are relevant to an understanding of markets in the Roman world. About the first there seems to be general agreement, though some of the proponents of the free-market model attempt to avoid its logical implication. A very large part of the economy, probably a little more than half, was consumed within the producing households of the peasant majority without ever entering the market.[67] The second factor concerns the many limits on the capacity of merchants to integrate markets in a pre-industrial society. Most markets in the empire were much, much smaller than Rome, with only a few thousand people, more or less. Combined with a technological regime where transport was relatively slow and prone to disruption by the vagaries of the weather, it would have been difficult to obtain information and coordinate the movement of goods between markets, to match shifting supply and demand closely. Even as goods moved around between markets, considerable local differences would have prevailed and integration remained fragmented – though not absent, it should be stressed.[68] Peasant households, a degree of local market fragmentation, and tributary empire need to be included in the institutional matrix on which we base our analysis of the Roman economy.

Comparative contextualization

Next, historical comparison. Peasant households and considerable local fragmentation can be found in most pre-industrial societies, as Erdkamp also points out, but not everywhere did extensive world empires like the Roman exist.[69] Notably, they were absent from later European history. No other empire managed again to unite the continent in similar fashion to Rome. Those that stress market integration like to draw parallels between the Roman Empire and the rise of the capitalist market system centered on Amsterdam and London in the seventeenth and eighteenth centuries. There is an irony here. For among economic historians, the absence, even the failure of attempts to recreate a new Europe-wide imperial hegemony is normally considered a key element in explanations of the rise of capitalism. Perpetual interstate competition drove some governments in search of new revenues to guarantee increasingly favorable conditions to merchants in return for tax payments.[70] The societies that pioneered capitalism witnessed a succession of commercial institutional innovations, regulated bourses, joint stock companies, state bonds, and stock exchanges, which vastly increased the organizational capacity of merchants to integrate markets and became key elements in the breakthrough to modern economic growth.[71]

I do not think that a similar dynamic can be claimed for the Roman Empire, and certainly not during the first two centuries CE when peace and unity might have been expected to have brought market integration to an unprecedented pitch.[72] Quite the reverse, in fact. Occasionally, the Roman companies of tax farmers are brought up as institutional forerunners of the business corporation. For a period during the last chaotic years of the republic, they even seem to have had "shares," though the details remain obscure. But the point is that these companies were first and foremost developed to tax imperial subjects, and their role in the imperial economy was significantly rolled back under the emperors, not promoted even further (see my discussion in Chapter 10). At the macro-economic level the differences become clear. When London during the eighteenth century began to approach the size-range that Rome is believed to have reached, stronger commercial integration compensated for a much smaller catchment area. If Rome drew resources from an empire of some 60 to 70 million, London in, say, 1750, even if we include colonies in the New World and international commerce, depended on perhaps a third as many people or fewer. By implication, economic integration must have been more intensive.[73]

Those in favor of the modernizing parallel need at least to produce a detailed argument for why the historians of capitalism are wrong and why empire did not produce a different scenario in the Roman case. In the meantime, I think it far more productive to search for closer analogues. The Ottoman Empire during the sixteenth to seventeenth centuries, with Istanbul receiving its grain from Egypt, would be an obvious candidate. In *The Roman Bazaar*, I used Mughal India where extensive, tributary empire presiding over a vast peasant population is also found to spawn developments that saw the increase of cities and growth of markets that benefited commercial groups. An important attraction of the Indian comparison was its ability to show the importance of markets for the mobilization of the agricultural surplus. The aim of the book was decidedly not to demonstrate that Roman trade was unimportant, but rather to place it in a more satisfactory historical context. This exercise included arguing that it was during Roman times that the system was consolidated, which later would come to be seen as the classic pattern of old-world trade, with precious metals being sent from the Mediterranean to India via Egypt or Syria in return for spices and fine textiles such as silk. It was this pattern that modern capitalist world trade began to transform when European companies penetrated the Indian Ocean by sailing around Africa.[74] Thus even if I do not think it appropriate to inscribe Rome in the narrative of modern capitalism, comparative history still affords us with an alternative that allows a "progressive" role to the Empire in the world history of trade.

Theoretical conflict

This leads me to some final theoretical observations. In the same book, I introduced the notion of the bazaar to account for the element of fragmentation and irregularity which any pre-industrial comparison would lead us to expect to have been part of the reality of the Roman trading world. For some of the most ardent supporters of the free market interpretation this was overly primitivizing.[75] But bazaars are certainly not primitive markets. One of the best attempts to date to conceptualize the characteristics of the bazaar, the study of the Moroccan suq in Sefrou by Clifford Geertz, was based on a city with some 25,000 inhabitants, in short well above what would have been the norm in most cities of the Roman Empire.[76] If anything, therefore, one could well argue that the parallel was too optimistic.

Involved in the debate here is also a question about the reach of modern economic theory, or rather a particular version of it. Some believe that one can employ the same concepts to analyze and describe the ancient economy as a modern economy. That project is obviously of far greater concern to economics as a discipline than it is to history. A historian cannot pretend that everything has always looked the same but needs to understand and explain how human societies have evolved and diverged through time. Of course, theory is simply a form of language and should therefore be adaptable to diverse situations. But this is not often the way it is used among that particular group of economists. For instance, an argument has been made that the Roman Empire constituted a free, unified labor market.[77] This is both implausible and incapable of demonstration, given the extreme paucity of price evidence. But in addition, slavery is not even seen as significantly modifying the overall picture. With slavery, however, people are forced, and routinely moved against their will, to supply labor that was not freely available either at all or at an "affordable" price. Either way, however, owners get to extract a rent from their slaves – a significant dimension which is not adequately conveyed by the notion of a free market in labor even if slaves were both bought and sold in the Roman world (see also above, Chapter 5). In similar fashion, the importance of peasant households for organizing economic activity has been downplayed. Although more than half of the economy in all probability remained within such households, it is still argued that the role of markets was not thereby significantly diminished in organizing economic activity. For, as it was claimed in the heat of argument, why should it be a significant difference between modern market economies and ancient peasant societies that the latter produced their primary subsistence within the household while "today's 'middle-class households' purchase raw steaks and only cook them at home."[78] My answer, in brief, would be the degree of the division of labor. The whole point about Adam Smith's *Wealth of Nations* was to advocate the advantages that could be derived from economic specialization and that if markets were expanded and allowed to coordinate the division of labor for a greater part of the economy, society stood to reap these rewards. But Smith's argument was in part descriptive and in part programmatic and prescriptive, intended to reform society. By implication, we also need to develop an analysis for situations before Britain took the first steps into modern economic conditions, in short where Smith's ideal types did not obtain. If a very large part of the population, perhaps three-quarters or four-fifths, produce their own main subsistence, this has serious implications for the extent that the market and the division of labor could penetrate the economy.

Interestingly, another school of economists are increasingly interested in exploring such issues. The New Institutional Economics has celebrated great triumphs during the last two decades. Incidentally, they cite Geertz' study of the bazaar and its obvious relevance for historical societies with approval;[79] and George Akerlof, who provided the theoretical underpinnings of Geertz's study, received the Nobel Prize for pointing out that, if information is unevenly distributed, then markets cannot be assumed to integrate.[80] His co-recipient, Joseph Stiglitz, has added to this insight the observation that while information asymmetries may be found in all markets, their effects were particularly felt in developing countries, and by implication pre-industrial societies, where markets consequently operated very differently from the textbook models of modern economics. The distribution of information is a function not merely of technological capacity, it must be emphasized, but also of hierarchies of power and societal organization.[81] There can be little doubt that information was very unevenly distributed across the Roman Empire due to the technological impediments to transport and travel;[82] it is also clear that imperial rule made the hierarchy of power much steeper and thereby reinforced asymmetries in the access to, as well as in the ability to act on, information.[83] Roman society had many features that make it unlikely that markets generally across the empire would have converged if left to themselves.

To conclude: the Roman economy was too complex to be reduced simply to the label market economy. The challenge is to explore the interplay of several modes of economic organization, market trade being only one important element among several in the institutional fabric of the empire.

14D: A Forum on Trade

Paul Erdkamp

The grain trade in the Roman world

It is beyond doubt that the Roman world saw more trade during the first centuries CE than at any time previous or – for a very long time – after. The impact of the increased levels of exchange on human life is clearly visible in written sources and archaeological findings. One reflection of this may be seen in the scale of urbanization, as most towns relied on market channels to feed their populace. Because grain was the largest single item of commercial exchange in the Roman world, and access to grain as the main staple food offered the basis for all economic activity, this section will concentrate on the trade in grain.[84] Despite all undeniable signs of growth, however, the emphasis here will be on cautioning against a tendency to overstress the degree of market integration in the Roman world.[85]

A distinction should be made between, on the one hand, the grain trade linking structural markets and structural suppliers and, on the other hand, the grain trade in response to the heavy fluctuation in production caused by the agricultural conditions and weather in the Mediterranean. Hopkins saw the precariousness of agriculture as one of the main stimulants of trade, as local gluts and shortages were thought to have almost automatically been evened out by traders "looking for some market which is badly stocked."[86] Also Horden and Purcell emphasized connectivity as a natural consequence of the micro-regions of the Mediterranean lands.[87] However, trade is neither an inevitable result of the imbalance between supply and demand, nor a natural response to environmental conditions. As far as there was connectivity, it consisted of a chain of smaller connectivities, in its simplest form between local producers and consumers, in its more complex and large-scale forms involving merchants and middlemen, transporters and shippers, specialized dealers and retail traders. Each segment of the chain acted in accordance with its own goals and considerations, which together determined the workings of the trade in grain.

It was not so much the imbalance in availability of grain that traders responded to as the opportunities for making a profit that the differing exchange values offered. However, two other interrelated elements come into play: costs and risk. The price-driven exchange between supply and demand was hampered by the costs of storage and transportation, and high costs were accepted only if risks were low. The volatility of harvests could be – and undoubtedly was to a small degree – evened out by storing surpluses in good years for consumption in bad years. However, because of its inherent uncertainties, so-called 'carryover' between harvest cycles was not an attractive option as a trading strategy. Price developments could be predicted with some certainty within the annual harvest cycle, as prices tended to be low just after harvest, rising gradually over the winter and reaching a high point just before the new harvest. This was the normal price cycle in early modern times, and ancient writers show that it was seen as the normal situation in Roman times too.[88] It was caused by the constraints on the behavior of most sellers and buyers. Need for cash and lack of storage facilities hampered the ability of small producers to delay selling their crop, while most consumers were short of sufficient cash to buy enough food at low prices to tide them over the expensive months. Large landowners and prosperous merchants, on the other hand, were able to delay the sale of their grain until prices reached their peak. There was little point, however, in holding on to their stores beyond the next harvest, as the drop in prices would diminish the value of their grain. Harvest failures would disrupt the usual price cycle, but were too unpredictable to provide the basis for a marketing strategy over the years. In sum, the extent of carryover in pre-industrial Europe was negligible, and this was certainly also the case in Roman times.[89]

Trading between various regions was a much more important response to fluctuations in production, because information was more readily available. However, marketing in space was not a simple case of connecting supply and demand, as any landowners who exported their stores in the face of local dearth realized. Markets offering high prices, low costs, and low risks were the preferred destinations.

A crucial factor in reducing risk and transaction costs was information, which was, in turn, based on the extent and speed of communication.[90] Early-modern grain traders reluctantly responded to old and unreliable information, because they ran the risk of investing capital and effort in an enterprise that turned out to be unprofitable.[91]

Ancient sources also show that trustworthy information was vital for the grain trade. Recent and reliable information was to be found mostly along the busy shipping lanes that connected the big markets and suppliers, like, for example, the route from Egypt and Asia Minor towards Rome. The conditions of seafaring and navigation favored certain routes, as a result of which some parts of the Mediterranean remained fairly isolated, at best frequented by small-scale traders operating within restricted zones.[92] Moreover, larger markets offered more stability of prices and thus more certainty, as the arrival of a few ships in a small town may have caused prices to collapse. Both elements favored large commercial centers as destinations of overseas grain merchants, as they had reliable contacts there, news travelled faster, and the market was more stable. Also the balance between profit and costs offered better marketing opportunities in some places than in others. Commercial centers provided infrastructure and banking facilities, offering the credit on which most overseas trade relied. The question whether there was a profitable return cargo to be found was another important element in the trader's calculations, as was the buying power of the people in need of grain. Even people threatened with starvation were not an attractive market if they lacked the means to pay high prices.

While these elements determined whether certain places were attractive destinations for traders wanting to sell grain, similar considerations apply to places trying to sell the surpluses stemming from an occasional good harvest. A region that in most years plays even and does not have surpluses to sell to outside markets will not be automatically a supplier in the overseas grain trade when it experiences a temporary glut. The absence of structural ties with traders and the lack of infrastructure in terms of logistical facilities increased transaction costs. Both on the supply side and on the demand side, conditions of trade favored those regions that participated in commercial exchange structurally.

The conclusion must be that while local glut and dearth as a result of the vagaries of the weather was a normal phenomenon in the Roman world, it did not automatically lead to trade. The idea that local harvest fluctuations averaged out at a total mean of zero is simply wrong, as supply and demand partly failed to connect. Obviously, the cost of transportation hampered any meaningful evening out of harvest shocks over land, but the point is that even when trade was within the range of the logistically possible, commercial considerations concerning risks and costs determined the workings of the interregional grain trade.

The nature of the grain market may explain several features of the food supply in the ancient world. In the first place, the nature of the commodity-chain reflects its economic conditions. The sparse evidence on grain traders in the Roman world complies with the model emerging for pre-industrial Europe, where the large investments and great risks inherent in the grain trade resulted in a lack of specialization and a high degree of diversification of activities.[93] In the Roman world we see diversification in the sense that ship-owners often also acted as captains and merchants and that traders often dealt in a variety of goods. Only the stability of the supply of large cities gave rise to specialized grain merchants. We see remarkably few senators and knights involved in the grain trade, which cannot be explained away as a result of considerations of social status, since we do find them in the olive and wine trade. The elite was involved in the grain market as landowners who sold their crop to merchants but not as businessmen specializing in the grain trade.[94] Moreover, the limitations of the grain market caused the direct involvement of the authorities in the distribution of grain in certain contexts, such as the supply of the city of Rome and of the armies.[95] Grain was the main staple food, with few alternative food stuffs available for the urban populace, and hence the ruling elite in the towns and cities of the Roman world was compelled to keep a close eye on the workings of the grain market, even if they were not able or willing to control it completely. On rare occasions Roman emperors and governors offered assistance in the form of grain shipments, but the general dependence on commercial channels tied the hands of town councillors when intervening in the urban grain market.

The emphasis on the limitations of the integration of the grain market does not only show us that part of the Roman world remained fairly isolated and profited little from improved market performance. It also sheds light on where the improvement of the grain trade came from: its causes have to be sought in information and communication, in the context of banking and logistical facilities, and in the reduction of violence and uncertainty. The strength of the grain market increased very much within the big cities and the commercial zones that were connected to these urban markets. The greater strength of the grain market boosted the economy in general. More trade in grain meant less risk in market reliance, as more market integration lessened price volatility. Hence, there was less risk in relying on the market and specializing in non-food producing sectors, which in turn increased labor productivity. Much of the above is meant as a caution against over-stressing ancient trade, but we may end with the conclusion that – even if only to a limited extent, not everywhere, and for just a few centuries – the strength of the grain trade allowed the economy to lift off the ground.

14E: A FORUM ON TRADE

Neville Morley

After more than a century of archaeological work, all discussions of Roman trade have to begin with the fact that the late Republic and early Principate saw an unprecedented expansion of the distribution of goods.[96] It was unprecedented certainly in terms of the volumes of amphorae and other pottery (which may also be taken as a proxy for goods that were carried in more perishable containers and so rarely appear in the material record) being shipped around the empire, and probably also in terms of the distances over which these containers were transported before their contents were consumed; the increase in the number of shipwrecks in this period – which is taken to indicate a dramatic increase in the sea journeys being made – is equally impressive.[97] As Andrew Wilson discusses, wine from Italy and Gaul, olive oil from Spain and North Africa, and fish sauce from coastal regions around the Mediterranean and up into the Atlantic could clearly be found almost anywhere in the western provinces of the Empire, and even in many parts of the east; meanwhile, literary sources, such as Aelius Aristides' praise of Rome as the common emporium of the world, give us an impression of the astonishing range of goods that could be obtained in the great cities of the Empire, drawn from every known region.[98] The expansion of the variety of consumption at a local level (as seen, for example, in patterns of pottery finds on Romano-British sites), the way in which different consumptive practices were extended downwards through the social hierarchy rather than being confined to a wealthy elite, and the trend towards increasing homogeneity at the regional, national, and global levels, all of which were dependent on the increased availability of imported goods across the empire, has led several historians to consider adopting the phrase 'Roman globalization' as a way of characterising these far-reaching developments.[99]

However, this celebration of the scale of Roman activity is the start rather than the conclusion of the debate; it is significant not so much in comparison to the level of activity in other pre-industrial societies – we lack the sort of detailed statistical evidence that would enable us to say whether Rome saw more or less distributive activity than, say, seventeenth-century Holland – but in comparison to an alternative historical tradition that took the likes of Cicero completely at face value in his condemnation of trade and so concluded that such activity can only ever have been small-scale and focused on luxuries.[100] Archaeology contradicts such pessimism by showing that relatively ordinary goods were widely distributed, and on a large scale – but it has, as yet, largely failed to engage with the other issues raised by that 'primitivist' tradition, or with any of the most important questions related to the importance of mass distribution in the Roman Empire.[101]

THE NATURE OF ACTIVITY

Was all the activity revealed by archaeological evidence 'trade', in the sense of profit-orientated market transactions? Clearly, archaeology tells us that amphorae and pottery were moved between regions, but it does not generally indicate by whom they were moved or why. It is clear from other sources that there was a continuing role in the Roman world for non-market exchanges: reciprocity (people exchanging gifts) and above all redistribution, with landowners moving goods between different estates and from their estates to their urban residences, and above all the Roman state moving goods under its control, like the grain collected as tax in kind from certain provinces and the products of state-owned mines, quarries, and estates. There is not necessarily an absolute divide between these different forms of distribution; there was no Roman state merchant fleet, for example, so the task of supplying the city of Rome with tax grain involved hiring private shippers to transport state-owned supplies.[102] Army provisions were frequently organized through the use of contractors, who would buy goods through the market and transport them to the frontiers on behalf of the Roman state. Public (redistributive) and private (market) activities overlapped and often supported one another – the state's need to ensure reliable supplies for the army and the capital effectively promoted private activity through the construction of harbors, subsidies for ship-building, and the like. The important historical questions concern the relative significance of public and private activity in the economy, and the nature of the relationship between them, rather than taking it for granted that all the evidence of the distribution of goods must be the result of market trade and private enterprise.

THE DYNAMICS OF ROMAN TRADE

The 'modernising' approach to the Roman economy not only assumes that almost all economic activity must be market-focused, it also takes trade for granted as a natural human instinct. If the question of why activity should have expanded dramatically under Rome is asked at all, it is answered by pointing to the establishment of peace and the unification of the Mediterranean, 'setting free' entrepreneurial instincts by reducing the risks and impediments, as Wilson implies (see above). It is certainly the case that the actions of the Roman state changed the context within which trade took place, not only through increasing security (though the empire's actual success in reducing piracy, as opposed to its claims to have done so, is disputed) but also by creating, for its own reasons, economic institutions like coinage and contract law that helped to reduce the costs of doing business and so made trade more viable.[103] However, was this sufficient impetus, in the face of the two great impediments to the development of trade in the ancient Mediterranean, the high cost of transport relative to the value of most goods, the relative ubiquity of most basic goods, and the limits of technological development, so that no region held any comparative advantage in production that could enable it to undercut other regions?

This suggests that we need to look for changes in the scale and nature of demand, and the ability to pay the costs of importing goods from elsewhere to meet that demand, in order to explain Roman developments, rather than focusing on changes in distribution or supply. The vagaries of the Mediterranean climate and the unreliability of agriculture meant that there were always regions with shortages and other regions with gluts, creating the possibility of profit in rectifying such imbalances – but the areas best placed to benefit were those already integrated into networks of distribution.[104] The Roman state created two great centres of demand that could be supported only through interregional distribution, the army and the city of Rome; in both cases, the costs of transport could be covered by state resources, because of the political imperative to keep both of them fed and hence content.[105] The expansion of Roman power in the west created, inadvertantly, further demands, by promoting cities as the preferred means of organizing space and society, and by presenting a template of 'Roman identity' that was defined in part by the consumption of particular sorts of goods; urban populations tended to depend on merchants for their food, while some aspiring Romans took to drinking wine and using *terra sigillata* pottery, which depended – until local production of such goods was established – on imports.[106] Of course, for cities to expand and for people to change their habits, some system of distribution had already to exist – and here again it seems most likely that it was the power of the Roman state, and the way in which it chose to deploy its resources, that was instrumental in creating an environment in which market trade could begin to flourish.

THE SIGNIFICANCE OF TRADE

The fact that the level of economic activity under the Roman Empire was much greater than historians in the 'primitivist' tradition were prepared to admit is frequently taken, without much discussion, as an indication that trade was therefore highly significant in absolute terms. This may have been the case, but it cannot be taken for granted. A substantial proportion of the empire's produce remained outside the market: it was not only poor peasants who consumed a significant proportion of what they produced, but the market-orientated villas of central Italy aimed to produce the bulk of their workforces' needs rather than focusing solely on cash crops – which offers an indication of the perceived dangers of dependence on a poorly integrated, unreliable and expensive market.[107] Meanwhile, the evidence suggests that the activities of the vast majority of merchants were of limited scope and scale, and that they remained relatively poor and socially inferior – which is to say, they were often substantially better off and wealthier than many of the peasants and ordinary townspeople who made up the bulk of the empire's population, but a long way from rivalling the political and social elites of the empire, for all the desire of some ancient historians to identify a powerful and confident class of entrepreneurs. The greatest profits from trading activity came into the hands of the landowners and the financiers – the same political and social elite that had dominated in earlier centuries.[108]

However, it is only the modernizing impulse that inclines us to evaluate the significance of trade solely in economic and monetary terms, and to look in vain for evidence of a Roman capitalist revolution parallel to that in early modern Europe. Trade was vital to the development of the Roman empire because of its role in sustaining the structures of imperialism, above all the dominant position of the land-owning elite, and in shaping the lives of millions of the empire's inhabitants by expanding their range of choice in consumptive practices and bringing them into contact with a wider range of goods, and thus a wider world.

'Roman globalization'

The Roman Empire depended on high levels of connectivity, and the movement of both goods and people; it also promoted increased connectivity and increased movement. Is it at all helpful to draw analogies with modern globalization?[109] On the one hand, there is no sign of 'time-space compression,' in which the world is effectively shrunk through developments in transport and communications technology; journey times in the empire remained slow, with serious consequences for the availability of information and hence the integration of markets, as both Bang and Erdkamp discuss in their contributions to this forum. But we do see changes in material practices, which can be interpreted (as in modern globalization theory) as the results of processes of relativization and reflexivity, as individuals in a globalizing world increasingly view themselves in relation to a global rather than local context and express their chosen social identity in their material practices.[110] This both depended on increased levels of trade, to provide the goods that enabled one to express 'Romanness' through consumption, and also promoted trade through the changing level of demand for goods that could not, at least at first, be obtained locally. Compared with the periods both before and after, the Roman Empire was more integrated, held together through shared practices and networks of exchange as well as through political structures and the threat of force.

Conclusion

Trade is one of the most fiercely disputed topics in the study of the Roman economy, because it is one of the elements that seems most familiar and modern. It is tempting to react to the naiveté of many 'modernizing' accounts, and their habit of interpreting all evidence in the most optimistic spirit possible, by over-emphasizing the primitive aspects of Rome – the continued emphasis on self-sufficiency, the dominant role of the state, the inefficiency and cost of transport, and so forth. Certainly the Roman economy was underdeveloped compared with the modern, but it is less clear that it was so inferior to the economies of other pre-industrial societies. We need to beware, as Peter Bang has noted, of using empty adjectives like 'complex' and 'sophisticated' without defining their meaning properly, but it is clear that there were significant developments in both the scale and the organization of exchange, redistribution, and trade under the Roman empire.[111] The task for the future is to explore the nature of these developments, in their historical context, rather than taking it for granted that an accumulation of supposed examples of 'large-scale commerce' tells us all we need to know.

Notes

1 Notably Finley 1999; Whittaker 1985. Bang 2008 also downplays the scale of long-distance private trade. None of these studies is properly aware of the range of archaeological evidence.
2 Arnaud 2011; Scheidel 2011a; Wilson 2011 a; b.
3 Cf. Harris 2000; Morley 2007a; b; Wilson 2008a: 181–6.
4 Loughton 2003.
5 Tchernia 1983; 1986; Panella and Tchernia 1994. Wrecks: Parker 1992: 249–50 no. 616 and 49–50 no. 28, with bibliography.
6 Pottery: e.g. Hayes 1972; Peacock 1982; Carandini 1983; Pucci 1983; Kenrick 1996; Oxé, Comfort, and Kenrick 2000; Poblome 2004; Bonifay 2004. Amphorae: many studies, see especially Peacock and Williams 1986; Borgard 2006 (alum). Cooking wares: Leitch 2010; 2011.
7 Foy 2003a; Nenna 2007; Wilson, Schörle and Rice forthcoming.
8 Wilson 2009a; 2011a.
9 Arnaud 2011.
10 Nieto 1997; Arnaud 2011. Cf. McCormick 2001 for the early medieval world.
11 Wilson 2011a; b.
12 Canals: Wikander 2000a: 321–30. Roads: e.g., Chevallier 1976; O'Connor 1993; Laurence 1999; Desanges et al. 2010.
13 Rickman 1980; Garnsey 1983; Aldrete and Mattingly 1999; *HA Sept. Sev.* 18.3; *Aurel.* 35.2, 48.1.
14 *HA Comm.* 17.7.
15 E.g., Bonifay 2003.
16 Rodríguez Almeida 1984; Blazquéz Martínez and Remesal Rodríguez 1999; M. Maischberger s.v. *Testaceus Mons*, *LTUR* V: 28–30.
17 Wilson 2008a: 187–8.
18 *HA Aurel.* 48; cf. *CIL* 6.1785 = 31931; Rougé 1957.
19 Cf. papers by J. B. Ward-Perkins collected in Dodge and Ward-Perkins 1992; Fant 1988; 2001; Russell 2009; 2011.
20 Mattingly 2002; 2003, 355–62; Mattingly et al. 2009; 2010; Mattingly and Wilson 2010; Fentress 2011.
21 Sidebotham 1986a; 1986b; 1996; 2011; Young 2001; De Romanis and Tchernia 2005; Tomber 2008; McLaughlin 2010; Seland 2010.
22 Tomber 2008, 16, 55, 174; Bowman 1994, 70; Cool 2006, 32, 64, 67.
23 Plin., *HN* 6.102–3; Sidebotham, Zitterkopf, and Riley 1991; Sidebotham, Zitterkopf, and Helm 1998; Bagnall, Bulow-Jacobsen, and Cuvigny 2001; Cuvigny 2003; Schörle 2010.
24 Villeneuve 2004.
25 Rathbone 2000.
26 Strabo 2.5.12.

27 Duncan-Jones 1994: 33–7, 45.
28 Strabo 2.5.8, 4.5.3.
29 Wilson 2006b: 233–4.
30 Whitehouse 1965; Wickham 2005: 735–6.
31 Hopkins 1995/6: 55–6; 1983: 88; Erdkamp 2005: 235.
32 *TPSulp.* 79; Casson 1980; Amm. Marc. 28.1.17–18.
33 Garnsey 1988: part IV.
34 Sirks 1991: 16–20.
35 Kelly 2004: 107–8, 138–40.
36 References in Silver 2009a.
37 Cic., *Font.* 5.11 (transl. Yonge).
38 Silver 2009a.
39 Strabo 4.4.3.111–19 (transl. Jones; emphasis added).
40 Strabo 4.1.7; Hitchner 1999: 378.
41 Silver 2006.
42 Carlsen 1995: 18–19.
43 Note Trimalchio in Petron. 76.3–5 and a banker/auctioneer at the Portus Vinarius Superior (Peña 1999: 11–12, 14–15).
44 De Sena 2005: Fig. 3–4.
45 Compare Peña 1999: 21.
46 Curchin 1991: 150–1; Sirks 1991: 388–9 with n. 5.
47 Broekaert 2008 (names); Peña 2007 (destruction); Rathbone 1991: 167 (costs); Peña 2007: 64–5; 1999: 11 with n. 88 (refills).
48 Silver 2008.
49 Silver 2008: 20 n. 41.
50 Morel 1993: 227.
51 *RGDA* 15. I would like give thanks to Walter Scheidel, who provoked me to write this piece; William Harris, whose seminar in New York was presented with the basic points presented here; and Peter Garnsey, who with his usual generosity read through and commented on the first draft.
52 Finley 1999: ch. 1 distinguishing the ancient economy of Greco-Roman society from that of the Middle East precisely because, to his mind, the former was a world of markets in contrast to the latter – an assessment which, as has become increasingly clear, was mistaken: market trade was well-developed in the ancient Near East, too. See, e.g., Bedford 2005.
53 Hopkins 1978: 96–8 is the best short discussion of the population of Rome and the evidence. Scheidel 2004a for a recent analysis of the demography of Roman Italy, including Rome.
54 Garnsey 1988: ch. 14, updated by Erdkamp 2005: ch. 5, for analyies of the Roman grain supply.
55 Temin 2001; Silver 2009a.
56 As is well brought out by the title of Polanyi, Arensberg and Pearson 1957.
57 Morley 1996 for an analysis.
58 Cf. Persson 1999 arguing that the Europe-wide integration of grain markets had to await the age of steam and railways.
59 Bang 2007. Cf. the similar assessment of the archaeologist André Tchernia (2011; 2010).
60 The best statement of this view is that of Lo Cascio 2007.

61 The basic pattern is surveyed by Wickham 2005 and Panella 1993. See Panella and Tchernia 2002 for a discussion of the interpretative problems of this evidence in relation to Roman imports. Carandini 1983 was an initial attempt to point to the significance of Africa in the late Roman economy.

62 Scheidel 2004b; Morley 1996.

63 Tchernia 1986 on Italian wine; Rauh 1993 on Delos; Harris 1999 and Scheidel 1997; 2005a debate the Roman slave trade.

64 Morley 2007b for the most recent discussion of import substitution.

65 E.g., capital exports (impossible to quantify or follow with any certainty). Silver 2009a: 438–40, thus imagines that Italian investment capital developed the economy of Gaul and thus presumably drew back profits to Italy. But Gaul had and developed its own aristocratic landowning elite which was quite capable of "developing" its own landholdings and the provincial economy. Left out of this mirage of Italian investment capital is any notion of imperialism, initial conquest, plunder, confiscation, and colonization followed by tribute (and rent). Finley 1978: 10 convincingly rejected this option in general.

66 Bang 2007 represents a first attempt to model the long-term development of the Roman imperial economy in terms of the sale of protection by the state. See also Bang 2008: ch. 2.

67 The best discussion remains that of Garnsey 1988: ch. 4.

68 Bang 2008: ch. 3; Erdkamp 2005: ch. 4.

69 Erdkamp 2005: e.g., 144, 205.

70 Some examples must suffice: Jones 2003; Landes 1998; Tilly 1992; Pearson 1991; Baechler, Hall and Mann 1988; Hall 1986; Wallerstein 1974.

71 Brewer 1989 on Britain; on Holland and Amsterdam, De Vries and Van der Woude 1997 and Lesger 2006.

72 As Scheidel 2009a points out, it is the Republican centuries of conquest that seem to reveal the most dynamic developments rather than the stable conditions of the Principate.

73 A point already made by Hume when he noted that London had in comparison to Rome grown by "uniting extensive commerce and middling empire" (1998: 265). See Wrigley 1987 for a classic analysis of London's economic and demographic base.

74 Bang 2008: Epilegomena.

75 Temin 2009; Silver 2009a.

76 Geertz 1979.

77 Temin 2004b.

78 Silver 2009a: 432; Temin 2001: 180.

79 North 1990: 11 and ch. 13, in particular subsection iii.

80 Akerlof 1970.

81 Stiglitz 1989.

82 Duncan-Jones 1990: ch. 1.

83 Garnsey and Humfress 2001 offer a good summary of the increasingly steep social hierarchies emerging as the Roman world moved towards late antiquity.

84 Much of the following is based on Erdkamp 2005.

85 Cf. Kessler and Temin 2007.

86 Philostr. *VA* 4.32. Hopkins 1980.

87 Horden and Purcell 2000.

88 Cic. 2 *Verr.* 3.214–15; Julian. *Mis.* 369b. Garnsey 1988: 24; Duncan-Jones 1990: 144ff.; Reger 1993: 308ff.
89 Hufton 1985: 122ff.; Persson 1996: 700f.; 1999: 67–70.
90 See also Bang 2006: 51–88; 2008: especially 131–201; Morley 2007a: 55–78.
91 For example, Braudel 1966: 575. See also Pelizzon 2000: 118f.
92 Cf. Gibbins 2001 regarding the Hellenistic world, McCormick 2001 on late antiquity.
93 On the grain trade and related sectors, see in particular Persson 1999: 67; Pelizzon 2000.
94 Cf. Rickman 1980; Kneissl 1983; Herz 1988; Pleket 1990: 124ff.
95 Regarding Rome, see in particular Aldrete and Mattingly 1999.
96 See Peacock and Williams 1986; Wilson 2009a.
97 Parker 1992.
98 Aristid. *Or.* 26.11–12.
99 On patterns of consumption, Pitts 2008; on globalization, Hingley 2005; Morley 2010: 107–27.
100 Cic., *Off.* 1.151; the tradition is summarized and criticized by D'Arms 1981.
101 For clear discussion of those issues, see Whittaker 1989 and Tchernia 1989.
102 On the grain supply, see Garnsey 1988; Sirks 1991; Erdkamp 2005.
103 On piracy, de Souza 1999; on transaction costs, Morley 2007a: 55–78.
104 Erdkamp 2005 and in the previous section of this forum.
105 Morley 2010: 70–101.
106 Woolf 1998: 1–23, 169–205.
107 On self-sufficiency in villas, Morley 1996: 75–6, 110–11; on market uncertainty and risk, Morley 2007a: 29–34; Bang 2008.
108 Andreau 1999.
109 Morley 2007a: 90–102; 2010: 115–27; on globalization generally, Waters 1995.
110 Hingley 2005.
111 Bang 2008: 32.

Part V

Outcomes

15: Physical Well-Being

Walter Scheidel

How did the Roman economy affect people's well-being? As I have noted in the opening chapter, there are many ways of assessing well-being, in terms of income and consumption and by considering goods such as education, security, or freedom. In this chapter I focus more narrowly on biological living standards.[1] Did the inhabitants of the Roman Empire live longer lives, grow to be taller, and enjoy better health and diets than the populations of earlier or later periods? As we will see, the relationship between any of these features and economic performance is complex, and economic interpretations of physical well-being are fraught with great difficulties. A growing body of pertinent evidence nevertheless merits our attention. Indeed, progress in the study of Roman health and nutrition has been so rapid that any attempt to summarize the current state of knowledge is bound to be out of date almost upon publication. The following survey cannot offer more than a snapshot of recent and ongoing developments that promise to put our understanding of the quality of life in the Roman world on a more solid footing.

Longevity and Mortality

Progress has primarily occurred in the study of skeletal remains. While this research has shed new light on stature, health, and nutrition, it has thus far failed to provide reliable new information on longevity. Until and unless this happens, our knowledge of this vital measure will not increase beyond what little we can say about it at present. The study of ancient life expectancy is severely constrained by our reliance on a relatively small amount of textual data.

Pride of place belongs to the census returns from Roman Egypt in the first three centuries CE that record the composition of several hundred households. The age distribution derived from these records has been fitted to model life tables that predict a mean life expectancy at birth of 22 years for women and 25+ years for men. However, the value of this exercise is undermined by reporting biases that distort urban census returns and information concerning males. All we can say with confidence is that these texts point to very high levels of mortality overall: mean life expectancy at birth for female villagers, the only group that appears to be reasonably reliably attested, was most likely in the twenties.[2]

The representative nature of these data is open to debate. It seems unwarranted to generalize from them to the Roman world more generally.[3] Instead, we must allow for a considerable degree of variation depending on ecological conditions. Egypt was exceptionally densely populated, hot, annually inundated, and until quite recently a hotbed of both endemic and epidemic disease and consequently subject to very high death rates.[4] The Fayyum, where many of the census data originate, may have been unhealthy even by the low standards of the region.[5]

Other ancient sources and comparative evidence give us a better idea of the probable range of variation. Depending on which model life tables we employ, the longevity upon accession of Roman emperors who died of natural causes translates to a mean life expectancy at birth of anywhere from 26 to 37 years.[6] The size, structure, and recruitment patterns of the Roman imperial senate and of a well-documented city council in Italy are consistent with corresponding values of 25 to 30 years.[7] A legal schedule for calculating annuities known as "Ulpian's Life Table" envisions survival rates that are likewise consistent with a mean life expectancy at birth in the twenties.[8]

Demographic information derived from the age distribution of skeletons found in Roman cemeteries is far less trustworthy. The age of adult bones remains difficult to determine with precision: existing methods tend to yield a surfeit of young and middle-aged adults and a grave scarcity or sometimes even complete absence of elderly individuals. While new and increasingly sophisticated ageing methods continue to be developed and debated, they have so far failed to build a firm base for 'paleodemography.'[9] Moreover, even if these technical problems could be fully resolved, we would also need to be able to account for differences between skeletal samples and actual populations that were caused by migration or funerary practice. This is particularly unfortunate given that deposits of skeletons provide a window to the distant past and, at least in theory, ought play a central role in demographic reconstructions: if large skeletal samples could legitimately be subjected to stable population analysis, they would answer our questions about local mortality and survival patterns in ways no other body of data can.[10]

Comparative evidence shows that the high rates of attrition implied by the Roman textual record were not historically uncommon. Average life expectancy at birth in the twenties is documented by data from places as diverse as China both in the first millennium CE and in the early twentieth century, India in the late nineteenth and early twentieth centuries, eighteenth-century France, and nineteenth-century Spain and Russia.[11] But we have also to allow for upward variation: Italian life expectancy at birth in the second half of the eighteenth century was mostly in the low thirties, and largely in the high thirties in eighteenth-century England.[12] While such evidence gives us a rough idea of what to expect in the Roman world – aggregate means somewhere in the high 20s or low 30s – they do not allow us empirically to compare the Roman experience to that of other periods, nor do they enlighten us about regional, class, and gender variation within the Roman world. In the most general terms, there is no indication that Roman elite longevity was much better than for the general population, a finding that is consistent with the observation that the health of elites did not greatly improve until the eighteenth century in England and China, at a time when growing knowledge finally began to enable them to parlay resources into longer lives.[13] We cannot empirically ascertain how urbanization, trade, and investment in infrastructure affected survival rates: we are limited to probabilistic conjecture regarding their potential demographic consequences – conjecture, which albeit (once again) informed by comparative evidence, cannot properly replace missing data.[14]

Epigraphic evidence offers greater opportunities for comparative demographic quantification. Epitaphs that report the day or at least the month of death can be used to reconstruct seasonal variation in mortality. Given that many or most deaths would have been associated with infectious disease and infection rates vary with the seasons, seasonal mortality profiles may shed some light on the underlying disease environment. In the present context, the implied *scale* of seasonal mortality variation is of great interest because it facilitates comparison with conditions in the more recent past. Relevant records come from a wide variety of settings, such as the city of Rome both in the late Republic and in late antiquity, from North and South Italy, from the Iberian peninsula, from Mauretania Caesariensis (now northern Algeria), and from Egypt, Israel, and Jordan. The majority of these regional samples suggest that death rates varied greatly over the course of the year.[15] This observation points to high disease loads. Broadly speaking, the scale of seasonal variability is inversely correlated with longevity: the stronger the fluctuations are, the lower life expectancy tends to be.[16] It is particularly striking that these mortality surges are documented in inscriptions that privilege teenagers and adults who, as a group, were more likely to be commemorated than small children. Massive seasonal mortality variation at these ages is without parallel in more recent data sets, where only babies display similarly strong vulnerability to fatal seasonal infection.[17] In the post-Roman period, only the most extreme circumstances produced comparable profiles at more mature ages, most notably epidemic outbreaks of plague or smallpox.[18]

Although seasonal mortality spikes are not universally attested, they were by no means confined to notoriously unhealthy regions such as Egypt. In the case of Rome and Italy, endemic malaria and its interaction with other diseases may have been a key factor; elsewhere we simply do not know about causation but must not assume that it was uniform across different regions.[19] If diverse environments were capable of generating substantial seasonal mortality variation at mature ages, this phenomenon may well have been of considerable significance for the demography of the Roman world as a whole. This alone casts doubt on optimistic views of Roman longevity based on evidence of economic growth and infrastructural investment.

NUTRITION AND HEALTH

Body height is an important marker of physical wellbeing.[20] Human growth is sustained by net nutrition, which is determined not only by food intake but also by energy-consuming activities such as work and by infections that mobilize immune responses or interfere with the processing of the diet. If net nutrition is inadequate for any of these reasons, the body prioritizes survival over growth. While growth may catch up if such stresses remain episodic, chronic net malnutrition inevitably results in stunting, an outcome that may also be caused by acute but severe deprivation. This permits us to view adult stature as a generic index of well-being in childhood and adolescence. Generally speaking, body height and life expectancy tend to be positively correlated in large population samples.[21]

Even so, many complexities complicate the interpretation of stature. Adult body height is the final product of a variety of interacting factors, such as diet, disease, pre-adult labor regimes, and the timing of resource stresses. These influences are impossible to disentangle if only stature is empirically known: in the words of a leading expert, "researchers face a huge identification problem in which there are far more determinants than outcomes."[22] It has even been conjectured that severe conditions may preferentially eliminate short individuals, thereby raising average height in the adult survivor population.[23]

What matters most for the purposes of this volume is that stature is not a reliable proxy of economic performance. For instance, the duration of breastfeeding or the contribution of dairy products to the diet can affect heights in ways that are unrelated to income. Such non-economic factors may account for the substantial body height of poor populations such as Plains Native Americans, the pre-famine Irish, or some contemporary African populations.[24] Conversely, child labor may raise income but curtail bodily growth. Western body heights famously decreased during the early stages of industrialization, when higher incomes were temporarily offset by worsening living conditions.[25]

Despite all these qualifications, stature does contribute to our understanding of overall living standards.[26] Several empirical issues are at stake: how body height developed during the Roman period; how Roman stature compared to conditions in the immediately preceding and following periods; and how it compares to conditions in the more recent past. In addition, we need to consider the question of how to relate empirical findings to Roman economic history.

In the absence of relevant statistics, the study of pre-modern body heights relies entirely on skeletal data, which pose distinct problems of analysis. Body height must be extrapolated from the length of long bones such as the femur, and different methods of varying reliability have long been used side by side. The resultant inconsistencies make it difficult to compare or consolidate large numbers of samples. Only studies of bone length that either avoid extrapolation to putative body height or consistently apply a single method can overcome these problems. A comparative diachronic study of long bone lengths in different parts of the Roman world has been undertaken by Geertje Klein Goldewijk. This project is still in progress, and the results may change as additional data are added. For now, her survey of more than ten thousand skeletons has yielded findings that are consistent with a Malthusian scenario of diminishing well-being in response to rising population pressure: in all regions under review, body height declined from the local onset of Roman-period evidence until the fourth century CE when this trend was for the most part reversed. Roman Italian body heights consistently lagged behind those at more northerly latitudes.[27]

Other surveys paint a similar picture. A recent study of 1,021 skeletons from seventy-four sites in central Italy reveals that mean stature in the Roman period was lower than both before (during the Iron Age) and after (in the Middle Ages). In the same vein, an alternative survey of 2,609 skeletons from twenty-six Italian sites ranging from the Roman period to the late Middle Ages shows a strong increase in body height in the late Roman and early medieval periods. An unpublished survey of 1,867 skeletons from sixty-one sites in Britain likewise documents an increase in body height after the end of Roman rule.[28] These findings reinforce the general impression conveyed by a more eclectic long-term survey of stature in different parts of Europe that identifies troughs during the Roman period and the High Middle Ages and peaks in the post-Roman period and in the wake of the Black Death.[29]

The fact that the inhabitants of north-western Europe were on average always taller than Mediterranean populations primarily reflects a diet richer in dairy (and meat) in the north but may also owe something to lower population densities and consequently lighter disease loads.[30] Yet it is the *direction* of change over time that is of special historical interest. All of the observed developments are logically consistent with a Malthusian perspective as outlined in earlier chapters.[31] In the heartland of the empire, high population density and perhaps also high social inequality depressed mean stature in the Roman period. Constraints on body growth were relaxed as population declined in late antiquity and especially in the post-Roman period, when both population densities and inequality appear to have been relatively low. (The late and post-Roman recovery in body height in Italy is consistent with evidence of expanding cattle farming and meat consumption, which points to reduced population density and inequality and better diet.[32]) Declining stature in Roman Gaul may be linked to growing population and inequality, and while the British post-Roman rise in stature fits the general pattern. From a comparative perspective, it is worth noting that after medieval population growth had come to depress heights by the thirteenth century, stature increased again in the aftermath of the Black Death, at a time when real incomes are known to have risen greatly in response to falling population pressure. This process may echo developments at the end of the Roman period.[33]

Systematic comparison of Roman body heights with anthropometric data from the last few centuries will have to await more comprehensive publication of internally consistent height estimates for the former period. All we can say at this point is that the population of the imperial heartland appears to have been fairly short by historical standards. The data that are currently available suggest that 164cm is a reasonable approximation of mean adult male height in Roman central Italy.[34] This corresponds to levels observed in France at various points in the eighteenth century or in Italy in the mid-nineteenth century, the latter marking that region's early modern nadir in stature at a time of particularly low real incomes.[35]

Long-term comparisons have yet to be undertaken for other regions. In addition, several other issues are worthy of investigation. One is the phenomenon of geographical height convergence observed in recent populations.[36] Did Roman imperial integration foster similar processes? Another question concerns inequality: class differences in body height can sometimes be considerable.[37] Does the same apply to the Roman world? While these questions require much more detailed analysis of the ancient skeletal record, answers need not be wholly beyond our reach.

Further insight into health and nutritional status is provided by other types of skeletal evidence. Telling markers of developmental stress can be found on human skulls. They appear in two varieties which may be linked to different causes, namely orbital lesions (*cribra orbitalia*) that are associated with chronic iron-deficiency anemia and other disorders, and porotic lesions of the cranial vault (*cribra cranii*).[38] The dental record is another important source of information, especially evidence of linear enamel hypoplasia, a dental condition arising from the temporary arrest of enamel matrix growth induced by infection, parasitism, or vitamin D deficiency. Just as in the case of body height, bone and tooth health are determined by a variety of factors from gross malnutrition to diseases that depress net nutrition. Yet again, their overall prevalence and distribution are indicative of the overall health status of affected populations. They also allow us to trace geographical, chronological, age, and gender differences in physical well-being.

Table 1 summarizes findings from a number of Roman-period burial sites, often from the Italian peninsula.[39] Owing to diverse reporting practices and classification standards, not all of these findings are

Table 15.1 *Incidence of skeletal lesions at Roman burial sites**

			Linear enamel hypoplasia in percentage of	
Site	Location	Cribra orbitalia	Teeth	Individuals
Casal Bertone	outside Rome	18	2	19
Via Collatina	outside Rome	77	42	80/92
Castellaccio Europarco	outside Rome	14	3	16
Osteria del Curato	outside Rome	79		70
Vallerano	outside Rome	69	64	93
Isola Sacra	Lazio, Italy		36	81
Lucus Feroniae	Lazio, Italy	32	46	82
Quadrella	Molise, Italy	23	59	92
Urbino	Marche, Italy	41		100
Herculaneum	Campania, Italy	34		27
Pompeii	Campania, Italy			88
Rimini/Ravenna	Romagna, Italy	56		84
Multiple sites	Coastal Croatia	20		63
Multiple sites	Continental Croatia		48	
Carthage	Tunisia	54		
Ancaster	Britain	12		7
Baldock 1	Britain	10		
Baldock 3	Britain	12	5	23
Cirencester	Britain	9		11
Colchester	Britain	5		18
Dorchester	Britain	3		
East London	Britain	2		
London	Britain	4		4
Poundbury	Britain	19		
Winchester	Britain	0		15
Mean for all sites	Britain	10	9	14
Kellis, Dakleh Oasis	Egypt	55		

* Sites listed according to distance from Rome

directly comparable: they merely add up to a very rough sketch of the emerging picture of physical well-being in different parts of the Roman Empire.

This patchwork of data supports only limited generalizations. The highest attested rates of cranial lesions are found near Rome, followed by sites in Romagna and the Egyptian desert. This pattern invites conjecture about the possible role of malaria, a disease that causes anemia and was a feature of both central Italy and the Egyptian oases.[40] With few exceptions outside Britain, dental problems were rife and often ubiquitous. More generally, the low rates of defects observed in Roman Britain match the greater heights of its population, a congruence that indicates better physical well-being overall. At the same time, the discovery of ostensibly healthy groups right outside Rome shows that any broad generalizations are hazardous and that local variation must have been considerable, even across small distances.

Adults tend to exhibit lower rates of active lesions than children. However, statistically significant differences between the sexes are usually absent. The study of socioeconomic differentiation requires an integrative approach to anthropometric data and their funerary contexts, with the latter often failing to provide reliable information.[41] Change over time is likewise difficult to ascertain unless samples from different periods are obtained from the same or adjacent locations, which has rarely been the case. A few comparative case studies of Roman and Lombard-period sites in central Italy point to a high degree of continuity.[42] For what it is worth, however, a geographically eclectic survey of twenty-three Italian cemeteries observes a decline in the incidence of cranial lesions between the Roman period and the Middle Ages, a finding that mirrors the concurrent increase in stature mentioned above and may reflect the benefits of lower population density and inequality.[43]

CONCLUSION

Evidence of longevity, health, and nutritional status is difficult to interpret because of the entanglement of economic, ecological, and cultural factors such as income, disease load, and dietary and breastfeeding practices. Straightforward extrapolation from physical well-being to economic performance is impossible. Economic growth may support a larger population but may also raise inequality; population growth, in turn, may exacerbate density-dependent diseases or depress real incomes. Yet economic growth may also boost investment in infrastructure that alleviates health hazards. In sum, the variables mediating between economy and well-being are complex and sometimes opaque.

Nevertheless, anthropometry sheds light on overall levels of physical well-being which, even if they defy comprehensive explication, provide a basis for comparative assessments both within the Roman world and with other periods. It appears that the imperial economy did not generally enhance biological living standards. Physical well-being was unevenly distributed, with more benefits accruing to peripheral areas than to the core. This pattern can be read in different ways. One is to assume that ecology may have mattered more than economic performance.[44] Comparative evidence leaves no doubt that differences in climate or altitude could play a major role in determining health and life expectancy.[45] Pliny the Younger already claimed to have observed unusual longevity in Tifernum Tiberinum, an Umbrian town located almost 300 meters above sea level that was described as temperate in the summer and cold in the winter.[46] Yet one would expect the majority of the imperial population to have been concentrated in more disease-prone areas – in coastal lowlands, along rivers, in areas that favored Mediterranean farming – potentially with unfavorable consequences for morbidity and mortality. Urban versus rural residence may have been another significant ecological divide. While we cannot tell to what extent the negative effects of urban crowding were offset by the beneficial consequences of Roman aqueducts, latrines, and sewers, the latter provisions speak against simplistic analogies with many better documented but less well endowed pre-modern societies.[47] Another way to make sense of the anthropometric evidence is by applying a Malthusian scenario of demographic pressure on marginal return on inputs and real incomes that would privilege peripheries over more densely populated cores. But all of these perspectives rely on ideal-typical conceptualizations of a more complex reality.

Scholars have begun to agree that there was no such thing as 'Roman life expectancy.'[48] Nor, as the skeletal data show, was there 'Roman stature' or 'Roman health.' The study of variation does not pose particular methodological challenges: more data will produce a more nuanced picture. It will be much more difficult to relate such findings to Roman economic history. For all we can tell, just like other pre-modern economies, the economy of the Roman Empire failed to deliver noticeably longer lives and better bodies to its subjects. But this is not to say that it had no effects on physical well-being at all: the true challenge lies in identifying the mechanisms and dynamics that were responsible for observed outcomes.

NOTES

1 This chapter draws on some of my earlier work, esp. Scheidel forthcoming b, c.
2 Scheidel 2001a: 142–62, on Bagnall and Frier 1994: 91–110, and now also Scheidel forthcoming c. Woods 1993; 2007; Scheidel 2001c discuss the shortcomings of modern model life tables.
3 *Pace* Bagnall and Frier 1994: 110. See also Frier 2000: 788–91.
4 See especially Scheidel 2001a: 178–9, and more generally *passim* for poor conditions up to the twentieth century.
5 Scheidel 2001a: 175, with 16–18, 82–9.
6 Scheidel 1999: 255–6 (26 years, based on the Princeton model life table "West"); 37 years derived by interpolation from Woods 2007: 379 (alternative model life table "South Europe").
7 Scheidel 1999: 258–65, revising Duncan-Jones 1990: 93–6.
8 Frier 1982; other scholars' doubts are referenced in Scheidel 2001b: 20 n. 70. Use of Woods' alternative model life table does not change the overall picture.
9 Scheidel 2001b: 19 n. 66 references the debate up to 2000. For more recent developments, see Hoppa and Vaupel (eds.) 2002 and now especially Chamberlain 2006: 81–132. Weise et al. 2009 may finally promise real progress.
10 Mortality patterns inferred from age distributions in epitaphs cannot be trusted: Scheidel 2001b: 17–19; 2001c: 11–12, 21–2; 2003: 161–2, *contra* Paine and Storey 1999; Frier 2000: 791. Cf. now also Paine and Storey 2006: 82–5 for growing skepticism.
11 Zhao 1997: 122; Bagnall and Frier 1994: 88; Livi Bacci 2000: 135.
12 Del Panta et al. 1996: 232 (but cf. 147); Wrigley et al. 1997: 295.
13 E.g., Hollingsworth 1977: 327–8; Lee, Wang and Campbell 1994: 401; and forthcoming work by S. R. Johansson.
14 *Contra* Kron forthcoming, who argues for better Roman longevity thanks to infrastructure and nutrition. For a critique, see Scheidel forthcoming c.
15 Shaw 1996: 2006; Scheidel 1994; 1996a: 139–63; 2001a: 1–117; 2003: 162; forthcoming a, b. Cases of muted seasonality are rare in the Roman record, limited in the first instance to late Roman Carthage: Scheidel 1996a: 157–61; and see also Scheidel 2001a: 20–1 for Alexandria in Egypt.
16 For a graphic illustration, see Scheidel 2001a: 52, drawing on Sakamoto-Momiyama 1977: 67 fig. 4.8 (Japan). Cf. also Shaw 1996: 111 fig. 3.
17 See most conveniently Shaw 1996: 119 fig. 10; Scheidel 1996a: 146–7; and especially Scheidel 2001a: 39–48.
18 For examples, see Hatcher 1986: 26 (plague in late medieval Canterbury); Scheidel 2001a: 95 fig. 1.41 (smallpox epidemics in seventeenth-century Geneva), 99 fig. 1.42 (plague in Cairo in 1801). By contrast, the Roman epigraphic documentation primarily reflects *endemic* conditions.
19 Malaria: Scheidel 1994b; 2003: 163–9. For malaria in Rome and Italy in general, see Sallares 2002. For the possible causes of seasonal mortality variation in Roman Egypt, see Scheidel 2001a: 51–117, esp. 110 table 1.19.

20 Steckel 1995 and 2009 reviews almost 500 recent social science studies on this topic.
21 Steckel 2009: 9.
22 Steckel 2009: 8.
23 Riley 1994; Deaton 2007.
24 Nicholas and Steckel 1997; Prince and Steckel 2003; Deaton 2007.
25 Steckel and Floud 1997; Steckel 2009: 12–13.
26 Steckel 2008; 2009: 14.
27 Klein Goldewijk forthcoming. Due to large differences between regional profiles, the composite graph based on a much earlier version of her data set in Jongman 2007b: 194 is misleading.
28 Giannecchini and Moggi-Cecchi 2008: 290 (and now also Paine et al. 2009: 201); Barbiera and Dalla Zuanna 2009: 375; Stephan 2008. See also Roberts and Cox 2003: 220.
29 Koepke and Baten 2005b: 76–7.
30 See Koepke and Baten 2008: 139–40.
31 See above, Chapters 1 and 3.
32 MacKinnon 2004, with Scheidel 2009a; Koepke and Baten 2008: 142–3. The count of animal bones in Jongman 2007a: 613–14 and 2007b: 191–3 conceals this shift.
33 For evidence of higher real wages (in Egypt) during the Justinianic Plague of the sixth to eighth centuries CE, see above, Chapter 1.
34 Giannecchini and Moggi-Cecchi 2008: 290, for a mean of 164.4 cm for Roman males, which is consistent with other relevant samples not included in their survey (Gowland and Garnsey 2010: 151 n. 174). This is significantly lower than the mean of 168.3cm for Italian males from 500 BCE to 500 CE computed by Kron 2005a: 72 using an extrapolation method which is shown to be unreliable by Giannecchini and Moggi-Cecchi 2008: 288–90; cf. also Gowland and Garnsey 2010: 151.
35 Komlos 2003: 168; Peracci 2008: 3 (cf. A'Hearn 2003: 370–1).
36 Steckel 2009: 7.
37 Komlos 2007; Steckel 2009: 13–14.
38 For discussion, see most recently Walker et al. 2009.
39 In order to avoid excessive bibliography, readers are referred to the convenient survey by Gowland and Garnsey 2010, which contains full references to the underlying scholarship (cf. also Scheidel forthcoming c). Their survey has been supplemented by data from Fornaciari et al. 1982; Killgrove 2010. All results for Britain are derived from the survey in Roberts and Cox 2003: 140–1. For preliminary findings from Roman Greece and Cyprus, see Fox 2005; for further studies of Roman North African data (which still await synthesis), see MacKinnon 2007, who (255) notes a high incidence of *cribra orbitalia*.
40 See Gowland and Garnsey 2010, and more generally Sallares 2002 (Italy); Scheidel 2001a: 80 (oases).
41 For some tentative analyses, see Manzi et al. 1999; Cucina et al. 2006; Pitts and Griffin 2012.
42 Manzi et al. 1999, on Latium (worse caries but less enamel hypoplasia in the seventh century CE); Salvadei, Ricci and Manzi 2001 and Belcastro et al. 2007, on Molise (similar rates of cranial and dental lesions but more meat consumption in the seventh century CE).

43 Barbiera and Dalla Zuanna 2009: 374.
44 Cf. Johansson 1994; 2005.
45 Dobson 1997: 224, with 148, 158, 495 (England); Del Panta 1989: 22, with Sallares 2002: 160–1 (Italy).
46 Sallares 2002: 269–71, on Plin. *Ep.* 5.6.6 and 46.
47 For the debate, see Scobie 1986; Laurence 1997; Scheidel 2003; Morley 2005; Lo Cascio 2006b; Kron forthcoming; Scheidel forthcoming c.
48 E.g., Scheidel 2001c: 25; Sallares 2002: 283–5.

16: Post-Roman Economies

Simon T. Loseby

Any attempt at providing a synthesis of the salient characteristics and chronological development of 'post-Roman' economies, which will be taken here to begin from the fifth century CE, is complicated by the extent to which change varied across space and time. The most meaningful and revealing approach to this infinite variety lies in extended and comparative regional study, as has recently been magisterially demonstrated.[1] Within the confines of an overview, however, one can only try to encapsulate this general pattern of fragmentation within a unitary framework of analysis, notwithstanding the schematic superficiality that this inevitably involves. In outline, a familiar distinction between the political destinies of the two halves of the empire, the fragmented, newly-barbarian West and the integrated and lately-flourishing East, can readily be carried over into the economic sphere because of the importance of the fiscal interests of the Roman state in shaping the dynamics of production and exchange. In neither case, however, was any radical economic transformation immediately and generally triggered by 'the fall of Rome.'[2] In the East, the late antique boom encouraged by the foundation of Constantinople, and implicit in the expansion of the extent and intensity of rural settlement in several regions, continued unabated.[3] In the West, with the notable exception of Britain, where the involution of the Roman system was complete within little more than a generation, the various successor-states entered upon a species of economic half-life, in the sense that they emitted Roman-ness in various aspects of their fiscal organization and patterns of exchange until the later seventh century, but in steadily diminishing quantities.[4] This fading but still recognizably post-Roman pattern would be significantly complicated, but not fundamentally altered, by the absorption of Africa and parts of Italy back into the imperial orbit as a result of Justinian's reconquests. In the seventh century, however, the eastern empire underwent a military-political crisis of its own, at once more concise in its nature and less decisive in its outcomes.[5] The Byzantine state survived, in shrunken form, and a variant of fiscal organization was maintained by the Umayads in the territories over which they had assumed control.[6] Even so, the Arab conquests appear more closely linked with the end of the Roman economic system than their barbarian precursors, if only because they anticipate decisive changes in long-established patterns of production and distribution in various regions of the Mediterranean that mark the point at which 'post-Roman' ceases to be a meaningful general description of contemporary patterns of exchange. Recent attempts either to downplay the significance of this break, or to accelerate the subsequent emergence of a new 'European' economy, fail to do justice to the scale and significance of the changes involved, and, indeed, to the exceptional economic integration and particular dynamics of exchange generated by the Roman world-system.

An empirical justification of this superficial narrative would ideally depend upon a host of factors, and a variety of evidence. But here particular emphasis will be laid upon one specific theme and one category of material, both for considerations of space, and because of their particular explanatory significance. The argument that follows is based primarily upon ceramic evidence, and derives from an understanding of the inextricable relationship between state-driven and commercial exchange within the ancient economic system that has in part been developed in response to the availability of such data. The classic accounts of late Roman, post-Roman, or early medieval economies had perforce relied upon textual sources, whether deployed to sustain the impressionistic sweep of Henri Pirenne, or the forensic precision of A. H. M. Jones.[7] This distinguished tradition has been carried forward more recently by Dietrich Claude's invaluable compendium of documentary evidence for trade in the sixth- and seventh-century western Mediterranean, and, in a very different style but across a similar thematic canvas, by Michael McCormick's rich study of Mediterranean communications and, by extension, exchange in the period from *c.* 700 to 900 CE.[8] But the evidence upon which these studies have to rely is in large measure anecdotal: a merchant going here, a commodity traded there, a trade-route linking this region with that. To be sure, these vignettes offer an appealing array of post-Roman possibilities, little dramas of exchange that the historian eschews for potsherds with some reluctance: a subdeacon in Lyon purloining Gaza wine for his personal consumption and offering his communicants vinegar instead, a hireling of Greek merchants chancing in Dickensian fashion upon distant relatives in Mérida, Gregory the Great trying for years without conspicuous success to send timber to Alexandria, Frankish ambassadors stopping off and getting killed in a street-fight in Carthage on their way to Constantinople, an unlucky Egyptian merchant whose consistently miserable fortunes changed to the extent that on his latest, church-backed venture he found himself blown all the way to Britain with a cargo of grain to sell in a time of famine.[9] In expert hands, the careful organization of such data into analytical categories has proved immensely revealing, perhaps most notably with regard to the persistence or otherwise of exchange-routes.[10] Even so, its frequently allusive and incidental character, its qualitative and quantitative limitations, and its random distribution generally make it difficult to get much sense of the scale of production or distribution, to draw convincing comparisons across space or time, to distinguish the typical from the possible, or to dig down from high-profile interregional or luxury traffic to the economic bedrock of local networks of production and exchange.[11] The inescapably distorted perspectives offered by the texts are nowhere more apparent than in regard to commodities, where high-value, low-volume luxury goods, marginal to the economy as a whole, tend to be privileged over staple items, the exchange of which is rendered visible primarily within institutional and redistributive contexts.[12]

These inherent deficiencies of the textual data can be rigorously controlled, but they cannot be easily transcended. *Faute de mieux*, the vagaries of the written record have often come either to be brushed to one side, or read as a meaningful reflection of contemporary realities. The single most influential historical study of the early medieval economy was therefore constructed around the availability or otherwise of luxury goods; the shortage of late Roman references to the circulation of staple commodities outside networks of redistribution was interpreted as one more indicator of the limited scale and significance of commercial exchange.[13] In recent decades, however, the parameters of our understanding of the ancient and early medieval economy have shifted thanks to the emergence of a wealth of archaeological evidence, particularly in the form of excavated ceramic material. Since pottery makes up the bulk of the finds on the majority of sites, whereas perishable items survive only in exceptional conditions, this might appear to be making a virtue of what Moses Finley once called "that great curse of archaeology."[14] But if we had to restrict ourselves to any single body of material from which to derive our understanding of ancient networks of exchange, then pottery would be a reasonable choice. First, it was in near-universal and continuous use throughout Antiquity, and survives in all archaeological contexts. Secondly, it was manufactured to a wide range of technological specifications, from rudimentary household wares to standardized mass-productions of superior quality and industrial scale. Thirdly, the study of ceramic kilns and fabrics and the increasingly sophisticated development of pottery typologies have allowed substantial proportions of this material to be classified, assigned to a specific region of production, and dated (with varying degrees of precision and confidence). Finally, the approximate productive quality of any given ware can be readily distinguished, as can the extent of its distribution; as one would expect, there is often some correlation to be observed between the two.[15]

For analytical purposes, therefore, the ceramic evidence provides much of what is missing from the texts: a measure of economic complexity that is generally and serially available, susceptible to meaningful statistical analysis, and readily comparable between regions and over centuries.[16] In societies where the pottery in circulation is restricted to basic local manufactures, we can assume the existence of relatively simple patterns of production and distribution. But where mass-produced, high-quality wares circulate within wide-ranging interregional distribution-networks that encompass remote or humble sites, as was the case in the Roman period, this must be indicative of the existence of an economic system sufficiently integrated and complex to make it possible for peasants to access and afford high-specification items manufactured hundreds of miles away across the Mediterranean, and for the producers and traders involved in these transactions to consider them worth their while. The elements of that system identifiable from the ceramic evidence are obviously specific to the pottery industry. However, the economic frameworks that made such complexity possible will not have been exclusively available to potters; it is a reasonable assumption that the production and exchange of comparable manufactured goods that can be made both widely and over a range of specifications, such as textiles, was taking place at a similar general level of sophistication.[17]

The interpretative potential of the ceramic evidence is, of course, enhanced further by the widespread use of amphorae in antiquity as containers for the maritime transport of a variety of foodstuffs, in particular olive oil and wine, two-thirds of the ancient trinity of agricultural staples.[18] Patterns of amphora production and distribution can therefore stand as proxy for the circulation of agricultural staples, and are similarly susceptible to comparative analysis across time.[19] We need to bear in mind that analysis of this data set is affected by more unknown variables than that of the pottery evidence, in general, for example, because we can never be sure how far alternative, perishable receptacles, such as barrels, skins, or sacks, were in circulation alongside amphorae, or more specifically because amphorae were multi-purpose and reusable containers, so that the identification of individual types with specific commodities is by no means as axiomatic as is often implied.[20] Even so, the recurrent correlation between archaeological evidence for the intensification of rural settlement and agricultural production in a given region, and the distribution of that region's amphora types to overseas markets suggests that such data can be especially revealing of phases of regional productive specialization and exchange complexity.

The ceramic evidence therefore offers either direct or proxy (and less comprehensive) access to the production and exchange of a number of staple commodities from both the manufacturing and agrarian sectors of the economy: pottery, olive oil, wine, and other foodstuffs. Although these make up but a fraction of the documented range of goods in circulation, there are good reasons for thinking that cumulatively they offer a tolerably representative basis for the characterization of the scale and sophistication of the economy at large. In the fifth century, pottery and foodstuffs produced in quantity in some regions of the Mediterranean were circulating very widely around and, to some extent, beyond its hinterlands within integrated networks of exchange. The primary markers of this system are African Red Slip pottery (ARS) and amphorae; their hegemony within networks of interregional exchange had been developing from the second century onwards, such that by late antiquity ARS had become so familiar and successful a brand as to spawn a host of local imitations.[21] However, this African dominance had lately come under challenge from producers in several regions of the eastern Mediterranean coast from the Aegean round to Egypt, whose distinct contributions to networks of interregional exchange can be identified from the various families of amphorae in which they commoditized their surplus oil and wine production. These begin to appear in quantity on western Mediterranean sites from the first half of the fifth century, closely pursued by eastern fine-ware pottery.[22] The overseas dissemination of these wares can be read as the latest phase in a sequence generated by the Roman world-system that had seen Italy, southern and central Gaul, Spain, Africa, and latterly the Near East successively take the lead in Mediterranean exchange. However, this final phase seems to be particularly polycentric in its focus and multifaceted in its nature, perhaps suggesting the interregional exchange-system had attained an unprecedented degree of maturity in late antiquity.[23] As we shall see, it would also be distinguished by its longevity.

The explanation of the persistence and eventual involution of this system, not to mention the integrity of the overarching narrative outlined above, hinges upon recognition of the entangled relationship between the state and commercial sectors of the Roman economic system that is discussed in more detail in other chapters in this volume. In general terms, the Roman state provided fiscal and transport infrastructures that made exchange easier, its tax-demands stimulated market activity, and its political authority assured a significant level of economic integration.[24] More specifically, the emperors found it politically expedient to command routine transports of staple foodstuffs to their armies and their capitals, where necessary over long distances, and came to resolve the considerable logistical implications through the mechanism of the *annona*, in effect a compulsory purchase- and distribution-system.[25] The willingness of the state to contract within this framework for the regular and direct supply of foodstuffs from designated regions to its chosen beneficiaries expanded the parameters of production and distribution in contributing regions by encouraging specialization and investment, guaranteeing demand, and sustaining the requisite infrastructural support, as is evident from the impact of this fiscal stimulus upon Africa, the main source of Rome's grain from the first century, and of its oil from the Severan era.[26]

By Late Antiquity, a growth in the numbers of state personnel and the range of commodities involved had ensured that the *annona*-system, like most components of the imperial machinery, was expanding in scale and significance. In 332, in particular, it was extended to the new imperial capital at Constantinople, building upon arrangements that had already been made to supply in similar fashion at least some of the needs of other major eastern cities such as Alexandria, and probably Antioch.[27] In the frontier zones, the requirements of the military appear as far as possible to have been met by producers in adjacent regions.[28] In the Mediterranean, however, where the interregional movement of goods was comparatively inexpensive, the demands of the major cities routinized massive transports of grain and other foodstuffs, in particular from Africa to Rome and from Egypt to Constantinople (but also from subsidiary sources of supply such as Sicily, Syria, and the Aegean), and carried out by shippers as part of their fiscal obligations.[29]

On the basis of the available textual evidence, dominated by the legal regulation of these arrangements, the shipment of staple foodstuffs within the context of the *annona* tended to be regarded as symptomatic of a command economy that effectively negated commercial enterprise.[30] However, the ceramic data made this proposition increasingly untenable by privileging the manifold outcomes of interregional exchange over the mechanisms through which it was achieved. The extraordinary diffusion of African fine-wares might have owed much to the *annona*, as we shall see, but it cannot conceivably have been a direct manifestation of the imperial will.[31] Similarly, while some proportion of excavated African and eastern Mediterranean amphorae will have carried foodstuffs bound for Rome or Constantinople, their circulation extends far beyond any narrowly circumscribed networks of redistribution. No less apparent, however, was the correlation between those Mediterranean regions involved in surplus production for the *annona* and those that dominate the ceramic record of contemporary interregional exchange. It was this above all that led to the reconception of state intervention as a catalyst rather than a barrier to commercial enterprise, through both its encouragement of surplus production, and its subsidizing of interregional transport.[32] The reconsideration of the late antique regulation of *annona*-transports in this newly entrepreneurial light has since emphasized the many benefits that shippers enjoyed in compensation for fulfilling their fiscal obligations and supplying the state's needs at significantly below the market rate. Not only did the state absorb some of the costs of shipbuilding and indemnify the *navicularii* against the risks of loss, it left them with the means, the opportunity, and a generous time-frame in which to conduct their own business on the side, duty-free.[33] Shippers from those regions involved in fiscal mechanisms of supply were thus able to exploit an embedded commercial advantage as they transported secondary cargoes – such as usefully heavy ceramics – alongside those they were routinely obliged to shift by the state, picked up others for their return voyages via the shores and islands of the Mediterranean, and created complex ceramic distributions through the variety of exchanges in which they engaged along the way.[34]

The Roman state has therefore become a necessary rather than a sufficient element in explaining the archaeologically visible patterns of the circulation of goods in the late antique Mediterranean. The demands of the *annona* were probably fundamental to the generation of enhanced surplus production geared specifically towards overseas exchange. Just as the African economy expanded in the context of its superseding Spain as Rome's main source of supply, so it is scarcely coincidental that surplus production for export around the eastern Mediterranean develops significantly over the century following the extension of the *annona* to Constantinople.[35] Even if our archaeological perception of such traffic, whether state-driven or commercial, is limited to the circulation of ceramics, the complexity of pottery and, in particular, amphora distributions alone is sufficient to emphasize the development alongside the axial *annona*-routes of multiple networks of exchange between various coastal regions and islands, particularly in the eastern Mediterranean.[36] But the ceramic evidence also shows how these networks had matured to the extent that they could survive the partial withdrawal of their original fiscal underpinning. The Vandal conquest of Carthage in 439 CE and the consequent ending of *annona*-transports probably disrupted established patterns of African ceramic production and distribution – and perhaps further encouraged the shipment of eastern goods to western consumers as a result – but it had no lasting structural impact upon their dominance of overseas markets.[37] The demands of the *annona* may have been instrumental in facilitating the African hegemony over interregional exchange in the first place, but its systems of production and distribution had become sufficiently established to endure without them.

In the Mediterranean, as a result, there was no fifth-century break between the late Roman and 'post-Roman' interregional exchange-systems, which constitute a unitary late antique phase running from the third century (in the West) and the fourth century (in the East) down to around 700 CE. Within the separate system of northwestern Europe, however, the economic legacy of the Roman state was much more short-lived. The principal driver of economic integration here had always been the fiscal cycle and in particular the military *annona*, which did not survive the disbanding of the centralized professional army. In Britain, the resulting meltdown was swift and absolute.[38] Across much of Gaul, however, the crisis was significantly less severe. Here, despite the supposedly devastating impact of barbarian warfare and violence, the sixth century dawned with many scions of established aristocratic families maintaining their status by lending their services directly to the rulers of the new successor-states, or doing so at one remove through the pursuit of office within the church, having more or less readily accommodated themselves to barbarian rule in exchange for the preservation of their landed wealth and social power.[39] The survival across the crisis period of the regional pottery industries of Argonne and Mayen, both of them in the hinterland of the collapsed frontier, tells a similar story; the reach of these wares was significantly reduced, in similar fashion to the horizons of the Gallic aristocracy, but not to the point of their disappearance.[40] Although it built in part upon such legacies, from the sixth century onwards the 'post-Roman' economy of Francia would redevelop within a fundamentally different framework, as its rulers relied on aristocratic followings rather than a professional army to guarantee the military security of their kingdoms, retained their loyalty with land, and eventually spared themselves the trouble of administering an increasingly residual Roman tax-system.[41] The regional exchange-networks that emerged were no longer geared to fiscal imperatives and, above all, to the supply of the military in the frontier zone, but came instead to be articulated along the main river-systems, and driven by the demand generated by landed aristocrats and ecclesiastical institutions. In the Frankish heartlands in particular, this was sufficient to foster an intensification of surplus production and exchange which, whether we prefer to regard bipartite estate organization as a Carolingian innovation or a late antique legacy, was visibly getting under way in the seventh century.[42] As these emerging riverine networks began to interlock and expand outwards, they did so in new directions, eastwards beyond the Roman frontier, and out into the northern seas.

The impact of the disintegration of the western empire upon the economies of its Mediterranean regions was more gradual. In the early fifth century most of these areas were neither closely integrated into the state system of supply, nor visibly engaged in the export of goods in bulk outside regional networks.[43] Southern Gaul and the Italian peninsula sustained an assortment of fine-ware and, in some cases, amphora productions, but with rare exceptions these wares normally circulated within distinct subregional orbits.[44] African fine-wares and amphorae, in marked contrast, were readily available right around the western Mediterranean (and the eastern besides), particularly in Italy, where their universal availability must have been subsidized to some degree by the *annona*, but also in Mediterranean Gaul and Spain, where their distribution can only have been commercial. In the latter region, a sharp distinction in material culture between the coast, where ARS was sufficiently available to negate any regional fine-wares altogether, and the upland Meseta, where it scarcely competed at all with local productions, highlights the scale, but also the limits, of this African domination of interregional exchange, and the truth of the observations of contemporaries elsewhere about the material divide between coastal and inland regions.[45]

This was largely a maritime hegemony, therefore, but, as far as it went, a comprehensive one, and it survived the ending of the fiscal underpinning provided by the *annona*. Indeed, the classic synthesis of late antique ceramics and interregional exchange argued for an essential continuity of African production and export across the period of the Vandal conquest, with the beginnings of its gradual involution postponed to the end of the fifth century.[46] This chronology has since been qualified by the later dating of some of the amphora types on which it relied, and by renewed recognition of a number of mid-fifth-century changes in patterns of African ceramic production and distribution.[47] In principle, it would hardly be surprising if the African economy suffered temporarily from the political upheaval associated with the Vandal takeover, and more generally from the withdrawal of the subsidizing effects of the *annona*, which may have led either to a drop in the volume of African exports or an increase in their price, creating opportunities for local or eastern producers to exploit.[48] On the other hand, African producers were now free to market their surplus as they pleased, which probably helped to ease their adjustment to the different exchange context in which they were now operating. The late fifth-century African ceramic data has recently been reinterpreted as indicative of something of a renewal in production, reflected in the distribution of new varieties of ARS and amphorae to overseas consumers in considerable quantities, notwithstanding the competition presented by the growing range and reach of eastern exports.[49] It may be going too far to suggest on this basis that there was 'a general boom in trade' in the decades around 500 (absolute volumes of exchange remain elusive, but in the absence of state involvement aggregate demand seems unlikely to have increased), but it is certain that the producers and distributors of African goods for overseas consumption had adapted to life without the *annona*, and that commercial demand for their wares was sufficient for them to renew their dominance of networks of interregional exchange.[50]

The economies of the 'post-Roman' western Mediterranean, insofar as they can be identified archaeologically through ceramics, might therefore be said to exhibit three consistent and, in general, abiding characteristics. The first is a certain persistence of existing traditions of production and distribution, particularly at the regional level, but also in interregional exchange-networks, enduringly dominated by African exports to the exclusion of significant western competition. Secondly, the political crises of the fifth century resonate only temporarily or locally within the ceramic record, even in regions where the interests of the state played a major part in the circulation of goods. At the regional level, the ceramic data consistently support an economic narrative of gradual transformation rather than the headlong collapse visible, exceptionally, in Britain. Finally, nothing suggests the development of significant new patterns of interregional exchange particular to the western Mediterranean; the original features of this period lie rather in the growing presence of eastern goods upon its shores, and the extension of such traffic beyond the Straits of Gibraltar and up to western Britain.[51] Instead, the economies of the sixth- and seventh-century Mediterranean West will be characterized by the involution of well-established networks of production and distribution.

The indications of this involution are already present before 500 in the Spanish interior, with a retreat in the distribution and quality of regional fine-wares, which become progressively more local, and usually less fine.[52] The equivalent southern Gallic wares suffer a similar fate, but over a longer time-frame; the Provençal variant of DS.P found in Marseille, a likely focus of its production and dissemination, stayed in production through the sixth century, for example, but declined steadily in quality and quantity to become increasingly indistinguishable from local common wares during the seventh.[53] In general, the ceramics manufactured in southern Gaul and Mediterranean Spain indicate the increasing localization of production and distribution over the sixth and seventh centuries. The scale of this involution (and the extent to which it has been studied) varies from one subregion to the next, but the simplification of internal exchange structures is clear.[54] In contrast, meanwhile, the major ports in these regions remained integrated into the wider Mediterranean economy, and continued to receive African and eastern imports in quantity well into the seventh century.[55] The Italian peninsula exhibits a broadly comparable pattern, though it unfolded along a more discontinuous route. Here the Gothic War and Lombard invasions shredded the political and fiscal integration that might otherwise have combined with the particular concentrations of wealth held by its elites to give Italy an advantage over other western regions, and replaced it with a lasting pattern of economic and political fragmentation.[56] Some regions emerged in better shape than others; a crude distinction might be drawn between a Lombard (or, perhaps just as importantly, less Mediterranean) north, where ceramic production had in many areas deteriorated to rudimentary levels by the mid-seventh century, and the Byzantine-held south, which sustained the production of semi-fine Red Painted wares on some scale, as well as its connections with the interregional exchange-system.[57] The regional pattern is more inconsistent here, therefore, than in southern Gaul or Spain, but exhibits a similar general combination of the simplification of internal networks of exchange alongside the participation of major coastal cities such as Rome and Naples, and other high-status sites, in wider Mediterranean networks, continuing long into the seventh century.[58] In Italy (and perhaps to some extent in Spain) the distribution of these wares privileged imperial-held territory, but the abundance of such imports in Visigothic

Tarragona and Frankish Marseille cautions against seeing their presence as fiscally- or politically- rather than commercially-driven; they appear indicative of particular concentrations of demand that persisted within the wider western context of economic simplification.[59]

The Justinianic reconquest and its precarious legacy clearly damaged the Italian economy. It is trickier to assess the Byzantine impact on Africa, where the resumption of *annona*-shipments, now heading for Constantinople rather than Rome, swiftly followed its smooth reentry into the imperial orbit. Whether or not the region's economy had been prospering outside imperial control, this renewal of guaranteed demand, combined with the temporary restoration of nine-tenths of the Mediterranean coastline to Byzantine rule might be expected to have enhanced the possibilities of African production and exchange. Ceramic distributions may suggest that this was indeed the case, as African exports show signs of picking up again in the later sixth century in the wake of the *annona*.[60] But within Africa, meanwhile, we see the beginnings of a localization and degeneration of ceramic production, a contraction in internal distribution-networks, and a retreat in rural settlement, all trends that will accelerate as the seventh century advances.[61] This is the familiar western pattern of abatement, but here it started late, and from a much higher baseline than elsewhere, and it did not affect the availability of African ceramics to overseas consumers on privileged sites for some time to come. Gradually, however, the distribution of such wares on western sites was becoming more restricted, and while this inexorable retreat was perhaps offset by exports to the East, such traffic may not have been sufficient to compensate either for declining western demand or for the reabsorption of a proportion of African agricultural surplus production by the state. The economy of Byzantine Africa was thus caught between two exchange-systems: a steadily declining western one, that it dominated for what were probably diminishing returns, and a still dynamic eastern one, to which its fiscal contribution apparently remained significant – hence Heraclius' prompt withholding of the African grain supply to Constantinople on his rebellion against Phocas in 608[62] – but within which it was geographically peripheral, and its commercial exports faced considerable competition from eastern producers.

On the other side of the Mediterranean pond, meanwhile, the economies of that eastern – and enduringly imperial – system had long been set upon an altogether different trajectory.[63] As has been discussed, their internal complexity and integration are likely to have been stimulated by the foundation of Constantinople, and the extension of the *annona* to the new capital.[64] Rural settlement was certainly expanding in several regions of the Near East from around the same time, as is revealed by the exploitation of hitherto marginal land and the development of substantial villages, most famously in the Limestone Massif northeast of Antioch, but similarly along the rugged coasts of Lycia and Cilicia, amid the basalt outcrops of the Hauran in southern Syria, and in the wadis of the Negev in the desert hinterland of Gaza.[65] These zones all have their distinctive characteristics, but the intensification of production and settlement within them is sufficiently consistent in nature and timing that it can legitimately be considered a unitary phenomenon, all the more so because this escalating rural prosperity coincides with the initial appearances upon overseas sites of amphora types manufactured along the coasts of the various regions concerned. The driver of this growth thereby emerges as surplus production for export of oil (supplied, for example, in Late Roman Amphora 1, widely manufactured around the northeastern quadrant of the Mediterranean) and wine (including, for example the Gaza *crus* singled out by several late antique writers that circulated in LRA 4).[66] By the later fifth century, these burgeoning eastern Mediterranean exchange-networks had reached maturity. Rural settlement in several regions was at an historic peak, and ceramic distributions reveal an intricate web of interregional exchanges, as all of the coastal regions from the shores of the Aegean round to Alexandria traded not only with each other, but also across to the West.[67] The general interplay of state and commercial interests in the expansion of this system is clearer than the detailed dynamics of their relationship, whether because the millions of *modii* of grain shipped annually from Egypt to Constantinople can obscure how little we know for sure about the extent to which the state regulated supplies to major eastern cities, or because our archaeological perception of the circulation of goods is, as ever, incomplete.[68] Egypt, for example, did not visibly dominate the eastern system on the back of its fiscal obligations to Constantinople in the way that Africa had the late antique West. In part, this was because it produced neither olive oil in any quantity, nor wine of any quality, such that its inhabitants looked to import them from the northeastern Mediterranean and Palestine respectively.[69] Less predictably, its voluminous fine-ware production was not widely exported either, leaving us to assume that if, by analogy with Africa, Egyptian shippers enjoyed commercial advantages by virtue of their service to the state, they must instead have exploited it to cram their holds with textiles, papyrus, and spices, or, perhaps likeliest of all, yet more grain. The leading fine-wares within the eastern system (though never approaching the dominance of ARS) were rather those produced down the Aegean coast from Constantinople at Phocaea, and the 'Cypriot' RS named for its abundance on an island that served as an exchange-hub for the produce of the adjacent coasts.[70] The circulation of these wares may owe something to their distribution by outward-bound or returning *annona*-fleets, but their fiscal underpinning is much less transparent than was the case with the rise of ARS, and the more capillary pattern of port-to-port exchange inferred from the distribution of the Phocaean wares would also fit the fiendish complexity of the various amphora distributions. In any case, however elusive the precise mix of fiscal and commercial interests involved, the patterns that resulted were altogether more diverse and polycentric than those generated by the sequential regional hegemonies that had previously characterized interregional Mediterranean exchange.

These polyfocal patterns of production and distribution remain broadly stable throughout the sixth century, when the obligation of African shippers to supply Constantinople consolidated flows of exchange between the two basins of the Mediterranean. Although renewed attempts have lately been made to seek harbingers of doom either in Justinian's autocratic rule, or in the demographic consequences of the outbreaks of plague that swirled repeatedly around the Mediterranean from the late 530s onwards, once again the potentially debilitating impact of such episodes upon the eastern economy at large is far from transparent in the archaeological evidence, whether with regard to rural settlement, where an end to the prolonged phase of intensification need not be equated with its immediate reverse into decline, or networks of interregional exchange, which continue much as before.[71] Instead, the onset of a generalized and substantive crisis is better postponed to the early seventh century, when civil war, a mutually destructive conflict with Persia, and the loss of most of its richest territories to the Arabs occurred in rapid and incremental succession within the space of four decades, and destroyed the political and fiscal integrity of the Byzantine empire.[72] One certain (but largely invisible) casualty of this disintegration will have been the *annona*, as the state lost its ability to command supplies from Egypt, Syria, and, ultimately, Africa. As in the fifth-century west, its disappearance did not automatically trigger the collapse of commercial circuits of ceramic production and distribution. The manufacture of familiar ceramic types initially continued without a break in the regions taken over by the Arabs, and Levantine amphorae went on reaching Constantinople and privileged western Mediterranean markets until the end of the century.[73] But by that time, as we shall see, many of the familiar fine-wares and amphorae characteristic of the eastern exchange-system were either ceasing to circulate outside their regions of production, or going out of production altogether. Its seventh-century crisis had rapidly imposed upon the East the regionalization and, in some of those regions, the simplification of exchange that had long been features of the post-Roman West.

An exceptionally sharp snapshot of the eventual demise of the integrated late antique Mediterranean exchange-system has been developed, appropriately enough, at Rome, through the study of a pair of closely-datable ceramic assemblages recovered from the massive dump at the Crypta Balbi.[74] In the first, from around 690, the tiny sample of fine-wares was predictably monopolized by ARS, although a scatter of African and eastern imports did also feature among the common wares, vastly outnumbered by much more local manufactures; the amphora assemblage was more heavily African-dominated, but also included a varied array of eastern and southern Italian containers, not to mention a significant proportion of amphorae the provenances of which are yet to be precisely determined. In total, around 80 percent of the identifiable ceramics in this late-seventh-century phase came from outside Italy, and their distant origins reflect long-established patterns. Despite the relentless contraction of participation in the interregional exchange-system, a diverse assortment of familiar African and eastern products was circulating within it until the end.[75] But by the time of the succeeding deposit at the Crypta Balbi, dating from around the 720s, imported amphorae and fine-wares are conspicuous by their absence. Instead, the assemblage consists almost entirely of central and southern Italian ceramics, from nowhere more distant than Sicily. The high-status users of this rubbish dump, plausibly associated with the monastery of S. Lorenzo in Pallacinis, had fallen back on local and regional suppliers for their oil, wine, and pottery, who, moreover, to judge from the significant decline in the total proportion of amphorae between the two samples, and Rome's subsequent ceramic history, were delivering their wares in other forms of container.[76]

For the vast majority of the inhabitants of the western Mediterranean coastal fringes, not to mention those living further inland, this final disappearance from the market of African and eastern pottery and foodstuffs would have been imperceptible, because they had long since ceased to be a part of their everyday experience. Unlike their ancestors, they will no longer have been accustomed to ARS, unless perhaps as an heirloom to be brought out like the best china on special occasions, while the renowned potency of Gaza wine had probably always been a more exclusive experience.[77] Only in exceptional cases might the impact of the change have been more keenly felt, as for example at Marseille, which, like Rome, had continued to be tied into the late antique system for as long as it existed. Marseille sustained this link by virtue of its role as the gateway through which Mediterranean imports were funnelled to distant but wealthy Frankish consumers via the Rhône corridor, in a striking reversion to its original *raison d'être* as an emporium.[78] The post-Roman renaissance of the port highlights the enduring cultural significance of such exchange in the West, but also the altogether different political and economic context in which it was now taking place, as imported foodstuffs from the Mediterranean increasingly resumed the status of luxuries, and rulers sought to exercise some measure of remote control over their distribution. When such imports finally stopped in around 700, Marseille ceased once again to matter, this time not because the Roman system had negated its liminal role in the mediation of interregional exchange, but because there was so little interregional exchange left to mediate.[79] As at Rome, the eventual western breakdown of this etiolated system was not driven exclusively by a failure of consumer demand – for there is every indication that in the late seventh century northern Frankish elites were still anxious to guarantee their access to such imports in some volume – but of supply.

The economic impact of the final disintegration of interregional exchange on exporting regions such as Africa must, of course, have been much more significant. Here the seventh century remains difficult to characterize, first because the growing internal evidence of economic involution contrasts with external indications of the tenacity of African exports, and second because of the uncertain contribution of the Arab conquests.[80] On the one hand, it can be argued that the contraction of rural settlement and the steady retreat and localization of the production and internal distribution of ceramics were all well under way before the Arabs arrived, and that the continuities in material culture across the conquest period in Egypt, Syria, and Palestine leave no reason to associate them with any swift transformation in material culture. On the other, it is hard to see how the intensification of their activity in the region in the 690s will not have been one contributory factor in the apparently abrupt cessation of centuries-old ceramic traditions within a generation of the fall of Carthage.[81] The negligible evidence as yet available for the eighth century suggests – in part by its very nature – that this productive break was accompanied by a further simplification of internal patterns of exchange. The region's agricultural potential was too great for this to last, but by the time its economy begins to show renewed signs of expansion, its potters had adopted the new fashion for polychrome glazed wares, which exhibit no transition from earlier ceramic traditions.[82]

Around the eastern Mediterranean, too, the disappearance of interregional exchange had wider ramifications, because of the greater economic integration that had ensured far more people were implicated in it in some way as producers or consumers. The impact of political crisis is perhaps most obvious in the vicinity of Constantinople in the later seventh century, as the fine-wares and amphora types most indicative of Aegean participation in interregional exchange (Phocaean Red Slip, LRA 2 and 3) all went out of production, much like their African equivalents, but within the wider context of a much more visible social and cultural transformation.[83] In Byzantine-held territory, nevertheless, the rupture was neither as complete nor as lasting, because a simpler regional exchange-network was rapidly reconstituted around the needs of Constantinople, as manifested in the eighth century by the circulation of the city's own Glazed White Wares, the production of which now expanded to fill the gap in the market left by the demise of PRS, and of various species of globular amphorae descended from LRA 2.[84] In its enduring devotion to the amphora, as in its flows of exchange to and from the capital, this Aegean-centered network is perhaps the only truly recognizable descendant of the ancient system, but one that was significantly reduced in scale and sophistication, and operating within a completely different world.[85]

In those areas of the eastern Mediterranean that were taken over by the Arabs in the seventh century, meanwhile, there are two telling contrasts, between coast and interior in Syria and Palestine, and, as so often, between Egypt and the rest. The oil and wine producers of the hinterlands of the Levantine coast, from Lycia round to Gaza, had been heavily implicated in the eastern Mediterranean exchange-system, and they suffered commensurately from its disintegration. Here again the diagnostic regional ceramic markers of their involvement, LRA 1 and 4, passed out of production, and this may well be connected with the beginnings of abatement in rural settlement in the marginal zones of the Negev and the Limestone Massif, in the Mediterranean-facing economic hinterlands of Gaza and Antioch respectively.[86] Not so far away, however, much of inland Syria and Palestine continued to prosper, in part because they were the core territories of the Umayyad regime, but also because their regional economies were far less exposed to the collapse of the ancient exchange-system. The ceramic evidence here suggests no marked break in material culture, but rather the ongoing evolution of existing patterns of production and distribution, as potters built upon vernacular traditions to often sophisticated effect, while increasingly looking eastwards for inspiration.[87] When a wider ceramic community of taste began to reemerge in the ninth century with the proliferation of polychrome glazed wares, its impetus would accordingly come from 'Abbasid Mesopotomia, and not from the Mediterranean.[88]

In Egypt, last but by no means least, where we might expect by analogy with Africa and the Levantine coast to find similar intimations of productive crisis indicative of the extent of its implication in the ancient system, it is telling that we see nothing of the sort. This discrepancy may in some measure be attributable to the familiar problem of the archaeological invisibility of much of Egypt's participation in interregional exchange, but the scale and sophistication of the Egyptian economy in its own right, fuelled and structured by the Nile, is probably much more significant. The regional system here was simply exceptional in its articulation and extent; the varieties of Red Slip ware produced on an industrial scale in workshops around Aswan, for example, circulated hundreds of miles downriver without even reaching the Mediterranean.[89] These levels of internal integration meant that in Egypt, unlike in Syria and Palestine, there was no great material contrast between coast and interior, and, in contrast to Africa, no fragile network of individual routes was required to link producers inland with coastal consumers or distributors. Most significantly of all, much of Egypt's prosperity was internally generated, and independent of overseas exchange, whether state-sponsored or commercial; under Arab rule, moreover, the fiscal system and its economically stimulating effects were so thoroughly maintained as to arouse visible discontent, even as Egypt's governors contrived to retain the surplus that it generated to fund the regional army rather than the caliphs in Damascus.[90] This continuation of business as usual is reflected in the long persistence, in contrast to other regions, of ancient traditions of ceramic manufacture; Egyptian potters did eventually adopt the new fashion for glaze, but its familiar amphora types would continue on into the Middle Ages.[91] In its capacity to sustain a complex internal economy outside the embrace of the Roman empire, Egypt in the eighth century was the opposite of Britain in the fifth.

Between those two geographical extremes of change and continuity, the timing of the end of the 'post-Roman' exchange-system across the Mediterranean heartlands of the empire is consistently located by the archaeological evidence in the decades around 700, when many of the long-established ceramic markers of interregional exchange went more or less abruptly out of production, and were not to be speedily superseded by substitutes with comparably extensive distributions. Since the first efforts to synthesise the excavated data in the 1980s, the development of ceramic typologies has steadily pushed this nadir in Mediterranean exchange later in time, such that it now corresponds closely to the chronology previously deduced, with particular reference to the West, from the more anecdotal indications of the textual sources, most systematically by Dietrich Claude, and rather more notoriously by Henri Pirenne.[92] This convergence is mutually reinforcing, and all the more compelling because of the different emphases, as previously outlined, of the two sets of data. But if the timing of this conclusive disintegration of the ancient economic system is relatively clear, the explanations for its demise must, as we have seen, vary from region to region. With some inevitable simplification, they might heuristically be divided into three broad geographical groups.

In northwestern Europe and down into the Spanish interior, Roman economic integration was underpinned by the fiscal system in general, and the demands of a professional army in particular. The latter disappeared within the fifth century, and the centralized taxation that had funded it did so much more gradually and unevenly thereafter, leaving early medieval polities whose rulers depended on a reciprocal relationship with elites and their military followings to secure their power.[93] The basic dynamic of this relationship was the distribution of land in exchange for service (a notion which also came to be extended to the spiritual sphere), whose recipients extracted rent from their tenants. Landowning was no longer a vehicle for gaining power within the state system, but the basis of power itself. Depending upon the scale of their holdings, rulers and aristocrats in these societies might still amass great wealth, but this shift to the 'politics of land' removed the fiscal integration of the Roman period, and simplified production and exchange down to the level directly sustainable by the demand of landed elites and institutions, which in turn was susceptible to regional geographical and political variables. These economies had already ceased to be 'post-Roman' in the sixth century.

In the late antique East, by contrast, we have seen how the integrative potential of the Roman system had arguably reached its peak around 500, as a result of the energizing impact of the state-backed and commercial demands of Constantinople upon rural production, and the exploitation of the greater possibilities of maritime networks for the interregional distribution of surplus foodstuffs and manufactured goods in bulk. Although this system rapidly disintegrated in the seventh century, it soon reformed along simpler lines in the Aegean and the Sea of Marmara to meet the demands of Constantinople, but within a commercial framework.[94] Other, as yet poorly characterized regional networks can now be glimpsed elsewhere in the eastern Mediterranean in the eighth century, but they exhibit little of the scale or complexity of the preceding period.[95] There was no swift revival of interregional exchange-networks once their underpinning by the *annona* had been removed. Despite the persistence of fiscal funding for salaried armies under the Arab rulers, tax generally stayed within the regions in which it was collected, and therefore no longer contributed to more extensive economic integration.[96] By the time the 'Abbasids did look to restore fiscal centralization in the later eighth century, their supremacy had also shifted the center of gravity of the Islamic world away from the Mediterranean towards Mesopotamia, taking the main focus of demand with it, and reorienting patterns of long-distance exchange accordingly. The regional exchange networks centered upon Constantinople and, especially, within Egypt, retained elements of the ancient economic legacy, but they were no longer part of a "post-Roman" economic system.

In the western Mediterranean, finally, the post-Roman pattern is less coherent, but arguably most revealing. The complications derive partly from the economic significance and historical liminality of Africa, but arise more generally because the neighboring regions progressively assumed the political dynamics characteristic of northwestern Europe while remaining integrated into the Mediterranean exchange-system. This meant that even as productive complexity withered within southern Gaul, Mediterranean Spain, and western Italy to varying degrees, their participation in interregional exchange was able to continue. On the one hand, this offers the clearest demonstration that some such exchange could exist on a purely commercial basis without the *annona*. On the other, it shows that no regional economies were sufficiently developed to foster any new overseas networks independent of the fiscal stimulus that the demands of the state had once provided. Although our ability to perceive the social meaning of imported staple foodstuffs and pottery is undermined by a shortage of suitable anecdotal (and especially pricing) data, they were never generally essential, since locally produced alternatives were widely available; as time went on, it seems reasonable to assume that they shifted increasingly into the luxury category. Access to such imports steadily contracted, to high-status sites and wealthy consumers, and might come to be channeled through dedicated emporia, as in the case of Marseille, under a measure of royal supervision. At this level, demand persisted till the last, because its logic was cultural rather than economic, and rooted in the enduring devotion of western elites to late antique and Byzantine practices, such as the use of oil-lamps rather than candle-wax for lighting purposes.[97] It was on this increasingly restricted basis, therefore, that interregional exchange of unmistakably 'post-Roman' type persisted in the western Mediterranean to around 700, even in the context of the ongoing involution of internal regional economies. When the end came, it was presumably because declining demand and rising transaction costs, compounded by the end of the *annona* and by political upheaval, combined to ensure that the profits to be derived from such exchange were no longer sufficient to sustain production and distribution of the scale and complexity that had always been required to make it possible.[98] Even so, it was only when their African and eastern sources of supply were definitively cut off that privileged consumers, such as the monastic communities of Rome or northern Francia, were compelled to fall back exclusively upon resources closer to home, and adopted alternative cultural practices.

In the eighth century, therefore, the fiscal integration, state-backed transfers of goods, and military or maritime exchange-networks that had all been characteristic of the Roman economy had either disappeared altogether, or become confined within specific regional systems which were, as ever, at varying stages of development. In the Frankish heartlands and, by now, across the Channel, they were intensifying and expanding outwards, as their Arab equivalents would too once their interconnections were accelerated by the revival of fiscal centralization under the 'Abbasids.[99] In each case, however, this momentum drew away from the Mediterranean, where the ceramic evidence suggests that the economies of most coastal regions were reduced in scale by comparison with earlier periods, and in places rudimentary.[100] Some caution is certainly required here, since the identification of eighth-century ceramics is by no means as advanced as that of earlier periods, and as the preference for the amphora as the Mediterranean container of choice diminishes, so does our archaeological access to the exchange of foodstuffs.[101] But these problems are in themselves symptomatic of the widespread changes that have taken place; ceramic typologies become harder to construct precisely because of the disappearance of many diagnostic wares and a subsequent decline in many regions in the sophistication of material culture, while one of the factors in the slow demise of the amphora may have been a reduction in the maritime bulk-transports for which they were preferred. The most extensive of the regional networks that remained were, as we have seen, those reconfigured around the particular needs of Rome and Constantinople.[102] But as far as interregional exchange is concerned, our archaeological evidence is as yet confined to vestigial traces of links between these southern Tyrrhenian and Aegean systems, along what the texts suggest was the only functioning eighth-century route between the two basins of the Mediterranean.[103] The integrated Mediterranean exchange-system still in operation in the seventh century had all but dissolved into its constituent parts, the various seas within a sea.

This does not mean that Mediterranean exchange ever ground to a complete halt. Small-scale cabotage traffic hopping between its coasts and islands will have carried on regardless, and likewise the movement of luxury goods over long distances. One recent reconsideration of the eighth- and ninth-century textual data has duly questioned the existence of an early medieval 'depression' by invoking the timeless 'connectivity' of the Mediterranean, and stressing cabotage.[104] An alternative approach has been to shorten it by grounding the origins of the European economy in a revival from the later eighth century onwards of long-distance communications, and, by proxy, exchange, emphasizing instead the interregional movement of persons and, in an inversion of Pirenne, of an eclectic assortment of high-value items.[105] But in their anxiety to get away from Pirenne's myth of a completely blocked Mediterranean, these more upbeat visions risk going too far the other way, because they minimize the impact of the eventual disappearance of a Roman world-system which had stimulated the interregional circulation of widely-available staple items within an integrated fiscal – and, no less significantly, cultural – framework to a remarkable extent.[106] To be sure, exchange at all levels remained possible throughout, and already by the ninth century interregional communications were getting under way again along an increasing variety of routes.[107] But the ceramic data consistently suggests that the integrated exchange-system of earlier periods had vanished, leaving in its wake a patchwork of local and regional networks of varying complexity, that were incidentally, but not structurally, connected.[108] In the absence of an overarching political and fiscal framework, such a system would not be easily revived. Such interregional traffic as did persist was now largely divorced from staple or mass production, and the Mediterranean focus of the ancient economy was economically and geographically marginal to the comparatively developed regional exchange-systems of northwestern and southeastern Europe. The origins of the emerging (western) European economy would lie not in long-distance exchange, but in an intensification of agrarian production, and the exploitation of the wealth it generated, within fiscal and political parameters far removed from those of the Roman empire. When exchange between the more dynamic of the Mediterranean regional systems does begin to show up more clearly in both the ceramic and the textual record again from the tenth century onwards, the inherent advantages of maritime transport come back into play, but this time to facilitate commercial traffic between independent states, with less emphasis on foodstuffs than on the manufactured goods in which they were coming to specialize.[109] This medieval economy, at long last, had ceased to be post-Roman.

Notes

1 Wickham 2005: especially chs. 1 and 12 for the difficulties of more general synthesis.
2 Ward-Perkins 2000; Loseby 2005. This is similarly the thrust of part II of Ward-Perkins 2005, notwithstanding the emphasis in part I on the directly destructive qualities of barbarian invasion.
3 Tate 1992; Foss 1995; Kingsley and Decker 2001; Wickham 2005: 443–54; Decker 2009.
4 Britain: Esmonde Cleary 1989, Mattingly 2006: pt. V; for the remainder, see below.
5 Haldon 1997; Whittow 2003.
6 Haldon 1993; Kennedy 1995.
7 Pirenne 1939; Jones 1964: especially chs. 20–21.
8 Claude 1985a (cf. Claude 1985b for the interior of Francia); McCormick 2001.
9 Gregory of Tours, *Glor.conf.* 64; *Vit. pat. Emeretensium* 4.3; Greg. I, *Reg.* 6.58, 7.37, 8.28, 9.176, 10.21, 13.43; Gregory of Tours, *Hist.* 10.2; Anon., *Life of John the Almsgiver* 10. These episodes and others like them are discussed further in Loseby 2005.
10 Claude 1985a: 131–66; McCormick 2001: pt. IV.
11 For Egypt, the substantive exception, see Banaji 2001 and Sarris 2006.
12 This problem leaps out from the catalogue of commodities by item in Claude 1985a: 71–120, which features orpiment, for example, but not pottery.
13 Pirenne 1939, notably his notorious 'disappearances,' with Lopez 1943 and Riising 1952; Jones 1964: especially 1039, with Ward-Perkins 2008.
14 Finley 1965: 41.
15 Peacock 1982 offers a classic typology of productive organization; see Ward-Perkins 2005: 87–108, 184–7, for crisp summaries of interpretative possibilities.
16 The classifications pioneered in Hayes 1972 and 1980, Riley 1979, and Keay 1984 are used in what follows. The field – and the level of typological discrimination – has since expanded well beyond the capacity of non-specialists to keep up, but see the ground-breaking synthesis of Panella 1993, and among regional studies Bonifay 2004 (Africa), Reynolds 2010 (Spain), and the papers assembled in Saguì (ed.) 1998a (Italy). Abadie-Reynal 1989 and Sodini 2000 provide overviews of the more intricate eastern Mediterranean patterns.

17 Jones 1964: 848–50, for a summary of the textual data, including recognition that cheap clothes could be exchanged over considerable distances; Avraméa 1991.

18 Trinity: e.g., Cassiod. *Var.* XII.22.1; for the third, grain, see most recently Erdkamp 2005.

19 Peacock and Williams 1986.

20 E.g. Bonifay 2003: 118–19, questioning the conventional association of African amphorae with oil.

21 Hegemony: Panella 1993: 625–41. Imitations: Bonifay 2004: 459–61.

22 Amphorae: Pieri 2005, 2007; Reynolds 2005a. Availability of eastern ceramics in the west: Reynolds 1995: 34–6, 73–4, updated in Reynolds 2010: 105–12.

23 Bang 2007: 15–25, and Wickham 2004: 163, come to a similar conclusion within different analytical frameworks.

24 Hopkins 1980; 1995/6.

25 Durliat 1990 and Sirks 1991 offer contrasting views of the relative importance of fiscal and commercial mechanisms in ensuring such supplies. Most historians accept a combination of the two.

26 Mattingly 1988. Bonifay 2003 questions the assumption that the overseas circulation of African goods was underpinned primarily by oil, rather than grain.

27 Carrié 1975; Durliat 1990: 323–81.

28 Wickham 2005: 77–8, with map 2. This is evident for the Gallic prefecture, which effectively formed a network apart, less so for the Danube and eastern frontier-zones, at least in part supplied from adjacent Mediterranean regions, as Karagiorgou 2001 shows for Aegean imports to the former.

29 Vera 1997–8, for Sicily in particular.

30 E.g. Jones 1964: 829: "[the service provided by the *navicularii*] no doubt became a positive burden." Durliat 1990 remains as resolutely pessimistic about any commercial implications of the *annona* as he is optimistic about its extent.

31 Bonifay 2004: 447–9, for the development over time of recognition of the extent of the distribution of ARS throughout the Mediterranean and beyond.

32 Wickham 1988: 189–93.

33 McCormick 1998: 65–107.

34 Late antique shipwrecks invariably carry heterogeneous cargoes: Parker 1992. For the likely importance of islands such as Cyprus or the Balearics as exchange-hubs, see, e.g., Rautman 2001, Reynolds 2005a, and more generally Horden and Purcell 2000: 137–43, 224–30.

35 This seems clear, though strictly it requires archaeological corroboration from Constantinople itself, as Reynolds 2005a: 576 points out.

36 Abadie-Reynal 1989; Sodini 2000; Kingsley and Decker 2001; Reynolds 1995: 70–83.

37 Bonifay 2004: 480–1; Reynolds 2005a: 419–23.

38 Esmonde Cleary 1989: 138–61.

39 Van Dam 1985. For the perils of taking graphic Gallic accounts of early fifth-century barbarian devastation at face value, see McLynn 2009.

40 Redknap 1988; Bayard 1993.

41 Goffart 1982; Wickham 2005: 102–15.

42 Internal networks: Claude 1985b. Varying perspectives on economic intensification: Devroey 2003, Lebecq 2000, Henning 2007b. The traditional view of the Carolingian origins of the bipartite estate summarized in Verhulst 2002: 33–49,

and upheld in Wickham 2005: 280–93, has been challenged by Sarris 2004; the problem lies in the poverty of pre-Carolingian data for productive organization.

43 Baetican oil, for example, was long past its export heyday, but remained available along the eastern Spanish seaboard for much of the fifth century: Reynolds 2005b: 387–8.

44 Saguì (ed.) 1998a for papers on various regional Italian fine-wares; Rigoir 1998 for southern Gallic DS.P, the Mediterranean variants of which were exported along the adjacent Catalonian and Ligurian coasts. The only non-African western amphora-type distributed interregionally in quantity in this period is the southern Italian Keay 52: Pacetti 1998.

45 Spanish divide: Reynolds 2005b; Wickham 2005: 741–6. Cf. Greg. Naz. *Or.* 43.34, Lyd. *Mag.* 3.61, both re Asia Minor.

46 Panella 1993: 641–54.

47 Keay 1998: 150–1; Bonifay 2004: 480–2.

48 E.g. Fontana 1998 for the proliferation of ARS imitations in Italy; Reynolds 2010: 105–12 for the steady fifth-century growth in eastern imports to the West, which nevertheless originates prior to the Vandal conquest.

49 Bonifay 2004: 482, Reynolds 2005a: 423–6. Merrills and Miles 2010: 176, offer more general grounds for thinking that the African economy enjoyed an 'Indian summer' under Vandal rule.

50 Boom: Reynolds 2010: 100.

51 Campbell and Bowles 2009.

52 Caballero Zoreda et al. 2003.

53 Mukai and Rigoir 2005.

54 Wickham 2005: 746–51 gives a convenient overview.

55 E.g., Marseille: Bonifay 2005a. Tarragona: Macias i Solé and Remolà i Vallverdú 2000.

56 Delogu 1994; Marazzi 1998.

57 Brogiolo and Gelichi 1998; Arthur and Patterson 1994; Zanini 2003; Wickham 2005: 728–39.

58 Rome: Panella and Saguì 2001. Naples: Arthur 2002: 122–33; Byzantine Spain: Reynolds 2010: 120–4.

59 Bonifay 2004: 447–9 for the futility of recurrent attempts to explain ceramic distributions primarily in terms of Byzantine political control.

60 Bonifay 2005b; Zanini 1996.

61 Mattingly and Leone 2004; Leone 2003; Bonifay 2003: 123–8; Wickham 2005: 723–4. The field survey data are not altogether independent of the decreasing circulation of diagnostic fine-wares.

62 Theophanes *Chron.* 6100, 1.296.

63 Ward-Perkins 2001; Morrisson and Sodini 2002.

64 Dagron 1974; for ceramic import patterns, Hayes 1992.

65 Limestone Massif: Tchalenko 1953–8, with Tate 1992. Wider syntheses: Gatier 1994; Foss 1995, Decker 2009: ch. 2.

66 Amphora types: Reynolds 2005a; Pieri 2005. Gaza wine in texts: Gatier 1988.

67 Overviews: Panella 1993: 657–73; Sodini 2000. For the west, Reynolds 2010: 84–90, 105–12.

68 The maximalist interpretation of the *annona* offered by Durliat 1990 postulates that many eastern cities were involved; if true, this would have significant

implications for the polycentric pattens of exchange visible in the archaeological data, but explicit textual confirmation of such arrangements is confined to Constantinople, Alexandria, and probably Antioch.

69 Bagnall 1993: 29–32; Ballet and Picon 1987; Bailey 1998.

70 PRS/Late Roman C: Abadie-Reynal 1989; Martin 1998. 'Cypriot' RS/Late Roman D, from a similar north-eastern Mediterranean orbit to LRA 1: Hayes 1972: 371–86; Rautman et al. 1999; Armstrong 2009, who points out recent kiln finds on the southern Turkish coast.

71 Justinian: most recently Sarris 2006. Plague: contrast Sarris 2002 and most of the papers in Little (ed.) 2007 with the doubts of Horden 2005. Its structural consequences remain harder to demonstrate than its immediate local impact.

72 Haldon 1997.

73 Sodini and Villeneuve 1992; Walmsley 2007; Pieri 2005.

74 Saguì 1998b.

75 Saguì 2002.

76 Panella and Saguì 2001: 804–15; Romei 2004.

77 The lack of references to pottery in our texts makes it impossible to do more than speculate about attitudes toward it, but for one Italian example of the hoarding of ARS see Wickham 2005: 209–10. For the power – be it spiritual or alcoholic – of Gaza wine, Greg. Tur. *Hist.* 7.29.

78 Loseby 1998; Bonifay 2005a; Bonifay, Carre and Rigoir 1998.

79 Loseby 2000.

80 Productive retreat: Mackensen and Schneider 2002, and n. 61 above.

81 Conquest: Brett 1978. Bonifay 2004: 484–5 prefers to play down any immediate Arab impact by emphasizing the persistence of overseas ceramic distributions into the early eighth century.

82 Louhichi 2003; Gelichi and Milanese 1998; Wickham 2005: 726–8.

83 Haldon 2000. LRA 2 would swiftly return in modified form.

84 Hayes 1992: 12–34, 71–3.

85 Laiou and Morrisson 2007: ch. 3. Amphorae still comprise 85% of the eighth-century ceramics at Saraçhane in Constantinople: Hayes 1992: 3, 61–79.

86 The timing of this abatement remains controversial, but ceramic redatings have tended to push its origins later than was concluded by Tate 1992: especially 335–42, or Dauphin 1998: especially 512–25. See Foss 1997, Magness 2003, and Wickham 2005: 454–9.

87 Overviews: Walmsley 2000, 2001; Sodini and Villeneuve 1992; Uscatescu 2003. See also Vokaer 2009, for the coarse Brittle Ware.

88 Northedge 2001.

89 Bailey 1998.

90 Wickham 2005: 133–44, 759–69; Kennedy 1998.

91 Gayraud 2003; 1997.

92 Claude 1985a, 299–309; Pirenne 1939.

93 Wickham 1984; Devroey 2003; Innes 2006.

94 Laiou 2002.

95 Armstrong 2009; Reynolds 2003.

96 Kennedy 1995.

97 Fouracre 1995.

98 Cf. Wickham 2005: ch. 11, with particular emphasis on the decisive importance of demand.

99 Verhulst 2002; Kennedy 2001.

100 E.g., southeastern Spain: Gutiérrez Lloret 1996: 170–203.

101 See Gelichi 2000 for an overview. Armstrong 2009 highlights the artificial termination of some eastern ceramic typologies in the seventh century.

102 Arthur 1993. The scale of the ninth-century Roman economy is qualified by Delogu 2007.

103 Wickham 2005: 788–9; McCormick 2001: 502–8.

104 Horden and Purcell 2000: 153–72, here, as Squatriti 2002 emphasizes, they downplay the archaeological evidence on which they otherwise prefer to rely.

105 McCormick 2001: especially pt. V.

106 World-system: Woolf 1990.

107 McCormick 2001: parts II-IV, appendix.

108 Loseby 2007: 10–12.

109 Wickham 2004.

Further reading*

There is no single up-to-date study of the Roman economy in English. Chapters 18–28 of W. Scheidel, I. Morris, and R. Saller (eds.), *The Cambridge Economic History of the Greco-Roman World* (Cambridge 2007; henceforth *CEHGRW*) cover the development of the Roman economy from its beginnings into late antiquity. M. I. Finley's classic *The Ancient Economy*, first published in 1973, expanded in 1985 and now available in an updated edition with a foreword by I. Morris (Berkeley 1999), is still required reading for its coherent (if contested) vision of the Greco-Roman economy as a whole. M. I. Rostovtzeff, *The Social and Economic History of the Roman Empire* (2nd edn. revised by P. Fraser, Oxford 1957) and A. H. M. Jones, *The Later Roman Empire 284–602: A Social, Economic and Administrative Survey* (3 vols., Oxford 1964) are ambitious works that focus more specifically on particular periods of Roman economic history. P. Garnsey and R. Saller, *The Roman Empire: Economy, Society and Culture* (London 1987), chapters 3–5 offer a convenient overview, and C. Wickham, *Framing the Early Middle Ages: Europe and the Mediterranean, 400–800* (Oxford 2005) traces the ending of the Roman economy. Recent treatments in other languages include H.-J. Drexhage, H. Konen and K. Ruffing, *Die Wirtschaft des Römischen Reiches (1.-3.Jahrhundert): Eine Einführung* (Berlin 2002) and J. Andreau, *L'économie du monde romain* (Paris 2010). W. Scheidel and S. von Reden (eds.), *The Ancient Economy* (Edinburgh 2002) reprint important contributions to this field and provide a more wide-ranging bibliographical essay (272–8). The most comprehensive relevant bibliography, with close to 3,400 titles, can be found in the aforementioned *CEHGRW* (769–917).

W. V. Harris, "Between archaic and modern: some current problems in the history of the Roman economy," in W. V. Harris (ed.), *The Inscribed Economy: Production and Distribution in the Roman Empire in the*

* This very brief survey privileges recent and accessible works published in English.

Light of instrumentum domesticum (Ann Arbor 1993), 11–29 discusses the state of research, as do I. Morris, "The ancient economy twenty years after *The Ancient Economy*," *Classical Philology* 89 (1994), 351–66 and J. Andreau, "Twenty years after Moses I. Finley's *The Ancient Economy*" in Scheidel and von Reden's aforementioned collection (33–49). In their introduction to J. G. Manning and I. Morris (eds.), *The Ancient Economy: Evidence and Models* (Stanford 2005), 1–44, the editors consider different approaches to the study of ancient economies.

For attempts to quantify Roman economic activity, see the materials in T. Frank (ed.) *An Economic Survey of Ancient Rome* (5 vols, Baltimore 1933–40), and most notably R. Duncan-Jones's trilogy *The Economy of the Roman Empire: Quantitative Studies* (2nd edn., Cambridge 1982), *Structure and Scale in the Roman Economy* (Cambridge 1990) and *Money and Government in the Roman Empire* (Cambridge 1994), as well as A. Bowman and A. Wilson (eds.) *Quantifying the Roman Economy: Problems and Methods* (Oxford 2009). K. Greene, *The Archaeology of the Roman Economy* (London 1986) has yet to be replaced as an introduction to the vital contribution of archaeology to the study of the Roman economy. The "Oxford Roman Economic Project" (http://oxrep.classics.ox.ac.uk/) promotes the use of material evidence. The ecological dimension of the Roman economy is still in need of greater attention: R. Sallares, *The Ecology of the Ancient Greek World* (London 1991) illustrates the potential of this approach. For now, see chapters 6–9 of P. Horden and N. Purcell, *The Corrupting Sea: A Study of Mediterranean History* (Oxford 2000). The role of demography has only recently begun to be appreciated by Roman historians: see W. Scheidel's chapter 3 in *CEHGRW* (38–86) and his survey "Progress and problems in Roman demography," in W. Scheidel (ed.), *Debating Roman Demography* (Leiden), 1–81. Much the same is true of the economic importance of institutions: see I. Morris and J. G. Manning, "The economic sociology of the ancient Mediterranean world," in N. J. Smelser and R. Swedberg (eds.), *The Handbook of Economic Sociology* (2nd edn. Princeton 2005), 131–59, B. W. Frier and D. P. Kehoe's chapter 5 in *CEHGRW*, and P. F. Bang, "The ancient economy and New Institutional Economics," *Journal of Roman Studies* 99 (2009), 194–206.

K. D. White, *Roman Farming* (London 1970) remains a classic study, and M. S. Spurr, *Arable Cultivation in Roman Italy c.200 B.C.-c.A.D.100* (London 1986) is likewise valuable. A. Launaro, *Peasants and Slaves: The Rural Population of Roman Italy (200 BC to AD 100)* (Cambridge 2011) reviews the rich evidence of field surveys. S. L. Dyson, *The Roman Countryside* (London 2003) offers a pithy overview. For the

Roman food supply, see P. Garnsey's two books on *Famine and Food Supply in the Graeco-Roman World: Responses to Risk and Crisis* (Cambridge 1988) and *Food and Society in Classical Antiquity* (Cambridge 1999), as well as J. M. Wilkins and S. Hill, *Food in the Ancient World* (Malden MA 2006). M. MacKinnon, *Production and Consumption of Animals in Roman Italy: Integrating the Zooarchaeological and Textual Evidence* (Portsmouth RI 2004) is an exemplary case study.

Roman rural labor relations have been studied by P. W. de Neeve, *Colonus: Private Farm-Tenancy in Italy during the Republic and the Early Principate* (Amsterdam 1984) and in a series of books by D. P. Kehoe (cited in this volume's bibliography), as well as D. Rathbone, *Economic Rationalism and Rural Society in Third-Century A.D. Egypt: The Heroninos Archive and the Appianus Estate* (Cambridge 1991), P. Sarris, *Economy and Society in the Age of Justinian* (Cambridge 2006), and J. Banaji, *Agrarian Change in Late Antiquity: Gold, Labour and Aristocratic Dominance* (updated edn. Oxford 2007).

K. Bradley, *Slavery and Society at Rome* (Cambridge 1994) is the best concise survey of Roman slavery, while the first two chapters of K. Hopkins, *Conquerors and Slaves: Sociological Studies in Roman History*, 1 (Cambridge 1978) remain a classic analysis of the Roman slave economy. For more detailed treatments, see now chapters 11–22 of K. Bradley and P. Cartledge (eds.), *The Cambridge World History of Slavery, Volume 1: The Ancient Mediterranean World* (Cambridge 2011) and K. Harper, *Slavery in the Late Roman World, AD 275–425* (Cambridge 2011). H. Mouritsen, *The Freedman in the Roman World* (Cambridge 2011) explores the practice of manumission.

On Roman technology, see K. D. White, *Greek and Roman Technology* (London 1984) and especially the contributions to J. P. Oleson (ed.), *The Oxford Handbook of Engineering and Technology in the Classical World* (New York 2008). For the debate on the relationship between technological and economic development, see K. Greene, "Technological innovation and economic progress in the ancient world: M. I. Finley re-considered," *Economic History Review* 53 (2000), 29–59, reacting to M. I. Finley's influential "Technical innovation and economic progress in the ancient world," *Economic History Review* 18 (1965), 29–45, and also A. Wilson, "Machines, power and the ancient economy," *Journal of Roman Studies* 92 (2002), 1–32 and, for balance, H. Schneider's chapter 6 in *CEHGRW*. V. Smil, *Energy in World History* (Boulder 1994) and chapter 3 of I. Morris, *The Measure of Civilization: How Social Development Decides the Fate of Nations* (Princeton 2013) provide vital context for our understanding of Roman energy generation.

N. Morley, *Trade in Classical Antiquity* (Cambridge 2007) offers an accessible overview. In "Taxes and trade in the Roman Empire (200 B.C.-A.D. 400)," *Journal of Roman Studies* 70 (1980), 101–25 and "Rome, taxes, rents and trade," *Kodai* 6/7 (1995/6), 41–75 (reprinted in Scheidel and von Reden's aforementioned *The Ancient Economy*, 190–230), K. Hopkins develops a model of the underlying dynamics of Roman exchange relations, now complemented by the comparativist perspectives of P. Erdkamp, *The Grain Market in the Roman Empire: A Social, Political, and Economic Study* (Cambridge 2005) and especially P. F. Bang's "Trade and empire – in search of organizing concepts for the Roman economy," *Past and Present* 195 (2007), 3–54 and *The Roman Bazaar: A Comparative Study of Trade and Markets in a Tributary Empire* (Cambridge 2008). J. H. D'Arms, *Commerce and Social Standing in Ancient Rome* (Cambridge MA 1981) is a revisionist study of the status of Roman traders, and L. de Ligt, *Fairs and Markets in the Roman Empire* (Amsterdam 1993) deals with Roman markets. Archaeological data have been crucial to the investigation of Roman exchange: see, e.g., D. P. S. Peacock and D. F. Williams, *Amphorae and the Roman Economy: An Introductory Guide* (London 1986), A. J. Parker, *Ancient Shipwrecks of the Mediterranean and the Roman Provinces* (Oxford 1992), and most recently D. Robinson and A. Wilson (eds.) *Maritime Archaeology and Ancient Trade in the Mediterranean* (Oxford 2011). *ORBIS: The Stanford geospatial network model of the Roman world* (http://orbis.stanford.edu) simulates the speed and cost of Roman transport by land, river and sea.

Monetary media of exchange are discussed by K. M. Harl, *Coinage in the Roman Economy, 300 BC – AD 700* (Baltimore 1996) and S. von Reden, *Money in Classical Antiquity* (Cambridge 2010). Other important contributions include C. Howgego, "The supply and use of money in the Roman world 200 BC to AD 300," *Journal of Roman Studies* 82 (1992), 1–31, R. Duncan-Jones's *Money and Government* (cited above), and C. Katsari, *The Roman Monetary System: The Eastern Provinces from the First to the Third Century AD* (Cambridge 2011). On Roman banking, see J. Andreau, *Banking and Business in the Roman World* (Cambridge 1999) and D. Jones, *The Bankers of Puteoli: Finance, Trade and Industry in the Roman World* (Stroud 2006). W. V. Harris, "A revisionist view of Roman money," *Journal of Roman Studies* 96 (2006), 1–24 and "The nature of Roman money," in W. V. Harris (ed.), *The Monetary Systems of the Greeks and Romans* (Oxford 2008), 174–207 stresses the importance of credit.

For applied models of the economy of Roman urbanism, see K. Hopkins, "Economic growth and towns in classical antiquity," in

P. Abrams and E. A. Wrigley (eds.), *Towns in Societies: Essays in Economic History and Historical Sociology* (Cambridge 1978), 35–77, W. Jongman, *The Economy and Society of Pompeii* (Amsterdam 1988), and N. Morley, *Metropolis and Hinterland: The City of Rome and the Italian Economy, 200 BC – AD 200* (Cambridge 1996). Endings are discussed by J. H. W. G. Liebeschuetz, *The Decline and Fall of the Roman City* (Oxford 2001) and in chapter 10 of C. Wickham's *Framing the Early Middle Ages*, cited above. Important forthcoming work includes A. Bowman and A. Wilson (eds.), *Settlement, Urbanization and Population* (Oxford) and A. Zuiderhoek's introduction to ancient urbanism for the present publisher's "Key Themes in Ancient History" series.

Bibliography

A'Hearn, B. (2003) "Anthropometric evidence on living standards in Northern Italy, 1730–1860," *Journal of Economic History* 63: 351–81.

Abadie-Reynal, C. (1989) "Céramique et commerce dans le bassin égéen du IVe au VIIe siècle," in *Hommes et richesses dans l'empire byzantin, I: IVe-VIIe siècle*. Paris: 143–59.

Acemoglu, D., Johnson, S., and Robinson, J. A. (2001) "The colonial origins of comparative development: an empirical investigation," *American Economic Review* 91: 1369–1401.

Acheson, J. M. (2002) "Transaction cost economics: accomplishments, problems, and possibilities," in *Theory in Economic Anthropology*, ed. J. Ensminger. Walnut Creek CA: 27–58.

Adams, C. E. P. (2001a) "There and back again: getting around in Roman Egypt," in *Travel and Geography in the Roman Empire*, ed. C. E. P. Adams and R. Laurence. London and New York: 138–66.

(2001b) "Who bore the burden? The organization of stone transport in Roman Egypt," in Mattingly and Salmon (eds.) 2001: 171–92.

(2007a) *Land Transport in Roman Egypt: A Study of Economics and Administration in a Roman Province*. Oxford.

(2007b) "War and society," in *The Cambridge History of Greek and Roman Warfare, Vol. 2: Rome from the Late Republic to the Late Empire*, ed. G. Sabin, H. Van Wees, and M. Whitby. Cambridge: 198–232.

Adams, J. N. (2003) *Bilingualism and the Latin Language*. Cambridge.

Akerlof, G. (1970) "The market for 'lemons'," *Quarterly Journal of Economics*, 84: 488–500.

Alcock, S. E. (1993) *Graecia Capta: The Landscapes of Roman Greece*. Cambridge.

(2007) "The eastern Mediterranean," in Scheidel, Morris and Saller (eds.) (2007): 671–97.

Aldrete, G. S. and Mattingly, D. J. (1999) "Feeding the city: the organization, operation and scale of the supply system for Rome," in *Life, Death and Entertainment in the Roman Empire*, ed. D. S. Potter and D. J. Mattingly. Ann Arbor: 171–204.

Alessio, G. (1889) "Alcune riflessioni intorno ai concetti del valore nell'antichità classica," *Archivio giuridico* 42: 379–423.

Alföldy, G. (1986) *Die römische Gesellschaft: Ausgewählte Beiträge*. Stuttgart.

(2000) "Economic structure and agricultural productivity in Europe, 1300–1800," *European Review of Economic History* 4: 1–26.

(2001) "The great divergence in European wages and prices from the Middle Ages to the First World War," *Explorations in Economic History* 38: 411–47.

(2008) "The nitrogen hypothesis and the English agricultural revolution: a biological analysis," *Journal of Economic History* 68: 182–210.

(2009a) *The British Industrial Revolution in Global Perspective*. Cambridge.

(2009b) "How prosperous were the Romans? Evidence from Diocletian's price edict (AD 301)," in Bowman and Wilson (eds.) (2009): 327–45.

Allen, R., Bengtsson, T., and Dribe, M. (eds.) (2005) *Living Standards in the Past: New Perspectives on Well-Being in Asia and Europe*. Oxford.

Ambrosoli, M. (1997) *The Wild and the Sown: Botany and Agriculture in Western Europe, 1350–1850*. Cambridge.

Amigues, S. (2007) "L'exploitation du monde végétal en Grèce classique et hellénistique," *Topoi* 15: 75–125.

Anderson, R. and Gallman, R. (1977) "Slaves as fixed capital: slave labor and Southern economic development," *Journal of American History* 64: 24–46.

André, J. (1961) *L'alimentation et la cuisine à Rome*. Paris.

Andreades, A. M. (1993) *A History of Greek Public Finance*. Cambridge MA.

Andreau, J. (1984) "Histoire des métiers bancaires et évolution économique," *Opus* 3: 99–114.

(1987) *La vie financière dans le monde romain. Les métiers de manieurs d'argent (IVe siècle av. J.-C. – IIIe siècle ap. J.-C.)*. Rome.

(1994a) "L'Italie impériale et les provinces: désequilibre des échanges et flux monétaires," in *L'Italie d'Auguste à Dioclétien*. Rome: 175–203.

(1994b) "La cité romaine dans ses rapports à l'échange et au monde de l'échange," in *Economie antique: Les échanges dans l'antiquité: le role de l'état*, ed. J. Andreau, P. Briant, and R. Descat. Saint Bertrand de Comminges: 83–98.

(1995), "Vingt ans d'après *L'économie antique* de Moses Finley," *Annales: Histoire, Sciences Sociales* 50: 947–60 (transl. as Andreau 2002).

(1999) *Banking and Business in the Roman World*. Cambridge.

(2002) "Twenty years after Moses I. Finley's *The Ancient Economy*," in Scheidel and von Reden (eds.) (2002): 33–49.

(2010) *L'économie du monde romain*. Paris.

Andreau, J. and Maucourant, J. (1999) "À propos de la 'rationalité économique' dans l'antiquité gréco-romaine: une interprétation des thèses de D. Rathbone [1991]," *Topoi Orient-Occident* 9.1: 48–102.

Armstrong, P. (2009) "Trade in the east Mediterranean in the 8th century," in Mango (ed.) (2009): 157–78.

Arnaud, P. (2005) *Les routes de la navigation antique: itinéraires en Méditerranée*. Paris.

(2007) "Diocletian's Price Edict: the prices of seaborne transport and the average duration of maritime travel," *Journal of Roman Archaeology* 20: 321–36.

(2011) "Ancient sailing-routes and trade patterns: the impact of human factors," in Robinson and Wilson (eds.) 2011: 61–80.

Arthur, P. (1993) "Early medieval amphorae, the duchy of Naples and the food supply of Rome," *Papers of the British School at Rome* 61: 231–44.

(2002) *Naples, from Roman Town to City-State*. London.

Arthur, P. and Patterson, H. (1994) "Ceramics and early medieval central and southern Italy: 'a potted history,'" in Francovich and Noyé (eds.) 1994: 409–41.

Aubert, J.-J. (1994) *Business Managers in Ancient Rome: A Social and Economic Study of Institores, 200 B.C. – A.D. 250*. Leiden.

Aubrion, E. (1989) "La 'correspondance' de Pline le Jeune: problèmes et orientations actuelles de la recherché," in *Aufstieg und Niedergang der Römischen Welt* 2.33.1. Berlin and New York: 304–74.

Avraméa, A. (1991) "Artisanat et commerce du textile dans le Bas-Empire oriental (IVe-VIIe siècles), " in *Cultural and Commercial Exchanges between the Orient and the Greek World*. Athens: 23–9.

Backhaus, W. (1989) "Servi vincti," *Klio* 71: 321–9.

Badian, E. (1968) *Roman Imperialism in the Late Republic*. Oxford.

(1972) *Publicans and Sinners: Private Enterprise in the Service of the Roman Republic*. Ithaca NY.

Baechler, J., Hall, J., and Mann, M. (eds.) (1988) *Europe and the Rise of Capitalism*. Cambridge.

Bagnall, R. S. (1985) "The camel, the wagon, and the donkey in Later Roman Egypt," *Bulletin of the American Society of Papyrologists* 22: 1–6.

(1993) *Egypt in Late Antiquity*. Princeton.

(2002) "The effects of plague: model and evidence," *Journal of Roman Archaeology* 15: 114–20.

(2005) "Evidence and models for the economy of Roman Egypt," in Manning and Morris 2005: 187–205.

Bagnall, R. and Bogaert, R. (1975) "Orders of payment from a banker's archive: papyri in the collection of Florida State University," *Ancient Society* 6: 79–108.

Bagnall, R., Bulow-Jacobsen, A., and Cuvigny, H. (2001) "Security and water on the Eastern Desert roads: the prefect Iulius Ursus and the construction of praesidia under Vespasian," *Journal of Roman Archaeology* 14: 325–33.

Bagnall, R. S. and Frier, B. W. (1994) *The Demography of Roman Egypt*. Cambridge (expanded edn. 2006).

Bagnall, R. S., Frier, B. W., and Rutherford, I. C. (1997) *The Census Register P.Oxy. 984: The Reverse of Pindar's Paeans*. Brussels.

Bailey, D. M. (1998) *Excavations at El-Ashmunein, V: Pottery, Lamps and Glass of the Late Roman and Early Arab Periods*. London.

Bakels, C. and Jacomet, S. (2003) "Access to luxury foods in Central Europe during the Roman Period: the archaeobotanical evidence," *World Archaeology* 34: 522–47.

Bakirtzis, C. (ed.) (2003) *VII Congrès international sur la céramique médiévale en Méditerranée*. Athens.

Ballet, P. and Picon, M. (1987) "Recherches préliminaires sur les origines de la céramique des Kellia (Égypte)," *Cahiers de la céramique égyptienne* 1: 17–48.

Banaji, J. (2001) *Agrarian Change in Late Antiquity: Gold, Labour and Aristocratic Dominance*. Oxford (updated edn. 2007).

(2003) "The fictions of free labour," *Historical Materialism* 11.3: 69–95.

Bang, P. F. (2006) "Imperial bazaar: towards a comparative understanding of markets in the Roman Empire," in: Bang, Ikeguchi and Ziche (eds.) 2006: 51–88.

(2007) "Trade and empire – in search of organizing concepts for the Roman economy," *Past and Present* 195: 3–54.

(2008) *The Roman Bazaar: A Comparative Study of Trade and Markets in a Tributary Empire*. Cambridge.

(2009a) "The ancient economy and New Institutional Economics," *Journal of Roman Studies* 99: 194–206.

(2009b), "Commanding and consuming the world: empire, tribute, and trade in Roman and Chinese history", in *Rome and China: Comparative Perspectives on Ancient World Empires*, ed. W. Scheidel. New York: 100–20.

Bang, P. F., Ikeguchi, M., and Ziche, H. (eds.) (2006) *Ancient Economies, Modern Methodologies: Archaeology, Comparative History, Models and Institutions*. Bari.

Bannon, C. J. (2009) *Gardens and Neighbors: Private Water Rights in Roman Italy*. Ann Arbor.

Barbiera, I. and Dalla-Zuanna, G. (2009) "Population dynamics in Italy in the Middle Ages: new insights from archaeological findings," *Population and Development Review* 35: 367–89.

Barker, G. W. W., Gilbertson, D. D., and Mattingly, D. J. (2007) *Archaeology and Desertification: The Wadi Faynan Landscape Survey, Southern Jordan*. Oxford.

Barro, R. J. and Lee, J.-W. (2010) *A New Data Set of Educational Attainment in the World, 1950–2010*. NBER Working Paper 15902.

Barzel, Y. (1977) "An economic analysis of slavery," *Journal of Law and Economics* 20: 87–110.

Basch, L. (1987) *Le musée imaginaire de la marine antique*. Athens.

Bayard, D. (1993) "La céramique dans le Nord de la Gaule à la fin de l'Antiquité (de la fin du IVème au VIème siècle," in *La céramique du Vème au Xème siècle dans l'Europe du Nord-Ouest*, ed. D. Piton. Arras: 107–28.

Beard, M. (2007) *The Roman Triumph*. Cambridge MA.

Becker, S. and Woessman, L. (2007) "Was Weber wrong? A human capital theory of Protestant economic history," Center for Economic Studies and Ifo Institute for Economic Research Working Paper no. 1987.

Bedford, P. (2005) "The economy of the Near East in the first millenium," in Manning and Morris (eds.) 2005: 58–83.

Bekker-Nielsen, T. (ed.) (2005) *Ancient Fishing and Fish Processing in the Black Sea Region*. Aarhus.

Belcastro, G., Rastelli, E., Mariotti, V., Consiglio, C., Facchini, F., and Bonfiglioni, B. (2007) "Continuity and discontinuity of the life-style in Central Italy during the Roman Imperial Age – Early Middle Ages transition: diet, health, and behavior," *American Journal of Physical Anthropology* 132: 381–94.

Bellen, H. (1971) *Studien zur Sklavenflucht im römischen Kaiserreich*. Wiesbaden.

Bellen, H. and Heinen, H. (eds.) (2003) *Bibliographie zur antiken Sklaverei*. 2 vols. Stuttgart.

Beltrán Lloris, F. (2006) "An irrigation decree from Roman Spain: the *Lex Rivis Hiberiensis*," *Journal of Roman Studies* 96: 147–96.

Benoist, S. (2006) "Les rapports sociaux dans l'oeuvre de Sénèque: l'homme dans la cité," in *Les régulations sociales dans l'antiquité*, Rennes: 55–70.

Berger, J.-F. (2008) "Étude géoarchéologique des réseaux hydrauliques romains en Gaule Narbonnaise (haute et moyenne vallée du Rhône): apports à la gestion des ressources en eau et à l'histoire agraire antique," in Hermon (ed.) 2008: 107–21.

Bernstein, L. (2001) "Private commercial law in the cotton industry: creating cooperation through rules, norms, and institutions," *Michigan Law Review* 99: 1724–90.

Biezunska-Malowist, I. (1977) *L'esclavage dans l'Égypte gréco-romaine II: Période romaine.* Wroclaw.

Billiard, R. (1913) *La vigne dans l'antiquité.* Lyon.

Blackmann, D. J. (1982) "Ancient harbours in the Mediterranean," *International Journal of Nautical Archaeology* 9: 79–104.

(2008) "Sea transport, 2. Harbors," in Oleson (ed.) 2008: 638–70.

Blázquez Martínez, J. M. and Remesal Rodríguez, J. (eds.) (1999) *Estudios sobre el Monte Testaccio (Roma)*, 1. Barcelona.

Bloch, M. (1935) "Avènement et conquête du moulin à eau," *Annales d'Histoire Economique et Sociale* 36: 538–63.

Blyth, H. (1995) "Economics of public baths," *Balnearia* 3.2: 2–4.

Bodel, J. (2005) "*Caveat emptor*: towards a study of Roman slave traders," *Jorunal of Roman Archaeology* 18: 181–95.

(2011) "Slave labour and Roman society," in Bradley and Cartledge (eds.) 2011: 311–36.

Boese, W. E. (1973) "A study of the slave trade and the sources of slaves in the Roman Republic and the Early Roman Empire." Dissertation. University of Washington.

Bonfante, P. (1976) *Diritto romano.* Milan.

Bonifay, M. (2003) "La céramique Africaine, un indice du développement économique?," *Antiquité Tardive* 11: 113–28.

(2004) *Études sur la céramique romaine tardive en Afrique.* Oxford.

(2005a) "La céramique en Provence à l'époque mérovingienne: un faciès résolument méditerranéen," in *La Méditerrannée et le monde Merovingien*, ed. X. Delestre et al. Aix-en-Provence: 85–97.

(2005b) "Observations sur la diffusion des céramiques africaines en Méditerranée orientale durant l'antiquité tardive," in *Mélanges Jean-Pierre Sodini. Travaux et Mémoires* 15: 565–81.

Bonifay, M., Carre, M.-B., Rigoir, Y. et al. (1998) *Fouilles à Marseille: les mobiliers (Ier-VIIe siècles ap. J.-C.).* Paris and Lattes.

Bonifay, M. and Tréglia, J.-C. (eds.) (2007) *LRCW 2: Late Roman Coarse Wares, Cooking Wares and Amphorae in the Mediterranean.* 2 vols. Oxford.

Bonner, S. F. (1977) *Education in Ancient Rome: From the Elder Cato to the Younger Pliny.* Los Angeles and Berkeley.

Booth, A. (1979). "The schooling of slaves in first-century Rome," *Transactions of the American Philological Association* 109: 11–19.

Borgard, P. (2006) "Les amphores à alun (Ier siècle avant J.-C.-IVe siècle après J.-C.), " in Borgard, Brun and Picon (eds.) 2006: 157–69.

Borgard, P., Brun, J.-P., and Picon, M. (eds.) (2006) *L'alun de Méditerranée (Actes du colloque international ≪L'alun de Méditerranée≫. Naples, Lipari. 4–8 juin 2003).* Naples.

Borgard, P. and Cavalier, M. (2003) "The Lipari origin of the 'Richborough 527.'" *Journal of Roman Pottery Studies* 10: 96–106.

Bourdieu, P. (2000) *Les structures sociales de l'économie.* Paris.

Bouvier, M. (2000) "Recherches sur les goûts des vins antiques," *Pallas* 53: 115–33.

Bowman, A. K. (1986) *Egypt after the Pharaohs, 332 B.C.-A.D. 642; From Alexander to the Arab conquest.* London.

(1994) *Life and Letters on the Roman Frontier: Vindolanda and its People.* London.

Bowman, A. and Wilson, A. (2009) "Quantifying the Roman economy: integration, growth, decline?," in Bowman and Wilson (eds.) 2009: 3–84.

Bowman, A. and Wilson, A. (eds.) (2009) *Quantifying the Roman Economy: Problems and Methods*. Oxford.

Bradley, K. R. (1987a) *Slaves and Masters in the Roman Empire: A Study in Social Control*. New York.

(1987b) "On the Roman slave supply and slavebreeding," in Finley (ed.) (1987): 42–64.

(1989) *Slavery and Rebellion in the Roman World, 140 B.C.-70 B.C.* Bloomington.

(1990) "*Servus onerosus*: Roman law and the troublesome slave," *Slavery and Abolition* 11: 135–57.

(1991) *Discovering the Roman Family*. Oxford.

(1994) *Slavery and Society at Rome*. Cambridge.

(2004) "On captives under the Principate," *Phoenix* 58: 298–318.

(2008) "Seneca and slavery," in *Seneca*, ed. J. G. Fitch. Oxford: 335–47.

(2011a) "Resisting slavery at Rome," in Bradley and Cartledge (eds.) (2011): 362–84.

(2011b) "Slavery in the Roman Republic," in Bradley and Cartledge (eds.) 2011: 241–64.

Bradley, K. and Cartledge, P. (eds.) (2011) *The Cambridge World History of Slavery, 1: The Ancient Mediterranean World*. Cambridge.

Brandon, C., Hohlfelder, R. L., Oleson, J. P., and Stern, C. (2005) "The Roman Maritime Concrete Study (ROMACONS): the harbour of Chersonisos in Crete and its Italian connection, " *Méditerranée: Revue Géographique des Pays Méditerranéens* 104: 25–9.

(1966) *The Mediterranean and the Mediterranean World in the Age of Philip II*. Vol. 1. New York.

(1985) *The Wheels of Commerce, Civilization and Capitalism: 15th-18th Century*. Vol. 2. London.

Brazzini, G. (1988) *Dall'economia aristotelica all'economia politica: saggio sul "Traicté" di Montchretien*. Pisa.

Bresson, A. (2005) "Ecology and beyond: the Mediterranean paradigm," in Harris (ed.) 2005: 94–114.

Bresson, A., Lo Cascio, E., and Velde, F. (eds.) (forthcoming) *The Oxford Handbook of Economies in the Classical World*. New York.

Brett, M. (1978) "The Arab conquest and the rise of Islam in North Africa," in *The Cambridge History of Africa*, II, ed. J. D. Fage and R. Olivier. Cambridge: 490–555.

Brewer, J. (1989) *The Sinews of Power: War, Money and the English State, 1688–1783*. London.

Broadhead, W. (2007) "Colonisation, land distribution, and veteran settlement," in *A Companion to the Roman Army*, ed. P. Erdkamp. Chichester: 148–63.

Broekaert, W. (2008) "Roman economic policies during the third century AD: the evidence of the *tituli picti* on oil amphorae," *Ancient Society* 38: 197–219.

Brogiolo, G.-P. and Gelichi, S. (1998) "La ceramica comune in Italia settentrionale tra IV e VIIs.," in Saguì (ed.) (1998a): 209–26.

Brousseau, E. and Glachant, J.-M. (eds.) (2008) *New Institutional Economics: A Guidebook*. Cambridge.

Brun, J.-P. (2000) "The production of perfumes in antiquity: the cases of Delos and Paestum," *American Journal of Archaeology* 104: 277–308.

(2003) *Le vin et l'huile dans la Méditerranée antique: viticulture, oléiculture et procédés de transformation*. Paris.

(2004a) *Archéologie du vin et de l'huile de la préhistoire à l'époque hellénistique*. Paris.

(2004b) *Archéologie du vin et de l'huile dans l'Empire romain*. Paris.

(2005) *Archéologie du vin et de l'huile en Gaule romaine*. Paris.

Brunet, M. (2008) "La gestion de l'eau en milieu urbain et rural à Delos dans l'antiquité," in Hermon (ed.) 2008: 25–40.

Brunt, P. A. (1972) Review of White 1970, *Journal of Roman Studies* 62: 153–8.

(1980) "Free labour and public works at Rome," *Journal of Roman Studies* 70: 81–100.

(1987) *Italian Manpower 225 B.C. – A.D. 14*. Rev. edn. Oxford.

(1990) *Roman Imperial Themes*. Oxford.

Burford, A. (1960) "Heavy transport in classical antiquity," *Economic History Review* 13: 1–18.

Bürge, A. (1980) "Vertrag und personale Abhängigkeiten im Rom der späten Republik und der frühen Kaiserzeit," *Zeitschrift der Savigny-Stiftung für Rechtsgeschichte, Romanistische Abteilung* 97: 105–56.

(1988) "Cum in familia nubas: Zur wirtschaftlichen und sozialen Bedeutung der familia libertorum," *Zeitschrift der Savigny-Stiftung für Rechtsgeschichte, Romanistische Abteilung* 105: 312–33.

Burnett, A. (1987) *Coinage in the Roman World*. London.

(2005) "The Roman West and the Roman East," in *Coinage and Identity in the Roman Provinces*, ed. C. Howgego, V. Heuchert and A. Burnett. Oxford: 171–80.

Burnett, A., Amandry, M., and Ripollès, P. P. (eds.) (1992) *Roman Imperial Coinage I: From the Death of Caesar to the Death of Vitellius (44 BC – AD 69)*. London.

Burnett, J. (1979) *Plenty and Want*. London.

Burnham, B. C. (1997) "Roman mining at Dolaucothi: the implications of the 1991–3 excavations near Carreg Pumsaint," *Britannia* 28: 325–36.

Caballero Zoreda, L. et al. (eds.) (2003) *Cerámicas tardoromanas y altomedievales en la península ibérica*. Madrid.

Caird, J. (1852) *English Agriculture in 1850–51* (2nd edn. 1968). London.

Calder, W. M. (1910) "A journey round the Proseilemmene," *Klio* 10: 232–42.

(1913) "A Roman imperial domain, " *Classical Review* 27.1: 9–11.

Caldwell, J. C. (2004) "Fertility control in the classical world: was there an ancient fertility transition?," *Journal of Population Research* 21: 1–17.

Caliri, E. (2005) "Dipendenza agraria, locazione e diffusione dello ius colonatus nel mondo romano," *Mediterraneo antico* 8:2: 795–809.

Camodeca, G. (2008) "La popolazione degli ultimi decenni di Ercolano," in *Ercolano: Tre Secoli di Scoperte*. Naples: 86–103.

Campbell, B. (1994) *The Roman Army 31 B.C – A.D. 337: A Sourcebook*. London.

Campbell, E. and Bowles, C. (2009) "Byzantine trade to the edge of the world: Mediterranean pottery imports to Atlantic Britain in the 6th century," in Mango (ed.) 2009: 297–313.

Canarella, G. and Tomaske, J. A. (1975) "The optimal utilization of slaves," *Journal of Economic History* 35: 621–9.

Capasso, L. (2001) *I fuggiaschi di ercolano: paleobiologia delle vittime dell'eruzione vesuviana del 79 d.C.* Rome.

Capogrossi Colognesi, L. (1981) "Proprietà agraria e lavoro subordinato nei giuristi e negli agronomi latini tra repubblica e principato," in *Società romana e produzione schiavistica*. Vol. 1, ed. A. Giardina and A. Schiavone, Bari: 445–54.

(1986) "Grandi proprietari contadini e coloni nell'Italia romana (I-III D.C.)" in *Società romana e impero tardoantico*, Vol. 1, ed. A. Giardina. Bari: 325–65.

(2000) *Max Weber e le economie del mondo antico*. Rome.

(2009) *Storia di Roma fra diritto e potere*. Bologna.

Cappers, R. J. T. (2006) *Roman Foodprints at Berenike. Archaeobotanical Evidence of Subsistence and Trade in the Eastern Desert of Egypt*. Los Angeles.

Carandini, A. (1983) "Pottery and the African economy," in Garnsey, Hopkins and Whittaker (eds.) 1983: 145–62.

(1988) *Schiavi in Italia: gli strumenti pensanti dei Romani fra tarda Repubblica e medio Impero*. Rome.

Carlsen, J. (1995) *Vilici and Roman Estate Managers until AD 284*. Rome.

Carlsen, J., Ørsted, P., and Skydsgaard, J.-E. (eds.) (1994) *Landuse in the Roman Empire*. Rome.

Carrié, J.-M. (1975) "Les distributions alimentaires dans les cités de l'empire romain tardif," *Mélanges de l'Ecole Française de Rome* 87: 995–1101.

(1983) "Un roman des origines: les généalogies du 'colonat du bas-empire,'" *Opus* 2: 205–51.

(1997) "'Colonato del Basso Impero': la resistenza del mito," in *Terre, proprietari e contadini dell'impero romano: Dall'affitto agrario al colonato tardoantico*, ed. E. Lo Cascio. Rome: 75–150.

Carter, M. (2003) "Gladiatorial ranking and the 'SC de Pretiis Gladiatorum Minuendis' (CIL II 6278 = ILS 5163)," *Phoenix* 57: 83–114.

Cartledge, P. (1993) *The Greeks: A Portrait of Self and Others*. Oxford.

(2002a) "The political economy of Greek slavery," in Cartledge, Cohen, and Foxhall (eds.) (2002): 156–66.

(2002b) "Greek civilisation and slavery," in *Classics in Progress: Essays on Ancient Greece and Rome*, ed. T. P. Wiseman. Oxford: 247–62.

Cartledge, P., Cohen, E. E., and Foxhall, L. (eds.) (2002) *Money, Labour and Land: Approaches to the Economies of Ancient Greece*. London.

Casavola, F. (1980) *Giuristi adrianei*. Naples.

Casson, L. (1950) "The Isis and her voyage," *Transactions of the American Philological Association* 81: 43–56.

(1971) *Ships and Seamanship in the Ancient World*. Princeton.

(1980) "The role of the state in Rome's grain trade," in *The Seaborne Commerce of Ancient Rome: Studies in Archaeology and History*, ed. J. H. D'Arms and E. C. Kopff. Rome: 21–33.

(1994) *Travel in the Ancient World*. 2nd edn. Baltimore.

Cauuet, B. (2005) "Les mines d'or antiques d'Europe hors peninsule ibérique: état des connaissances et travaux recents, " *Pallas* 67: 241–91.

Chamberlain, A. (2006) *Demography in Archaeology*. Cambridge.

Chase-Dunn, C., Hall, T. D., and Turchin, P. (2007) "World-systems in the biogeosphere: urbanization, state formation, and climate change since the Iron Age," in *The World System and the Earth System: Global Socioenvironmental Change and Sustainability since the Neolithic*, ed. A. Hornborg and C. Crumley. Walnut Creek: 132–48.

Chaudhuri, K. N. (1985) *Trade and Civilisation in the Indian Ocean*. Cambridge.

Chaumartin, F. R. (1989) "Les désillusions de Sénèque devant l'évolution de la politique néronienne et l'aspiration à la retraite: le 'de vita beata' et le 'de beneficiis' de Sénèque," in *Aufstieg und Niedergang der Römischen Welt* 2.36.3. Berlin and New York: 1686–723.

Chevallier, R. (1976) *Roman Roads*. London.

Chouquer, G. and Favory, F. (2001) *L'arpentage romain: histoire des textes - droit - techniques*. Paris.

Christiansen, E. (1984) "On denarii and other coin-terms in the papyri," *Zeitschrift für Papyrologie und Epigraphik*: 54: 271–99.

Ciaraldi, M. (2007) *People and Plants from Ancient Pompeii: A New Approach to Urbanism from the Microscope Room*. London.

Cimma, M. R. (1981) *Ricerche sulle società di publicani*. Milan.

Clapham, C. (1985) *Third World Politics*. Madison WI.

Clark, G. (2007a) "The long march of history: farm wages, population, and economic growth, England, 1209–1869," *Economic History Review* 60: 136–89.

(2007b) *A Farewell to Alms: A Brief Economic History of the World*. Princeton.

Claude, D. (1985a) *Untersuchungen zu Handel und Verkehr der vor- und frühgeschichtlichen Zeit in Mittel- und Nordeuropa, II: Der Handel im westlichen Mittelmeer während des Frühmittelalters*. Göttingen.

(1985b) "Aspekte des Binnenhandels im Merowingerreich auf Grund der Schriftquellen," in *Der Handel des frühen Mittelalters*, ed. K. Düwel et al. Göttingen: 9–99.

Coase, R. H. (1937) "The nature of the firm," *Economica* 4.16: 386–405.

(1988) *The Firm, the Market, and the Law*. Chicago.

Cockle, H. (1981) "Pottery manufacture in Roman Egypt: a new papyrus," *Journal of Roman Studies* 71: 87–95.

Cohen, B. (2004) *The Future of Money*. Princeton.

Cohen, D. J. (1991) *Law, Sexuality, and Society: The Enforcement of Morals in Classical Athens*. Cambridge.

Collin-Bouffier, S. (2008) "L'organisation des territoires grecs antiques et le gestion de l'eau," in Hermon (ed.) 2008: 41–54.

Connolly, S. (2010) *Lives behind the Laws: The World of the Codex Hermogenianus*. Bloomington IN.

Constantokopoulou, C. (2002) "Connectivity in the Aegean: the practice of *porthmeutice* and its importance for small-scale interaction," *Journal of Mediterranean Studies* 12: 223–26.

Cool, H. E. M. (2006) *Eating and Drinking in Roman Britain*. Cambridge.

Cotterell, B. and Kaminga, J. (1990) *Mechanics of Pre-Industrial Technology*. Cambridge.

Cottier, M., Crawford, M. H., Crowther, C. V., Ferrary, J.-L., Levick, B. M., Salomies, O., and Wörrle, M. (eds.) (2008) *The Customs Law of Asia*. Oxford.

Coulston, J. and Dodge, H. (eds.) (2000) *Ancient Rome: The Archaeology of the Eternal City*. Oxford.

Crawford, M. (1970) "Money and exchange in the Roman world," *Journal of Roman Studies* 60: 40–8.

(1971) "Le problème des liquidités dans l'antiquité classique," *Annales ESC* 26: 1228–33.

(1974) *Roman Republican Coinage*. 2 vols. Cambridge.

(1985) *Coinage and Money under the Roman Republic*. London.
Crone, P. (1989) *Pre-Industrial Societies*. Oxford.
Cucina, A. et al. (2006) "The necropolis of Vallerano (Rome, 2nd-3rd century AD): an anthropological perspective on the ancient Romans in the *suburbium*," *International Journal of Osteoarchaeology* 16: 104–17.
Curchin, L. A. (1991) *Roman Spain: Conquest and Assimilation*. London.
Curtis, R. I. (1991) *Garum and Salsamenta: Production and Commerce in Materia Medica*. Leiden.
(2001) *Ancient Food Technology*. Leiden.
(2008) "Food processing and preparation," in Oleson (ed.) 2008: 369–92.
Cuvigny, H. (1996) "The amount of wages paid to the quarry-workers at Mons Claudianus," *Journal of Roman Studies* 86: 139–45.
(ed.) (2003) *La route de Myos Hormos: l'armée romaine dans le désert oriental d'Égypte*. Cairo.
D'Arms, J. H. (1977) "M. I. Rostovtzeff and M. I. Finley: the status of traders in the ancient world," in *Ancient and Modern: Essays in Honor of G. F. Else*, ed. J. H. D'Arms and J. W. Eadie. Ann Arbor: 159–79.
(1981) *Commerce and Social Standing in Ancient Rome*. Cambridge MA.
Dagron, G. (1974) *Naissance d'une capitale: Constantinople et ses institutions de 330 à 451*. Paris.
Dal Lago, E. and Katsari, C. (eds.) (2008) *Slave Systems: Ancient and Modern*. Cambridge.
Dalby, A. (2000) *Empire of Pleasures: Luxury and Indulgence in the Roman World*. London and New York.
Dauphin, C. (1998) *La Palestine byzantine: peuplement et populations*. Oxford.
Davies, J. K. (2007) "Classical Greece: production," in Scheidel, Morris and Saller (eds.) 2007: 333–61.
De Callataÿ, F. (1995) "Calculating ancient coin production: what we may hope," *Numismatic Chronicle* 155: 289–311.
(2005) "The Graeco-Roman economy in the super-long run: lead, copper, and shipwrecks," *Journal of Roman Archaeology* 18: 361–72.
De Caro, S. and Boriello, M. (eds.) (2002) *La natura morta nelle pitture e nei mosaici delle città vesuviane*. Naples.
De Cecco, M. (1985) "Monetary theory and Roman history," *Journal of Economic History* 45: 809–822.
De Laet, S. (1949) *Portorium: études sur l'organisation douanière chez les Romains*. Bruges.
De Ligt, L. (1990) "Demand, supply, distribution: the Roman peasantry between town and countryside: rural monetization and peasant demand," *Münstersche Beiträge zur Antiken Handelsgeschichte* 9.2: 24–56.
(2000) "Studies in legal and agrarian history II: tenancy under the Republic," *Athenaeum* 88: 377–91.
(2004) "Poverty and demography: the case of the Gracchan land reforms," *Mnemosyne* 57: 725–57.
De Ligt, L. and Northwood, S. J. (eds.) (2008) *People, Land, and Politics: Demographic Developments and the Transformation of Roman Italy, 300 BC – AD 14*. Leiden.
De Martino, F. (1958) *Storia della costituzione romana*. Naples.
(1979–80) *Storia economica di Roma antica*. 2 vols. Florence.
De Neeve, P. W. (1984) *Colonus: Private Farm-Tenancy in Italy during the Republic and the Early Principate*. Amsterdam.

(1990) "A Roman landowner and his estates: Pliny the Younger," *Athenaeum* 78: 363–402.

De Romanis, F. and Tchernia, A. (eds.) (2005) *Crossings: Early Mediterranean Contacts with India*. New Delhi.

De Sena, E. C. (2005) "An assessment of wine and oil production in Rome's hinterland: ceramic, literary, art historical and modern evidence," in *Roman Villas around the Urbs: Interaction with Landscape and Environment. Proceedings of a Conference at the Swedish Institute in Rome, September 17–18*, 2004, ed. B. Santillo Frizell and A. Klynne. Rome: 1–15.

De Vries, A. and Van Der Woude, A. (1997) *The First Modern Economy. Success, Failure, and Perseverance of the Dutch Economy 1500–1800*. Cambridge.

Dearne, M. J. and Branigan, K. (1995) "The use of coal in Roman Britain," *Antiquities Journal* 75: 71–105.

Deaton, A. (2007) "Height, health, and development," *Proceedings of the National Academy of Sciences* 104: 13232–7.

Decker, M. (2009) *Tilling the Hateful Earth: Agricultural Production and Trade in the Late Antique East*. Oxford.

Del Panta, L. (1989) *Malaria e regime demografico: la maremma grossetana nell'ottocento preunitario*. Messina.

Del Panta, L., Livi Bacci, M., Pinto, G., and Sonnino, E. (1996) *La popolazione italiana dal medioevo a oggi*. Bari.

DeLaine, J. (1997) *The Baths of Caracalla: A Study in the Design, Construction, and Economics of Large-Scale Building Projects in Imperial Rome*. Portsmouth RI.

Delogu, P. (1994) "La fine del mondo antico e l'inizio del medioevo: nuovi dati per un vecchio problema," in Francovich and Noyé (eds.) 1994: 7–29.

(2007) "Rome in the ninth century: the economic system," in Henning (ed.) 2007a: 105–22.

Demandt, A. (1984) *Der Fall Roms: Die Auflösung des römischen Reiches im Urteil der Nachwelt*. Munich.

Depeyrot, G. (2006) "Economy and society," in *The Cambridge Companion to the Age of Constantine*, ed. N. Lenski. Cambridge, 226–52.

Desanges, J., Duval, N., Lepelley, C., and Saint-Amans, S. (eds.) (2010) *Carte des routes et des cités de l'est de l'Africa à la fin de l'antiquité d'après le tracé de Pierre Salama*. Turnhout.

Devroey, J.-P. (2003) *Economie rurale et société dans l'Europe franque (VIe-IXe siècles)*. Vol. 1. Paris.

Dickson, A. (1788) *The Husbandry of the Ancients in Two Volumes*. Edinburgh.

Dimitriev, S. (2009) "The rise and quick fall of the theory of ancient economic imperialism," *Economic History Review* 62: 785–801.

Dobbin, F. (2005) "Comparative and historical approaches to Economic Sociology," in Smelser and Swedberg (eds.) 2005: 26–48.

Dobson, M. J. (1997) *Contours of Death and Disease in Early Modern England*. Cambridge.

Dodge, H. and Ward-Perkins, B. (1992) *Marble in Antiquity: Collected Papers of J. B. Ward-Perkins*. London.

Domergue, C. (1983) "La mine antique d'Aljustrel (Portugal) et les tables de bronze de Vipasca," *Conimbriga* 22: 5–193.

(1990) *Les mines de la péninsule ibérique dans l'antiquité romaine*. Rome.

(2008) *Les mines antiques: la production des métaux aux époques grecque et romaine*. Paris.

Domergue, C. and Hérail, G. (1977) "Une méthode pour l'étude des mines antiques en alluvion: l'exemple des mines d'or romaines de la Valduerna (León, Espagne)," *Mélanges de la Casa de Velázquez* 13: 9–29.

Drexhage, H.-J. (1991) *Preise, Pieten/Pachten, Kosten und Löhne im Römischen Ägypten bis zum Regierungsantritt Diokletians*. St. Katharinen.

Drexhage, H.-J., Konen, H., and Ruffing, K. (2002) *Die Wirtschaft des Römischen Reiches (1.-3.Jahrhundert): Eine Einführung*. Berlin.

Drinkwater, J. F. (2001) "The Gallo-Roman woollen industry and the great debate: the Igel column revisited," in Mattingly and Salmon (eds.) 2001: 297–308.

Du Coudray la Blanchère, R. M. and Gauckler, P. (1897) *Catalogue du Musée Alaoui*. Paris.

Du Plessis, P. J. (2003) *A History of Remissio Mercedis and Related Legal Institutions*. Rotterdam.

Dumont, J. C. (1987) *Servus: Rome et l'esclavage sous la république*. Rome.

Duncan-Jones, R. (1982) *The Economy of the Roman Empire: Quantitative Studies*. 2nd edn. Cambridge.

(1984) "Problems of the Delphic manumission payments 200–1 B.C.," *Zeitschrift für Papyrologie und Epigraphik* 57: 203–9.

(1990) *Structure and Scale in the Roman Economy*. Cambridge.

(1994) *Money and Government in the Roman Empire*. Cambridge.

Dupont, F. (1997) "*Recitatio* and the reorganization of the space of public discourse," in *The Roman Cultural Revolution*, ed. T. Habinek and A. Schiesaro. Cambridge: 44–59.

Durliat, J. (1990) *De la ville antique à la ville byzantine: le problème des subsistences*. Rome.

Easterlin, R. (1981) "Why isn't the whole world developed?," *Journal of Economic History* 41: 1–19.

Eck, W. (2000) "Emperor, senate and magistrates," in *The Cambridge Ancient History, 2nd edn. Vol. 11: The High Empire, A.D. 70–192*, ed. A. Bowman, P. Garnsey, and D. Rathbone. Cambridge: 214–37.

Edwards, C. and Woolf, G. (eds.) (2003) *Rome the Cosmopolis*. Cambridge.

Eggertsson, T. (1990) *Economic Behavior and Institutions*. Cambridge.

Eisner, R. (1989) *The Total Incomes System of Accounts*. Chicago.

Elvin, M. (1973) *The Pattern of the Chinese Past: A Social and Economic Interpretation*. Stanford.

Engelmann, H. and Knibbe, D. (eds.) (1989) *Das Zollgesetz der Provinz Asia: Eine neue Inschrift aus Ephesos*. Bonn.

Eppig, C., Fincher, C. L., and Thornhill, R. (2010) "Parasite prevalence and the worldwide distribution of cognitive ability," *Proceedings of the Royal Society B: Biological Sciences* 277: 3801–8.

Erdkamp, P. (1999) "Agriculture, underemployment, and the cost of rural labor in the Roman world," *Classical Quarterly* 49: 556–72.

(2001) "Beyond the limits of the 'consumer city': a model of the urban and rural economy in the Roman world," *Historia* 50: 332–56.

(2005) *The Grain Market in the Roman Empire: A Social, Political, and Economic Study*. Cambridge.

Esmonde Cleary, S. (1989) *The Ending of Roman Britain*. London.

Evenari, M., Shanan, L., and Tadmor, N. (1982) *The Negev: The Challenge of a Desert*. 2nd edn. Cambridge MA.

Fabre, G. (1981) *Libertus: recherches sur les rapports patron-affranchi à la fin de la République romaine*. Rome.

(1992) "Mobilité et stratification: le cas des serviteurs imperiaux", in *La mobilité sociale dans le monde romain*. Strasbourg.

Fagan, G. G. (1999) *Bathing in Public in the Roman World*. Ann Arbor.

Fant, J. C. (ed.) (1988) *Ancient Marble Quarrying and Trade: Papers from a Colloquium held at the Annual Meeting of the Archaeological Institute of America, San Antonio, Texas, December, 1986*. Oxford.

(2001) "Rome's marble yards," *Journal of Roman Archaeology* 14: 167–98.

Farr, J. R. (2000) *Artisans in Europe, 1300–1914*. Cambridge.

Farrar, L. (1998) *Ancient Roman Gardens*. Phoenix Mill.

Faulkner, N. (2000) *The Decline and Fall of Roman Britain*. Stroud.

Fear, A. T. (1989) "Isis and Igabrum," *Habis* 20: 193–203.

Fenoaltea, S. (1984) "Slavery and supervision in comparative perspective: a model," *Journal of Economic History* 44: 635–68.

Fentress, E. (1990) "The economy of an inland city: Sétif," in *L'Afrique dans l'occident romain*. Rome: 117–28.

(2001) "Villas, wine and kilns: the landscape of Jerba in the late Hellenistic period," *Journal of Roman Archaeology* 14: 249–68.

(2011) "Slavers on chariots: the Garamantes between Siwa and the Niger Bend," in *Money, Trade and Trade Routes in Pre-Islamic North Africa*, ed. A. Dowler and E. R. Galvin. London.

Findlay, R. (1975) "Slavery, incentives, and manumission: a theoretical model," *Journal of Political Economy* 83: 923–34.

Findlay, R. and Lundahl, M. (2006) "Demographic shocks and the factor proportion model: from the Plague of Justinian to the Black Death," in *Eli Heckscher, International Trade, and Economic History*, ed. R. Findlay, R.G. Henriksson, H. Lindgren, and M. Lundahl. Cambridge MA: 157–98.

Fink, Z. S. (1945) *The Classical Republicans: An Essay in the Recovery of a Pattern of Thought in Seventeenth-Century England*. Evanston IL.

Finkelman, P. and Miller, J. C. (eds.) (1998) *Macmillan Encyclopedia of World Slavery*. 2 vols. New York.

Finley, M. I. (1965) "Technical innovation and economic progress in the ancient world," *Economic History Review* 18: 29–45.

(1978) "Empire in the Greco-Roman world," *Greece and Rome* 25: 1–15.

(1981) *Economy and Society in Ancient Greece*, ed. B. D. Shaw and R. P. Saller. London.

(ed.) (1987) *Classical Slavery*. London.

(1998) *Ancient Slavery and Modern Ideology*, ed. B. D. Shaw. Princeton (expanded from London 1980 edn.).

(1999) *The Ancient Economy*. Updated edn. by I. Morris. Berkeley.

Flach, D. (1990) *Römische Agrargeschichte*. Munich.

Flaig, E. (2009) *Weltgeschichte der Sklaverei*. Munich.

Fogel, R. W. (2004) *The Escape from Hunger and Premature Death, 1700–2100: Europe, America, and the Third World*. Cambridge.

Fontana, S. (1998) "Le 'imitazioni' della sigillata africana e le ceramiche da mensa italiche tardo-antiche," in Saguì (ed.) 1998a: 83–100.

Forabosci, A. and Gara, L. (1982) "L'economia dei crediti in natura (Egitto)," *Athenaeum* 70: 69–83.

Fornaciari, G., Mallegni, F., Bertini, D., and Nuti, V. (1982) "Cribra orbitalia and elemental bone iron in the Punics of Carthage," *Ossa* 8: 63–77.

Forni, G. (2002) "Colture, lavori, tecniche, rendimenti," in Forni and Marcone (eds.) 2002: 62–156.

(2006) "Innovazione e progresso nel mondo romano. Il caso del agricoltura," in E. Lo Cascio (ed.) 2006a: 145–79.

Forni, G. and Marcone, A. (eds.) (2002) *Storia dell'agricoltura italiana I.2: l'età romana*. Florence.

Foss, C. (1995) "The Near Eastern countryside in late antiquity: a review article," in *The Roman and Byzantine Near East: Some Recent Archaeological Research*, ed. J. Humphrey. Ann Arbor: 213–34.

(1997) "Syria in transition, A.D. 550–750: an archaeological approach," *Dumbarton Oaks Papers* 51: 189–269.

Foucher, L. (1957) *Navires et barques: figures sur des mosaiques déouvertes à Sousse et aux environs*. Tunis.

Fouracre, P. (1995) "Eternal light and earthly needs: practical aspects of the development of Frankish immunities," in *Property and Power in the Early Middle Ages*, ed. P. Fouracre and W. Davies. Cambridge: 53–81.

Fox, S. C. (2005) "Health in Hellenistic and Roman times: the case studies of Paphos, Cyprus and Corinth, Greece," in King (ed.) (2005): 59–82.

Foxhall, L. (1990) "The dependent tenant: land leasing and labour in Italy and Greece," *Journal of Roman Studies* 80: 97–114.

Foy, D. (ed.) (2003a) *Coeur de verre: production et diffusion du verre antique*. Gollion.

(2003b) "Une chaine de fabrication segmentée," in Foy (ed.) (2003a): 26–7.

(2003c) "*Quid* de l'occident?, " in Foy (ed.) (2003a): 34–5.

Foy, D. and Nenna, M.-D. (2001) *Tout feu tout sable: mille ans de verre antique dans le Midi de la France*. Marseille.

France, J. (2007) "Deux questions sur la fiscalité provinciale d'après Cicéron Ver. 3.12," in *La Sicile de Cicéron. Lectures des Verrines*, ed. J. Dubouloz and S. Pittia. Franche-Comté: 169–87.

Franceschini, M. (1998) *Le ville romane della X Regio (Venetia et Histria)*. Rome.

Francovich, R. and Noyé, G. (eds.) (1994) *La storia dell'alto medioevo italiano (VI-X secolo) alla luce dell'archeologia*. Florence.

Frank, A. G. and Thompson, W. R. (2006) "Early Iron Age economic expansion and contraction revisited," in *Globalization and Global History*, ed. B. K. Gills and W. R. Thompson. London: 139–62.

Frank, T. (ed.) (1933–40) *An Economic Survey of Ancient Rome*. 5 vols. Baltimore.

Frass, M. (2006) *Antike römische Gärten: Soziale und wirtschaftliche Funktionen der Horti Romani*. Horn.

Freyberg, H.-U. von (1989) *Kapitalverkehr und Handel im römischen Kaiserreich (27 v. Chr. – 235 n. Chr.)*. Freiburg.

Frier, B. W. (1979a) *Landlords and Tenants in Imperial Rome*. Princeton.

(1979b) "Law, technology, and social change: the equipping of Italian farm tenancies," *Zeitschrift der Savigny-Stiftung für Rechtsgeschichte, Romanistische Abteilung* 96: 204–28.

(1982) "Roman life expectancy: Ulpian's evidence," *Harvard Studies in Classical Philology* 86: 213–51.
(1989–90) "Law, economics, and disasters down on the farm: 'remissio mercedis' revisited," *Bullettino di Istituto di Diritto Romano* 31–32: 237–70.
(2000) "Demography," in *The Cambridge Ancient History, 2nd edn., vol. 11: The High Empire, A.D.70–192*, ed. A. K. Bowman, P. Garnsey, and D. Rathbone. Cambridge: 787–816.
Frier, B. W. and Kehoe, D. P. (2007) "Law and economic institutions," in Scheidel, Morris and Saller (eds.) 2007: 113–43.
Frigo, D. (1985) *Il padre di famiglia: governo della casa e governo civile nella tradizione dell' "economica" tra Cinque e Seicento*. Rome.
Frost, F. (1999) "Sausage and meat preservation in antiquity," *Greek, Roman and Byzantine Studies* 40: 241–52.
Fukuyama, F. (2004) *State Building: Governance and World Order in the Twenty-First Century*. Ithaca NY.
Fülle, G. (1997) "The internal organization of the Arretine *terra sigillata* industry: problems of evidence and interpretation," *Journal of Roman Studies* 87: 111–55.
Furubotn, E. and Richter, R. (1997) *Institutions and Economic Theory: The Contribution of New Institutional Economics*. Ann Arbor.
Gabba, E. (1988) *Del buon uso della ricchezza*. Milan.
(1991) "Seneca e l'impero," in *Storia di Roma*, ed. G. Clemente, F. Coarelli, and E. Gabba, Vol. 2.2. Turin: 253–63.
Gabrielsen, V. (1997) *The Naval Aristocracy of Rhodes*. Aarhus.
Galloway, P. R. (1986) "Long-term fluctuations in climate and population in the preindustrial era," *Population and Development Review* 12: 1–24.
Galor, O. (2005) "From stagnation to growth: unified growth theory," in *Handbook of Economic Growth*, ed. P. Aghion and S. Durlauf. Amsterdam: 171–294.
Gara, A. (1992) "Progresso tecnico e mentalità classicista," in *Storia di Roma*, ed. E. Gabba and A. Schiavone, Vol. 2.3. Turin: 361–80.
Garcìa MacGaw, C. G. (2006) "La transiciòn del esclavismo al feudalismo y la 'villa esclavista,'" *Dialogues d'histoire ancienne* 32.2: 27–41.
Garnsey, P. (ed.) (1980) *Non-Slave Labour in the Greco-Roman World*. Cambridge.
(1983) "Grain for Rome," in Garnsey, Hopkins and Whittaker (eds.) 1983: 118–30.
(1988) *Famine and Food Supply in the Graeco-Roman World: Responses to Risk and Crisis*. Cambridge.
(1996) *Ideas of Slavery from Aristotle to Augustine*. Cambridge.
(1998) *Cities, Peasants and Food in Classical Antiquity: Essays in Social and Economic History*, ed. W. Scheidel. Cambridge.
Garnsey, P., Hopkins, K., and Whittaker, C. R. (eds.) (1983) *Trade in the Ancient Economy*. Cambridge.
Garnsey, P. and Humfress, C. (2001) *The Evolution of the Late Antique World*. Cambridge.
Garnsey, P. and Saller, R. (1987) *The Roman Empire: Economy, Society and Culture*. London.
Gatier, P.-L. (1988) "Le commerce maritime de Gaza au VIe siècle," in *Navires et commerces de la Méditerranée antique: hommage à J. Rougé*. Lyon: 361–70.
(1994) "Villages du Proche-Orient protobyzantin (4ème-7ème s.)," in *The Byzantine and Early Islamic Near East*, Vol. 2, ed. G. D. R. King and A. Cameron. Princeton: 17–48.

Gayraud, R.-P. (1997) "Les céramiques égyptiennes à glaçure, IXe-XIIe siècles," in *La céramique médiévale en Méditerranée*. Aix-en-Provence: 261–70.

(2003) "La transition céramique en Egypte. VIIe – IXe siècles," in Bakirtzis 2003: 558–62.

Geertz, C. (1979) "Suq: the bazaar economy in Sefrou," in C. Geertz, H. Geertz, and L. Roan (eds.), *Meaning and Order in Moroccan Society: Three Essays in Cultural Analysis*. Cambridge: 123–310.

Gelderen, M. van and Skinner, Q. (2002) *Republicanism: a shared European heritage*. Cambridge.

Gelichi, S. (2000) "Ceramic production and distribution in the early medieval Mediterranean basin (seventh to tenth centuries AD): between town and countryside," in *Towns and their Territories Between Late Antiquity and the Early Middle Ages*, ed. G. P. Brogiolo et al. Leiden: 115–39.

Gelichi, S. and Milanese, M. (1998) "Problems in the transition towards the medieval in the *Ifriqya*," in *L'Africa Romana*. Vol. 12. Sassari: 457–84.

Geraghty, R. M. (2007) "The impact of globalization in the Roman Empire, 200 BC – AD 100," *Journal of Economic History* 67: 1036–61.

Giannecchini, M. and Moggi-Cecchi, J. (2008) "Stature in archaeological samples from Central Italy: methodological issues and diachronic changes," *American Journal of Physical Anthropology* 135: 284–92.

Giardina, A. and Schiavone, A. (eds.) (1981) *Società romana e produzione schiavistica*. 3 vols. Bari.

Gibbins, D. (2001) "Shipwrecks and Hellenistic trade," in: *Hellenistic Economies*, ed. Z. H. Archibald, J. Davies, V. Gabrielsen, and G. J. Oliver. London: 273–312.

Goffart, W. (1982) "Old and new in Merovingian taxation," *Past and Present* 96: 3–21.

Goldsmith, R. W. (1984) "An estimate of the size and structure of the national product of the early Roman empire," *Review of Income and Wealth* 30: 263–88.

(1987) *Premodern Financial Systems: A Historical Comparative Study*. Cambridge.

Gonzales, A. (1997) "Esclaves, affranchis et 'familia' dans la 'correspondance' de Pline le Jeune," in *Schiavi e dipendenti nell'ambito dell' "oikos" e della familia*, ed. M. Moggi and G. Cordiano. Pisa: 329–76.

Goodchild, H. (2007) "Modelling Roman agricultural production in the Middle Tiber Valley, Central Italy." PhD dissertation. University of Birmingham.

Goodman, M. (1987) *The Ruling Class of Judea: The Origins of the Jewish Revolt Against Rome, A.D. 66–70*. Cambridge.

Gowland, R. and Garnsey, P. (2010) "Skeletal evidence for health, nutritional status and malaria in Rome and the empire," in H. Eckardt (ed.), *Roman Diasporas: Archaeological Approaches to Mobility and Diversity in the Roman Empire*. Portsmouth RI: 131–56.

Graham, A., Jacobsen, K. W., and Kassianidou, V. (2006) "Ayia Marina Mavrovouni: preliminary report on the Roman settlement and smelting workshop in the central northern foothills of the Troodos Mountains, Cyprus," *Report of the Department of Antquities, Cyprus*: 345–67.

Granovetter, M. (1985) "Economic action and social structure: the problem of embeddedness," *American Journal of Sociology* 91: 481–510.

(1992) "Economic institutions as social constructions: a framework for analysis," *Acta Sociologica* 35: 3–11.

Grantham, G. W. (1993) "Division of labour: agricultural productivity and occupational specialization in pre-industrial France," *Economic History Review* 46: 478–502.

Greene, K. (1990) "Perspectives on Roman technology," *Oxford Journal of Archaeology* 9.2: 209–19.

(2000) "Technological innovation and economic progress in the ancient world: M. I. Finley re-considered," *Economic History Review* 53: 29–59.

Greif, A. (2006) *Institutions and the Path to the Modern Economy: Lessons from Medieval Trade*. Cambridge.

Grey, C. (2007) "Contextualizing *colonatus*: the *origo* of the Late Roman Empire," *Journal of Roman Studies* 97: 155–75.

Griffin, M. (1976) *Seneca, a Philosopher in Politics*. Oxford.

(2003a) "Seneca as a sociologist: *De beneficiis*," in *Seneca uomo politico e l'età di Claudio e Nerone*, ed. A. De Vivo and E. Lo Cascio. Bari: 89–122.

(2003b) "*De beneficiis* and Roman society," *Journal of Roman Studies* 93: 92–113.

Grimal, P. (1989) "Sénèque et le stoicisme romain," in *Aufstieg und Niedergang der Römischen Welt* 2.36.3. Berlin and New York: 1962–92.

Gundlach, R. (1994) *Die Zwangsumsiedlung auswärtiger Bevölkerung als Mittel ägyptischer Politik bis zum Ende des Mittleren Reiches*. Stuttgart.

Gurt I Esparraguera, J. M., Buxeda I Garrigós, J., and Cau Ontiveros, M. A. (eds.) (2005) *LRCW I: Late Roman Coarse Wares, Cooking Wares and Amphorae in the Mediterranean*. Oxford.

Gutiérrez Lloret, S. (1996) *La Cora de Tudmir de la antigüedad tardía al mundo islámico*. Madrid.

Haas, J. (2006) *Die Umweltkrise des 3. Jahrhunderts n.Chr. im Nordwesten des Imperium Romanum: Interdisziplinäre Studien zu einem Aspekt der allgemeinen Reichskrise im Bereich der beiden Germaniae sowie der Belgica und der Raetia*. Stuttgart.

Habinek, T. N. (1998) *The Politics of Latin Literature: Writing, Identity and Empire in Ancient Rome*. Princeton.

Haldon, J. F. (1993) "Military service, military lands, and the status of soldiers," *Dumbarton Oaks Papers* 47: 1–67.

(1997) *Byzantium in the Seventh Century: The Transformation of a Culture*. 2nd edn. Cambridge.

(2000) "Production, distribution and demand in the Byzantine world, *c*.660–840," in Wickham and Hansen (eds.) 2000: 225–64.

(2008) "Framing transformation, transforming the framework," *Millennium* 5: 327–51.

Haley, E. W. (2003) *Baetica Felix: People and Prosperity in Southern Spain from Caesar to Septimius Severus*. Austin TX.

Hall, A. J., Fallick, A. E., Perdikatsis, V., and Photos-Jones, E. (2003) "A model for the origin of Al-rich efflorescences near fumaroles, Melos, Greece: enhanced weathering in a geothermal setting," *Mineralogical Magazine* 67: 363–79.

Hall, J. A. (1986) *Powers and Liberties: The Causes and Consequences of the Rise of the West*. London.

Halstead, P. (1997) Review of M-C. Amouretti and J.-P. Brun, *La production du vin et de l'huile en Méditerranée*, *Journal of Hellenic Studies* 117: 242–4.

(2002) "Traditional and ancient rural economy in Mediterranean Europe: plus ça change?," in Scheidel and von Reden (eds.) 2002: 53–70.

Hanes, C. (1996) "Turnover cost and the distribution of slave labor in Anglo-America," *Journal of Economic History* 56: 307–29.
Hansen, M. H. (2006) *The Shotgun Method: The Demography of the Ancient Greek City-State Culture*. Columbia MO and London.
Hanson, V. D. (1999) *The Other Greeks: The Family Farm and the Agrarian Roots of Western Civilization*. 2nd edn. New York.
Harl, K. W. (1996) *Coinage in the Roman Economy 300 BC to AD 700*. Baltimore and London.
Harland, P. A. (2003) *Associations, Synagogues, and Congregations: Claiming a Place in Ancient Mediterranean Society*. Minneapolis MN.
Harper, K. (2008) "The Greek census inscriptions of late antiquity," *Journal of Roman Studies* 98: 83–119.
(2010) "Slave prices in late antiquity (and in the very long run)," *Historia* 59: 206–38.
(2011) *Slavery in the Late Roman World, AD 275–425*. Cambridge.
Harris, W. V. (1979), *War and Imperialism in Republican Rome 327–70 B.C.* Oxford.
(1980) "Towards a study of the Roman slave trade," in *The Seaborne Commerce of Ancient Rome: Studies in Archaeology and History*, eds. J. H. D'Arms and E. C. Kopff. Rome: 117–40.
(1989) *Ancient Literacy*. Cambridge MA.
(1993) "Between archaic and modern: some current problems in the history of the Roman economy," in *The Inscribed Economy: Production and Distribution in the Roman Empire in the Light of* instrumentum domesticum, ed. W. V. Harris. Ann Arbor: 11–29.
(1999) "Demography, geography and the sources of Roman slaves," *Journal of Roman Studies* 89: 62–75.
(2000) "Trade," in *The Cambridge Ancient History, 2nd edn., XI: The High Empire, A.D. 70–192*, ed. A. K. Bowman, P. D. A. Garnsey, and D. Rathbone. Cambridge: 710–40.
(2003) "Roman governments and commerce, 300 B.C. – A.D. 300," in *Mercanti e politica nel mondo antico*, ed. C. Zaccagnini. Rome: 275–305.
(ed.) (2005) *Rethinking the Mediterranean*. Oxford.
(2006) "A revisionist view of Roman money," *Journal of Roman Studies* 96: 1–24.
(ed.) (2008a) *The Monetary Systems of the Greeks and Romans*. Oxford.
(2008b) "The nature of Roman money," in Harris (ed.) 2008: 174–207.
(2011a) *Rome's Imperial Economy: Twelve Essays*. Oxford.
(2011b) "Bois et déboisement dans la Méditerranée antique," *Annales: Histoire, Sciences Sociales* 66: 105–40.
Hasegawa, K. (2005) *The Familia Urbana during the Early Empire: A Study of Columbaria Inscriptions*. Oxford.
Hass, J. (2007) *Economic Sociology: An Introduction*. London.
Hassall, M. (2000) "The army," in *The Cambridge Ancient History, 2nd edn., XI: The High Empire, A.D. 70–192*, ed. A. K. Bowman, P. Garnsey, and D. Rathbone. Cambridge: 320–43.
Hatcher, J. (1986) "Mortality in the fifteenth century: some new evidence," *Economic History Review* 39: 19–38.
Hatcher, J. and Bailey, M. (2001) *Modelling the Middle Ages: The History and Theory of England's Economic Development*. Oxford.

Hauken, T. (1998) *Petition and Response: An Epigraphic Study of Petitions to Roman Emperors 181–249*. Bergen.

Hawkins, C. (2006) "Work in the city: Roman artisans and the urban economy." PhD dissertation. University of Chicago.

(forthcoming) "Labour and employment," in *The Cambridge Companion to Ancient Rome*, ed. P. Erdkamp. Cambridge.

Hayes, J. W. (1972) *Late Roman Pottery*. London.

(1980) *A Supplement to Late Roman Pottery*. London.

(1992) *Excavations at Saraçhane in Istanbul*, II. Princeton.

Hazzard, R. (1984) "The silver standard of Ptolemaic coinage," *Révue Numismatique* 1984: 231–9.

Hemelrijk, E. (2008) "Patronesses and 'mothers' of Roman collegia," *Classical Antiquity* 27: 115–62.

Henig, M. (1988) "The chronology of Roman engraved gemstones," *Journal of Roman Archaeology* 1: 142–52.

Henning, J. (ed.) (2007a) *Post-Roman Towns, Trade and Settlement in Europe and Byzantium*. 2 vols. Berlin and New York.

(2007b) "Early European towns: the development of the economy in the Frankish realm between dynamism and deceleration, AD 500–1100," in Henning 2007a: 3–40.

(2008) "Strong rulers – weak economy? Rome, the Carolingians and the archaeology of slavery in the first millennium AD," in *The Long Morning of Early Medieval Europe*, ed. J. R. Davis and M. McCormick. Burlington VT: 33–53.

Hermon, E. (ed.) (2008) *Vers une gestion intégrée de l'eau dans l'Empire romain*. Rome.

Herrmann-Otto, E. (1994) *Ex ancilla natus: Untersuchungen zu den "hausgeborenen" Sklaven und Sklavinnen im Westen des römischen Kaiserreiches*. Stuttgart.

Herz, P. (1988) *Studien zur römischen Wirtschaftsgesetzgebung: Die Lebensmittelversorgung*. Wiesbaden.

Hezser, C. (2001) *Jewish Literacy in Roman Palestine*. Tübingen.

(2005) *Jewish Slavery in Antiquity*. Oxford.

Higginbotham, J. (1997) *Piscinae - Artificial Fishponds in Roman Italy*. Chapel Hill NC.

Hin, S. (forthcoming) *The Demography of Roman Italy*. Cambridge.

Hingley, R. (2005) *Globalizing Roman Culture: Unity, Diversity and Empire*. London and New York.

Hirt, A. M. (2010) *Imperial Mines and Quarries in the Roman World: Organizational Aspects 27 BC – AD 235*. Oxford.

Hitchner, R. B. (1999) "More Italy than province? Archaeology, texts, and culture change in Roman Provence," *Transactions of the American Philological Association* 129: 375–79.

(2005) "'The advantages of wealth and luxury': the case for economic growth in the Roman Empire," in Manning and Morris (eds.) 2005: 207–22.

Hobson, J. A. (1902) *Imperialism: A Study*. London.

Hodges, R. and Bowden, W. (eds.) (1998) *The Sixth Century: Production, Distribution and Demand*. Leiden.

Hodges, R. and Whitehouse, D. (1983) *Mohammed, Charlemagne and the Origins of Europe: Archaeology and the Pirenne thesis*. London.

Hodkinson, S. (1988) "Animal husbandry in the Greek polis," in *Pastoral Economies in Classical Antiquity*, ed. C. R. Whittaker. Cambridge: 35–74.

Hollander, D. (2005) "Veterans, agriculture, and monetization in the Late Roman Republic," in *A Tall Order: Writing the Social History of the Ancient World. Essays in Honour of William V. Harris*, ed. Z. Varhelji and J.-J. Aubert. Munich and Leipzig: 229–39.

(2007) *Money in the Late Republic*. Leiden.

Hollingsworth, T. H. (1977) "Mortality in the British peerage families since 1600," *Population* 32: 323–52.

Holum, K. G. (2005) "The classical city in the sixth century: survival and transformation," in *The Cambridge Companion to the Age of Justinian*, ed. M. Maas. Cambridge: 87–112.

Honoré, T. (2002) *Ulpian, Pioneer of Human Rights*. Oxford.

Hopkins, K. (1978) *Conquerors and Slaves: Sociological Studies in Roman History*. Vol. 1. Cambridge.

(1980) "Taxes and trade in the Roman Empire (200 B.C.-A.D. 400)," *Journal of Roman Studies* 70: 101–25.

(1982) "The transport of staples in the Roman Empire," in *Eighth International Economic History Congress, Budapest*. Budapest: 80–7.

(1983) "Models, ships and staples," in *Trade and Famine in Classical* Antiquity, ed. P. D. A. Garnsey and C. R. Whittaker. Cambridge: 84–109.

(1995/6) "Rome, taxes, rents and trade," *Kodai* 6/7: 41–75 (repr. in Scheidel and von Reden [eds.] 2002: 190–230).

(2000), "Rents, taxes, trade and the city of Rome," in *Mercati permanenti e mercati periodici nel mondo romano*, ed. E. Lo Cascio. Bari: 253–67.

(2009) "The political economy of the Roman empire," in *The Dynamics of Ancient Empires*, ed. I. Morris and W. Scheidel. New York: 178–204.

Hoppa, R. D. and Vaupel, J. W. (eds.) (2002) *Paleodemography: Age Distributions from Skeletal Samples*. Cambridge.

Horden, P. (2005) "Mediterranean plague in the age of Justinian," in *The Cambridge Companion to the Age of Justinian*, ed. M. Maas. Cambridge: 134–60.

Horden, P. and Purcell, N. (2000) *The Corrupting Sea: A Study of Mediterranean History*. Oxford.

Howgego, C. (1992) "The supply and use of money in the Roman world: 200 BC to AD 300," *Journal of Roman Studies* 82: 1–31.

(1994) "Coin circulation and the integration of the Roman economy," *Journal of Roman Archaeology* 7: 5–21.

(1995) *Ancient History from Coins*. London.

Hufton, O. (1985) "Social conflict and the grain supply in eighteenth-century France," in *Hunger and History: The Impact of Changing Food Production and Consumption Patterns on Society*, ed. R. I. Rotberg and T. K. Rabb. Cambridge: 105–33.

Hume, D. (1998) *Selected Essays*, ed. S. Copley and A. Edgar. Oxford.

Innes, M. (2006) "Land, freedom and the making of the medieval West," *Transactions of the Royal Historical Society* 16: 39–74.

International Monetary Fund (2010) *World Economic Outlook Database*, April 2010.

Jacobs, J. (1969) *The Economy of Cities*. New York.

Jézégou, M.-P. (2007) "L'épave *Ouest-Embiez* 1: proposition d'un modèle de reexportation de produits verriers et du vin à la charnière des IIe/IIIe siècles après J.C.," in *Comercio, redistribución y fondeaderos: la navegación a vela en el Mediterráneo*, ed. J. Pérez Ballester and G. Pascual. Valencia: 451–60.

Johansson, S. R. (1994) "Food for thought: rhetoric and reality in modern mortality history," *Historical Methods* 27: 101–25.

(2005) "The pitfalls of policy history: writing the past to change the present," *International Journal of Epidemiology* 34: 526–9.

Johnson, A. C. (1936) *Roman Egypt to the Reign of Diocletian*. Baltimore.

Johnson, H. (1971) *The World Atlas of Wine: A Complete Guide to the Wines and Spirits of the World*. London.

Johnston, D. (1999) *Roman Law in Context*. Cambridge.

Jones, A. H. M. (1964) *The Later Roman Empire 284–602: A Social, Economic and Administrative Survey*. 3 vols. Oxford.

(1974) *The Roman Economy: Studies in Ancient Economic and Administrative History*, ed. P. A. Brunt. Oxford.

Jones, D. (2006) *The Bankers of Puteoli: Finance, Trade and Industry in the Roman World*. Stroud.

Jones, E. L. (2000) *Growth Recurring: Economic Change in World History*. 2nd edn. Ann Arbor.

Jones, E. L. (2003) *The European Miracle: Environments, Economies and Geopolitics in the History of Europe and Asia*. 3rd edn. Cambridge.

Jones, G. D. B. and Mattingly, D. J. (1990) *An Atlas of Roman Britain*. London.

Jones, H. (ed.) (1998) *Le monde antique et les droits de l'homme*. Brussels.

Jones, M. J. (2007) "Cities and urban life," in *A Companion to Roman Britain*, ed. M. Todd. Oxford: 162–92.

Jones, R. F. J. and Bird, D. G. (1972) "Roman gold-mining in North-West Spain, II: Workings on the Rio Duerna," *Journal of Roman Studies* 62: 59–74.

Jones, R. F. J. (1987) "A false start? The Roman urbanization of western Europe," *World Archaeology* 19: 47–57.

Jones, W. H. S. (1909) "Dea febris: a study of malaria in ancient Italy," *Liverpool Annals of Archaeology and Anthropology* 2: 97–124.

Jongman, W. (2003) "Slavery and the growth of Rome: the transformation of Italy in the second and first centuries BCE," in Edwards and Woolf (eds.) 2003: 100–22.

(2006) "The rise and fall of the Roman economy: population, rents and entitlement," in Bang, Ikeguchi, and Ziche (eds.) 2006: 237–54.

(2007a) "The early Roman empire: consumption," in Scheidel, Morris, and Saller (eds.) 2007: 592–618.

(2007b) "Gibbon was right: the decline and fall of the Roman economy," in *Crises and the Roman Empire*, ed. O. Hekster, G. De Kleijn, and D. Slootjes. Leiden: 183–99.

Jördens, A. (1990) *Vertragliche Regelungen von Arbeiten im späten griechischsprachigen Ägypten (P.Heid. V)*. Heidelberg.

Joshel, S. R. (1992) *Work, Identity, and Legal Status at Rome: A Study of the Occupational Inscriptions*. Norman, OK.

Joskow, P. L. (2008) "Introduction to New Institutional Economics: a report card," in Brousseau and Glachant (eds.) 2008: 1–19.

Kaltenstadler, W. (1978) *Arbeitsorganisation und Führungssystem bei den römischen Agrarschriftstellern (Cato, Varro, Columella)*. Stuttgart.

Kaplan, S. (1976) *Bread, Politics and Political Economy in the Reign of Louis XIV*. The Hague.

Karagiorgou, O. (2001) "LR2: a container for the military *annona* on the Danubian border," in Kingsley and Decker (eds.) 2001: 129–66.

Kaser, M. (1971) *Das römische Privatrecht. Erster Abschnitt: Das altrömische, das vorklassische und klassische Recht.* 2nd ed. Munich.

Kassianidou, V. (2004) "Recording Cyprus' mining history through archaeological survey," in *Archaeological Field Survey in Cyprus: Past History, Future Potentials*, ed. M. Iacovou. London: 95–104.

Katsari, C. (2005) "The monetization of Roman Asia Minor in the third century AD," in *Patterns in the Economy of Asia Minor*, ed. S. Mitchell and K. Katsari. Swansea: 261–88.

(2008) "The monetization of the Roman frontier provinces," in Harris (ed.) 2008: 242–66.

Keay, S. J. (1984) *Late Roman Amphorae in the Western Mediterranean. A Typology and Economic Study: The Catalan Evidence.* Oxford.

(1991) "The ager Tarraconensis in the late empire: a model for the economic relations of town and country in eastern Spain?," in *Roman Landscapes: Archaeological Survey in the Mediterranean Region*, ed. G. Barker and J. Lloyd. London: 79–87.

(1998) "African amphorae," in Saguì (ed.) 1998a: 141–55.

Kehoe, D. P. (1988a) "Allocation of risk and investment on the estates of Pliny the Younger," *Chiron* 18: 15–42.

(1988b) *The Economics of Agriculture on Roman Imperial Estates in North Africa.* Göttingen.

(1989) "Approaches to economic problems in the 'Letters' of Pliny the Younger: the question of risk in agriculture," in *Aufstieg und Niedergang der Römischen Welt.* Berlin and New York. Vol. 2.33.1: 555–90.

(1992) *Management and Investment on Estates in Roman Egypt during the Early Empire.* Bonn.

(1997) *Investment, Profit and Tenancy: The Jurists and the Roman Agrarian Economy.* Ann Arbor.

(2007a) *Law and the Rural Economy in the Roman Empire.* Ann Arbor.

(2007b) "The early Roman empire: production," in Scheidel, Morris and Saller (eds.) 2007: 543–69.

Kelly, C. (2004) *Ruling the Later Roman Empire.* Cambridge MA.

Kennedy, H. (1995) "The financing of the military in the early Islamic state," in *The Byzantine and Early Islamic Near East*, III, ed. A. Cameron. Princeton: 361–78.

(1998) "Egypt as a province in the Islamic caliphate, 641–868," in *The Cambridge History of Egypt*, I, ed. C. F. Petry. Cambridge: 62–85.

(2001) *The Armies of the Caliphs.* London.

Kenrick, P. (1993) "Italian terra sigillata: a sophisticated Roman industry," *Oxford Journal of Archaeology* 12: 235–42.

(1996) "The importation of Italian sigillata to Algeria," *Antiquités Africaines* 32: 37–44.

Ker, J. (2006) "Seneca, man of many genres," in *Seeing Seneca Whole: Perspectives on Philosophy, Poetry and Politics*, ed. K. Volk and G. D. Williams. Leiden: 19–41.

Kessler, D. and Temin, P. (2007) "The organization of the grain trade in the early Roman Empire," *Economic History Review* 60: 313–32.

(2008) "Money and prices in the early Roman Empire," in Harris (ed.) 2008: 137–59.

Kießling, G. (1924) "Giroverkehr," in *Paulys Realencyclopädie der Classischen Altertumswissenschaft*, Suppl. IV. Stuttgart: 696–709.

Killgrove, K. (2010) "Migration and mobility in imperial Rome." PhD dissertation. University of North Carolina.

King, A. (1999) "Diet in the Roman world: a regional inter-site comparison of the mammal bones," *Journal of Roman Archaeology* 12: 168–202.

King, H. (ed.) (2005) *Health in Antiquity*. London.

Kingsley, S. and Decker, M. (eds.) (2001) *Economy and Exchange in the East Mediterranean during Late Antiquity*. Oxford.

Kirschenbaum, A. (1987) *Sons, Slaves and Freedmen in Roman Commerce*. Jerusalem.

Kiser, E. and Sacks, A. (2009) "Improving tax administration in contemporary African states: lessons from history," in *The New Fiscal Sociology*, ed. I. W. Martin, A. K. Mehrotra and M. Prasad. Cambridge: 183–201.

Kleijwegt, M. (1991) *Ancient Youth*. Amsterdam.

Klein Goldewijk, G. (forthcoming) "Stature and the standard of living in the Roman Empire." PhD dissertation. University of Groningen.

Kneissl, P. (1983) "*Mercator – negotiator*: römische Geschäftsleute und die Terminologie ihrer Berufe," *Münstersche Beiträge zur antiken Handelsgeschichte* 2: 73–90.

Koepke, N. and Baten, J. (2005a) "Climate and its impact on the biological standard of living in North-East, Centre-West and South Europe during the last 2000 years," *History of Meteorology* 2: 147–59.

(2005b) "The biological standard of living in Europe during the last two millennia," *European Review of Economic History* 9: 61–95.

(2008) "Agricultural specialization and height in ancient and medieval Europe," *Explorations in Economic History* 45: 127–46.

Kolb, A. (2000) *Transport und Nachrichtentransfer im Römischen Reich*. Berlin.

Kolendo, J. (1980) *L'agricoltura nell'Italia romana: tecniche agrarie e progresso economico dalla tarda repubblica al principato*. Rome.

(1985) "Le attività agricole degli abitanti di Pompei e gli atrezzi agricoli ritrovati all'interno della città," *Opus* 4: 111–24.

(1994) "Praedia suburbana e loro redditività," in Carlsen, Ørsted, and Skydsgaard (eds.) 1994: 59–71.

Komlos, J. (2003) "An anthropometric history of early modern France," *European Review of Economic History* 7: 159–89.

(2007) "In English pygmies and giants: the physical stature of English youth in the late-18th and early-19th centuries," *Research in Economic History* 25: 149–68.

Kron, G. (2000) "Roman Ley-farming," *Journal of Roman Archaeology* 13: 277–87.

(2002) "Archaeozoological evidence for the productivity of Roman livestock farming," *Münstersche Beiträge zur antiken Handelsgeschichte* 21: 53–73.

(2004) "A deposit of carbonized hay from Oplontis and Roman fodder quality," *Mouseion* 4: 275–331.

(2005a) "Anthropometry, physical anthropology, and the reconstruction of ancient health, nutrition, and living standards," *Historia* 54: 68–83.

(2005b) "The Augustan census figures and the population of Italy," *Athenaeum* 93: 441–95.

(2005c) "Sustainable Roman intensive mixed farming methods: water conservation and erosion control," in *Concepts, pratiques et enjeux environnementaux dans l'empire romain*, ed. R. Bedon and E. Hermon. Limoges: 285–308.

(2008a) "Animal husbandry, hunting, fishing and pisciculture," in Oleson (ed.) 2008: 176–222.

(2008b) "The much maligned peasant: comparative perspectives on the productivity of the small farmer in classical antiquity," in De Ligt and Northwood (eds.) 2008: 71–119.

(forthcoming) "Nutrition, hygiene and mortality: setting parameters for Roman health and life expectancy consistent with our comparative evidence," in Lo Cascio (ed.) forthcoming.

Kuniholm, P. I. (2002) "Dendrochronological investigations at Herculaneum and Pompeii," in *The Natural History of Pompeii*, ed. W. M. F. Jashemski and F. G. Meyer. Cambridge: 235–9.

Lachiver, M. (1988) *Vins, vignes et vignerons: histoire du vignoble français*. Paris.

Laes, C. (2008) "Child slaves at work in Roman antiquity," *Ancient Society* 38: 235–83.

Laiou, A. E. (2002) "Exchange and trade, seventh-twelfth centuries," in *The Economic History of Byzantium*, III, ed. A. E. Laiou et al. Washington, DC: 697–770.

Laiou, A. E. and Morrisson, C. (2007) *The Byzantine Economy*. Cambridge.

Landes, D. (1998) *The Wealth and Poverty of Nations* (London).

Lane, F. C. (1966) *Venice and History*. Baltimore.

Langholm, O. (1979) *Price and Value in the Aristotelian Tradition*. Bergen.

(1983) *Wealth and Money in the Aristotelian Tradition*. Bergen.

(1984) *The Aristotelian Analysis of Usury*. Bergen.

(1998) *The Legacy of Scholasticism in Economic Thought: Antecedents of Choice and Power*. Cambridge.

Launaro, A. (2011) *Peasants and Slaves: The Rural Population of Roman Italy (200 BC to AD 100)*. Cambridge.

Laurence, R. (1997) "Writing the Roman metropolis," in *Roman Urbanism: Beyond the Consumer City*, ed. H. Parkins. London and New York: 1–20.

(1999) *The Roads of Roman Italy*. London and New York.

Lavan, L. and Bowden, W. (eds.) (2003) *Theory and Practice in Late Antique Archaeology*. Leiden.

Lebecq, S. (2000) "The role of the monasteries in the systems of production and exchange of the Frankish world between the seventh and the beginning of the ninth centuries," in Wickham and Hansen (eds.) (2000): 121–48.

Lee, J. Z., Wang, F., and Campbell, C. (1994) "Infant and child mortality among the Qing nobility: implications for two types of positive check," *Population Studies* 48: 395–411.

Lee, R. (1980) "An historical perspective on economic aspects of the population explosion," in *Population and Economic Change in Developing Countries*, ed. R. Easterlin. Chicago: 517–57.

(1986a) "Malthus and Boserup: A Dynamic Synthesis," in *The State of Population Theory: Forward from Malthus*, ed. D. Coleman and R. Schofield. Oxford: 96–130.

(1986b) "Population homeostasis and English demographic history," in *Population and Economy: Population and Economy from the Traditional to the Modern World*, ed. R. I. Rotberg and T. K. Rabb. Cambridge: 75–100.

Lefebvre des Noëttes, C. (1931) *L'attelage: le cheval de selle à travers les ages: contribution à l'histoire de l'esclavage*. Paris.

Leguilloux, M. (2002) "Les salaisons de viande: l'apport de l'archéozoologie," in *Animali tra uomini e dei. Archeozoologica del mondo preromano. Atti del Convegno internazionale 8–9 novembre 2002*. Bologna: 139–52.

Leitch, V. (2010) "Production and trade of Roman and Late Roman North African cookwares." DPhil thesis, University of Oxford.

(2011) "Location, location, location: characterizing coastal and inland production and distribution of Roman African cooking wares," in Robinson and Wilson (eds.) 2011: 169–95.

Leone, A. (2003) "Topographies of production in the cities of late antique North Africa," in Lavan and Bowden (eds.) 2003: 257–87.

Lesger, C. (2006) *The Rise of the Amsterdam Market and Information Exchange: Merchants, Commercial Expansion and Change in the Spatial Economy of the Low Countries, c.1550–1630*. Burlington VT.

Leveau, P. (1993) "Mentalité economique et grandes travaux: le drainage du lac Fucin. Aux origines d'un modèle," *Annales ESC* 48: 3–16.

(1995) "Les moulins romains de Barbegal, les ponts-aqueducs du Vallon de l'Arc, et l'histoire naturelle de la vallée des Baux (Bilan de six ans de fouilles programmées)," *Comptes Rendus de l'Academie des Inscriptions et Belles-Lettres* 1995: 116–44.

Levi, M. (1988) *Of Rule and Revenue*. Berkeley.

Levick, B. (2003) "Seneca and money," in *Seneca uomo politico e l'età di Claudio e Nerone*, ed. A. De Vivo and E. Lo Cascio. Bari: 211–28.

Levy, E. (1951) *West Roman Vulgar Law: The Law of Property*. Philadelphia.

(1956) *Weströmisches Vulgarrecht: Das Obligationenrecht*. Weimar.

Lewis, M. J. T. (1997) *Millstone and Hammer: The Origins of Water Power*. Hull.

Lewit, T. (2004) *Villas, Farms, and the Late Roman Rural Economy: Third to Fifth Centuries AD*. Oxford.

Liebeschuetz, J. H. W. G. (2001) *The Decline and Fall of the Roman City*. Oxford.

Liou, B. and Pomey, P. (1985) "Direction des recherches archéologiques sous-marines," *Gallia* 43: 547–76.

Little, L. K. (ed.) (2007) *Plague and the End of Antiquity: The Pandemic of 541–750*. Cambridge.

Livi Bacci, M. (2000) *The Population of Europe: A History*. Oxford and Malden MA.

Ljungqvist, F. C. (2009) "Temperature proxy records covering the last two millennia: a tabular and visual overview," *Geografiska Annaler* 91A: 11–29.

(2010) "A new reconstruction of temperature variability in the extra-tropical Northern Hemisphere during the last two millennia," *Geografiska Annaler* 92A: 339–51.

Lo Cascio, E. (1978) "Oro e moneta in età traianea," *Annali dell'istituto italiano di numismatica* 25: 75–95.

(1981) "State and coinage in the late Republic and early Empire," *Journal of Roman Studies* 71: 76–86.

(1986) "Teoria e politica monetaria a Roma tra III e IVs. d.C.," in *Società romana e impero tardoantico*, ed. A. Giardina, I. Bari: 535–57.

(1991a) "Le tecniche dell'amministrazione," in *Storia di Roma*, II.2, ed. G. Clemente, F. Coarelli, and E. Gabba. Turin: 119–91.

(1991b) "Forme dell'economia imperiale," in *Storia di Roma*. II.2, ed. G. Clemente, F. Coarelli, and E. Gabba. Turin: 313–65.

(ed.) (2006a) *Innovazione tecnica e progresso economico nel mondo romano*. Bari.
(2006b) "Did the population of imperial Rome reproduce itself?," in Storey (ed.) 2006: 52–68.
(2006c) "The role of the state in the Roman economy – making use of the New Institutional Economics," in Bang, Ikeguchi, and Ziche (eds.) 2006: 215–34.
(2007) "The early Roman Empire: the state and the economy," in Scheidel, Morris, and Saller (eds.) 2007: 619–47.
(2009) *Crescita e declino: studi di storia dell'economia romana*. Rome.
(2010) "Thinking slave and free in coordinates," in *By the Sweat of Your Brown: Roman Slavery in its Socio-Economic Setting*, ed. U. Roth. London.
(ed.) (forthcoming) *L'impatto della "peste antonina."* Bari.
Lo Cascio, E. and Malanima, P. (2005) "Cycles and stability: Italian population before the demographic transition," *Rivista di Storia Economica* 21: 5–40.
(2009) "GDP in pre-modern agrarian economies (1–1820 AD): a revision of the estimates," *Rivista di Storia Economica* 25: 391–420.
Lopez, R. S. (1943) "Mohammed and Charlemagne: a revision," *Speculum* 18: 14–38.
Los, A. (1995) "La condition sociale des affranchis privés au 1er siècle aprés J.-C.," *Annales: Histoire, Sciences Sociales* 50: 1011–43.
Loseby, S. T. (1998) "Marseille and the Pirenne thesis, I: Gregory of Tours, the Merovingian kings, and 'un grand port'," in Hodges and Bowden (eds.) 1998: 203–29.
(2000) "Marseille and the Pirenne thesis, II: 'ville morte,'" in Wickham and Hansen (eds.) 2000: 167–93.
(2005) "The Mediterranean economy," in *The New Cambridge Medieval History, I, c.500-c.700*, ed. P. Fouracre. Cambridge: 605–38.
(2007) "The ceramic data and the transformation of the Roman world," in Bonifay and Tréglia (eds.) 2007: 1–14.
Loughton, M. E. (2003) "The distribution of Republican amphorae in France," *Oxford Journal of Archaeology* 22.2: 177–207.
Louhichi, A. (2003) "Ifriqiya (VIIIe-IXe siècles)," in Bakirtzis (ed.) 2003: 569–71.
Love, J. R. (1991) *Antiquity and Capitalism: Max Weber and the Sociological Foundations of Roman Civilization*. London.
Lovejoy, P. E. (1979) "The characteristics of plantations in the nineteenth-century Sokoto Caliphate," *The American Historical Review* 84: 1267–92.
(1981) "Slavery in the Sokoto caliphate," in *The Ideology of Slavery in Africa*, ed. P. E. Lovejoy. Beverly Hills CA: 201–43.
(2000) *Transformations in Slavery: A History of Slavery in Africa*. 2nd edn. Cambridge.
Lowe, B. (2009) *Roman Iberia: Economy, Society and Culture*. London.
Lucas, A. R. (2006) *Wind, Water, Work: Ancient and Medieval Milling Technology*. Leiden.
Macias i Solé, J. M. and Remolà i Vallverdú, J. A. (2000) "Tarraco visigoda: caracterisacion del material ceramico del siglo VII dC," in *V Reunió d'arqueologia cristiana hispànica*. Barcelona: 485–97.
Mackensen, M. (1993) *Die spätantiken Sigillata- und Lampentöpfereien von El Mahrine*. Munich.
Mackensen, M. and Schneider, G. (2002) "Production centres of African red slip ware (3rd – 7th c.) in northern and central Tunisia," *Journal of Roman Archaeology* 15: 121–58.
MacKinnon, M. (2004) *Production and Consumption of Animals in Roman Italy: Integrating the Zooarchaeological and Textual Evidence*. Portsmouth RI.

(2007) "Peopling the mortuary landscape of North Africa: an overview of the human osteological evidence," in *Mortuary Landscapes of North Africa*, ed. D. L. Stone and L. M. Stirling. Toronto: 204–40.

MacMullen, R. (1963) *Soldier and Civilian in the Later Roman Empire*. Cambridge MA.

(1987) "Late Roman slavery," *Historia* 36: 359–82.

Maddison, A. (2007) *Contours of the World Economy, 1–2030 AD*. Oxford.

Magness, J. (2003) *The Archaeology of the Early Islamic Settlement in Palestine*. Winona Lake IN.

Maisano, R. (1979) *Olimpiodoro Tebano: frammenti storici. Introduzione, traduzione e note con in appendice il testo greco*. Naples.

Malanima, P. (forthcoming) "The long ancient growth 1000 BC – 200 AD," *Studi Storici*.

Malmendier, U. (2002) *Societas publicanorum: staatliche Wirtschaftsaktivitäten in den Händen privater Unternehmer*. Cologne.

(2005), "Roman shares," in *The Origins of Value: The Financial Innovations that Created Modern Capital Markets*, ed. W. Goetzmann and G. Rouwenhorst. Oxford: 31–42.

Maloney, R. P. (1971) "Usury in Greek, Roman and Rabbinic thought," *Traditio* 27: 79–95.

Malthus, T. R. (2004) *An Essay on the Principle of Population*. New York.

Manca Masciardi, M. and Montevecchi, O. (1984) *I contratti di baliatico*. Milano.

Mangartz, F. (2006) "Zur Rekonstruktion der wassergetriebenen byzantinischen Steinsägemaschine von Ephesos, Türkei – Vorbericht," *Archäologisches Korrespondenzblatt* 36: 573–90.

Mango, M. M. (ed.) (2009) *Byzantine Trade, 4th – 12th Centuries: The Archaeology of Local, Regional and International Exchange*. Farnham.

Manning, C. E. (1989) "Stoicism and slavery in the Roman Empire," in *Aufstieg und Niedergang der Römischen Welt* 2.36.3. Berlin and New York: 1518–43.

(2007) "Hellenistic Egypt," in: Scheidel, Morris and Saller (eds.) 2007: 434–59.

Manning, J. G. and Morris, I. (eds.) (2005) *The Ancient Economy: Evidence and Models*. Stanford.

Manzi, G. et al. (1999) "Discontinuity of life conditions at the transition from the Roman imperial age to the early Middle Ages: examples from Central Italy evaluated by pathological dento-alveolar lesions," *American Journal of Human Biology* 11: 327–41.

Marache, R. (1989) "Juvenal, peintre de la société de son temps," in *Aufstieg und Niedergang der Römischen Welt* 2.33.1. Berlin and New York: 592–639.

Marazzi, F. (1998) "The destinies of the late antique Italies: politico-economic developments of the sixth century," in Hodges and Bowden (eds.) 1998: 119–59.

Marcone, A. (1997) *Storia dell'agricoltura romana: dal mondo arcaico all'età imperiale*. Rome.

(2006) "Le innovazione nell'agricoltura romana," in Lo Cascio (ed.) 2006a: 181–95.

Maresch, K. (1996) *Bronze und Silber: Papyrologische Beiträge zur Geschichte der Währung im ptolemäischen und römischen Ägypten bis zum 2. Jh. n. Chr.* Cologne.

Marinovic, L. P., Golubcova, E. S., Sifman, I. S., and Pavlovskaja, A. I. (1992) *Die Sklaverei in den östlichen Provinzen des römischen Reiches im 1.-3. Jahrhundert*. Stuttgart.

Martin, A. (1998) "La sigillata focese (Phocaean Red-Slip/Late Roman C ware)," in Saguì (ed.) 1998a: 109–22.

Martin, P. (2000) "La tradition sur l'integration des peuples vaincus aux origines de Rome et son utilisation politique," in *Integrazione mescolanza e rifiuto*, ed. G. Urso. Rome: 65–88.

Martin, R. (1967) "Pline le jeune et les problèmes économiques de son temps," *Revue des Études Anciennes* 69: 62–97.

Martin, S. D. (1989) *The Roman Jurists and the Organization of Private Building in the Late Republic and Early Empire*. Brussels.

(2002) "Roman law and the study of Roman land transportation," in *Speculum Iuris: Roman Law as a Reflection of Social and Economic Life in Antiquity*, ed. J.-J. Aubert and B. Sirks. Ann Arbor: 151–68.

Marzano, A. (2007) *Roman Villas in Central Italy: A Social and Economic History*. Leiden.

Mastrorosa, I. (2006) "Condizione e ruoli della donna nella realtà agraria romana: il contributo degli *Scriptores rei rusticate*," *Euphrosyne* 34: 135–48.

Matías Rodríguez, R. (2006) "La Minería Aurífera Romana del Nordest de Hispania: Ingeniería minera y gestión de las explotaciones auríferas romanas en la Sierra del Teleno (León-España)", in *Nuevos elementos de ingeniería romana. III Congreso de las Obras Públicas Romanas*. Astorga: 213–63.

Mattingly, D. (1988) "Oil for export? A comparison of Libyan, Spanish, and Tunisian olive oil production in the Roman empire," *Journal of Roman Archaeology* 1: 33–56.

(2002) "Impacts beyond empire: Rome and the Garamantes of the Sahara," in *The Transformation of Economic Life under the Roman Empire*, ed. L. De Blois and J. Rich. Amsterdam: 184–203.

(2003) (ed.) *The Archaeology of Fazzan*, I: *Synthesis*. London.

(2006) *An Imperial Possession: Britain in the Roman Empire, 54 BC – AD 409*. London.

Mattingly, D., al-Aghab, S., Ahmed, M., Moussa, F., Sterry, M., and Wilson, A. (2010) "DMP X: Survey and landscape conservation issues around the Taqallit headland," *Libyan Studies* 41: 105–32.

Mattingly, D. and Aldrete, G. (2000) "The feeding of imperial Rome: the mechanics of the food supply system," in Coulston and Dodge (eds.) 2000: 142–65.

Mattingly, D. J., Daniels, C. M., Dore, J. N., Edwards, D. N., Hawthorne, J. W. J. et al. (2010) *The Archaeology of Fazzan*, III: *Excavations of C. M. Daniels*. London.

Mattingly, D., Lahr, M. M., and Wilson, A. I. (2009) "DMP V: Investigations in 2009 of cemeteries and related sites on the west side of the Taqallit Promontory," *Libyan Studies* 40: 95–131.

Mattingly, D. and Leone, A. (2004) "Vandal, Byzantine and Arab rural landscapes in North Africa," in *Landscapes of Change: the Evolution of the Countryside in Late Antiquity and the Early Middle Ages*, ed. N. Christie. Aldershot: 135–62.

Mattingly, D. J. and Salmon, J. (eds.) (2001) *Economies Beyond Agriculture in the Classical World*. London.

Mattingly, D. J., Stone, D., Stirling, L., and Ben Lazreg, N. (2001) "Leptiminus (Tunisia): A 'producer' city?," in Mattingly and Salmon (eds.) 2001: 66–89.

Mattingly, D. J. and Wilson, A. I. (2010) "Concluding thoughts: Made in Fazzan?," in *The Archaeology of Fazzan*, III, ed. D. J. Mattingly. London: 523–30.

Maucourant, J. (1996) "Une analyse économique de la redistribution: est-elle possible? Eléments de comparaison entre la 'new institutional economics' et l'approche substantive," *Topoi* 6: 131–58.

(2004) "Rationalité économique ou comportements socioéconomiques?," in *Mentalités et choix économiques des romains*, ed. J. Andreau, J. France, and S. Pittia. Bordeaux: 228–40.

Mayer-Maly, T. (1956) *Locatio-Conductio: Eine Untersuchung zum klassischen römischen Recht*. Vienna and Munich.

Mazzoli, G. (1989) "Le 'epistulae morales ad Lucilium' di Seneca," in *Aufsteig und Niedergang der Römischen Welt* 2.36.3. Berlin and New York: 1823–77.

McCormick, M. (1998) "Bateaux de vie, bateaux de mort: maladie, commerce, transports annonaires et le passage économique du bas-empire au moyen âge," in *Morfologie sociali e culturali in Europa fra tarda antichità e alto medioevo*. Spoleto: 35–118.

(2001) *Origins of the European Economy: Communications and Commerce, AD 300–900*. Cambridge.

McKeown, N. (2007) *The Invention of Ancient Slavery?* London.

McLaughlin, R. (2010) *Rome and the Distant East: Trade Routes to the Ancient Lands of Arabia, India and China*. London and New York.

McLynn, N. (2009) "Poetic creativity and political crisis in early fifth-century Gaul," *Journal of Late Antiquity* 2: 60–74.

Meiggs, R. (1971) *Roman Ostia*. 2nd edn. Oxford.

(1982) *Trees and Timber in the Ancient Mediterranean World*. Oxford.

Meltzer, D. O. (1992) "Mortality decline, the demographic transition, and economic growth." PhD dissertation, University of Chicago.

Merrills, A. and Miles, R. (2010) *The Vandals*. Oxford.

Metzler, J. (1975) "Rational management, modern business practices, and economies of scale in the ante-bellum southern plantations," *Explorations in Economic History* 12: 123–50.

Meyer-Termeer, A. J. M. (1978) *Die Haftung der Schiffer im griechischen und römischen Recht*. Zutphen.

Michel, J. (1962) *Gratuité en droit romain*. Brussels.

Milani, P. A. (1972) *La schiavitù nel pensiero politico dei Greci al basso medio evo*. Milan.

Milanovic, B., Lindert, P. H., and Williamson, J. G. (2007) "Measuring ancient inequality," NBER Working Paper 13550.

Millar, F. (1993) *The Roman Near East, 31 B.C.-A.D. 337*. Cambridge MA.

Miller, J. C. (2008) "Slaving as historical process: examples from the ancient Mediterranean and the modern Atlantic," in Dal Lago and Katsari (eds.) (2008): 70–102.

Miller, J. I. (1969) *The Spice Trade of the Roman Empire, 29 BC to AD 641*. Oxford.

Millett, P. (1991) *Lending and Borrowing in Ancient Athens*. Cambridge.

(2001) "Productive to Some Purpose? The Problem of Ancient Economic Growth," in Mattingly and Salmon (eds.) 2001: 17–48.

Minaud, G. (2005) *La comptabilité à Rome: essai d'histoire économique sur la pensée comptable commerciale et privée dans le monde antique romain*. Lausanne.

Mitchell, S. (1993) *Anatolia*. 2 vols. Oxford.

(2007) *A History of the Later Roman Empire, AD 284–641*. Oxford.

Mladenovic, D. (2009) "Roman Moesia Superior: the creation of a new provincial entity and processes of multicultural adjustment." DPhil thesis, University of Oxford.

Mols, S. (1999) *Wooden Furniture in Herculaneum: Form, Technique and Function*. Amsterdam.

(2002) "Identification of the woods used in the furniture at Herculaneum," in *The Natural History of Pompeii*, ed. W. M. F. Jashemski and F. G. Meyer. Cambridge: 225–34.

Monson, A. (2006) "The ethics and economics of Ptolemaic religious associations," *Ancient Society* 36: 221–38.

Morel, J.-P. (1993) "The craftsman," in *The Romans*, ed. Andrea Giardina. Chicago: 214–44.

(2007) "Early Rome and Italy," in Scheidel, Morris, and Saller (eds.) (2007): 487–510.

Morley, N. (1996) *Metropolis and Hinterland: The City of Rome and the Italian Economy, 200 BC – AD 200*. Cambridge.

(2005) "The salubriousness of the Roman city," in King (ed.) 2005: 192–204.

(2006) "Narrative economy," in Bang, Ikeguchi and Ziche (eds.) 2006: 27–47.

(2007a) *Trade in Classical Antiquity*. Cambridge.

(2007b) "The early Roman Empire: distribution," in Scheidel, Morris, and Saller (eds.) 2007: 570–91.

(2009) *Antiquity and Modernity*. Malden MA.

(2010) *The Roman Empire: Roots of Imperialism*. London.

(2011) "Slavery under the Principate," in Bradley and Cartledge (eds.) 2011: 265–86.

Morris, I. (2002) "Hard surfaces," in Cartledge, Cohen and Foxhall (eds.) 2002: 8–43.

(2004) "Economic growth in ancient Greece," *Journal of Institutional and Theoretical Economics* 160: 709–42.

(2005) "Archaeology, standards of living, and Greek economic history," in Manning and Morris (eds.) 2005: 91–126.

(2010) *Why the West Rules – For Now: The Patterns of History, and What They Reveal about the Future*. New York.

Morris, I. and Manning, J. G. (2005) "The economic sociology of the ancient Mediterranean world," in *The Handbook of Economic Sociology*, ed. N. J. Smelser and R. Swedberg. 2nd edn. Princeton: 131–59.

Morris, I., Scheidel, W., and Saller, R. (2010) "Introduction," in Scheidel, Morris, and Saller (eds.) 2007: 1–12.

Morrisson, C. and Sodini, J.-P. (2002) "The sixth-century economy," in *The Economic History of Byzantium*, ed. A. E. Laiou. Washington DC: 171–220.

Morton, J. (2001) *The Role of the Environment in Ancient Greek Seafaring*. Leiden.

Morvillez, É., Chevalier, P., Mardesic, J., Pender, B., Topic, M., and Causevic, M. (2005) "La noria découverte à proximité de 'L'oratoire A,' dans le quartier épiscopal de Salone (mission archéologique franco-croate de Salone)," in *Aquam in altum exprimere. Les machines élévatrices d'eau dans l'Antiquité*, ed. A. Bouet. Bordeaux: 153–69.

Mouritsen, H. (2005) "Freedmen and decurions: epitaphs and social history in imperial Italy," *Journal of Roman Studies* 95: 38–63.

(2007) "*CIL* X 1403: the *album* from Herculaneum and the nomenclature of the Latini Iuniani," *Zeitschrift für Papyrologie und Epigraphik* 161: 288–90.

(2011) *The Freedman in the Roman World*. Cambridge.

(forthcoming) "Slavery and manumission in the Roman elite: a study of the *columbaria* of the Volusii Saturnini and the Statilii Tauri," in *Ancient Slavery and Material Culture*, ed. M. George.

Mukai, T. and Rigoir, Y. (2005) "Les dérivées-des-sigillées paléochrétiennes (DS.P)," in *Carte archéologique de la Gaule 13/3: Marseille et ses alentours*, ed. M.-P. Rothé and H. Tréziny. Paris: 261–4.

Murray, G. W. (1914) "Notes (Bir Kareim; Amethysts)," *Cairo Scientific Journal* 8: 179.

Nafissi, M. (2005) *Ancient Athens and Modern Ideology: Value, Theory and Evidence in Historical Sciences. Max Weber, Karl Polyani and Moses Finley*. London.

Neal, L. (1990) "The Dutch and English East India companies compared: evidence from the stock and foreign exchange markets," in Tracy (ed.) 1990: 195–223.

Nee, V. (2005) "The New Institutionalisms in Economics and Sociology," in Smelser and Swedberg (eds.) 2005: 49–74.

Neesen, L. (1980) *Untersuchungen zu den direkten Staatsabgaben der römischen Kaiserzeit (27 v. Chr. – 284 n. Chr.* Bonn.

Nenna, M.-D. (2003) "Les ateliers égyptiens à l'époque greco-romaine," in *Coeur de verre: production et diffusion du verre antique*, ed. D. Foy. Gollion: 32–3.

(2007) "Production et commerce du verre à l'époque impériale," *Facta* 1: 125–48.

Nicholas, S. and Steckel, R. H. (1997) "Tall but poor: living standards of men and women in pre-famine Ireland," *Journal of European Economic History* 26: 105–34.

Nicolet, C. (1966) *L'ordre équestre à l'époque républicaine 312–43 av. J.-C.*, I. Paris.

(1971) "Les variations des prix et la 'théorie quantitative de la monnaie' à Rome, de Cicéron à Pline l'Ancien," *Annales ESC* 26: 1203–27.

(1980) *The World of the Citizen in Republican Rome*. Berkeley.

(1982) "Il pensiero economico dei romani," in *Storia delle idee politiche, economiche, sociali*, ed. L. Firpo. Turin: 877–960.

(1984) "Pline, Paul et la théorie de la monnaie," *Athenaeum* 72: 105–35.

(1988a) *L'inventaire du monde: géographie et politique aux origines de l'Empire romain*. Paris.

(1988b) *Rendre à César*. Paris.

(1994) "Economy and society, 133–43 BC," in *The Cambridge Ancient History*, 2nd edn., *Vol. 9: The Last Age of the Roman Republic 146–43 B.C.*, ed. J. A. Crook, Lintott, A., and Rawson, E. Cambridge: 599–643.

(2000) *Censeurs et publicains: économie et fiscalité dans la Rome antique*. Paris.

Nieto, X. (1997) "Le commerce de cabotage et de redistribution," in *La navigation dans l'antiquité*, ed. P. Pomey. Aix-en-Provence: 146–59.

North, D. C. (1977) "Markets and other allocation systems in history: the challenge of Karl Polanyi," *Journal of European Economic History* 6: 703–16.

(1981) *Structure and Change in Economic History*. New York.

(1984) "Government and the cost of exchange in history," *Journal of Economic History* 44: 255–64.

(1990) *Institutions, Institutional Change, and Economic Performance*. Cambridge.

North, D. C., Wallis, J. J., and Weingast, B. R. (2009) *Violence and Social Orders: A Conceptual Framework for Interpreting Recorded Human History*. Cambridge.

Northedge, A. (2001) "Thoughts on the introduction of polychrome glazed pottery in the Middle East," in *La céramique byzantine et proto-islamique en Syrie-Jordanie (IVe-VIIIe siècles apr. J.-C.)*, ed. E. Villeneuve and P. Watson. Beirut: 207–14.

Nussbaum, M. C. (2000) *Women and Human Development: The Capabilities Approach*. Cambridge.
Nutton, V. (1969) "Medicine and the Roman army: a further reconsideration," *Medical History* 13: 260–70.
Nye, J. (2008) "Institutions and the institutional environment," in Brousseau and Glachant (eds.) 2008: 67–80.
Oakes, J. (1990) *Slavery and Freedom: An Interpretation of the Old South*. New York.
Ober, J. (2010) "Wealthy Hellas," *Transactions of the American Philological Association* 140: 241–86.
O'Connor, C. (1993) *Roman Bridges*. Cambridge.
Oded, B. (1979) *Mass Deportations and Deportees in the Neo-Assyrian Empire*. Wiesbaden.
Oleson, J. P. (1984) *Greek and Roman Mechanical Water-Lifting Devices: The History of a Technology*. Toronto.
(1988) "The technology of Roman harbours," *International Journal of Nautical Archaeology* 17: 147–57.
(2000) "Water-lifting," in *Handbook of Ancient Water Technology*, ed. Ö. Wikander. Leiden: 207–302.
(ed.) (2008) *The Oxford Handbook of Engineering and Technology in the Classical World*. New York.
Oliver, J. H. (1989) *Greek Constitutions of Early Roman Emperors from Inscriptions and Papyri*. Philadelphia.
Olson, M. (2000) *Power and Prosperity: Outgrowing Communist and Capitalist Dictatorships*. Oxford.
Ortalli, J. (2006) "Parva luxuria: qualità residenziali dell'insediamento rustico minore norditalico," in: *Vivere in villa: le qualità delle residenze agresti in età romana. Atti del convegno, Ferrara, gennaio 2003*. Florence: 261–83.
Osborne, R. (1991) "Pride and prejudice, sense and subsistence: exchange and society in the Greek city," in *City and Country in the Ancient World*, ed. J. Rich and A. Wallace-Hadrill. London: 119–45.
Östenberg, I. (2009) *Staging the World: Spoils, Captives, and Representations in the Roman Triumphal Procession*. Oxford.
Oxé, A., Comfort, H., and Kenrick, P. (2000) *Corpus Vasorum Arretinorum: A Catalogue of the Signatures, Shapes and Chronology of Italian Sigillata*. 2nd edn. Bonn.
Pacetti, F. (1998) "La questione delle Keay LII nell'ambito della produzione anforica in Italia," in Saguì (ed.) 1998a: 185–208.
Paine, R. R. and Storey, G. R. (1999) "Latin funerary inscriptions: another attempt at demographic analysis," in *Atti XI congresso internazionale di epigrafia greca e Latina*. Rome: 847–62.
(2006) "Epidemics, age at death, and mortality in ancient Rome," in Storey (ed.) 2006: 69–85.
Paine, R. R., Vargiu, R., Signoretti, C., and Coppa, A. (2009) "A health assessment for imperial Roman burials recovered from the necropolis of San Donato and Bivio CH, Urbino, Italy," *Journal of Anthropological Sciences* 87: 193–210.
Palmer, R. G. (1953) *Seneca's* De remediis fortuitorum *and the Elizabethans*. Chicago.
Pamuk, S. (2007) "The Black Death and the origins of the 'Great Divergence' across Europe, 1300–1600," *European Review of Economic History* 11: 289–317.
Panella, C. (1993) "Merci e scambi nel Mediterraneo tardoantico," in *Storia di Roma*, III.2, ed. A. Schiavone. Turin: 613–97.

Panella, C. and Saguì, L. (2001) "Consumo e produzione a Roma tra tardoantico e altomedioveo: le merci, i contesti," in *Roma nell'alto medioevo*. Spoleto: 757–820.
Panella, C. and Tchernia, A. (1994) "Produits agricoles transportés en amphores: l'huile et surtout le vin," in *L'Italie d'Auguste à Dioclétien*. Rome: 145–65 (English transl. in Scheidel and von Reden [eds.] [2002]: 173–89).
(2002) "Agricultural products transported in amphorae: oil and wine," in Scheidel and von Reden (eds.) 2002: 173–89.
Papathomas, A. (2006) "Zu den Luxusspeisen und -getränken in griechischen Papyri," *Zeitschrift für Papyrologie und Epigraphik* 158: 193–200.
Parker, A. J. (1992) *Ancient Shipwrecks of the Mediterranean and the Roman Provinces*. Oxford.
Paterson, A. M. and Broad, W. H. (1909) "Human skulls from Asia Minor," *Liverpool Annals of Archaeology and Anthropology* 2: 91–3.
Paterson, J. (1998) "Trade and traders in the Roman world: scale, structure and organization," in *Trade, Traders and the Ancient City*, ed. H. Parkins and C. Smith. London and New York: 149–67.
Patterson, O. (1982) *Slavery and Social Death: A Comparative Study*. Cambridge MA.
(1991) *Freedom. Vol. I: Freedom in the Making of Western Culture*. London.
Pavis d'Escurac, H. (1992) "Pline le Jeune et les lettres de recommandation," in *La mobilité sociale dans le monde romain*. Strasbourg: 55–69.
Peacock, D. P. S. (1982) *Pottery in the Roman World: An Ethnoarchaeological Approach*. London.
Peacock, D. P. S. and Williams, D. F. (1986) *Amphorae and the Roman Economy: An Introductory Guide*. London.
Pearson, M. N. (1991) "Merchants and states," in Tracy (ed.) 1991: 41–116.
Pecirka, D. (1970) "Excavations of farms and farmhouses in the chora of Chersonesus in the Crimea," *Eirene* 8: 123–74.
Pelizzon, S. (2000) "Grain flour, 1590–1790," *Review* 23: 87–195.
Peña, J. T. (1999) *The Urban Economy during the Early Dominate: Pottery Evidence from the Palatine Hill*. Oxford.
(2007) *Roman Pottery in the Archaeological Record*. Cambridge.
Peracci, F. (2008) "Height and economic development in Italy, 1730–1930," CEIS Tor Vergata Research Paper Series 108.
Persson, K. G. (1988) *Pre-Industrial Economic Growth: Social Organization and Technological Progress in Europe*. Oxford.
(1996) "The seven lean years, elasticity traps, and intervention in grain markets in pre-industrial Europe," *Economic History Review* 49: 692–714.
(1999) *Grain markets in Europe, 1500–1900: Integration and Deregulation*. Cambridge.
Phang, S. E. (2007) "Military documents, languages, and literacy," in *A Companion to the Roman Army*, ed. P. Erdkamp, Oxford: 286–305.
Photos-Jones, E., Hall, A. J., Atkinson, J. A., Tompsett, G., Cottier, A., and Sanders, G. D. R. (1999) "The Aghia Kyriaki, Melos Survey: prospecting for the elusive earths in the Roman period in the Aegean," *Annual of the British School at Athens* 94: 377–413.
Pieri, D. (2005) *Le commerce du vin oriental à l'époque byzantine (Ve – VIIe siècle): le temoignage des amphores en Gaule*. Paris.
(2007) "Les centres de production d'amphores en Méditerrannée orientale durant l'antiquité tardive," in Bonifay and Tréglia (eds.) 2007: 611–25.

Pikoulas, Y. (2007) "Travelling by land in Ancient Greece," in *Travel, Geography and Culture in Ancient Greece, Egypt and the Near East*, ed. C. E. P. Adams and J. Roy. Oxford: 78–87.

Pirenne, H. (1939) *Mohammed and Charlemagne*. London.

Pitts, M. (2008) "Globalizing the local in Roman Britain: an anthropological approach to social change," *Journal of Anthropological Archaeology* 27: 493–506.

Pitts, M. and Griffin, R. (2012) "Exploring health and social well-being in late Roman Britain: an intercemetery approach," *American Journal of Archaeology* 116: 253–76.

Pleket, H. (1983) "Urban elites and business in the Greek part of the Roman empire," *Münstersche Beiträge zur antiken Handelsgeschichte* 3: 3–35.

(1990) "Wirtschaft," in *Handbuch der Europäischen Wirtschafts- und Sozialgeschichte I: Europäische Wirtschafts- und Sozialgeschichte in der Kaiserzeit*, ed. F. Vittinghoff. Stuttgart: 25–160.

(1993a) "Agriculture in the Roman empire in comparative perspective," in *De Agricultura: In Memoriam Pieter Willem de Neeve (1945–1990)*, ed. H. van Sancisi-Weerdenburg, R. J. van der Spek, H. C. Teitler, and H. T. Wallinga. Amsterdam: 317–42.

(1993b) "Rome: a pre-industrial megalopolis," in: *Megalopolis. The Giant City in History*, ed. T. Barker and A. Sutcliffe. London: 14–35.

(1998) "Models and inscriptions: export of textiles in the Roman Empire," *Epigraphica Anatolica* 30: 117–28.

Poblome, J. (2004) "Italian sigillata in the Eastern Mediterranean," in *Early Italian Sigillata: The Chronological Framework and Trade Patterns. Proceedings of the First International ROCT-Congress, Leuven, May 7 and 8, 1999*, ed. J. Poblome, P. Talloen, R. Brulet, and M. Waelkens. Leuven: 17–30.

Pocock, J. G. A. (1975) *The Machiavellian Moment: Florentine Political Thought and the Atlantic Republican Tradition*. Princeton.

Pöhlmann, R. (1884) *Die Überbevölkerung der antiken Großstädte im Zusammenhange mit der Gesamtentwicklung städtischer Civilisation dargestellt*. Leipzig.

Polanyi, K. (1957) "The economy as instituted process," in Polanyi, Arensberg, and Pearson (eds.) (1957): 243–69.

(1977) *The Livelihood of Man*. New York.

Polanyi, K., Arensberg, C., and Pearson, H. (eds.) (1957) *Trade and Market in the Early Empires*. New York.

Pollard, N. (2000) *Soldiers, Cities and Civilians in Roman Syria*. Ann Arbor.

Polverini, L. (1964–5) "L'aspetto sociale del passaggio dalla repubblica al principato," *Aevum* 38–39: 241–85, 439–67, 77–100.

Pomey, P. and Tchernia, A. (1977) "Le tonnage maximum des navires de commerce romains," *Archaeonautica* 2: 233–51.

(1978) "Le tonnage maximum des navires de commerce romains," *Archaeonautica* 2: 233–51.

Ponsich, M. (1988) *Aceite de oliva y salazones de pescado. Factores geo-económicos de Bética y Tingitania*. Madrid.

Prachner, G. (1995) "Untersuchungen zum Verhältnis von Lösegeld-Forderungen für Kriegsgefangene im 4. und 3. Jahrhundert v.Chr., zu den Verkaufserlösen bei einer Auktion im Jahre 293 v.Chr. und Sklavenpreisen im italisch-sizilischen und griechischen Raum sowie in Ägypten," *Laverna* 6: 1–40.

Prag, J. R. W. (ed.) (2007) *Sicilia Nutrix Plebis Romanae: Rhetoric, Law, and Taxation in Cicero's Verrines*. London.

Prakash, O. (1999) "The Portuguese and the Dutch in Asian maritime trade: a comparative analysis," in *Merchants, Companies, and Trade: Europe and Asia in the Early Modern Era*, ed. S. Chaudhuri and M. Morineau. Cambridge: 175–88.

Prince, J. M. and Steckel, R. H. (2003) "Nutritional success on the Great Plains: nineteenth-century equestrian nomads," *Journal of Interdisciplinary History* 33: 353–84.

Pringsheim, F. (1950) *The Greek Law of Sale*. Weimar.

Pryor, J. H. (1988) *Geography, Technology and War: Studies in the Maritime History of the Mediterranean, 649–1571*. Cambridge.

Pucci, G. (1983) "Pottery and trade in the Roman period," in Garnsey, Hopkins and Whittaker (eds.) 1983: 105–17.

Pugliese, G. (1992) "Il diritto privato," in *Storia di Roma*, ed. E. Gabba and A. Schiavone, II.3. Turin: 153–210.

Purcell, N. (1990) "The creation of a provincial landscape: the Roman impact on Cisalpine Gaul," in *The Early Roman Empire in the West*, ed. T. Blagg and M. Millett. Oxford: 6–29.

(2005) "The ancient Mediterranean: the view from the customs house," in Harris (ed.) 2005: 200–32.

Quilici, L. (2008) "Land transport, part 1: roads and bridges," in Oleson (ed.) 2008: 551–79.

Quilici, L. and Quilici-Gigli, S. (eds.) (1995) *Interventi di bonifica agraria nell'Italia romana*. Rome.

Quilici-Gigli, S. (1992) "Opere di bonifica in relazione a tracciati viari," in *Tecnica stradale romana*. Rome: 73–81.

(1994) "The changing landscape of the Roman Campagna: lo sfruttamento del territorio in età imperiale," in Carlsen, Ørsted, and Skydsgaard (eds.) 1994: 135–43.

Raaflaub, K. (1996) "Born to be wolves? Origins of Roman imperialism," in *Transitions to Empire*, ed. R. W. Wallace and E. M. Harris. Norman OK: 273–314.

Raepsaet, G. (2002) *Attelages et techniques de transport dans le monde gréco-romaine*. Brussels.

Ramin, J. and Veyne, P. (1981) "Droit romain et société: les hommes libres qui passent pour esclaves et l'esclavage volontaire," *Historia* 30: 472–97.

Raskolnikoff, M. (1982) "La 'rivoluzione romana' e gli storici sovietici," in *La rivoluzione romana: inchiesta fra gli antichisti*. Naples: 51–65.

Rathbone, D. W. (1981) "The development of agriculture in the 'Ager Cosanus' during the Roman Republic: problems of evidence and interpretation," *Journal of Roman Studies* 71: 10–23.

(1983) "The slave mode of production in Italy," *Journal of Roman Studies* 73: 160–8.

(1989) "The ancient economy and Graeco-Roman Egypt," in *Egitto e storia antica dall'ellenismo all'età araba*, ed. L. Criscuolo and G. Geraci. Bologna: 159–76 (repr. in Scheidel and von Reden (eds.) 2002: 155–69).

(1990) "Villages, land, and population in Graeco-Roman Egypt," *Proceedings of the Cambridge Philological Society* 36: 103–42.

(1991) *Economic Rationalism and Rural Society in Third-Century A.D. Egypt: The Heroninos Archive and the Appianus Estate*. Cambridge.

(1996a) "The imperial finances," in *The Cambridge Ancient History*. 2nd edn. Vol. 10, ed. A. Bowman, E. Champlin, and A. Lintott. Cambridge: 309–23.

(1996b) "Monetization not price inflation," in *Coin Finds and Coin Use in the Roman World*, ed. C. E. King and D. G. Wigg. Frankfurt: 321–39.

(2000) "The 'Muziris' papyrus (*SB* XVIII 13167): financing Roman trade with India," *Bulletin de la Société Archéologique à Alexandrie* 46: 39–50.

(2003) "The financing of maritime commerce in the Roman Empire, I-II AD," in *Credito e moneta nel mondo Romano*, ed. E. Lo Cascio. Bari: 197–231.

(2005) "Economic rationalism and the Heroninos Archive," *Topoi Orient-Occident* 12–13: 261–9.

(2007) "Roman Egypt," in Scheidel, Morris, and Saller (eds.) 2007: 698–719.

(2009) "Earnings and costs: living standards and the Roman economy (first to third centuries AD)," in Bowman and Wilson (eds.) 2009: 299–326.

(2008) "Nero's reforms of *vectigalia* and the inscription of the *lex portorii Asiae*," in Cottier et al. (eds.) 2008: 251–78.

Rathbone, D. and Temin, P. (2008) "Financial intermediation in 1st-century AD Rome and 18th-century England," in *Bankers, Loans and Archives in the Ancient World*, ed. K. Verboven. Leuven: 371–419.

Rauh, N. (1986), "Cicero's business friendships: economics and politics in the Late Roman Republic," *Aevum* 60: 3–30.

(1993) *The Sacred Bonds of Commerce: Religion, Economy, and Trade Society at Hellenistic Roman Delos, 166–87 B.C.* Amsterdam.

Rautman, M. (2001) "Rural society and economy in late Roman Cyprus," in *Urban Centers and Rural Contexts in Late Antiquity*, ed. T. S. Burns and J. W. Eadie. East Lansing MI: 241–62.

Rautman, M. et al. (1999) "Amphoras and rooftiles from Late Roman Cyprus: a compositional study of calcareous ceramics from Kalavasos-Kopetra," *Journal of Roman Archaeology* 12: 377–91.

Rawls, J. (1971) *A Theory of Justice*. Cambridge MA.

Rawson, B. (2003) *Children and Childhood in Roman Italy*. Oxford.

Redknap, M. 1988. "Medieval pottery production at Mayen," in *Zur Keramik des Mittelalters und der beginnenden Neuzeit im Rheinland*, ed. D. R. M. Gaimster et al. Oxford: 3–37.

Redman, C. L., Crumley, C. L., Hassan, F. A., Hole, F., Morais, J., Riedel, F., Scarborough, V. L., Tainter, J. A., Turchin, P., and Yasuda, Y. (2007) "Group report: Millennial perspectives on the dynamic interactions of climate, people, and resources," in *Sustainability or Collapse? An Integrated History and Future of People on Earth*, ed. R. Costanza, L. J. Graumlich, and W. Steffen. Cambridge MA: 115–50.

Reduzzi Merola, F. (1990) *"Servo Parere": studi sulla condizione giuridica degli schiavi vicari e dei sottoposti a schiavi nelle esperienze greca e romana*. Camerino.

Reger, G. (1993) "The public purchase of grain on independent Delos," *Classical Antiquity* 12: 300–34.

(1994) *Regionalism and Exchange in the Economy of Independent Delos, 314–167 BC*. Berkeley.

Reynolds, P. (1995) *Trade in the Western Mediterranean A.D. 400–700: The Ceramic Evidence*. Oxford.

(2003) "Pottery and the economy in eighth-century Beirut: an Umayyad assemblage from the Roman imperial baths," in Bakirtzis (ed.) 2003: 725–35.

(2005a) "Levantine amphorae from Cilicia to Gaza: a typology and analysis of regional production trends from the 1st to 7th centuries," in J. Ma. Gurt I Esparraguera, J. Buxeda I Garrigós, and M. A. Cau Ontiveros (eds.), *LRCW I. Late Roman Coarse Wares, Cooking Wares and Amphorae in the Mediterranean: archaeology and archaeometry*. 2005: 563–611.

(2005b) "Hispania in the late Roman Mediterranean: ceramics and trade," in *Hispania in Late Antiquity*, ed. M. Kulikowski and K. Bowes. Leiden: 369–486.

(2010) *Hispania and the Roman Mediterranean AD 100–700. Ceramics and Trade*. London.

Richman, B. D. (2004) "Firms, courts, and reputation mechanisms: towards a positive theory of private ordering," *Columbia Law Review* 104: 2328–67.

(2006) "How communities create economic advantage: Jewish diamond merchants in New York," *Law and Social Inquiry* 31: 383–420.

Rickman, G. E. (1980) *The Corn Supply of Ancient Rome*. Oxford.

(2008) "Ports, ships, and power in the Roman world," in *The Maritime World of Ancient Rome*, ed. R. L. Hohlfelder. Ann Arbor: 5–20.

Rigoir, Y. (1998) "Les dérivées-des-sigillées paléochrétiennes," in Saguì (ed.) 1998a: 101–7.

Riising, A. (1952) "The fate of Henri Pirenne's thesis on the consequences of Islamic expansion," *Classica et Mediaevalia* 13: 87–130.

Riley, J. A. (1979) "The coarse pottery," in *Excavations at Sidi Khrebish Benghazi (Berenice)*, II, ed. J. A. Lloyd. Tripoli: 91–467.

Riley, J. C. (1994) "Height, nutrition, and mortality risk reconsidered," *Journal of Interdisciplinary History* 24: 465–92.

Ringrose, D. R. (1970) *Transportation and Economic Stagnation in Spain, 1750–1850*. Durham NC.

Ritti, T., Grewe, K., and Kessener, P. (2007) "A relief of a water-powered stone saw mill on a sarcophagus at Hierapolis and its implications," *Journal of Roman Archaeology* 20: 138–63.

Rizzelli, G. (1998–9) "Lo schiavo romano: immaginario sociale e diritto," *Bullettino dell'Istituto di Diritto Romano* 101–2: 227–51.

Roberts, C. and Cox, M. (2003) *Health and Disease in Britain: From Prehistory to the Present Day*. Thrupp.

Robinson, D. M. (1924) "A Preliminary Report on the Excavations at Pisidian Antioch and at Sizma," *American Journal of Archaeology* 28: 435–44.

Robinson, D. and Wilson, A. (eds.) (2011) *Maritime Archaeology and Ancient Trade in the Mediterranean*. Oxford.

Rodríguez Almeida, E. (1984) *Il Monte Testaccio: ambiente, storia, materiali*. Roma.

Romei, D. (2004) "Produzione e circolazione dei manufatti ceramici a Roma nell'alto medioevo," in *Roma dall'antichità al medioevo, II, Contesti tardoantichi e altomedievali*, ed. L. Paroli and L. Venditelli. Milan: 278–311.

Rook, T. (1993a) "How to fire a Roman bath; or, the confessions of a fornacator," *Current Archaeology*, August/September: 114–7.

(1993b) "'X' marks the spot: fuel trials at Xanten," *Balnearia* 1.2: 3–6.

(1994) "Fuel corrections," *Current Archaeology* 2: 7.

Rosenstein, N. (2008) "Aristocrats and agriculture in the Middle and Late Republic," *Journal of Roman Studies* 98: 1–26.

Rosenzweig, M. (1994) "Human capital accumulation, the family, and economic development," in *Human Capital and Economic Development*, ed. S. Asefa and W.-C. Huang. Kalamazoo MI: 63–90.

Rosivach, V. (1993) "Agricultural slavery in the Northern colonies and in classical Athens: some comparisons," *Comparative Studies in Society and History* 35: 551–67.

Rosser, G. (1997) "Crafts, guilds, and the negotiation of work in the medieval town," *Past and Present* 154: 3–31.

Rossiter, J. J. (1978) *Roman Farm Buildings in Italy*. Oxford.

Rostovtzeff, M. I. (1957) *The Social and Economic History of the Roman Empire*. 2nd edn. revised by P. Fraser. Oxford.

Roth, U. (2007) *Thinking Tools: Agricultural Slavery between Evidence and Models*. London.

Rotman, Y. (2009) *Byzantine Slavery and the Mediterranean World*. Cambridge MA.

Rougé, J. (1957) "Ad ciconias nixas," *Revue des Études Anciennes* 59: 320–8.

(1966) *Recherches sur l'organisation du commerce maritime en Méditerranée sous l'empire romaine*. Paris.

Rowlandson, J. (1996) *Landowners and Tenants in Roman Egypt: The Social Relations of Agriculture in the Oxyrhynchite Nome*. Oxford.

Ruffing, K. and Drexhage, H.-J. (2008) "Antike Sklavenpreise," in *Antike Lebenswelten: Konstanz – Wandel – Wirkungsmacht*, ed. P. Mauritsch et al. Wiesbaden: 321–51.

Rupprecht, H.-A. (1994) *Kleine Einführung in die Papyruskunde*. Darmstadt.

Russell, B. (2009) "The dynamics of stone transport between the Roman Mediterranean and its hinterland," *Facta* 2: 107–26.

(2011) "Lapis transmarinus: stone-carrying ships and the maritime distribution of stone in the Roman empire," in Robinson and Wilson (eds.) 2011: 139–55.

Russu, I. I. (1975) *Inscritile Daciei Romane:* Vol. I: *Introducere Istorica si Epigraphica Diplomele Militare & Tablitele Cerate*. Bucarest.

Sachs, J. and Malaney, P. (2002) "The economic and social burden of malaria," *Nature* 415: 680–5.

Sadori, L. et al. (2009) "The introduction and diffusion of the peach in ancient Italy," in *Plants and Culture: Seeds of the Cultural Heritage of Europe*. Bari: 45–61.

Safrai, Z. (1994) *The Economy of Roman Palestine*. London.

Saguì, L. (ed.) (1998a) *Ceramica in Italia: VI-VII secolo: atti del convegno in onore di John Hayes*. Florence.

(1998b) "Il deposito della Crypta Balbi: una testimonianza imprevedibile sulla Roma del VII secolo," in Saguì (ed.) 1998a: 305–30.

(2002) "Roma, i centri privilegiati e la lunga durata della tarda antichità," *Archeologia Medievale* 29: 7–42.

Ste Croix, G. E. M. de (1956) "Greek and Roman accounting," in *Studies in the History of Accounting*, ed. A. C. Littleton and B. S. Yamey. London: 14–74.

(1981) *The Class Struggle in the Ancient World from the Archaic Age to the Arab Conquests*. London.

Sakamoto-Momiyama, M. (1997) *Seasonality in Human Mortality: A Medico-Geographical Study*. Tokyo.

Salinas, A. (1900) "Racalmuto - scoperta di forme romane inscritte, per lastroni di zolfo," *Notizie degli scavi di antichità 1900*: 659–60.

Sallares, R. (1991) *The Ecology of the Ancient Greek World*. London.
(2002) *Malaria and Rome: A History of Malaria in Ancient Italy*. Oxford.
(2007) "Ecology," in Scheidel, Morris, and Saller (eds.) 2007: 15–37.
Saller, R. P. (2002) "Framing the debate over growth in the ancient economy," in Scheidel and von Reden (eds.) 2002: 251–69 (repr. in Manning and Morris [eds.] 2005: 223–38).
(2003) "Women, slaves, and the economy of the Roman household," in *Early Christian Families in Context: An Interdisciplinary Dialogue*, ed. D. L. Balch and C. Osiek. Grand Rapids MI: 185–204.
(2007) "Household and gender," in Scheidel, Morris, and Saller (eds.) 2007: 87–112.
Salmeri, G. (2011) "The emblematic province – Sicily from the Roman Empire to the Kingdom of the Two Sicilies," in *Tributary Empires in Global History*, ed. P. F. Bang and C. A. Bayly. Basingstoke and New York: 151–68.
Salvadei, L, Ricci, F., and Manzi, G. (2001) "Porotic hyperostosis as a marker of health and nutritional conditions during childhood: studies at the transition between imperial Rome and the early Middle Ages," *American Journal of Human Biology* 13: 709–17.
Sarris, P. (2002) "The Justinianic plague: origins and effects," *Continuity and Change* 17: 169–82.
(2004) "The origins of the manorial economy: new insights from late antiquity," *English Historical Review* 119: 279–311.
(2006) *Economy and Society in the Age of Justinian*. Cambridge.
Scheidel, W. (1994a) "Grain cultivation in the villa economy of Roman Italy," in Carlsen, Ørsted, and Skydsgaard (eds.) 1994: 159–66.
(1994b) "Libitina's bitter gains: seasonal mortality and endemic disease in the ancient city of Rome," *Ancient Society* 25: 151–175.
(1996a) *Measuring Sex, Age and Death in the Roman Empire: Explorations in Ancient Demography*. Ann Arbor.
(1996b) "Reflections on the differential valuation of slaves in Diocletian's price edict and in the United States," *Münstersche Beiträge zur Antiken Handelsgeschichte* 15: 67–79.
(1997) "Quantifying the sources of slaves in the early Roman empire," *Journal of Roman Studies* 87: 156–69.
(1999) "Emperors, aristocrats and the Grim Reaper: towards a demographic profile of the Roman élite," *Classical Quarterly* 49: 254–281.
(2001a) *Death on the Nile: Disease and the Demography of Roman Egypt*. Leiden.
(2001b) "Progress and problems in Roman demography," in *Debating Roman Demography*, ed. W. Scheidel. Leiden: 1–81.
(2001c) "Roman age structure: evidence and models," *Journal of Roman Studies* 91: 1–26.
(2002) "A model of demographic and economic change in Roman Egypt after the Antonine Plague," *Journal of Roman Archaeology* 15: 97–114.
(2003) "Germs for Rome," in Edwards and Woolf (eds.) 2003: 158–76.
(2004a) "Human mobility in Roman Italy, I: the free population," *Journal of Roman Studies* 94: 1–26.
(2004b) "Creating a metropolis: a comparative demographic perspective," in *Ancient Alexandria between Egypt and Greece*, ed. W. V. Harris and G. Ruffini. Leiden: 1–31.

(2005a) "Human mobility in Roman Italy, II: the slave population," *Journal of Roman Studies* 95: 64–79.

(2005b) "Real slave prices and the relative cost of slave labor in the Greco-Roman world," *Ancient Society* 35: 1–17.

(2007a) "Demography," in Scheidel, Morris, and Saller (eds.) (2007): 38–86.

(2007b) "A model of real income growth in Roman Italy," *Historia* 56: 322–46.

(2007c) "Roman funerary commemoration and the age at first marriage," *Classical Philology* 102: 389–402.

(2008a) "Roman population size: the logic of the debate," in De Ligt and Northwood (eds.) 2008: 17–70.

(2008b) "The comparative economics of slavery in the Greco-Roman world," in Dal Lago and Katsari (eds.) 2008: 105–26.

(2009a) "In search of Roman economic growth," *Journal of Roman Archaeology* 22: 46–70.

(2009b) "The monetary systems of the Han and Roman empires," in *Rome and China: Comparative Perspectives on Ancient World Empires*, ed. W. Scheidel. New York: 137–207.

(2010) "Real wages in early economies: evidence for living standards from 1800 BCE to 1300 CE," *Journal of the Economic and Social History of the Orient* 53: 425–62.

(2011a) "A comparative perspective on the determinants of the scale and productivity of maritime trade in the Roman Mediterranean," in *Maritime Technology in the Ancient Economy: Ship Design and Navigation*, ed. W. V. Harris and K. Iara. Portsmouth RI: 21–38.

(2011b) "The Roman slave supply," in Bradley and Cartledge (eds.) (2011): 287–310.

(forthcoming a) "Epigraphy and demography: birth, marriage, family, and death," in *Epigraphy and the Historical Sciences*, ed. J. Davies and J. Wilkes. Oxford.

(forthcoming b) "Disease and death," in *The Cambridge Companion to Ancient Rome*, ed. P. Erdkamp. Cambridge.

(forthcoming c) "Roman wellbeing and the economic consequences of the Antonine Plague," in Lo Cascio (ed.) forthcoming.

Scheidel, W. and Friesen, S. J. (2009) "The size of the economy and the distribution of income in the Roman empire," *Journal of Roman Studies* 99: 61–91.

Scheidel, W., Morris, I., and Saller, R. (eds.) (2007) *The Cambridge Economic History of the Greco-Roman World*. Cambridge.

Scheidel, W. and von Reden, S. (eds.) (2002) *The Ancient Economy*. Edinburgh.

Schiavone, A. (1992) "Il pensiero giuridico fra scienza del diritto e potere imperiale," in *Storia di Roma* II.3, ed. E. Gabba and A. Schiavone. Turin: 7–84.

(1996) *La storia spezzata*. Bari (Engl. transl as Schiavone [2000]).

(2000) *The End of the Past: Ancient Rome and the Modern West*. Cambridge MA.

Schneider, H. (2007) "Technology," in Scheidel, Morris, and Saller (eds.) 2007: 144–71.

Schörle, K. (2008) "The Roman exploitation of the Eastern Desert of Egypt." MPhil thesis, University of Oxford.

(2011) "From harbour to desert: an integrated interface on the Red Sea and its impact on the Eastern Egyptian Desert," *Bolletino di Archeologia Online* 2011: http://151.12.58.75/archeologia/.

Schumpeter, J. A. (2010 [1942]) *Capitalism, Socialism and Democracy*. Abingdon.

Schwarz, L. D. (1992) *London in the Age of Industrialisation: Entrepreneurs, Labour Force, and Living Conditions, 1700–1850*. Cambridge.

Scobie, A. (1986) "Slums, sanitation, and mortality in the Roman world," *Klio* 68: 399–433.

Seigne, J. (2002) "A sixth-century waterpowered sawmill at Jerash," *Annual of the Department of Antiquities of Jordan* 46: 205–13.

Seland, E. H. (2010) *Ports and Political Power in the* Periplus*: Complex Societies and Maritime Trade on the Indian Ocean in the First Century AD*. Oxford.

Setälä, P. (1977) *Private* Domini *in Roman Brick Stamps of the Empire: A Historical and Prosopographical Study of Landowners in the District of Rome*. Helsinki.

Shatzman, I. (1975) *Senatorial Wealth and Roman Politics*. Brussels.

Shaw, B. D. (1996) "Seasons of death: aspects of mortality in imperial Rome," *Journal of Roman Studies* 86: 100–38.

(1998) "'A wolf by the ears': M. I. Finley's *Ancient Slavery and Modern Ideology* in historical context," in Finley 1998: 3–74.

(2001) "Challenging Braudel: a new vision of the Mediterranean," *Journal of Roman Archaeology* 14: 419–53.

(2006) "Seasonal mortality in imperial Rome and the Mediterranean: three problem cases," in Storey (ed.) 2006: 86–109.

(2008) "After Rome: transformations of the early Mediterranean world," *New Left Review* 51: 89–114.

Shaw, I., Bunbury, J., and Jameson, R. (1999) "Emerald mining in Roman and Byzantine Egypt," *Journal of Roman Archaeology* 12: 203–15.

Shaw, I. and Jameson, R. (1993) "Amethyst mining in the Eastern Desert: a preliminary survey at Wadi el-Hudi," *Journal of Egyptian Archaeology* 79: 81–97.

Sherk, R. K. (1988) *The Roman Empire: Augustus to Hadrian*. Cambridge.

Sherwin-White, A. N. (1972) "The Roman citizenship: a survey of its development into a world franchise," in *Aufstieg und Niedergang der Römischen Welt*, 1.2. Berlin and New York: 23–58.

(1985) *The Letters of Pliny*. Oxford.

Shortland, A., Schachner, L., Freestone, I., and Tite, M. (2006) "Natron as a flux in the early vitreous materials industry: sources, beginnings and reasons for decline," *Journal of Archaeological Science* 33: 521–30.

Sidebotham, S. E. (1986a) "Ports of the Red Sea and the Arabia-India trade," *MBAH* 5.2: 16–36.

(1986b) *Roman Economic Policy in the Erythra Thalassa 30 B.C.-A.D. 217*. Leiden.

(1996) "Roman interests in the Red Sea and Indian Ocean," in J. E. Reade (ed.), *The Indian Ocean in Antiquity* (London) 290–308.

(2011) *Berenike and the Ancient Maritime Spice Route*. Berkeley.

Sidebotham, S. E., Hense, M., and Nouwens, H. M. (2008) *The Red Land: The Illustrated Archaeology of Egypt's Eastern Desert*. Cairo.

Sidebotham, S. E. and Zitterkopf, R. E. (1995) "Routes through the Eastern Desert of Egypt," *Expedition* 37: 39.

Sidebotham, S. E., Zitterkopf, R. E., and Helm, C. C. (1998) "Survey of the Via Hadriana: the 1998 season," *Journal of the American Research Center in Egypt* 37: 115.

Sidebotham, S. E., Zitterkopf, R. E., and Riley, J. A. (1991) "Survey of the Abu Sha'ar-Nile road," *American Journal of Archaeology* 95: 571–622.

Sijpesteijn, P. (1987) *Customs Duties in Graeco-Roman Egypt*. Zutphen.

Sillièrres, P. (1990) *Les voies de communication de l'Hispanie méridionale*. Paris.

Silver, M. (2006) "Skilled slaves, tenants and market information in the transformation of agricultural organization in Late Republican Rome," *Münstersche Beiträge zur Antiken Handelsgeschichte* 25: 29–48.

(2007) "Roman economic growth and living standards: perceptions versus evidence," *Ancient Society* 37: 191–252.

(2008) "The rise, demise, and (partial) rehabilitation of the peasant in Hopkins' model of Roman trade and taxes," *Classics Ireland* 15: 1–33.

(2009a) "Historical otherness, the Roman bazaar, and primitivism: P. F. Bang on the Roman economy," *Journal of Roman Archaeology* 22: 421–43.

(2009b) "Must frequently performed economic services have distinctive names? A probe of Finley's hypothesis," *Historia* 58: 246–56.

Sion, J. (1935) "Quelques problèmes de transports dans l'antiquité: le point de vue d'une géographie méditerranéenne," *Annales d'histoire économique et sociale* 6: 628–33.

Sippel, D. V. (1987) "Some observations on the means and cost of transport of bulk commodities in the Late Republic and Early Empire," *Ancient World* 16: 35–45.

Sirks, B. (1991) *Food for Rome: The Legal Structure of the Transportation and Processing of Supplies for the Imperial Distributions in Rome and Constantinople*. Amsterdam.

Skinner, Q. (2009) "Making history: the discipline in perspective: interview with Professor Quentin Skinner," *Storia e Politica* 1: 113–34.

(1989) "Ausonius' saw-mills – once more," *ORom* 17: 185–90.

Smelser, N. J. and Swedberg, R. (eds.) (2005a) *The Handbook of Economic Sociology*. 2nd edn. Princeton.

(2005b) "Introducing Economic Sociology," in Smelser and Swedberg (eds.) (2005): 3–25.

Smith, A. (1976) *An Inquiry into the Nature and Causes of the Wealth of Nations*. 2 vols. Oxford.

Smith, W. (2001) "Environmental sampling (1990–94)," in *Leptiminus (Lamta): A Roman Port City in Tunisia*, ed. L. M. Stirling, D. J. Mattingly, and N. Ben Lazreg. Ann Arbor: 420–41.

Smuts, W. and Stromback, T. (2001) *The Economics of the Apprenticeship System*. Cheltenham.

Sodini, J.-P. (2000) "Productions et échanges dans le monde protobyzantin (IVe-VIIe s.): le cas de la céramique," in *Byzanz als Raum*, ed. K. Belke et al. Vienna: 181–208.

Sodini, J.-P. and Villeneuve, E. (1992) "Le passage de la céramique byzantine à la céramique omeyyade en Syrie du Nord, en Palestine et en Transjordanie," in *La Syrie de Byzance à l'Islam, VIIe-VIIIe siècles*, ed. P. Canivet and J.-P. Rey-Coquais. Damascus: 195–218.

Sonenscher, M. (1989) *Work and Wages: Natural Law, Politics, and the Eighteenth-Century French Trades*. Cambridge.

Souza, P. de (1999) *Piracy in the Graeco-Roman World*. Cambridge.

Spagnuolo Vigorita, T. (1993) "Cittadini e sudditi tra II e III secolo," in *Storia di Roma* III.1, ed. A. Carandini, L. Cracco Ruggini, and A. Giardina. Turin: 5–50.

Sperber, D. (1998) *The City in Roman Palestine*. Oxford.

Spruytte, J. (1983) *Early Harness Systems: Experimental Studies: Contribution to the Study of the Ancient Horse*. London.

Spurr, M. S. (1986) *Arable Cultivation in Roman Italy c.*200 B.C.-*c.A.D.100*. London.

Squatriti, P. (2002) "Review article: Mohammed, the early medieval Mediterranean, and Charlemagne," *Early Medieval Europe* 11: 263–79.

Staerman, E. and Trofimova, M. (1975) *La schiavitù nell'Italia imperiale*. Rome.

Staerman, E. M., Smirin, V. M., Belova, N. N., and Kolosovskaja, J. K. (1987) *Die Sklaverei in den westlichen Provinzen des römischen Reiches im 1.-3. Jahrhundert*. Stuttgart.

Steckel, R. H. (1995) "Stature and standard of living," *Journal of Economic Literature* 33: 1903–40.

(2008) "Biological measures of the standard of living," *Journal of Economic Perspectives* 22: 129–52.

(2009) "Heights and human welfare: recent developments and new directions," *Explorations in Economic History* 46: 1–23.

Steckel, R. H. and Floud, R. (1997) *Health and Welfare during Industrialization*. Chicago.

Steensgard, N. (1973) *Carracks, Caravans and Companies: The Structural Crisis in the European-Asian Trade in the Early 17th century*. Copenhagen.

(1981) "Violence and the rise of capitalism: Frederic C. Lane's theory of protection and tribute," *Review* 5.2: 247–73.

(1990) "The growth and composition of the long-distance trade of England and the Dutch Republic before 1750," in Tracy (ed.) 1990: 102–52.

Stephan, R. S. (2008) "The height of the Romans: stature and standards of living in ancient Britain." Seminar paper, Stanford University.

Stiglitz, J. E. (1989) "Markets, market failures, and development," *American Economic Review* 79: 197–210.

Stirling, L. M. and Ben Lazreg, N. (2001) "A Roman kiln complex (Site 290): preliminary results of excavations, 1995–98," in *Leptiminus (Lamta): A Roman Port City in Tunisia*, ed. L. M. Stirling, D. J. Mattingly, and N. Ben Lazreg. Ann Arbor: 220–35.

Storey, G. R. (ed.) (2006) *Urbanism in the Preindustrial World: Cross-Cultural Approaches*. Tuscaloosa AL.

Straus, J. A. (1973) "Deux notes sur l'affranchissement," *Zeitschrift für Papyrologie und Epigraphik* 11: 143–6.

Strong, D. E. (1966) *Greek and Roman Gold and Silver Plate*. Ithaca NY.

Subrahmanyam, S. and Thomas, L. F. F. R. (1991) "Evolution of empire: the Portuguese in the Indian Ocean during the sixteenth century," in Tracy (ed.) 1991: 298–331.

Tate, G. (1992) *Les campagnes de la Syrie du Nord du IIe au VIIe siècle: un exemple d'expansion démographique et économique à la fin de l'antiquité*, I. Paris.

Tchalenko, G. (1953–8) *Villages antiques de la Syrie du Nord: le massif du Bélus à l'époque romaine*. 3 vols. Paris.

Tchernia, A. (1983) "Italian wine in Gaul at the end of the Republic," in Garnsey, Hopkins, and Whittaker (eds.) 1983: 87–104.

(1986) *Le vin de l'Italie romaine: essai d'histoire économique d'après les amphores*. Rome.

(1989) "Encore sur les modèles économiques et les amphores," in *Amphores romaines et histoire économique: dix ans de recherche*. Rome: 529–36.

(1992) "Le dromadaire des Peticii," *Mélanges de l'École Francaise de Rome* 104: 293–301.

(2010) "L'exportation du vin : interpretations actuelles de l'exception gauloise," in *Agricoltura e scambi nell'Italia Tardo-Repubblicana*, ed. J. Carlsen and E. Lo Cascio. Bari: 91–114.

(2011) *Les Romains et le commerce*. Naples.

Temin, P. (1980) "Modes of behavior," *Journal of Economic Behavior and Organization* 1: 175–95.

(2001) "A market economy in the early Roman empire," *Journal of Roman Studies* 91: 169–81.

(2002) "Price behavior in ancient Babylon," *Explorations in Economic History* 39: 46–60.

(2004a) "Financial intermediation in the early Roman empire," *Journal of Economic History* 64: 705–33.

(2004b) "The labor market of the early Roman empire," *Journal of Interdisciplinary History* 34: 513–38.

(2006a) "Estimating GDP in the early Roman Empire," in Lo Cascio (ed.) 2006a: 31–54.

(2006b) "Mediterranean Trade in Biblical Times," in *Eli Heckscher, International Trade, and Economic History*. eds. R. Findlay, R. G. H. Henriksson, H. Lindgren, and M. Lundahl. Cambridge MA: 141–56.

(2009) Review of Bang 2008, *Journal of Economic History* 69: 1165–6.

(forthcoming a) *The Economics of Antiquity*. Princeton.

(forthcoming b) "Growth theory for ancient economies," in *Economic Growth in Classical Antiquity*, ed. W. Jongman.

Terrenato, N. (2001) "The Auditorium site in Rome and the origins of the villa," *Journal of Roman Archaeology* 14: 5–32.

Thompson, F. H. (2003) *The Archaeology of Greek and Roman Slavery*. London.

Thurmond, D. (2006) *A Handbook of Ancient Food Processing: For Her Bounty No Winter*. Leiden.

Tilly, C. (1992) *Coercion, Capital, and European States, AD 990–1992*. Oxford.

Toman, J. T. (2005) "The gang system and comparative advantage," *Explorations in Economic History* 42: 310–23.

Tomber, R. (2008) *Indo-Roman Trade: From Pots to Pepper*. London.

Tozzi, G. (1961) *Economisti greci e romani*. Milan.

Tracy, J. (ed.) (1990) *The Rise of Merchant Empires: Long-Distance Trade in the Early Modern World 1350–1750*. Cambridge.

(ed.) (1991) *The Political Economy of Merchant Empires: State Power and World Trade 1350–1750*. Cambridge.

Treggiari, S. (1969) *Roman Freedmen during the Late Republic*. Oxford.

(1975) "Jobs in the household of Livia," *Papers of the British School at Rome* 43: 48–77.

(1979) "Lower class women in the Roman economy," *Florilegium* 1: 65–86.

(1980) "Urban Labour in Rome: Mercennarii and Tabernarii," in Garnsey (ed.) 1980: 48–64.

Trombley, F. R. (1987) "Korykos in Cilicia Trachis: the economy of a small coastal city in late antiquity (saec. V-VI)," *Ancient History Bulletin* 1: 16–23.

True, A. C. (1929) *A History of Agricultural Education in the United States 1875–1925*. Washington, D.C.

Turchin, P. and Nefedov, S. A. (2009) *Secular Cycles*. Princeton.

Turley, D. (2000) *Slavery*. Oxford.

Turner, E. G. (1954) "Tiberius Julius Alexander," *Journal of Roman Studies* 44: 54–64.
Udovitch, A. L. (1978) "Time, the sea and society: duration of commercial voyages on the southern shores of the Mediterranean during the high Middle Ages," *Settimane di Studio del Centro Italiano di Studi sull Alto Medioevo*, 25. Spoleto: 503–46, with 547–63.
Uggeri, G. (1987) "La navigazione interna della Cisalpina in età romana," *Antichità Alto-Adriatiche* 19: 305–54.
Uscatescu, A. (2003) "Report on the Levant pottery (5th-9th century AD)," in Bakirtzis (ed.) 2003: 546–58.
Van Dam, R. (1985) *Leadership and Community in Late Antique Gaul*. Berkeley.
Van der Veen, M. (1998) "A life of luxury in the desert? The food and fodder supply to Mons Claudianus," *Journal of Roman Archaeology* 11: 101–16.
Van Gelderen, M. and Skinner, Q. (2002) *Republicanism: A Shared European Heritage*. Cambridge.
Van Minnen, P. (1987) "Urban craftsmen in Roman Egypt," *Münstersche Beiträge zur antiken Handelgeschichte* 6: 31–88.
Van Nijf, O. M. (2002) "*Collegia* and civic guards: two chapters in the history of sociability," in *After the Past: Essays in Ancient History in Honour of H. W. Pleket*, ed. W. Jongman and M. Kleijwegt. Leiden: 305–39.
(2008) "The social world of tax farmers and their personnel," in Cottier et al. (eds.) 2008: 279–311.
Van Rengen, W. (1995) "A new Paneion at Mons Porphyrites," *Chronique d'Egypte* 70: 139–140, 240–5.
Van Wees, H. (2003) "Conquerors and serfs: wars of conquest and forced labour in archaic Greece," in *Helots and their Masters in Laconia and Messenia: Histories, Ideologies, Structures*, ed. N. Luraghi and S. E. Alcock. Cambridge MA: 33–80.
Vélissaropoulos, J. (1980) *Les nauclères Grecs: recherches sur les institutions maritimes en Grèce et dans l'Orient hellénisé*. Geneva.
Vera, V. (1995) "Dalla villa perfecta alla villa di Palladio: sulle trasformazioni del sistema agrario in Italia fra principato e dominato," *Athenaeum* 83: 189–211, 331–56.
Vera, D. (1997–8) "Fra Egitto ed Africa, fra Roma e Costantinopoli, fra annona e commercio: la Sicilia nel Mediterraneo tardoantico," *Kokalos* 43–4: 33–72.
Verboven, K. (2002) *The Economy of Friends: Economic Aspects of Amicitia and Patronage in the Late Republic*. Brussels.
(2007) "The associative order: status and ethos among Roman businessmen in the late Republic and early Empire," *Athenaeum* 95: 861–93.
Verhulst, A. (2002) *The Carolingian Economy*. Cambridge.
Veyne, P. (1961) "Vie de Trimalcion," *Annales ESC* 16: 213–47.
(1991) *La société romaine*. Paris.
(2003) *Seneca: The Life of a Stoic*. New York and London.
Vidman, L. (1960) *Étude sur la correspondance de Pline le jeune avec Trajan*. Prague.
Villeneuve, F. (2004) "Une inscription latine sur l'archipel Farasan, Arabie Séoudite, sud de la Mer Rouge," *Comptes Rendus de l'Académie des Inscriptions et Belles-Lettres* 2004: 419–29.
Viner, J. (1960) "The intellectual history of laissez faire," *Journal of Law and Economics* 3: 45–69.

Vivenza, G. (1994) *Divisioni agrimensore e tributi fondiari nel mondo antico*. Padua.
(1998a) "Geminiano Montanari e l'eredità di Aristotele," *Nuova Economia e Storia* 4: 69–79.
(1998b) "Roman thought on economics and justice," in *Ancient and Medieval Economic Ideas and Concepts of Social Justice*, ed. S.T. Lowry and B. Gordon. Leiden: 269–331.
(1999) "Translating Aristotle: at the origin of the terminology and content of economic value," in *Incommensurability and Translation: Kuhnian Perspectives on Scientific Communication and Theory Change*, ed. R. Rossini Favretti, G. Sandri, and R. Scazzieri. Cheltenham: 131–56.
(2000) "La terra e l'agricoltura: i molti aspetti della "risorsa" di base nel mondo romano," in *Agricoltura, musei, trasmissione dei saperi*, ed. G. Volpato. Verona: 87–101.

Vokaer, A. (2009) "Brittle ware trade in Syria between the 5th and 8th centuries," in Mango (ed.) 2009: 121–36.

Volkmann, H. (1990) *Die Massenversklavungen der Einwohner eroberter Städte in der hellenistisch-römischen Zeit*. 2nd edn. Stuttgart.

Von Petrikovits, H. (1981) "Die Spezialisierung des römischen Handwerks," in *Das Handwerk in vor- und frühgeschichtlicher Zeit, I: Historische und rechtshistorische Beiträge und Untersuchungen zur Frühgeschichte der Gilde*, ed. H. von Jankuhn. Göttingen: 63–132.

Von Reden, S. (2007) *Money in Ptolemaic Egypt*. Cambridge.
(2010) *Money in Classical Antiquity*. Cambridge.

Wagner-Hasel, B. (2011) *Die Arbeit des Gelehrten: Der Nationalökonom Karl Bücher (1847–1930)*. Frankfurt.

Waldstein, W. (1986) *Operae Libertorum: Untersuchungen zur Dienstpflicht freigelassener Sklaven*. Stuttgart.

Walker, P. L., Bathurst, R. R., Richman, R., Gjerdrum, T., and Andrushko, V. A. (2009) "The causes of porotic hyperostosis and cribra orbitalia: a reappraisal of the iron deficiency-anemia hypothesis," *American Journal of Physical Anthropology* 139: 109–25.

Wallace-Hadrill, A. (1997) "*Mutatio morum*: the idea of cultural revolution," in *The Roman Cultural Revolution*, ed. T. Habinek and A. Schiesaro. Cambridge: 3–22.
(2008) *Rome's Cultural Revolution*. Cambridge.

Wallerstein, I. (1974) *The Modern World-System, Vol. 1: Capitalist Agriculture and the Origins of the European World-Economy in the Sixteenth Century*. New York.

Walmsley, A. (1996) "Byzantine Palestine and Arabia: urban prosperity in late antiquity," in *Towns in Transition: Urban Evolution in Late Antiquity and the Early Middle Ages*, ed. N. Christie and S. T. Loseby. Aldershot: 126–58.
(2000) "Production, exchange and regional trade in the Islamic east Mediterranean: old structures, new systems?," in Wickham and Hansen (eds.) 2000: 265–343.
(2001) "Turning east: the appearance of Islamic Cream Ware in Jordan: the 'end of antiquity,'" in *La céramique byzantine et proto-islamique en Syrie-Jordanie (IVe – VIIIe siècles après J.-C.)*, ed. E. Villeneuve and P. Watson. Beirut: 305–13.
(2007) *Early Islamic Syria*. London.

Waltzing, J. P. (1895–1900) *Étude historique sur les corporations professionnelles chez les Romains depuis les origines jusqu'à la chute de l'Empire d'Occident*. 4 vols. Louvain.

Ward-Perkins, B. (2000) "Specialised production and exchange," in *The Cambridge Ancient History*, 2nd edn., Vol. 14, ed. A. Cameron, B. Ward-Perkins, and M. Whitby. Cambridge: 346–91.

(2001) "Specialisation, trade, and prosperity: an overview of the economy of the late antique eastern Mediterranean," in Kingsley and Decker (eds.) 2001: 167–78.

(2005) *The Fall of Rome and the End of Civilization*. Oxford.

(2008) "Jones and the late Roman economy," in *A. H. M. Jones and the Later Roman Empire*, ed. D. M. Gwynn. Leiden: 193–211.

Waters, M. (1995) *Globalization*. London and New York.

Watson, J. L. (1980) "Slavery as an institution: open and closed systems," in *Asian and African Systems of Slavery*, ed. J. L. Watson. Berkeley: 1–15.

Weaver, P. R. C. (1972) *Familia Caesaris: A Social Study of the Emperor's Freedmen and Slaves*. Cambridge.

Webber, R. (1972) *Market Gardening: The History of Commercial Flower, Fruit and Vegetable Growing*. London.

Weber, M. (1924) "Agrarverhältnisse im Altertum," in M. Weber, *Gesammelte Aufsätze zur Sozial- und Wirtschaftsgeschichte*. Tübingen: 1–288.

Webster, G. (1998) *The Roman Imperial Army of the First and Second Centuries A.D.* 3rd edn. Norman OK.

Weise, S., Boldsen, J. L., Gampe, J., and Milner, G. R. (2009) "Calibrated expert inference and the construction of unbiased paleodemographic mortality profiles," *American Journal of Physical Anthropology* 138: S269.

Weiss, A. (2004) *Sklave der Stadt: Untersuchungen zur öffentlichen Sklaverei in den Städten des Römischen Reiches*. Stuttgart.

Welwei, K.-W. (1988) *Unfreie im antiken Kriegsdienst, Dritter Teil: Rom*. Stuttgart.

(2000) *Sub corona vendere: Quellenkritische Studien zu Kriegsgefangenschaft und Sklaverei in Rom bis zum Ende des Hannibalkrieges*. Stuttgart.

Wessely, C. (1894) *Papyrus Erzherzog Rainer: Führer durch die Ausstellung*. Vienna.

Westermann, W. L. (1928) "On inland transportation and communication in antiquity," *Political Science Quarterly* 43: 364–87.

(1955) *The Slave Systems of Greek and Roman Antiquity*. Philadelphia.

White, K. D. (1967) *Agricultural Implements of the Roman World*. Cambridge.

(1970) *Roman Farming*. London.

(1984) *Greek and Roman Technology*. London.

Whitehouse, D. (1965) "Forum ware: a distinctive type of early medieval glazed pottery in the Roman Campagna," *Medieval Archaeology* 9: 55–63.

Whittaker, C. R. (1985 [1987]) "Trade and the aristocracy in the Roman empire," *Opus* 4: 49–75.

(1987) "Circe's pigs: from slavery to serfdom in the later Roman world," in Finley (ed.) 1987: 88–122.

(1989) "Amphorae and trade," in *Amphores romaines et histoire économique: dix ans de recherche*. Rome: 537–9.

(1993) *Land, City and Trade in the Roman Empire*. Aldershot.

Whittow, M. (2003) "Decline and fall? Studying long-term change in the east," in Lavan and Bowden (eds.) 2003: 404–23.

Wickham, C. (1984) "The other transition: from the ancient world to feudalism," *Past and Present* 103: 3–36 (repr. in Wickham 1994: 7–42).

(1988) "Marx, Sherlock Holmes, and late Roman commerce," *Journal of Roman Studies* 78: 183–93 (repr. in Wickham 1994: 77–98).
(1994) *Land and Power: Studies in Italian and European Social History, 400–1200*. London.
(2004) "The Mediterranean around 800: on the brink of the second trade cycle," *Dumbarton Oaks Papers* 58: 161–74.
(2005) *Framing the Early Middle Ages: Europe and the Mediterranean, 400–800*. Oxford.
Wickham, C. and Hansen, I. L. (eds.) (2000) *The Long Eighth Century: Production, Distribution and Demand*. Leiden.
Wickson, E. J. (1891) *The California Fruits and How to Grow Them*. San Francisco.
Wiedemann, T. E. J. (1985) "The regularity of manumission at Rome," *Classical Quarterly* 35: 162–75.
(1989) *Adults and Children in the Roman Empire*. New Haven CT.
(1996) "Servi senes: the role of old slaves at Rome," *Polis* 8: 275–93.
Wikander, Ö. (1981) "The use of water-power in classical antiquity," *Opuscula Romana* 13: 91–104.
(1984) *Exploitation of Water-Power or Technological Stagnation? A Reappraisal of the Productive Forces in the Roman Empire*. Lund.
(1985) "Archaeological evidence for early water-mills - an interim report," *History of Technology* 10: 151–79.
(2000a) "Canals," in *Handbook of Ancient Water Technology*, ed. Ö. Wikander. Leiden: 321–30.
(2000b) "The water-mill," in *Handbook of Ancient Water Technology*, ed. Ö. Wikander. Leiden: 371–400.
(2008) "Sources of energy and exploitation of power," in Oleson 2008: 136–57.
Wild, J.-P. (1999) "Textile manufacture: a rural craft?," in *Artisanat et productions artisanales en milieu rural dans les provinces du nord-ouest de l'Empire romain*, ed. M. Polfer. Montagnac: 29–37.
Williamson, O. E. (2000) "The New Institutional Economics: taking stock, looking ahead," *Journal of Economic Literature* 38: 595–613.
Wilson, A. (2001) "Timgad and textile production," in: Mattingly and Salmon (eds.) 2001: 271–96.
(2002) "Machines, power and the ancient economy," *Journal of Roman Studies* 92: 1–32.
(2003) "Classical water technology in the early Islamic world," in *Technology, Ideology, Water: From Frontinus to the Renaissance and Beyond*, ed. C. Bruun and A. Saastamoinen. Rome: 115–41.
(2006a) "Fishy business: Roman exploitation of marine resources," *Journal of Roman Archaeology* 19: 525–37.
(2006b) "The economic impact of technological advances in the Roman construction industry," in Lo Cascio (ed.) (2006): 225–36.
(2007) "The metal supply of the Roman Empire," in *Supplying Rome and the Roman Empire*, ed. E. Papi. Portsmouth RI: 109–25.
(2008a) "Economy and trade," in *The Roman Era*, ed. E. Bispham. Oxford: 170–202.
(2008b) "Large-scale manufacturing, standardization, and trade," in Oleson (ed.) 2008: 393–417.
(2008c) "Machines in Greek and Roman technology," in Oleson (ed.) 2008: 337–66.

(2009a) "Approaches to quantifying Roman trade," in Bowman and Wilson (eds.) 2009: 213–49.

(2009b) "Indicators for Roman economic growth: a response to Walter Scheidel," *Journal of Roman Archaeology* 22: 71–82.

(2009c) "Villas, horticulture and irrigation infrastructure in the Tiber Valley," in *Mercator Placidissimus: The Tiber Valley in Antiquity. New research in the Upper and Middle River Valley*, ed. F. Coarelli and H. Patterson. Rome: 731–68.

(2011a) "Developments in Mediterranean shipping and maritime trade from 200 BC to AD 1000," in Robinson and Wilson (eds.) 2011: 33–59.

(2011b) "The economic influence of developments in maritime technology in antiquity," in *Maritime Technology in the Ancient Economy: Ship Design and Navigation*, ed. W. V. Harris and K. Iara. Portsmouth RI: 211–34.

(forthcoming a) "Ancient technology and economic growth," in *Economic Growth in Classical Antiquity*, ed. W. Jongman.

(forthcoming b) "City sizes and urbanization in the Roman empire," in *Settlement, Urbanization and Population*, ed. A. Bowman and A. Wilson. Oxford.

Wilson, A. I. and Malouta, M. (forthcoming) "Mechanical irrigation: water-lifting devices in the archaeological evidence and in the Egyptian papyri," in A. K. Bowman and A. I. Wilson (eds.), *The Roman Agricultural Economy: Organisation, Investment, and Production* (Oxford Studies on the Roman Economy 3). Oxford.

Wilson, A. I., Schörle, K., and Rice, C. (forthcoming) "Roman ports and Mediterranean connectivity," in *Portus and the Ports of the Roman Mediterranean*, ed. S. Keay. London.

Wilson, R. J. A. (1990) *Sicily under the Roman Empire: The Archaeology of a Roman Province, 36 BC – AD 535*. Warminster.

Wolters, R. (1999) *Nummi Signati: Untersuchungen zur römischen Münzprägung und Geldwirtschaft*. Munich.

Wood, J. W. (1998) "A theory of preindustrial population dynamics," *Current Anthropology* 39: 99–135.

Woodruff, D. (1996) "Barter of the bankrupt: the politics of demonetization in Russia's Federal State," in *Uncertain Transition: Ethnographies of Change in the Postsocialist World*, ed. M. Burawoy and K. Verdery. Lanham MD: 83–124.

Woods, R. I. (1993) "On the historical relationship between infant and adult mortality," *Population Studies* 47: 195–219.

(2007) "Ancient and early modern mortality: experience and understanding," *Economic History Review* 60: 373–99.

Woolf, G. (1990) "World systems analysis and the Roman empire," *Journal of Roman Archaeology* 3: 44–58.

(1992) "Imperialism, empire and the integration of the Roman economy," *World Archaeology* 23: 283–93.

(1998) *Becoming Roman: The Origins of Provincial Civilization in Gaul*. Cambridge.

(2001) "Regional productions in early Roman Gaul," in Mattingly and Salmon (eds.) 2001: 49–65.

Wright, G. (2006) *Slavery and American Economic Development*. Baton Rouge LA.

Wrigley, E. A. (1987) *Peoples, Cities and Wealth: The Transformation of Traditional Society*. Oxford.

(2004) *Poverty, Progress and Population*. Cambridge.

(2010) *Energy and the English Industrial Revolution*. Cambridge.

Wrigley, E. A., Davies, R. S., Oeppen, J. E., and Schofield, R. S. (1997) *English Population History from Family Reconstitution 1580–1837*. Cambridge.

Yacoub, M. (1970) *Musée du Bardo. Musée antique*. Tunis.

Yeo, C. A. (1946) "Land and sea transport in imperial Italy," *Transactions of the American Philological Association* 77: 221–44.

Young, G. (2001) *Rome's Eastern Trade: International Commerce and Imperial Policy 31 BC-AD 305*. London and New York.

Zanini, E. (1996) "Ricontando la terra sigillata africana," *Archeologia Medievale* 23: 677–88.

(2003) "La ceramica bizantina in Italia tra VI e VII secolo: un sistema informativo territoriale per lo studio della distribuzione e del consumo," in Bakirtzis (ed.) 2003: 381–94.

Zecchini, G. (1998) "La *constitutio antoniniana* e l'universalismo politico di Roma," in *L'ecumenismo politico nella coscienza dell'Occidente*, ed. L. Aigner Foresti, A. Barzano, C. Bearzot, L. Prandi, and G. Zecchini. Rome: 349–58.

(2005) "Economie a confronto: Roma e gli Stati Uniti," in *Storia romana e storia moderna*, ed. M. Pani. Bari: 155–66.

Zehnacker, H. (1979) "Pline l'ancien et l'histoire de la monnaie romaine," *Ktema* 4: 169–81.

Zelener, Y. (2003) "Smallpox and the disintegration of the Roman economy after 165 A.D." PhD dissertation, Columbia University.

Zhang, D. D., Brecke, P., Lee, H. F., He, Y.-Q., and Zhang, J. (2007) "Global climate change, war, and population decline in recent human history," *Proceedings of the National Academy of Sciences* 104: 19214–9.

Zhao, Z. (1997) "Long-term mortality patterns in Chinese history: evidence from a recorded clan population," *Population Studies* 51: 117–27.

Zimmermann, R. (1990) *The Law of Obligations: Roman Foundations of the Civilian Tradition*. Cape Town.

Ziolkowski, A. (1986) "The plundering of Epirus in 167 BC: economic considerations," *Papers of the British School at Rome* 54: 69–80.

INDEX